Opera for All Seasons

Opera

Marianne Williams Tobias

George Calder,
Nancy J. Guyer,
C. David Higgins, and
Charles H. Webb

contributing editors

for All Seasons

60 YEARS OF INDIANA UNIVERSITY OPERA THEATER

Indiana University Press

Bloomington and Indianapolis

This book is a publication of

Indiana University Press
601 North Morton Street
Bloomington, Indiana 47404-3797 USA

www.iupress.indiana.edu

Telephone orders 800-842-6796
Fax orders   812-855-7931
Orders by e-mail iuporder@indiana.edu

☉ The paper used in this publication meets
the minimum requirements of the American National Standard for Information
Sciences—Permanence of Paper for Printed
Library Materials, ANSI Z39.48-1992.

Manufactured in China

Library of Congress Cataloging-in-
Publication Data

Tobias, Marianne Williams.
 Opera for all seasons : 60 years of
Indiana University Opera Theater /
Marianne Williams Tobias ; George
Calder ... [et al.], contributing editors.
   p. cm.
 ISBN 978-0-253-35340-5 (cloth : alk. paper)
1. Indiana University Opera Theater—
History. 2. Opera—Indiana—Bloomington.
I. Calder, George (George A.) II. Title.
ML28.B635I534 2010
792.509772'255—dc22

                    2009049154

1 2 3 4 5 15 14 13 12 11 10

Contents

Preface

It gives me great pleasure to welcome you to *Opera for All Seasons,* a voyage through more than sixty years of Indiana University Opera Theater productions.

More than anything, *Opera for All Seasons* is about a devotion to repertoire—a central element in the development of the Jacobs School of Music. Repertoire is a measure of our capacity and potential, a manifestation of what we can achieve pedagogically and artistically, and a statement to the world about the extraordinary abilities of the collegiate musician.

For Dean Wilfred C. Bain, opera's allure was its ability to synthesize the instrumental, the vocal, and the balletic and—when combined with the visual and the dramatic—to move the audience in a singular way. Thus he began to create an opera program in the collegiate realm unlike any imagined before that time or since.

In these 500 pages and 300 images, we strive to capture the triumph of Bain's inspired vision and identify many of the creative individuals who made it possible. A number of our alumni who now populate orchestras and grace the stages of this country and throughout the world can be seen here in some of their very first roles.

However remarkable, Dean Bain could not have realized his dream without the efforts and financial contributions of many individuals, foundations, and corporations as well as the citizens of the state of Indiana. Most notably, recent support from the Barbara M. and David H. Jacobs family and the Lilly Endowment makes it possible for us to reflect upon our role in global society and to imagine a future that was until now unthinkable.

Many people have worked diligently to make this publication a reality, and we thank all of them for their passion in capturing this commemoration of Indiana University Opera Theater. We also express our profound appreciation to Indiana University Press.

The photos in this publication are the primary means to connect to much of IU Opera Theater's past. But our present and future efforts are being captured in digital sound and images as the IU Jacobs School of Music moves to take performances beyond the walls of the Musical Arts Center. Join us now for a glimpse of that past, and then connect to our present at www.music .indiana.edu/opera.

Gwyn Richards, Dean
Jacobs School of Music
Indiana University, Bloomington
January 2010

Acknowledgments

Among those to whom we are indebted for assistance with preparation of the book are Neha Martin, Andrew Aders, David Altenhof, Philip Ponella, and Bradley Cook. Student assistants were Daniel Shirley, Audrey Snyder, Steven Hrycelak, Heather Youngquist, Caitlin Andrews, Lindsay Kerrigan, and Cody Medina.

Opera for All Seasons

Introduction

*I*ndiana University Opera Theater is just about the most serious and consistently satisfying of all American opera companies," concluded Andrew Porter, then music critic of *The New Yorker* magazine, in a review of Wagner's *Parsifal* performed on April 18, 1976—the last of twenty-three productions of the work staged by Indiana University Opera Theater. *Opera for All Seasons* presents an illustrated account of how IU Opera Theater earned such an esteemed assessment in its sixty-year history.

A treasury of production photos and drawings illuminates six decades of opera performance at Indiana University, from the first production of Offenbach's *The Tales of Hoffmann* in 1948, when orchestra members and choristers were recruited by the new dean's wife at the local A & P supermarket, to the 2008 production of Puccini's *La Bohème,* the first opera live-streamed on the internet from Indiana University to a worldwide audience. Seven chapters take a thematic approach to the phenomenon that is Indiana University Opera Theater.

The first chapter chronicles the many premieres and commissioned opera productions, as well as American and collegiate first performances presented by Indiana University Opera Theater throughout its history. Indiana University Opera Theater, for example, was instrumental in bringing many new operas to American audiences. The second chapter, "The Core of the Matter" catalogs the performance history of IU Opera Theater's core repertoire, which consists of twenty-nine operas, including classics like Puccini's *La Bohème* as well as others unique to IU's opera tradition, such as Wagner's *Parsifal*. Though *Parsifal* presented many challenges in staging, IU Opera Theater maintained it as part of its core repertoire as a demonstration of its growing reputation.

The third chapter, "Other Classics," documents performances of operas that are relatively standard and would normally be seen in any major opera company's season, but for a variety of reasons are less common fare for Indiana University Opera Theater. Other operas in this chapter are less-performed masterworks, such as Wagner's *Die Meistersinger von Nürnberg* and Britten's *A Midsummer Night's Dream,* which have been mounted by Indiana University Opera Theater but were not performed with the frequency of the core repertoire.

During the sixty-year history of Indiana University Opera Theater there have been many tours to other venues. Chapter 4, "On the Road," documents them chronologically. Early on, most traveling performances were within the state of Indiana as part of an audience-building initiative. More recently the tours have been to significant national and international destinations, the most noteworthy being the tour in 1981 of Martinů's *The Greek Passion* to the Metropolitan Opera at Lincoln Center in New York City. Indiana University Opera Theater is the only collegiate opera company ever to perform at the Met.

"Musicals and the Light" shows the long tradition of light opera and musical theater offered by Indiana University Opera Theater. From its very beginning, productions of this genre, including Gilbert and Sullivan, have been included in the repertoire, usually in the summer. Often not as vocally demanding as opera, these works offer a wide variety of roles, as well as acting and dance training, and are suitable for younger singers.

"Off the Beaten Path" documents the more obscure operas, both early and contemporary, that have been performed over the years, such as *Doktor Faust* by Ferruccio Busoni and Leoš Janáček's *Jenůfa*. Some noted works are by IU faculty, such as Edwin Penhorwood's *Too Many Sopranos*, while other projects involve IU's Early Music Institute or Choral Department. Taken as a body of work, these operas not only make up a significant part of the IU Opera Theater's history, but also show the great depth and variety of performances and abilities at IU Opera Theater.

The final chapter, "Behind the Scenes," provides a look at the teams that help create IU Opera Theater productions, including designers of stage, sound, light, and costume.

Tradition

When Wilfred C. Bain arrived at Indiana University in 1947 from Denton, Texas, to serve as dean of the Indiana University School of Music, his charge from the visionary and charismatic university president Herman B Wells was to transform the School of Music into an institution with a national, even international, reputation for excellence. Dean Bain set about bringing to campus the very best faculty selected from the finest conservatories, orchestras, and opera houses of Europe and America. Many were European-trained, eager for the stability that academia in the United States provided in the post–World War II era, as well as for the opportunity to be part of a unique operatic educational experience. Bain saw a future full of possibilities and had every intention of meeting President Wells's expectations.

Dean Bain's vision was to make opera the central performance focus of the music school. He believed that opera performance drew upon all the components of a world-class music school. If providing a world-class education was the overriding objective, then opera performance would consolidate all the forces required to accomplish that mission. Music theory, history, and literature, as well as other academic disciplines, would be essential. Vocal training, coaching, and knowledge of musical styles would be needed. Orchestras requiring excellence in applied music training in all instruments would be conducted by accomplished professionals, assuring excellence in the pit and on stage. Ballet, an important component of romantic operas, would be a key element along with study in stage direction and scenic design.

The vision came true. During Bain's tenure of more than twenty-five years, the international reputation of the Indiana University School of Music was established, with Indiana University Opera Theater playing an important role in that success. Bain's administration laid the foundation for IU Opera Theater with such innovative decisions as the annual production of *Parsifal,* which became IU Opera Theater's signature piece. George Calder, Executive Administrator of Indiana University Opera Theater from 1968 to 1997, remembers that, when he was working in Germany as a répétiteur before coming to IU, people in the German opera world would refer to this phenomenon as "*Parsifal* in Bloomington University."

There were also four outdoor arena productions during the 1960s, including Puccini's *Turandot,* which was performed at the New York World's Fair in 1964. It was the building of the Musical Arts Center, however, that was the crowning achievement of this period. It provided a state-of-the-art home for opera and other School of Music performance activities, and firmly established the Indiana University School of Music as an important world leader in music education. It is also noteworthy that the opening of the Musical Arts Center in 1972 predates the formation of all other Midwest regional opera companies except the Lyric Opera of Chicago. Indiana University Opera Theater became, in fact, the only fully operational opera company within two hundred miles of Bloomington and was consequently a magnet for opera audiences throughout the region.

Charles Webb succeeded Wilfred C. Bain as dean of the Indiana University School of Music in 1973. While in this role he also became artistic director of Indiana University Opera Theater, as Bain had been before him. Primarily, the dean has ultimate artistic control over productions and approves all of the repertoire choices, production teams, and casting decisions presented by the executive administrator of IU Opera Theater. Dean Webb had been associated with the school during Bain's administration as an associate dean, and certainly had first-hand knowledge of the developments in IU Opera Theater during that period. He embraced his administrative role and understood well the mission and core purpose of the program. Dean Webb has stated that this mission "was to give our students the kinds of experiences they need, so that when they graduate and become professionals, they will have the background to enter a professional company and be qualified to do what is asked of them."

Webb's tenure as dean of the Indiana University School of Music spanned twenty-four years and is punctuated by many accomplishments that built on the reputation of Indiana University Opera Theater. Dean Webb was a tireless advocate for the School of Music with the central administration of IU, facilitating growth and expansion in both the School of Music and IU Opera Theater. He increased the number of world-class faculty members and the level of funding to the school, both of which made the continuation of high production standards possible. Webb was successful in bringing Leonard Bernstein to Bloomington for an extended artistic residency during which Bernstein composed his second opera, *A Quiet Place.* Indiana University Opera Theater also gave the first staged performance of the rewritten *1600 Pennsylvania Avenue.* In 1981 Webb negotiated an IU Opera Theater production of Martinů's *The Greek Passion,* to be performed at the Metropolitan Opera as part of a week-long celebration in New York City of the Indiana University School of Music. In 1988 IU Opera Theater had the honor of performing Bernstein's *Mass* at Tanglewood in celebration of the composer's 70th birthday. Many of IU Opera Theater's premieres and firsts are due to Dean Webb's leadership—with this and the school's record of past accomplishments, IU Opera Theater realized a great period of growth, and productions were routinely compared to those of the largest American opera companies.

During the Webb administration, many changes took place within the university, as well. Reductions in state funding increased the importance of developing the school's private endowment, while the then new responsibility-centered budgeting system at IU placed greater emphasis on faculty governance. These major shifts in finance and administration presented new challenges to the school's efforts to maintain its high standards and excellence in the performing arts—especially for opera.

Upon Charles Webb's retirement in 1997, David Woods, a specialist in music education, was appointed dean of the music school. He left the position after a brief two-year tenure, but in that short time he encouraged the Opera Theater to develop a long-range strategic plan, emphasizing corporate and individual gifts as part of IU's institution-wide fundraising campaign.

Gwyn Richards, who served as Associate Dean for Admissions under Charles Webb and David Woods, was appointed Interim Dean of the School of Music in 1999. Not only familiar with the institution and the faculty, he had worked with Dean Webb in navigating the recent changes in the culture of the university. Richards was the logical bridge between the previous administrations and the new academic climate. In 2001, he received a continuing appointment, and became the sixth dean to serve the Indiana University School of Music.

The Future

The School of Music was recently renamed in honor of Barbara and David Jacobs of Cleveland, Ohio, both graduates of Indiana University in the late forties. This act was a form of thanks and acknowledgment for a large endowment that will help secure the School of Music's future as one of the top schools of music in the United States and the world. The Jacobs' generous gift grew out of a friendship that began under Dean Webb's tenure. With these funds, Dean Richards will be able to initiate several projects that had previously only been dreams.

The Jacobs' endowment has increased the school's level of scholarship funding, which has in turn helped the school to recruit top-quality students. It has also enabled Dean Richards to bring a greater number of guest conductors and stage directors to IU Opera Theater, thus providing more opportunities for students to interact with professionals who are working outside of academia. The dean has championed renovations for the Musical Arts Center to return it to a state-of-the-art facility, including an initiative to install a seat-back title system, which will better serve the needs of the audience and will keep the school in the forefront of performance innovations. Dean Richards has also redefined the mission of IU Opera Theater as it moves into the age of new technologies:

Indiana University Opera Theater serves two constituents: first the students of The Jacobs School of Music and Indiana University and, second, the audiences

INTRODUCTION

7

both on campus and elsewhere who attend our performances. I am interested in developing new technologies to extend our productions beyond the walls of The Musical Arts Center to a broader and more accessible worldwide audience. Consider the possibilities of live opera from Indiana University on your own computer.

Indiana University Opera Theater is well situated to take advantage of emerging technologies to better serve both aspects of its mission, and Dean Richards is committed to making these possibilities become realities.

The Scene

This book contains more than three hundred photographs of Indiana University Opera Theater productions.

Prior to the opening of the Musical Arts Center, during Dean Bain's administration, it was not uncommon for faculty to perform in major opera roles. This was a matter of practicality, since many operas programmed during this period contained roles beyond the capabilities of the usual student singer—*Parsifal* serves as a prime example. The photographs from the 1950s and 1960s illustrate this practice. Most of the photographs after this period are of student performers, and show many graduates of the opera program who went on to have impressive careers both in the United States and abroad.

In the early decades of IU Opera Theater, it was the school's policy to present operas in English. This reflected a trend to perform opera in the language of the audience in order to make it more accessible. In the beginning years of Dean Webb's administration, with the decision to use primarily student singers, this policy was modified to include some productions staged in the original language. The administration and voice faculty believed that this approach was more pedagogically sound. Also, this change was in keeping with the worldwide trend in the 1970s to perform in the opera's original language, providing supertitles for greater audience comprehension. IU Opera Theater now wholeheartedly embraces this practice, performing as many operas as possible in their original language.

Many of the photographs feature wide-angle stage shots of designs executed by the faculty scenic designers. These images are included to show the visual impact and the varied artistic style of the productions. Dean Bain aimed for professionalism in every aspect of the productions, and it was he who enticed first Andreas Nomikos then C. Mario Cristini to join the faculty as resident designers. Professor Cristini is of particular importance in terms of the program's history because his designs for *Parsifal* and, later, *Turandot* for the 1964 New York World's Fair, helped establish IU Opera Theater as a major player on the world opera scene. Cristini's designs reflect the romantic-realist tradition from which he came (by way of La Scala Opera, Milan) and they established the first visual style for IU Opera Theater.

Cristini was also the architect of the scenic design degree program that was offered by the School of Music starting in 1962. Harold Mack, a product of that program, became the technical director for Indiana University Opera Theater in 1968, as well as a contributing set designer. C. David Higgins, who now serves as principal designer for IU Opera Theater, was also a protégé of Cristini. Examples of their work are represented in several chapters. Higgins's designs show a clear romantic influence from his teacher but also reflect a more eclectic and contemporary visual style.

Antonin Dimitrov joined the faculty for a short residence after Cristini's death in 1971, and served through the opening of the Musical Arts Center. He designed the inaugural production of *Don Giovanni,* along with most of the first regular season in the new Musical Arts Center. Max Röthlisberger, from the Staatsoper Zurich, joined the faculty in 1973 and was a major contributor to the reputation of the school for impressive, high-quality productions. Röthlisberger's more Germanic Impressionist visual style provided a striking contrast to that of Cristini's. Professor Röthlisberger's appointment was the last made by Dean Bain.

The designers and others appointed by Bain were European by birth, bringing a particular sensibility to IU Opera Theater. Dean Bain's first permanent appointment for stage director was Hans Busch, son of the famous European conductor Fritz Busch. He also appointed Ernst Hoffman, Wolfgang Vacano, and Tibor Kozma to serve as primary operatic conductors. Later, Dean Webb appointed Thomas Baldner and Brian Balkwill as principal conductors. All were seasoned professionals with European credentials and all brought a decidedly European attitude to the production of opera. Even the design of the Musical Arts Center reflects this philosophy, with its European-style seating.

It was 1988 before a designer of purely American origin became associated with Indiana University Opera Theater. That year Robert O'Hearn, well known for his work at the Metropolitan Opera and other major venues, joined the faculty. His designs illustrate yet another major visual style now associated with IU Opera Theater and represent an important American perspective in stage design.

Ross Allen was appointed Professor of Music and Stage Director for IU Opera Theater in 1953. He was an interesting counterpoint to Hans Busch, exhibiting a decidedly American attitude in his productions, and many of the readers of this book will remember his encyclopedic knowledge of all things associated with opera. He was American-born and -trained and had a significant impact on the development of Indiana University Opera Theater. After the retirements of Hans Busch and Ross Allen and following a short period of reorganization, during which James Lukas held a brief appointment, Vincent Liotta joined the staff of Indiana University Opera Theater in 1995. A graduate of the IU School of Music and a former student of Ross Allen, Liotta developed an impressive career before coming to IU as a stage director and producer. He has for many years been closely associated with the Lyric Opera of Chicago as well as many other important venues.

The sixtieth anniversary of IU Opera Theater's unique and impressive tradition is celebrated with this book—a tradition that has been created and maintained by many of the people who grace its pages and certainly many more not found in front of the camera. Today the Jacobs School of Music is world renowned, not only for opera but for a host of other musical disciplines, all of which evolved from the vision and unique academic climate originally created by Dean Wilfred C. Bain and which continue to flourish under his successors.

Premieres and Firsts

Facing. The Tales of Hoffmann (Les Contes d'Hoffmann, J. Offenbach), May 15, 1948. The Olympia Scene (L to R, front): William Geiser, Howard Kahl, Anne Weeks, Joan Merriman, Louis Vanelle, and chorus. This was the first IU Opera Theater production. IU Archives, 48-622.

*O*ver the course of its sixty-year history, Indiana University Opera Theater produced an impressive number of world premieres, in addition to many American and collegiate first performances. Some of the entries in this chapter were milestones in the development of Indiana University Opera Theater, including the first opera produced at IU, the first opera to travel, the first opera sung in its original language. Other firsts represent programming choices on the part of the School of Music administration—choices that reflected the growing importance and prestige of Indiana University Opera Theater. In the early years it was not difficult to claim the right to collegiate first performances since there were virtually no other universities producing fully staged operas in the late 1940s and 1950s. Menotti's *Amahl and the Night Visitors* is an example of such a first. It was commissioned by the NBC TV Opera Theater in 1951 and then came to Indiana University Opera Theater for the first theatrically staged production in 1952.

American premieres make up an important part of this chapter as well, and show that Indiana University Opera Theater has been instrumental in bringing many new operas to American audiences. *Elegy for Young Lovers,* by Hans Werner Henze, is a prime example. Several of the productions listed are the premiere of works by faculty composers, such as *Heracles,* by John Eaton, or of works commissioned by the school to commemorate important events. In 1966, *A Hoosier Tale,* by faculty member Walter Kaufmann, was presented to commemorate the sesquicentennial of the state of Indiana. More recently IU Opera Theater commissioned *Our Town,* by Ned Rorem, co-producing it with several other regional opera companies and presenting the world premiere as part of its 2006 opera season. Taken all together, the photographs in this chapter reveal the impressive scope and vitality of Indiana University Opera Theater over the past sixty years and demonstrate the school's commitment to new and contemporary operatic works.

Parsifal (R. Wagner), April 10, May 8, 1949. Good Friday Scene (*L to R*): Mary Alice Hensley, Guy Owen Baker, Thomas Merriman. This was the first performance of *Parsifal* at Indiana University. It has been performed a total of 23 times by IU Opera Theater. *IU Archives, 49-617.*

The Jumping Frog of Calaveras County (L. Foss), May 18,
19, 20, 1950. As a night of world premieres, Foss's opera
was paired with Bernard Rogers's *The Veil*. Virgil Thomson,
reviewing for the New York *Herald Tribune* praised both as
"distinguished compositions and excellent Indiana productions;
they set each other off to an advantage." *IU Archives, 50-443.*

Facing. The Veil (B. Rogers), May 18, 19, 20, 1950.
Peter Smith (*seated*), Lee Fiser (*standing center*),
Juliana Larson (*seated*). *IU Archives, 50-451.*

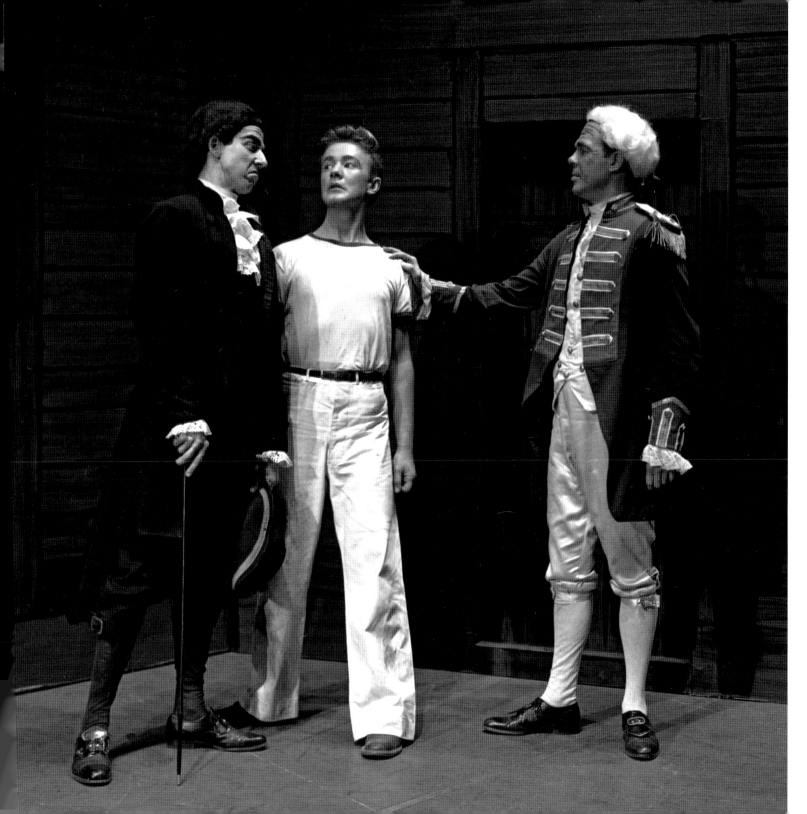

Facing top. A Parfait for Irene (W. Kaufmann), February 21, 22, 23, 24, 1952. The world premiere of *A Parfait for Irene* was paired with the first stage performance of Gian-Carlo Menotti's *Amahl and the Night Visitors*. *IU Archives, 52-842.*

Facing bottom. Amahl and the Night Visitors (G.-C. Menotti), February 21, 22, 23, 24, 1952. This was the first stage performance of the opera, which was originally written for television broadcast. *IU Archives, 52-846.*

Billy Budd (B. Britten), December 7, 1952. (*L to R*): Donald Vogel, John Gillaspy, Eugene Bayless. This American premiere was also the first IU Opera Theater production of an opera by Benjamin Britten. *IU Archives, 52-1781.*

The Ruby (N. Dello Joio),
May 13, 14, 1955. Millicent
McConochy, Ticho Parly. IU
staged the world premiere of
Norman Dello Joio's opera in a
double bill with Leoncavallo's
I Pagliacci. *IU Archives, 55-1218*.

*Facing. The Land Between the
Rivers* (C. Van Buskirk), May 18,
19, 1956. Van Buskirk was a member of the voice faculty and this
production was the first opera
composed by a faculty member
to be premiered at Indiana
University. *IU Archives, 56-1180*.

Die Kluge (*The Clever Girl,* C. Orff),
May 13, 14, 19, 1960. Musicians (*on left*):
Albert Holub, Mary Ann Renne, Cecile
Schneller, Thomas Waechter; (*on right*):
John Large, Dorothea Brown. This
American premiere was presented as
a double bill with *The Spanish Hour*
by Ravel. *IU Archives, 60-796.*

Facing top. The Scarlet Letter (W. Kaufmann), May 6, 13, 16, 1961. Thomas
East, Dorothea Brown. This was the world premiere of Walter Kaufmann's
opera, presented as part of Indiana University's celebration of the Bicentennial
of 1976–77. The opera was produced again in early 1962; that production also
traveled to North Central High School in Indianapolis. *IU Archives, 61-650.*

Facing bottom. The Darkened City (B. Heiden), February 23, March 2, 30, 1963.
Roy Samuelsen. Both the music and libretto for this world premiere were
composed by IU faculty members Bernhard Heiden and Robert Glynn Kelly
respectively. The new opera was received enthusiastically, despite its morbid
subject matter—the coming of the Black Plague to England in 1348. On a
lighter note, in the final rehearsal, as the populace sang "Give us bread,"
a loaf of bread was tossed from the pit onto the stage, causing a dead stop.
No one, to this day, has confessed to being the "tosser." *IU Archives, 63-379.*

Aida (G. Verdi), July 27, 31, August 3, 7, 1963. This
was the first outdoor opera production in the Indiana
University Memorial Stadium. *IU Archives, 63-827.*

Facing. Aida (G. Verdi), July 27, 31, August 3, 7, 1963.
Rendering of the Triumphal Scene by set designer
C. Mario Cristini. The Memorial Stadium bleachers
and turf are clearly depicted. *IU Art Museum.*

I.U. MEMORIAL STADIUM.
-AIDA-
JULY 27-31 AUGUST 3-8

C. M. Cristini

A Hoosier Tale (W. Kaufmann), July 30, August 3, 6, 1966.
(August 6, 1966: Clowes Memorial Hall, Indianapolis). This was
the world premiere of the opera written by Kaufmann to "honor
the State of Indiana and its citizens." The work was commissioned by the School of Music. *IU Archives, 66-983.*

Elegy for Young Lovers (H. W. Henze), March 2, 9, 16, 23, 1968. Joelyn McGowan, David Martin. This was the American premiere of Henze's opera, which, according to Dean Bain, "marked a peak in the artistic performance of opera at Indiana University. . . . The Bloomington audience accepted this unusual work with much aplomb." *IU Archives, 68-628.*

Facing. The Musical Arts Center on opening night, January 29, 1972. The theater and orchestra pit from the stage. For this, the 135th production of the IU Opera Theater, the hall was filled with an audience of 1,500 people. Dean Bain began: "Ladies and gentlemen, the reason I am out here is to attract your attention so the photographers can record for permanence your presence here. . . . We believe that in a measure we hope we have achieved excellence in this wonderful house. And you who are sitting here, you are the people who have made this possible. . . . I extend to you very hearty and very warm thanks." *IU Archives, 72-435.3.*

Facing. Don Giovanni (W. A. Mozart), January 29, February 11, 12, 1972. (*L to R*): Elaine Pavlick, Bert Neely, LaVergne Monette, Joseph Frank, Caroline Murdoch. This was the first production to grace the stage of the Musical Arts Center, soon to be known as "The Met of the Midwest." *IU Archives, 72-472.7.*

Heracles (J. Eaton), April 22, 29, 1972. This world premiere was the opening performance of the Dedication Week Festival. The performance was followed by a dinner on the stage. *IU Archives, 72-663.4.*

PREMIERES
AND FIRSTS

Rigoletto (G. Verdi), April 5, 12, 19, 26, 1975. (*L to R*): Bruce Hubbard, William McGraw. This production of *Rigoletto* was the first opera to be performed in an original language other than English by the IU Opera Theater. *IU Archives, C75-160.1.*

Danton and Robespierre (J. Eaton), April 21, 22, 29,
1978. This was the world premiere of the fifth opera
by faculty member John Eaton. *IU Archives, 78-83.8.*

The Cry of Clytaemnestra (J. Eaton),
March 1, 8, 15, 1980. This world
premiere cast included Nelda
Nelson. *IU Archives, 80-48.2.*

Jakob Lenz (W. Rihm),
July 11, 18, 1981. The American
premiere of Rihm's opera.
IU Archives, 81-173.11.

The Greek Passion (*Řecké pašije*, B. Martinů), April 4, 10, 11, 18, 26, 1981. Larry Paxton as Manolios and Rebecca Field as Katerina. The American premiere occurred at the Musical Arts Center and this production also toured to the Metropolitan Opera on April 26, 1981. *IU Archives, 81-86.1.*

The Excursions of Mr. Broucek (*Výlety pana Broučka*, L. Janáček),
November 21, December 5, 12, 1981. American premiere. *IU Archives, 81-313.7.*

Facing. Soldier Boy, Soldier (T. J. Anderson), October 23, 30, November 6, 1982.
William Johnson (*holding bass*). This was a world premiere commissioned by
the Indiana University Foundation in conjunction with the School of Music
and Office of Afro-American Affairs. *IU Archives, 82-266.6.*

Das Rheingold (R. Wagner),
March 31, April 7, 14, 21, 1984.
(*L to R*): Ann Benson, Peter Volpe,
Stephen Skinner. *IU Archives, 84-81.2.*

Murder in the Cathedral (*Assassinio nella cattedrale,* I. Pizzetti), March 30, April 6, 13, 20, 1985. (*L to R*): Peter Volpe, Thomas Murphy, Victor Ledbetter, James Moore, Ron Peo. This was the American premiere of the Italian composer Pizzetti's opera, based on the poetic drama by T. S. Eliot, an American expatriate and British citizen. The production was staged and directed by the famous bass and IU faculty member, Nicola Rossi-Lemeni. *IU Archives, 85-77.12.*

The Tempest (J. Eaton), March 8, 29, April 5, 1986.
Nelda Nelson. This was the collegiate premiere
of Eaton's last opera. *IU Archives, 86-96.8.*

The Legend of Tsar Saltan (*Skazka o Tsare Saltane,* N. Rimsky-Korsakov),
April 4, 11, 18, 25, 1987. Collegiate premiere. *The Legend of Tsar Saltan* featured
one of IU Opera Theater's most complicated sets. Ceilings backstage were only
28 feet high, so the sets had to be moved out and then telescoped to their
ultimate heights after being placed on stage. *IU Archives, 87-89.20.*

Facing. The Legend of Tsar Saltan (*Skazka o Tsare Saltane,* N. Rimsky-Korsakov),
April 4, 11, 18, 25, 1987. The model of the set designed by Max Röthlisberger in 1987.

The Dawn of the Poor King (J. Orrego-Salas),
November 10, 17, 18, December 1, 1990. The IU
Opera Theater staged the world premiere of
Orrego-Salas's opera-oratorio. *IU Archives, slide 28.*

1600 Pennsylvania Avenue
(L. Bernstein), July 11, 17, 18, 25
(MAC), August 11, 12, 13 (Kennedy
Center), 1992. Kathryn Foss-Pittman,
Angela M. Brown. This collegiate
premiere traveled to the Kennedy
Center in Washington, D.C., for
three performances. *IU Archives,
slide 46.*

The Devils of Loudun
(K. Penderecki), February 20,
27, March 6, 1993. This was
the American premiere of the
revised version of Penderecki's
work. *IU Archives, slide 120.*

Nixon in China
(J. Adams), February 18,
24, 25, March 4, 1995.
Collegiate premiere.
IU Archives, slide 22.

Facing. Nixon in China
(J. Adams), February 18,
24, 25, March 4, 1995.
(*L to R*): Brian Horne,
Kreg Gottschall,
C. Louis Brooks.
IU Archives, slide 39.

PREMIERES
AND FIRSTS

45

McTeague (W. Bolcom), February 17, 23, 24, March 2, 1996.
(*L to R*): Kimberly Fuselier, Maria Izzo, Deborah Poyner, Kevin
Eckard (*in background*), Allen Saunders, Michael Sheehan,
Michael Belnap. Collegiate premiere. *IU Archives, 96-0266.34A.*

The Ghosts of Versailles (J. Corigliano), April 12, 18, 19, 26, 1997. Collegiate premiere. *IU Archives, 97-0387.3A.*

Little Women (M. Adamo), February 2,
3, 8, 9, 2002. Color rendering by set
designer Robert O'Hearn.

Little Women (M. Adamo),
February 2, 3, 8, 9, 2002.
(*L to R*): Leslie Mutchler,
Anita Rollo, Tiffany Rosenquist, Kate Mangiameli.
Collegiate premiere. The set
for *Little Women* has been
rented frequently to outside
opera companies. *IU Photographic Services, 02-0015.*

Jeppe (S.-D. Sandström),
February 7, 8, 14, 15, 2003.
This was the American
premiere of the opera by
IU faculty member Sven-
David Sandström. *IU Pho-
tographic Services, 03-4609.*

A View from the Bridge (W. Bolcom), February 4, 5, 11, 12, 2005. Colleen Brooks, Todd Wieczorek. Collegiate premiere. *IU Photographic Services, 05-5838.*

Our Town (N. Rorem), February 24, 25, March 3, 4, 2006.
Opening night celebration reception in the Musical Arts Center lobby
with the composer, Ned Rorem, at the podium and the opera's librettist,
J. D. McClatchy, to his right. (*L to R*): C. David Higgins, Daniel Shirley,
Daniel J. Yarzebinski, J. D. McClatchy, Ned Rorem, Carmund White,
Jamie Barton, David Effron, Juliet Gilchrist, Jennifer Bilfield, Dean
Gwyn Richards, Helane Anderson, Sarah Mabary, Kevin Murphy.

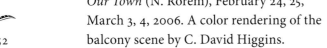

Our Town (N. Rorem), February 24, 25,
March 3, 4, 2006. A color rendering of the
52   balcony scene by C. David Higgins.

Our Town (N. Rorem), February 24, 25, March 3, 4, 2006. Anna Steenerson, Marc Schapman in the Balcony Scene. IU Opera Theater staged the world premiere of Ned Rorem's adaptation of the quintessentially American play by Thornton Wilder. *IU Photographic Services, 06-4907.*

Facing. A Wedding (W. Bolcom),
February 1, 2, 8, 9, 2008. Joshua Whitener,
Robin Federici. Collegiate premiere.
IU Photographic Services, 08-9381.

The Core of the Matter 2

*A*s the materials for this book were compiled, it became evident that certain operas have been systematically and continuously produced over the years. The number of roles, size of the chorus, style of the music, and a host of other production considerations have all been important factors in the decision to mount these operas. Most of the operas covered in this chapter will be familiar standards and perennial audience favorites, as well as practical educational choices.

Some of the operas in this chapter, however, are not considered standard programming choices for most professional companies, let alone schools, and yet they have a special place in the history of IU Opera Theater. The significance of *Parsifal* to the development of the Jacobs School of Music's opera program is well-known—IU Opera Theater has produced *Parsifal* twenty-three times since its first staging in 1948. Puccini's *Tosca* is another example of non-standard fare for a university opera program.

Facing. The Abduction from the Seraglio (Die Entführung aus dem Serail, W. A. Mozart), October 15, 22, 29, 1966. Roger Havranek, Fulton Gallagher. IU Archives, 66-1280.8.

Early in the history of Indiana University Opera Theater, the nonstandard operas were more easily programmed since faculty members were regularly cast in the most demanding lead roles. In later years, when appropriate student talent has been available, these operas were and are programmed not only to provide a performance opportunity to those student singers who are ready for the challenge, but also to provide chorus and orchestra students, as well as the general public, the performance experience of these great operas.

Facing. The Abduction from the Seraglio (Die Entführung aus dem Serail, W. A. Mozart), September 25, October 1, 2, 9, 1993. Curtis Cook, James Dalfonso. *IU Archives, slide 346.*

The Abduction from the Seraglio (Die Entführung aus dem Serail, W. A. Mozart), September 26, 27, October 3, 4, 2003. James Neff (*center*), Alison Bates (*on platform at right*), and chorus. *IU Photographic Services, 03-7437.*

Facing. The Barber of Seville (Il Barbiere di Siviglia, G. Rossini), October 29, 30, November 3, 1971; February 5, 1972. Act I of the production designed by Antonin Dimitrov, 1971.

The Barber of Seville (Il Barbiere di Siviglia, G. Rossini). Pablo Elvira, Janice Redick. This was the last opera performed in the IU Auditorium before IU Opera Theater moved into the Musical Arts Center. The stage designer was Antonin Dimitrov, a new member of the staff from Czechoslovakia whose wife, Olga, was costume designer for the production. *IU Archives, 71-1261.6.*

THE CORE OF
THE MATTER

Facing. The Barber of Seville
(*Il Barbiere di Siviglia,* G. Rossini),
February 3, 4, 10, 11, 2006. Florin
Olimpio Ormenisan, Jason Plourde.
IU Photographic Services, 06-1940.

The Bartered Bride
(*Prodaná nevěsta*, B. Smetana),
February 10, 17, 24, March 6, 1968.
Roger Havranek, Emily Rawlins,
and chorus. This production
traveled to Purdue University's
Elliott Hall of Music after three
performances in Bloomington.
IU Archives, 68-573.14.

The Bartered Bride
(*Prodaná nevěsta,* B. Smetana),
September 27, October 3, 4, 11,
1986. Dancers. *IU Archives,*
86-310.28.

Facing. The Bartered Bride
(*Prodaná nevěsta,* B. Smetana),
July 30, August 5, 6, 1994.
Jonathan Schrader, Curtis
Cook, Rebecca Cullison.
IU Archives, slide 216.

Facing. La Bohème (G. Puccini), March 2, 3, 4, 1950. This was the first production to be performed in East Hall. This audience favorite among Puccini's operas went on to be staged every five years. *IU Archives, 50-171.*

La Bohème (G. Puccini), November 3, 10, 20, December 1, 1962; January 12, 1963. Bernadine Oliphint, David Arnold, and others. This production was presented successfully at North Central High School in Indianapolis on November 20; the other performances were in East Hall. *IU Archives, 62-1487.*

La Bohème (G. Puccini), February 16, 23, March 1, 2, 1985. (*L to R*): Carol Ann Edwards, Jorge Pita, Marilyn Mims. *IU Archives, 85-40.18.*

Facing. La Bohème (G. Puccini), July 30, 31,
August 6, 7, 1999. Michael Belnap, Kristine
Biller. *IU Archives, 99-706.35.*

La Bohème (G. Puccini), September 24, 25,
October 1, 2, 2004. Matthew Mindrum, Angela
Mannino. *IU Photographic Services, 04-1901A.*

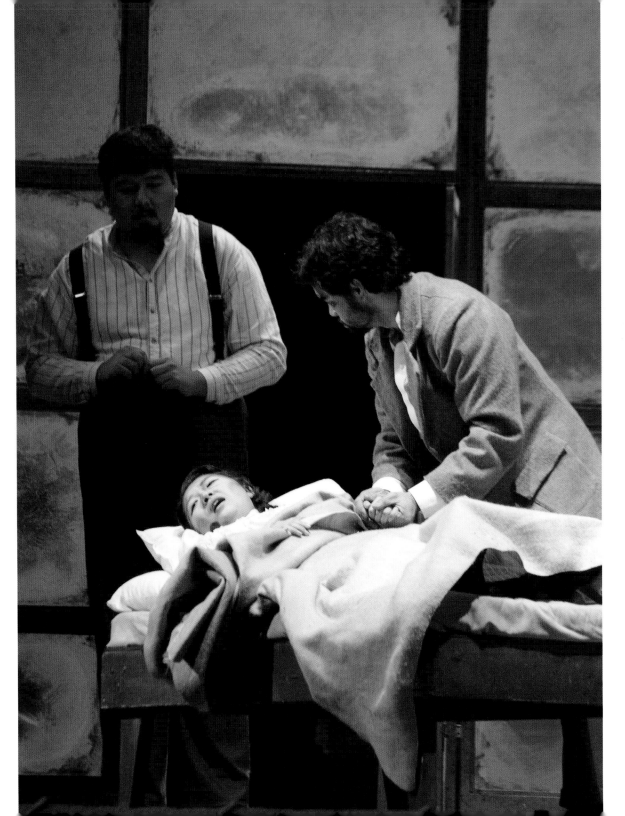

La Bohème (G. Puccini),
November 9, 10, 16, 17, 2007.
(*L to R*): Adonis Abuyen,
Jung Nan Yoon (*lying on bed*),
Brian Arreola. This set utilized
three turntables with scenery
that moved forward and back-
ward, which coordinated with
complicated lighting, snow
effects, and projections that
panned when the turntables
moved. *IU Photographic
Services, 07-3377.*

Facing. La Bohème (G. Puccini),
November 9, 10, 16, 17, 2007.
Act III. *IU Photographic
Services, 07-3296.*

Candide (L. Bernstein), December 16, 17, 1957.
Ronald Hedlund (*seated*) and group.
IU Archives, 57-1943.

Facing. Candide (L. Bernstein), October 17, 24,
31, 1987. Laura Aikin. *IU Archives, 87-232.20.*

Candide (L. Bernstein), October 16, 23, 30, November 6, 1993.
Andrew Hendricks (*center*), Amy Kraabel. *IU Archives, slide 141.*

Carmen (G. Bizet), July 28, 31, August 1, 4, 6, 7, 1965. Chorus. These six performances of the opera were staged in IU Memorial Stadium, now the Arboretum. *IU Archives, 65-960.6.*

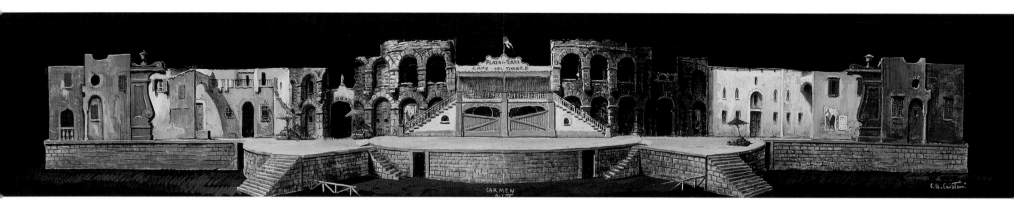

Facing top, Carmen (G. Bizet), Act IV, and *facing bottom,*
Carmen (G. Bizet), July 27, August 2, 3, 1985. Christine
Meadows, Mark Baker. *Photo, IU Archives, 85-144.10.*

Above. Carmen (G. Bizet). Rendering of
Act I by Robert O'Hearn.

Carmen (G. Bizet), October 23, 24, 30, 31, 1998. April Golliver as Carmen. *IU Archives, 98-1008.36.*

Carmen (G. Bizet), April 7, 8, 14, 15, 2006. John Sumners. *IU Photographic Services, 06-7127.*

THE CORE OF
THE MATTER

79

Così fan tutte (W. A. Mozart), October 20, 27, November 3, 1984. (*R to L*): Tod Kowallis, Victor Ledbetter, Laura Beyer, Janine Hawley. *IU Archives, 84-310.12.*

Così fan tutte (W. A. Mozart), September 23, 30, October 7, 1989. (*L to R*): Thomas Barrett, Danielle Strauss, Berkley Stutts, Philip Zawisza. *IU Archives, slide 271.*

Così fan tutte (W. A. Mozart), September 23, 29, 30,
October 7, 1995. (*L to R*): Andrew Hendricks, Alan
Bennett, Daniel Cole. *IU Archives, C-95-1018-17.*

Così fan tutte (W. A. Mozart), October 20, 21, 27, 28, 2000.
(*L to R*): Corey McKern, Sheila Murphy, Rachel Holland,
Heidi Vanderford, Charles Blandy. *IU Archives, 00-797.8.*

Don Giovanni (W. A. Mozart), February 8, 14, 15, 22, 1986. (*L to R*):
Yun-Yi Chen, Randal Turner, Victor Ledbetter, Solrun Bragadottir,
Previn Moore, Marilyn Mims. This production was taken to Clowes
Memorial Hall in Indianapolis on February 18, 1986. *IU Archives, 86-23.3.*

Don Giovanni (W. A. Mozart), October 26, November 1,
2, 9, 1991. (*L to R*): Emily Magee, Michael Rorex,
Christopher Schaldenbrand. *IU Archives, slide 198.*

Facing. Don Giovanni (W. A. Mozart), September 28, October 5, 12, 19, 1996. (*L to R*): Twyla Robinson, Sheri Jackson, Kevin Eckard, Jonathan Hodel, Amy Cope, Jeffrey Byers (*kneeling*), Brian Banion (*front*). *IU Archives, C-96-0913.21.*

Don Giovanni (W. A. Mozart), September 22, 23, 29, 30, 2006. John Paul Huckle. *IU Photographic Services, 06-0097.*

Facing. Don Giovanni (W. A. Mozart).
Model of the set designed by
Max Röthlisberger, 1979.

Don Pasquale (G. Donizetti), October 12,
13, 1957. Don Yule (*seated*), Barbara Stevens,
William Arnholt (*far right*). *IU Archives, 57-1631.*

"DON PASQUALE"

Don Pasquale (G. Donizetti).
Rendering of Act I, Scene 1 and Act III,
Scene 2 set by C. Mario Cristini.

Don Pasquale (G. Donizetti), September 24,
October 1, 8, 1988. Elizabeth Futral.
IU Archives, slide 126.

The Elixir of Love (*L'Elisir d'amore*, G. Donizetti),
May 11, 12, July 7, 14, 21, 28, August 4, 1962. Rendering of Act III, scene I by C. Mario Cristini.

The Elixir of Love (*L'Elisir d'amore,* G. Donizetti),
May 11, 12, July 7, 14, 21, 28, August 4, 1962.
(*Near well*): George Osborne, Rachel Day,
William McDonald. *IU Archives, 62-795.*

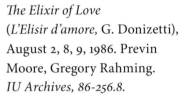

The Elixir of Love
(*L'Elisir d'amore*, G. Donizetti),
August 2, 8, 9, 1986. Previn
Moore, Gregory Rahming.
IU Archives, 86-256.8.

The Elixir of Love
(*L'Elisir d'amore*, G. Donizetti),
January 26, February 1, 2, 9,
1991. William Burden, Kathlyn
Fries. *IU Archives, slide 78.*

The Elixir of Love (*L'elisir d'amore*, G. Donizetti),
July 27, 28, August 3, 4, 2007. Chorus.
IU Photographic Services, 07-7999.

Falstaff (G. Verdi),
April 11, 17, 18, 25, 1998.
Timothy Noble as Falstaff.
IU Archives, 98-360.

Falstaff (G. Verdi), November 14, 15, 21, 22, 2003.
(*L to R*): Lindsey Falduto, Hee Jung Yoo, Sophie Roland,
Juliet Gilchrist. *IU Photographic Services, 03 1771.*

Facing. Faust (C. Gounod), November 18, 19,
20, 1955. David Starkey, Anna Lee Hamilton.
IU Archives, 55-1934.

Above. Faust (C. Gounod), February 19, 26,
March 4, 1972. Janice Redick. *IU Archives, 75-526.*

Faust (C. Gounod), January 27,
February 3, 9, 10, 1990. Jane Dutton,
Bradley Garvin. *IU Archives, slide 176.*

Die Fledermaus (*The Bat*, J. Strauss), September 28,
October 4, 5, 12, 1985. (*L to R*): Carol Ann Edwards,
Tod Kowallis, Alan Cemore. *IU Archives, 85-169.4.*

Facing. Die Fledermaus
(*The Bat,* J. Strauss), October 26,
November 1, 2, 9, 1996. (*L to R*):
Raymond Fellman, Nicole
Lyndes, Matthew Chambers.
IU Archives, 85-169.4.

Die Fledermaus
(*The Bat,* J. Strauss),
July 27, 28, August 2, 3, 2002.
Howard Swyers, Michael Deleget.
IU Photographic Services, 02-0082.

Hansel and Gretel (E. Humperdinck), November 10, 11, 16, 17, 2001. *IU Photographic Services, 01-2120.*

Facing. Hansel and Gretel (E. Humperdinck), November 10, 11, 17, 18, 2006. (*L to R*): Kathryn Leemhuis, Michael Match, Marie Masters. *IU Photographic Services, 06-3614.*

Facing. Hansel and Gretel
(E. Humperdinck). The Act II model
designed by Max Röthlisberger, 1982.

The Love for Three Oranges (*Lyubov k Tryom Apelsinam,*
S. Prokofiev), May 15, 16, 19, 1959. (*Top row*): Don Yule, Maribeth
Ostertag, Carlyle Weiss, and chorus. *IU Archives, 59-971.*

Facing. The Love for Three Oranges (*Lyubov k Tryom Apelsinam,*
S. Prokofiev), October 18, 25, November 1, 8, 1975. Set designed
by Max Röthlisberger. *IU Archives, 75-327.8.*

Facing. The Love for Three Oranges (Lyubov k Tryom Apelsinam, S. Prokofiev), April 2, 9, 16, 23, 1994. Set designed by C. David Higgins.

Above. Madama Butterfly (G. Puccini), November 7, 8, 15, 22, 1958. (*L to R*): Frankie Weathers, Ami Pressler, William Arnholt. This opera was presented in commemoration of the centenary of Puccini's birth. *IU Archives, 58-2242.*

Madama Butterfly (G. Puccini), August 1,
2, 8, 9, 1975. Malcolm Webb, Suzette
Wankier. *IU Archives, C75-267.2.*

Madama Butterfly (G. Puccini), September 26,
October 3, 10, 17, 1981. (*L to R*): Gayletha Nichols, Lewis
Schlanbusch, Nova Thomas. *IU Archives, 81-253.2.*

Madama Butterfly (G. Puccini), July 28, 29,
August 3, 4, 2001. Chorus. *IU Archives, 01-190.13.*

Madama Butterfly (G. Puccini), April 6, 7, 13, 14, 2007.
Jing Zhang. *IU Photographic Services, 07-1044.*

The Magic Flute (*Die Zauberflöte*, W. A. Mozart),
December 3, 10, 1960; January 7, April 8, 1961.
(*Center*): Malcolm Smith. *IU Archives, 60-1559.*

The Magic Flute (*Die Zauberflöte,* W. A. Mozart), February 3,
10, 17, 24, 1973. (*L to R*): Gordon Greer, Kyung Sook Bang,
Jerry Norman, Roy King. *IU Archives, 73-0062.*

The Magic Flute (*Die Zauberflöte*, W. A. Mozart), October 15, 22, 29, November 5, 1988. Christopher Schaldenbrand, Clare Mueller. *IU Archives, slide 134.*

The Magic Flute (*Die Zauberflöte*, W. A. Mozart), April 8, 9, 15, 16, 2005. John Huckle as Sarastro (*center*) with the priests of the temple. *IU Photographic Services, 05-2993.*

Facing. The Magic Flute (*Die Zauberflöte*, W. A. Mozart), October 15, 22, 29, November 5, 1994. Simone Nold, Matthias Klink. *IU Archives, slide 248.*

Facing. Manon (J. Massenet), November 4, 11, 18,
December 2, 1967. Carole Farley, David Arnold.
IU Archives, 67-1381.1.

Above. Manon (J. Massenet), April 5, 12, 19, 26, 1980.
Gran Wilson, Sylvia McNair. *IU Archives, 80-86.5.*

Manon (J. Massenet), October 20, 21, 27, 28, 2006.
Chorus. *IU Photographic Services, 06-1582.*

Manon (J. Massenet), 1994. Rendering of Act II by Robert O'Hearn.

Facing. The Marriage of Figaro (*Le Nozze di Figaro*, W. A. Mozart),
December 7, 14, 1968; January 11, February 8, 15, 1969. (*L to R*): Harriet
Karlsond, Donna Dalton, Roy Samuelsen. *IU Archives, 68-1548.8.*

Above. The Marriage of Figaro (*Le Nozze di Figaro*, W. A.
Mozart), October 25, 31, November 1, 8, 1980. Set designed
by Max Röthlisberger. *IU Archives, 80-391.4.*

Facing. The Marriage of Figaro
(*Le Nozze di Figaro,* W. A. Mozart),
January 31, February 6, 7, 14, 1998.
(*L to R*): Stephanie Johnson,
Kirsten Blasé, Kimberly
Fuselier. *IU Archives, 98-98.12.*

The Marriage of Figaro
(*Le Nozze di Figaro,* W. A. Mozart),
February 22, 23, 29, March 1, 2008.
Thomas Florio. *IU Photographic
Services, 08-0886.*

Facing. The Merry Widow (Die lustige Witwe,
F. Lehár), Summer 1949; March 10, 11, 15,
16, 17, 18, 1950. Chorus. *IU Archives, 49-1337.*

Above. The Merry Widow (Die lustige Witwe,
F. Lehár), October 13, 20, 27, November 3,
1990. The cast. *IU Archives, slide 65.*

Facing. The Merry Widow (*Die lustige Witwe*, F. Lehár), July 27, August 2, 3, 1996. Patricia Wise and chorus men. *IU Archives, C-96-0691.33.*

The Merry Widow (*Die lustige Witwe*, F. Lehár), October 24, 25, 31, November 1, 2003. Vera Savage, Jeremy Hunt. *IU Photographic Services, 03-0900.*

Facing. Parsifal (R. Wagner),
March 18, 1951. Eugene
Bayless, Diane Griffith.
IU Archives, 51-91.

Parsifal (R. Wagner),
April 11, 1954. Father and
daughter, Kay and George
Krueger of the IU Choral
faculty. *IU Archives, 54-0199.*

THE CORE OF
THE MATTER

135

- PARSIFAL - ACT I SC. 2 - ACT III SC. 2

Parsifal (R. Wagner). Rendering of Act I, Scene 2
and Act III, Scene 2 by C. Mario Cristini.

Facing. Parsifal (R. Wagner), April 14, 1957. Charles
Kullman, Ralph Appelman. *IU Archives, 57-904.*

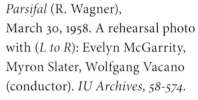

Parsifal (R. Wagner),
March 30, 1958. A rehearsal photo
with (*L to R*): Evelyn McGarrity,
Myron Slater, Wolfgang Vacano
(conductor). *IU Archives, 58-574.*

Parsifal (R. Wagner),
April 7, 1963. Charles Kullman,
Margaret Harshaw. *IU Archives,
63-519.1.*

Facing. Parsifal (R. Wagner),
April 10, 17, 24, 1976. Flower Maidens
and Michael Ballam. This production
was last in a series of 23 performances
of *Parsifal,* which featured the first
student to perform the title role,
Michael Ballam. *IU Archives, 76-98.3.*

Peter Grimes (B. Britten), April 25, May 2, 9, 15, 1964.
Richard Knoll, David Knoll. *IU Archives, 64-669.3.*

Peter Grimes (B. Britten), November 7, 14,
December 5, 1987. Adam Klein. *IU Archives, 87-289.6.*

Peter Grimes (B. Britten), April 9, 10, 16, 17,
2004. *IU Photographic Services, 04-17.*

Facing. Rigoletto
(G. Verdi), February 11,
18, 25, March 11, 1967.
IU Archives, C67-503.

Rigoletto
(G. Verdi), September 27,
October 4, 11, 18, 1980.
Gran Wilson, Sylvia McNair.
IU Archives, 80-329.8.

Rigoletto (G. Verdi),
February 7, 13, 14, 21, 1987.
Carlos Montané, Kristine Jepson.
IU Archives, 87-21.23.

THE CORE OF
THE MATTER

Rigoletto (G. Verdi), February 23, 24, March 2, 3,
2001. Kristine Winkler. *IU Archives, 01-45.29.*

Facing. Rigoletto (G. Verdi), September 21, 22, 28, 29, 2007.
Jonathan R. Green. *IU Photographic Services, 07-0887.*

Facing. The Tales of Hoffmann (*Les Contes d'Hoffmann,*
J. Offenbach), May 15, 1948. Vera Scammon,
Louis Vanelle. *IU Archives, 48-620.*

Above. The Tales of Hoffmann (*Les Contes d'Hoffmann,*
J. Offenbach), July 28, August 3, 4, November 17,
December 1, 8, 1973. Chorus. *IU Archives, 73-0486.1.*

The Tales of Hoffmann (*Les Contes d'Hoffmann,*
J. Offenbach), April 8, 14, 15, 22, 1989. Rendering
of the Prologue by C. David Higgins.

The Tales of Hoffmann (*Les Contes d'Hoffmann*,
J. Offenbach), March 30, April 6, 13, 20, 1996.
Tod Kowallis and chorus. *IU Archives, C-960441.26.*

The Tales of Hoffmann
(*Les Contes d'Hoffmann,* J. Offenbach),
November 15, 16, 22, 23, 2002. The
Olympia scene. (*L to R*): Mi Young
Park (*behind curtain*), Michael Rees
Davis, Timothy Birt. Set design by
C. David Higgins. *IU Photographic
Services, 02-2695.*

Facing. The Tales of Hoffmann
(*Les Contes d'Hoffmann,* J. Offenbach),
April 4, 5, 11, 12, 2008. Carolina
Castells, Adam Cioffari. This set
featured vast sets of gears and
clocks that were interlinked and
revolved in tandem. *IU Photographic
Services, 02-337.*

Tosca (G. Puccini), November 1, 8, 15,
22, 1969. Rendering of Act I by Harold Mack.

Facing. Tosca (G. Puccini), September 24,
October 1, 8, 15, November 2, 1977. Jean Deis,
Rebecca Cook. *IU Archives, 77-527.2.*

Tosca (G. Puccini), July 31, August 6, 7, 1993.
Katharine Morgan, James Cornelison.
IU Archives, slide 191.

Tosca (G. Puccini), July 30, 31, 2004. Jeffrey Springer. *IU Photographic Services, 04-9599.*

Facing. La Traviata (G. Verdi), November 9, 16, 20, 23, 1968; April 12, 18, 1969. (*L to R*): Emily Rawlins, Richard McComb, and chorus. This production traveled to Purdue University and to North Central High School in Indianapolis. *IU Archives, 68-1429.3.*

Above. La Traviata (G. Verdi), February 18, 25, March 2, 3, 1984. William Johnson, Luis Felix. *IU Archives, 84-44.1.*

La Traviata (G. Verdi), September 22, 28, 29,
October 6, 1990. Chorus. *IU Archives, slide 172.*

La Traviata (G. Verdi), August 2, 8, 9, 1997.
Dawn Waggener. *IU Archives, 97-645.27.*

Il Trittico: Il Tabarro (*A Triptych: The Cloak,* G. Puccini),
December 16, 17, 1955. The first part of Puccini's triptych, *Il Tabarro,*
was paired with Ravel's *The Bewitched Child. IU Archives, 55-2127.*

Facing. Il Trittico: Suor Angelica (*A Triptych: Sister Angelica,* G. Puccini),
July 26, 29, 31, August 2, 1969. The second part of Puccini's triptych,
Suor Angelica. Nancy Shade, Barbara Lockard. *IU Archives, 69-897.8.*

Facing. Il Trittico: Gianni Schicchi (A Triptych: Gianni Schicchi, G. Puccini), February 25, March 4, 25, 1989. The third part of Puccini's *Il Trittico, Gianni Schicchi* was presented as a double bill with *Bluebeard's Castle* by Béla Bartók. *IU Archives, slide 18.*

Other Classics

*T*here has existed almost from the beginning of Indiana University Opera Theater the desire to include in each season's repertoire diverse examples of operatic style. This goal has driven many programming decisions over the years. Each season optimally includes an example of Italian, French, and German origin. Each also ideally has a classical, bel canto, and romantic example, with perhaps a twentieth-century opera representing more contemporary composers, or an opera from the earlier pre-classical period. The aim of this inclusive approach is to effectively educate the students in as many performance styles as is feasible during their studies at IU, and to provide the patrons of IU Opera Theater with a theatrical experience as varied and interesting as possible. "Other Classics" is a collection of historical productions that represent this array of operatic literature but that have not been performed with the frequency of IU Opera Theater's standard repertoire.

Many of these operas are certainly classics and are often performed in the professional world. Others are lesser-known works by great composers, such as *La Finta Giardiniera,* by W. A. Mozart. Some are emerging American classics such as Carlisle Floyd's *Susannah* and Robert Ward's *The Crucible.* These diverse works represent a significant portion of the IU Opera Theater performance history and, along with the core repertoire, make up the bulk of the operas depicted in this book. Taken as a whole these operas show the depth of programming and the great diversity of literature that have been a part of Indiana University Opera Theater.

Facing. Albert Herring (B. Britten), May 16, 17, 1958. (*L to R*): Evelyn Kaufmann, Virgil Hale, Ronald Hedlund, Susan Cullen, Ted Jones. *IU Archives, 58-965.2.*

Above. Amahl and the Night Visitors
(G.-C. Menotti), November 10, 17, 18,
December 1, 1990. Set by C. David
Higgins. *IU Archives, slide 23.*

Facing. Andrea Chénier (U. Giordano),
April 27, May 4, 11, 1968. Roy Samuelsen (*center*).
The conductor for this production was
Dean Charles H. Webb. *IU Archives, 68-748.12.*

Facing. Arabella (R. Strauss), February 26, 27, March 5, 6, 1999. Twyla Robinson as Arabella. *IU Archives, 99-258.4.*

Above. Arabella (R. Strauss), February 23, 24, March 2, 3, 2007. Chorus. *IU Photographic Services, 07-8051.*

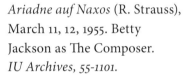

Ariadne auf Naxos (R. Strauss), March 11, 12, 1955. Betty Jackson as The Composer. *IU Archives, 55-1101.*

Ariadne auf Naxos (R. Strauss), April 25, May 2, 9, 16, 1970. (*L to R*): Joseph Frank, Peter Schuba, Kyung Wook Shin as Zerbinetta. *IU Archives, 70-781.10.*

Ariadne auf Naxos
(R. Strauss), November 16,
22, 23, December 7, 1996.
Angela M. Brown as Ariadne.
IU Archives, 96-1223.2A.

Facing. The Ballad of Baby Doe (D. Moore), February 26, March 4, 5, 1983. Reri Grist, Walter Cassel (*center*). This production was conducted by Dean Charles H. Webb. *IU Archives, 83-35.7.*

Above. The Ballad of Baby Doe (D. Moore), February 6, 7, 13, 14, 2004. (*L to R*): Benjamin Czarnota, Ian Paul, Christopher Sponseller, David Swain, Jessica Vanderhoof. *IU Photographic Services, 04-4023.*

A Masked Ball
(*Un Ballo in Maschera*, G. Verdi),
August 2, 4, September 19, 21, 1958.
(*L to R*): William Appel, Frankie
Weathers, Phillip Cohen.
IU Archives, 58-1963.

Béatrice et Bénédict (H. Berlioz), February 27,
March 4, 5, 1988. Chorus. *IU Archives, slide 8.*

Facing. Bluebeard's Castle (B. Bartók), February 25,
March 4, 25, 1989. Stephen Meyer, Caroline Dowd,
Michelle Boyle, Lisa Riegel. *IU Archives, slide 15.*

Above. Boris Godunov (M. Musorgsky),
February 12, 13, 26, 27, 1965.
Linda Matousek, Franklin Lusk.
IU Archives, 65-401.8.

Below. Boris Godunov (M. Musorgsky),
March 17, April 7, 14, 21, 1979. Nova Thomas,
Ralph Appelman. Injured during the final
dress rehearsal, Ralph Appelman sang
all four performances with a broken
collarbone. *IU Archives, 79-60.5.*

Facing. Boris Godunov (M. Musorgsky),
October 22, 29, November 5, 12, 1983.
Nicola Rossi-Lemeni. *IU Archives, 83-224.14.*

Cavalleria Rusticana (*Rustic Chivalry*, P. Mascagni),
February 7, 8, 1958. Chorus. *IU Archives, 58-487.*

Facing. La Cenerentola (*Cinderella*, G. Rossini), February 1,
7, 8, 15, 1992. Cenerentola was played by Patricia Risley
and Kathryn Krasovec. *IU Archives, slide 44.*

La Cenerentola (*Cinderella,* G. Rossini), February 5, 6, 12, 13, 1999. (*L to R, front row*): Kyle Ketelsen, Helen Allen, Erin Coats, Andrew Hendricks. *IU Archives, 99-104.12.*

Facing. La Cenerentola (*Cinderella,* G. Rossini), November 12, 13, 19, 20, 2004. (*L to R*): Kristen Robinson, Benjamin Gelfand, Kristin Brouwer. *IU Photographic Services, 04-3908.*

The Crucible (R. Ward), August 1, 7, 8, 1987.
Tod Kowallis, Elizabeth Futral. *IU Archives, 87-155.3.*

Facing left. The Dialogues of the Carmelites (*Dialogues des Carmélites,* F. Poulenc), February 21, 27, 28, March 7, 1998.
(*L to R*): René Harrison, Kerrin Dunbar. *IU Archives, 98-166.24.*

Right. The Dialogues of the Carmelites
(*Dialogues des Carmélites,* F. Poulenc),
February 25, 26, March 4, 5, 2005.
Eileen Bora. *IU Photographic
Services, 05-8779.*

187

Facing. Don Carlos (G. Verdi), August 5, 9, 12, September 23, 29, 30, October 14, 1972. Linda Healy, Kathryn Montgomery. This opera was presented for the Metropolitan Opera National Council's Central Opera Service Regional Conference, which was held in Bloomington so that its members could see the newly opened Musical Arts Center. *IU Archives, 72-947.9.*

Eugene Onegin (P. I. Tchaikovsky),
October 25, 31, November 1, 8, 1997.
Chorus. *IU Archives, 97-1025.13.*

Facing. Eugene Onegin (P. I. Tchaikovsky),
October 22, 23, 29, 30, 2004. Michelle Auslander,
Scott Skiba. *IU Photographic Services, 04-2960.*

Facing. Fidelio (L. Beethoven), July 25, 29, August 1, 1970. (*Center*): Donna Dalton, David Aiken. Presented in commemoration of the two-hundredth anniversary of Beethoven's birth, this production of *Fidelio* "served as a landmark in achievement to the credit of the Indiana University Opera Theater forces—cast, chorus, [and] orchestra . . ." (Dean Wilfred C. Bain). *IU Archives, 70-1048.4.*

Above. The Daughter of the Regiment (*La Fille du régiment*, G. Donizetti), July 28, August 3, 4, 1984. (*L to R, front*): Stephen Chambers, Susan Patterson, Ray Liddle. *IU Archives, 84-195.3.*

La Finta Giardiniera (The Pretend Gardener,
W. A. Mozart), April 12, 13, 20, May 8, 1991. Set
designed by Robert O'Hearn. *IU Archives, slide 191.*

Facing. L'Heure espagnole (The Spanish Hour, M. Ravel), November 10, 17,
December 1, 8, 1984. (*L to R*): David Little, Andrea Adkins, Mark-
Bowman Hester, Brian Scott, Gregory Rahming. *IU Archives, 84-337.5.*

Facing. Idomeneo
(W. A. Mozart), October 16,
23, 30, November 6, 1976. Set
designed by Max Röthlisberger.
IU Archives, 76-339.4.

Idomeneo (W. A. Mozart),
November 13, 14, 20, 21, 1998.
(*L to R*): Cynthia Watters,
Michael Lee (*kneeling*), Joshua
Vincent (*standing*), Stephanie
Johnson. *IU Archives, 98-1136.3.*

Facing. The Italian Girl in Algiers (L'Italiana in Algeri, G. Rossini), October 12, 19, 26, November 2, 1968. Judith Schwenzfeier (Judith Christin), William Oberholtzer. IU Archives, 68-1286.8.

Giulio Cesare (Julius Caesar, G. F. Handel), October 25, 26, November 1, 2, 2002. Rebecca Ball as Cleopatra. IU Photographic Services, 02-1772.

Facing. L'Incoronazione di Poppea (The Coronation of Poppea, C. Monteverdi), October 14, 21, 28, 1967. Jorge Enrique Guberna, Emily Rawlins. Poppea was presented in celebration of the 400th anniversary of Monteverdi's birth and was the first opera performed at the University School Auditorium after East Hall burned. IU Archives, 67-1312.7.

Facing. Love on Trial (*La pietra del paragone*, G. Rossini), December 6, 13, 1969; January 10, 17, February 7, April 11, 1970. (*L to R*): Judith Schwenzfeier (Judith Christin), Ann Swedish, William Pell, William McDonald. *Love on Trial* opened a seven-opera series in honor of Indiana University's sesquicentennial year (1820–1970). *IU Archives, 69-1373.5.*

Lucia di Lammermoor (G. Donizetti), October 17, 20, 24, 31, November 7, 1970; March 21, 25, 1971. Gianna d'Angelo (*back to viewer*). *IU Archives, 70-1297.5.*

Lucia di Lammermoor (G. Donizetti), April 5, 6, 12, 13, 2002. Scott Six, Evelyn Pollock. *IU Photographic Services, 02-79.*

Manon Lescaut (G. Puccini), November 14, 21, December 5, 12, 1970. Chorus. C. Mario Cristini's set design was executed and painted by his students shortly after his death. *IU Archives, 70-1421.*

Mass (L. Bernstein), April 16, 17, 23, 24, 1999. Stage. *IU Archives, 99-471.4.*

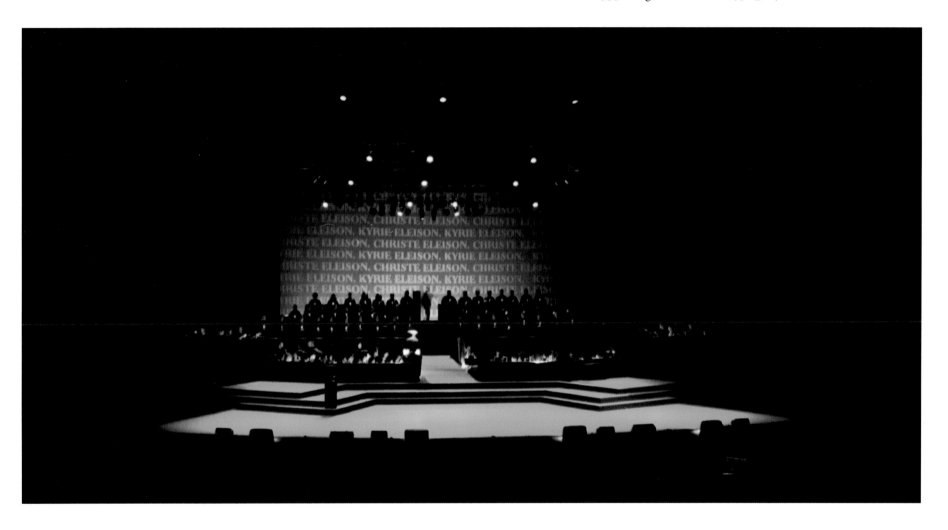

Die Meistersinger von Nürnberg (*The Mastersingers of Nuremberg*, R. Wagner),
July 29, August 5, 1961. Shoemakers' Guild. *IU Archives, 61-1042.*

Facing. Die Meistersinger von Nürnberg (*The Mastersingers of Nuremberg*,
R. Wagner), July 27, 30, August 1, 3, 1968. (*L to R, front*): David Aiken, Linda
Anderson, Ralph Appelman, Roger Havranek. Corbin Patrick of the *Indianapolis
Star* lauded Ralph Appelman's singing as "mellow and golden" and acknowledged
David Aiken, a new faculty member, for handling a "taxing role with fluent
ease and heraldic tone quality." *IU Archives, 68-1071.1.*

The Merry Wives of Windsor (*Die lustigen Weiber von Windsor,*
O. Nicolai), October 24, 31, November 7, 14, 1981. Kathryn
Case, Jan Prokop, Christine Ross. *IU Archives, 81-277.4.*

A Midsummer Night's Dream (B. Britten),
November 11, 12, 18, 19, 2005. Robert Samels,
Natalie Ford. *IU Photographic Services, 05-8545.*

Facing. *L'Orfeo* (L. Rossi), April 2, 9, 23, 1988. (*L to R, front*): Suzanne Galer, Gina d'Alessio. *IU Archives, slide 75.*

Orfeo ed Euridice (C. W. Gluck), October 24, 31, November 7, 8, 1992. Set shot. *IU Archives, slide 27.*

Orpheus in the Underworld (Orphée aux enfers,
J. Offenbach), January 30, February 5, 6, 13, 1993.

Andrew Hendricks as Orpheus. *IU Archives, slide 70.*

Orpheus in the Underworld
(*Orphée aux enfers*, J. Offenbach),
September 25, 26, October 2,
3, 1998. Kimberly Fuselier.
IU Archives, 98-789.20.

Otello (G. Verdi), October 14, 21, 28, November 4, 1989. James King, Michael Krueger. *IU Archives, NBd24.*

Facing. Otello (G. Verdi), October 14, 21, 28, November 4, 1989. Jeanne-Michèle Charbonnet, Erwin Stephan. *IU Archives, slide 12.*

I Pagliacci (R. Leoncavallo), November 16, 23,
December 7, 1991. Michael Bellnap, Leann
Sandel. *IU Archives, slide 5.*

Pelléas et Mélisande (C. Debussy), January 29,
February 5, 12, 1977. Set designed by Max
Röthlisberger. *IU Archives, 77-27.2.*

Pelléas et Mélisande
(C. Debussy), September 24,
30, October 1, 8, 1994. Branch
Fields (*standing*), Kathryn Lang.
IU Archives, slide 13.

Facing. The Queen of Spades
(*La Pique Dame*, P. I. Tchaikovsky),
April 26, May 3, 10, 17, 1969.
Douglas Murdock (*front left*),
William Oberholtzer (*center*).
IU Archives, 69-644.3.

Facing. Porgy and Bess (G. Gershwin),
November 13, 19, 20, December 4, 5,
6, 1976. Michael Smartt (*kneeling*).
IU Archives, 76-395.6.

The Rake's Progress
(I. Stravinsky), February 22,
March 1, 8, 15, 1969. Holly Day,
Elizabeth Mannion. *IU Archives,
69-558.8.*

The Rake's Progress
(I. Stravinsky), February 22, 29,
March 7, 1992. (*L to R*): Mary
Kruger, James Cornelison, Charles
Davidson. *IU Archives, slide 226.*

OTHER
CLASSICS

221

Roméo et Juliette (C. Gounod),
November 5, 12, 19, December 3, 1966. (*L to R,
on stairs*): Roy Samuelsen, Linda Woodruff,
Linda Phillips. *IU Archives, 66-1402.*

Facing. Roméo et Juliette (C. Gounod),
October 21, 22, 28, 29, 2005. Besty Uschkrat,
Brian Arreola. *IU Photographic Services, 05-7536.*

La Rondine (*The Swallow,* G. Puccini), February 20,
27, 1960. Rendering of Act I by A. Nomikos.

La Rondine (*The Swallow*, G. Puccini), February 20, 27, 1960.
Karen Crowley, William Holley (*couple on right*). This opera
ushered in the tradition of Saturday night performances, a
practice which continues to this day. *IU Archives, 60-456.*

Der Rosenkavalier (*The Knight of the Rose*, R. Strauss), April 15,
May 5, 1966. Opening the IU Auditorium's 25th anniversary
celebration. (*L to R*): Joan Volek Gersten (*far left*), Marian
Krajewska, Roger Havranek (*center*), Val Stuart, Carolyne James.
George Calder notes that performing *Der Rosenkavalier* was
"a huge achievement for any University production." The set
designer was Robert O'Hearn. *IU Archives, 66-552.*

Facing. Salome (R. Strauss), May 15, 1971. Nancy
Shade as Salome. According to Charles Staff of
the *Indianapolis News,* "the evening belonged
to Miss Shade." *IU Archives, 74-641.*

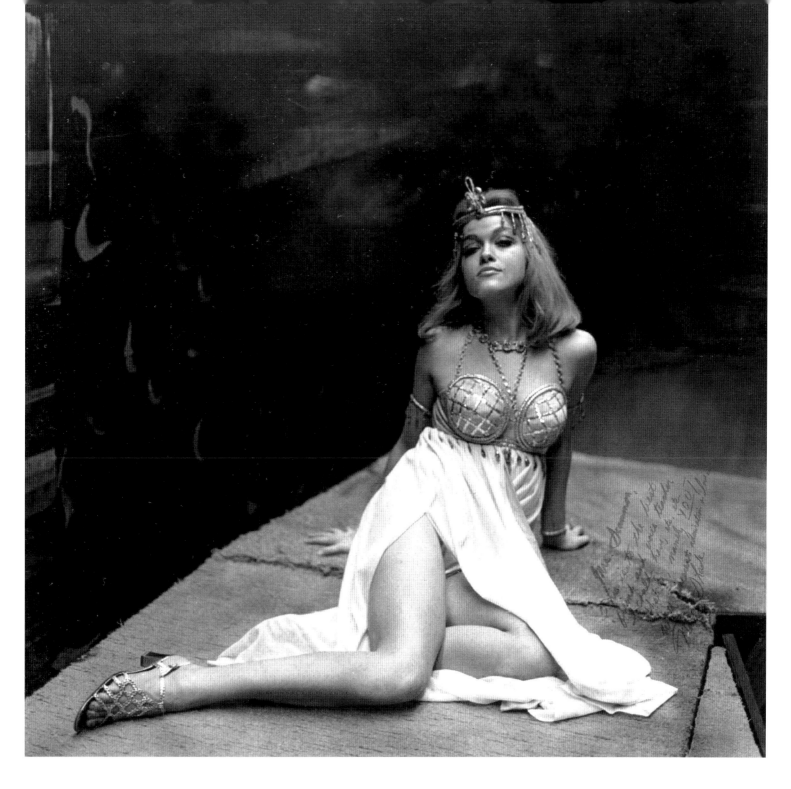

La Sonnambula (*The Sleepwalker*, V. Bellini),
October 19, 26, November 2, 1985. Barbara Gilbert,
Mark Bowman Hester. *IU Archives, 85-199.15.*

Facing. Susannah (C. Floyd), August 6, 7, 8, 1976.
Jack Clay (*center*). *IU Archives, 76-233.5.*

Facing. Susannah (C. Floyd),
October 19, 20, 26, 27, 2007.
Aleksey Bogdanov, Elizabeth
Ashantiva. *IU Photographic
Services, 07-2368.*

The Turk in Italy
(*Il Turco in Italia*, G. Rossini),
February 27, 28, March 5, 6,
2004. Robert Samels, Marcy
Richardson. *IU Photographic
Services, 04-4608.*

Facing. Vanessa (S. Barber), March 1,
8, 15, 1975. Patricia Johnson Gilliland,
Michael Ballam. *IU Archives, 75-73.3.*

Above. Die Walküre (*The Valkyrie,* R. Wagner),
March 22, 1970. (*L to R*): Elliot Palay, Peter
Schuba, Roy Samuelsen. *IU Archives, C70-637.*

Werther (J. Massenet), November 15, 22, December 6, 1975. Clark Watters (*front*). Children: Stephanie Erb, Doug Lathom, Alexandra Smith, Bettina Winold, Hans Peter Winold, Charles Webb III. *IU Archives, 75-371.3.*

Below. Wozzeck (A. Berg), February 16, 22, 23, March 2, 1991. Steven LaCosse, Jeff Morrissey. *IU Archives, slide 79.*

Right. Wozzeck (A. Berg), October 22, 23, 29, 30, 1999. Michael Lee, Matthew Curran. *IU Archives, 99-1175.13.*

On the Road

4

Facing. Tosca (G. Puccini), December 9, 1961; January 27, February 3, April 28, 1962. This production traveled for two additional performances: December 12, 1961 (North Central High School, Indianapolis); March 24, 1962 (Indiana University, South Bend campus). Elizabeth Wrancher, Thomas East. *IU Archives, 61-2434.*

*O*ver the years operatic tours were effective in promoting IU Opera Theater, Indiana University, and by association the state of Indiana, as well as in providing unique educational opportunities for the student musicians and crews. Possibly the most historically important tour was the 1955 production of *Parsifal,* which was taken to the Kiel Municipal Opera House in St. Louis. This was the first tour of the emerging Indiana University Opera Theater and generated national exposure for Indiana University. Publicity generated by the performance catapulted the School of Music into the international limelight. In 1964 the tour to the New York World's Fair with a mammoth arena-stage production of Puccini's *Turandot* further solidified a growing international reputation.

The record shows that there was much more touring within the state in the earlier years of IU Opera Theater, a practice which has been largely abandoned.

However, in the recent past there have been some very important special tours to distant venues. In 1981 the School of Music traveled to New York City with a week of musical performances intended to showcase student talent in major music venues. The culmination was a production of Martinů's *The Greek Passion* at the Metropolitan Opera House at Lincoln Center. IU Opera Theater remains the only student production company to have performed at the MET.

In the last decade of his life Leonard Bernstein had a close relationship with the Indiana University School of Music, and spent 1982 in residence in Bloomington composing his last opera, *A Quiet Place*. Although IU Opera Theater didn't have the opportunity to perform this work, it did mount a production of Bernstein's *Mass* and performed it at Tanglewood in 1988 to commemorate his 70th birthday. The photographic record of the many occasions when Indiana University Opera Theater has toured productions bears testimony to the importance of opera at IU and the importance of IU Opera Theater to other communities.

Don Carlos (G. Verdi), February 10, 17, March 3, 15,
1962. This production was presented in Indianapolis
(at North Central High School) for its final performance.
Set designed by Andreas Nomikos. *IU Archives, 61-496.*

A Midsummer Night's Dream (B. Britten), March 10, 17, April 7, 17, 1962.
The final performance was at North Central High School in Indianapolis.
(*Center*): Katherine Fisher (Tatiana), William McDonald (Oberon).
The set was designed by C. Mario Cristini. *IU Archives, 62-539.*

The Force of Destiny (*La Forza del Destino,* G. Verdi), March 16,
23, 26, April 20, 1963. This production traveled to Indianapolis
for a performance on March 26th at North Central High School.
Spotlighted: Roy Samuelsen. *IU Archives, 63-444.*

The Girl of the Golden West (*La Fanciulla del West,* G. Puccini),
December 14, 1963; January 11, 14, February 8, 15, 1964. The January 14
performance was in Indianapolis at North Central High School.
Richard Knoll (*on platform*), Joyce Shealy (*center*). *IU Archives, 64-466.*

Facing. Turandot (G. Puccini), July 29, August 1, 5, 8, 1964 (IU Memorial
Stadium); August 17, 18, 1964 (New York World's Fair Singer Bowl).
The opera went to the New York World's Fair. Corbin Patrick of the
Indianapolis Star commented: "The Indiana University Opera Theater
marshaled a huge cast of 300 singers, dancers, musicians, and gorgeously
costumed supernumeraries. . . . It fills the great expanse of a stage 250
feet wide and 30 feet high. . . ." *IU Archives, 64-1106.*

Il Trovatore (*The Troubadour,* G. Verdi), December 9, 16, 1967; January 6, 13, 1968. The production later traveled within Indiana: January 26 (Kokomo), January 27 (Gary), January 28 (South Bend), 1968. Nancy Shade, Jean Deis. *IU Archives, 67-1549.6.*

Facing. The World on the Moon (*Il Mondo della Luna,* F. J. Haydn), September 20, 27, October 4, 11, 1975. This rarely performed opera was taken to the Kennedy Center in Washington, D.C., during the Hadyn Festival and performed on September 29. *IU Archives, 75-293.4.*

The Greek Passion (Řecké pašije, B. Martinů), April 4, 10, 11, 18, 1981.
This production appeared at the Met in New York City on April 26.
Set in a small village in Greece during the Turkish occupation, this
IU Opera Theater production was designed by Max Röthlisberger.
Painting for his sets tended toward the minimal. Rather than
painted textures, sets featured many textured surfaces, which
received and reflected light. *IU Archives, 81-82.6.*

Mass (L. Bernstein), September 3, 1988; January 16, 1989. This production appeared on August 27, 1988, at the Tanglewood Music Festival in Lenox, Massachusetts. Leonard Bernstein receiving applause. *IU Archives, Bernstein-88a.*

Facing. The Cry of Clytaemnestra (J. Eaton), March 31, April 7, 14, 21, 1990. On May 16th and 19th, this production was performed in Moscow, USSR. It was a double bill with *Francesca da Rimini. IU Archives, slide 70.*

Below. Francesca da Rimini (S. Rachmaninoff), March 31, April 7, 14, 21, 1990. On May 16th and 19th, this production was performed in Moscow, USSR. *IU Archives, slide 3.*

Right. 1600 Pennsylvania Avenue (L. Bernstein), July 11, 17, 18, 25, August 11, 12, 13, 1992. This photo features the cast and production team in front of the U.S. Capitol while on tour to the Kennedy Center in August.

Musicals and the Light

Facing. The Mikado (Gilbert and Sullivan), July 13, 14, 15, 20, 21, 22, 1951. *The Mikado* was performed in a series of summer musicals that included *The Chocolate Soldier* and *Lost in the Stars*. *IU Archives, 51-1631.*

*I*U Opera Theater typically offers two productions during the summer, one of which is traditionally a musical or an operetta, though there were some summers when several small-scale productions were mounted in various venues around the Bloomington campus. The dual approach to summer programming accomplishes two goals. First, it addresses a faculty concern that musicals and operettas were under-represented and also that they are more appropriate training vehicles for younger students and students whose voices are more suited to lighter fare. Second, from the perspective of audience reception, summer opera-goers tend to be more interested in musicals and light opera as an alternative to the more serious repertoire of the regular academic season. "Musicals and the Light" presents a photographic record of these summer productions.

These works were an important part of the earliest Indiana University Opera Theater seasons. Although the first one listed is *The Mikado,* by Gilbert and Sullivan, in 1951, there have been relatively few Gilbert and Sullivan productions offered by IU Opera Theater; *The Mikado, The Gondoliers,* and a recent production of *HMS Pinafore* represent the total output. The majority of this material represents the American musical and European operettas. Both of these genres are important components of musical training and it is important to note that IU Opera Theater has a long tradition of including them as part of its overall mission to both students and the public.

Lost in the Stars (K. Weill), July 27, 28, 29, August 3, 4, 5, 1951. Ralph Appelman (*kneeling*). Kurt Weill attended all five performances of his opera. *IU Archives, 51-1748.*

Kiss Me, Kate (C. Porter), August 1, 2, 8, 9, 1952. The cast. *IU Archives, 52-1371.*

Facing. The King and I (Rodgers and Hammerstein), July 19, 20, 21, 26, 27, 28, August 3, 4, 1957. Gilbert and Nancy Reed, who were the entire ballet faculty at the time. The August performances were located at the Mesker Memorial Amphitheater in Evansville, Indiana. *IU Archives, 57-1227.*

Above. The Most Happy Fella (F. Loesser), July 24, 25, 31, August 1, 3, 1959; January 9, 13, February 5, 6, 13, 1960. Featuring Ralph Appelman (*left*). *IU Archives, 59-1533.*

Brigadoon (Lerner and Loewe),
June 30, July 1, 2, 8, 10, 13, 18, 31, August 1,
8, November 10, 19, December 3, 10, 1961;
January 7, 14, 21, 28, February 18, 1962.
Alan Bergman (*left front*), William
McDonald (*right front*). This performance was in the oval Frangipani Room
of the Indiana Memorial Union, which
provided a small stage at one end and
the opportunity to perform as a theater
in the round. *IU Archives, 61-875.*

Facing. 110 in the Shade (Schmidt and
Jones), March 22, 23, 24, June 28, 29,
July 6, 12, 13, 1968. Kevin Kline,
Elaine Pavlick. *IU Archives, PS68-653.3.*

Facing. Finian's Rainbow (Lane and Harburg), October 17, 19, 22, 24, 1969. George Bledsoe, Mary Wakefield. This musical was produced in Alumni Hall in the Indiana Memorial Union. *IU Archives, 69-1166.7.*

Facing. Fiddler on the Roof (Bock and Harnick),
July 14, 15, 21, 22, 1972. *IU Archives, 72-860.*

Above. Kiss Me, Kate (C. Porter), July 13, 14, 19,
20, 1973. (*L to R*): Melanie Young, Thomas
Holliday, Clark Watters. *IU Archives, 73-0304.5.*

The Gondoliers
(Gilbert and Sullivan),
July 12, 13, 19, 20, 1974.
IU Archives, 74-473.2.

*Facing. A Little Night
Music* (S. Sondheim),
July 11, 12, 18, 19, 1975.
Harold Mack's set design.
IU Archives, 75-232.1.

Carousel (Rodgers and Hammerstein),
July 10, 17, 24, 1976. A chorus number.
IU Archives, 76-193.10.

Facing. Naughty Marietta (V. Herbert),
July 22, 23, 30, 31, 1977. Mark Baker,
Maria Bernazzani. *IU Archives, 77-285.11.*

The Canterbury Tales (Hill and Hawkins),
June 30, July 1, 7, 8, 1978. *IU Archives, 78-162.5.*

Showboat (J. Kern), July 13, 14, 20, 21, 1984.
Bruce Hubbard. *IU Archives, 84-168.3.*

Man of La Mancha (Leigh and Darion), July 5, 6, 13, 19, 20, 1985. (*L to R*): Victor Ledbetter, Previn Moore, Brian Scott. *IU Archives, 86-137.14.*

West Side Story (L. Bernstein),
April 12, 18, 19, 26, 1986.
IU Archives, 86-137.14.

Camelot (Lerner and Loewe),
July 12, 18, 19, 26, 1986.
IU Archives, 86-239.16.

Man of La Mancha (Leigh and Darion),
January 28, February 4, 11, 18, 1989. Colleen
McCarthy (*center*). *IU Archives, slide 87.*

Kismet
(Wright and Forrest),
July 8, 9, 15, 22, 1989.
Heidi Clark.
IU Archives, slide 144.

Facing. Company
(S. Sondheim),
July 7, 13, 14, 21, 1990.
IU Archives, slide 37.

Hello, Dolly! (J. Herman), July 6, 12, 13, 20, 1991.
Vivica Genaux as Dolly. *IU Archives, slide 28.*

Jubilee (C. Porter), September 28, October 5, 12, 19, 1991. (*L to R*): Cheryl Martin, Robert Gallagher, Steven LaCosse, Heidi Clark, and chorus. *IU Archives, slide 6.*

West Side Story (L. Bernstein), April 3,
9, 10, 17, 24, 1993. The Jets and the Sharks.
IU Archives, slide 104.

Facing. Carousel (Rodgers and Hammerstein),
July 10, 16, 17, 24, 1993. *IU Archives, slide 146.*

Fiddler on the Roof (Bock and Harnick),
July 9, 15, 16, 23, 1994. Giorgio Tozzi
as Tevye. *IU Archives, slide 14.*

The King and I (Rodgers and Hammerstein), July 6, 12, 13, 20, 1996. Lee Lofton, Seung-Ah Chae. *IU Archives, C-96-0664.7.*

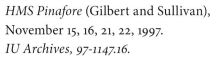

HMS Pinafore (Gilbert and Sullivan),
November 15, 16, 21, 22, 1997.

IU Archives, 97-1147.16.

Candide (L. Bernstein), April 6, 7, 13, 14,
2001. David Ray, Michael Deleget.
IU Archives, 01-93.30.

Putting It Together
(S. Sondheim), July 6, 7, 12, 13, 2002.
(*L to R*): Jeremy Truhel, Corey McKern,
Nicholas Provenzale, Trent Casey.
IU Photographic Services.

The Secret Garden (L. Simon),
July 12, 18, 19, 2003. (*L to R*):
Matthew Gailey, David Sievers,
Nathan Pratt, Jordan Goodmon,
Jennifer Feinstein. *IU Archives, 03-5180.*

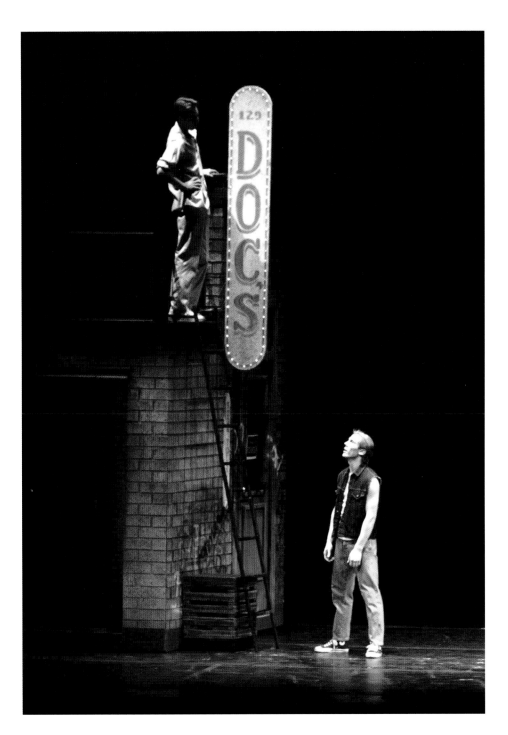

West Side Story (L. Bernstein),
April 11, 12, 18, 19, 2003.
Nathan Bick (*above*),
Christopher Gobles. *IU
Photographic Services.*

Facing. She Loves Me
(Bock and Harnick), July 9,
10, 11, 2004. Diane Tychsen,
Roger Henry, Noriko Hashimoto,
Kristen Robinson, Barron Breland.
IU Photographic Services.

HMS Pinafore
(Gilbert and Sullivan),
July 29, 30, August 5, 6, 2005.
Anna Steenerson, Marc Schapman.
IU Photographic Services.

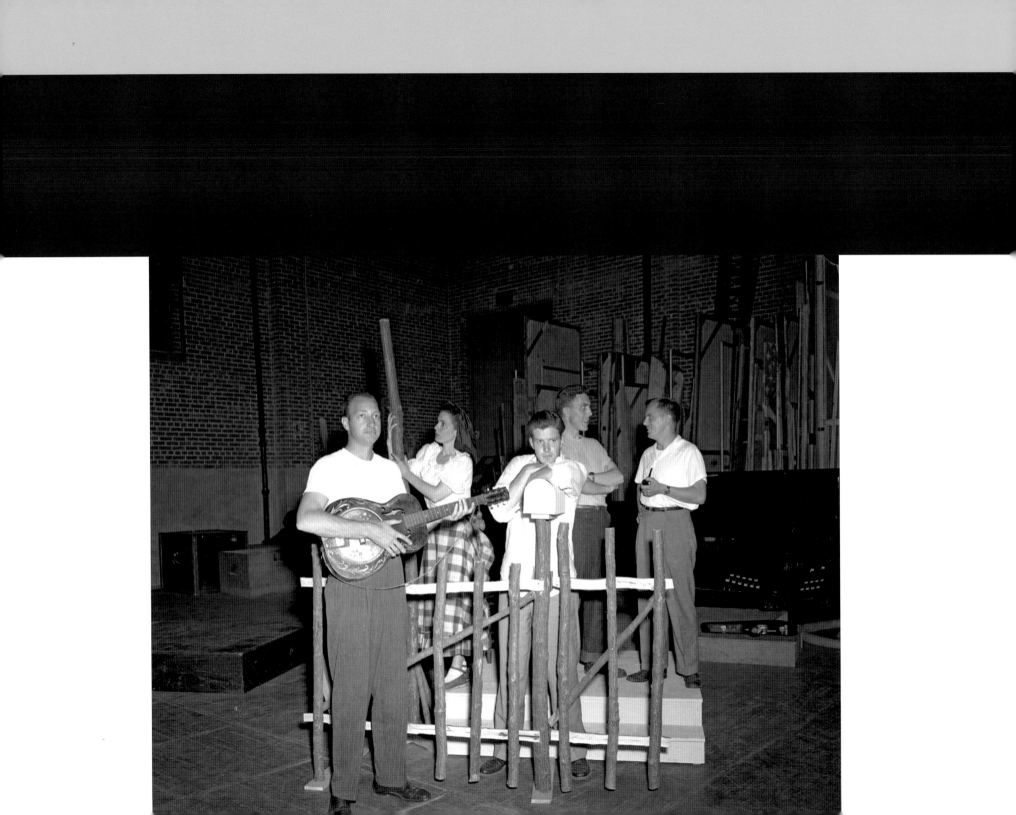

Off the Beaten Path

Facing. Down in the Valley
(K. Weill), July 15, 1948.
David Aiken (*holding guitar*),
Marion Bell. *IU Archives, 48-1002.*

*I*t has always been a goal of Indiana University Opera Theater to provide students and audiences with well-rounded programs, representing diverse aspects of the varied history of opera. In fact this is at the center of the mission of IU Opera Theater, as stated by Dean Richards. Frequently, IU Opera Theater programs operas that are historically or artistically important but not the kind of productions that would be offered by a company that relied solely on box office revenue. This is an example of how Indiana University Opera Theater is markedly different from professional companies. It is free to make programming decisions based on criteria that are not governed solely by profitability.

Production photographs in this chapter represent some of IU Opera Theater's more obscure programming choices, from *Down in the Valley,* by Kurt Weill, produced in 1948, to *Too Many Sopranos,* by faculty member Edwin Penhorwood, produced in 2007. These interesting operas do not fall easily into the categories of the other chapters in this book but are nonetheless an important segment of the history of IU Opera Theater.

Facing. Down in the Valley (K. Weill), July 15, 1948.
(*L to R*): Marion Bell, Kurt Weill, Hans Busch.
Composer Kurt Weill was also a part-time
faculty member. *IU Archives, 48-1013.*

Above. Street Scene (K. Weill), August 2, 3,
4, 5, 6, 1950. *IU Archives, 50-1801.*

Song of Norway (Wright and Forrest),
July 4, 5, 11, 12, 1952. *IU Archives, 52-1271.*

L'Enfant et les Sortilèges (*The Bewitched Child*, M. Ravel), December 16, 17, 1955. *IU Archives, 55-2119.*

Roberta (J. Kern), June 27, 28, July 5, 6,
1958. Lillian Garabedian (*center*).
IU Archives, 58-1344.

Capriccio (R. Strauss), December 12, 13, 1958. Grace Trester (*left*), Carolyn Whitmer (*dancer*). *IU Archives, 58-2087.*

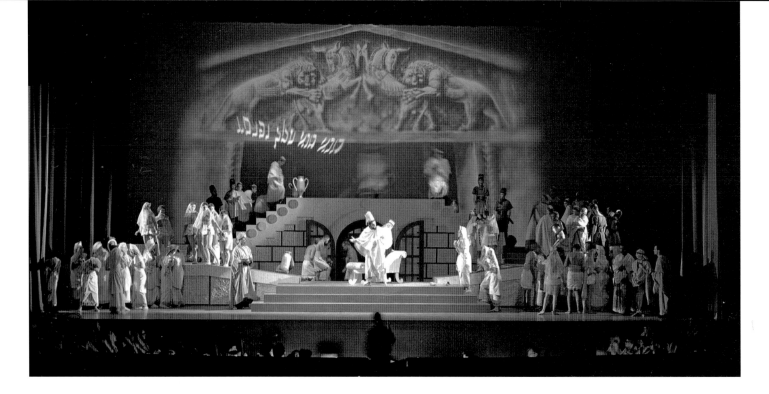

Facing top. Belshazzar (G. F. Handel), November 22, 1959. A projected Hebrew text scrolls across the wall continually and reads "thou art weighed in the balances and found wanting." *IU Photographic Services, 59-2003.*

Facing bottom. Le Coq d'or (*The Golden Cockerel,* N. Rimsky-Korsakoff), July 29, 30, August 5, 6, October 15, 22, November 12, 1960; January 21, 28, 1961. Astrologer: Allen R. White. *IU Archives, 60-1151.*

Above. Oedipus Rex (I. Stravinsky), November 7, 14, 21, 1964. Rendering by A. Nomikos.

Simon Boccanegra (G. Verdi),
December 5, 12, 1964; January 9,
16, 1965. Roy Samuelsen (*seated*).
IU Archives, 64-1663.6.

Facing. Deidamia (G. F. Handel),
October 11, 18, 25, 1969. Signe Landoe
as Nerea. *IU Archives, 69-1092.4.*

Jenůfa (L. Janáček), October 21, 28, November 4, 11, 1972.
Authenticity has always been a primary concern in costuming
IU Opera Theater. For *Jenůfa,* the last opera produced under
Dean Bain, many costumes came from personal friends of
Olga Dimitrov, the wife of Czech set designer Antonin
Dimitrov. *IU Archives, 72-1074.5.*

Facing. Jenůfa (L. Janáček), October 21, 28, November 4, 11,
1972. Act I of the production designed by Antonin Dimitrov.

Facing. The Mother of Us All (V. Thomson),
October 20, 26, 27, November 3, 1973. Jack Clay,
Melanie Young-Holliday. *IU Archives, 73-0436.11.*

Above. Doktor Faust (F. Busoni), November 16,
23, December 7, 1974. *IU Archives, 74-712.1.*

The Night Before Christmas (N. Rimsky-
Korsakov), November 19, December 2,
3, 10, 1977. *IU Archives, 77-594.5.*

The Turn of the Screw (B. Britten),
February 24, March 3, 10, 1979.
IU Archives, 79-20.13.

Arlecchino (*The Windows,* F. Busoni),
March 1, 8, 15, 1980. *IU Archives, 80-44.18.*

Facing. Prince Igor (A. Borodin), November 15,
22, December 6, 13, 1980. *IU Archives, 80-430.17.*

Tom Jones (F.-A. Philidor), January 28, February 4, 11, 1984.
(*L to R, front row*): chorus member, Randall Black, Richard
Rebilas, Heidi Geddert, Mary Dombek. *IU Archives, 84-6.17.*

L'Enfant et les Sortilèges (*The Bewitched Child*, M. Ravel),
November 10, 17, December 1, 8, 1984. Brian Scott,
Nancy Loshkajian. This was presented as a double
bill with another Ravel opera, *L'Heure espagnole*
(*The Spanish Hour*). *IU Archives, 84-342.11.*

Tamerlano (G. F. Handel), January 26, February 2, 9, 1985. (*L to R*): Gloria Nathan, Victoria Atwater, Previn Moore, Scott Gruoner. *IU Archives, 85-27.17.*

Too Many Sopranos (E. Penhorwood), February 2, 3, 9, 10, 2007. (*L to R*): Alan Dunbar, Lindsay Ammann, Siân Davies, Jacqueline Brecheen, Angela Mannino, Jacob Sentgeorge. *IU Photographic Services.*

David Effron, conductor (*on left*), and Tito Capobianco, stage director, in action during a staging rehearsal for *La Bohème.* A typical rehearsal schedule includes three weeks of coachings, one week of musical rehearsals with only the conductor, three weeks of staging rehearsals, and a final week of dress rehearsals.

Behind the Scenes

*I*t takes an army to produce an opera.

Since the very beginning of Indiana University Opera Theater, the Jacobs School of Music has invested in high production values. Dean Bain's successors have thoroughly embraced his philosophy of professionalism, realizing the importance of impressive opera productions in providing both quality education and entertainment. Thus far *Opera for All Seasons* has chronicled the public face of IU Opera Theater's first sixty years. We now turn to the many individuals who worked behind the scenes, some for the better part of the time covered by this book.

Because of the seamless appearance of IU Opera Theater productions onstage, the general public is often unaware of the large number of people required to produce an opera. At least 350 people were behind the scenes to support the triumphant 2008 production of *La Bohème*. Several technical production departments—construction, painting and properties, rigging, lighting, costuming and makeup—comprise a workforce of dozens of people, most of whom are students. Students provide not only nearly all the backstage support, but commit to extraordinarily long hours in doing so. After a Saturday night performance, it is not unusual that they will strike the set and set up a shell for a concert the next day, keeping them at the Musical Arts Center through the middle of the night.

In the early years of IU Opera Theater, technical support made do with carpenters, stagehands, and painters recruited from the student body or the university community, but by the mid-fifties, IU Opera Theater had evolved to the point of requiring professional staff in technical direction, costuming, construction, and lighting to support both the resident or guest designers and more sophisticated productions. Mario Cristini's years at IU Opera Theater truly launched the production infrastructure, culminating in the construction of the Musical Arts Center.

East Hall was the original home of Indiana University Opera Theater and was located at the site of the MAC. The hall itself had been used during World War II as a military training facility and was acquired by the growing Jacobs School as an additional performance space. It had a seating capacity of about 600 and a small stage intended for movies rather than theatrical use. Richard Scammon (1949–55) and Ed Gallagher (1955–58) are the earliest designers on record in IU Opera Theater. Paul Martin (1959–63) was known for his lighting in many early productions.

By the end of the fifties, a number of IU alumni were recruited as technical support for IU Opera Theater. Sigrid Insull (1958–67) joined the staff as set designer and costumer for the *Turandot* World's Fair tour. Ted Jones (1958–61) served as lighting designer and technical director. Richard Snyder (1964–68) served as technical director and left just before construction began on the MAC. Ted Jones returned in 1964 from a Fulbright fellowship to resume his duties as executive assistant to the general manager. He also developed and administered the Technical Studies Program (1971–96), which served for many years as a training ground for theater technicians and was the major source of skilled labor for IU Opera Theater.

When East Hall burned to the ground in the winter of 1968, it marked the end of the formative years of IU Opera Theater. The Musical Arts Center had already been designed and mostly funded, and was becoming a reality that would literally rise from the ashes of East Hall in just two and a half years. During construction, IU Opera Theater was housed at University Middle School, on the eastern border of the IU campus in Bloomington. This presented some logistical challenges since construction and painting was housed at the old Trees Center—now the site of the School of Education—and scenery was stored in the former Showers Furniture Company complex. IU Opera Theater now has a newer storage facility on the east side of campus.

George Calder was the first full-time IU Opera Theater Administrator, appointed by Dean Bain and serving the entirety of Dean Webb's tenure. Ted Jones and Richard Snyder had assisted Dean Bain with administrative duties beginning in 1964, but their primary responsibilities were as technical director and lighting designer. Calder was present for the transition from the limited East Hall to the even more restrictive University Middle School, and then to the new and modern Musical Arts Center. He coordinated the operas at University Middle School with all the challenges associated with that venue, while planning and preparing for productions in the new and impressively large MAC. Before coming to IU, Calder had been studying and working in Germany and Austria, where he served as a répétiteur in Mannheim. These experiences prepared him for the role of vocal coach, and in 1968 he became the executive assistant to the general manager. Calder had a tremendous impact on the success of IU Opera Theater. He retired in 1997 and graciously returned from retirement to serve as acting Opera Administrator in 2001.

Ted Jones's close involvement with the University Architect's office as the Jacobs School liaison during the construction of the MAC relieved him of his production responsibilities, creating the need for a new staff lighting designer. Allen R. White, who gained production experience serving in the armed forces, was recruited to serve as resident lighting designer in 1966. White served the Jacobs School of Music for thirty-seven years, distinguishing himself not only in lighting design for IU Opera Theater but also as an important national and international designer and producer. He retired in 2003 and was succeeded by Michael Schwandt.

Harold Mack also joined the staff during the transitional time leading up to the opening of the Musical Arts Center. Mack came to Indiana University in 1962 to study with Mario Cristini and had exhibited a true talent for technical design. In the years leading up to his appointment in 1968, he studied scenic design and painting. During his career at IU he designed several unforgettable productions before retiring in 2003. Kent Cyr, who had worked for several years as an assistant to Harold Mack, held the position of Technical Director from 2003 to 2005. Paul Brunner was appointed to the post in 2006.

Costumes have been made in-house since 1955, and at present, approximately 20,000 costumes are stored on the fourth floor of the Musical Arts Center. In 1971 Patricia Vanderbeke became the second costume coordinator for IU Opera Theater. Until then, Sigrid Insull had been costumer along with her other duties. Vanderbeke was the first costumer to deal with the enlarged demands for costuming brought about by moving into the MAC, and served until 1977. She was followed by Margaret Vincent (1977–79) and Marsha Le Boeuf (1979–80). Nancy Steele became head of costumes and makeup in 1980 and served until 1992, at which point Alice Bristow joined the company and served until 1997. Mary (Grusak) Cyr held the position from 1997 to 2002, when Parwin Farzad, a long-time employee in the IU Opera Theater costume shop, was appointed head of costuming and makeup.

Mario Cristini, IU Opera Theater's most influential designer, was trained as a scenographer in the European tradition, which means he took responsibility for all visual aspects of a production, including set design, costumes, and scenic painting. This philosophy was at the center of his design program and his teaching. Cristini was particularly well known for his painting ability and he emphasized this with his students. Dean Bain was especially interested in his painting technique, mainly because so much scenic information could be communicated in relatively little space. When Cristini passed away the summer before the opening of the Musical Arts Center, his former student C. David Higgins was appointed Master Scenic Artist. His addition to the staff was an effort to continue the painted illusionism for which Cristini was known. Higgins, as Harold Mack had done, became part of the resident design staff while retaining his other duties. In 1990 Tim Stebbins joined the staff as Assistant Scenic Artist and in 2002 was promoted to Head Scenic Artist. Higgins now serves the opera as Principal Designer.

Of course successful opera programs require more than high-quality visual aesthetics. There is a saying in the opera world: "Conductors come and go, but coaches go on forever." Coaches help the singers learn their parts and accompany the stage rehearsals on the piano. Some of our most dedicated coaches, who gave literally decades to IU Opera Theater, have included Carl Fuerstner, Elmar Burrows, Mark Phelps, and Shuichi Umeyama, plus innumerable student coaches such as Patrick Summers.

Another important aspect of Indiana University Opera Theater is not behind the scenes at all but at the "front of the house." These workers manage the interface between stage and public. Many readers will remember Richard Lathom as the long-time House Manager of the Musical Arts Center. He worked tirelessly to provide IU Opera Theater patrons with a welcoming environment. He joined the staff of the MAC in 1971 and was present at virtually every performance until his retirement in 2000. Tridib Pal joined the staff as House Manager in 2003 and carries on the long tradition of attentive audience service.

When George Calder retired in 1997, his responsibilities were split into two positions—Opera Executive Administrator and Instrumental Ensembles Coordinator. Tom Wieligman became Instrumental Ensembles Executive Administrator at that time, overseeing the instrumental forces of all student ensembles in the Jacobs School of Music. Mark R. Clark served as Opera Administrator from 1997 to 2001 and in 2002 Maria Levy took over that important role with marked success.

All of the people mentioned in this chapter have contributed to the success of Indiana University Opera Theater. Their professionalism and dedication to producing the very best opera performances possible have served the students and patrons of IU Opera Theater by providing both high-quality professional education and top-notch productions. The Jacobs School of Music is dedicated to providing both constituencies a meaningful and enriching theatrical experience far into the future.

Facing. A midnight set change from *The Merry Wives of Windsor* (*hanging on left*) to *The Love for Three Oranges* (*scenic elements lying on the floor*).

A "lighting hang" (installation) for *La Traviata*.
Theaters with multiple light bridges, common
in Europe, are more rare in the United States.

One of three full-time carpenters, Ken D'Eliso measures the interior of the carriage unit, a part of C. David Higgins's set for Massenet's *Cendrillon,* prior to painting. Scenic conception and construction for new productions begin two years prior to the opening.

After construction, scenery is laid out on the paint floor. Here, Assistant Scenic Artist Mark Smith applies the final touches to the house unit for *Cendrillon.*

Facing. Assembly of the *Falstaff* set. For scts that have been stored off site at the warehouse, paint touch-ups occur after assembly.

New sets, such as this world-class set for *La Bohème,* are assembled over the course of many days. Such large-scale productions take a year to construct and paint prior to assembly on stage.

The fly system allows scenic elements to be changed quickly during a performance. Since the scenic elements are very heavy, a system of counterweights balances each piece so that one person is able to "fly" it at any given moment. Here, two crew members are loading these counterweights, or "throwing bricks."

Facing. The Musical Arts Center stage proscenium opening is completely adjustable with a minimum width of 48 feet and a maximum width of 68 feet. Likewise, the height can be adjusted anywhere up to 36 feet. The large dimensions and adjustability make the MAC stage truly one-of-a-kind, as an average theater would be set at around 32 feet wide and 24 feet high. In this picture, the proscenium is lowered to its working level so that the attached elements may be changed.

After receiving costume renderings, the first step in the process is "swatching," or choosing suitable fabrics for each costume. Here, First Hand Dana Tzvetkov swatches the fairy chorus for *Cendrillon*.

Once costume construction is complete, final fittings are conducted in the presence of the designer to ensure proper fit, not only physically, but also according to the vision of the designer. This costume is worn by Fata Morgana in *The Love for Three Oranges*. (*L to R*): Dana Tzvetkov, Nancy Guyer, Soraya Noorzad.

Appendix 1

*Operas Performed, by Season,
with Composer, Venue, and
Performance Dates*

Academic Year	Opera Name	Composer Name	Venue*	Performance Date
1947–1948	*Down in the Valley*	Kurt Weill	IU Auditorium	Jul 15
1947–1948	*Hin und Zurück (There and Back)*	Paul Hindemith	IU Auditorium	Jul 15
1947–1948	*Les Contes d'Hoffmann (The Tales of Hoffmann)*	Jacques Offenbach	IU Auditorium	May 15
1948–1949	*Parsifal*	Richard Wagner	IU Auditorium	Apr 10, May 8
1949–1950	*Die lustige Witwe (The Merry Widow)*	Franz Lehár	The University Theater	Mar 10, 11, 15, 16, 17, 18
1949–1950	*The Firefly*	Rudolf Friml	East Hall	Jul 13, 14, 20, 21, 22
1949–1950	*The Jumping Frog of Calaveras County*	Lukas Foss	East Hall	May 18, 19, 20
1949–1950	*La Bohème*	Giacomo Puccini	East Hall	Mar 2, 3, 4
1949–1950	*The New Moon*	Sigmund Romberg	East Hall	Jun 29, 30, Jul 6, 7, 8
1949–1950	*Parsifal*	Richard Wagner	IU Auditorium	Apr 2
1949–1950	*Street Scene*	Kurt Weill	East Hall	Aug 2, 3, 4, 5, 6
1949–1950	*The Veil*	Bernard Rogers	East Hall	May 18, 19, 20
1950–1951	*The Chocolate Soldier*	Oscar Straus	East Hall	Jul 6, 7, 8
1950–1951	*Lost in the Stars*	Kurt Weill	East Hall	Jul 27, 28, 29, Aug 3, 4, 5
1950–1951	*The Mikado*	Arthur Sullivan	East Hall	Jul 13, 14, 15, 20, 21, 22

*All venues are located in Bloomington, Indiana, unless otherwise indicated.

Academic Year	Opera Name	Composer Name	Venue*	Performance Date
1950–1951	*Parsifal*	Richard Wagner	IU Auditorium	Mar 18
1950–1951	*Rigoletto*	Giuseppe Verdi	East Hall	Apr 27, 28, May 4, 5
1951–1952	*Amahl and the Night Visitors*	Gian-Carlo Menotti	East Hall	Feb 21, 22, 23, 24
1951–1952	*Die Entführung aus dem Serail (The Abduction from the Seraglio)*	Wolfgang Amadeus Mozart	East Hall	May 23, 24
1951–1952	*Kiss Me, Kate*	Cole Porter	East Hall	Aug 1, 2, 8, 9
1951–1952	*On the Town*	Leonard Bernstein	East Hall	Jul 18, 19, 25, 26
1951–1952	*A Parfait for Irene*	Walter Kaufmann	East Hall	Feb 21, 22, 23, 24
1951–1952	*Parsifal*	Richard Wagner	IU Auditorium	Apr 6
1951–1952	*Song of Norway*	Edvard Grieg. Adapted by Robert Wright and George Forrest	East Hall	Jul 4, 5, 11, 12
1952–1953	*Billy Budd*	Benjamin Britten	IU Auditorium	Dec 7
1952–1953	*Blossom Time*	Sigmund Romberg	East Hall	Jul 17, 18, 24, 25
1952–1953	*Brigadoon*	Frederick Loewe	East Hall	Jul 31, Aug 1, 7, 8
1952–1953	*Carousel*	Richard Rodgers	East Hall	Jul 9, 10, 11, 12
1952–1953	*Parsifal*	Richard Wagner	IU Auditorium	Mar 29
1953–1954	*Boris Godunov*	Modest Musorgsky	IU Auditorium	May 26
1953–1954	*Brigadoon*	Frederick Loewe	East Hall	Nov 13, 14
1953–1954	*Die Zauberflöte (The Magic Flute)*	Wolfgang Amadeus Mozart	East Hall	Jan 15, 16
1953–1954	*Finian's Rainbow*	Burton Lane	East Hall	Jul 2, 3, 4, 9, 10, 11
1953–1954	*Parsifal*	Richard Wagner	IU Auditorium	Apr 11
1953–1954	*Show Boat*	Jerome Kern	East Hall	Jul 30, 31, Aug 1, 6, 7, 8
1953–1954	*Where's Charley?*	Frank Loesser	East Hall	Jul 16, 17, 18, 23, 24, 25
1954–1955	*Ariadne auf Naxos*	Richard Strauss	East Hall	Mar 11, 12
1954–1955	*Die Fledermaus (The Bat)*	Johann Strauss Jr.	East Hall	Oct 22, 23, 24
1954–1955	*I Pagliacci*	Ruggiero Leoncavallo	East Hall	May 13, 14
1954–1955	*La Traviata*	Giuseppe Verdi	East Hall	Jan 14, 15
1954–1955	*Oklahoma!*	Richard Rodgers	East Hall	Jul 1, 2, 3, 8, 9, 10
1954–1955	*Oklahoma!*	Richard Rodgers	Mesker Memorial Amphitheater—Evansville, Ind.	Jul 16, 17
1954–1955	*Parsifal*	Richard Wagner	IU Auditorium	Apr 3

Academic Year	Opera Name	Composer Name	Venue*	Performance Date
1954–1955	*The Ruby*	Norman Dello Joio	East Hall	May 13, 14
1954–1955	*Wonderful Town*	Leonard Bernstein	East Hall	Jul 22, 23, 24, 29, 30, 31
1954–1955	*Wonderful Town*	Leonard Bernstein	Mesker Memorial Amphitheater—Evansville, Ind.	Aug 6, 7
1955–1956	*The Bartered Bride (Prodaná nevěsta)*	Bedřich Smetana	East Hall	Oct 14, 15
1955–1956	*Faust*	Charles Gounod	East Hall	Nov 18, 19, 20
1955–1956	*Il Tabarro (The Cloak)* 1st part of *Il Trittico (A Triptych)*	Giacomo Puccini	East Hall	Dec 16, 17
1955–1956	*The Land Between the Rivers*	Carl Van Buskirk	East Hall	May 18, 19
1955–1956	*L'Enfant et les Sortilèges (The Bewitched Child)*	Maurice Ravel	East Hall	Dec 16, 17
1955–1956	*Le Nozze di Figaro (The Marriage of Figaro)*	Wolfgang Amadeus Mozart	East Hall	Feb 24, 25
1955–1956	*Parsifal*	Richard Wagner	IU Auditorium	Mar 25
1955–1956	*Parsifal*	Richard Wagner	Kiel Municipal Opera House—St. Louis, Mo.	Apr 15
1956–1957	*Annie Get Your Gun*	Irving Berlin	East Hall	Jul 20, 21, 22, 27, 28, 29
1956–1957	*Annie Get Your Gun*	Irving Berlin	Mesker Memorial Amphitheater—Evansville, Ind.	Aug 4, 5
1956–1957	*Carmen*	Georges Bizet	East Hall	Mar 8, 9
1956–1957	*Così fan tutte (The School for Lovers)*	Wolfgang Amadeus Mozart	East Hall	May 17, 18, 21
1956–1957	*Falstaff*	Giuseppe Verdi	East Hall	Nov 18, 19
1956–1957	*Hänsel und Gretel (Hansel and Gretel)*	Engelbert Humperdinck	East Hall	Jan 11, 12, 14
1956–1957	*Il Barbiere di Siviglia (The Barber of Seville)*	Gioachino Rossini	East Hall	Oct 12, 13
1956–1957	*Parsifal*	Richard Wagner	IU Auditorium	Apr 14
1956–1957	*South Pacific*	Richard Rodgers	East Hall	Jun 29, 30, Jul 1, 6, 7, 8
1957–1958	*Albert Herring*	Benjamin Britten	East Hall	May 16, 17
1957–1958	*Amelia Goes to the Ball*	Gian-Carlo Menotti	East Hall	Feb 7, 8
1957–1958	*Candide*	Leonard Bernstein	East Hall	Dec 16, 17
1957–1958	*Cavalleria Rusticana (Rustic Chivalry)*	Pietro Mascagni	East Hall	Feb 7, 8

Academic Year	Opera Name	Composer Name	Venue*	Performance Date
1957–1958	*Don Pasquale*	Gaetano Donizetti	East Hall	Oct 12, 13
1957–1958	*The King and I*	Richard Rodgers	East Hall	Jul 19, 20, 21, 26, 27, 28
1957–1958	*The King and I*	Richard Rodgers	Mesker Memorial Amphitheater—Evansville, Ind.	Aug 3, 4
1957–1958	*La Bohème*	Giacomo Puccini	East Hall	Nov 15, 16, 17
1957–1958	*La Cenerentola (Cinderella)*	Gioachino Rossini	East Hall	Mar 7, 8
1957–1958	*Parsifal*	Richard Wagner	IU Auditorium	Mar 30
1957–1958	*Tosca*	Giacomo Puccini	East Hall	Jul 5, 6, 12, 13
1958–1959	*Capriccio*	Richard Strauss	East Hall	Dec 12, 13
1958–1959	*Die lustigen Weiber von Windsor (The Merry Wives of Windsor)*	Otto Nicolai	East Hall	Oct 10, 11
1958–1959	*Don Giovanni*	Wolfgang Amadeus Mozart	East Hall	Feb 20, 21, 28
1958–1959	*The Love for Three Oranges (Lyubov k Tryom Apelsinam)*	Sergei Prokofiev	East Hall	May 15, 16, 19
1958–1959	*Madama Butterfly*	Giacomo Puccini	East Hall	Nov 7, 8, 15, 22
1958–1959	*Parsifal*	Richard Wagner	IU Auditorium	Mar 22
1958–1959	*Roberta*	Jerome Kern	East Hall	Jun 27, 28, Jul 5, 6
1958–1959	*Un Ballo in Maschera (A Masked Ball)*	Giuseppe Verdi	East Hall	Aug 2, 4, Sep 19, 21
1959–1960	*Belshazzar*	George Frideric Handel	IU Auditorium	Nov 22
1959–1960	*Die Kluge (The Clever Girl)*	Carl Orff	East Hall	May 13, 14, 19
1959–1960	*La Rondine (The Swallow)*	Giacomo Puccini	East Hall	Feb 20, 27
1959–1960	*Les Contes d'Hoffmann (The Tales of Hoffmann)*	Jacques Offenbach	East Hall	Mar 18, 19, 26
1959–1960	*L'Heure espagnole (The Spanish Hour)*	Maurice Ravel	East Hall	May 13, 14, 19
1959–1960	*Manon Lescaut*	Giacomo Puccini	East Hall	Jul 3, 4, 10, 11
1959–1960	*The Most Happy Fella*	Frank Loesser	East Hall	Jul 24, 25, 31, Aug 1, 3, Jan 9, 13, Feb 5, 6, 13
1959–1960	*Parsifal*	Richard Wagner	IU Auditorium	Apr 10
1959–1960	*Rigoletto*	Giuseppe Verdi	East Hall	Oct 17, 19, 21, Nov 7
1959–1960	*Rigoletto*	Giuseppe Verdi	Indiana University campus—Gary, Ind.	Oct 30
1959–1960	*Rigoletto*	Giuseppe Verdi	Ripon, Wisc.	Oct 29

Academic Year	Opera Name	Composer Name	Venue*	Performance Date
1960–1961	*Die Zauberflöte (The Magic Flute)*	Wolfgang Amadeus Mozart	East Hall	Dec 3, 10, Jan 7, Apr 8
1960–1961	*Don Carlos*	Giuseppe Verdi	East Hall	Mar 4, 11, Apr 8
1960–1961	*La Traviata*	Giuseppe Verdi	East Hall	Oct 29, Nov 5, 19, Feb 4, Apr 22, 29
1960–1961	*Le Coq d'or (The Golden Cockerel)*	Nikolai Rimsky-Korsakov	East Hall	Jul 29, 30, Aug 5, 6, Oct 15, 22, Nov 12, Jan 21, 28
1960–1961	*Parsifal*	Richard Wagner	IU Auditorium	Mar 26
1960–1961	*The Scarlet Letter*	Walter Kaufmann	East Hall	May 6, 13, 16
1960–1961	*Street Scene*	Kurt Weill	East Hall	Jul 8, 9, 15, 16, 22, 23, Feb 11, 18, 25
1961–1962	*Brigadoon*	Frederick Loewe	Frangipani Room—Indiana Memorial Union	Jun 30, Jul 1, 2, 8, 10, 13, 18, 31, Aug 1, 8, Nov 10, 19, Dec 3, 10, Jan 7, 14, 21, 28, Feb 18
1961–1962	*Die Entführung aus dem Serail (The Abduction from the Seraglio)*	Wolfgang Amadeus Mozart	East Hall	Oct 14, 21, 28, Nov 18
1961–1962	*Die Entführung aus dem Serail (The Abduction from the Seraglio)*	Wolfgang Amadeus Mozart	North Central High School—Indianapolis	Feb 13
1961–1962	*Die Meistersinger von Nürnberg (The Mastersingers of Nuremberg)*	Richard Wagner	IU Auditorium	Jul 29, Aug 5
1961–1962	*Don Carlos*	Giuseppe Verdi	East Hall	Feb 10, 17, Mar 3
1961–1962	*Don Carlos*	Giuseppe Verdi	North Central High School—Indianapolis	Mar 15
1961–1962	*L'Elisir d'amore (The Elixir of Love)*	Gaetano Donizetti	East Hall	May 11, 12, Jul 7, 14, 21, 28, Aug 4
1961–1962	*A Midsummer Night's Dream*	Benjamin Britten	East Hall	Mar 10, 17, Apr 7
1961–1962	*A Midsummer Night's Dream*	Benjamin Britten	North Central High School—Indianapolis	Apr 17
1961–1962	*Parsifal*	Richard Wagner	IU Auditorium	Apr 15
1961–1962	*The Scarlet Letter*	Walter Kaufmann	East Hall	Jan 13, 20, Feb 24, Mar 31
1961–1962	*The Scarlet Letter*	Walter Kaufmann	North Central High School—Indianapolis	Jan 30
1961–1962	*Tosca*	Giacomo Puccini	East Hall	Dec 9, Jan 27, Feb 3, Apr 28

Academic Year	Opera Name	Composer Name	Venue*	Performance Date
1961–1962	*Tosca*	Giacomo Puccini	Indiana University Extension Center—South Bend, Ind.	Mar 24
1961–1962	*Tosca*	Giacomo Puccini	North Central High School—Indianapolis	Dec 12
1961–1962	*Werther*	Jules Massenet	East Hall	Nov 4, 11, Mar 31
1962–1963	*Carmen*	Georges Bizet	East Hall	Feb 2, 9, 16, Mar 9
1962–1963	*Carmen*	Georges Bizet	North Central High School—Indianapolis	Feb 12
1962–1963	*The Darkened City*	Bernhard Heiden	East Hall	Feb 23, Mar 2, 30
1962–1963	*Der Fliegende Holländer (The Flying Dutchman)*	Richard Wagner	IU Auditorium	Jul 29, Aug 5
1962–1963	*Die Fledermaus (The Bat)*	Johann Strauss Jr.	East Hall	Oct 13, 20, 27, Nov 17
1962–1963	*Die Fledermaus (The Bat)*	Johann Strauss Jr.	North Central High School—Indianapolis	Oct 16
1962–1963	*La Bohème*	Giacomo Puccini	East Hall	Nov 3, 10, Dec 1, Jan 12
1962–1963	*La Bohème*	Giacomo Puccini	North Central High School—Indianapolis	Nov 20
1962–1963	*La Forza del Destino (The Force of Destiny)*	Giuseppe Verdi	East Hall	Mar 16, 23, Apr 20
1962–1963	*La Forza del Destino (The Force of Destiny)*	Giuseppe Verdi	North Central High School—Indianapolis	Mar 26
1962–1963	*Le Nozze di Figaro (The Marriage of Figaro)*	Wolfgang Amadeus Mozart	East Hall	Dec 8, 15, Jan 19, 26
1962–1963	*Le Nozze di Figaro (The Marriage of Figaro)*	Wolfgang Amadeus Mozart	North Central High School—Indianapolis	Jan 8
1962–1963	*Parsifal*	Richard Wagner	IU Auditorium	Apr 7
1962–1963	*Ruddigore (The Witch's Curse)*	Arthur Sullivan	Frangipani Room—Indiana Memorial Union	Jul 13, 15, 18, 22, 30, Aug 1, 4, 5, 6, 7
1963–1964	*Aida*	Giuseppe Verdi	Memorial Stadium	Jul 27, 31, Aug 3, 7
1963–1964	*Così fan tutte (The School for Lovers)*	Wolfgang Amadeus Mozart	East Hall	Feb 22, 29, Apr 4, 11
1963–1964	*Così fan tutte (The School for Lovers)*	Wolfgang Amadeus Mozart	North Central High School—Indianapolis	Apr 14
1963–1964	*The Fair at Sorochinsk*	Modest Musorgsky	East Hall	Jul 6, 13, 20, Apr 27, May 4, 11
1963–1964	*The Fair at Sorochinsk*	Modest Musorgsky	Purdue University—W. Lafayette, Ind.	Jul 17

Academic Year	Opera Name	Composer Name	Venue*	Performance Date
1963–1964	*The Fantasticks*	Harvey L. Schmidt	Frangipani Room—Indiana Memorial Union	Jul 10, 14, 17, 21, 24, 28, Aug 5, Oct 16, 23, 25, 30, Nov 6, 13, 20
1963–1964	*Il Barbiere di Siviglia (The Barber of Seville)*	Gioachino Rossini	East Hall	Oct 12, 19, 26, Nov 2
1963–1964	*Il Barbiere di Siviglia (The Barber of Seville)*	Gioachino Rossini	North Central High School—Indianapolis	Oct 15
1963–1964	*Il Campanello di Notte (The Night Bell)*	Gaetano Donizetti	East Hall	Jul 6, 13, 20, Apr 27, May 4, 11
1963–1964	*Il Campanello di Notte (The Night Bell)*	Gaetano Donizetti	Purdue University—W. Lafayette, Ind.	Jul 17
1963–1964	*Kismet*	Alexander Borodin. Adapted by Robert Wright and George Forrest	East Hall	May 4
1963–1964	*La Fanciulla del West (The Girl of the Golden West)*	Giacomo Puccini	East Hall	Dec 14, Jan 11, Feb 8, 15
1963–1964	*La Fanciulla del West (The Girl of the Golden West)*	Giacomo Puccini	North Central High School—Indianapolis	Jan 14
1963–1964	*Lucia di Lammermoor*	Gaetano Donizetti	East Hall	Nov 9, 16, 23, Jan 11
1963–1964	*Lucia di Lammermoor*	Gaetano Donizetti	North Central High School—Indianapolis	Nov 12
1963–1964	*Parsifal*	Richard Wagner	IU Auditorium	Mar 15
1963–1964	*Peter Grimes*	Benjamin Britten	East Hall	Apr 25, May 2, 9, 15
1964–1965	*Boris Godunov*	Modest Musorgsky	East Hall	Feb 12, 13, 26, 27
1964–1965	*Die lustige Witwe (The Merry Widow)*	Franz Lehár	East Hall	May 1, 8, 15
1964–1965	*Don Giovanni*	Wolfgang Amadeus Mozart	East Hall	Mar 13, 19, 20, 27
1964–1965	*Don Giovanni*	Wolfgang Amadeus Mozart	MENC—North Central Division Conference—Indianapolis	Mar 22
1964–1965	*Gianni Schicchi*	Giacomo Puccini	East Hall	Nov 7, 14, 21
1964–1965	*Madama Butterfly*	Giacomo Puccini	East Hall	Oct 10, 17, 24, 31
1964–1965	*Oedipus Rex*	Igor Stravinsky	East Hall	Nov 7, 14, 21
1964–1965	*Simon Boccanegra*	Giuseppe Verdi	East Hall	Dec 5, 12, Jan 9, 16
1964–1965	*Turandot*	Giacomo Puccini	Memorial Stadium	Jul 29, Aug 1, 5, 8

Academic Year	Opera Name	Composer Name	Venue*	Performance Date
1964–1965	*Turandot*	Giacomo Puccini	New York World's Fair—Singer Bowl	Aug 17, 18
1965–1966	*Carmen*	Georges Bizet	Memorial Stadium	Jul 28, 31, Aug 1, 4, 6, 7
1965–1966	*Der Rosenkavalier (The Knight of the Rose)*	Richard Strauss	IU Auditorium	Apr 15, May 5
1965–1966	*Dialogues des Carmélites (The Dialogues of the Carmelites)*	Francis Poulenc	East Hall	Nov 13, 20, Dec 4, 6
1965–1966	*Die lustige Witwe (The Merry Widow)*	Franz Lehár	East Hall	Jul 3, 10, 16, 17
1965–1966	*Die Zauberflöte (The Magic Flute)*	Wolfgang Amadeus Mozart	East Hall	Jan 8, 15, Feb 12, 19
1965–1966	*Don Pasquale*	Gaetano Donizetti	Cressy Thomas Havens Auditorium—Kokomo, Ind.	Nov 12
1965–1966	*Macbeth*	Giuseppe Verdi	East Hall	Feb 26, Mar 5, 12, Apr 9
1965–1966	*Parsifal*	Richard Wagner	IU Auditorium	Mar 20
1966–1967	*Albert Herring*	Benjamin Britten	East Hall	Dec 10, 17, Jan 7, 14
1966–1967	*Boris Godunov*	Modest Musorgsky	East Hall	Jul 16, 20, 23
1966–1967	*Cavalleria Rusticana*	Pietro Mascagni	East Hall	Apr 4, 8, 15
1966–1967	*Die Entführung aus dem Serail (The Abduction from the Seraglio)*	Wolfgang Amadeus Mozart	East Hall	Oct 15, 22, 29
1966–1967	*A Hoosier Tale*	Walter Kaufmann	Clowes Memorial Hall—Indianapolis	Aug 6
1966–1967	*A Hoosier Tale*	Walter Kaufmann	IU Auditorium	Jul 30, Aug 3
1966–1967	*I Pagliacci*	Ruggiero Leoncavallo	East Hall	Mar 4, Apr 8, 15
1966–1967	*Parsifal*	Richard Wagner	IU Auditorium	Mar 19
1966–1967	*Quattro rusteghi (The Four Ruffians)*	Ermanno Wolf-Ferrari	East Hall	Apr 29, May 3, 6, 13
1966–1967	*Rigoletto*	Giuseppe Verdi	Clowes Memorial Hall—Indianapolis	Mar 11
1966–1967	*Rigoletto*	Giuseppe Verdi	East Hall	Feb 11, 18, 25
1966–1967	*Roméo et Juliette*	Charles Gounod	East Hall	Nov 5, 12, 19, Dec 3
1967–1968	*110 in the Shade*	Tom Jones, Harvey Schmidt	Frangipani Room—Indiana Memorial Union	Mar 22, 23, 24
1967–1968	*Albert Herring*	Benjamin Britten	East Hall	Jul 7, 8, 14, 15
1967–1968	*Andrea Chénier*	Umberto Giordano	University School Auditorium	Apr 27, May 4, 11
1967–1968	*The Bartered Bride (Prodaná nevěsta)*	Bedřich Smetana	Elliott Hall of Music, Purdue University—W. Lafayette, Ind.	Mar 6
1967–1968	*The Bartered Bride (Prodaná nevěsta)*	Bedřich Smetana	University School Auditorium	Feb 10, 17, 24

Academic Year	Opera Name	Composer Name	Venue*	Performance Date
1967–1968	*Elegy for Young Lovers*	Hans Werner Henze	University School Auditorium	Mar 2, 9, 16, 23
1967–1968	*Il Trovatore (The Troubadour)*	Giuseppe Verdi	Indiana University campus—Gary, Ind.	Jan 27
1967–1968	*Il Trovatore (The Troubadour)*	Giuseppe Verdi	Indiana University campus— Kokomo, Ind.	Jan 26
1967–1968	*Il Trovatore (The Troubadour)*	Giuseppe Verdi	Indiana University campus—South Bend, Ind.	Jan 28
1967–1968	*Il Trovatore (The Troubadour)*	Giuseppe Verdi	University School Auditorium	Dec 9, 16, Jan 6, 13
1967–1968	*L'Incoronazione di Poppea (The Coronation of Poppea)*	Claudio Monteverdi	University School Auditorium	Oct 14, 21, 28
1967–1968	*Manon*	Jules Massenet	University School Auditorium	Nov 4, 11, 18, Dec 2
1967–1968	*Mefistofele*	Arrigo Boito	Memorial Stadium	Jul 28, 29, Aug 4, 5
1967–1968	*Parsifal*	Richard Wagner	IU Auditorium	Mar 31
1968–1969	*110 in the Shade*	Tom Jones, Harvey Schmidt	Frangipani Room—Indiana Memorial Union	Jun 28, 29, Jul 6, 12, 13
1968–1969	*The Boys from Syracuse*	Richard Rodgers	Frangipani Room—Indiana Memorial Union	Jul 19, 20, 26, Aug 2, Oct 31, Nov 1, 6, 8
1968–1969	*Camelot*	Frederick Loewe	Alumni Hall—Indiana Memorial Union	Mar 2
1968–1969	*Die Meistersinger von Nürnberg (The Mastersingers of Nuremberg)*	Richard Wagner	IU Auditorium	Jul 27, 30, Aug 1, 3
1968–1969	*La Pique Dame (The Queen of Spades)*	Peter Ilyitch Tchaikovsky	University School Auditorium	Apr 26, May 3, 10, 17
1968–1969	*La Traviata*	Giuseppe Verdi	Indianapolis Showcase Series at North Central High School—Indianapolis	Apr 18
1968–1969	*La Traviata*	Giuseppe Verdi	Purdue University—W. Lafayette, Ind.	Nov 20
1968–1969	*La Traviata*	Giuseppe Verdi	University School Auditorium	Nov 9, 16, 23, Apr 12
1968–1969	*Le Nozze di Figaro (The Marriage of Figaro)*	Wolfgang Amadeus Mozart	University School Auditorium	Dec 7, 14, Jan 11, Feb 8, 15
1968–1969	*L'Italiana in Algeri (The Italian Girl in Algiers)*	Gioachino Rossini	University School Auditorium	Oct 12, 19, 26, Nov 2
1968–1969	*Parsifal*	Richard Wagner	IU Auditorium	Mar 23
1968–1969	*The Rake's Progress*	Igor Stravinsky	University School Auditorium	Feb 22, Mar 1, 8, 15

Academic Year	Opera Name	Composer Name	Venue*	Performance Date
1969–1970	*Ariadne auf Naxos*	Richard Strauss	University School Auditorium	Apr 25, May 2, 9, 16
1969–1970	*Camelot*	Frederick Loewe	Alumni Hall—Indiana Memorial Union	Jul 11, 12, 17, 19, Aug 1
1969–1970	*Deidamia*	George Frideric Handel	University School Auditorium	Oct 11, 18, 25
1969–1970	*Die Walküre (The Valkyrie)*	Richard Wagner	IU Auditorium	Mar 22
1969–1970	*Finian's Rainbow*	Burton Lane	Alumni Hall—Indiana Memorial Union	Oct 17, 19, 22, 24
1969–1970	*Love on Trial (La Pietra del Paragone)*	Gioachino Rossini	North Central High School—Indianapolis	Apr 11
1969–1970	*Love on Trial (La Pietra del Paragone)*	Gioachino Rossini	University School Auditorium	Dec 6, 13, Jan 10, 17, Feb 7
1969–1970	*Suor Angelica (Sister Angelica)*	Giacomo Puccini	IU Auditorium	Jul 26, 29, 31, Aug 2
1969–1970	*Tosca*	Giacomo Puccini	University School Auditorium	Nov 1, 8, 15, 22
1969–1970	*Un Ballo in Maschera (A Masked Ball)*	Giuseppe Verdi	Clowes Memorial Hall—Indianapolis	Feb 19, 20, 21
1969–1970	*Un Ballo in Maschera (A Masked Ball)*	Giuseppe Verdi	University School Auditorium	Feb 14, 28, Mar 7, 14, Apr 18
1970–1971	*Carousel*	Richard Rodgers	IU Auditorium	Mar 27, 28
1970–1971	*Così fan tutte (The School for Lovers)*	Wolfgang Amadeus Mozart	University School Auditorium	Feb 27, Mar 6, 13, 20
1970–1971	*Fidelio*	Ludwig van Beethoven	IU Auditorium	Jul 25, 29, Aug 1
1970–1971	*La Bohème*	Giacomo Puccini	University School Auditorium	Jan 9, 16, 23, Feb 20
1970–1971	*La Bohème*	Giacomo Puccini	Vanderburgh Auditorium—Evansville, Ind.	Feb 6
1970–1971	*Lucia di Lammermoor*	Gaetano Donizetti	Indiana University campus—South Bend, Ind.	Mar 21, 25
1970–1971	*Lucia di Lammermoor*	Gaetano Donizetti	North Central High School—Indianapolis	Oct 20
1970–1971	*Lucia di Lammermoor*	Gaetano Donizetti	University School Auditorium	Oct 17, 24, 31, Nov 7
1970–1971	*Manon Lescaut*	Giacomo Puccini	University School Auditorium	Nov 14, 21, Dec 5, 12
1970–1971	*Salome*	Richard Strauss	IU Auditorium	May 15
1971–1972	*Die Walküre (The Valkyrie)*	Richard Wagner	Musical Arts Center	Mar 25, Apr 1
1971–1972	*Don Giovanni*	Wolfgang Amadeus Mozart	Musical Arts Center	Jan 29, Feb 11, 12
1971–1972	*Falstaff*	Giuseppe Verdi	IU Auditorium	Jul 17, 21, 24, Sep 29, Oct 1
1971–1972	*Faust*	Charles Gounod	Musical Arts Center	Feb 19, 26, Mar 4
1971–1972	*Heracles*	John Eaton	Musical Arts Center	Apr 22, 29

Academic Year	Opera Name	Composer Name	Venue*	Performance Date
1971–1972	*Il Barbiere di Siviglia (The Barber of Seville)*	Gioachino Rossini	Indiana University Extension Center—South Bend, Ind.	Apr 28, 30, May 5, 6, 7
1971–1972	*Il Barbiere di Siviglia (The Barber of Seville)*	Gioachino Rossini	IU Auditorium	Oct 29, 30
1971–1972	*Il Barbiere di Siviglia (The Barber of Seville)*	Gioachino Rossini	Mesker Memorial Amphitheater—Evansville, Ind.	Feb 5
1971–1972	*Il Barbiere di Siviglia (The Barber of Seville)*	Gioachino Rossini	North Central High School—Indianapolis	Nov 3
1972–1973	*Arabella*	Richard Strauss	Musical Arts Center	Apr 7, 14, 21, 28
1972–1973	*Die Zauberflöte (The Magic Flute)*	Wolfgang Amadeus Mozart	Musical Arts Center	Feb 3, 10, 17, 24
1972–1973	*Don Carlos*	Giuseppe Verdi	Musical Arts Center	Aug 5, 9, 12, Sep 23, 29, 30
1972–1973	*Fiddler on the Roof*	Jerry Bock, Sheldon Harnick	Musical Arts Center	Jul 14, 15, 21, 22
1972–1973	*Il Trittico (A Triptych)*	Giacomo Puccini	Musical Arts Center	Nov 18, Dec 2, Jan 20, 27
1972–1973	*Il Trittico (A Triptych)*	Giacomo Puccini	North Central High School—Indianapolis	Nov 29
1972–1973	*Jenůfa*	Leoš Janáček	Musical Arts Center	Oct 21, 28, Nov 4, 11
1972–1973	*The Lion and Androcles*	John Eaton	Musical Arts Center Foyer*	Oct 24, 25
1972–1973	*Parsifal*	Richard Wagner	Musical Arts Center	Mar 3, 24, 31
1973–1974	*Carmen*	Georges Bizet	Musical Arts Center	Feb 2, 9, 16, 23
1973–1974	*Kiss Me, Kate*	Cole Porter	Musical Arts Center	Jul 13, 14, 19, 20
1973–1974	*Le Nozze di Figaro (The Marriage of Figaro)*	Wolfgang Amadeus Mozart	Musical Arts Center	Mar 2, 23, 30
1973–1974	*Les Contes d'Hoffmann (The Tales of Hoffmann)*	Jacques Offenbach	Musical Arts Center	Jul 28, Aug 3, 4, Nov 17, Dec 1, 8
1973–1974	*The Mother of Us All*	Virgil Thomson	Musical Arts Center	Oct 20, 26, 27, Nov 3
1973–1974	*Tosca*	Giacomo Puccini	Musical Arts Center	Sep 22, 29, Oct 6, 13
1973–1974	*Wozzeck*	Alban Berg	Musical Arts Center	Apr 13, 20, 27
1974–1975	*Die Entführung aus dem Serail (The Abduction from the Seraglio)*	Wolfgang Amadeus Mozart	Musical Arts Center	Oct 19, 26, Nov 2, 9
1974–1975	*Doktor Faust*	Ferruccio Busoni	Musical Arts Center	Nov 16, 23, Dec 7

*Opera taped in foyer for Public Television.

Academic Year	Opera Name	Composer Name	Venue*	Performance Date
1974–1975	*Eugene Onegin*	Peter Ilyich Tchaikovsky	Musical Arts Center	Feb 1, 8, 15, 22, Aug 3, 9, 10
1974–1975	*The Gondoliers*	Arthur Sullivan	Musical Arts Center	Jul 12, 13, 19, 20
1974–1975	*La Bohème*	Giacomo Puccini	Musical Arts Center	Sep 21, 28, Oct 5, 12
1974–1975	*Rigoletto*	Giuseppe Verdi	Musical Arts Center	Apr 5, 12, 19, 26
1974–1975	*Vanessa*	Samuel Barber	Musical Arts Center	Mar 1, 8, 15
1975–1976	*The Ballad of Baby Doe*	Douglas Moore	Musical Arts Center	Feb 28, Mar 5, 6, 13
1975–1976	*Il Mondo della Luna* (The World on the Moon)	Franz Joseph Haydn	Kennedy Center—Washington, D.C.	Sep 29
1975–1976	*Il Mondo della Luna* (The World on the Moon)	Franz Joseph Haydn	Musical Arts Center	Sep 20, 27, Oct 4, 11
1975–1976	*A Little Night Music*	Stephen Sondheim	Musical Arts Center	Jul 11, 12, 18, 19
1975–1976	*The Love for Three Oranges* (Lyubov k Tryom Apelsinam)	Sergei Prokofiev	Musical Arts Center	Oct 18, 25, Nov 1, 8
1975–1976	*Madama Butterfly*	Giacomo Puccini	Musical Arts Center	Aug 1, 2, 8, 9
1975–1976	*Parsifal*	Richard Wagner	Musical Arts Center	Apr 10, 17, 24
1975–1976	*Un Ballo in Maschera (A Masked Ball)*	Giuseppe Verdi	Musical Arts Center	Jan 31, Feb 7, 14, 21
1975–1976	*Werther*	Jules Massenet	Musical Arts Center	Nov 15, 22, Dec 6
1976–1977	*Bernstein on Broadway/Trouble in Tahiti*	Leonard Bernstein	Esco Music Centre—Ein-Gev, Israel	Apr 3
1976–1977	*Bernstein on Broadway/Trouble in Tahiti*	Leonard Bernstein	Hechal Hatarbut Ha'Ironi—Kfar Saba, Israel	Mar 30
1976–1977	*Bernstein on Broadway/Trouble in Tahiti*	Leonard Bernstein	Jerusalem Theatre—Jerusalem, Israel	Apr 6, 9
1976–1977	*Bernstein on Broadway/Trouble in Tahiti*	Leonard Bernstein	Kongresshaus Villach—Austria	Aug 21
1976–1977	*Bernstein on Broadway/Trouble in Tahiti*	Leonard Bernstein	Ljubljana, Slovenia	Aug 23
1976–1977	*Bernstein on Broadway/Trouble in Tahiti*	Leonard Bernstein	Megiddo Regional Theatre—Ein-Hashofet, Israel	Mar 29
1976–1977	*Bernstein on Broadway/Trouble in Tahiti*	Leonard Bernstein	Musical Arts Center	Mar 14
1976–1977	*Bernstein on Broadway/Trouble in Tahiti*	Leonard Bernstein	Nachmani Theatre—Tel Aviv, Israel	Apr 5, 7
1976–1977	*Bernstein on Broadway/Trouble in Tahiti*	Leonard Bernstein	Slovenia	Aug 25
1976–1977	*Carousel*	Richard Rodgers	IU Auditorium	Jul 10, 17, 24
1976–1977	*Falstaff*	Giuseppe Verdi	Musical Arts Center	Feb 19, 26, Mar 5, 12
1976–1977	*Idomeneo*	Wolfgang Amadeus Mozart	Musical Arts Center	Oct 16, 23, 30, Nov 6

Academic Year	Opera Name	Composer Name	Venue*	Performance Date
1976–1977	*Madama Butterfly*	Giacomo Puccini	Musical Arts Center	Sep 18, 25, Oct 2, 9
1976–1977	*Pelléas et Mélisande*	Claude Debussy	Musical Arts Center	Jan 29, Feb 5, 12
1976–1977	*Porgy and Bess*	George Gershwin	Musical Arts Center	Nov 13, 19, 20, Dec 4, 5, 6
1976–1977	*The Scarlet Letter*	Walter Kaufmann	Musical Arts Center	Apr 2, 9, 16, 23
1976–1977	*Susannah*	Carlisle Floyd	Musical Arts Center	Aug 6, 7, 8
1977–1978	*Carmen*	Georges Bizet	Musical Arts Center	Jan 28, Feb 3, 4, 11, 17, 18
1977–1978	*Così fan tutte (The School for Lovers)*	Wolfgang Amadeus Mozart	Musical Arts Center	Jul 2, 9, 15
1977–1978	*Danton and Robespierre*	John Eaton	Musical Arts Center	Apr 21, 22, 29
1977–1978	*Die Zauberflöte (The Magic Flute)*	Wolfgang Amadeus Mozart	Musical Arts Center	Oct 22, 29, Nov 4, 12
1977–1978	*Don Pasquale*	Gaetano Donizetti	Musical Arts Center	Feb 25, 26, Mar 3, 4
1977–1978	*Naughty Marietta*	Victor Herbert	Musical Arts Center	Jul 22, 23, 30, 31
1977–1978	*The Night Before Christmas*	Nicolai Rimsky-Korsakov	Musical Arts Center	Nov 19, Dec 2, 3, 10
1977–1978	*Peter Grimes*	Benjamin Britten	Musical Arts Center	Jul 22, 23
1977–1978	*Tosca*	Giacomo Puccini	Musical Arts Center	Sep 24, Oct 1, 8, 15, Nov 2
1978–1979	*Boris Godunov*	Modest Musorgsky	Musical Arts Center	Mar 17, Apr 7, 14, 21
1978–1979	*The Canterbury Tales*	Richard Hill	Musical Arts Center	Jun 30, Jul 1, 7, 8
1978–1979	*Così fan tutte (The School for Lovers)*	Wolfgang Amadeus Mozart	Musical Arts Center	Sep 23, 30, Oct 7, 14
1978–1979	*The Darkened City*	Bernhard Heiden	Musical Arts Center	Nov 18, Dec 2, 9
1978–1979	*Der Fliegende Holländer (The Flying Dutchman)*	Richard Wagner	Musical Arts Center	Jul 22, 29, Aug 5
1978–1979	*La Traviata*	Giuseppe Verdi	Musical Arts Center	Oct 21, 28, Nov 3, 4, 11
1978–1979	*Les Contes d'Hoffmann (The Tales of Hoffmann)*	Jacques Offenbach	Musical Arts Center	Jan 27, Feb 3, 9, 10, 17
1978–1979	*The Turn of the Screw*	Benjamin Britten	Musical Arts Center	Feb 24, Mar 3, 10
1979–1980	*Arlecchino*	Ferruccio Busoni	Musical Arts Center	Mar 1, 8, 15
1979–1980	*The Bartered Bride (Prodaná nevěsta)*	Bedřich Smetana	Musical Arts Center	Oct 27, Nov 2, 3, 10
1979–1980	*The Cry of Clytaemnestra*	John Eaton	Musical Arts Center	Mar 1, 8, 15
1979–1980	*Don Giovanni*	Wolfgang Amadeus Mozart	Musical Arts Center	Nov 17, Dec 1, 8, 15
1979–1980	*La Bohème*	Giacomo Puccini	Musical Arts Center	Jul 28, Aug 3, 4
1979–1980	*Manon*	Jules Massenet	Musical Arts Center	Apr 5, 12, 19, 26
1979–1980	*My Fair Lady*	Frederick Loewe	Musical Arts Center	Jul 13, 14, 20, 21

Academic Year	Opera Name	Composer Name	Venue*	Performance Date
1979–1980	*Porgy and Bess*	George Gershwin	Musical Arts Center	Feb 2, 9, 15, 16, 22, 23
1979–1980	*Susannah*	Carlisle Floyd	Musical Arts Center	Sep 29, Oct 5, 6, 13
1980–1981	*Don Pasquale*	Gaetano Donizetti	Musical Arts Center	Feb 28, Mar 7, 14
1980–1981	*The Greek Passion (Řecké pašije)*	Bohuslav Martinů	Metropolitan Opera—New York City	Apr 26
1980–1981	*The Greek Passion (Řecké pašije)*	Bohuslav Martinů	Musical Arts Center	Apr 4, 10, 11, 18
1980–1981	*Il Barbiere di Siviglia (The Barber of Seville)*	Gioachino Rossini	Musical Arts Center	Jul 26, Aug 2, 9
1980–1981	*Le Nozze di Figaro (The Marriage of Figaro)*	Wolfgang Amadeus Mozart	Musical Arts Center	Oct 25, 31, Nov 1, 8
1980–1981	*The Love for Three Oranges (Lyubov k Tryom Apelsinam)*	Sergei Prokofiev	Musical Arts Center	Jan 31, Feb 7, 14, 21
1980–1981	*The Music Man*	Meredith Willson	Musical Arts Center	Jul 11, 12, 18, 19
1980–1981	*Prince Igor*	Alexander Borodin	Musical Arts Center	Nov 15, 22, Dec 6, 13
1980–1981	*Rigoletto*	Giuseppe Verdi	Musical Arts Center	Sep 27, Oct 4, 11, 18
1981–1982	*Die Entführung aus dem Serail (The Abduction from the Seraglio)*	Wolfgang Amadeus Mozart	Musical Arts Center	Jan 30, Feb 6, 13, 20
1981–1982	*Die lustigen Weiber von Windsor (The Merry Wives of Windsor)*	Otto Nicolai	Musical Arts Center	Oct 24, 31, Nov 7, 14
1981–1982	*Faust*	Charles Gounod	Musical Arts Center	Feb 27, Mar 6, 12, 13
1981–1982	*Jakob Lenz*	Wolfgang Rihm	Musical Arts Center	Jul 11, 18
1981–1982	*Madama Butterfly*	Giacomo Puccini	Musical Arts Center	Sep 26, Oct 3, 10, 17
1981–1982	*Oklahoma!*	Richard Rodgers	Musical Arts Center	Jul 31, Aug 1, 7, 8
1981–1982	*Výlety pana Broučka (The Excursions of Mr. Broucek)*	Leoš Janáček	Musical Arts Center	Nov 21, Dec 5, 12
1981–1982	*Wozzeck*	Alban Berg	Musical Arts Center	Apr 3, 17, 24
1982–1983	*The Ballad of Baby Doe*	Douglas Moore	Musical Arts Center	Feb 26, Mar 4, 5
1982–1983	*Die Fledermaus (The Bat)*	Johann Strauss Jr.	Musical Arts Center	Jul 30, 31, Aug 6, 7
1982–1983	*Die Zauberflöte (The Magic Flute)*	Wolfgang Amadeus Mozart	Musical Arts Center	Jan 29, Feb 5, 12, 19
1982–1983	*Hänsel und Gretel (Hansel and Gretel)*	Engelbert Humperdinck	Musical Arts Center	Nov 13, 20, Dec 4, 11
1982–1983	*Il Barbiere di Siviglia (The Barber of Seville)*	Gioachino Rossini	Musical Arts Center	Sep 25, Oct 2, 9, 16,
1982–1983	*Il Trittico (A Triptych)*	Giacomo Puccini	Musical Arts Center	Apr 9, 16, 23
1982–1983	*The Most Happy Fella*	Frank Loesser	Musical Arts Center	Jul 9, 10, 16, 17
1982–1983	*Passion Play—Carmina Burana*	[anonymous]	First United Methodist Church	Mar 6, 7, 8

Academic Year	Opera Name	Composer Name	Venue*	Performance Date
1982–1983	*Soldier Boy, Soldier*	T. J. Anderson	Musical Arts Center	Oct 23, 30, Nov 6
1983–1984	*Boris Godunov*	Modest Musorgsky	Musical Arts Center	Oct 22, 29, Nov 5, 12
1983–1984	*Candide*	Leonard Bernstein	Musical Arts Center	Jul 30, Aug 5, 6
1983–1984	*Das Rheingold*	Richard Wagner	Musical Arts Center	Mar 31, Apr 7, 14, 21
1983–1984	*Die lustige Witwe (The Merry Widow)*	Franz Lehár	Musical Arts Center	Sep 24, Oct 1, 8, 15
1983–1984	*La Traviata*	Giuseppe Verdi	Musical Arts Center	Feb 18, 25, Mar 2, 3
1983–1984	*A Midsummer Night's Dream*	Benjamin Britten	Musical Arts Center	Dec 2, 3, 10
1983–1984	*Sweeney Todd*	Stephen Sondheim	Musical Arts Center	Jul 16, 22, 23
1983–1984	*Tom Jones*	François-André Philidor	Musical Arts Center	Jan 28, Feb 4, 11
1984–1985	*Assassinio nella cattedrale (Murder in the Cathedral)*	Ildebrando Pizzetti	Musical Arts Center	Mar 30, Apr 6, 13, 20
1984–1985	*Carmen*	Georges Bizet	Musical Arts Center	Jul 27, 28, Aug 2, 3
1984–1985	*Così fan tutte (The School for Lovers)*	Wolfgang Amadeus Mozart	Musical Arts Center	Oct 20, 27, Nov 3
1984–1985	*La Bohème*	Giacomo Puccini	Musical Arts Center	Feb 16, 23, Mar 1, 2
1984–1985	*La Fille du régiment (The Daughter of the Regiment)*	Gaetano Donizetti	Musical Arts Center	Jul 28, Aug 3, 4
1984–1985	*L'Enfant et les Sortilèges (The Bewitched Child)*	Maurice Ravel	Musical Arts Center	Nov 10, 17, Dec 1, 8
1984–1985	*L'Heure espagnole (The Spanish Hour)*	Maurice Ravel	Musical Arts Center	Nov 10, 17, Dec 1, 8
1984–1985	*Orphée aux enfers (Orpheus in the Underworld)*	Jacques Offenbach	Musical Arts Center	Sep 22, 29, Oct 6, 13
1984–1985	*Show Boat*	Jerome Kern	Musical Arts Center	Jul 13, 14, 20, 21
1984–1985	*Tamerlano*	George Frideric Handel	Musical Arts Center	Jan 26, Feb 2, 9
1985–1986	*Der Fliegende Holländer (The Flying Dutchman)*	Richard Wagner	Musical Arts Center	Nov 9, 16, Dec 7
1985–1986	*Die Fledermaus (The Bat)*	Johann Strauss Jr.	Musical Arts Center	Sep 28, Oct 4, 5, 12
1985–1986	*Don Giovanni*	Wolfgang Amadeus Mozart	Clowes Memorial Hall—Indianapolis	Feb 18
1985–1986	*Don Giovanni*	Wolfgang Amadeus Mozart	Musical Arts Center	Feb 8, 14, 15, 22
1985–1986	*La Sonnambula (The Sleepwalker)*	Vincenzo Bellini	Musical Arts Center	Oct 19, 26, Nov 2
1985–1986	*Man of La Mancha*	Mitch Leigh	Musical Arts Center	Jul 5, 6, 13, 19, 20
1985–1986	*The Tempest*	John Eaton	Musical Arts Center	Mar 8, 29, Apr 5

Academic Year	Opera Name	Composer Name	Venue*	Performance Date
1985–1986	*West Side Story*	Leonard Bernstein	Musical Arts Center	Apr 12, 18, 19, 26
1986–1987	*The Bartered Bride (Prodaná nevěsta)*	Bedřich Smetana	Musical Arts Center	Sep 27, Oct 3, 4, 11
1986–1987	*Camelot*	Frederick Loewe	Musical Arts Center	Jul 12, 18, 19, 26
1986–1987	*Dialogues des Carmélites (The Dialogues of the Carmelites)*	Francis Poulenc	Musical Arts Center	Feb 28, Mar 7, 27, 28
1986–1987	*The Legend of Tsar Saltan (Skazka o Tsare Saltane)*	Nicolai Rimsky-Korsakov	Musical Arts Center	Apr 4, 11, 18, 25
1986–1987	*L'Elisir d'amore (The Elixir of Love)*	Gaetano Donizetti	Musical Arts Center	Aug 2, 8, 9
1986–1987	*Le Nozze di Figaro (The Marriage of Figaro)*	Wolfgang Amadeus Mozart	Musical Arts Center	Nov 8, 14, 15, Dec 6
1986–1987	*The Rake's Progress*	Igor Stravinsky	Musical Arts Center	Oct 18, 25, 31, Nov 1
1986–1987	*Rigoletto*	Giuseppe Verdi	Musical Arts Center	Feb 7, 13, 14, 21
1987–1988	*Béatrice et Bénédict*	Hector Berlioz	Musical Arts Center	Feb 27, Mar 4, 5
1987–1988	*Candide*	Leonard Bernstein	Musical Arts Center	Oct 17, 24, 31
1987–1988	*The Crucible*	Robert Ward	Musical Arts Center	Aug 1, 7, 8
1987–1988	*Die Entführung aus dem Serail (The Abduction from the Seraglio)*	Wolfgang Amadeus Mozart	Musical Arts Center	Feb 6, 13, 20
1987–1988	*L'Orfeo*	Luigi Rossi	Musical Arts Center	Apr 2, 9, 23
1987–1988	*Madama Butterfly*	Giacomo Puccini	Musical Arts Center	Sep 26, Oct 2, 3, 10
1987–1988	*Mass*	Leonard Bernstein	Musical Arts Center	Apr 28
1987–1988	*Of Thee I Sing*	George Gershwin	Musical Arts Center	Jul 11, 18, 24, 25
1987–1988	*Peter Grimes*	Benjamin Britten	Musical Arts Center	Nov 7, 14, Dec 5
1988–1989	*Bluebeard's Castle*	Béla Bartók	Musical Arts Center	Feb 25, Mar 4, 25
1988–1989	*Die Zauberflote (The Magic Flute)*	Wolfgang Amadeus Mozart	Musical Arts Center	Oct 15, 22, 29, Nov 5
1988–1989	*Don Pasquale*	Gaetano Donizetti	Musical Arts Center	Sep 24, Oct 1, 8
1988–1989	*Eugene Onegin*	Peter Ilyich Tchaikovsky	Musical Arts Center	Nov 12, 19, Dec 3
1988–1989	*Gianni Schicchi* 3rd part of *Il Trittico (A Triptych)*	Giacomo Puccini	Musical Arts Center	Feb 25, Mar 4, 25
1988–1989	*Il Barbiere di Siviglia (The Barber of Seville)*	Gioachino Rossini	Musical Arts Center	Jul 30, Aug 5, 6
1988–1989	*Les Contes d'Hoffmann (The Tales of Hoffmann)*	Jacques Offenbach	Musical Arts Center	Apr 8, 14, 15, 22
1988–1989	*A Little Night Music*	Stephen Sondheim	Musical Arts Center	Jul 9, 16, 22, 23

Academic Year	Opera Name	Composer Name	Venue*	Performance Date
1988–1989	*Man of La Mancha*	Mitch Leigh	Musical Arts Center	Jan 28, Feb 4, 11, 18
1988–1989	*Mass*	Leonard Bernstein	Musical Arts Center	Sep 3
1988–1989	*Mass*	Leonard Bernstein	Tanglewood Music Center—Lenox, Mass.	Aug 27
1989–1990	*Così fan tutte (The School for Lovers)*	Wolfgang Amadeus Mozart	Musical Arts Center	Sep 23, 30, Oct 7
1989–1990	*The Cry of Clytaemnestra*	John Eaton	Moscow Conservatory, USSR	May 16, 19
1989–1990	*The Cry of Clytaemnestra*	John Eaton	Musical Arts Center	Mar 31, Apr 7, 14, 21
1989–1990	*Faust*	Charles Gounod	Musical Arts Center	Jan 27, Feb 3, 9, 10
1989–1990	*Francesca da Rimini*	Sergei Rachmaninoff	Musical Arts Center	Mar 31, Apr 7, 14, 21
1989–1990	*Francesca da Rimini*	Sergei Rachmaninoff	Moscow Conservatory, USSR	May 16, 19
1989–1990	*Hänsel und Gretel (Hansel and Gretel)*	Engelbert Humperdinck	Musical Arts Center	Nov 11, 18, 19, Dec 2
1989–1990	*Kismet*	Robert Wright, George Forrest	Musical Arts Center	Jul 8, 9, 15, 22
1989–1990	*La Bohème*	Giacomo Puccini	Musical Arts Center	Jul 29, Aug 4, 5
1989–1990	*La Rondine (The Swallow)*	Giacomo Puccini	Musical Arts Center	Feb 17, 24, Mar 3
1989 1990	*Otello*	Giuseppe Verdi	Musical Arts Center	Oct 14, 21, 28, Nov 4
1990–1991	*Amahl and the Night Visitors*	Gian-Carlo Menotti	Musical Arts Center	Nov 10, 17, 18, Dec 1
1990–1991	*Company*	Stephen Sondheim	Musical Arts Center	Jul 7, 13, 14, 21
1990–1991	*The Dawn of the Poor King*	Juan Orrego-Salas	Musical Arts Center	Nov 10, 17, 18, Dec 1
1990–1991	*Die Fledermaus (The Bat)*	Johann Strauss Jr.	Musical Arts Center	Jul 28, Aug 3, 4
1990–1991	*Die lustige Witwe (The Merry Widow)*	Franz Lehár	Musical Arts Center	Oct 13, 20, 27, Nov 3
1990–1991	*La Finta Giardiniera (The Pretend Gardener)*	Wolfgang Amadeus Mozart	Musical Arts Center	Apr 12, 13, 20
1990–1991	*La Traviata*	Giuseppe Verdi	Musical Arts Center	Sep 22, 28, 29, Oct 6
1990–1991	*L'Elisir d'amore (The Elixir of Love)*	Gaetano Donizetti	Musical Arts Center	Jan 26, Feb 1, 2, 9
1990–1991	*Wozzeck*	Alban Berg	Musical Arts Center	Feb 16, 22, 23, Mar 2
1991–1992	*Carmen*	Georges Bizet	Musical Arts Center	Apr 4, 11, 18, 25
1991–1992	*Carmina Burana*	Carl Orff	Musical Arts Center	Nov 16, 23, Dec 7
1991–1992	*Don Giovanni*	Wolfgang Amadeus Mozart	Musical Arts Center	Oct 26, Nov 1, 2, 9
1991–1992	*Hello, Dolly!*	Jerry Herman	Musical Arts Center	Jul 6, 12, 13, 20
1991–1992	*Jubilee*	Cole Porter	Musical Arts Center	Sep 28, Oct 5, 12, 19
1991–1992	*Madama Butterfly*	Giacomo Puccini	Musical Arts Center	Jul 27, Aug 2, 3
1991–1992	*I Pagliacci*	Ruggiero Leoncavallo	Musical Arts Center	Nov 16, 23, Dec 7

Academic Year	Opera Name	Composer Name	Venue*	Performance Date
1991–1992	*La Cenerentola (Cinderella)*	Gioachino Rossini	Musical Arts Center	Feb 1, 7, 8, 15
1991–1992	*The Rake's Progress*	Igor Stravinsky	Musical Arts Center	Feb 22, 29, Mar 7
1992–1993	*1600 Pennsylvania Avenue*	Leonard Bernstein	Kennedy Center—Washington, D.C.	Aug 11, 12, 13
1992–1993	*1600 Pennsylvania Avenue*	Leonard Bernstein	Musical Arts Center	Jul 11, 17, 18, 25
1992–1993	*Die Teufel von Loudun (The Devils of Loudun)*	Krzysztof Penderecki	Musical Arts Center	Feb 20, 27, Mar 6
1992–1993	*Falstaff*	Giuseppe Verdi	Musical Arts Center	Nov 14, 20, 21, Dec 5
1992–1993	*Le Nozze di Figaro (The Marriage of Figaro)*	Wolfgang Amadeus Mozart	Musical Arts Center	Sep 26, Oct 3, 10, 17
1992–1993	*Orfeo ed Euridice*	Christoph Willibald Gluck	Musical Arts Center	Oct 24, 31, Nov 7, 8
1992–1993	*Orphée aux enfers (Orpheus in the Underworld)*	Jacques Offenbach	Musical Arts Center	Jan 30, Feb 5, 6, 13
1992–1993	*Rigoletto*	Giuseppe Verdi	Musical Arts Center	Aug 1, 7, 8
1992–1993	*West Side Story*	Leonard Bernstein	Musical Arts Center	Apr 3, 9, 10, 17, 24
1993–1994	*Candide*	Leonard Bernstein	Musical Arts Center	Oct 16, 23, 30, Nov 6
1993–1994	*Carousel*	Richard Rodgers	Musical Arts Center	Jul 10, 16, 17, 24
1993–1994	*Die Entführung aus dem Serail (The Abduction from the Seraglio)*	Wolfgang Amadeus Mozart	Musical Arts Center	Sep 25, Oct 1, 2, 9
1993–1994	*Gianni Schicchi*	Giacomo Puccini	Musical Arts Center	Feb 19, 25, 26, Mar 5
1993–1994	*The Love for Three Oranges (Lyubov k Tryom Apelsinam)*	Sergei Prokofiev	Musical Arts Center	Apr 2, 9, 16, 23
1993–1994	*Lucia di Lammermoor*	Gaetano Donizetti	Musical Arts Center	Nov 19, 20, Dec 4
1993–1994	*Manon*	Jules Massenet	Musical Arts Center	Jan 29, Feb 4, 5, 12
1993–1994	*Tosca*	Giacomo Puccini	Musical Arts Center	Jul 31, Aug 6, 7
1994–1995	*The Bartered Bride (Prodaná nevěsta)*	Bedřich Smetana	Musical Arts Center	Jul 30, Aug 5, 6
1994–1995	*Die Zauberflöte (The Magic Flute)*	Wolfgang Amadeus Mozart	Musical Arts Center	Oct 15, 22, 29, Nov 5
1994–1995	*Fiddler on the Roof*	Jerry Bock	Musical Arts Center	Jul 9, 15, 16, 23
1994–1995	*Il Barbiere di Siviglia (The Barber of Seville)*	Gioachino Rossini	Musical Arts Center	Apr 1, 8, 15, 22
1994–1995	*La Bohème*	Giacomo Puccini	Musical Arts Center	Jan 28, Feb 3, 4, 11
1994–1995	*Nixon in China*	John Adams	Musical Arts Center	Feb 18, 24, 25, Mar 4
1994–1995	*Pelléas et Mélisande*	Claude Debussy	Musical Arts Center	Sep 24, 30, Oct 1, 8
1994–1995	*Peter Grimes*	Benjamin Britten	Musical Arts Center	Nov 12, 18, 19, Dec 3

Academic Year	Opera Name	Composer Name	Venue*	Performance Date
1995–1996	*Agrippina*	George Frideric Handel	Musical Arts Center	Nov 4, 10, 11, Dec 2
1995–1996	*Così fan tutte (The School for Lovers)*	Wolfgang Amadeus Mozart	Musical Arts Center	Sep 23, 29, 30, Oct 7
1995–1996	*Hänsel und Gretel (Hansel and Gretel)*	Engelbert Humperdinck	Musical Arts Center	Jan 27, Feb 2, 3, 10
1995–1996	*La Périchole*	Jacques Offenbach	Musical Arts Center	Jul 29, Aug 4, 5
1995–1996	*Les Contes d'Hoffmann (The Tales of Hoffmann)*	Jacques Offenbach	Musical Arts Center	Mar 30, Apr 6, 13, 20
1995–1996	*McTeague*	William Bolcom	Musical Arts Center	Feb 17, 23, 24, Mar 2
1995–1996	*Rigoletto*	Giuseppe Verdi	Musical Arts Center	Oct 14, 20, 21, 28
1995–1996	*South Pacific*	Richard Rodgers	Musical Arts Center	Jul 8, 14, 15, 22
1996–1997	*Ariadne auf Naxos*	Richard Strauss	Musical Arts Center	Nov 16, 22, 23, Dec 7
1996–1997	*Die Fledermaus (The Bat)*	Johann Strauss Jr.	Musical Arts Center	Oct 26, Nov 1, 2, 9
1996–1997	*Die lustige Witwe (The Merry Widow)*	Franz Lehár	Musical Arts Center	Jul 27, Aug 2, 3
1996–1997	*Don Giovanni*	Wolfgang Amadeus Mozart	Musical Arts Center	Sep 28, Oct 5, 12, 19
1996–1997	*The Ghosts of Versailles*	John Corigliano	Musical Arts Center	Apr 12, 18, 19, 26
1996–1997	*Il Turco in Italia (The Turk in Italy)*	Gioachino Rossini	Musical Arts Center	Feb 1, 7, 8, 15
1996–1997	*The King and I*	Richard Rodgers	Musical Arts Center	Jul 6, 12, 13, 20
1996–1997	*Madama Butterfly*	Giacomo Puccini	Musical Arts Center	Feb 22, 23, 28, Mar 1, 8
1997–1998	*Dialogues des Carmélites (The Dialogues of the Carmelites)*	Francis Poulenc	Musical Arts Center	Feb 21, 27, 28, Mar 7
1997–1998	*Don Pasquale*	Gaetano Donizetti	Musical Arts Center	Sep 27, Oct 4, 11, 18
1997–1998	*Eugene Onegin*	Peter Ilyich Tchaikovsky	Musical Arts Center	Oct 25, 31, Nov 1, 8
1997–1998	*Falstaff*	Giuseppe Verdi	Musical Arts Center	Apr 11, 17, 18, 25
1997–1998	*HMS Pinafore*	Arthur Sullivan	Musical Arts Center	Nov 15, 16, 21, 22
1997–1998	*Oklahoma!*	Richard Rodgers	Musical Arts Center	Jul 12, 18, 19, 26
1997–1998	*La Traviata*	Giuseppe Verdi	Musical Arts Center	Aug 2, 8, 9
1997–1998	*Le Nozze di Figaro (The Marriage of Figaro)*	Wolfgang Amadeus Mozart	Musical Arts Center	Jan 31, Feb 6, 7, 14
1998–1999	*Arabella*	Richard Strauss	Musical Arts Center	Feb 26, 27, Mar 5, 6
1998–1999	*Carmen*	Georges Bizet	Musical Arts Center	Oct 23, 24, 30, 31
1998–1999	*Die Zauberflöte (The Magic Flute)*	Wolfgang Amadeus Mozart	Musical Arts Center	Jul 31, 1, Aug 7, 8
1998–1999	*Down in the Valley*	Kurt Weill	Creative Arts Auditorium	Jan 15
1998–1999	*Down in the Valley*	Kurt Weill	Musical Arts Center	Jan 16

Academic Year	Opera Name	Composer Name	Venue*	Performance Date
1998–1999	*Idomeneo*	Wolfgang Amadeus Mozart	Musical Arts Center	Nov 13, 14, 20, 21
1998–1999	*Kiss Me, Kate*	Cole Porter	Musical Arts Center	Jul 10, 11, 17, 18
1998–1999	*La Cenerentola (Cinderella)*	Gioachino Rossini	Musical Arts Center	Feb 5, 6, 12, 13
1998–1999	*Mass*	Leonard Bernstein	Musical Arts Center	Apr 16, 17, 23, 24
1998–1999	*Orphée aux enfers (Orpheus in the Underworld)*	Jacques Offenbach	Musical Arts Center	Sep 25, 26, Oct 2, 3
1999–2000	*Gianni Schicchi*	Giacomo Puccini	Musical Arts Center	Nov 12, 13, 19, 20
1999–2000	*La Bohème*	Giacomo Puccini	Musical Arts Center	Jul 30, 31, Aug 6, 7
1999–2000	*The Love for Three Oranges (Lyubov k Tryom Apelsinam)*	Sergei Prokofiev	Musical Arts Center	Apr 7, 8, 14, 15
1999–2000	*Man of La Mancha*	Mitch Leigh	Musical Arts Center	Jul 9, 10, 16, 17
1999–2000	*The Rake's Progress*	Igor Stravinsky	Musical Arts Center	Feb 25, 26, Mar 3, 4
1999–2000	*The Rape of Lucretia*	Benjamin Britten	Musical Arts Center	Feb 4, 5, 11, 12
1999–2000	*Suor Angelica (Sister Angelica)* 2nd part of *Il Trittico (A Triptych)*	Giacomo Puccini	Musical Arts Center	Nov 12, 13, 19, 20
1999–2000	*Vanessa*	Samuel Barber	Musical Arts Center	Sep 24, 25, Oct 1, 2
1999–2000	*Wozzeck*	Alban Berg	Musical Arts Center	Oct 22, 23, 29, 30
2000–2001	*Candide*	Leonard Bernstein	Musical Arts Center	Apr 6, 7, 13, 14
2000–2001	*Così fan tutte (The School for Lovers)*	Wolfgang Amadeus Mozart	Musical Arts Center	Oct 20, 21, 27, 28
2000–2001	*Faust*	Charles Gounod	Musical Arts Center	Feb 2, 3, 9, 10
2000–2001	*Il Barbiere di Siviglia (The Barber of Seville)*	Gioachino Rossini	Musical Arts Center	Jul 28, 29, Aug 4, 5
2000–2001	*L'Elisir d'amore (The Elixir of Love)*	Gaetano Donizetti	Musical Arts Center	Sep 22, 23, 29, 30
2000–2001	*Rigoletto*	Giuseppe Verdi	Musical Arts Center	Feb 23, 24, Mar 2, 3
2000–2001	*The Sound of Music*	Richard Rodgers	Musical Arts Center	Jul 7, 8, 14, 15
2000–2001	*Susannah*	Carlisle Floyd	Musical Arts Center	Nov 10, 11, 17, 18
2001–2002	*The Bartered Bride (Prodaná nevěsta)*	Bedřich Smetana	Musical Arts Center	Feb 22, 23, Mar 1, 2
2001–2002	*Hänsel und Gretel (Hansel and Gretel)*	Engelbert Humperdinck	Musical Arts Center	Nov 10, 11, 16, 17
2001–2002	*Le Nozze di Figaro (The Marriage of Figaro)*	Wolfgang Amadeus Mozart	Musical Arts Center	Sep 21, 22, 28, 29
2001–2002	*Little Women*	Mark Adamo	Musical Arts Center	Feb 2, 3, 8, 9
2001–2002	*Lucia di Lammermoor*	Gaetano Donizetti	Musical Arts Center	Apr 5, 6, 12, 13
2001–2002	*Madama Butterfly*	Giacomo Puccini	Musical Arts Center	Jul 28, 29, Aug 3, 4

Academic Year	Opera Name	Composer Name	Venue*	Performance Date
2001–2002	*Manon*	Jules Massenet	Musical Arts Center	Oct 19, 20, 26, 27
2001–2002	*The Music Man*	Meredith Willson	Musical Arts Center	Jul 7, 8
2002–2003	*Die Fledermaus (The Bat)*	Johann Strauss Jr.	Musical Arts Center	Jul 27, 28, Aug 2, 3
2002–2003	*Don Giovanni*	Wolfgang Amadeus Mozart	Musical Arts Center	Sep 27, 28, Oct 4, 5
2002–2003	*Giulio Cesare (Julius Caesar)*	George Frideric Handel	Musical Arts Center	Oct 25, 26, Nov 1, 2
2002–2003	*Jeppe*	Sven-David Sandström	Musical Arts Center	Feb 7, 8, 14, 15
2002–2003	*La Traviata*	Giuseppe Verdi	Musical Arts Center	Feb 28, Mar 1, 7, 8
2002–2003	*Les Contes d'Hoffmann (The Tales of Hoffmann)*	Jacques Offenbach	Musical Arts Center	Nov 15, 16, 22, 23
2002–2003	*Putting It Together*	Stephen Sondheim	Musical Arts Center	Jul 6, 7, 12, 13
2002–2003	*West Side Story*	Leonard Bernstein	Musical Arts Center	Apr 11, 12, 18, 19
2003–2004	*The Ballad of Baby Doe*	Douglas Moore	Musical Arts Center	Feb 6, 7, 13, 14
2003–2004	*Die Entführung aus dem Serail (The Abduction from the Seraglio)*	Wolfgang Amadeus Mozart	Musical Arts Center	Sep 26, 27, Oct 3, 4
2003–2004	*Die lustige Witwe (The Merry Widow)*	Franz Lehár	Musical Arts Center	Oct 24, 25, Oct 31, Nov 1
2003–2004	*Don Pasquale*	Gaetano Donizetti	Musical Arts Center	Aug 1, 2, 8, 9
2003–2004	*Falstaff*	Giuseppe Verdi	Musical Arts Center	Nov 14, 15, 21, 22
2003–2004	*Il Turco in Italia (The Turk in Italy)*	Gioachino Rossini	Musical Arts Center	Feb 27, 28, Mar 5, 6
2003–2004	*Peter Grimes*	Benjamin Britten	Musical Arts Center	Apr 9, 10, 16, 17
2003–2004	*The Secret Garden*	Lucy Simon	Musical Arts Center	Jul 12, 18, 19
2004–2005	*Dialogues des Carmélites (The Dialogues of the Carmelites)*	Francis Poulenc	Musical Arts Center	Feb 25, 26, Mar 4, 5
2004–2005	*Die Zauberflöte (The Magic Flute)*	Wolfgang Amadeus Mozart	Musical Arts Center	Apr 8, 9, 15, 16
2004–2005	*Eugene Onegin*	Peter Ilyich Tchaikovsky	Musical Arts Center	Oct 22, 23, 29, 30
2004–2005	*La Bohème*	Giacomo Puccini	Musical Arts Center	Sep 24, 25, Oct 1, 2
2004–2005	*La Cenerentola (Cinderella)*	Gioachino Rossini	Musical Arts Center	Nov 12, 13, 19, 20
2004–2005	*She Loves Me*	Jerry Bock	Ruth N. Halls Theater	Jul 9, 10, 11
2004–2005	*Tosca*	Giacomo Puccini	IU Auditorium	Jul 30, 31
2004–2005	*A View from the Bridge*	William Bolcom	Musical Arts Center	Feb 4, 5, 11, 12
2005–2006	*Carmen*	Georges Bizet	Musical Arts Center	Apr 7, 8, 14, 15
2005–2006	*Così fan tutte (The School for Lovers)*	Wolfgang Amadeus Mozart	Musical Arts Center	Sep 23, 24, 30, Oct 1

Academic Year	Opera Name	Composer Name	Venue*	Performance Date
2005–2006	*HMS Pinafore*	Arthur Sullivan	Musical Arts Center	Jul 29, 30, Aug 5, 6
2005–2006	*Il Barbiere di Siviglia (The Barber of Seville)*	Gioachino Rossini	Musical Arts Center	Feb 3, 4, 10, 11
2005–2006	*A Midsummer Night's Dream*	Benjamin Britten	Musical Arts Center	Nov 11, 12, 18, 19
2005–2006	*Our Town*	Ned Rorem	Musical Arts Center	Feb 24, 25, Mar 3, 4
2005–2006	*Roméo et Juliette*	Charles Gounod	Musical Arts Center	Oct 21, 22, 28, 29
2006–2007	*Arabella*	Richard Strauss	Musical Arts Center	Feb 23, 24, Mar 2, 3
2006–2007	*Arlecchino*	Ferruccio Busoni	Musical Arts Center	Feb 2, 3, 9, 10
2006–2007	*Don Giovanni*	Wolfgang Amadeus Mozart	Musical Arts Center	Sep 22, 23, 29, 30
2006–2007	*Hänsel und Gretel (Hansel and Gretel)*	Engelbert Humperdinck	Musical Arts Center	Nov 10, 11, 17, 18
2006–2007	*Madama Butterfly*	Giacomo Puccini	Musical Arts Center	Apr 6, 7, 13, 14
2006–2007	*Manon*	Jules Massenet	Musical Arts Center	Oct 20, 21, 27, 28
2006–2007	*The Mikado*	Arthur Sullivan	Musical Arts Center	Jul 28, 29, Aug 4, 5
2006–2007	*Too Many Sopranos*	Edwin Penhorwood	Musical Arts Center	Feb 2, 3, 9, 10
2007–2008	*La Bohème*	Giacomo Puccini	Musical Arts Center	Nov 9, 10, 16, 17
2007–2008	*L'Elisir d'amore (The Elixir of Love)*	Gaetano Donizetti	Musical Arts Center	Jul 27, 28, Aug 3, 4
2007–2008	*Le Nozze di Figaro (The Marriage of Figaro)*	Wolfgang Amadeus Mozart	Musical Arts Center	Feb 22, 23, 29, Mar 1
2007–2008	*Les Contes d'Hoffmann (The Tales of Hoffmann)*	Jacques Offenbach	Musical Arts Center	Apr 4, 5, 11, 12
2007–2008	*Rigoletto*	Giuseppe Verdi	Musical Arts Center	Sep 21, 22, 28, 29
2007–2008	*Susannah*	Carlisle Floyd	Musical Arts Center	Oct 19, 20, 26, 27
2007–2008	*A Wedding*	William Bolcom	Musical Arts Center	Feb 1, 2, 8, 9
2008–2009	*Cendrillon*	Jules Massenet	Musical Arts Center	Feb 6, 7, 13, 14
2008–2009	*Die lustigen Weiber von Windsor (The Merry Wives of Windsor)*	Otto Nicolai	Musical Arts Center	Oct 24, 25, 31, Nov 1
2008–2009	*Giulio Cesare (Julius Caesar)*	George Frideric Handel	Musical Arts Center	Feb 27, 28, Mar 6, 7
2008–2009	*La Traviata*	Giuseppe Verdi	Musical Arts Center	Sep 26, 27, Oct 3, 4
2008–2009	*The Love for Three Oranges (Lyubov k Tryom Apelsinam)*	Sergei Prokofiev	Musical Arts Center	Nov 14, 15, 21, 22
2008–2009	*The Most Happy Fella*	Frank Loesser	Musical Arts Center	Apr 10, 11, 17, 18
2009–2010	*Die Zauberflöte (The Magic Flute)*	Wolfgang Amadeus Mozart	Musical Arts Center	Nov 13, 14, 20, 21
2009–2010	*La Rondine (The Swallow)*	Giacomo Puccini	Musical Arts Center	Feb 26, 27, Mar 5, 6

Academic Year	Opera Name	Composer Name	Venue*	Performance Date
2009–2010	*L'Italiana in Algeri (The Italian Girl in Algiers)*	Gioachino Rossini	Musical Arts Center	Sep 25, 26, Oct 2, 3
2009–2010	*Lucia di Lammermoor*	Gaetano Donizetti	Musical Arts Center	Feb 5, 6, 12, 13
2009–2010	*Roméo et Juliette*	Charles Gounod	Musical Arts Center	Oct 23, 24, 30, 31
2009–2010	*West Side Story*	Leonard Bernstein	Musical Arts Center	Apr 9, 10, 16, 17

Appendix 2

Operas Performed, by Title

Opera Name	Academic Years of Production	Opera Name	Academic Years of Production
110 in the Shade	1967–1968, 1968–1969	*Bernstein on Broadway*	1976–1977
1600 Pennsylvania Avenue	1992–1993	*Billy Budd*	1952–1953
Agrippina	1995–1996	*Blossom Time*	1952–1953
Aida	1963–1964	*Bluebeard's Castle*	1988–1989
Albert Herring	1957–1958, 1966–1967, 1967–1968	*La Bohème*	1949–1950, 1957–1958, 1962–1963, 1970–1971, 1974–1975, 1979–1980, 1984–1985, 1989–1990, 1994–1995, 1999–2000, 2004–2005, 2007–2008
Amahl and the Night Visitors	1951–1952, 1990–1991		
Amelia Goes to the Ball	1957–1958		
Andrea Chénier	1967–1968	*Boris Godunov*	1953–1954, 1964–1965, 1966–1967, 1978–1979, 1983–1984
Annie Get Your Gun	1956–1957		
Arabella	1972–1973, 1998–1999, 2006–2007	*The Boys from Syracuse*	1968–1969
		Brigadoon	1952–1953, 1953–1954, 1961–1962
Ariadne auf Naxos	1954–1955, 1969–1970, 1996–1997	*Camelot*	1968–1969, 1969–1970, 1986–1987
		Il Campanello di Notte (The Night Bell)	1963–1964
Arlecchino	1979–1980, 2006–2007		
The Ballad of Baby Doe	1975–1976, 1982–1983, 2003–2004	*Candide*	1957–1958, 1976–1977, 1983–1984, 1987–1988, 1993–1994, 2000–2001
Un Ballo in Maschera (A Masked Ball)	1958–1959, 1969–1970, 1975–1976		
		Canterbury Tales	1978–1979
Il Barbiere di Siviglia (The Barber of Seville)	1956–1957, 1963–1964, 1971–1972, 1980–1981, 1982–1983, 1988–1989, 1994–1995, 2000–2001, 2005–2006	*Capriccio*	1958–1959
		Carmen	1956–1957, 1962–1963, 1965–1966, 1973–1974, 1977–1978, 1991–1992, 1998–1999, 2005–2006
The Bartered Bride	1955–1956, 1967–1968, 1979–1980, 1986–1987, 1994–1995, 2001–2002		
Béatrice et Bénédict	1987–1988	*Carmina Burana*	1991–1992

Opera Name	Academic Years of Production	Opera Name	Academic Years of Production
Carousel	1952–1953, 1970–1971, 1976–1977, 1993–1994	*Down in the Valley*	1947–1948, 1998–1999
Cavalleria Rusticana	1957–1958, 1966–1967	*Elegy for Young Lovers*	1967–1968
Cendrillon	2008–2009	*Die Entführung aus dem Serail (The Abduction from the Seraglio)*	1951–1952, 1961–1962, 1966–1967, 1974–1975, 1981–1982, 1987–1988, 1993–1994, 2003–2004
La Cenerentola (Cinderella)	1957–1958, 1991–1992, 1998–1999, 2004–2005		
The Chocolate Soldier	1950–1951	*Eugene Onegin*	1974–1975, 1988–1989, 1997–1998, 2004–2005
Company	1990–1991	*The Excursions of Mr. Broucek*	1981–1982
Les Contes d'Hoffmann (The Tales of Hoffmann)	1947–1948, 1959–1960, 1973–1974, 1978–1979, 1988–1989, 1995–1996, 2002–2003, 2007–2008	*The Fair at Sorochinsk*	1963–1964
		Falstaff	1956–1957, 1971–1972, 1976–1977, 1992–1993, 1997–1998, 2003–2004
Le Coq d'or (The Golden Cockerel)	1960–1961	*La Fanciulla del West (The Girl of the Golden West)*	1963–1964
Così fan tutte	1956–1957, 1963–1964, 1970–1971, 1977–1978, 1978–1979, 1984–1985, 1989–1990, 1995–1996, 2000–2001, 2005–2006	*The Fantasticks*	1963–1964
		Faust	1955–1956, 1971–1972, 1981–1982, 1989–1990, 2000–2001
The Crucible	1987–1988	*Fiddler on the Roof*	1972–1973, 1994–1995
The Cry of Clytaemnestra	1979–1980, 1989–1990	*Fidelio*	1970–1971
Danton and Robespierre	1977–1978	*La Fille du Régiment (The Daughter of the Regiment)*	1984–1985
The Darkened City	1962–1963, 1978–1979		
The Dawn of the Poor King	1990–1991	*Finian's Rainbow*	1953–1954, 1969–1970
Deidamia	1969–1970	*La Finta Giardiniera (The Pretend Gardener)*	1990–1991
Dialogues des Carmélites	1965–1966, 1986–1987, 1997–1998, 2004–2005		
		The Firefly	1949–1950
Doktor Faust	1974–1975	*Die Fledermaus (The Bat)*	1954–1955, 1962–1963, 1982–1983, 1985–1986, 1990–1991, 1996–1997, 2002–2003
Don Carlos	1960–1961, 1961–1962, 1972–1973		
Don Giovanni	1958–1959, 1964–1965, 1971–1972, 1979–1980, 1985–1986, 1991–1992, 1996–1997, 2002–2003, 2006–2007	*Der Fliegende Holländer (The Flying Dutchman)*	1962–1963, 1978–1979, 1985–1986
		La Forza del Destino (The Force of Destiny)	1962–1963
Don Pasquale	1957–1958, 1965–1966, 1977–1978, 1980–1981, 1988–1989, 1997–1998, 2003–2004	*Francesca da Rimini*	1989–1990

Opera Name	Academic Years of Production	Opera Name	Academic Years of Production
The Ghosts of Versailles	1996–1997	L'Incoronazione di Poppea (The Coronation of Poppea)	1967–1968
Gianni Schicchi	1964–1965, 1988–1989, 1993–1994, 1999–2000	The Lion and Androcles	1972–1973
Giulio Cesare	2002–2003, 2008–2009	L'Italiana in Algeri (The Italian Girl in Algiers)	1968–1969, 2009–2010
The Gondoliers	1974–1975		
The Greek Passion	1980–1981	A Little Night Music	1975–1976, 1988–1989
Hänsel und Gretel	1956–1957, 1982–1983, 1989–1990, 1995–1996, 2001–2002, 2006–2007	Little Women	2001–2002
		L'Orfeo	1987–1988
Hello, Dolly!	1991–1992	Lost in the Stars	1950–1951
Heracles	1971–1972	The Love for Three Oranges (Lyubov k Tryom Apelsinam)	1958–1959, 1975–1976, 1980–1981, 1993–1994, 1999–2000, 2008–2009
Hin und Zurück (There and Back)	1947–1948		
HMS Pinafore	1997–1998, 2005–2006		
A Hoosier Tale	1966–1967	Love on Trial (La Pietra del Paragone)	1969–1970
Idomeneo	1976–1977, 1998–1999	Lucia di Lammermoor	1963–1964, 1970–1971, 1993–1994, 2001–2002, 2009–2010
Jakob Lenz	1981–1982		
Jenůfa	1972–1973	Die Lustige Witwe (The Merry Widow)	1949–1950, 1964–1965, 1965–1966, 1983–1984, 1990–1991, 1996–1997, 2003–2004
Jeppe	2002–2003		
Jubilee	1991–1992		
The Jumping Frog of Calaveras County	1949–1950	Die Lustigen Weiber von Windsor (The Merry Wives of Windsor)	1958–1959, 1981–1982, 2008–2009
The King and I	1957–1958, 1996–1997	Macbeth	1965–1966
Kismet	1963–1964, 1989–1990	Madama Butterfly	1958–1959, 1964–1965, 1975–1976, 1976–1977, 1981–1982, 1987–1988, 1991–1992, 1996–1997, 2001–2002, 2006–2007
Kiss Me, Kate	1951–1952, 1973–1974, 1998–1999		
Die Kluge (The Clever Girl)	1959–1960		
The Land Between the Rivers	1955–1956		
The Legend of Tsar Saltan	1986–1987	Man of La Mancha	1985–1986, 1988–1989, 1999–2000
L'Elisir d'amore (The Elixir of Love)	1961–1962, 1986–1987, 1990–1991, 2000–2001, 2007–2008		
		Manon	1967–1968, 1979–1980, 1993–1994, 2001–2002, 2006–2007
L'Enfant et les Sortilèges (The Bewitched Child)	1955–1956, 1984–1985	Manon Lescaut	1959–1960, 1970–1971
		Mass	1987–1988, 1988–1989, 1998–1999
L'Heure espagnole (The Spanish Hour)	1959–1960, 1984–1985	McTeague	1995–1996

Opera Name	Academic Years of Production	Opera Name	Academic Years of Production
Mefistofele	1967–1968	*A Parfait for Irene*	1951–1952
Die Meistersinger von Nürnberg (The Mastersingers of Nuremberg)	1961–1962, 1968–1969	*Parsifal*	1948–1949, 1949–1950, 1950–1951, 1951–1952, 1952–1953, 1953–1954, 1954–1955, 1955–1956, 1956–1957, 1957–1958, 1958–1959, 1959–1960, 1960–1961, 1961–1962, 1962–1963, 1963–1964, 1964–1965, 1965–1966, 1966–1967, 1967–1968, 1968–1969, 1972–1973, 1975–1976
A Midsummer Night's Dream	1961–1962, 1983–1984, 2005–2006		
The Mikado	1950–1951, 2006–2007		
Il Mondo della Luna (The World on the Moon)	1975–1976		
The Most Happy Fella	1959–1960, 1982–1983, 2008–2009		
The Mother of us All	1973–1974	*Passion Play—Carmina Burana*	1981–1982, 1982–1983
Murder in the Cathedral	1984–1985	*Pelléas et Mélisande*	1976–1977, 1994–1995
The Music Man	1980–1981, 2001–2002	*La Périchole*	1995–1996
My Fair Lady	1979–1980	*Peter Grimes*	1963–1964, 1977–1978, 1987–1988, 1994–1995, 2003–2004
Myshkin	1972–1973		
Naughty Marietta	1977–1978	*La Pietra del Paragone (Love on Trial)*	1969–1970
The New Moon	1949–1950		
The Night Before Christmas	1977–1978	*La Pique Dame (The Queen of Spades)*	1968–1969
Nixon in China	1994–1995		
Le Nozze di Figaro (The Marriage of Figaro)	1955–1956, 1962–1963, 1968–1969, 1973–1974, 1980–1981, 1986–1987, 1992–1993, 1997–1998, 2001–2002, 2007–2008	*Porgy and Bess*	1976–1977, 1979–1980
		Prince Igor	1980–1981
		Putting It Together	2002–2003
		Quattro Rusteghi (The Four Ruffians)	1966–1967
Oedipus Rex	1964–1965		
Of Thee I Sing	1987–1988	*The Rake's Progress*	1968–1969, 1986–1987, 1991–1992, 1999–2000
Oklahoma!	1954–1955, 1981–1982, 1997–1998		
On the Town	1951–1952	*The Rape of Lucretia*	1999–2000
Orfeo ed Euridice	1992–1993	*Das Rheingold*	1983–1984
Orphée aux Enfers (Orpheus in the Underworld)	1984–1985, 1992–1993, 1998–1999	*Rigoletto*	1950–1951, 1959–1960, 1966–1967, 1974–1975, 1980–1981, 1986–1987, 1992–1993, 1995–1996, 2000–2001, 2007–2008
Otello	1989–1990		
Our Town	2005–2006, 2005–2006		
I Pagliacci	1954–1955, 1966–1967, 1991–1992	*Roberta*	1958–1959

Opera Name	Academic Years of Production	Opera Name	Academic Years of Production
Roméo et Juliette	1966–1967, 2005–2006, 2009–2010	*La Traviata*	1954–1955, 1960–1961, 1968–1969, 1978–1979, 1983–1984, 1990–1991, 1997–1998, 2002–2003, 2008–2009
La Rondine (The Swallow)	1959–1960, 1989–1990, 2009–2010		
Der Rosenkavalier	1965–1966	*Il Trittico (A Triptych)*	1969–1970, 1972–1973, 1982–1983
The Ruby	1954–1955	*Trouble in Tahiti*	1976–1977
Ruddigore (The Witch's Curse)	1962–1963	*Il Trovatore*	1967–1968
Salome	1970–1971	*Turandot*	1964–1965
The Scarlet Letter	1960–1961, 1961–1962, 1976–1977	*Il Turco in Italia (The Turk in Italy)*	1996–1997, 2003–2004
The Secret Garden	2003–2004	*The Turn of the Screw*	1978–1979
She Loves Me	2004–2005	*Vanessa*	1974–1975, 1999–2000
Show Boat	1953–1954, 1984–1985	*The Veil*	1949–1950
Simon Boccanegra	1964–1965	*A View from the Bridge*	2004–2005
Soldier Boy, Soldier	1982–1983	*Die Walküre*	1969–1970, 1971–1972
Song of Norway	1951–1952	*A Wedding*	2007–2008
La Sonnambula (The Sleepwalker)	1985–1986	*Werther*	1961–1962, 1975–1976
The Sound of Music	2000–2001	*West Side Story*	1985–1986, 1992–1993, 2002–2003, 2009–2010
South Pacific	1956–1957, 1995–1996		
Street Scene	1949–1950, 1960–1961	*Where's Charley?*	1953–1954
Suor Angelica (Sister Angelica)	1999–2000	*Wonderful Town*	1954–1955
Susannah	1976–1977, 1979–1980, 2000–2001, 2007–2008	*Wozzeck*	1973–1974, 1981–1982, 1990–1991, 1999–2000
Sweeney Todd	1983–1984	*Die Zauberflöte (The Magic Flute)*	1953–1954, 1960–1961, 1965–1966, 1972–1973, 1977–1978, 1982–1983, 1988–1989, 1994–1995, 1998–1999, 2004–2005, 2009–2010
Il Tabarro (The Cloak)	1955–1956		
Tamerlano	1984–1985		
The Tempest	1985–1986		
Die Teufel von Loudun (The Devils of Loudun)	1992–1993		
Tom Jones	1983–1984		
Too Many Sopranos	2006–2007		
Tosca	1957–1958, 1961–1962, 1969–1970, 1973–1974, 1977–1978, 1993–1994, 2004–2005		

Appendix 3

Singers, Roles Performed, and Operas

Singer Name, Opera Roles Performed, Opera Name, Academic Year of Performance

Abel, Albert: Constable, *Der Rosenkavalier,* 1965–66

Abram, Cathy: Kate Pinkerton, *Madama Butterfly,* 1975–76; Mary, *The Ballad of Baby Doe,* 1975–76; Girl on the street, *Trouble in Tahiti,* 1976–77; Player, *Bernstein on Broadway,* 1976–77

Abram, Rebecca: Gilda, *Rigoletto,* 1986–87; Constanza, *Die Entführung aus dem Serail (The Abduction from the Seraglio),* 1987–88; Rosina, *Il Barbiere di Siviglia (The Barber of Seville),* 1988–89

Abrams, Dick: Intern, *Street Scene,* 1960–61

Abuyen, Adonis Duque: M. Javelinot, *Dialogues des Carmélites,* 2004–05; Abbate Cospicuo, *Arlecchino,* 2006–07; Peter, *Hänsel und Gretel,* 2006–07; Lindorf, *Les Contes d'Hoffmann (The Tales of Hoffmann),* 2007–08; Schaunard, *La Bohème,* 2007–08

Acker, Anne: Margarita, *West Side Story,* 2002–03

Ackerman, David: Mercurio (Mercury), *L'Orfeo,* 1987–88; Odysseus, *The Cry of Clytaemnestra,* 1989–90; Dr. Blind, *Die Fledermaus (The Bat),* 1990–91; Poet, *The Dawn of the Poor King,* 1990–91; Tenor, *Carmina Burana,* 1991–92; Budgen, *1600 Pennsylvania Avenue,* 1992–93; Pennsylvannia Delegate, *1600 Pennsylvania Avenue,* 1992–93

Adamczyk, Jane: Genevieve, *Pelléas et Mélisande,* 1976–77

Adams, Camille: Little Eva, *The King and I,* 1957–58

Adams, Darin: Lt. Joseph Cable, *South Pacific,* 1995–96; Marcus Schouler, *McTeague,* 1995–96; Marullo, *Rigoletto,* 1995–96; Count Danilo Danilovitch, *Die lustige Witwe (The Merry Widow),* 1996–97; Pierre-Augustin de Beaumarchais, *The Ghosts of Versailles,* 1996–97; Curly, *Oklahoma!,* 1997–98

Adams, David: Marschallin's Hairdresser, *Der Rosenkavalier,* 1965–66; First Prisoner, *Fidelio,* 1970–71

Adams, James: Endimione, *L'Orfeo,* 1987–88

Adams, Jay: Amantio di Nicolao, *Gianni Schicchi,* 1988–89; The Barber, *Man of La Mancha,* 1988–89; Njegus, *Die lustige Witwe (The Merry Widow),* 1990–91; Mowgli (Charles Rausmiller), *Jubilee,* 1991–92; Don Curzio, *Le Nozze di Figaro (The Marriage of Figaro),* 1992–93; Schrank, *West Side Story,* 1992–93; Pasha Selim, *Die Entführung aus dem Serail (The Abduction from the Seraglio),* 1993–94; Alcindoro, *La Bohème,* 1994–95

Adams, Katherine: Madame Khadja, *Die lustige Witwe (The Merry Widow),* 1949–50; Mrs. Olga Olsen, *Street Scene,* 1949–50

Adams, Mark: A Tree, *L'Enfant et les Sortilèges (The Bewitched Child),* 1984–85; Bernardo, *West Side Story,* 1985–86; Arthur, *Camelot,* 1986–87; Third Sailor, *The Legend of Tsar Saltan,* 1986–87

Adams, Nancy: Amelia Grimaldi (Maria Boccanegra), *Simon Boccanegra,* 1964–65; Donna Elvira, *Don Giovanni,* 1964–65; Hostess of the Inn, *Boris Godunov,* 1964–65; La Ciesca, *Gianni Schicchi,* 1964–65; First Lady, *Die Zauberflöte (The Magic Flute),* 1965–66; Lady Macbeth, *Macbeth,* 1965–66; Praskovia, *Die lustige Witwe (The Merry Widow),* 1965–66; Lady Billows, *Albert Herring,* 1966–67

Adams, Philip: The Padre, *Man of La Mancha,* 1988–89

Adams, Ruth: Pearl, *The Scarlet Letter,* 1976–77; Yniold, *Pelléas et Mélisande,* 1976–77

Adams, Sam: Andrew MacLaren, *Brigadoon,* 1961–62

Adams, Sheri: Ado Annie Carnes, *Oklahoma!,* 1997–98

Adamson, Philip: Marco, *Il Trittico (A Triptych),* 1969–70; Sciarrone, *Tosca,* 1969–70

Adamson, Spencer: Hermann, *Les Contes d'Hoffmann (The Tales of Hoffmann),* 2002–03; Schlemil, *Les Contes d'Hoffmann (The Tales of Hoffmann),* 2002–03

Adkins, Andrea: Emily, *The Ballad of Baby Doe,* 1982–83; Woglinde, *Das Rheingold,* 1983–84; Xenia, *Boris Godunov,* 1983–84; Concepcion, *L'Heure espagnole (The Spanish Hour),* 1984–85; Coryphee, *Murder in the Cathedral,* 1984–85; Magnolia, *Show Boat,* 1984–85; Aldonza / Dulcinea, *Man of La Mancha,* 1985–86; Anita, *West Side Story,* 1985–86; Rosalinda, *Die Fledermaus (The Bat),* 1985–86; Anne Trulove, *The Rake's Progress,* 1986–87; Blanche, *Dialogues des Carmélites,* 1986–87; Cio-Cio San, *Madama Butterfly,* 1987–88

Adkins, Ted: Ajax, *The Cry of Clytaemnestra,* 1979–80; Colline, *La Bohème,* 1979–80; Commendatore, *Don Giovanni,* 1979–80; Count des Grieux, *Manon,* 1979–80; Policeman, *Porgy and Bess,* 1979–80; An Old Man, *The Greek Passion,* 1980–81; Celio, *The Love for Three Oranges,* 1980–81; Olin Britt, *The Music Man,* 1980–81; Sparafucile, *Rigoletto,* 1980–81; Jud Fry, *Oklahoma!,* 1981–82; Mephistopheles, *Faust,* 1981–82; The Bonze, *Madama Butterfly,* 1981–82; Don Basilio, *Il Barbiere di Siviglia (The Barber of Seville),* 1982–83; Pimen, *Boris Godunov,* 1983–84

Aguiar, Marcos: Don Jose, *Carmen,* 2005–06; Lt. Pinkerton, *Madama Butterfly,* 2006–07

Aiken, David: Dappertutto, *Les Contes d'Hoffmann (The Tales of Hoffmann),* 1947–48; Dr. Miracle, *Les Contes d'Hoffmann (The Tales of Hoffmann),* 1947–48; Lindorf, *Les Contes d'Hoffmann (The Tales of Hoffmann),* 1947–48; The Leader, *Down in the Valley,* 1947–48; Amfortas, *Parsifal,* 1948–49; Mr. Frank Maurant, *Street Scene,* 1949–50; Parsifal, *Parsifal,* 1968–69; Walther Von Stolzing, *Die Meistersinger von Nürnberg (The Mastersingers of Nuremberg),* 1968–69; Bacchus/Tenor, *Ariadne auf Naxos,* 1969–70; Florestan, *Fidelio,* 1970–71; Herod, *Salome,* 1970–71; Lichas, *Heracles,* 1971–72; Parsifal, *Parsifal,* 1972–73; Mephistopheles, *Doktor Faust,* 1974–75

Aikin, Laura: Cunegonde, *Candide,* 1987–88; Madame Merville, *A Little Night Music,* 1988–89; Mrs. Nordstrom, *A Little Night Music,* 1988–89; Olympia, *Les Contes d'Hoffmann (The Tales of Hoffmann),* 1988–89; Gretel, *Hänsel und Gretel,* 1989–90

Aker, Linda: First Maid, *The Boys from Syracuse,* 1968–69

Akers, William: Old Astrologer, *Le Coq d'or (The Golden Cockerel),* 1960–61

Aladren, Eduardo: Rodolpho, *A View from the Bridge,* 2004–05

Albright, Jan: Lauretta, *Il Trittico (A Triptych),* 1969–70

Alderson, Alan: Ike Skidmore, *Oklahoma!,* 1981–82

Alewine, Jeffrey: A-Rab, *West Side Story,* 2002–03

Alex, Gene: Hermann, *Les Contes d'Hoffmann (The Tales of Hoffmann),* 1973–74; Sciarrone, *Tosca,* 1973–74; The Duke of Plaza-Toro, *The Gondoliers,* 1974–75;

Zaretsky, *Eugene Onegin,* 1974–75; Johann, *Werther,* 1975–76; Prince Yamadori, *Madama Butterfly,* 1975–76; Silvano, *Un Ballo in Maschera (A Masked Ball),* 1975–76; The Beadle (and Jailer), *The Scarlet Letter,* 1976–77; Etienne Grandet, *Naughty Marietta,* 1977–78

Alexander, Daniel: Masetto, *Don Giovanni,* 1996–97; The King, *The King and I,* 1996–97

Alexander, Ivan: Tom of Warwick, *Camelot,* 1986–87

Alexander, John: Man in Armor, *Die Zauberflöte (The Magic Flute),* 1965–66

Alexander, Ralph: Frank, *Brigadoon,* 1961–62; Townsman, *Kismet,* 1963–64

Al-Jabir, Mohammed: Vallon, *Show Boat,* 1984–85

Allard, Maurice: A mute, *Die Entführung aus dem Serail (The Abduction from the Seraglio),* 1951–52; Page, *Parsifal,* 1951–52; Novice's Friend, *Billy Budd,* 1952–53; Page, *Parsifal,* 1952–53

Allardice, Robin: Aspen, *The Veil,* 1949–50; Clotilde, *The New Moon,* 1949–50; Mrs. Greta Fiorentino, *Street Scene,* 1949–50

Allbritten, James: Rev. Horace Adams, *Peter Grimes,* 1987–88; Nathanael, *Les Contes d'Hoffmann (The Tales of Hoffmann),* 1988–89; Triquet, *Eugene Onegin,* 1988–89; Alfredo Germont, *La Traviata,* 1990–91; Don Ottavio, *Don Giovanni,* 1991–92; Don Ramiro, *La Cenerentola (Cinderella),* 1991–92; Chevalier des Grieux, *Manon,* 1993–94; Jenik, *The Bartered Bride,* 1994–95; Piquillo, *La Périchole,* 1995–96

Allen, Barry: Photographer, *Albert Herring,* 1966–67; Policeman, *Albert Herring,* 1966–67

Allen, Cheryl: Voice of the Mother, *Les Contes d'Hoffmann (The Tales of Hoffmann),* 1978–79; Mrs. Ott, *Susannah,* 1979–80

Allen, Ferris: Ser Metteo del Sarto, *Arlecchino,* 2006–07; Jules, *A Wedding,* 2007–08

Allen, Gail: Luciana, *The Boys from Syracuse,* 1968–69

Allen, Helen: Clorinda, *La Cenerentola (Cinderella),* 1998–99

Allen, Lindsey: Pauline, *West Side Story,* 2002–03

Allicock, Aubrey: Unnamed Bass, *Too Many Sopranos,* 2006–07; Figaro, *Le Nozze di Figaro (The Marriage of Figaro),* 2007–08; Marullo, *Rigoletto,* 2007–08

Allison, Linda: Fortune, *L'Incoronazione di Poppea (The Coronation of Poppea),* 1967–68

Almond, Christopher: Player, *Mass,* 1987–88; Blues Singer, *Mass,* 1988–89

Almquist, Nancy: Mary, *The Ballad of Baby Doe,* 1982–83

Alt, Evelyn: Meg, *The Ballad of Baby Doe,* 1975–76

Althof, Stephanie: Dame Quickly, *Falstaff,* 1992–93

Altizer, Dennis: Gastone, *La Traviata,* 1983–84; Missail, *Boris Godunov,* 1983–84; Hortensius, *La Fille du régiment (The Daughter of the Regiment),* 1984–85; Knight, *Murder in the Cathedral,* 1984–85; Pluto, *Orphée aux enfers (Orpheus in the Underworld),* 1984–85; Dr. Sanson Carrasco / The Duke, *Man of La Mancha,* 1985–86

Altobello, Katherine: Maid, *Manon,* 2001–02; Mrs. Winthrop, *The Secret Garden,* 2003–04; Mrs. Wright, *The Secret Garden,* 2003–04; Silver Dollar (grown up), *The Ballad of Baby Doe,* 2003–04; Madame Larina, *Eugene Onegin,* 2004–05

Alvarez, Maria: Pauline, *La Pique Dame (The Queen of Spades),* 1968–69; The Monitor of the Convent, *Il Trittico (A Triptych),* 1969–70

Amaize, Odekhiren: Teucer, *The Cry of Clytaemnestra,* 1989–90; Balthasar, *Amahl and the Night Visitors,* 1990–91; The Doctor, *Wozzeck,* 1990–91; Sparafucile, *Rigoletto,* 1992–93

Ambrose, Holmes: Baron Schober, *Blossom Time,* 1952–53

Ambs, Ceil: Ensign Cora McRae, *South Pacific,* 1956–57; Winnie Tate, *Annie Get Your Gun,* 1956–57; Tuptim, *The King and I,* 1957–58; Amelia, *Amelia Goes to the Ball,* 1957–58; French Lady, *Candide,* 1957–58; Norina, *Don Pasquale,* 1957–58; Venetian Lady, *Candide,* 1957–58

Amend, Laura: Osa, *A Little Night Music,* 1988–89

Ames, Courtney: Eine Kartenaufschlaegerin, *Arabella,* 1998–99; La Suor Zelatrice, *Suor Angelica (Sister Angelica),* 1999–2000; Gertrude, *Hänsel und Gretel,* 2001–02

Ames, John: Lottery Agent/Health Inspector, *McTeague,* 1995–96; Sparafucile, *Rigoletto,* 1995–96; Commendatore, *Don Giovanni,* 1996–97; The Bonze, *Madama Butterfly,* 1996–97; Truffaldino, *Ariadne auf Naxos,* 1996–97

Amini, Nancy: Princess Ninetta, *The Love for Three Oranges,* 1975–76; Nanetta, *Falstaff,* 1976–77; Susannah Polk, *Susannah,* 1976–77; Micaëla, *Carmen,* 1977–78

Ammann, Lindsay: Dame Doleful, *Too Many Sopranos,* 2006–07; Maddalena, *Rigoletto,* 2007–08; Nettie/Aunt Bea, *A Wedding,* 2007–08

Amore, Vincent: Slave, *Die Zauberflöte (The Magic Flute),* 1982–83; The McCourt family, *The Ballad of Baby Doe,* 1982–83; Waiter, *The Ballad of Baby Doe,* 1982–83; Alcindoro, *La Bohème,* 1984–85

Amoretti, Ruben: Beppe, *I Pagliacci,* 1991–92

Amos, Gloria: Alisa, *Lucia di Lammermoor,* 1963–64; Handmaiden, *Simon Boccanegra,* 1964–65; Liu, *Turandot,* 1964–65

Andersen, Kevin: A Footman, *Vanessa,* 1999–2000; A Herald, *The Love for Three Oranges,* 1999–2000; Elder Ott, *Susannah,* 2000–01

Anderson, Alfred: A Gypsy, *Il Trovatore,* 1967–68; Foquier-Tinville, *Andrea Chénier,* 1967–68; Major-domo, *Andrea Chénier,* 1967–68; Count Tomsky, *La Pique Dame (The Queen of Spades),* 1968–69; Keeper of the Madhouse, *The Rake's Progress,* 1968–69; Marquis D'Obigny, *La Traviata,* 1968–69; Count Renato, *Un Ballo in Maschera (A Masked Ball),* 1969–70; Woody, *Finian's Rainbow,* 1969–70; Mr. Daniel Buchanan, *Street Scene,* 1949–50; Page, *Parsifal,* 1949–50; Parpignol, *La Bohème,* 1949–50; Pietro, *The Firefly,* 1949–50; Tavern Keeper, *The New Moon,* 1949–50; Page, *Parsifal,* 1951–52

Anderson, Dayton: A Guide, *Wonderful Town,* 1954–55; Drunk, *Wonderful Town,* 1954–55; Ruth's escort, *Wonderful Town,* 1954–55

Anderson, James: Cecco, *Il Mondo della Luna (The World on the Moon),* 1975–76; Doorman at the Tabor Grand Theatre, *The Ballad of Baby Doe,* 1975–76; Father Chapelle, *The Ballad of Baby Doe,* 1975–76; Henrik Egerman, *A Little Night Music,* 1975–76; Master of Ceremonies, *The Love for Three Oranges,* 1975–76; Old Silver Miner, *The Ballad of Baby Doe,* 1975–76; Page, *Parsifal,* 1975–76; Elder Hayes, *Susannah,* 1976–77; Enoch Snow, *Carousel,* 1976–77; Idamante, *Idomeneo,* 1976–77; Player, *Bernstein on Broadway,* 1976–77; Danton, *Danton and Robespierre,* 1977–78; Ferrando, *Così fan tutte,* 1977–78; The Deacon, *The Night Before Christmas,* 1977–78; Alfredo Germont, *La Traviata,* 1978–79; Grigori (Dimitri, the Pretender), *Boris Godunov,* 1978–79; Minstrel, *The Darkened City,* 1978–79

Anderson, Linda: Pamina, *Die Zauberflöte (The Magic Flute),* 1965–66; Sister Constance, *Dialogues des Carmélites,* 1965–66; Constanza, *Die Entführung aus dem Serail (The Abduction from the Seraglio),* 1966–67; Drusilla, *L'Incoronazione di Poppea (The Coronation of Poppea),* 1967–68; Hilda Mack, *Elegy for Young Lovers,* 1967–68; Anne Trulove, *The Rake's Progress,* 1968–69; Eva, *Die Meistersinger von Nürnberg (The Mastersingers of Nuremberg),* 1968–69; Violetta Valery, *La Traviata,* 1968–69; Iole, *Heracles,* 1971–72; Marguerite, *Faust,* 1971–72; Arabella, *Arabella,* 1972–73; Elizabeth of Valois, *Don Carlos,* 1972–73; Nastasia, *Myshkin,* 1972–73; Floria Tosca, *Tosca,* 1973–74; Marie, *Wozzeck,* 1973–74

Anderson, Norman: Celio, *The Love for Three Oranges,* 1975–76; Tom, *Un Ballo in Maschera (A Masked Ball),* 1975–76; Arkel, *Pelléas et Mélisande,* 1976–77

Andrews, Caitlin: Mrs. Hayes, *Susannah,* 2007–08

Andrews, Cameron: Eric Dare, *Jubilee,* 1991–92; Georgia Delegate, *1600 Pennsylvania Avenue,* 1992–93; Glieg, *1600 Pennsylvania Avenue,* 1992–93; Mr.

Greenback the Right End Man, *1600 Pennsylvania Avenue,* 1992–93; Enoch Snow, Jr., *Carousel,* 1993–94; Juggler, *Carousel,* 1993–94

Andrews, Roger: The Bonze, *Madama Butterfly,* 1976–77

Angell, Julie: Esmeralda, *The Bartered Bride,* 1967–68

Anstine, Erik: Crespel, *Les Contes d'Hoffmann (The Tales of Hoffmann),* 2007–08; Snooks, *A Wedding,* 2007–08

Antenbring, Christine: Olga, *Eugene Onegin,* 1997–98

Appel, William: Charlie Davenport, *Annie Get Your Gun,* 1956–57; Dr. Caius, *Falstaff,* 1956–57; Ferrando, *Così fan tutte,* 1956–57; Major Gordon Lillie, *Annie Get Your Gun,* 1956–57; Radio Operator, *South Pacific,* 1956–57; Remendado, *Carmen,* 1956–57; Albert Herring, *Albert Herring,* 1957–58; Candide, *Candide,* 1957–58; Don Ramiro, *La Cenerentola (Cinderella),* 1957–58; Lun Tha, *The King and I,* 1957–58; Count Riccardo, *Un Ballo in Maschera (A Masked Ball),* 1958–59

Appelman, Ralph: Stephan Kumalo, *Lost in the Stars,* 1950–51; Gurnemanz, *Parsifal,* 1951–52; Gurnemanz, *Parsifal,* 1952–53; Boris Godunov, *Boris Godunov,* 1953–54; Gurnemanz, *Parsifal,* 1954–55; Gurnemanz, *Parsifal,* 1955–56; Gurnemanz, *Parsifal,* 1956–57; Tony, *The Most Happy Fella,* 1959–60; Grand Inquisitor, *Don Carlos,* 1961–62; Gurnemanz, *Parsifal,* 1962–63; Gurnemanz, *Parsifal,* 1963–64; Ramphis, *Aida,* 1963–64; Boris Godunov, *Boris Godunov,* 1964–65; Boris Godunov, *Boris Godunov,* 1966–67; Gurnemanz, *Parsifal,* 1966–67; Mephistopheles, *Mefistofele,* 1967–68; Gurnemanz, *Parsifal,* 1968–69; Hans Sachs, *Die Meistersinger von Nürnberg (The Mastersingers of Nuremberg),* 1968–69; Wotan, *Die Walküre,* 1971–72; Gurnemanz, *Parsifal,* 1972–73; King Philip II, *Don Carlos,* 1972–73; Gurnemanz, *Parsifal,* 1975–76; Boris Godunov, *Boris Godunov,* 1978–79

Applewhite, James: Intern, *Street Scene,* 1960–61

Ard, Martha: Niece, *Peter Grimes,* 1963–64

Arment, Gwen: Luciana, *The Boys from Syracuse,* 1968–69

Armstrong, John: Gremio, *Kiss Me, Kate,* 1998–99

Armstrong, Sean: Leon, *The Ghosts of Versailles,* 1996–97; Scaramuccio, *Ariadne auf Naxos,* 1996–97; Curly, *Oklahoma!,* 1997–98

Arnholt, William: Knight, *Parsifal,* 1952–53; Doctor Bartolo, *Il Barbiere di Siviglia (The Barber of Seville),* 1956–57; Zuniga, *Carmen,* 1956–57; Atheist, *Candide,* 1957–58; Croupier, *Candide,* 1957–58; Dandini, *La Cenerentola (Cinderella),* 1957–58; Doctor, *Candide,* 1957–58; Dr. Malatesta, *Don Pasquale,* 1957–58; Husband, *Amelia Goes to the Ball,* 1957–58; Masetto, *Don Giovanni,* 1958–59; Sharpless, *Madama Butterfly,* 1958–59

Arnold, David: Monk, *Don Carlos,* 1961–62; Starveling, *A Midsummer Night's Dream,* 1961–62; Leader of Penitents, *The Darkened City,* 1962–63; Morales, *Carmen,* 1962–63; Schaunard, *La Bohème,* 1962–63; Figaro, *Il Barbiere di Siviglia (The Barber of Seville),* 1963–64; Guglielmo, *Così fan tutte,* 1963–64; Messenger, *Aida,* 1963–64; The Sidney Duck, *La Fanciulla del West (The Girl of the Golden West),* 1963–64; Schelkalov, *Boris Godunov,* 1964–65; Sharpless, *Madama Butterfly,* 1964–65; The Messenger, *Oedipus Rex,* 1964–65; Morales, *Carmen,* 1965–66; Second Chief, *A Hoosier Tale,* 1966–67; Schelkalov, *Boris Godunov,* 1966–67; Silvio, *I Pagliacci,* 1966–67; Klingsor, *Parsifal,* 1967–68; Lescaut, *Manon,* 1967–68; Ottone, *L'Incoronazione di Poppea (The Coronation of Poppea),* 1967–68; Count Almaviva, *Le Nozze di Figaro (The Marriage of Figaro),* 1968–69; Klingsor, *Parsifal,* 1968–69; Prince Yeletsky, *La Pique Dame (The Queen of Spades),* 1968–69; Count Renato, *Un Ballo in Maschera (A Masked Ball),* 1969–70; Harlequin, *Ariadne auf Naxos,* 1969–70

Arnold, Henry: Count Ceprano, *Rigoletto,* 1959–60; Maitre d'hotel, *La Rondine (The Swallow),* 1959–60

Aronis, Andrew: Gherardino, *Gianni Schicchi,* 1993–94

Arreola, Brian: Romeo, *Roméo et Juliette,* 2005–06; Chevalier des Grieux, *Manon,* 2006–07; Nelson Deadly, *Too Many Sopranos,* 2006–07; Rodolfo, *La Bohème,* 2007–08; The Duke of Mantua, *Rigoletto,* 2007–08

Arst, Gregg: Ali Hakim, *Oklahoma!,* 1997–98

Arvin, Gary: Guillot, *Eugene Onegin,* 1974–75; The Young Pastor, *Vanessa,* 1974–75; Pasquino, *Il Mondo della Luna (The World on the Moon),* 1975–76; Washington Dandy, *The Ballad of Baby Doe,* 1975–76

Ashantiva, Elizabeth: Kate Pinkerton, *Madama Butterfly,* 2006–07; Susannah Polk, *Susannah,* 2007–08

Asher, Nadine: Old woman, *Heracles,* 1971–72; Schwertleite, *Die Walküre,* 1971–72; Eine Kartenaufschlaegerin, *Arabella,* 1972–73; Grandmother Buryja, *Jenůfa,* 1972–73; The Princess, *Il Trittico (A Triptych),* 1972–73; Voice from Heaven, *Parsifal,* 1972–73; Marcellina, *Le Nozze di Figaro (The Marriage of Figaro),* 1973–74; Shepherd Boy, *Tosca,* 1973–74; Voice of the Mother, *Les Contes d'Hoffmann (The Tales of Hoffmann),* 1973–74; Old Baroness, *Vanessa,* 1974–75

Astraquillo, Corbelita: Mrs. Greta Fiorentino, *Street Scene,* 1960–61

Astrup, Margaret: Hippolyta, *A Midsummer Night's Dream,* 1983–84

Atchinson, Kathy: Annunziata, *Arlecchino,* 1979–80

Atchison, Dawn: Soprano, *Carmina Burana,* 1991–92

Atkins, Barbara: Musetta, *La Bohème*, 1949–50; Natalie, *Die lustige Witwe (The Merry Widow)*, 1949–50

Atkins, Shallen: Cunegonde, *Candide*, 2000–01

Atwater, Victoria: Johanna, *Sweeney Todd*, 1983–84; Jou-Jou, *Die lustige Witwe (The Merry Widow)*, 1983–84; Tytania, *A Midsummer Night's Dream*, 1983–84; Asteria, *Tamerlano*, 1984–85; Eurydice, *Orphée aux enfers (Orpheus in the Underworld)*, 1984–85; Adele, *Die Fledermaus (The Bat)*, 1985–86; Adina, *L'Elisir d'amore (The Elixir of Love)*, 1986–87; Swan-Bird, *The Legend of Tsar Saltan*, 1986–87; Cunegonde, *Candide*, 1987–88

August, Veronica: Adelaide, *Arabella*, 1972–73; Grandmother Buryja, *Jenůfa*, 1972–73; The Princess, *Il Trittico (A Triptych)*, 1972–73; Anne, *The Mother of Us All*, 1973–74; Jenny Reefer, *The Mother of Us All*, 1973–74; Marcellina, *Le Nozze di Figaro (The Marriage of Figaro)*, 1973–74; Margaret, *Wozzeck*, 1973–74; Maddalena, *Rigoletto*, 1974–75; Old Baroness, *Vanessa*, 1974–75; Madame Armfeldt, *A Little Night Music*, 1975–76

Augustine, Paul: Player, *Mass*, 1987–88; Player, *Mass*, 1988–89; Harry, *Company*, 1990–91; Don Magnifico, *La Cenerentola (Cinderella)*, 1991–92; Horace Vandergelder, *Hello, Dolly!*, 1991–92; Mannoury, *Die Teufel von Loudun (The Devils of Loudun)*, 1992–93; Billy Bigelow, *Carousel*, 1993–94; Enrico Ashton, *Lucia di Lammermoor*, 1993–94

Auslander, Michelle: Donna Elvira, *Don Giovanni*, 2002–03; Tatyana, *Eugene Onegin*, 2004–05

Austin, Karla: Gracie Shinn, *The Music Man*, 1980–81; Effie, *The Ballad of Baby Doe*, 1982–83; Second Lay Sister, *Il Trittico (A Triptych)*, 1982–83; Hermia, *A Midsummer Night's Dream*, 1983–84

Axelrod, Lenny: Constable, *Fiddler on the Roof*, 1972–73

Axsom, Edgar: Haberdasher, *Kiss Me, Kate*, 1951–52

Ayers, Angela: Mama Sieppe, *McTeague*, 1995–96

Ayers, Vanessa: Maria, *Porgy and Bess*, 1976–77

Azar, David: A-Rab, *West Side Story*, 1985–86; Louis Lippman, *Of Thee I Sing*, 1987–88

Baccus, John: Orpheus, *Orphée aux enfers (Orpheus in the Underworld)*, 1992–93

Bader, Susan: Second Mourner, *The Darkened City*, 1978–79

Badolato, Anthony: Schmidt, *Werther*, 1961–62; Alfred, *Die Fledermaus (The Bat)*, 1962–63; Don Alvaro, *La Forza del Destino (The Force of Destiny)*, 1962–63

Baer, Elisabeth: Somewhere solo, *West Side Story*, 2002–03

Baer, Nathan: Erik, *Jeppe*, 2002–03; Tolomeo, *Giulio Cesare (Julius Caesar)*, 2002–03; Quince, *A Midsummer Night's Dream*, 2005–06

Bailey, Alfred: Keeper of the Madhouse, *The Rake's Progress*, 1991–92; Lud Simmons, *1600 Pennsylvania Avenue*, 1992–93; Judge of the Inquisition, *Candide*, 1993–94; Schaunard, *La Bohème*, 1994–95

Bailey, Mike: Frazier, *Porgy and Bess*, 1976–77

Bailey, Wayne: The Bonze, *Madama Butterfly*, 1975–76

Bain, Stephanie: Mother Marie of the Incarnation, *Dialogues des Carmélites*, 2004–05

Bainbridge, Jonathan: Betto, *Gianni Schicchi*, 1993–94; Hobson, *Peter Grimes*, 1994–95; Marcello, *La Bohème*, 1994–95; Count Monterone, *Rigoletto*, 1995–96; Peter, *Hänsel und Gretel*, 1995–96; Njegus, *Die lustige Witwe (The Merry Widow)*, 1996–97; Ford, *Falstaff*, 1997–98; Escamillo, *Carmen*, 1998–99; Mandryka, *Arabella*, 1998–99; Valentin, *Faust*, 2000–01; Lavitsky, *Boris Godunov*, 1964–65; Pietro, *Simon Boccanegra*, 1964–65; Simone, *Gianni Schicchi*, 1964–65

Baker, Guy Owen: Parsifal, *Parsifal*, 1948–49; Count Danilo Danilovitch, *Die lustige Witwe (The Merry Widow)*, 1949–50; Parsifal, *Parsifal*, 1949–50; Parsifal, *Parsifal*, 1950–51

Baker, Mark: High Priest, *Idomeneo*, 1976–77; Reverend Master Arthur Dimmesdale, *The Scarlet Letter*, 1976–77; Captain Richard Warrington, *Naughty Marietta*, 1977–78; Man in Armor, *Die Zauberflöte (The Magic Flute)*, 1977–78; Bajazet, *Tamerlano*, 1984–85; Don Jose, *Carmen*, 1984–1985

Baker, Sonya: Madame Armfeldt, *A Little Night Music*, 1988–89; Minstrel, *The Dawn of the Poor King*, 1990–91

Baldridge, Annabelle: Patricia, *Where's Charley?*, 1953–54; The Princess in the Storybook, *L'Enfant et les Sortilèges (The Bewitched Child)*, 1955–56

Baldvinsson, Magnus: Osmin, *Die Entführung aus dem Serail (The Abduction from the Seraglio)*, 1987–88; Plutone (Pluto), *L'Orfeo*, 1987–88; Bluebeard, *Bluebeard's Castle*, 1988–89; Don Basilio, *Il Barbiere di Siviglia (The Barber of Seville)*, 1988–89; Prince Gremin, *Eugene Onegin*, 1988–89

Baldwin, Elizabeth: Cousin Hebe, *HMS Pinafore*, 2005–06; Mrs. Webb, *Our Town*, 2005–06; Arabella, *Arabella*, 2006–07; Countess Almaviva, *Le Nozze di Figaro (The Marriage of Figaro)*, 2007–08

Balke, Maureen: Clarissa, *Il Mondo della Luna (The World on the Moon)*, 1975–76; Ilia, *Idomeneo*, 1976–77; Flora, *The Turn of the Screw*, 1978–79; Susanna, *Le Nozze di Figaro (The Marriage of Figaro)*, 1986–87

Ball, Rebecca: Page, *Rigoletto*, 2000–01; Barbarina, *Le Nozze di Figaro (The Marriage of Figaro)*, 2001–02; Cleopatra, *Giulio Cesare (Julius Caesar)*, 2002–03; Norina, *Don Pasquale*, 2003–04

Ballam, Michael: Andres, *Wozzeck*, 1973–74; Hoffmann, *Les Contes d'Hoffmann (The Tales of Hoffmann)*, 1973–74; Anatol, *Vanessa*, 1974–75; Mephistopheles, *Doktor Faust*, 1974–75; Rodolfo, *La Bohème*, 1974–75; Ecclitico, *Il Mondo della Luna (The World on the Moon)*, 1975–76; Lt. Pinkerton, *Madama Butterfly*, 1975–76; Parsifal, *Parsifal*, 1975–76; Pelleas, *Pelléas et Mélisande*, 1976–77; Danton, *Danton and Robespierre*, 1977–78

Ballard, Blaine: Fiorello, *Il Barbiere di Siviglia (The Barber of Seville)*, 1956–57; Officer, *Il Barbiere di Siviglia (The Barber of Seville)*, 1956–57; Alidoro, *La Cenerentola (Cinderella)*, 1957–58; First Officer, *Candide*, 1957–58

Ballard, Michael: Priest, *Die Zauberflöte (The Magic Flute)*, 1977–78; Third Suitor, *The Darkened City*, 1978–79

Ballenger, Julie: Proserpina, *L'Orfeo*, 1987–88

Ballotti, Jill: Kate Pinkerton, *Madama Butterfly*, 1976–77

Banford, Amy: Eileen, *West Side Story*, 1992–93

Bang, Kyung Sook: Pamina, *Die Zauberflöte (The Magic Flute)*, 1972–73; Theobald, *Don Carlos*, 1972–73; Susanna, *Le Nozze di Figaro (The Marriage of Figaro)*, 1973–74; Thierry, *Dialogues des Carmélites*, 1997–98

Banion, Brian: Schlemil, *Les Contes d'Hoffmann (The Tales of Hoffmann)*, 1995–96; Leporello, *Don Giovanni*, 1996–97; The Bonze, *Madama Butterfly*, 1996–97; Count Almaviva, *Le Nozze di Figaro (The Marriage of Figaro)*, 1997–98; Eugene Onegin, *Eugene Onegin*, 1997–98; Jud Fry, *Oklahoma!*, 1997–98; Nick Shadow, *The Rake's Progress*, 1999–2000; The Doctor, *Vanessa*, 1999–2000; Don Basilio, *Il Barbiere di Siviglia (The Barber of Seville)*, 2000–01

Barabino, Fernando: Giorgio Germont, *La Traviata*, 1968–69; Baron Scarpia, *Tosca*, 1969–70; Gianni Schicchi, *Il Trittico (A Triptych)*, 1969–70; Michele, *Il Trittico (A Triptych)*, 1969–70

Barber, Rebecca: Effie, *The Ballad of Baby Doe*, 1975–76; Servant of Buonafede, *Il Mondo della Luna (The World on the Moon)*, 1975–76; Baker's Wife, *Danton and Robespierre*, 1977–78; Lizette, *Naughty Marietta*, 1977–78; First Mourner, *The Darkened City*, 1978–79; Marina Mnishek, *Boris Godunov*, 1978–79; Colombina, *Arlecchino*, 1979–80

Bardwell, E. P.: Vicomte Ribaud, *The New Moon*, 1949–50

Bare, Betsy Ann: Countess Ceprano, *Rigoletto*, 2000–01; Mrs. Hayes, *Susannah*, 2000–01; Gertrude, *Hänsel und Gretel*, 2001–02; Giulietta, *Les Contes d'Hoffmann (The Tales of Hoffmann)*, 2002–03; Player, *Putting It Together*, 2002–03

Barker, Laura: Sister Mathilde, *Dialogues des Carmélites*, 2004–05

Barley, Douglas: Monostatos, *Die Zauberflöte (The Magic Flute)*, 1998–99; The Captain, *Wozzeck*, 1999–2000

Barnes, Ben: Sportin' Life, *Porgy and Bess*, 1976–77; Sportin' Life, *Porgy and Bess*, 1979–80

Barnes, Judith: Prince Orlofsky, *Die Fledermaus (The Bat)*, 1990–91

Barnes-Kerrigan, Judith: Mercedes, *Carmen*, 1991–92; Ninon, *Die Teufel von Loudun (The Devils of Loudun)*, 1992–93

Barnet, Nancy: Spirit, *Die Zauberflöte (The Magic Flute)*, 1960–61

Barras, Ann: Maddalena, *Rigoletto*, 1959–60; Mrs. Emma Jones, *Street Scene*, 1960–61

Barrett, John: Tenorio / a Muleteer, *Man of La Mancha*, 1985–86

Barrett, Richard: Man in Armor, *Die Zauberflöte (The Magic Flute)*, 2004–05

Barrett, Thomas: Benedict, *The Tempest*, 1985–86; Second Commissioner, *Dialogues des Carmélites*, 1986–87; Krushina, *The Bartered Bride*, 1986–87; Second Sailor, *The Legend of Tsar Saltan*, 1986–87; Player, *Mass*, 1987–88; The Imperial Commissioner, *Madama Butterfly*, 1987–88; Thomas Putnam, *The Crucible*, 1987–88; Gianni Schicchi, *Gianni Schicchi*, 1988–89; Player, *Mass*, 1988–89; Agamemnon, *The Cry of Clytaemnestra*, 1989–90; Don Alfonso, *Così fan tutte*, 1989–90; Marcello, *La Bohème*, 1989–90; Mephistopheles, *Faust*, 1989–90; Public Poet, *Kismet*, 1989–90; Dr. Dulcamara, *L'Elisir d'amore (The Elixir of Love)*, 1990–91; Melchior, *Amahl and the Night Visitors*, 1990–91

Barry, Kathleen: Mrs. Gleaton, *Susannah*, 1979–80

Bartlemay, Diane: Assistant Courtesan, *The Boys from Syracuse*, 1968–69

Bartley, Kevin: Couthon, *Danton and Robespierre*, 1977–78; The Friar, *Canterbury Tales*, 1978–79

Barton, Ann: Dodo, *Die lustige Witwe (The Merry Widow)*, 1949–50

Barton, Jamie: Thisbe, *La Cenerentola (Cinderella)*, 2004–05; Buttercup, *HMS Pinafore*, 2005–06; Mrs. Soames, *Our Town*, 2005–06; The Witch, *Hänsel und Gretel*, 2006–07

Bartow, Caryn: Mrs. Mullin, *Carousel*, 1970–71

Barzilay, Guy: Notary, *Don Pasquale*, 1988–89; Marquis D'Obigny, *La Traviata*, 1990–91

Basile, Frank: Marullo, *Rigoletto*, 1986–87

Basinski, Anne: The Child, *L'Enfant et les Sortilèges (The Bewitched Child)*, 1984–85; Estella, *West Side Story*, 1985–86; Morgan le Fey, *Camelot*, 1986–87;

Giunone, *L'Orfeo*, 1987–88; Niece, *Peter Grimes*, 1987–88; Papagena, *Die Zauberflöte (The Magic Flute)*, 1988–89; Cassandra, *The Cry of Clytaemnestra*, 1989–90; Susanna, *Le Nozze di Figaro (The Marriage of Figaro)*, 1992–93

Bates, Alison: Amy, *Little Women*, 2001–02; Cleopatra, *Giulio Cesare (Julius Caesar)*, 2002–03; Constanza, *Die Entführung aus dem Serail (The Abduction from the Seraglio)*, 2003–04; Catherine, *A View from the Bridge*, 2004–05

Bates, Linda: A young girl, *Heracles*, 1971–72

Baube, Margaret: Lolette, *La Rondine (The Swallow)*, 1989–90; Jou-Jou, *Die lustige Witwe (The Merry Widow)*, 1990–91; Clorinda, *La Cenerentola (Cinderella)*, 1991–92

Bauman, Kenneth: Morales, *Carmen*, 1977–78; Sciarrone, *Tosca*, 1977–78; Soldier, *Danton and Robespierre*, 1977–78

Bauman, Lynne: Gretl, *The Sound of Music*, 2000–01

Baumer, Bruce: Commendatore, *Don Giovanni*, 1991–92; The Bonze, *Madama Butterfly*, 1991–92; Zuniga, *Carmen*, 1991–92; Dr. Bartolo, *Le Nozze di Figaro (The Marriage of Figaro)*, 1992–93; Father Barre, *Die Teufel von Loudun (The Devils of Loudun)*, 1992–93

Baxter, Tiffany: Mercedes, *Carmen*, 1998–99; Second Lady, *Die Zauberflöte (The Magic Flute)*, 1998–99

Bayless, Eugene: Bumerli, *The Chocolate Soldier*, 1950–51; Parsifal, *Parsifal*, 1950–51; Edvard Grieg, *Song of Norway*, 1951–52; First Man, *Kiss Me, Kate*, 1951–52; Parsifal, *Parsifal*, 1951–52; Captain Edward Fairfax Vere, *Billy Budd*, 1952–53; Parsifal, *Parsifal*, 1952–53; Parsifal, *Parsifal*, 1953–54; Albert, *The Ruby*, 1954–55; Parsifal, *Parsifal*, 1954–55; Walther Von Stolzing, *Die Meistersinger von Nürnberg (The Mastersingers of Nuremberg)*, 1961–62; Peter Grimes, *Peter Grimes*, 1963–64; Parsifal, *Parsifal*, 1967–68; Lescaut, *Manon Lescaut*, 1970–71

Bayless, Kay: A Princess of Ababu, *Kismet*, 1963–64

Beall, Charles: Banquo, *Macbeth*, 1965–66; Fleance, *Macbeth*, 1965–66; Priest, *Die Zauberflöte (The Magic Flute)*, 1965–66; Cancian, *Quattro rusteghi (The Four Ruffians)*, 1966–67; Father Zeisberger, *A Hoosier Tale*, 1966–67; Pasha Selim, *Die Entführung aus dem Serail (The Abduction from the Seraglio)*, 1966–67; A Night Watchman, *Die Meistersinger von Nürnberg (The Mastersingers of Nuremberg)*, 1968–69; Simone, *Il Trittico (A Triptych)*, 1969–70; Talpa, *Il Trittico (A Triptych)*, 1969–70; Second Prisoner, *Fidelio*, 1970–71; A Monk, *Don Carlos*, 1972–73; Lazar Wolf, *Fiddler on the Roof*, 1972–73

Bean, Amanda: Javotte, *Manon*, 2006–07

Bean, Matthew: Messenger, *The Legend of Tsar Saltan*, 1986–87

Beane, James: Betto, *Gianni Schicchi*, 1964–65; Prince Yamadori, *Madama Butterfly*, 1964–65; Schelkalov, *Boris Godunov*, 1964–65

Beard, David: The "Horses", *Man of La Mancha*, 1988–89

Beatty, F. Scott: Soldier of the Praetorian Guard, *L'Incoronazione di Poppea (The Coronation of Poppea)*, 1967–68

Bechtelheimer, John: Captain, *Carousel*, 1952–53

Beck, Mary: Fiordiligi, *Così fan tutte*, 1956–57; Mrs. Alice Ford, *Falstaff*, 1956–57

Beckendorf, Sharon: Floria Tosca, *Tosca*, 1973–74; Giulietta, *Les Contes d'Hoffmann (The Tales of Hoffmann)*, 1973–74; Stella, *Les Contes d'Hoffmann (The Tales of Hoffmann)*, 1973–74; Duchess of Parma, *Doktor Faust*, 1974–75; Tatyana, *Eugene Onegin*, 1974–75

Becklenberg, James: Diesel, *West Side Story*, 1992–93

Beddow, Sara: Niece #1, *Peter Grimes*, 2003–04

Behr, Clarissa: Gilda, *Rigoletto*, 1980–81; Constanza, *Die Entführung aus dem Serail (The Abduction from the Seraglio)*, 1981–82; Lauretta, *Il Trittico (A Triptych)*, 1982–83; Violetta Valery, *La Traviata*, 1983–84

Behrmann, Beth: Player, *Mass*, 1988–89

Beikman, Sharon: Eva Standing, *Jubilee*, 1991–92; Mrs. Mullin, *Carousel*, 1993–94

Belisle, John: Cord Elam, *Oklahoma!*, 1954–55

Bell, Marion: Jennie Parsons, *Down in the Valley*, 1947–48

Bellner, Monica: Mother Goose, *The Rake's Progress*, 1991–92; Maddalena, *Rigoletto*, 1992–93; Ninon, *Die Teufel von Loudun (The Devils of Loudun)*, 1992–93

Belnap, Michael: Canio, *I Pagliacci*, 1991–92; De Laubardemont, *Die Teufel von Loudun (The Devils of Loudun)*, 1992–93; Dr. Caius, *Falstaff*, 1992–93; Edgardo, *Lucia di Lammermoor*, 1993–94; Mario Cavaradossi, *Tosca*, 1993–94; Peter Grimes, *Peter Grimes*, 1994–95; Rodolfo, *La Bohème*, 1994–95; McTeague, *McTeague*, 1995–96; Bacchus/Tenor, *Ariadne auf Naxos*, 1996–97

Beman, Dwight: First Apprentice, *Wozzeck*, 1973–74; Thaddeus Stevens, *The Mother of Us All*, 1973–74; Duke of Parma, *Doktor Faust*, 1974–75; Gretchen's Brother, *Doktor Faust*, 1974–75; Chester A. Arthur, *The Ballad of Baby Doe*, 1975–76; Parsifal, *Parsifal*, 1975–76

Benish, Jeff: Bulgarian Soldier, *Candide*, 1993–94; Sailor, *Candide*, 1993–94

Benner, Jennifer: Blessed Spirit, *Orfeo ed Euridice*, 1992–93

Bennett, Alan: Belmonte, *Die Entführung aus dem Serail (The Abduction from the Seraglio)*, 1993–94; Ferrando, *Così fan tutte*, 1995–96

Bennett, Betty: Countess Ceprano, *Rigoletto*, 1959–60; Stella, *Les Contes d'Hoffmann (The Tales of Hoffmann)*, 1959–60; Waitress, *The Most Happy Fella*,

1959–60; Blonde, *Die Entführung aus dem Serail (The Abduction from the Seraglio)*, 1961–62; Micaëla, *Carmen*, 1962–63

Bennett, Elijah: Celio, *The Love for Three Oranges*, 1958–59; Knight, *Parsifal*, 1958–59; The Bonze, *Madama Butterfly*, 1958–59

Benson, Ann: Alison, *Canterbury Tales*, 1978–79; Despina, *Così fan tutte*, 1978–79; Marenka, *The Bartered Bride*, 1979–80; Mrs. Hayes, *Susannah*, 1979–80; Gretel, *Hänsel und Gretel*, 1982–83; Freia, *Das Rheingold*, 1983–84

Benson, Leila: Frasquita, *Carmen*, 1965–66

Bentley, Julia: Cat, *L'Enfant et les Sortilèges (The Bewitched Child)*, 1984–85; Mercedes, *Carmen*, 1984–85; Muse, *Les Contes d'Hoffmann (The Tales of Hoffmann)*, 1988–89; Nicklausse, *Les Contes d'Hoffmann (The Tales of Hoffmann)*, 1988–89; Second Lady, *Die Zauberflöte (The Magic Flute)*, 1988–89; Hansel, *Hänsel und Gretel*, 1989–90

Berger, Brigid: Mary, *The Ballad of Baby Doe*, 2003–04

Bergman, Alan: Harry Beaton, *Brigadoon*, 1961–62

Bermingham, Ronald: Doctor, *Macbeth*, 1965–66; Zuniga, *Carmen*, 1965–66; Guillot de Morfontaine, *Manon*, 1979–80; Jenik, *The Bartered Bride*, 1979–80; Count Almaviva, *Il Barbiere di Siviglia (The Barber of Seville)*, 1980–81; Faust, *Faust*, 1981–82; Goro, *Madama Butterfly*, 1981–82; Ciccio, *The Most Happy Fella*, 1982–83; Gabriel von Eisenstein, *Die Fledermaus (The Bat)*, 1982–83; Prince Tamino, *Die Zauberflöte (The Magic Flute)*, 1982–83

Bernardini, Don: Jenik, *The Bartered Bride*, 1979–80; Count Almaviva, *The Barber of Seville*, 1980–81; Goro, *Madame Butterfly*, 1981–82; Faust, *Faust*, 1981–82; Ciccio, *The Most Happy Fella*, 1981–82; Gabriel, *Die Fledermaus*, 1982–83; Tamino, *The Magic Flute*, 1982–93; Alfredo Germont, *La Traviata*, 1983–84; Martin, *Candide*, 1983–84; The Governor of Cartagena, *Candide*, 1983–84

Bernath, Jesse: Anxious, *West Side Story*, 2002–03

Bernazzani, Maria: An elegant lady, *The Scarlet Letter*, 1976–77; Marietta, *Naughty Marietta*, 1977–78

Bernbach, Daniel: Diesel, *West Side Story*, 2002–03

Bernens, Celia: Flora Bervoix, *La Traviata*, 1978–79; Maddalena, *Rigoletto*, 1980–81; Marian Paroo, *The Music Man*, 1980–81

Bernhardt, Don: Player, *Bernstein on Broadway*, 1976–77

Berns, Christopher: Jacob, *The Ballad of Baby Doe*, 1982–83; Baron Thunder-Ten-Tronck, *Candide*, 1983–84; The Grand Inquisitor, *Candide*, 1983–84

Berry, Kathleen: Fata Morgana, *The Love for Three Oranges*, 1980–81; Yaroslavna's nurse, *Prince Igor*, 1980–81

Best, Ross: Conductor, *The Music Man*, 2001–02; Peter, *Hänsel und Gretel*, 2001–02

Beversdorf, Anne: Violin Student, *Street Scene*, 1960–61

Beyer, John: The Interpreter, *The King and I*, 1957–58; Hermann, *Les Contes d'Hoffmann (The Tales of Hoffmann)*, 1959–60

Beyer, Laura: Maid, *Manon*, 1979–80; A young Polovtsian maiden, *Prince Igor*, 1980–81; Lenio, *The Greek Passion*, 1980–81; Marguerite, *Faust*, 1981–82; Fiordiligi, *Così fan tutte*, 1984–85; Miranda, *The Tempest*, 1985–86; Marie Antoinette, *The Ghosts of Versailles*, 1996–97

Bhatt, Sachin: Toro, *West Side Story*, 2002–03

Bianning, Frank: Pisoni, *Song of Norway*, 1951–52

Bick, Nathan: Master of Ceremonies, *The Love for Three Oranges*, 1999–2000; Little Bat McLean, *Susannah*, 2000–01; Rolf, *The Sound of Music*, 2000–01; The Ringmaster, *The Bartered Bride*, 2001–02; Josh, *Jeppe*, 2002–03; Tony, *West Side Story*, 2002–03; Bushy, *The Ballad of Baby Doe*, 2003–04; The Father Confessor, *Dialogues des Carmélites*, 2004–05

Bickel, Kory: Masetto, *Don Giovanni*, 2002–03; Dr. Malatesta, *Don Pasquale*, 2003–04; The Poet, Prosdocimo, *Il Turco in Italia (The Turk in Italy)*, 2003–04; Dandini, *La Cenerentola (Cinderella)*, 2004–05; Mercutio, *Roméo et Juliette*, 2005–06

Biesterfeld, Mark: First Apprentice, *Wozzeck*, 1990–91; Servant, *Amahl and the Night Visitors*, 1990–91; Ape, *Jubilee*, 1991–92; Cabinet Minister, *Jubilee*, 1991–92; Masetto, *Don Giovanni*, 1991–92; The Drunk, *Jubilee*, 1991–92; Antonio, *Le Nozze di Figaro (The Marriage of Figaro)*, 1992–93

Biever, Richard: Diesel, *West Side Story*, 1985–86

Bigbee, Rosemarie: Judith, *Bluebeard's Castle*, 1988–89

Biggers, Stephen: Leporello, *Don Giovanni*, 1979–80; An Old Man, *The Greek Passion*, 1980–81; Count Ceprano, *Rigoletto*, 1980–81; Figaro, *Le Nozze di Figaro (The Marriage of Figaro)*, 1980–81; Jacob, *The Ballad of Baby Doe*, 1982–83; Simone, *Il Trittico (A Triptych)*, 1982–83

Biggs, Amanda: Berta (Marcellina), *Il Barbiere di Siviglia (The Barber of Seville)*, 2005–06

Biller, Kristine: Micaëla, *Carmen*, 1998–99; Mimi, *La Bohème*, 1999–2000; Princess Ninetta, *The Love for Three Oranges*, 1999–2000; Adina, *L'Elisir d'amore (The Elixir of Love)*, 2000–01; Manon Lescaut, *Manon*, 2001–02

Bills, John: Arturo Bucklaw, *Lucia di Lammermoor*, 1970–71; Enoch Snow, *Carousel*, 1970–71; Bardolph, *Falstaff*, 1971–72; Radomsky, *Myshkin*, 1972–73

Binfield, Sharon: Praskovia, *Die lustige Witwe (The Merry Widow),* 1964–65; Hostess of the Inn, *Boris Godunov,* 1966–67

Bingman, Steven: Tommy Djilas, *The Music Man,* 1980–81; Jake, *The Most Happy Fella,* 1982–83; The Cashier, *The Most Happy Fella,* 1982–83; Frank, *Show Boat,* 1984–85; Rubberface, *Show Boat,* 1984–85; Mordred, *Camelot,* 1986–87

Binkley, Leonor: John, *Peter Grimes,* 1987–88; Page, *L'Orfeo,* 1987–88

Birkland, Nicole: Giulietta, *Les Contes d'Hoffmann (The Tales of Hoffmann),* 2007–08; Maddalena, *Rigoletto,* 2007–08

Birt, Timothy: Andres, *Les Contes d'Hoffmann (The Tales of Hoffmann),* 2002–03; Cochenille, *Les Contes d'Hoffmann (The Tales of Hoffmann),* 2002–03; Franz, *Les Contes d'Hoffmann (The Tales of Hoffmann),* 2002–03; Pittichinaccio, *Les Contes d'Hoffmann (The Tales of Hoffmann),* 2002–03; Ernesto, *Don Pasquale,* 2003–04

Bisch, Jordan: Count Ceprano, *Rigoletto,* 2000–01; Antonio, *Le Nozze di Figaro (The Marriage of Figaro),* 2001–02; Micha, *The Bartered Bride,* 2001–02; Crespel, *Les Contes d'Hoffmann (The Tales of Hoffmann),* 2002–03; Curio, *Giulio Cesare (Julius Caesar),* 2002–03; Luther, *Les Contes d'Hoffmann (The Tales of Hoffmann),* 2002–03; Osmin, *Die Entführung aus dem Serail (The Abduction from the Seraglio),* 2003–04; Swallow, *Peter Grimes,* 2003–04; Prince Gremin, *Eugene Onegin,* 2004–05

Biss, Daniel: Gherardino, *Gianni Schicchi,* 1988–89

Bissinger, Stephani: Dewman, *Hänsel und Gretel,* 1989–90

Black, Randall: Orestes, *The Cry of Clytaemnestra,* 1979–80; The Ringmaster, *The Bartered Bride,* 1979–80; Ernesto, *Don Pasquale,* 1980–81; Michelis, *The Greek Passion,* 1980–81; Tom Jones, *Tom Jones,* 1983–84; Vicomte Camille di Rosillon, *Die lustige Witwe (The Merry Widow),* 1983–84; Ferrando, *Così fan tutte,* 1984–85

Black, Thomas: Jim, *Porgy and Bess,* 1976–77

Blackburn, David: A Monk, *Don Carlos,* 1960–61; Doctor Grenville, *La Traviata,* 1960–61

Blackburn, Royce: Grandier, *Die Teufel von Loudun (The Devils of Loudun),* 1992–93; Lescaut, *Manon,* 1993–94; Sciarrone, *Tosca,* 1993–94; An Indian, *The Bartered Bride,* 1994–95; Chou En-lai, *Nixon in China,* 1994–95; Papageno, *Die Zauberflöte (The Magic Flute),* 1994–95; Don Andres, *La Périchole,* 1995–96; Pierre-Augustin de Beaumarchais, *The Ghosts of Versailles,* 1996–97

Blackburn, Walter: Snout, *A Midsummer Night's Dream,* 1961–62

Blackhall, Jack: Spalanzani, *Les Contes d'Hoffmann (The Tales of Hoffmann),* 1973–74

Blackshire, Richard: Lancelot, *Camelot,* 1986–87; Marullo, *Rigoletto,* 1986–87; John P. Wintergreen, *Of Thee I Sing,* 1987–88; Maximilian, *Candide,* 1987–88

Blackshire, Scott: Anxious, *West Side Story,* 1985–86

Blair, Julia: Bess, *Porgy and Bess,* 1979–80; Susanna, *Le Nozze di Figaro (The Marriage of Figaro),* 1980–81

Blair, Lynn: Mistress Page (Frau Reich), *Die lustigen Weiber von Windsor (The Merry Wives of Windsor),* 1958–59; Zerlina, *Don Giovanni,* 1958–59; Antonia, *Les Contes d'Hoffmann (The Tales of Hoffmann),* 1959–60; Rosabella, *The Most Happy Fella,* 1959–60; Pamina, *Die Zauberflöte (The Magic Flute),* 1960–61; Queen of Shemakha, *Le Coq d'or (The Golden Cockerel),* 1960–61; Rose Maurant, *Street Scene,* 1960–61

Blandy, Charles: Master of Ceremonies, *The Love for Three Oranges,* 1999–2000; Ferrando, *Così fan tutte,* 2000–01

Blank, Johanne: Public Opinion, *Orphée aux enfers (Orpheus in the Underworld),* 1992–93

Blank, Julie: Himeneo, *L'Orfeo,* 1987–88

Blanning, Frank: Pooh-Bah, *The Mikado,* 1950–51; Mr. Redburn, *Billy Budd,* 1952–53

Blase, Kirsten: Despina, *Così fan tutte,* 1995–96; Adele, *Die Fledermaus (The Bat),* 1996–97; Valencienne, *Die lustige Witwe (The Merry Widow),* 1996–97; Cherubino, *Le Nozze di Figaro (The Marriage of Figaro),* 1997–98

Bledsoe, George: Pellinore, *Camelot,* 1968–69; Finian, *Finian's Rainbow,* 1969–70; Pellinore, *Camelot,* 1969–70

Blevins, Jeremy: A Lackey, *Ariadne auf Naxos,* 1996–97; Captain Orton, *The King and I,* 1996–97; M. Javelinot, *Dialogues des Carmélites,* 1997–98

Block, Melissa: Barbarina, *Le Nozze di Figaro (The Marriage of Figaro),* 2007–08

Blossom, Larry: First Prisoner, *Fidelio,* 1970–71

Bluth, Jordan: Archibald Craven, *The Secret Garden,* 2003–04; Chester A. Arthur, *The Ballad of Baby Doe,* 2003–04; Mayor of Leadville, *The Ballad of Baby Doe,* 2003–04; Old Silver Miner, *The Ballad of Baby Doe,* 2003–04; Prince Tamino, *Die Zauberflöte (The Magic Flute),* 2004–05; Count Almaviva, *Il Barbiere di Siviglia (The Barber of Seville),* 2005–06; Ferrando, *Così fan tutte,* 2005–06

Boardman, Una: Miss Bore, *A Parfait for Irene,* 1951–52

Bobb, Hildegard: Annina, *La Traviata,* 1968–69

Boesing, Paul: Bassett, *Where's Charley?,* 1953–54; First Gospeleer, *Finian's Rainbow,* 1953–54; Frank, *Show Boat,* 1953–54; Geologist, *Finian's Rainbow,* 1953–54; Slave, *Die Zauberflöte (The Magic Flute),* 1953–54

Bogdanov, Aleksey: Abbate Cospicuo, *Arlecchino*, 2006–07; Coppelius, *Les Contes d'Hoffmann (The Tales of Hoffmann)*, 2007–08; Dappertutto, *Les Contes d'Hoffmann (The Tales of Hoffmann)*, 2007–08; Dr. Miracle, *Les Contes d'Hoffmann (The Tales of Hoffmann)*, 2007–08; Lindorf, *Les Contes d'Hoffmann (The Tales of Hoffmann)*, 2007–08; Olin Blitch, *Susannah*, 2007–08

Bohannon, Kenneth: Messenger, *The Legend of Tsar Saltan*, 1986–87; Aegisthus, *The Cry of Clytaemnestra*, 1989–90; Count Danilo Danilovitch, *Die lustige Witwe (The Merry Widow)*, 1990–91; Gabriel von Eisenstein, *Die Fledermaus (The Bat)*, 1990–91; Gastone, *La Traviata*, 1990–91

Bolden, Diane: Micaëla, *Carmen*, 1973–74; Mimi, *La Bohème*, 1974–75

Bolduc, Chris: Papageno, *Die Zauberflöte (The Magic Flute)*, 2004–05; Demetrius, *A Midsummer Night's Dream*, 2005–06

Bolza-Schunemann, Irene: Shepherd Figure in the Wallpaper, *L'Enfant et les Sortilèges (The Bewitched Child)*, 1984–85

Bond, Carl: Marquis D'Obigny, *La Traviata*, 1960–61

Bond, Nancy: Cleo, *The Most Happy Fella*, 1959–60; Theobald, *Don Carlos*, 1960–61

Bond, Vicki: Miss Wordsworth, *Albert Herring*, 1966–67

Bonk, Rachel: Nero, *Agrippina*, 1995–96

Bonner, June: The Dragonfly, *L'Enfant et les Sortilèges (The Bewitched Child)*, 1955–56; Dorabella, *Così fan tutte*, 1956–57; Angelina (Cinderella), *La Cenerentola (Cinderella)*, 1957–58; Lola, *Cavalleria Rusticana*, 1957–58; Nancy, *Albert Herring*, 1957–58

Bono, Dallas: Hoffmann, *Les Contes d'Hoffmann (The Tales of Hoffmann)*, 1995–96; Vicomte Camille di Rosillon, *Die lustige Witwe (The Merry Widow)*, 1996–97

Bonsall, Christina: Hanna Glawari, *Die lustige Witwe (The Merry Widow)*, 2003–04; Norina, *Don Pasquale*, 2003–04; Blanche, *Dialogues des Carmélites*, 2004–05

Booth, Luctrician: Second Lady, *Die Zauberflöte (The Magic Flute)*, 1988–89

Bora, Eileen Marie: Niece #2, *Peter Grimes*, 2003–04; Madame Lidoine, *Dialogues des Carmélites*, 2004–05; Helena, *A Midsummer Night's Dream*, 2005–06

Borden, Addai: Scipio, *Porgy and Bess*, 1979–80

Bork, Robert: Schlemil, *Les Contes d'Hoffmann (The Tales of Hoffmann)*, 1978–79; Second Bearer, *The Darkened City*, 1978–79; Agamemnon, *The Cry of Clytaemnestra*, 1979–80; Elder McLean, *Susannah*, 1979–80; Fotis, *The Greek Passion*, 1980–81; Prince Galitsky, *Prince Igor*, 1980–81; The King of Clubs, *The Love for Three Oranges*, 1980–81; Oberlin, *Jakob Lenz*, 1981–82; Wozzeck, *Wozzeck*, 1981–82; A Denver Politician, *The Ballad of Baby Doe*, 1982–83; Bouncer at the saloon, *The Ballad of Baby Doe*, 1982–83; Michele, *Il Trittico (A Triptych)*, 1982–83

Bornemen, John: First Crap Shooter, *The Jumping Frog of Calaveras County*, 1949–50; Novakovich, *Die lustige Witwe (The Merry Widow)*, 1949–50; Borsa, *Rigoletto*, 1950–51; Knight, *Parsifal*, 1950–51; Nicholas, *A Parfait for Irene*, 1951–52; Pedrillo, *Die Entführung aus dem Serail (The Abduction from the Seraglio)*, 1951–52; Squeak, *Billy Budd*, 1952–53

Bos, Margot: Prince Orlofsky, *Die Fledermaus (The Bat)*, 1985–86

Bossort, Thomas: Photographer, *The Ballad of Baby Doe*, 1975–76

Botkin, Virginia: Irina, *Lost in the Stars*, 1950–51; Fiona MacLaren, *Brigadoon*, 1952–53

Boudreaux, Ron: Graf Dominik, *Arabella*, 1972–73; Marco, *Il Trittico (A Triptych)*, 1972–73; Perchik, *Fiddler on the Roof*, 1972–73; Priest, *Die Zauberflöte (The Magic Flute)*, 1972–73; Cesare Angelotti, *Tosca*, 1973–74; Figaro, *Le Nozze di Figaro (The Marriage of Figaro)*, 1973–74; Fred Graham, *Kiss Me, Kate*, 1973–74; Petruchio, *Kiss Me, Kate*, 1973–74; Ernesto, *Il Mondo della Luna (The World on the Moon)*, 1975–76; Sharpless, *Madama Butterfly*, 1975–76; Billy Bigelow, *Carousel*, 1976–77; Elder McLean, *Susannah*, 1976–77; Sharpless, *Madama Butterfly*, 1976–77; Worshipful Master Bellingham, *The Scarlet Letter*, 1976–77; Drunk, *Danton and Robespierre*, 1977–78; Guglielmo, *Così fan tutte*, 1977–78

Bourne, Michael: Frosch, *Die Fledermaus (The Bat)*, 1982–83; Bacchus, *Orphée aux enfers (Orpheus in the Underworld)*, 1984–85

Bowers, Jeanne: Shepherd Boy, *Tosca*, 1969–70; A Page, *Manon Lescaut*, 1970–71; Dorabella, *Così fan tutte*, 1970–71; Page, *Salome*, 1970–71; Waltraute, *Die Walküre*, 1971–72

Bowman, Bliss: Widow Yussef, *Kismet*, 1963–64

Bowman-Hester, Mark: Belmonte, *Die Entführung aus dem Serail (The Abduction from the Seraglio)*, 1981–82; Fenton, *Die lustigen Weiber von Windsor (The Merry Wives of Windsor)*, 1981–82; Judge of the Inquisition, *Candide*, 1983–84; Lysander, *A Midsummer Night's Dream*, 1983–84; Pirelli, *Sweeney Todd*, 1983–84; Gonzalvo, *L'Heure espagnole (The Spanish Hour)*, 1984–85; Tempter, *Murder in the Cathedral*, 1984–85; Tonio, *La Fille du régiment (The Daughter of the Regiment)*, 1984–85; Elvino, *La Sonnambula (The Sleepwalker)*, 1985–86

Boyle, Mary: Giovanna, *Rigoletto*, 1974–75; The Duchess of Plaza-Toro, *The Gondoliers*, 1974–75; Princess Clarissa, *The Love for Three Oranges*, 1975–76; Ulrica, *Un Ballo in Maschera (A Masked Ball)*, 1975–76

Boyle, Michelle: Second Wife, *Bluebeard's Castle*, 1988–89; Claire, *Die Teufel von Loudun (The Devils of Loudun)*, 1992–93; Gertie Cummings, *Oklahoma!*, 1997–98

Bradbury, Virginia: Christa, *Song of Norway*, 1951–52; Madam Dilly, *On the Town*, 1951–52; Miss Norden, *Song of Norway*, 1951–52

Bradley, Everett: A Muleteer, *Man of La Mancha*, 1985–86; The "Horses," *Man of La Mancha*, 1985–86

Bradley, Jaclyn: Cousin Hebe, *HMS Pinafore*, 1997–98; Venus, *Orphée aux enfers (Orpheus in the Underworld)*, 1998–99; La Conversa, *Suor Angelica (Sister Angelica)*, 1999–2000; Maid, *Vanessa*, 1999–2000; Sister Margaretta, *The Sound of Music*, 2000–01

Bragadottir, Solrun: Donna Anna, *Don Giovanni*, 1985–86; Younger Sister, later Tsaritsa Militrisa, *The Legend of Tsar Saltan*, 1986–87

Branch, Jean: Pamina, *Die Zauberflöte (The Magic Flute)*, 1960–61

Brand, Matthew: Mustardseed, *A Midsummer Night's Dream*, 1983–84

Brandes, Jeanie: Seeress of the Temple, *The Boys from Syracuse*, 1968–69

Brandt, Robert: Alfieri, *A View from the Bridge*, 2004–05; Demetrius, *A Midsummer Night's Dream*, 2005–06; Sir Joseph Porter, *HMS Pinafore*, 2005–06; Mandryka, *Arabella*, 2006–07; Pooh-Bah, *The Mikado*, 2006–07

Brassfield, Lori Kay: Anybodys, *West Side Story*, 1992–93; Liat, *South Pacific*, 1995–96; Lolo, *Die lustige Witwe (The Merry Widow)*, 1996–97

Braun, Judith: Rossweisse, *Die Walküre*, 1971–72

Brautigam, Keith: Curly, *Oklahoma!*, 1981–82; Valentin, *Faust*, 1981–82; Fiorello, *Il Barbiere di Siviglia (The Barber of Seville)*, 1982–83; The Doctor, *The Most Happy Fella*, 1982–83; Gaylord Ravenal, *Show Boat*, 1984–85; Guglielmo, *Così fan tutte*, 1984–85; Gabriel von Eisenstein, *Die Fledermaus (The Bat)*, 1985–86; The Marquis de la Force, *Dialogues des Carmélites*, 1986–87

Braxton, Moses: Frazier, *Porgy and Bess*, 1979–80; Innkeeper, *Manon*, 1979–80; Kreonte, *The Love for Three Oranges*, 1980–81; Skula, *Prince Igor*, 1980–81; First Apprentice, *Wozzeck*, 1981–82; Osmin, *Die Entführung aus dem Serail (The Abduction from the Seraglio)*, 1981–82

Bray, David: A Herald, *The Love for Three Oranges*, 1975–76; Samuel, *Un Ballo in Maschera (A Masked Ball)*, 1975–76; Voice of Neptune, *Idomeneo*, 1976–77

Brecheen, Jacqueline: Just Jeanette, *Too Many Sopranos*, 2006–07; Adina, *L'Elisir d'amore (The Elixir of Love)*, 2007–08; Susanna, *Le Nozze di Figaro (The Marriage of Figaro)*, 2007–08

Brehm, Jill: Maria / The Innkeeper's Wife, *Man of La Mancha*, 1985–86; Joanne, *Company*, 1990–91; Eva Standing, *Jubilee*, 1991–92

Brennan, Kevin: Notary, *La Sonnambula (The Sleepwalker)*, 1985–86; Pepe, *West Side Story*, 1985–86

Brewer, Alice: Shirley Kaplan, *Street Scene*, 1949–50

Brewer, Daniel: Missail, *Boris Godunov*, 1978–79; Giuseppe, *La Traviata*, 1978–79; Achilles, *The Cry of Clytaemnestra*, 1979–80; Parpignol, *La Bohème*, 1979–80; Sam Polk, *Susannah*, 1979–80; Eroshka, *Prince Igor*, 1980–81; Manolios, *The Greek Passion*, 1980–81; The Prince, *The Love for Three Oranges*, 1980–81; Faust, *Faust*, 1981–82; The Harper, *The Excursions of Mr. Broucek*, 1981–82; Ambrogio, *Il Barbiere di Siviglia (The Barber of Seville)*, 1982–83

Brewer, Wendi: Majordomo, *La Rondine (The Swallow)*, 1989–90

Brewster, Bobby: A Lamplighter, *Manon Lescaut*, 1959–60; The Doctor, *The Most Happy Fella*, 1959–60

Brice, Beverly: Mrs. Frohn, *The Veil*, 1949–50

Bridgewater, Thomas: Intern, *Street Scene*, 1960–61

Brier, Corinne: Spirit, *Die Zauberflöte (The Magic Flute)*, 1998–99; Nella, *Gianni Schicchi*, 1999–2000

Brilla, Marianne: The McCourt family, *The Ballad of Baby Doe*, 1975–76; Ulrica, *Un Ballo in Maschera (A Masked Ball)*, 1975–76; Mistress Hibbins, *The Scarlet Letter*, 1976–77

Brimm, Jeremy: Max Detweiler, *The Sound of Music*, 2000–01; Marcellus Washburn, *The Music Man*, 2001–02

Brindley, Susan: Paquette, *Candide*, 1983–84; Ellie, *Show Boat*, 1984–85

Brinkerhoff, Gayle: Second Lay Sister, *Il Trittico (A Triptych)*, 1972–73; Adah, *Naughty Marietta*, 1977–78

Brinson, Anthony: Tiger, *West Side Story*, 1992–93

Brint, Cassandra: Prostitute, *Danton and Robespierre*, 1977–78

Broadaway, Andrew: Lillas Pastia, *Carmen*, 1998–99; Mercury, *Orphée aux enfers (Orpheus in the Underworld)*, 1998–99; Rock Singer, *Mass*, 1998–99; Second Apprentice, *Wozzeck*, 1999–2000; Second Footman, *Vanessa*, 1999–2000

Brookes, Gregory: Leporello, *Don Giovanni*, 2002–03; Lindorf, *Les Contes d'Hoffmann (The Tales of Hoffmann)*, 2002–03; Don Geronio, *Il Turco in Italia (The Turk in Italy)*, 2003–04; Bottom, *A Midsummer Night's Dream*, 2005–06; Leporello, *Don Giovanni*, 2006–07; The Mikado of Japan, *The Mikado*, 2006–07

Brooks, C. Louis: Doctor Bartolo, *Il Barbiere di Siviglia (The Barber of Seville)*, 1994–95; Henry Kissinger, *Nixon in China*, 1994–95; Man in Armor, *Die Zauberflöte (The Magic Flute)*, 1994–95; Swallow, *Peter Grimes*, 1994–95; Lesbo, *Agrippina*, 1995–96; Venus, *Agrippina*, 1995–96; Dick Deadeye, *HMS Pinafore*, 1997–98; Jud Fry, *Oklahoma!*, 1997–98

Brooks, Carri Jane: Ayah to Princess Samaris, *Kismet*, 1963–64

Brooks, Colleen: Kate, *The Ballad of Baby Doe*, 2003–04; Sylviane, *Die lustige Witwe (The Merry Widow)*, 2003–04; Catherine, *A View from the Bridge*, 2004–05

Brooks, David: Old Silver Miner, *The Ballad of Baby Doe*, 1982–83

Brooks, Jane: Zozo, *Die lustige Witwe (The Merry Widow)*, 1964–65; Zozo, *Die lustige Witwe (The Merry Widow)*, 1965–66

Brooks, Jill: Lolo, *Die lustige Witwe (The Merry Widow)*, 1964–65

Brooks, Tom: The Pardoner, *Canterbury Tales*, 1978–79; Thisbe, *La Cenerentola (Cinderella)*, 2004–05; Hermia, *A Midsummer Night's Dream*, 2005–06

Brower, Angela: Kate Pinkerton, *Madama Butterfly*, 2006–07; Cherubino, *Le Nozze di Figaro (The Marriage of Figaro)*, 2007–08

Brown, Angela M.: Seena, *1600 Pennsylvania Avenue*, 1992–93; Fata Morgana, *The Love for Three Oranges*, 1993–94; Ariadne/Prima Donna, *Ariadne auf Naxos*, 1996–97

Brown, Cristy Lynn: Auntie, *Peter Grimes*, 1994–95; Bloody Mary, *South Pacific*, 1995–96; The Witch, *Hänsel und Gretel*, 1995–96; Praskovia, *Die lustige Witwe (The Merry Widow)*, 1996–97; Suzuki, *Madama Butterfly*, 1996–97; Aunt Eller, *Oklahoma!*, 1997–98; Buttercup, *HMS Pinafore*, 1997–98; The Old Prioress, *Dialogues des Carmélites*, 1997–98

Brown, Dorothea: Giulietta, *Les Contes d'Hoffmann (The Tales of Hoffmann)*, 1959–60; Magda de Civry, *La Rondine (The Swallow)*, 1959–60; Manon Lescaut, *Manon Lescaut*, 1959–60; The Peasant's Daughter, *Die Kluge (The Clever Girl)*, 1959–60; Elizabeth of Valois, *Don Carlos*, 1960–61; First Lady, *Die Zauberflöte (The Magic Flute)*, 1960–61; Hester Prynne, *The Scarlet Letter*, 1960–61; Mrs. Anna Maurant, *Street Scene*, 1960–61; Queen of Shemakha, *Le Coq d'or (The Golden Cockerel)*, 1960–61; Violetta Valery, *La Traviata*, 1960–61

Brown, Dorothy: Mistress Hibbins, *The Scarlet Letter*, 1960–61; Third Lady, *Die Zauberflöte (The Magic Flute)*, 1960–61; Hermia, *A Midsummer Night's Dream*, 1961–62; Mistress Hibbins, *The Scarlet Letter*, 1961–62; Shepherd Boy, *Tosca*, 1961–62

Brown, Heidi: Hannah, *Carousel*, 1993–94; Bluma, *Fiddler on the Roof*, 1994–95

Brown, J. Riley: Second Commissioner, *Dialogues des Carmélites*, 1965–66

Brown, Jenna: Elizabeth Tabor, *The Ballad of Baby Doe*, 2003–04

Brown, Lauren: Princess Ying Yaowlak, *The King and I*, 1996–97; Gracie Shinn, *The Music Man*, 2001–02

Brown, Lyle: Pirate, *Candide*, 1993–94; Westphalian Soldier, *Candide*, 1993–94

Brown, Mark: Ned Keene, *Peter Grimes*, 1987–88; Scrivener, *Béatrice et Bénédict*, 1987–88; Rinuccio, *Gianni Schicchi*, 1988–89; 3rd Muezzin, *Kismet*, 1989–90; Bangle Man, *Kismet*, 1989–90; Cassio, *Otello*, 1989–90; Imam, *Kismet*, 1989–90; Menelaus, *The Cry of Clytaemnestra*, 1989–90; Alfred, *Die Fledermaus (The Bat)*, 1990–91; Count Danilo Danilovitch, *Die lustige Witwe (The Merry Widow)*, 1990–91; The Contino Belfiore, *La Finta Giardiniera*, 1990–91; Don Jose, *Carmen*, 1991–92; Lt. Pinkerton, *Madama Butterfly*, 1991–92; The Duke of Mantua, *Rigoletto*, 1992–93

Brown, Maxwilliam: Nikolios, *The Greek Passion*, 1980–81; The Imperial Commissioner, *Madama Butterfly*, 1981–82

Brown, Melanie: Maid, *Vanessa*, 1999–2000; Esmeralda, *The Bartered Bride*, 2001–02

Brown, Michael: Moose, *West Side Story*, 1985–86

Brown, Nathan: Breedley, *A Wedding*, 2007–08; Count Ceprano, *Rigoletto*, 2007–08; Hermann, *Les Contes d'Hoffmann (The Tales of Hoffmann)*, 2007–08

Brown, Paul: Count Monterone, *Rigoletto*, 1992–93; Sharpless, *Madama Butterfly*, 1996–97; Ford, *Falstaff*, 1997–98; Giorgio Germont, *La Traviata*, 1997–98

Brown, Raylene: Maria, *West Side Story*, 1992–93

Brown, Stephen: Ruggero Lastouc, *La Rondine (The Swallow)*, 1989–90

Brown, William: Clarence Cratwell, *Soldier Boy, Soldier*, 1982–83

Brown, Willie: Gastone, *La Traviata*, 1960–61; Monostatos, *Die Zauberflöte (The Magic Flute)*, 1960–61; A slave, *Die Entführung aus dem Serail (The Abduction from the Seraglio)*, 1961–62; Flute, *A Midsummer Night's Dream*, 1961–62; Reverend Master John W. Wilson, *The Scarlet Letter*, 1961–62; Schmidt, *Werther*, 1961–62

Browne, Phyllis: Cinders, *L'Enfant et les Sortilèges (The Bewitched Child)*, 1955–56

Browning, David: Parpignol, *La Bohème*, 1984–85

Brownlee, Lawrence: Brighella, *Ariadne auf Naxos*, 1996–97; The Dancing Master, *Ariadne auf Naxos*, 1996–97; Ernesto, *Don Pasquale*, 1997–98; Don Ramiro, *La Cenerentola (Cinderella)*, 1998–99; Prince Tamino, *Die Zauberflöte (The Magic Flute)*, 1998–99; The Prince, *The Love for Three Oranges*, 1999–2000; Count Almaviva, *Il Barbiere di Siviglia (The Barber of Seville)*, 2000–01; Faust, *Faust*, 2000–01

Bruce, Beverly: Louise, *Carousel*, 1976–77

Bruce, Linda: Porter of the Convent, *Il Trittico (A Triptych)*, 1982–83; Sarah, *The Ballad of Baby Doe*, 1982–83; The Monitor of the Convent, *Il Trittico (A Triptych)*, 1982–83

Brundick, Melissa: The Housekeeper for Alonso, *Man of La Mancha*, 1985–86

Bryan, Elizabeth: Sandman, *Hänsel und Gretel,* 1989–90; Arminda, *La Finta Giardiniera,* 1990–91; Donna Anna, *Don Giovanni,* 1991–92; Countess Almaviva, *Le Nozze di Figaro (The Marriage of Figaro),* 1992–93; Floria Tosca, *Tosca,* 1993–94; Manon Lescaut, *Manon,* 1993–94

Bryant, Eloise: Bloody Mary, *South Pacific,* 1956–57

Bryant, Melville: Paul, *Kiss Me, Kate,* 1951–52

Brylyova, Elena: Francesca, *Francesca da Rimini,* 1989–90

Bubb, John: Ambrose Kemper, *Hello, Dolly!,* 1991–92; Cabinet Minister, *Jubilee,* 1991–92; Morales, *Carmen,* 1991–92; Official Registrar, *Madama Butterfly,* 1991–92; The Imperial Commissioner, *Madama Butterfly,* 1991–92; Riff, *West Side Story,* 1992–93

Bubeck, Daniel: Oberon, *A Midsummer Night's Dream,* 2005–06

Buchanan, Shelly: Mother, *Amahl and the Night Visitors,* 1990–91; Carmen, *Carmen,* 1991–92; Suzuki, *Madama Butterfly,* 1991–92; Juno, *Agrippina,* 1995–96; Maria Miranda Macapa, *McTeague,* 1995–96; Narciso, *Agrippina,* 1995–96; Zaida, *Il Turco in Italia (The Turk in Italy),* 1996–97

Bucher, Terry: A Herald, *The Love for Three Oranges,* 1980–81; Fred, *Oklahoma!,* 1981–82; Al, *The Most Happy Fella,* 1982–83; Washington Dandy, *The Ballad of Baby Doe,* 1982–83

Buchholz, Teresa: Mrs. Meg Page, *Falstaff,* 1992–93; Javotte, *Manon,* 1993–94; Smeraldina, *The Love for Three Oranges,* 1993–94; Melisande, *Pelléas et Mélisande,* 1994–95; Dorabella, *Così fan tutte,* 1995–96; Muse, *Les Contes d'Hoffmann (The Tales of Hoffmann),* 1995–96; Nicklausse, *Les Contes d'Hoffmann (The Tales of Hoffmann),* 1995–96

Buckingham, Kenneth: Furniture Mover, *Street Scene,* 1949–50

Buckwalter, Henry: Official Registrar, *Madama Butterfly,* 1975–76

Buerkert, Eileen: Fruma-Sarah, *Fiddler on the Roof,* 1994–95; Secretary II, *Nixon in China,* 1994–95; Giovanna, *Rigoletto,* 1995–96; Muse, *Les Contes d'Hoffmann (The Tales of Hoffmann),* 1995–96; Nicklausse, *Les Contes d'Hoffmann (The Tales of Hoffmann),* 1995–96; Cherubino, *The Ghosts of Versailles,* 1996–97

Bulli, Marilyn: Mistress Alice Ford (Frau Fluth), *Die lustigen Weiber von Windsor (The Merry Wives of Windsor),* 1981–82; First Lady, *Die Zauberflöte (The Magic Flute),* 1982–83; Maidservant, *Passion Play—Carmina Burana,* 1982–83; Helena, *A Midsummer Night's Dream,* 1983–84; Pink Sheep, *Candide,* 1983–84; The Princess in the Storybook, *L'Enfant et les Sortilèges (The Bewitched Child),* 1984–85

Bultman, Betty Jo: Sister Osmina, *Il Trittico (A Triptych),* 1969–70

Bumbaugh, Rainelle: Page, *Rigoletto,* 2007–08

Bunting, Campbell: Matthew Kumalo, *Lost in the Stars,* 1950–51

Burchett, Christopher: Nick Shadow, *The Rake's Progress,* 1999–2000; Don Basilio, *Il Barbiere di Siviglia (The Barber of Seville),* 2000–01; Dr. Dulcamara, *L'Elisir d'amore (The Elixir of Love),* 2000–01; Olin Blitch, *Susannah,* 2000–01; Figaro, *Le Nozze di Figaro (The Marriage of Figaro),* 2001–02; Raimondo Bidebent, *Lucia di Lammermoor,* 2001–02; Coppelius, *Les Contes d'Hoffmann (The Tales of Hoffmann),* 2002–03; Dappertutto, *Les Contes d'Hoffmann (The Tales of Hoffmann),* 2002–03; Dr. Miracle, *Les Contes d'Hoffmann (The Tales of Hoffmann),* 2002–03; Lindorf, *Les Contes d'Hoffmann (The Tales of Hoffmann),* 2002–03

Burchett, Jacqueline: First Waitress, *Candide,* 2000–01; Ethel Toffelmier, *The Music Man,* 2001–02; Javotte, *Manon,* 2001–02; Kate Pinkerton, *Madama Butterfly,* 2001–02; Violetta Valery, *La Traviata,* 2002–03

Burden, William: Don Curzio, *Le Nozze di Figaro (The Marriage of Figaro),* 1986–87; Candide, *Candide,* 1987–88; Giles Corey, *The Crucible,* 1987–88; Pedrillo, *Die Entführung aus dem Serail (The Abduction from the Seraglio),* 1987–88; Count Almaviva, *Il Barbiere di Siviglia (The Barber of Seville),* 1988–89; Prince Tamino, *Die Zauberflöte (The Magic Flute),* 1988–89; Rinuccio, *Gianni Schicchi,* 1988–89; Ferrando, *Così fan tutte,* 1989–90; Nemorino, *L'Elisir d'amore (The Elixir of Love),* 1990–91

Burdett, Robert: Guide, *Carmen,* 1962–63; Happy Haliday, *La Fanciulla del West (The Girl of the Golden West),* 1963–64; Ned Keene, *Peter Grimes,* 1963–64; Notary, *Il Barbiere di Siviglia (The Barber of Seville),* 1963–64; Doctor Spinelloccio, *Gianni Schicchi,* 1964–65; Novakovich, *Die lustige Witwe (The Merry Widow),* 1964–65; Dancaire, *Carmen,* 1965–66; Notary, *Don Pasquale,* 1965–66; Novakovich, *Die lustige Witwe (The Merry Widow),* 1965–66; The Witch Doctor, *A Hoosier Tale,* 1966–67

Burdick, Barbara: Stella, *Les Contes d'Hoffmann (The Tales of Hoffmann),* 1973–74; The Duchess of Plaza-Toro, *The Gondoliers,* 1974–75; Sarah, *The Ballad of Baby Doe,* 1975–76

Burdsall, Timothy: Prunier, *La Rondine (The Swallow),* 1989–90; Andres, *Wozzeck,* 1990–91; Gastone, *La Traviata,* 1990–91

Burgess, Gary: Alfredo Germont, *La Traviata,* 1968–69; Page, *Parsifal,* 1968–69; Chevalier des Grieux, *Manon Lescaut,* 1970–71

Burgin, John: Fenton, *Falstaff,* 1956–57; Spoletta, *Tosca,* 1957–58

Burgtorf, Carol: Madrigal Singer, *Manon Lescaut,* 1970–71

Burke, Caitlin: Somewhere solo, *West Side Story,* 2002–03; The Ayah, *The Secret Garden,* 2003–04

Burke, Derek: Vladimir, *Fiddler on the Roof,* 1994–95

Burke, Jason: Newsboy, *Jubilee,* 1991–92; Connecticut Delegate, *1600 Pennsylvania Avenue,* 1992–93; Mercury, *Orphée aux enfers (Orpheus in the Underworld),* 1992–93; Ordway, *1600 Pennsylvania Avenue,* 1992–93; Riff, *West Side Story,* 1992–93; Benoit, *La Bohème,* 1994–95; Marcus Schouler, *McTeague,* 1995–96

Burns, Lynn: Diana, *Orphée aux enfers (Orpheus in the Underworld),* 1984–85; Ida, *Die Fledermaus (The Bat),* 1985–86; Adina's aunt, *L'Elisir d'amore (The Elixir of Love),* 1986–87; Sister Constance, *Dialogues des Carmélites,* 1986–87; Attendant to Cunegonde, *Candide,* 1987–88; Niece, *Peter Grimes,* 1987–88; Pink Sheep, *Candide,* 1987–88; Anne Egerman, *A Little Night Music,* 1988–89

Burns, Stephen: A Captain, *Eugene Onegin,* 1988–89

Burr, Charles: Hermann, *Les Contes d'Hoffmann (The Tales of Hoffmann),* 1947–48; Peters, *Down in the Valley,* 1947–48; The Intern, *Hin und Zurück (There and Back),* 1947–48; Von Schwind, *Blossom Time,* 1952–53

Burrell, Amy: A Princess of Ababu, *Kismet,* 1989–90

Burrows, Elmar: The Major Domo, *Ariadne auf Naxos,* 1969–70

Bursky, Jay: Count Ceprano, *Rigoletto,* 1974–75; Barney, *The Ballad of Baby Doe,* 1975–76

Burt, Mary: Mrs. Alice Ford, *Falstaff,* 1976–77; Third Lady, *Die Zauberflöte (The Magic Flute),* 1977–78

Burton, Donna: Xenia, *Boris Godunov,* 1953–54

Burton, Larry: Angus MacGregor, *Brigadoon,* 1961–62; First Ancestor, *Ruddigore (The Witch's Curse),* 1962–63

Burton, Matthew: Oberon, *A Midsummer Night's Dream,* 2005–06

Bushard, Suzanne: Xenia, *Boris Godunov,* 1964–65

Bushfield, Mary: Giovanna, *Rigoletto,* 1950–51

Busse, Robert: Yeoman Herbert Quale, *South Pacific,* 1956–57

Bustin, Paul: Innkeeper, *Manon,* 1993–94; Leandro, *The Love for Three Oranges,* 1993–94; Golaud, *Pelléas et Mélisande,* 1994–95

Butler, Cameron: Moth, *A Midsummer Night's Dream,* 2005–06

Butler, Kate: Orpheus, *Orfeo ed Euridice,* 1992–93

Butler, Kevin: Silas Slick, *Naughty Marietta,* 1977–78; Page, *Canterbury Tales,* 1978–79; Robin, *Canterbury Tales,* 1978–79; Will Parker, *Oklahoma!,* 1981–82; The Postman, *The Most Happy Fella,* 1982–83; Father Bernard, *Candide,* 1983–84; Judge of the Inquisition, *Candide,* 1983–84; Frank, *Show Boat,* 1984–85; Rubberface, *Show Boat,* 1984–85

Butterman, Michael: Jupiter, *Orphée aux enfers (Orpheus in the Underworld),* 1992–93

Bybee, Brooklyn: Trouble, *Madama Butterfly,* 1991–92

Byers, Carol: Spirit, *Die Zauberflöte (The Magic Flute),* 1977–78; Coryphee, *Murder in the Cathedral,* 1984–85; Irene, *Tamerlano,* 1984–85

Byers, Jeffrey: Coppelius, *Les Contes d'Hoffmann (The Tales of Hoffmann),* 1995–96; Dappertutto, *Les Contes d'Hoffmann (The Tales of Hoffmann),* 1995–96; Dr. Miracle, *Les Contes d'Hoffmann (The Tales of Hoffmann),* 1995–96; Rigoletto, *Rigoletto,* 1995–96; Don Giovanni, *Don Giovanni,* 1996–97; Sharpless, *Madama Butterfly,* 1996–97

Byers, Joy: Fluff, *The Veil,* 1949–50

Byler, Christopher: Washington Dandy, *The Ballad of Baby Doe,* 1975–76; Prince Yamadori, *Madama Butterfly,* 1976–77; Etienne Grandet, *Naughty Marietta,* 1977–78; Roland, *Danton and Robespierre,* 1977–78; The Mayor of Dikanka, *The Night Before Christmas,* 1977–78; Carpenter, *Canterbury Tales,* 1978–79; January, *Canterbury Tales,* 1978–79; The Steward, *Canterbury Tales,* 1978–79

Byrd, Avance: Giuseppe, *La Traviata,* 1983–84

Byrne, Sandra: Amazon, *The Boys from Syracuse,* 1968–69

Byun, Jin Hwan: Arturo Bucklaw, *Lucia di Lammermoor,* 2001–02; Alfredo Germont, *La Traviata,* 2002–03; Fenton, *Falstaff,* 2003–04; Rodolfo, *La Bohème,* 2004–05

Cacciola, Nicholas: Bernardo, *West Side Story,* 2002–03

Cahill, Timothy: Nireno, *Giulio Cesare (Julius Caesar),* 2002–03; Bogdanowitsch, *Die lustige Witwe (The Merry Widow),* 2003–04

Cain, Bruce: Guglielmo, *Così fan tutte,* 1978–79; Schelkalov, *Boris Godunov,* 1978–79; Krushina, *The Bartered Bride,* 1979–80

Caldwell, Jeff: Bulgarian Soldier, *Candide,* 1987–88; Don Pedro, *Béatrice et Bénédict,* 1987–88; Enforcer, *Candide,* 1987–88; Sam Jenkins, *Of Thee I Sing,* 1987–88; Player, *Mass,* 1988–89

Caldwell, Robin: Irene, *Tamerlano,* 1984–85

Call, Amy: Annina, *La Traviata,* 2002–03

Callahan, Tiffany: Whore, *Candide,* 1993–94; Pamina, *Die Zauberflöte (The Magic Flute),* 1994–95; La Périchole, *La Périchole,* 1995–96

Callan, Tatiana: Countess of Eremberg, *Don Carlos,* 1972–73; The Aunt, *Jenůfa,* 1972–73

Cameron, Margie: Greta, *Blossom Time,* 1952–53

Camp, Dewey: Don Alfonso, *Così fan tutte*, 1956–57; Figaro, *Il Barbiere di Siviglia (The Barber of Seville)*, 1956–57; Sir John Falstaff, *Falstaff*, 1956–57; Sacristan, *Tosca*, 1957–58; Fra Melitone, *La Forza del Destino (The Force of Destiny)*, 1962–63; Juggler, *The Darkened City*, 1962–63; Don Annibale Pistachio, *Il Campanello di Notte (The Night Bell)*, 1963–64; Gypsy, *The Fair at Sorochinsk*, 1963–64; A Mandarin, *Turandot*, 1964–65; Gianni Schicchi, *Gianni Schicchi*, 1964–65; Officer of the Border Guard, *Boris Godunov*, 1964–65; Ping, *Turandot*, 1964–65; Prince Yamadori, *Madama Butterfly*, 1964–65; Dancaire, *Carmen*, 1965–66

Camp, Michael: Westphalian Soldier, *Candide*, 1987–88; Larry, *Company*, 1990–91

Camp, Rex: Sheriff, *Finian's Rainbow*, 1969–70

Campbell, Charles: Coppelius, *Les Contes d'Hoffmann (The Tales of Hoffmann)*, 1947–48; Luther, *Les Contes d'Hoffmann (The Tales of Hoffmann)*, 1947–48; The Preacher, *Down in the Valley*, 1947–48; Thomas Bouche, *Down in the Valley*, 1947–48; Klingsor, *Parsifal*, 1948–49; Captain Duval, *The New Moon*, 1949–50; Colline, *La Bohème*, 1949–50; Herr Franz, *The Firefly*, 1949–50; Klingsor, *Parsifal*, 1949–50; Mr. Carl Olsen, *Street Scene*, 1949–50; Popoff, *Die lustige Witwe (The Merry Widow)*, 1949–50; Stranger, *The Jumping Frog of Calaveras County*, 1949–50

Campbell, Cynthia: Jean MacLaren, *Brigadoon*, 1952–53; Louise, *Carousel*, 1952–53; Jean MacLaren, *Brigadoon*, 1953–54; Susan, *Finian's Rainbow*, 1953–54

Canady, James: Player, *Bernstein on Broadway*, 1976–77

Canfield, Nanette: Sarah, *The Ballad of Baby Doe*, 1982–83; Prospective Slave, *Candide*, 1983–84; The Baroness, *Candide*, 1983–84; Victim of the Inquisition, *Candide*, 1983–84; Parthy Ann Hawkes, *Show Boat*, 1984–85

Capell, Matthew: Detective, *Porgy and Bess*, 1976–77; Lillas Pastia, *Carmen*, 1977–78

Capelle, Madelene: Electra, *Idomeneo*, 1976–77

Caperton, Callie: A Princess of Ababu, *Kismet*, 1989–90

Caplinger, Carmon: Cascada, *Die lustige Witwe (The Merry Widow)*, 1949–50; Uncle Henry, *The Jumping Frog of Calaveras County*, 1949–50

Capps, Kay: Lover, *Il Trittico (A Triptych)*, 1982–83; Dodo, *Die lustige Witwe (The Merry Widow)*, 1983–84; The Landlord's Daughter, *Tom Jones*, 1983–84; Despina, *Così fan tutte*, 1984–85

Cappuccilli, Mark: Miroslav the Goldsmith, *The Excursions of Mr. Broucek*, 1981–82; Priest, *Murder in the Cathedral*, 1984–85; Anselmo / a Muleteer, *Man of La Mancha*, 1985–86

Cardenas, Nestor: Gherardo, *Il Trittico (A Triptych)*, 1982–83; Pritschitsch, *Die lustige Witwe (The Merry Widow)*, 1983–84; Remendado, *Carmen*, 1984–85

Carducci, Chris: Hermann, *Les Contes d'Hoffmann (The Tales of Hoffmann)*, 2002–03; Schlemil, *Les Contes d'Hoffmann (The Tales of Hoffmann)*, 2002–03; Dr. Malatesta, *Don Pasquale*, 2003–04; Prosdocimo, *Il Turco in Italia (The Turk in Italy)*, 2003–04; Papageno, *Die Zauberflöte (The Magic Flute)*, 2004–05; Guglielmo, *Così fan tutte*, 2005–06

Carey, Brian: Scipio, *Porgy and Bess*, 1976–77

Carey, Joan: Serena, *Porgy and Bess*, 1976–77

Carey, Phil: Zanni, *Il Mondo della Luna (The World on the Moon)*, 1975–76

Carguill, Reyna: Suor Genovieffa, *Suor Angelica (Sister Angelica)*, 1999–2000; Mrs. Hayes, *Susannah*, 2000–01; Beatrice, *Jeppe*, 2002–03; Rosalinda, *Die Fledermaus (The Bat)*, 2002–03; Floria Tosca, *Tosca*, 2004–05

Carlock, William: Man, *Street Scene*, 1949–50; Workman, *Street Scene*, 1949–50

Carlton, Christine: Violetta Valery, *La Traviata*, 1983–84; Fiordiligi, *Così fan tutte*, 1984–85

Carlton, Grant: Captain, *Carousel*, 1993–94

Carmack, Dee: Count of Lerma, *Don Carlos*, 1972–73; Gherardo, *Il Trittico (A Triptych)*, 1972–73; Lover, *Il Trittico (A Triptych)*, 1972–73; Page, *Parsifal*, 1972–73; Jo the Loiterer, *The Mother of Us All*, 1973–74; Luiz, *The Gondoliers*, 1974–75; Pedrillo, *Die Entführung aus dem Serail (The Abduction from the Seraglio)*, 1974–75; Goro, *Madama Butterfly*, 1975–76

Carpenter, Floyd: Guard, *Down in the Valley*, 1947–48

Carpenter, John: Soldier of the Praetorian Guard, *L'Incoronazione di Poppea (The Coronation of Poppea)*, 1967–68; Toni Reischmann, *Elegy for Young Lovers*, 1967–68

Carr, Sharon: The Queen, *Jubilee*, 1991–92

Carr, William: City Marshall, *Street Scene*, 1949–50

Carra, Lawrence, Jr.: Alex, *Lost in the Stars*, 1950–51

Carroll, Mike: Aunt Emma, *Hin und Zurück (There and Back)*, 1947–48

Carroll, Richard: Second Deputy, *Finian's Rainbow*, 1969–70

Carsey, Richard: Player, *Mass*, 1987–88; Player, *Mass*, 1988–89

Carson, Patrick: Newcomer, *Street Scene*, 1960–61; Captain, *The Scarlet Letter*, 1961–62; Count di Lerma, *Don Carlos*, 1961–62

Cart, Robert: Westphalian Soldier, *Candide*, 1987–88

Carter, Kay: Moth, *A Midsummer Night's Dream*, 1961–62; Musetta, *La Bohème*, 1962–63; The Girl, *The Fantasticks*, 1963–64

Carter, Ruth: Micaëla, *Carmen*, 1956–57; Rosina, *Il Barbiere di Siviglia (The Barber of Seville)*, 1956–57

Casbon, Carissa: Princess Ninetta, *The Love for Three Oranges*, 1993–94; Berille, *Fiddler on the Roof*, 1994–95; Pat Nixon, *Nixon in China*, 1994–95

Case, Kathryn: Norina, *Don Pasquale*, 1980–81; Mistress Alice Ford (Frau Fluth), *Die lustigen Weiber von Windsor (The Merry Wives of Windsor)*, 1981–82

Casey, Barry Lawrence: Count Monterone, *Rigoletto*, 1986–87; Captain Balstrode, *Peter Grimes*, 1987–88; The Imperial Commissioner, *Madama Butterfly*, 1987–88; Zaretsky, *Eugene Onegin*, 1988–89

Casey, Trent: Gideon March, *Little Women*, 2001–02; Innkeeper, *Manon*, 2001–02; Don Giovanni, *Don Giovanni*, 2002–03; Dr. Miracle, *Les Contes d'Hoffmann (The Tales of Hoffmann)*, 2002–03; Player, *Putting It Together*, 2002–03; Horace Tabor, *The Ballad of Baby Doe*, 2003–04

Cassard, Francesca: Kundry, *Parsifal*, 1960–61; Floria Tosca, *Tosca*, 1961–62

Cassel, Walter: Horace Tabor, *The Ballad of Baby Doe*, 1975–76; Baron Scarpia, *Tosca*, 1977–78; Horace Tabor, *The Ballad of Baby Doe*, 1982–83

Cassimatis, Paul: An Indian, *The Bartered Bride*, 1955–56

Castellan, Caryn: Clo-clo, *Die lustige Witwe (The Merry Widow)*, 1990–91; Ermengarde, *Hello, Dolly!*, 1991–92

Castells, Carolina: Emily, *Our Town*, 2005–06; Donna Elvira, *Don Giovanni*, 2006–07; Antonia, *Les Contes d'Hoffmann (The Tales of Hoffmann)*, 2007–08

Casto, Carmen: Gossip 1, *The Ghosts of Versailles*, 1996–97

Castronuovo, David: Porter of the Seminary, *Manon*, 1979–80

Cave, Susan: Himeneo, *L'Orfeo*, 1987–88; Mary Turner, *Of Thee I Sing*, 1987–88

Cawood, Elizabeth: Dame Hannah, *Ruddigore (The Witch's Curse)*, 1962–63

Cawood, Marion: Mimi, *La Bohème*, 1962–63; Rosalinda, *Die Fledermaus (The Bat)*, 1962–63; Fiordiligi, *Così fan tutte*, 1963–64; Donna Anna, *Don Giovanni*, 1964–65; Hanna Glawari, *Die lustige Witwe (The Merry Widow)*, 1964–65

Cemore, Alan: Footman at the wedding, *The Ballad of Baby Doe*, 1982–83; Papageno, *Die Zauberflöte (The Magic Flute)*, 1982–83; Count Danilo Danilovitch, *Die lustige Witwe (The Merry Widow)*, 1983–84; Giorgio Germont, *La Traviata*, 1983–84; Police Chief, *Candide*, 1983–84; Señor of Cadiz, *Candide*, 1983–84; Marcello, *La Bohème*, 1984–85; Dr. Falke, *Die Fledermaus (The Bat)*, 1985–86

Cercy, Joseph: The Priest, *The Most Happy Fella*, 1982–83; Flute, *A Midsummer Night's Dream*, 1983–84; Torquemada, *L'Heure espagnole (The Spanish Hour)*, 1984–85

Cesbron, Jean-Jacques: Choir boy, *Candide*, 1987–88

Cha, Jong-Hun: M. Javelinot, *Dialogues des Carmélites*, 2004–05; Prince of Verona, *Roméo et Juliette*, 2005–06; Masetto, *Don Giovanni*, 2006–07; Prince Yamadori, *Madama Butterfly*, 2006–07

Chae, Seung-Ah: Tuptim, *The King and I*, 1996–97

Chaffin, Brad: Chip, *On the Town*, 1951–52

Chakos, Gigi: Anita, *West Side Story*, 1985–86; Esmeralda, *The Bartered Bride*, 1986–87; Older Sister, later Povarikha, *The Legend of Tsar Saltan*, 1986–87

Chamberlain, Gail: Smeraldina, *The Love for Three Oranges*, 1980–81; Kedruta, *The Excursions of Mr. Broucek*, 1981–82; Martha, *Faust*, 1981–82; Berta (Marcellina), *Il Barbiere di Siviglia (The Barber of Seville)*, 1982–83; Marie, *The Most Happy Fella*, 1982–83

Chambers, Matthew: Sheriff, *McTeague*, 1995–96; Count Almaviva, *The Ghosts of Versailles*, 1996–97; Gabriel von Eisenstein, *Die Fledermaus (The Bat)*, 1996–97; Don Basilio, *Le Nozze di Figaro (The Marriage of Figaro)*, 1997–98; Graf Elemer, *Arabella*, 1998–99

Chambers, Stephen: Lover, *Il Trittico (A Triptych)*, 1982–83; Song Vendor, *Il Trittico (A Triptych)*, 1982–83; Blifil, *Tom Jones*, 1983–84; Candide, *Candide*, 1983–84; Flute, *A Midsummer Night's Dream*, 1983–84; Maximilian, *Candide*, 1983–84; Tonio, *La Fille du régiment (The Daughter of the Regiment)*, 1984–85

Champ, Christi: Annina, *La Traviata*, 1997–98; Beth, *Little Women*, 2001–02

Champagne, Salvatore: Ernesto, *Don Pasquale*, 1988–89; Hoffmann, *Les Contes d'Hoffmann (The Tales of Hoffmann)*, 1988–89; Rodolfo, *La Bohème*, 1989–90

Chandler, Janice: Giulietta, *Les Contes d'Hoffmann (The Tales of Hoffmann)*, 1988–89; Marguerite, *Faust*, 1989–90

Chaney, Michael: Pete, *Show Boat*, 1984–85; Steve, *Show Boat*, 1984–85; Sir Dinadan, *Camelot*, 1986–87

Chaney, Philip: Bushy, *The Ballad of Baby Doe*, 1982–83; Monostatos, *Die Zauberflöte (The Magic Flute)*, 1982–83; Froh, *Das Rheingold*, 1983–84

Chang, Michael: Gherardo, *Gianni Schicchi*, 1964–65; Goro, *Madama Butterfly*, 1964–65; Missail, *Boris Godunov*, 1964–65; Count Riccardo, *Quattro rusteghi (The Four Ruffians)*, 1966–67

Charbonnet, Jeanne-Michele: Countess Almaviva, *Le Nozze di Figaro (The Marriage of Figaro)*, 1986–87; Ellen Orford, *Peter Grimes*, 1987–88; Tatyana, *Eugene Onegin*, 1988–89; Desdemona, *Otello*, 1989–90

Chasteen, Terry: Lodovico, Court Gentleman, *The Tempest*, 1985–86; First Commissioner, *Dialogues des Carmélites*, 1986–87; Don Basilio, *Le Nozze di Figaro (The Marriage of Figaro)*, 1986–87; Bob Boles, *Peter Grimes*, 1987–88; Goro, *Madama Butterfly*, 1987–88; Prince Tamino, *Die Zauberflöte (The Magic*

Flute), 1988–89; Poet, *The Dawn of the Poor King*, 1990–91; Candide, *Candide*, 1993–94; Rinuccio, *Gianni Schicchi*, 1993–94

Cheatham, Jill: Mrs. Gleaton, *Susannah*, 2007–08

Cheek, Sher Lee: Katinka, *The Chocolate Soldier*, 1950–51; Pitti-Sing, *The Mikado*, 1950–51; Rose, *Lost in the Stars*, 1950–51

Chen, Rong-Kwei: Leader of Penitents, *The Darkened City*, 1978–79

Chen, Yun-Yi: Zerlina, *Don Giovanni*, 1985–86

Cheron, Carrie: Sister Mathilde, *Dialogues des Carmélites*, 1997–98; Player, *Mass*, 1998–99

Cherry, Alphonso: Don Issachar, *Candide*, 2000–01; Figaro, *Le Nozze di Figaro (The Marriage of Figaro)*, 2001–02; Krushina, *The Bartered Bride*, 2001–02; Prince Yamadori, *Madama Butterfly*, 2001–02; The Imperial Commissioner, *Madama Butterfly*, 2001–02

Chertkoff, Darren: Cobweb, *A Midsummer Night's Dream*, 1983–84; Orange Merchant, *Kismet*, 1989–90

Cheung, Chris: Don Curzio, *Le Nozze di Figaro (The Marriage of Figaro)*, 2007–08

Chiarelli, Angelo: Don Curzio, *Le Nozze di Figaro (The Marriage of Figaro)*, 1973–74; Triquet, *Eugene Onegin*, 1974–75; Schmidt, *Werther*, 1975–76

Chisenhall, Richard: Spalanzani, *Les Contes d'Hoffmann (The Tales of Hoffmann)*, 1978–79

Chitwood, Trent: Gee-Tar, *West Side Story*, 2002–03

Choi, In: Prince Yamadori, *Madama Butterfly*, 1976–77

Chreste, William: Hessian, *Candide*, 1957–58; Very Old Inquisitor, *Candide*, 1957–58

Christenson, Ann: Myrtle, *Street Scene*, 1949–50

Christenson, Jane: Arnalta, *L'Incoronazione di Poppea (The Coronation of Poppea)*, 1967–68; Carolina von Kirchstettin, *Elegy for Young Lovers*, 1967–68; Ludmila, *The Bartered Bride*, 1967–68; Madelon, *Andrea Chénier*, 1967–68; Mother Goose, *The Rake's Progress*, 1968–69; The Abbess, *Il Trittico (A Triptych)*, 1969–70

Christiansen, Philip: Captain of the Inquisition, *Man of La Mancha*, 1988–89; Guccio, *Gianni Schicchi*, 1988–89; Hermann, *Les Contes d'Hoffmann (The Tales of Hoffmann)*, 1988–89; Notary, *Il Barbiere di Siviglia (The Barber of Seville)*, 1988–89; Slave, *Die Zauberflöte (The Magic Flute)*, 1988–89; The Wazir of Police, *Kismet*, 1989–90; Kronkov, *Die lustige Witwe (The Merry Widow)*, 1990–91; A Sandwich Man, *Jubilee*, 1991–92; Cabinet Minister, *Jubilee*, 1991–92; Cornelius Hackl, *Hello, Dolly!*, 1991–92; Dandini, *La Cenerentola (Cinderella)*, 1991–92; Lifeguard, *Jubilee*, 1991–92; Master of Ceremonies, *Jubilee*, 1991–92;

Police Officer, *Jubilee*, 1991–92; The Bonze, *Madama Butterfly*, 1991–92; The Imperial Commissioner, *Madama Butterfly*, 1991–92; Count Monterone, *Rigoletto*, 1992–93; Jupiter, *Orphée aux enfers (Orpheus in the Underworld)*, 1992–93; New Hampshire Delegate, *1600 Pennsylvania Avenue*, 1992–93; Pimms, *1600 Pennsylvania Avenue*, 1992–93; Billy Bigelow, *Carousel*, 1993–94; Leandro, *The Love for Three Oranges*, 1993–94; Maximilian, *Candide*, 1993–94

Christiansen, William: Guillot, *Eugene Onegin*, 1988–89; Governor, *Candide*, 1993–94; The Governor of Cartagena, *Candide*, 1993–94

Chu, George: Enoch Snow, Jr., *Carousel*, 1976–77

Cioffari, Adam: Photographer, *The Ballad of Baby Doe*, 2003–04; Customs Officer, *La Bohème*, 2004–05; Man in Armor, *Die Zauberflöte (The Magic Flute)*, 2004–05; Snug, *A Midsummer Night's Dream*, 2005–06; Guardsman, *Manon*, 2006–07; Masetto, *Don Giovanni*, 2006–07; Orson, *Too Many Sopranos*, 2006–07; The Imperial Commissioner, *Madama Butterfly*, 2006–07; Welko, *Arabella*, 2006–07; Coppelius, *Les Contes d'Hoffmann (The Tales of Hoffmann)*, 2007–08; Count Monterone, *Rigoletto*, 2007–08; Dr. Miracle, *Les Contes d'Hoffmann (The Tales of Hoffmann)*, 2007–08; Elder Ott, *Susannah*, 2007–08

Ciolek, Lynda: Spirit, *Die Zauberflöte (The Magic Flute)*, 1972–73; Anna Hope, *The Mother of Us All*, 1973–74; Mercedes, *Carmen*, 1973–74

Claffey, Dianne: Filipyevna, *Eugene Onegin*, 1974–75

Clark, Andrea: Fredel, *Fiddler on the Roof*, 1994–95

Clark, Catherine: Lauretta, *Il Trittico (A Triptych)*, 1972–73; Constance Fletcher, *The Mother of Us All*, 1973–74; Constanza, *Die Entführung aus dem Serail (The Abduction from the Seraglio)*, 1974–75; Gianetta, *The Gondoliers*, 1974–75; Musetta, *La Bohème*, 1974–75; Flaminia, *Il Mondo della Luna (The World on the Moon)*, 1975–76; Mrs. Nordstrom, *A Little Night Music*, 1975–76

Clark, Cheryl: Louise, *Carousel*, 1970–71

Clark, David: Don Basilio, *Le Nozze di Figaro (The Marriage of Figaro)*, 1968–69; Sellem, *The Rake's Progress*, 1968–69

Clark, Dennis: Jerome, *South Pacific*, 1956–57; Louis Leonowens, *The King and I*, 1957–58

Clark, Heidi: Attendant to Cunegonde, *Candide*, 1987–88; Countess Celimene, *A Little Night Music*, 1988–89; Desiree Armfeldt, *A Little Night Music*, 1988–89; Lalume, *Kismet*, 1989–90; Hanna Glawari, *Die lustige Witwe (The Merry Widow)*, 1990–91; Rosalinda, *Die Fledermaus (The Bat)*, 1990–91; The Queen, *Jubilee*, 1991–92

Clark, Keith: Cap'n Andy, *Show Boat*, 1984–85; Windy, *Show Boat*, 1984–85

Clark, Kristin: Bianca, *Kiss Me, Kate*, 1998–99; Lois Lane, *Kiss Me, Kate*, 1998–99

Clark, Lawrence: Count Almaviva, *Le Nozze di Figaro (The Marriage of Figaro)*, 1955–56; Michele, *Il Tabarro (The Cloak)*, 1955–56; Wagner, *Faust*, 1955–56; Emile DeBeque, *South Pacific*, 1956–57

Clark, Leslie: Bloodhound, *The King and I*, 1957–58

Clark, Mark: Sergeant, *Manon Lescaut*, 1970–71; Messenger, *Heracles*, 1971–72; Antonio, *Le Nozze di Figaro (The Marriage of Figaro)*, 1973–74; Alcindoro, *La Bohème*, 1974–75

Clark, Mozelle: Page, *Parsifal*, 1953–54

Clark, Randy: Drunkard, *The Darkened City*, 1978–79

Clark, Sarah: Praskovia, *Die lustige Witwe (The Merry Widow)*, 2003–04; The McCourt family, *The Ballad of Baby Doe*, 2003–04

Clarke, Grant: Priest, *Die Zauberflöte (The Magic Flute)*, 2004–05

Clay, Jack: Indiana Elliott's Brother, *The Mother of Us All*, 1973–74; Zuniga, *Carmen*, 1973–74; Colline, *La Bohème*, 1974–75; Prince Gremin, *Eugene Onegin*, 1974–75; Sparafucile, *Rigoletto*, 1974–75; Wagner, *Doktor Faust*, 1974–75; The Imperial Commissioner, *Madama Butterfly*, 1975–76; Olin Blitch, *Susannah*, 1976–77

Claycombe, Robert: Ralph, the Stage Manager, *Kiss Me, Kate*, 1998–99

Clayton, Jeffrey: Barney, *The Ballad of Baby Doe*, 1982–83; Gianni Schicchi, *Il Trittico (A Triptych)*, 1982–83; Tony, *The Most Happy Fella*, 1982–83; Anthony Hope, *Sweeney Todd*, 1983–84; Bogdanowitsch, *Die lustige Witwe (The Merry Widow)*, 1983–84; Demetrius, *A Midsummer Night's Dream*, 1983–84; Morales, *Carmen*, 1984–85; Arthur, *Camelot*, 1986–87

Clements, Henry: Alidoro, *La Cenerentola (Cinderella)*, 1957–58; Ferone, *Candide*, 1957–58; Hessian General, *Candide*, 1957–58; Junkman, *Candide*, 1957–58; Schaunard, *La Bohème*, 1957–58; Ship's Captain, *Candide*, 1957–58

Clendening, Bob: Prosecutor at the Wazir's Court, *Kismet*, 1989–90; Court Clerk, *Hello, Dolly!*, 1991–92

Cleveland, Beatrice: Queenie, *Show Boat*, 1953–54

Cleveland, John: Sailor, *Street Scene*, 1949–50

Cline, David: Lover, *Il Trittico (A Triptych)*, 1972–73; Don Curzio, *Le Nozze di Figaro (The Marriage of Figaro)*, 1973–74

Clopper, Jansen: Drunkard, *The Darkened City*, 1962–63; Voice from Inside, *The Darkened City*, 1962–63

Clough, Thomas: Dancaire, *Carmen*, 1962–63; Second Suitor, *The Darkened City*, 1962–63; Trabucco, *La Forza del Destino (The Force of Destiny)*, 1962–63; Nick, *La Fanciulla del West (The Girl of the Golden West)*, 1963–64; Normanno, *Lucia di Lammermoor*, 1963–64; Page, *Parsifal*, 1963–64

Clugstone, Scott: Guide, *Carmen*, 1977–78

Coats, Erin: Cousin Hebe, *HMS Pinafore*, 1997–98; Juno, *Orphée aux enfers (Orpheus in the Underworld)*, 1998–99; Spirit, *Die Zauberflöte (The Magic Flute)*, 1998–99; Thisbe, *La Cenerentola (Cinderella)*, 1998–99; Bianca, *The Rape of Lucretia*, 1999–2000; Berta (Marcellina), *Il Barbiere di Siviglia (The Barber of Seville)*, 2000–01

Cobb, John: A Lamplighter, *Manon Lescaut*, 1959–60; Gobin, *La Rondine (The Swallow)*, 1959–60; Gus, *The Most Happy Fella*, 1959–60; The Doctor, *The Most Happy Fella*, 1959–60

Cobb, Susan: Aida, *Aida*, 1963–64; Ellen Orford, *Peter Grimes*, 1963–64; Minnie, *La Fanciulla del West (The Girl of the Golden West)*, 1963–64; Cio-Cio San, *Madama Butterfly*, 1964–65

Cockrum, James: Amfortas, *Parsifal*, 1951–52; Amfortas, *Parsifal*, 1952–53; Mr. Flint, *Billy Budd*, 1952–53; Amfortas, *Parsifal*, 1953–54

Cody, David: Vecchia, *L'Orfeo*, 1987–88; Doctor Spinelloccio, *Gianni Schicchi*, 1988–89; The Barber, *Man of La Mancha*, 1988–89; Calchas, *The Cry of Clytaemnestra*, 1989–90; Andres, *Wozzeck*, 1990–91; Marquis de Cascada, *Die lustige Witwe (The Merry Widow)*, 1990–91; Borsa, *Rigoletto*, 1992–93; Orpheus, *Orphée aux enfers (Orpheus in the Underworld)*, 1992–93; Bob Boles, *Peter Grimes*, 1994–95; Monostatos, *Die Zauberflöte (The Magic Flute)*, 1994–95; Rev. Horace Adams, *Peter Grimes*, 1994–95

Coffey, Deanna: Friend, *Amelia Goes to the Ball*, 1957–58; Lady Toothly, *Candide*, 1957–58; Mistress Page (Frau Reich), *Die lustigen Weiber von Windsor (The Merry Wives of Windsor)*, 1958–59

Coffin, Phil: Man in Armor, *Die Zauberflöte (The Magic Flute)*, 1953–54

Coffman, Karen: Charlotte, *Werther*, 1975–76; Kate Pinkerton, *Madama Butterfly*, 1975–76

Cogswell, Joshua: The Kralahome, *The King and I*, 1996–97; Andrew Carnes, *Oklahoma!*, 1997–98

Cohen, Devin: 3rd Beggar, *Kismet*, 1989–90

Cohen, Phillip: Giorgio Germont, *La Traviata*, 1954–55; Silvio, *I Pagliacci*, 1954–55; Amfortas, *Parsifal*, 1955–56; Cat, *L'Enfant et les Sortilèges (The Bewitched Child)*, 1955–56; Valentin, *Faust*, 1955–56; Alfio, *Cavalleria Rusticana*, 1957–58; Klingsor, *Parsifal*, 1957–58; Marcello, *La Bohème*, 1957–58; Count Renato, *Un Ballo in Maschera (A Masked Ball)*, 1958–59

Coku, Alexandra: Maria, *West Side Story*, 1985–86; Swan-Bird, *The Legend of Tsar Saltan*, 1986–87; Constanza, *Die Entführung aus dem Serail (The Abduction from the Seraglio)*, 1987–88

Colaner, Daniel: Slim, *Oklahoma!*, 1981–82; Pinellino, *Il Trittico (A Triptych)*, 1982–83

Colbert, Rusty: Charlie Hildebrand, *Street Scene*, 1960–61

Colburn, William: Chevalier de St. Brioche, *Die lustige Witwe (The Merry Widow)*, 1964–65

Cole, Daniel: Doctor Spinelloccio, *Gianni Schicchi*, 1993–94; Farfarello, *The Love for Three Oranges*, 1993–94; Henry Kissinger, *Nixon in China*, 1994–95; Krushina, *The Bartered Bride*, 1994–95; Physician, *Pelléas et Mélisande*, 1994–95; Don Alfonso, *Così fan tutte*, 1995–96; Hermann, *Les Contes d'Hoffmann (The Tales of Hoffmann)*, 1995–96; Leporello, *Don Giovanni*, 1996–97; Figaro, *Le Nozze di Figaro (The Marriage of Figaro)*, 1997–98; Colline, *La Bohème*, 1999–2000

Cole, Robert: Prince Shuisky, *Boris Godunov*, 1983–84; Priest, *Murder in the Cathedral*, 1984–85

Collins, Richard: Ford, *Falstaff*, 1956–57; Baron Scarpia, *Tosca*, 1957–58; Captain Orton, *The King and I*, 1957–58

Coloton, Diane: Baker's Wife, *Danton and Robespierre*, 1977–78; Fiordiligi, *Così fan tutte*, 1977–78; First Lady, *Die Zauberflöte (The Magic Flute)*, 1977–78; Miss Jessel, *The Turn of the Screw*, 1978–79; Wife of Lazarus, *The Darkened City*, 1978–79; Donna Anna, *Don Giovanni*, 1979–80; Old Lady, *Candide*, 2000–01; The Witch, *Hänsel und Gretel*, 2001–02

Colwell, Nora: Alma Hix, *The Music Man*, 2001–02

Concoran, Byron: Flamand, *Capriccio*, 1958–59

Conn, Gary: Mr. Frank Maurant, *Street Scene*, 1960–61

Conner, Nick: Newsboy, *The Ballad of Baby Doe*, 2003–04

Constantakos, Evangelia: Old Lady, *Candide*, 1993–94

Conwell, Julia: Norina, *Don Pasquale*, 1977–78; Oksana, *The Night Before Christmas*, 1977–78

Cook, Cheri: Pauline, *West Side Story*, 1985–86; Gianetta, *L'Elisir d'amore (The Elixir of Love)*, 1986–87; Paquette, *Candide*, 1987–88; Spirit, *Die Zauberflöte (The Magic Flute)*, 1988–89; Marsinah, *Kismet*, 1989–90; Yvette, *La Rondine (The Swallow)*, 1989–90; Don Pasquale, *Don Pasquale*, 1997–98

Cook, Christine: Giovanna, *Rigoletto*, 1966–67; Pantalis, *Mefistofele*, 1967–68; Rosette, *Manon*, 1967–68; Frugola, *Il Trittico (A Triptych)*, 1969–70; Grimgerde, *Die Walküre*, 1969–70; Alisa, *Lucia di Lammermoor*, 1970–71; Mrs. Mullin, *Carousel*, 1970–71; Dame Quickly, *Falstaff*, 1971–72; Princess Eboli, *Don Carlos*, 1972–73

Cook, Curtis: Father Barre, *Die Teufel von Loudun (The Devils of Loudun)*, 1992–93; Pistol, *Falstaff*, 1992–93; Kreonte, *The Love for Three Oranges*, 1993–94; Osmin, *Die Entführung aus dem Serail (The Abduction from the Seraglio)*, 1993–94; Raimondo Bidebent, *Lucia di Lammermoor*, 1993–94; Don Basilio, *Il Barbiere di Siviglia (The Barber of Seville)*, 1994–95; Kezal, *The Bartered Bride*, 1994–95; Sarastro, *Die Zauberflöte (The Magic Flute)*, 1994–95; Baron Mirko Zeta, *Die lustige Witwe (The Merry Widow)*, 1996–97; Commendatore, *Don Giovanni*, 1996–97; Selim, *Il Turco in Italia (The Turk in Italy)*, 1996–97; The Major Domo, *Ariadne auf Naxos*, 1996–97; Don Pasquale, *Don Pasquale*, 1997–98; Sarastro, *Die Zauberflöte (The Magic Flute)*, 1998–99; Don Basilio, *Il Barbiere di Siviglia (The Barber of Seville)*, 2005–06

Cook, Edward: Arbace, *Idomeneo*, 1976–77; Captain, *Carousel*, 1976–77; Doctor Seldon, *Carousel*, 1976–77; Physician, *Pelléas et Mélisande*, 1976–77; Player, *Bernstein on Broadway*, 1976–77; Principal, *Carousel*, 1976–77; Starkeeper, *Carousel*, 1976–77; Panas, *The Night Before Christmas*, 1977–78; Zuniga, *Carmen*, 1977–78; Don Giovanni, *Don Giovanni*, 1979–80; Henry Higgins, *My Fair Lady*, 1979–80; Olin Blitch, *Susannah*, 1979–80; Herald, *Murder in the Cathedral*, 1984–85

Cook, Natalie: Louise, *Carousel*, 1993–94

Cook, Rebecca: Amelia, *Un Ballo in Maschera (A Masked Ball)*, 1975–76; Cio-Cio San, *Madama Butterfly*, 1976–77; Hester Prynne, *The Scarlet Letter*, 1976–77; Susannah Polk, *Susannah*, 1976–77; Floria Tosca, *Tosca*, 1977–78; Antonia, *Les Contes d'Hoffmann (The Tales of Hoffmann)*, 1978–79; Violetta Valery, *La Traviata*, 1978–79

Cook, Samuel: Don Ottavio, *Don Giovanni*, 1979–80; Mingo, *Porgy and Bess*, 1979–80; Count Almaviva, *Il Barbiere di Siviglia (The Barber of Seville)*, 1980–81; Ernesto, *Don Pasquale*, 1980–81; Nikolios, *The Greek Passion*, 1980–81; Belmonte, *Die Entführung aus dem Serail (The Abduction from the Seraglio)*, 1981–82; Mazal, *The Excursions of Mr. Broucek*, 1981–82

Cooke, Richard: Dr. Blind, *Die Fledermaus (The Bat)*, 1962–63; Remendado, *Carmen*, 1962–63; Wagner, *Mefistofele*, 1967–68; Gherardo, *Il Trittico (A Triptych)*, 1969–70

Cooklis, Ramon: Fabrizio, *Il Mondo della Luna (The World on the Moon)*, 1975–76; Frid, *A Little Night Music*, 1975–76

Coop, Allison: Flora Bervoix, *La Traviata*, 1997–98; Player, *Mass*, 1998–99; Spirit, *Die Zauberflöte (The Magic Flute)*, 1998–99; La Ciesca, *Gianni Schicchi*, 1999–2000; La Suora Infermiera, *Suor Angelica (Sister Angelica)*, 1999–2000

Coopman, John: Sir Despard Murgatroyd, *Ruddigore (The Witch's Curse)*, 1962–63

Cope, Amy: Juno, *Orphée aux enfers (Orpheus in the Underworld)*, 1992–93; Gertrude, *Hänsel und Gretel*, 1995–96; Donna Anna, *Don Giovanni*, 1996–97; Marie, *Wozzeck*, 1999–2000

Cope, Anne-Marie: Concepcion, *L'Heure espagnole (The Spanish Hour)*, 1959–60; Lolette, *La Rondine (The Swallow)*, 1959–60; Page, *Parsifal*, 1959–60; Rosabella, *The Most Happy Fella*, 1959–60; Papagena, *Die Zauberflöte (The Magic Flute)*, 1960–61; Rose Maurant, *Street Scene*, 1960–61; Voice of the Cockerel, *Le Coq d'or (The Golden Cockerel)*, 1960–61

Cope, Marianne: Olympia, *Les Contes d'Hoffmann (The Tales of Hoffmann)*, 1995–96; Zerbinetta, *Ariadne auf Naxos*, 1996–97

Cope, Sam: Merchant of Ephesus, *The Boys from Syracuse*, 1968–69

Copeland, Rachel: Peep-Bo (Ward of Ko-Ko), *The Mikado*, 2006–07; Zdenka, *Arabella*, 2006–07

Coppolo, Nicholas: The Young Pastor, *Vanessa*, 1999–2000; Adm. Von Schreiber, *The Sound of Music*, 2000–01; Sam Polk, *Susannah*, 2000–01; Alfred, *Die Fledermaus (The Bat)*, 2002–03; Alfredo Germont, *La Traviata*, 2002–03; Mario Cavaradossi, *Tosca*, 2004–05

Cora, Pablo: Nathanael, *Les Contes d'Hoffmann (The Tales of Hoffmann)*, 1995–96; Frosch, *Die Fledermaus (The Bat)*, 1996–97; Marquis, *The Ghosts of Versailles*, 1996–97

Corbin, Patricia: Giovanna, *Rigoletto*, 1992–93; Louise, *Die Teufel von Loudun (The Devils of Loudun)*, 1992–93

Corcoran, Byron: Buster, *The Land Between the Rivers*, 1955–56; Don Basilio, *Le Nozze di Figaro (The Marriage of Figaro)*, 1955–56; Conjurer, *Candide*, 1957–58; Rodolfo, *La Bohème*, 1957–58; Turiddu, *Cavalleria Rusticana*, 1957–58

Corcoran, Kenneth: Don Jose, *Carmen*, 1956–57; Dr. Caius, *Falstaff*, 1956–57; Mario Cavaradossi, *Tosca*, 1957–58

Cornelison, James: Man in Armor, *Die Zauberflöte (The Magic Flute)*, 1988–89; Speaker of the Temple, *Die Zauberflöte (The Magic Flute)*, 1988–89; Chief Policeman, *Kismet*, 1989–90; Diomedes, *The Cry of Clytaemnestra*, 1989–90; Schaunard, *La Bohème*, 1989–90; Leporello, *Don Giovanni*, 1991–92; Trulove, *The Rake's Progress*, 1991–92; Count Almaviva, *Le Nozze di Figaro (The Marriage of Figaro)*, 1992–93; Baron Scarpia, *Tosca*, 1993–94

Cornelison, Rebecca: Sally, *1600 Pennsylvania Avenue*, 1992–93

Cornell, Christine: Buffy, *A Wedding*, 2007–08

Corpening, Elizabeth: Beryl, *Where's Charley?*, 1953–54

Corrigan, Ann: Second Lady, *Die Zauberflöte (The Magic Flute)*, 1972–73; Tzeital, *Fiddler on the Roof*, 1972–73

Corso, Charles: Hermann, *Les Contes d'Hoffmann (The Tales of Hoffmann)*, 1978–79; Messenger/Commissioner, *La Traviata*, 1978–79; Mityukh, *Boris Godunov*, 1978–79; Servant, *The Darkened City*, 1978–79; Alcindoro, *La Bohème*, 1979–80; Masetto, *Don Giovanni*, 1979–80; Farfarello, *The Love for Three Oranges*, 1980–81; Fiorello, *Il Barbiere di Siviglia (The Barber of Seville)*, 1980–81; Pasquale, *The Most Happy Fella*, 1982–83

Cortright, Robert: Don Basilio, *Le Nozze di Figaro (The Marriage of Figaro)*, 1962–63; First Suitor, *The Darkened City*, 1962–63; Gabriel von Eisenstein, *Die Fledermaus (The Bat)*, 1962–63; Afansy Ivanovich, *The Fair at Sorochinsk*, 1963–64; Bob Boles, *Peter Grimes*, 1963–64; Edgardo, *Lucia di Lammermoor*, 1963–64; Jose Castro, *La Fanciulla del West (The Girl of the Golden West)*, 1963–64; Knight, *Parsifal*, 1963–64; Count Danilo Danilovitch, *Die lustige Witwe (The Merry Widow)*, 1964–65; Pang, *Turandot*, 1964–65; Prince Shuisky, *Boris Godunov*, 1964–65; Count Danilo Danilovitch, *Die lustige Witwe (The Merry Widow)*, 1965–66

Costantakos, Evangelia: Zita, *Gianni Schicchi*, 1993–94; Page, *The Dawn of the Poor King*, 1990–91

Coulson, Nancy: Velma, *West Side Story*, 1985–86; Player, *Mass*, 1987–88; Antonia / Alonso's Niece, *Man of La Mancha*, 1988–89; Papagena, *Die Zauberflöte (The Magic Flute)*, 1988–89; Player, *Mass*, 1988–89

Coursey, Herbert: Ulysses, *Deidamia*, 1969–70; Enoch Snow, *Carousel*, 1970–71; Jaquino, *Fidelio*, 1970–71; Normanno, *Lucia di Lammermoor*, 1970–71; The Dancing Master, *Manon Lescaut*, 1970–71; Third Jew, *Salome*, 1970–71

Couts, Wendell: Dr. Wilson, *Street Scene*, 1960–61

Cowan, Richard: Leader of Penitents, *The Darkened City*, 1978–79; Varlaam, *Boris Godunov*, 1978–79; De Bretigny, *Manon*, 1979–80; Kezal, *The Bartered Bride*, 1979–80; Teucer, *The Cry of Clytaemnestra*, 1979–80; Igor, *Prince Igor*, 1980–81

Cowan, Tom: H.C. Curry, *110 in the Shade*, 1967–68; H.C. Curry, *110 in the Shade*, 1968–69; Master of Ceremonies, *La Pique Dame (The Queen of Spades)*, 1968–69; Avram, *Fiddler on the Roof*, 1972–73

Cox, Kenneth: Bailiff, *Werther*, 1975–76; Celio, *The Love for Three Oranges*, 1975–76; Gurnemanz, *Parsifal*, 1975–76; Samuel, *Un Ballo in Maschera (A Masked Ball)*, 1975–76; Arkel, *Pelléas et Mélisande*, 1976–77; Roger Chillingworth, *The Scarlet Letter*, 1976–77; Voice of Neptune, *Idomeneo*, 1976–77; Chub Korny, *The Night Before Christmas*, 1977–78; Don Pasquale, *Don Pasquale*, 1977–78; Sarastro, *Die Zauberflöte (The Magic Flute)*, 1977–78

Cox Williams, Joyce: Zorah, *Ruddigore (The Witch's Curse)*, 1962–63

Crafts, Edward: Klingsor, *Parsifal,* 1975–76; Leandro, *The Love for Three Oranges,* 1975–76; Golaud, *Pelléas et Mélisande,* 1976–77

Craig, Philip: Jake, *Porgy and Bess,* 1979–80; Undertaker, *Porgy and Bess,* 1979–80

Cramer, Stewart: Dr. Caius, *Falstaff,* 1997–98; Player, *Mass,* 1998–99

Cramer, William: Fred, *Oklahoma!,* 1954–55

Crane, April: Stella, *Les Contes d'Hoffmann (The Tales of Hoffmann),* 1995–96

Crane, Marilyn: Irene, *A Parfait for Irene,* 1951–52; Fiona MacLaren, *Brigadoon,* 1953–54; Kitty Verdun, *Where's Charley?,* 1953–54; Magnolia, *Show Boat,* 1953–54; Rosalinda, *Die Fledermaus (The Bat),* 1954–55

Cranor, Cinda: Anna Hope, *The Mother of Us All,* 1973–74; Madame Larina, *Eugene Onegin,* 1974–75

Crawley, Douglas: The Imperial Commissioner, *Madama Butterfly,* 1976–77; Citizen, *Danton and Robespierre,* 1977–78; Priest, *Die Zauberflöte (The Magic Flute),* 1977–78

Cray, Richard: Count Almaviva, *Le Nozze di Figaro (The Marriage of Figaro),* 1980–81

Creek, Leah: Eurydice, *Orphée aux enfers (Orpheus in the Underworld),* 1992–93; Javotte, *Manon,* 1993–94; Smeraldina, *The Love for Three Oranges,* 1993–94; Rosina, *Il Barbiere di Siviglia (The Barber of Seville),* 1994–95; Third Lady, *Die Zauberflöte (The Magic Flute),* 1994–95

Creekmore, Charles: Slave, *Die Zauberflöte (The Magic Flute),* 1960–61

Cristescu, Emil: Don Magnifico, *La Cenerentola (Cinderella),* 1991–92; Leporello, *Don Giovanni,* 1991–92; Father Ambrose, *Die Teufel von Loudun (The Devils of Loudun),* 1992–93; Figaro, *Le Nozze di Figaro (The Marriage of Figaro),* 1992–93; Gianni Schicchi, *Gianni Schicchi,* 1993–94; Sacristan, *Tosca,* 1993–94

Crouse, Courtney: Blues Singer, *Mass,* 1998–99; La Cercatrice (Seconda), *Suor Angelica (Sister Angelica),* 1999–2000; Amalia Balash, *She Loves Me,* 2004–05; Second Lady, *Die Zauberflöte (The Magic Flute),* 2004–05; Josephine, *HMS Pinafore,* 2005–06; Mrs. Gibbs, *Our Town,* 2005–06; Colombina, *Arlecchino,* 2006–07; Victoria, *A Wedding,* 2007–08

Crowley, Karen: Mistress Anne Page (Anna Reich), *Die lustigen Weiber von Windsor (The Merry Wives of Windsor),* 1958–59; Magda de Civry, *La Rondine (The Swallow),* 1959–60

Culbertson, Edwin: The Narrator, *Oedipus Rex,* 1964–65

Cullen, Susan: Miss Wordsworth, *Albert Herring,* 1957–58; Page, *Parsifal,* 1957–58

Cullison, Rebecca: Diana, *Orphée aux enfers (Orpheus in the Underworld),* 1992–93; Alisa, *Lucia di Lammermoor,* 1993–94; Ludmila, *The Bartered Bride,* 1994–95; Queen of the Night, *Die Zauberflöte (The Magic Flute),* 1994–95

Cultice, Thomas: Escamillo, *Carmen,* 1962–63; Marcello, *La Bohème,* 1962–63; Priest, *The Darkened City,* 1962–63; Enrico, *Il Campanello di Notte (The Night Bell),* 1963–64; Marquis de Croissant, *Die lustige Witwe (The Merry Widow),* 1965–66; Morales, *Carmen,* 1965–66; Mercutio, *Roméo et Juliette,* 1966–67; Sid, *Albert Herring,* 1966–67; Sid, *Albert Herring,* 1967–68

Cummines, Kevin: Ike Skidmore, *Oklahoma!,* 1997–98; Phillip, *Kiss Me, Kate,* 1998–99; The Barber, *Man of La Mancha,* 1999–2000

Cummings, Joel: The Father Confessor, *Dialogues des Carmélites,* 2004–05

Cummings, Michael: Gabriel, *Too Many Sopranos,* 2006–07; Andres, *Les Contes d'Hoffmann (The Tales of Hoffmann),* 2007–08; Cochenille, *Les Contes d'Hoffmann (The Tales of Hoffmann),* 2007–08; Franz, *Les Contes d'Hoffmann (The Tales of Hoffmann),* 2007–08; Little Bat McLean, *Susannah,* 2007–08; Pittichinaccio, *Les Contes d'Hoffmann (The Tales of Hoffmann),* 2007–08

Cunio, Thaxter: Gherardo, *Il Trittico (A Triptych),* 1982–83; Mayor of Leadville, *The Ballad of Baby Doe,* 1982–83; Slave, *Die Zauberflöte (The Magic Flute),* 1982–83; Washington Dandy, *The Ballad of Baby Doe,* 1982–83

Curling, Ashley: Samantha, *The Ballad of Baby Doe,* 2003–04

Curran, Matthew: Graf Waldner, *Arabella,* 1998–99; Collatinus, *The Rape of Lucretia,* 1999–2000; The Doctor, *Wozzeck,* 1999–2000; Don Alfonso, *Così fan tutte,* 2000–01

Currie, Maija: Vivienne, *Oklahoma!,* 1997–98; Manon Lescaut, *Manon,* 2001–02; Beatrice, *Jeppe,* 2002–03; Manon Lescaut, *Manon,* 2006–07

Curry, Lawrence: Ralph, the Stage Manager, *Kiss Me, Kate,* 1973–74

Curtis, Brandt: Grigori (Dimitri, the Pretender), *Boris Godunov,* 1953–54; Third Gospeleer, *Finian's Rainbow,* 1953–54; Gabriel von Eisenstein, *Die Fledermaus (The Bat),* 1954–55; Sniggers, *The Ruby,* 1954–55; The Dancing Master, *Ariadne auf Naxos,* 1954–55; Flute, *A Midsummer Night's Dream,* 1961–62; Pedrillo, *Die Entführung aus dem Serail (The Abduction from the Seraglio),* 1961–62; Gabriel von Eisenstein, *Die Fledermaus (The Bat),* 1962–63; Remendado, *Carmen,* 1962–63; The Emperor Altoum, *Turandot,* 1964–65

Curtis, Craig: Player, *Mass,* 1987–88; Player, *Mass,* 1988–89

Czarnota, Benjamin: Njegus, *Die lustige Witwe (The Merry Widow),* 2003–04; Washington Dandy, *The Ballad of Baby Doe,* 2003–04; Schaunard, *La Bohème,* 2004–05; Guglielmo, *Così fan tutte,* 2005–06; Mr. Webb, *Our Town,* 2005–06

Czuba, Victoria: Flora Bervoix, *La Traviata*, 1978–79; Cassandra, *The Cry of Clytaemnestra*, 1979–80

Dailey, William: Morales, *Carmen*, 1956–57; Peter, *Hänsel und Gretel*, 1956–57

Dalal, Zane: Agent of the Inquisition, *Candide*, 1987–88

Dales, Richard: Rigoletto, *Rigoletto*, 1950–51

d'Alessio, Gina: Euridice, *L'Orfeo*, 1987–88

Dalfonso, James: Belcore, *L'Elisir d'amore (The Elixir of Love)*, 1990–91; Roberto (Nardo), *La Finta Giardiniera*, 1990–91; Tom Rakewell, *The Rake's Progress*, 1991–92; Tony, *West Side Story*, 1992–93; Pedrillo, *Die Entführung aus dem Serail (The Abduction from the Seraglio)*, 1993–94

Dallas, Ellen: Spirit, *Die Zauberflöte (The Magic Flute)*, 1953–54

Dallas, Lorna: Page, *Parsifal*, 1963–64; Hanna Glawari, *Die lustige Witwe (The Merry Widow)*, 1964–65; Lauretta, *Gianni Schicchi*, 1964–65; Zerlina, *Don Giovanni*, 1964–65; Papagena, *Die Zauberflöte (The Magic Flute)*, 1965–66; Sophie, *Der Rosenkavalier*, 1965–66

Dalton, Donna: Countess de Coigny, *Andrea Chénier*, 1967–68; Manon Lescaut, *Manon*, 1967–68; Countess Almaviva, *Le Nozze di Figaro (The Marriage of Figaro)*, 1968–69; Eva, *Die Meistersinger von Nürnberg (The Mastersingers of Nuremberg)*, 1968–69; Floria Tosca, *Tosca*, 1969–70; Giorgetta, *Il Trittico (A Triptych)*, 1969–70; Leonore, *Fidelio*, 1970–71

Dalton, Truman: A Wig Maker, *Ariadne auf Naxos*, 1969–70; Guglielmo, *Così fan tutte*, 1970–71; Second Prisoner, *Fidelio*, 1970–71; Knight, *Parsifal*, 1972–73

Dammrich, Mary: Mitzi Kranz, *Blossom Time*, 1952–53; Page, *Parsifal*, 1952–53; Spirit, *Die Zauberflöte (The Magic Flute)*, 1953–54

Danforth, Kathryn: Widow Yussef, *Kismet*, 1989–90

d'Angelo, Gianna: Lucia, *Lucia di Lammermoor*, 1970–71

Daniels, Brian: Concierge, *Arabella*, 2006–07

Danto, Joanne: Princess Zubbediya of Zanzibar, *Kismet*, 1963–64

Dantzler, Zanice: Bersi, *Andrea Chénier*, 1967–68; The Mistress of the Novices, *Il Trittico (A Triptych)*, 1969–70

Danziger, Sebastian: Notary, *La Sonnambula (The Sleepwalker)*, 1985–86; An Officer, *Dialogues des Carmélites*, 1986–87

Darling, Andrew: Achilla, *Giulio Cesare (Julius Caesar)*, 2002–03; Barney, *The Ballad of Baby Doe*, 2003–04; Sciarrone, *Tosca*, 2004–05; The Marquis de la Force, *Dialogues des Carmélites*, 2004–05; Fiorello, *Il Barbiere di Siviglia (The Barber of Seville)*, 2005–06

Darling, Neil: Gherardo, *Gianni Schicchi*, 1999–2000; Sellem, *The Rake's Progress*, 1999–2000; Governor, *Candide*, 2000–01; Don Basilio, *Le Nozze di Figaro (The Marriage of Figaro)*, 2001–02; Andres, *Les Contes d'Hoffmann (The Tales of Hoffmann)*, 2002–03; Cochenille, *Les Contes d'Hoffmann (The Tales of Hoffmann)*, 2002–03; Franz, *Les Contes d'Hoffmann (The Tales of Hoffmann)*, 2002–03; Pittichinaccio, *Les Contes d'Hoffmann (The Tales of Hoffmann)*, 2002–03

Daugherty, Joy: The Abbess, *Il Trittico (A Triptych)*, 1982–83

David, Marilee: Queen of the Night, *Die Zauberflöte (The Magic Flute)*, 1982–83

Davidson, Ann: Fortune, *L'Incoronazione di Poppea (The Coronation of Poppea)*, 1967–68; Siegrune, *Die Walküre*, 1969–70

Davidson, Charles: Customs Officer, *La Bohème*, 1984–85; Stephano, *The Tempest*, 1985–86; Don Issachar, *Candide*, 1987–88; Official Registrar, *Madama Butterfly*, 1987–88; Owner of the Gambling House, *Candide*, 1987–88; Player, *Mass*, 1987–88; Dr. Sanson Carrasco / The Duke, *Man of La Mancha*, 1988–89; Gherardo, *Gianni Schicchi*, 1988–89; Henrik Egerman, *A Little Night Music*, 1988–89; Player, *Mass*, 1988–89; Orestes, *The Cry of Clytaemnestra*, 1989–90; Cascada, *Die lustige Witwe (The Merry Widow)*, 1990–91; Dr. Blind, *Die Fledermaus (The Bat)*, 1990–91; Marquis de Cascada, *Die lustige Witwe (The Merry Widow)*, 1990–91; The Captain, *Wozzeck*, 1990–91; Tom Rakewell, *The Rake's Progress*, 1991–92; Fenton, *Falstaff*, 1992–93; Tony, *West Side Story*, 1992–93

Davies, Brian: Page, *Parsifal*, 1953–54; Priest, *Die Zauberflöte (The Magic Flute)*, 1953–54; Page, *Parsifal*, 1954–55; Michele, *Il Tabarro (The Cloak)*, 1955–56

Davies, Mark: Schaunard, *La Bohème*, 2007–08

Davies, Siân: Donna Anna, *Don Giovanni*, 2006–07; Madame Pompous, *Too Many Sopranos*, 2006–07; Countess Almaviva, *Le Nozze di Figaro (The Marriage of Figaro)*, 2007–08

Davis, Agnes: Kundry, *Parsifal*, 1956–57

Davis, Eugene: Harry Easter, *Street Scene*, 1960–61; Messenger/Commissioner, *La Traviata*, 1960–61; Page, *Parsifal*, 1960–61; Cesare Angelotti, *Tosca*, 1961–62; Charlie Dalrymple, *Brigadoon*, 1961–62; Johann, *Werther*, 1961–62; Page, *Parsifal*, 1961–62; Morales, *Carmen*, 1962–63; The Boy, *The Fantasticks*, 1963–64

Davis, Marcia: Prince Orlofsky, *Die Fledermaus (The Bat)*, 1962–63

Davis, Michael Rees: Hoffmann, *Les Contes d'Hoffmann (The Tales of Hoffmann)*, 2002–03

Davis, Neil: Mr. Carl Olsen, *Street Scene*, 1960–61

Davis, Rick: Andreas, *Carmen*, 1973–74; Herman Atlan, *The Mother of Us All*, 1973–74; Morales, *Carmen*, 1973–74; Customs Officer, *La Bohème*, 1974–75; Marullo, *Rigoletto*, 1974–75; Zaretsky, *Eugene Onegin*, 1974–75; Leandro, *The Love for Three Oranges*, 1975–76; Prospero, *Il Mondo della Luna (The World on the Moon)*, 1975–76; The Beadle (and Jailer), *The Scarlet Letter*, 1976–77; Dr. Malatesta, *Don Pasquale*, 1977–78; The Mayor of Dikanka, *The Night Before Christmas*, 1977–78

Davis, William: Robbins, *Porgy and Bess*, 1976–77

Davis, Kenneth, Jr.: Ciccio, *The Most Happy Fella*, 1959–60; First Tramp, *Die Kluge (The Clever Girl)*, 1959–60; Ulrich Eisslinger, *Die Meistersinger von Nürnberg (The Mastersingers of Nuremberg)*, 1961–62

Dawson, Margaret: Jou-Jou, *Die lustige Witwe (The Merry Widow)*, 1964–65

Day, Holly: Lady in Waiting, *Macbeth*, 1965–66; Madame Lidoine, *Dialogues des Carmélites*, 1965–66; Nedda, *I Pagliacci*, 1966–67; Elizabeth Zimmer, *Elegy for Young Lovers*, 1967–68; Virtue, *L'Incoronazione di Poppea (The Coronation of Poppea)*, 1967–68; Anne Trulove, *The Rake's Progress*, 1968–69; Countess Almaviva, *Le Nozze di Figaro (The Marriage of Figaro)*, 1968–69

Day, Marilyn: Newcomer, *Street Scene*, 1960–61

Day, Rachel: Adina, *L'Elisir d'amore (The Elixir of Love)*, 1961–62; Constanza, *Die Entführung aus dem Serail (The Abduction from the Seraglio)*, 1961–62; Eva, *Die Meistersinger von Nurnberg (The Mastersingers of Nuremberg)*, 1961–62, Micaëla, *Carmen*, 1962–63

Day-Kessler, Rachel: Fiordiligi, *Così fan tutte*, 1963–64

de Anguera, Marguerite: Maggie Anderson, *Brigadoon*, 1953–54

De Coudres, Neil: Old Clothes Man, *Street Scene*, 1949–50; Tramp, *Street Scene*, 1949–50

De Oliveira, Mazias: Sebastian, *The Tempest*, 1985–86; Spalanzani, *Les Contes d'Hoffmann (The Tales of Hoffmann)*, 1988–89; Hattie, *Kiss Me, Kate*, 1998–99

de Oliviera, Edlyn: Jennie Parsons, *Down in the Valley*, 1998–99

Deaderick, Joy: Farfarello, *The Love for Three Oranges*, 1958–59

Deaton, Christina: Princess Ninetta, *The Love for Three Oranges*, 1993–94; Boy, *Die Zauberflöte (The Magic Flute)*, 1994–95

Debenport, Sylvia: Greta, *Song of Norway*, 1951–52; Prince Orlofsky, *Die Fledermaus (The Bat)*, 1954–55; Cherubino, *Le Nozze di Figaro (The Marriage of Figaro)*, 1955–56; Frugola, *Il Tabarro (The Cloak)*, 1955–56; Martha, *Faust*, 1955–56

Debro, Mike: Henry, *Finian's Rainbow*, 1969–70

Deckard, Jerry Lyn: Clarice, *West Side Story*, 1985–86

deCoverly, Mary: Ruth Sherwood, *Wonderful Town*, 1954–55

Deeg, David: Footman, *Der Rosenkavalier*, 1965–66; Waiter, *Der Rosenkavalier*, 1965–66

Deen, Hugh: Second Waiter, *On the Town*, 1951–52; Andy, *On the Town*, 1951–52; Butler, *Song of Norway*, 1951–52; Sailor, *On the Town*, 1951–52; Binder, *Blossom Time*, 1952–53; Charlie Dalrymple, *Brigadoon*, 1952–53; Brighella, *Ariadne auf Naxos*, 1954–55

DeFries, Stanley: Italian Singer, *Capriccio*, 1958–59; Borsa, *Rigoletto*, 1959–60

Degen, Sharon: Countess Charlotte Malcolm, *A Little Night Music*, 1975–76; Emily, *The Ballad of Baby Doe*, 1975–76; First Woman of Paris, *Danton and Robespierre*, 1977–78; Sixth Woman of Paris, *Danton and Robespierre*, 1977–78; The Tsaritsa, *The Night Before Christmas*, 1977–78

Degler, Kathryn: Mrs. Segstrom, *A Little Night Music*, 1975–76; Page, *Parsifal*, 1975–76; Servant of Buonafede, *Il Mondo della Luna (The World on the Moon)*, 1975–76

Deis, Jean: Grigori (Dimitri, the Pretender), *Boris Godunov*, 1966–67; Andrea Chénier, *Andrea Chénier*, 1967–68; Faust, *Mefistofele*, 1967–68; Manrico, *Il Trovatore*, 1967–68; Alfredo Germont, *La Traviata*, 1968–69; Count Riccardo, *Un Ballo in Maschera (A Masked Ball)*, 1969–70; Luigi, *Il Trittico (A Triptych)*, 1969–70; Mario Cavaradossi, *Tosca*, 1969–70; Rinuccio, *Il Trittico (A Triptych)*, 1969–70; Chevalier des Grieux, *Manon Lescaut*, 1970–71; Florestan, *Fidelio*, 1970–71; Rodolfo, *La Bohème*, 1970–71; Faust, *Faust*, 1971–72; Luigi, *Il Trittico (A Triptych)*, 1972–73; Rodolfo, *La Bohème*, 1974–75; Mario Cavaradossi, *Tosca*, 1977–78; Hoffmann, *Les Contes d'Hoffmann (The Tales of Hoffmann)*, 1978–79

Deis, Lila: Pousette, *Manon*, 1967–68

del Legno, Asino: A Donkey, *Arlecchino*, 1979–80

Deleget, Michael: The Host of the Garter Inn, *Falstaff*, 1997–98; Bill Calhoun, *Kiss Me, Kate*, 1998–99; Celebrant, *Mass*, 1998–99; Lucentio, *Kiss Me, Kate*, 1998–99; Pluto, *Orphée aux enfers (Orpheus in the Underworld)*, 1998–99; Amantio di Nicolao, *Gianni Schicchi*, 1999–2000; Miguel de Cervantes / Don Quixote, *Man of La Mancha*, 1999–2000; Voltaire (Pangloss, Cacambo, Martin, Galley Slave), *Candide*, 2000–01; Harold Hill, *The Music Man*, 2001–02; The Witch, *Hänsel und Gretel*, 2001–02; Gabriel von Eisenstein, *Die Fledermaus (The Bat)*, 2002–03

Delk, Skylar: Guide, *Carmen*, 2005–06; Lillas Pastia, *Carmen*, 2005–06

Dell, Tiffany: Blues Singer, *Mass*, 1998–99; Frasquita, *Carmen*, 1998–99

Della Porta, Francesca: First Lay Sister, *Il Trittico (A Triptych)*, 1969–70

Delon, Jack: Abraham Kaplan, *Street Scene*, 1949–50; Leader, *Lost in the Stars*, 1950–51; The Duke of Mantua, *Rigoletto*, 1950–51; Belmonte, *Die Entführung aus dem Serail (The Abduction from the Seraglio)*, 1951–52; Kaspar, *Amahl and the Night Visitors*, 1951–52; Alfred, *Die Fledermaus (The Bat)*, 1954–55; Alfredo Germont, *La Traviata*, 1954–55; Canio, *I Pagliacci*, 1954–55

Demetropolis, Phyllis: Melisande, *Pelléas et Mélisande*, 1976–77

Demirmen, Sibel: Chana, *Fiddler on the Roof*, 1994–95

Denhart, Jay: Sancho Panza, *Man of La Mancha*, 1988–89

Denne, Judith: Maid, *Il Campanello di Notte (The Night Bell)*, 1963–64

Dennie, Roberta: Pamina, *Die Zauberflöte (The Magic Flute)*, 1972–73

Denzin, Roger: Thierry, *Dialogues des Carmélites*, 1965–66

DePew, Shari: A Princess of Ababu, *Kismet*, 1963–64

Derby, Kenneth: Pasha Selim, *Die Entführung aus dem Serail (The Abduction from the Seraglio)*, 1981–82; Will Parker, *Oklahoma!*, 1981–82; Bushy, *The Ballad of Baby Doe*, 1982–83; Doctor Spinelloccio, *Il Trittico (A Triptych)*, 1982–83; Dr. Blind, *Die Fledermaus (The Bat)*, 1982–83; Baron Douphol, *La Traviata*, 1983–84; Dr. Pangloss, *Candide*, 1983–84; The Clock, *L'Enfant et les Sortilèges (The Bewitched Child)*, 1984–85; Dr. Bartolo, *Le Nozze di Figaro (The Marriage of Figaro)*, 1986–87

Derryberry, Rory: Winthrop Paroo, *The Music Man*, 2001–02

Deschamps, Elise: Sandman, *Hänsel und Gretel*, 1995–96; Cherubino, *The Ghosts of Versailles*, 1996–97; Lady Thiang, *The King and I*, 1996–97; Mother Jeanne, *Dialogues des Carmélites*, 1997–98; Smeraldina, *The Love for Three Oranges*, 1999–2000

DeSelms, James: First Priest of the Temple, *Die Zauberflöte (The Magic Flute)*, 1994–95

DeVaughn, Alteouise: Priscilla Jones, *Soldier Boy, Soldier*, 1982–83

DeVerger, Angela: Giulietta, *Les Contes d'Hoffmann (The Tales of Hoffmann)*, 1995–96

Dewald, Meghan: Diana, *A Wedding*, 2007–08

Dewese, Scott: Count Ceprano, *Rigoletto*, 1995–96; Bogdanowitsch, *Die lustige Witwe (The Merry Widow)*, 1996–97; A Jailer, *Dialogues des Carmélites*, 1997–98; Harrison Howell, *Kiss Me, Kate*, 1998–99; Captain Corcoran, *HMS Pinafore*, 2005–06

Dewey, Patricia: Diana Devereaux, *Of Thee I Sing*, 1987–88; Player, *Mass*, 1987–88; Player, *Mass*, 1988–89; Suzy, *La Rondine (The Swallow)*, 1989–90

di Rocco, Sister Theresa: Mrs. Herring, *Albert Herring*, 1967–68; Ottavia, *L'Incoronazione di Poppea (The Coronation of Poppea)*, 1967–68; Voice from Heaven, *Parsifal*, 1967–68; Marcellina, *Le Nozze di Figaro (The Marriage of Figaro)*, 1968–69; Voice from Heaven, *Parsifal*, 1968–69

di Toro, Nicholas: Ernesto, *Il Mondo della Luna (The World on the Moon)*, 1975–76; Fredrik Egerman, *A Little Night Music*, 1975–76; Horace Tabor, *The Ballad of Baby Doe*, 1975–76; Olin Blitch, *Susannah*, 1976–77; Sir John Falstaff, *Falstaff*, 1976–77

Diaz, Milka: Lucia, *Cavalleria Rusticana*, 1966–67; Arnalta, *L'Incoronazione di Poppea (The Coronation of Poppea)*, 1967–68; Madelon, *Andrea Chénier*, 1967–68

Dibner, Steven: Annibale, *The Gondoliers*, 1974–75

DiCarlo, Rita: Ciesca, *Il Trittico (A Triptych)*, 1982–83; Player, *Mass*, 1987–88; Scrubwoman, *Of Thee I Sing*, 1987–88; Player, *Mass*, 1988–89

Dick, Charlotte: Cunegonde, *Candide*, 1993–94; Gilda, *Rigoletto*, 1995–96

Dickinson, Thomas: Lindorf, *Les Contes d'Hoffmann (The Tales of Hoffmann)*, 1995–96; Pallante, *Agrippina*, 1995–96

Diddle, Laura: Minerva, *Orphée aux enfers (Orpheus in the Underworld)*, 1984–85; April, *Company*, 1990–91

Diehl, Joe: Tony, *A View from the Bridge*, 2004–05; A Doctor, *Arabella*, 2006–07; Enrico Carouser, *Too Many Sopranos*, 2006–07

Diemer, Maliwan: Little Eva, *The King and I*, 1996–97; Graziella, *West Side Story*, 2002–03

Diggory, Edith: Fiordiligi, *Così fan tutte*, 1978–79; Cassandra, *The Cry of Clytaemnestra*, 1979–80

Dilger, Amber: Le Novizie (Prima), *Suor Angelica (Sister Angelica)*, 1999–2000

Dillon, Marcelene: Edith, *Where's Charley?*, 1953–54; Maude, *Finian's Rainbow*, 1953–54; Lt. Genevieve Marshall, *South Pacific*, 1956–57

Dionne, Sarah: Princess Ninetta, *The Love for Three Oranges*, 1999–2000

Ditson, Rayma: Dryad, *Ariadne auf Naxos*, 1954–55; Frugola, *Il Tabarro (The Cloak)*, 1955–56; Marcellina, *Le Nozze di Figaro (The Marriage of Figaro)*, 1955–56

Dittmar, Heidi: Consuelo, *West Side Story*, 1985–86

Ditto, Charlotte: Sweet Seller, *The Darkened City*, 1962–63; Madame Rosa, *Il Campanello di Notte (The Night Bell)*, 1963–64

Dixon, Curtis: Guard, *The Darkened City*, 1978–79; Servant, *The Darkened City*, 1978–79

Dixon, Mary: Aunt Eller, *Oklahoma!*, 1997–98

Dixon, Michael: Don Curzio, *Le Nozze di Figaro (The Marriage of Figaro)*, 1980–81

Dixon, Thomas: Captain in the Navy, *Manon Lescaut,* 1970–71; Customs Officer, *La Bohème,* 1970–71; Schaunard, *La Bohème,* 1970–71

Dobbs, Sara: Velma, *West Side Story,* 2002–03

Dobins, Pat: Jou-Jou, *Die lustige Witwe (The Merry Widow),* 1949–50

Dolinger, Lesley: Spirit, *Die Zauberflöte (The Magic Flute),* 1988–89

Dolter, Gerald: Albert, *Werther,* 1975–76; Knight, *Parsifal,* 1975–76; Silvano, *Un Ballo in Maschera (A Masked Ball),* 1975–76; The Chief Magistrate, *Un Ballo in Maschera (A Masked Ball),* 1975–76; Worshipful Master Bellingham, *The Scarlet Letter,* 1976–77

Dolz, Francisco: Second Gambler, *Candide,* 2000–01; Second Officer, *Candide,* 2000–01; Juano, *West Side Story,* 2002–03

Dombek, Mary: Princess Nicoletta, *The Love for Three Oranges,* 1980–81; Mistress Anne Page (Anna Reich), *Die lustigen Weiber von Windsor (The Merry Wives of Windsor),* 1981–82; Rosalinda, *Die Fledermaus (The Bat),* 1982–83; Cunegonde, *Candide,* 1983–84; Mrs. Honour, *Tom Jones,* 1983–84; Magnolia, *Show Boat,* 1984–85; Anne Trulove, *The Rake's Progress,* 1986–87

Domengeaux, Patricia: Ermengarde, *Hello, Dolly!,* 1991–92; Cupid, *Orphée aux enfers (Orpheus in the Underworld),* 1992–93

Dominiak, Debra: Fish Wife, *Danton and Robespierre,* 1977–78; Rosette, *Manon,* 1979–80

Donahue, Angela: Graziella, *West Side Story,* 1985–86

Donahue, Carrie: Mercy Lewis, *The Crucible,* 1987–88

Donenfeld, Ron: James, *Candide,* 2000–01; Guardsman, *Manon,* 2001–02

Donovan, Jamie: Madame Merville, *A Little Night Music,* 1975–76; Osa, *A Little Night Music,* 1975–76

Dooling, Paige: Mary, *The Ballad of Baby Doe,* 1982–83; Silver Dollar (grown up), *The Ballad of Baby Doe,* 1982–83; Valencienne, *Die lustige Witwe (The Merry Widow),* 1983–84

Doren, Carol: Nurse of the Children, *Boris Godunov,* 1966–67

Dorfman, Phillip: Knight, *Murder in the Cathedral,* 1984–85; Master of the Ship, *The Tempest,* 1985–86

Doria, Paula: Madame Larina, *Eugene Onegin,* 1997–98; The Old Prioress, *Dialogues des Carmélites,* 1997–98

Dorminy, Larry: Achilles, *Deidamia,* 1969–70; Scaramuccio, *Ariadne auf Naxos,* 1969–70; Edmondo, *Manon Lescaut,* 1970–71; Totsky, *Myshkin,* 1972–73

Doss, Mark: Don Pasquale, *Don Pasquale,* 1980–81; Khan Konchak, *Prince Igor,* 1980–81; Mephistopheles, *Faust,* 1981–82; The Sacristan of St. Vitus's Cathedral, *The Excursions of Mr. Broucek,* 1981–82; Doctor Bartolo, *Il Barbiere di Siviglia (The Barber of Seville),* 1982–83; Speaker of the Temple, *Die Zauberflöte (The Magic Flute),* 1982–83

Dothard, Phillip: Ford, *Falstaff,* 2003–04; Marcello, *La Bohème,* 2004–05; Figaro, *Il Barbiere di Siviglia (The Barber of Seville),* 2005–06

Douglas, Deborah: Inez, *Il Trovatore,* 1967–68; The nursing sister from the infirmary, *Il Trittico (A Triptych),* 1969–70

Dowd, Caroline: First Wife, *Bluebeard's Castle,* 1988–89; Stella, *Les Contes d'Hoffmann (The Tales of Hoffmann),* 1988–89; Susan, *Company,* 1990–91; Kate Pinkerton, *Madama Butterfly,* 1991–92

Dowd, Jeffrey: Antonio, *The Tempest,* 1985–86; Erik, *Der Fliegende Holländer (The Flying Dutchman),* 1985–86; Krupke, *West Side Story,* 1985–86; First Sailor, *The Legend of Tsar Saltan,* 1986–87; Jenik, *The Bartered Bride,* 1986–87; The Chevalier, *Dialogues des Carmélites,* 1986–87; Peter Grimes, *Peter Grimes,* 1987–88; Fredrik Egerman, *A Little Night Music,* 1988–89

Downey, Freddie Fay: Woman, *Down in the Valley,* 1947–48

Downing, Eldon: Vincent Jones, *Street Scene,* 1960–61

Downing, Karen: Martha Sheldon, *The Crucible,* 1987–88

Downs, Ross: Willie Maurant, *Street Scene,* 1949–50

Doyle, David: Chevalier des Grieux, *Manon,* 1979–80

Dronkers, Marcelle: Smeraldina, *The Love for Three Oranges,* 1980–81

DuBois, Michael: Fred Cullen, *Street Scene,* 1960–61; Count di Lerma, *Don Carlos,* 1961–62; Spoletta, *Tosca,* 1961–62; Third Suitor, *The Darkened City,* 1962–63

DuBon, Ulises: Priest, *Die Zauberflöte (The Magic Flute),* 2004–05; Remendado, *Carmen,* 2005–06; Tybalt, *Roméo et Juliette,* 2005–06

Dueñas-Arbide, José: Executioner, *Candide,* 1993–94

Duffin, Mark: Peter Grimes, *Peter Grimes,* 2003–04

Duffy, Deborah: Praskovia, *Die lustige Witwe (The Merry Widow),* 1996–97

Dugan, Thomas: Mohamed, *Der Rosenkavalier,* 1965–66

Dugas, Ted: Citizen, *Danton and Robespierre,* 1977–78; Baron Douphol, *La Traviata,* 1978–79; Krushina, *The Bartered Bride,* 1979–80

Duhon, Russell: Robin, *Falstaff,* 1992–93

Dumski, Mara: The Nun, *Canterbury Tales,* 1978–79; Xenia, *Boris Godunov,* 1978–79; Pousette, *Manon,* 1979–80; Lenio, *The Greek Passion,* 1980–81; Princess Ninetta, *The Love for Three Oranges,* 1980–81

Dunbar, Alan: Alcindoro, *La Bohème,* 2004–05; Louis, *A View from the Bridge,* 2004–05; Dick Deadeye, *HMS Pinafore,* 2005–06; Doctor Bartolo, *Il Barbiere di Siviglia (The Barber of Seville),* 2005–06; Don Alfonso, *Così fan tutte,* 2005–06;

Leporello, *Don Giovanni*, 2006–07; Pish-Tush, *The Mikado*, 2006–07; Saint Peter, *Too Many Sopranos*, 2006–07; Dr. Dulcamara, *L'Elisir d'amore (The Elixir of Love)*, 2007–08; Jules, *A Wedding*, 2007–08

Dunbar, Ann: Sister Dolcina, *Il Trittico (A Triptych)*, 1982–83

Dunbar, Kerrin: Sister Constance, *Dialogues des Carmélites*, 1997–98; Cupid, *Orphée aux enfers (Orpheus in the Underworld)*, 1998–99; Papagena, *Die Zauberflöte (The Magic Flute)*, 1998–99; Zdenka, *Arabella*, 1998–99; Anne Trulove, *The Rake's Progress*, 1999–2000; Musetta, *La Bohème*, 1999–2000; Gilda, *Rigoletto*, 2000–01

Duncan, Thomas: Mohamed, *Der Rosenkavalier*, 1965–66

Duncanson, Nancy: Schwertleite, *Die Walküre*, 1971–72

Dunn, Eloise: Second Musician, *On the Town*, 1951–52; Hattie, *Kiss Me, Kate*, 1951–52

Dunn, Micki: Princess Linetta, *The Love for Three Oranges*, 1975–76

Dunn, Susan: Fish Wife, *Danton and Robespierre*, 1977–78; Mrs. Grose, *The Turn of the Screw*, 1978–79; Ludmila, *The Bartered Bride*, 1979–80; Mrs. Gleaton, *Susannah*, 1979–80

Dunston, Daphne: Margaret, *Wozzeck*, 1990–91; Rachel, *1600 Pennsylvania Avenue*, 1992–93

DuPont, Carl: Graf Lamoral, *Arabella*, 2006–07; Dr. Dulcamara, *L'Elisir d'amore (The Elixir of Love)*, 2007–08; Elder Ott, *Susannah*, 2007–08; Randolph, *A Wedding*, 2007–08

Dupuis, Catherine: Sweet Seller, *The Darkened City*, 1978–79

Durnbaugh, Kenneth: Master Ford (Herr Fluth), *Die lustigen Weiber von Windsor (The Merry Wives of Windsor)*, 1981–82; Schaunard, *La Bohème*, 1984–85; Alonso, King of Naples, *The Tempest*, 1985–86; Miguel de Cervantes / Don Quixote, *Man of La Mancha*, 1985–86; Schrank, *West Side Story*, 1985–86

Dusdieker, Carol: Antonia, *Les Contes d'Hoffmann (The Tales of Hoffmann)*, 2002–03; Mrs. Alice Ford, *Falstaff*, 2003–04; Musetta, *La Bohème*, 2004–05; Fiordiligi, *Così fan tutte*, 2005–06; Arabella, *Arabella*, 2006–07

Dustin, Mollie: The Baroness, *Candide*, 1993–94; Grandma Tzeitel, *Fiddler on the Roof*, 1994–95; Shaindel, *Fiddler on the Roof*, 1994–95; Public Opinion, *Orphée aux enfers (Orpheus in the Underworld)*, 1998–99; Elsa Schrader, *The Sound of Music*, 2000–01

Dutton, Jane: Ceres, *The Tempest*, 1985–86; Teresa, *La Sonnambula (The Sleepwalker)*, 1985–86; Giovanna, *Rigoletto*, 1986–87; Ludmila, *The Bartered Bride*, 1986–87; Player, *Mass*, 1987–88; Ursula, *Béatrice et Bénédict*, 1987–88; Filipyevna, *Eugene Onegin*, 1988–89; Player, *Mass*, 1988–89; Dorabella, *Così*

fan tutte, 1989–90; Siebel, *Faust*, 1989–90; Flora Bervoix, *La Traviata*, 1990–91; Minstrel, *The Dawn of the Poor King*, 1990–91; The Cavaliere Ramiro, *La Finta Giardiniera*, 1990–91; Carmen, *Carmen*, 1991–92; Cherubino, *Le Nozze di Figaro (The Marriage of Figaro)*, 1992–93; Maddalena, *Rigoletto*, 1992–93

Duvall, William: Hans Foltz, *Die Meistersinger von Nürnberg (The Mastersingers of Nuremberg)*, 1968–69

Dwyer, Terry: Fifth Jew, *Salome*, 1970–71; Wagner, *Faust*, 1971–72; Gloster Heming, *The Mother of Us All*, 1973–74; Schlemil, *Les Contes d'Hoffmann (The Tales of Hoffmann)*, 1973–74; Sciarrone, *Tosca*, 1973–74; Zuniga, *Carmen*, 1973–74

Dzubay, Laura: Silver Dollar Tabor, *The Ballad of Baby Doe*, 2003–04

Eakle, Robert: A Cappadocian, *Salome*, 1970–71; Innkeeper, *Manon Lescaut*, 1970–71

Earnest, Josephine: Mrs. Black Tooth, *Annie Get Your Gun*, 1956–57

Earp, Garée: Tailor, *The Boys from Syracuse*, 1968–69

East, Thomas: Alfredo Germont, *La Traviata*, 1960–61; Reverend Master Arthur Dimmesdale, *The Scarlet Letter*, 1960–61; Don Carlos, *Don Carlos*, 1961–62; Mario Cavaradossi, *Tosca*, 1961–62; Reverend Master Arthur Dimmesdale, *The Scarlet Letter*, 1961–62; Erik, *Der Fliegende Holländer (The Flying Dutchman)*, 1962–63

Eastridge, Ann: Laurey, *Oklahoma!*, 1981–82

Eaton, Julian: Orestes as a child, *The Cry of Clytaemnestra*, 1989–90

Eberhart, Annalise: Georgette, *La Rondine (The Swallow)*, 1989–90; Philippe, *Die Teufel von Loudun (The Devils of Loudun)*, 1992–93; Pousette, *Manon*, 1993–94

Ebersole, Joel: Grocery Boy, *Street Scene*, 1949–50; Leader, *Lost in the Stars*, 1950–51; Ozzie, *On the Town*, 1951–52; Charlie Dalrymple, *Brigadoon*, 1952–53; Heavenly Friend, *Carousel*, 1952–53; Policeman, *Carousel*, 1952–53; Vogl, *Blossom Time*, 1952–53; Charlie Dalrymple, *Brigadoon*, 1953–54; Gaylord Ravenal, *Show Boat*, 1953–54; Lavitsky, *Boris Godunov*, 1953–54; Sam Kaplan, *Street Scene*, 1960–61

Eckard, Kevin: Amantio di Nicolao, *Gianni Schicchi*, 1993–94; Micha, *The Bartered Bride*, 1994–95; Second Priest of the Temple, *Die Zauberflöte (The Magic Flute)*, 1994–95; Shloime, *Fiddler on the Roof*, 1994–95; Count Monterone, *Rigoletto*, 1995–96; Masetto, *Don Giovanni*, 1996–97

Eddy, Steven: Count Ceprano, *Rigoletto*, 2007–08

Edgerton, Robert: Roisterer, *The Darkened City*, 1962–63

Edgeworth, Amy: Hodel, *Fiddler on the Roof*, 1972–73

Edmundson, Stephen: Betto, *Il Trittico (A Triptych)*, 1972–73; Haberdasher, *Kiss Me, Kate*, 1973–74

Edwards, Carol Ann: Xenia, *Boris Godunov*, 1983–84; Musetta, *La Bohème*, 1984–85; Venus, *Orphée aux enfers (Orpheus in the Underworld)*, 1984–85; Frasquita, *Carmen*, 1984–85; Miranda, *The Tempest*, 1985–86; Rosalinda, *Die Fledermaus (The Bat)*, 1985–86; Blanche, *Dialogues des Carmélites*, 1986–87; Guenevere, *Camelot*, 1986–87

Edwards, Dilawar: Song Vendor, *Il Trittico (A Triptych)*, 1969–70

Edwards, Jan: Olga, *Eugene Onegin*, 1974–75; Mama McCourt, *The Ballad of Baby Doe*, 1975–76

Edwards, Linda: Sophie, *Werther*, 1975–76; Cunegonde, *Candide*, 1976–77; Nanetta, *Falstaff*, 1976–77; Player, *Bernstein on Broadway*, 1976–77; Norina, *Don Pasquale*, 1977–78

Edwards, Nancy: Olga, *Die lustige Witwe (The Merry Widow)*, 1990–91

Edwards, Richard: Phillippe, *The New Moon*, 1949–50; Rodolfo, *La Bohème*, 1949–50; Sam Kaplan, *Street Scene*, 1949–50

Egger, Chandra: Countess Ceprano, *Rigoletto*, 2000–01; Countess Almaviva, *Le Nozze di Figaro (The Marriage of Figaro)*, 2001–02; Antonia, *Les Contes d'Hoffmann (The Tales of Hoffmann)*, 2002–03; Rosalinda, *Die Fledermaus (The Bat)*, 2002–03

Eggleston, Alan: Francisco, *The Tempest*, 1985–86; Antonio, *Le Nozze di Figaro (The Marriage of Figaro)*, 1986–87; The Buffoon, *The Legend of Tsar Saltan*, 1986–87; Hobson, *Peter Grimes*, 1987–88; Satyr, *L'Orfeo*, 1987–88

Eguchi, Takumi: Achilles, *The Cry of Clytaemnestra*, 1989–90

Ehrlich, Michael: Ali Hakim, *Oklahoma!*, 1981–82

Eich, Craig: Horse Guard, *Jubilee*, 1991–92

Eikum, Rex: Count Danilo Danilovitch, *Die lustige Witwe (The Merry Widow)*, 1964–65; Don Ottavio, *Don Giovanni*, 1964–65; Oedipus, *Oedipus Rex*, 1964–65; Count Danilo Danilovitch, *Die lustige Witwe (The Merry Widow)*, 1965–66; Parsifal, *Parsifal*, 1965–66; Prince Tamino, *Die Zauberflöte (The Magic Flute)*, 1965–66; The Chevalier, *Dialogues des Carmélites*, 1965–66; Belmonte, *Die Entführung aus dem Serail (The Abduction from the Seraglio)*, 1966–67; Canio, *I Pagliacci*, 1966–67; John Conner, *A Hoosier Tale*, 1966–67; Walther Von Stolzing, *Die Meistersinger von Nürnberg (The Mastersingers of Nuremberg)*, 1968–69

Einarsson, Adalsteinn: Herald, *Otello*, 1989–90; Doctor Grenville, *La Traviata*, 1990–91; Servant, *Amahl and the Night Visitors*, 1990–91; Masetto, *Don Giovanni*, 1991–92; Sparafucile, *Rigoletto*, 1992–93; Antonio, *Le Nozze di Figaro (The Marriage of Figaro)*, 1997–98; Dick Deadeye, *HMS Pinafore*, 1997–98

Einhorn, Ellen: Frou-Frou, *Die lustige Witwe (The Merry Widow)*, 1965–66

Eisner, Jeffrey: Krupke, *West Side Story*, 2002–03

Eissler, David: Belmonte, *Die Entführung aus dem Serail (The Abduction from the Seraglio)*, 1974–75; Borsa, *Rigoletto*, 1974–75; Ecclitico, *Il Mondo della Luna (The World on the Moon)*, 1975–76; Truffaldino, *The Love for Three Oranges*, 1975–76

Eissler, Lisa: Alma Hix, *The Music Man*, 1980–81

Elder, Louisa: Angel (adult), *The Dawn of the Poor King*, 1990–91; Sarah, *Company*, 1990–91

Eldredge, Joan: Amazon, *The Boys from Syracuse*, 1968–69; Madrigal Singer, *Manon Lescaut*, 1970–71

Eley, Benjamin: Benoit, *La Bohème*, 2004–05; Mr. Maraczek, *She Loves Me*, 2004–05; Bill Bobstay, *HMS Pinafore*, 2005–06; Dancaire, *Carmen*, 2005–06

Eley, Elem: Prince Yamadori, *Madama Butterfly*, 1981–82; The Apparition of the Poet, Svatopluk Cech, *The Excursions of Mr. Broucek*, 1981–82; Valentin, *Faust*, 1981–82; Figaro, *Il Barbiere di Siviglia (The Barber of Seville)*, 1982–83; Sulpice, *La Fille du régiment (The Daughter of the Regiment)*, 1984–85

Elias, Diane: Mrs. McLean, *Susannah*, 1979–80; Maddalena, *Rigoletto*, 1980–81; Rosina, *Il Barbiere di Siviglia (The Barber of Seville)*, 1980–81; Widow Katerina, *The Greek Passion*, 1980–81

Elkins, Judy: Page, *Parsifal*, 1960–61; Spirit, *Die Zauberflöte (The Magic Flute)*, 1960–61; Page, *Parsifal*, 1961–62; Page, *Parsifal*, 1962–63

Ellenberger, Katherine: Malla, *A Little Night Music*, 1988–89

Elliott, Kenneth: Amantio di Nicolao, *Gianni Schicchi*, 1988–89; Simone, *Gianni Schicchi*, 1993–94; Colline, *La Bohème*, 1994–95; Sarastro, *Die Zauberflöte (The Magic Flute)*, 1994–95; Lottery Agent/Health Inspector, *McTeague*, 1995–96; Kronkov, *Die lustige Witwe (The Merry Widow)*, 1996–97

Elliott, Paul: Belmonte, *Die Entführung aus dem Serail (The Abduction from the Seraglio)*, 1987–88

Elmer, Nathaniel: Spirit, *Die Zauberflöte (The Magic Flute)*, 2004–05

Elvira, Pablo: Alfio, *Cavalleria Rusticana*, 1966–67; Rigoletto, *Rigoletto*, 1966–67; Tonio, *I Pagliacci*, 1966–67; Charles Gérard, *Andrea Chénier*, 1967–68; Count di Luna, *Il Trovatore*, 1967–68; Gregor Mittenhofer, *Elegy for Young Lovers*, 1967–68; Count Tomsky, *La Pique Dame (The Queen of Spades)*, 1968–69; Giorgio Germont, *La Traviata*, 1968–69; Taddeo, *L'Italiana in Algeri (The Italian Girl in Algiers)*, 1968–69; Baron Scarpia, *Tosca*, 1969–70; Count

Asdrubale, *Love on Trial (La Pietra del Paragone)*, 1969–70; Count Renato, *Un Ballo in Maschera (A Masked Ball)*, 1969–70; Figaro, *Il Barbiere di Siviglia (The Barber of Seville)*, 1971–72; Heracles, *Heracles*, 1971–72; Mandryka, *Arabella*, 1972–73; Michele, *Il Trittico (A Triptych)*, 1972–73; Escamillo, *Carmen*, 1973–74

Embree, Marianne: Antonia / Alonso's Niece, *Man of La Mancha*, 1988–89

Emmerich, Gerry: Margot, *Die lustige Witwe (The Merry Widow)*, 1964–65; Margot, *Die lustige Witwe (The Merry Widow)*, 1965–66

Enders, Randy: Thomas Putnam, *The Crucible*, 1987–88; Robert, *Company*, 1990–91

Engel, Nancy: Jeanne, the Prioress, *Die Teufel von Loudun (The Devils of Loudun)*, 1992–93; Old Lady, *Candide*, 1993–94; Gertrude, *Hänsel und Gretel*, 1995–96

Ensinger, Lisa: Filipyevna, *Eugene Onegin*, 1997–98

Ensor, Thomas: Corporal of Police, *The Boys from Syracuse*, 1968–69; Dromio of Syracuse, *The Boys from Syracuse*, 1968–69; Sir Lionel, *Camelot*, 1969–70

Enzinger, Gary: Enoch Snow, *Carousel*, 1993–94; Spoletta, *Tosca*, 1993–94; Guard, *The Darkened City*, 1978–79; Juggler, *The Darkened City*, 1978–79; Sir Lionel, *Camelot*, 1986–87; Customs Officer, *La Bohème*, 1989–90; Dr. Crabbe, *Peter Grimes*, 1994–95

Eppley, Garth: Man in Armor, *Die Zauberflöte (The Magic Flute)*, 2004–05; Frank, *Our Town*, 2005–06; Lysander, *A Midsummer Night's Dream*, 2005–06

Erb, James: Prince Tamino, *Die Zauberflöte (The Magic Flute)*, 1953–54; Simpleton, *Boris Godunov*, 1953–54

Erway, Kevin: Henchman, *Arlecchino*, 1979–80

Espada, Jose: Andrew, *Passion Play—Carmina Burana*, 1982–83

Espina, Noni: Henry Davis, *Street Scene*, 1949–50; Rigoletto, *Rigoletto*, 1950–51

Evanoff, Karl: Toro, *West Side Story*, 1992–93

Evans, Dorothy: The Squirrel, *L'Enfant et les Sortilèges (The Bewitched Child)*, 1984–85; Countess Ceprano, *Rigoletto*, 1986–87

Evans, James: Merlyn, *Camelot*, 1968–69; Robust, *Finian's Rainbow*, 1969–70; Parpignol, *La Bohème*, 1970–71

Evans, Joan: Lauretta, *Gianni Schicchi*, 1964–65

Evans, Juli: Sarah, *Company*, 1990–91

Evans, Nicholas: Fred Cullen, *Street Scene*, 1960–61; Slave, *Die Zauberflöte (The Magic Flute)*, 1960–61

Everett, Rex: First Bearer, *The Darkened City*, 1978–79

Everett, Virginia: Ida, *Die Fledermaus (The Bat)*, 1962–63

Everton, Jack: Amfortas, *Parsifal*, 1972–73; Rodrigo, *Don Carlos*, 1972–73; Coppelius, *Les Contes d'Hoffmann (The Tales of Hoffmann)*, 1973–74; Dappertutto, *Les Contes d'Hoffmann (The Tales of Hoffmann)*, 1973–74; Dr. Miracle, *Les Contes d'Hoffmann (The Tales of Hoffmann)*, 1973–74; Lindorf, *Les Contes d'Hoffmann (The Tales of Hoffmann)*, 1973–74

Eves, Rosemary: Kitzi Kranz, *Blossom Time*, 1952–53; Adele, *Die Fledermaus (The Bat)*, 1954–55; Zerbinetta, *Ariadne auf Naxos*, 1954–55; Fire, *L'Enfant et les Sortilèges (The Bewitched Child)*, 1955–56; Susanna, *Le Nozze di Figaro (The Marriage of Figaro)*, 1955–56

Ewing, Adam: Elder McLean, *Susannah*, 2007–08; Schlemil, *Les Contes d'Hoffmann (The Tales of Hoffmann)*, 2007–08; Spalanzani, *Les Contes d'Hoffmann (The Tales of Hoffmann)*, 2007–08

Ewing, Scott: Gherardino, *Il Trittico (A Triptych)*, 1982–83

Ewing, William: Anselmo / a Muleteer, *Man of La Mancha*, 1988–89; Hassan-Ben, *Kismet*, 1989–90; Schlemil, *Les Contes d'Hoffmann (The Tales of Hoffmann)*, 2007–08; Spalanzani, *Les Contes d'Hoffmann (The Tales of Hoffmann)*, 2007–08

Facer, Charles: Ali Hakim, *Oklahoma!*, 1981–82

Falduto, Lindsey: Princess Linetta, *The Love for Three Oranges*, 1999–2000; Giovanna, *Rigoletto*, 2000–01; Mrs. McLean, *Susannah*, 2000–01; Sister Berthe, *The Sound of Music*, 2000–01; Cherubino, *Le Nozze di Figaro (The Marriage of Figaro)*, 2001–02; Dolly, *Jeppe*, 2002–03; Mrs. Meg Page, *Falstaff*, 2003–04

Falker, Regina Marie: Hodel, *Fiddler on the Roof*, 1972–73; Vittoria, *The Gondoliers*, 1974–75; Lily, *Porgy and Bess*, 1979–80

Fallen, Sean: Nathanael, *Les Contes d'Hoffmann (The Tales of Hoffmann)*, 1995–96; Don Narciso, *Il Turco in Italia (The Turk in Italy)*, 1996–97; Ernesto, *Don Pasquale*, 1997–98; Don Ramiro, *La Cenerentola (Cinderella)*, 1998–99

Fang, Carly: Princess Linetta, *The Love for Three Oranges*, 1999–2000

Farabee, Allen: A mute, *Die Entführung aus dem Serail (The Abduction from the Seraglio)*, 1966–67; A skipper, *Die Entführung aus dem Serail (The Abduction from the Seraglio)*, 1966–67; Benvolio, *Roméo et Juliette*, 1966–67; Page, *Parsifal*, 1966–67

Faracco, Thomas: Leandro, Cavalier, *Arlecchino*, 1979–80

Faris, Scott: Winthrop Paroo, *The Music Man*, 1980–81

Farley, Carole: Second Lady, *Die Zauberflöte (The Magic Flute)*, 1965–66; Countess Ceprano, *Rigoletto*, 1966–67; Felice, *Quattro rusteghi (The Four Ruffians)*, 1966–67; Nedda, *I Pagliacci*, 1966–67; Page, *Parsifal*, 1966–67; Manon Lescaut, *Manon*, 1967–68

Farrell, Brian: Angelo, *The Boys from Syracuse*, 1968–69; Merlyn, *Camelot*, 1969–70

Farris, Jon: Arlecchino, *Arlecchino*, 1979–80

Farris, Willis: Ferdinand, *The Tempest*, 1985–86; Tony, *West Side Story*, 1985–86; Jenik, *The Bartered Bride*, 1986–87

Farrokh, Nasrin: A Moorish Girl, *Man of La Mancha*, 1985–86; Nella, *Gianni Schicchi*, 1988–89; Yvette, *La Rondine (The Swallow)*, 1989–90; The Marchesa Violante Onesti (Sandrina), *La Finta Giardiniera*, 1990–91

Faulkner, Julie: Annina, *La Traviata*, 1978–79; Countess Almaviva, *Le Nozze di Figaro (The Marriage of Figaro)*, 1980–81; Sister Angelica, *Il Trittico (A Triptych)*, 1982–83

Faust, Henry: Doctor Grenville, *La Traviata*, 1968–69; Trulove, *The Rake's Progress*, 1968–69; Jailer, *Tosca*, 1969–70; Simone, *Il Trittico (A Triptych)*, 1969–70; Tom, *Un Ballo in Maschera (A Masked Ball)*, 1969–70

Fay, Jon: Sir Sagramore, *Camelot*, 1969–70; High Priest, *Idomeneo*, 1976–77; Reverend Master Arthur Dimmesdale, *The Scarlet Letter*, 1976–77; Sam Polk, *Susannah*, 1976–77; Captain Richard Warrington, *Naughty Marietta*, 1977–78; Don Jose, *Carmen*, 1977–78; Grigori (Dimitri, the Pretender), *Boris Godunov*, 1978–79; Nicholas, *Canterbury Tales*, 1978–79; The Student, *Canterbury Tales*, 1978–79; Achilles, *The Cry of Clytaemnestra*, 1979–80; Sam Polk, *Susannah*, 1979–80

Fay, Rebecca: Mrs. Hayes, *Susannah*, 2007–08; Musetta, *La Bohème*, 2007–08

Featheringill, Jack: Harry Beaton, *Brigadoon*, 1952–53; Harry Beaton, *Brigadoon*, 1953–54

Federici, Robin: Die Fiakermilli, *Arabella*, 2006–07; Muffin, *A Wedding*, 2007–08

Fee, Constance: Giulietta, *Les Contes d'Hoffmann (The Tales of Hoffmann)*, 1973–74; Mercedes, *Carmen*, 1973–74; Shepherd Boy, *Tosca*, 1973–74; Voice of the Mother, *Les Contes d'Hoffmann (The Tales of Hoffmann)*, 1973–74; Madame Larina, *Eugene Onegin*, 1974–75; Augusta Tabor, *The Ballad of Baby Doe*, 1975–76; Charlotte, *Werther*, 1975–76; Suzuki, *Madama Butterfly*, 1975–76

Feiertag, Dorothy: Nancy, *Annie Get Your Gun*, 1956–57; Lisbon Woman, *Candide*, 1957–58

Feinstein, Jennifer: Flora Bervoix, *La Traviata*, 2002–03; Mama McCourt, *The Ballad of Baby Doe*, 2003–04; Martha, *The Secret Garden*, 2003–04; Angelina (Cinderella), *La Cenerentola (Cinderella)*, 2004–05; Ilona Ritter, *She Loves Me*, 2004–05; Rosina, *Il Barbiere di Siviglia (The Barber of Seville)*, 2005–06; Dame Doleful, *Too Many Sopranos*, 2006–07; Katisha, *The Mikado*, 2006–07

Felberg, Kathleen: Bianca, *La Rondine (The Swallow)*, 1959–60

Felix, Luis: Luigi, *Il Trittico (A Triptych)*, 1982–83; Alfredo Germont, *La Traviata*, 1983–84; Grigori (Dimitri, the Pretender), *Boris Godunov*, 1983–84; Rodolfo, *La Bohème*, 1984–85; The Duke of Mantua, *Rigoletto*, 1986–87

Fell, Eleanor: Diane, *Finian's Rainbow*, 1953–54

Fellman, Raymond: Dr. Falke, *Die Fledermaus (The Bat)*, 1996–97; Dr. Malatesta, *Don Pasquale*, 1997–98; Sir John Falstaff, *Falstaff*, 1997–98; Mandryka, *Arabella*, 1998–99; Marcello, *La Bohème*, 1999–2000; Tarquinius, *The Rape of Lucretia*, 1999–2000; Figaro, *Il Barbiere di Siviglia (The Barber of Seville)*, 2000–01; Rigoletto, *Rigoletto*, 2000–01

Fenske, Jerrad: Marquis, *The Ghosts of Versailles*, 1996–97; The Drum Major, *Wozzeck*, 1999–2000

Fenty, Maria: Mother Jeanne, *Dialogues des Carmélites*, 1986–87

Ferrantelli, Sal: Flora's Servant, *La Traviata*, 1968–69

Fetters, Susan: Sheila, *Where's Charley?*, 1953–54

Fey, Richard: Marco, *Il Trittico (A Triptych)*, 1972–73; Pinellino, *Il Trittico (A Triptych)*, 1972–73

Field, Rebecca: Donna Elvira, *Don Giovanni*, 1979–80; Electra, *The Cry of Clytaemnestra*, 1979–80; Widow Katerina, *The Greek Passion*, 1980–81; Marina Mnishek, *Boris Godunov*, 1983–84

Fielder, Aubrey: Silver Dollar (grown up), *The Ballad of Baby Doe*, 2003–04

Fielder, Raymond: Count Almaviva, *Le Nozze di Figaro (The Marriage of Figaro)*, 1980–81

Fields, Branch: Bernardo, *West Side Story*, 1992–93; Father Rangier, *Die Teufel von Loudun (The Devils of Loudun)*, 1992–93; David Bascomb, *Carousel*, 1993–94; Jailer, *Tosca*, 1993–94; Jonathan, *Carousel*, 1993–94; Pasha Selim, *Die Entführung aus dem Serail (The Abduction from the Seraglio)*, 1993–94; Raimondo Bidebent, *Lucia di Lammermoor*, 1993–94; The King of Clubs, *The Love for Three Oranges*, 1993–94; Arkel, *Pelléas et Mélisande*, 1994–95; Constable, *Fiddler on the Roof*, 1994–95; Don Basilio, *Il Barbiere di Siviglia (The Barber of Seville)*, 1994–95; Kezal, *The Bartered Bride*, 1994–95; Lindorf, *Les Contes d'Hoffmann (The Tales of Hoffmann)*, 1995–96; Sparafucile, *Rigoletto*, 1995–96

Fields, Sharon: Lady Soothly, *Candide*, 1957–58

Figura, Marcia: Nurse of the Children, *Boris Godunov*, 1978–79

Filak, Carolyn: Barbarina, *Le Nozze di Figaro (The Marriage of Figaro)*, 1992–93; Julie Jordan, *Carousel*, 1993–94

Filosa, Mark: Slave Merchant, *Kismet*, 1989–90; Announcer, *Jubilee*, 1991–92; Barnaby Tucker, *Hello, Dolly!*, 1991–92; Keeper of Zoo, *Jubilee*, 1991–92;

Broom, *1600 Pennsylvania Avenue*, 1992–93; D'Armagnac, *Die Teufel von Loudun (The Devils of Loudun)*, 1992–93; Doc, *West Side Story*, 1992–93; Mercury, *Orphée aux enfers (Orpheus in the Underworld)*, 1992–93; New Jersey Delegate, *1600 Pennsylvania Avenue*, 1992–93; Ross, *1600 Pennsylvania Avenue*, 1992–93; Senator Roscoe Conkling, *1600 Pennsylvania Avenue*, 1992–93; Doctor Seldon, *Carousel*, 1993–94; Don Issachar, *Candide*, 1993–94; Starkeeper, *Carousel*, 1993–94; Hermann, *Les Contes d'Hoffmann (The Tales of Hoffmann)*, 1995–96; Frosch, *Die Fledermaus (The Bat)*, 1996–97

Findlay, Mark: Chauffeur, *My Fair Lady*, 1979–80

Findley, Cynthia: Gertrude, *Hänsel und Gretel*, 1956–57

Fink, Mary Jane: Elvira, *L'Italiana in Algeri (The Italian Girl in Algiers)*, 1968–69; Deidamia, *Deidamia*, 1969–70; Nella, *Il Trittico (A Triptych)*, 1969–70; Marzelline, *Fidelio*, 1970–71

Finke, Alyssa: Suor Osmina, *Suor Angelica (Sister Angelica)*, 1999–2000

Fischer, Rebecca: Yente, *Fiddler on the Roof*, 1972–73

Fischer, Robert: Michele, *Il Trittico (A Triptych)*, 1972–73

Fiser, Lee: Dr. Keane, *The Veil*, 1949–50; Knight, *Parsifal*, 1949–50; Rodolfo, *La Bohème*, 1949–50

Fisguss, Marilyn: Laurey, *Oklahoma!*, 1954–55

Fisher, Jane: Morgan le Fey, *Camelot*, 1969–70

Fisher, Katherine: Miss Wordsworth, *Albert Herring*, 1957–58; Musetta, *La Bohème*, 1957–58; Donna Anna, *Don Giovanni*, 1958–59; Mistress Anne Page (Anna Reich), *Die lustigen Weiber von Windsor (The Merry Wives of Windsor)*, 1958–59; Sophie Teale, *Roberta*, 1958–59; Concepcion, *L'Heure espagnole (The Spanish Hour)*, 1959–60; Lisette, *La Rondine (The Swallow)*, 1959–60; Celestial Voice, *Don Carlos*, 1960–61; Queen of the Night, *Die Zauberflöte (The Magic Flute)*, 1960–61; Adina, *L'Elisir d'amore (The Elixir of Love)*, 1961–62; Celestial Voice, *Don Carlos*, 1961–62; Constanza, *Die Entführung aus dem Serail (The Abduction from the Seraglio)*, 1961–62; Jane Ashton, *Brigadoon*, 1961–62; Tytania, *A Midsummer Night's Dream*, 1961–62

Fisher, Paul: The Hairdresser, *Manon Lescaut*, 1970–71

Fisher, Robert: Billy Bigelow, *Carousel*, 1970–71; Figaro, *Il Barbiere di Siviglia (The Barber of Seville)*, 1971–72; Sir John Falstaff, *Falstaff*, 1971–72; Valentin, *Faust*, 1971–72; Mandryka, *Arabella*, 1972–73; Rodrigo, *Don Carlos*, 1972–73

Fisher, Sally: Geraldine Van Dare, *The Firefly*, 1949–50

Fisher, Sara Ann: Musetta, *La Bohème*, 1949–50; Rose Maurant, *Street Scene*, 1949–50; Sonia, *Die lustige Witwe (The Merry Widow)*, 1949–50

Fisher, Susan: Spirit, *Die Zauberflöte (The Magic Flute)*, 1953–54

Fisher, Zeal: Frank, *Brigadoon*, 1953–54

Fitzpatrick, Thomas: Don Jose, *Carmen*, 1962–63

Flaherty, Hope: Princess Zubbediya of Zanzibar, *Kismet*, 1989–90

Flake, Uta-Maria: Die Fiakermilli, *Arabella*, 1972–73; Queen of the Night, *Die Zauberflöte (The Magic Flute)*, 1972–73

Flores, Carelle: Maria, *West Side Story*, 2002–03; Constanza, *Die Entführung aus dem Serail (The Abduction from the Seraglio)*, 2003–04; Mimi, *La Bohème*, 2004–05

Flores, Paul: Guglielmo, *Così fan tutte*, 1956–57; Cesare Angelotti, *Tosca*, 1957–58; Dandini, *La Cenerentola (Cinderella)*, 1957–58; Dr. Malatesta, *Don Pasquale*, 1957–58; Husband, *Amelia Goes to the Ball*, 1957–58; Marcello, *La Bohème*, 1957–58; Second Officer, *Candide*, 1957–58; Sultan, *Candide*, 1957–58; The King, *The King and I*, 1957–58; Don Giovanni, *Don Giovanni*, 1958–59; Sharpless, *Madama Butterfly*, 1958–59; Rigoletto, *Rigoletto*, 1959–60; The Cashier, *The Most Happy Fella*, 1959–60

Flores, Sara: Frasquita, *Carmen*, 2005–06

Florio, Thomas: Figaro, *Le Nozze di Figaro (The Marriage of Figaro)*, 2007–08

Flower, Beverly: Lizzie Curry, *110 in the Shade*, 1967–68; Donna Fulvia, *Love on Trial (La Pietra del Paragone)*, 1969–70

Flowers, Blalock: Tinca, *Il Trittico (A Triptych)*, 1969–70

Flowles, Jay: Editor, *Wonderful Town*, 1954–55

Floyd, Brian: Jamie, *My Fair Lady*, 1979–80; Marcellus Washburn, *The Music Man*, 1980–81; Joe, *Oklahoma!*, 1981–82; Bus Driver, *The Most Happy Fella*, 1982–83; Juan / a Muleteer, *Man of La Mancha*, 1985–86

Floyd, Victor: The Father Confessor, *Dialogues des Carmélites*, 1986–87; Pedrillo, *Die Entführung aus dem Serail (The Abduction from the Seraglio)*, 1987–88; Andres, *Les Contes d'Hoffmann (The Tales of Hoffmann)*, 1988–89; Cochenille, *Les Contes d'Hoffmann (The Tales of Hoffmann)*, 1988–89; Count Almaviva, *Il Barbiere di Siviglia (The Barber of Seville)*, 1988–89; Franz, *Les Contes d'Hoffmann (The Tales of Hoffmann)*, 1988–89; Pittichinaccio, *Les Contes d'Hoffmann (The Tales of Hoffmann)*, 1988–89

Follman, Robin: Consuelo, *West Side Story*, 1992–93; Diana, *Orphée aux enfers (Orpheus in the Underworld)*, 1992–93; Paquette, *Candide*, 1993–94; Musetta, *La Bohème*, 1994–95

Foncannon, Linda: Micaëla, *Carmen*, 1956–57; Nanetta, *Falstaff*, 1956–57

Forbes, Michael: Guillot, *Eugene Onegin*, 2004–05

Ford, Bruce: Robbins, *Porgy and Bess*, 1976–77

Ford, Natalie: Tytania, *A Midsummer Night's Dream*, 2005–06; Zerlina, *Don Giovanni*, 2006–07

Fordyce, Robert: Trainman, *Annie Get Your Gun*, 1956–57

Foreman, Blanche: Mary, *Der Fliegende Holländer (The Flying Dutchman)*, 1978–79; Voice of the Mother, *Les Contes d'Hoffmann (The Tales of Hoffmann)*, 1978–79

Forkner, Terry: Enoch Snow, Jr., *Carousel*, 1970–71

Fosdick, Cody: Dandini, *La Cenerentola (Cinderella)*, 2004–05; Captain Corcoran, *HMS Pinafore*, 2005–06; George Gibbs, *Our Town*, 2005–06

Fosselman, Joseph: A Steersman, *Der Fliegende Holländer (The Flying Dutchman)*, 1985–86; Adrian, *The Tempest*, 1985–86; Tom Rakewell, *The Rake's Progress*, 1986–87; Belmonte, *Die Entführung aus dem Serail (The Abduction from the Seraglio)*, 1987–88; Lt. Pinkerton, *Madama Butterfly*, 1987–88; Lensky, *Eugene Onegin*, 1988–89; Mr. Erlanson, *A Little Night Music*, 1988–89; The Caliph, *Kismet*, 1989–90

Foss-Pittman, Kathryn: The President's Wife, *1600 Pennsylvania Avenue*, 1992–93

Foster, Bob: Gil, *Street Scene*, 1960–61

Foster, Justin: Little Jake, *Annie Get Your Gun*, 1956–57; Prince Chulalongkorn, *The King and I*, 1957–58

Foster, Renee: Surcha, *Fiddler on the Roof*, 1994–95

Foster Strebing, Mary: Juliet, *Roméo et Juliette*, 1966–67; Marina, *Quattro rusteghi (The Four Ruffians)*, 1966–67; Margaret, *Mefistofele*, 1967–68

Fowles, Jay: Chernikofsky, *Boris Godunov*, 1953–54; Bacchus/Tenor, *Ariadne auf Naxos*, 1954–55; Joe, *Oklahoma!*, 1954–55; Knight, *Parsifal*, 1955–56; Luigi, *Il Tabarro (The Cloak)*, 1955–56

Fox, Cassandra: Countess Ceprano, *Rigoletto*, 1986–87; Sister Mathilde, *Dialogues des Carmélites*, 1986–87; Svatia Babarikha, *The Legend of Tsar Saltan*, 1986–87

Fox, Sarah: Olympia, *Les Contes d'Hoffmann (The Tales of Hoffmann)*, 2007–08

Francis, Mardene: Golde, *Fiddler on the Roof*, 1994–95

Francis, Nelson: Preacher, *Finian's Rainbow*, 1953–54; Trainman, *Annie Get Your Gun*, 1956–57

Frank, Joseph: An Incroyable, *Andrea Chénier*, 1967–68; Valetto, *L'Incoronazione di Poppea (The Coronation of Poppea)*, 1967–68; Chekalinsky, *La Pique Dame (The Queen of Spades)*, 1968–69; Don Curzio, *Le Nozze di Figaro (The Marriage of Figaro)*, 1968–69; Page, *Parsifal*, 1968–69; Spoletta, *Tosca*, 1969–70; The Dancing Master, *Ariadne auf Naxos*, 1969–70; Arturo Bucklaw, *Lucia di Lammermoor*, 1970–71; Ferrando, *Così fan tutte*, 1970–71; Count Almaviva,

Il Barbiere di Siviglia (The Barber of Seville), 1971–72; Don Ottavio, *Don Giovanni*, 1971–72; Hyllus, *Heracles*, 1971–72

Frankforter, Lynelle: Emily, *The Ballad of Baby Doe*, 1975–76; Page, *Parsifal*, 1975–76; Kate Pinkerton, *Madama Butterfly*, 1976–77; Mrs. Meg Page, *Falstaff*, 1976–77; Dorabella, *Così fan tutte*, 1977–78; Oksana, *The Night Before Christmas*, 1977–78

Frankforter-Wiens, Lynelle: Hansel, *Hänsel und Gretel*, 1982–83

Franklin, Frances: Javotte, *Manon*, 1979–80; Marian Paroo, *The Music Man*, 1980–81; Emily, *The Ballad of Baby Doe*, 1982–83; Flora Bervoix, *La Traviata*, 1983–84; Concepcion, *L'Heure espagnole (The Spanish Hour)*, 1984–85; Abigail Williams, *The Crucible*, 1987–88; Player, *Mass*, 1988–89

Franklin, Janet: Helen, *Annie Get Your Gun*, 1956–57

Franklin, John: Ambulance Driver, *Street Scene*, 1949–50; Policeman, *Street Scene*, 1949–50; Rosabella, *The Most Happy Fella*, 1959–60

Frankson, Heidi: Marsinah, *Kismet*, 1989–90; Jenny, *Company*, 1990–91

Fredell, Karla: Mother Goose, *The Rake's Progress*, 1986–87; Svatia Babarikha, *The Legend of Tsar Saltan*, 1986–87; Old Lady, *Candide*, 1987–88; Rebecca Nurse, *The Crucible*, 1987–88; Berta (Marcellina), *Il Barbiere di Siviglia (The Barber of Seville)*, 1988–89; Zita, *Gianni Schicchi*, 1988–89; The Witch, *Hänsel und Gretel*, 1989–90

Fredericks, Steven: Third Thug, *Danton and Robespierre*, 1977–78; Doctor Grenville, *La Traviata*, 1978–79; Luther, *Les Contes d'Hoffmann (The Tales of Hoffmann)*, 1978–79; Nikitich, *Boris Godunov*, 1978–79; Officer of the Border Guard, *Boris Godunov*, 1978–79; Alcindoro, *La Bohème*, 1979–80; Colonel Pickering, *My Fair Lady*, 1979–80; Elder McLean, *Susannah*, 1979–80; Guardsman, *Manon*, 1979–80; Kezal, *The Bartered Bride*, 1979–80; Doctor Bartolo, *Il Barbiere di Siviglia (The Barber of Seville)*, 1980–81; Sir John Falstaff, *Die lustigen Weiber von Windsor (The Merry Wives of Windsor)*, 1981–82; Priest, *Die Zauberflöte (The Magic Flute)*, 1982–83; Talpa, *Il Trittico (A Triptych)*, 1982–83; Varlaam, *Boris Godunov*, 1983–84

Frederiksen, Paul: A.A., *The Mother of Us All*, 1973–74; Francesco, *The Gondoliers*, 1974–75; Claudio, *Il Mondo della Luna (The World on the Moon)*, 1975–76

Fredricks, Olive: Curra, *La Forza del Destino (The Force of Destiny)*, 1962–63; Mercedes, *Carmen*, 1962–63; Page, *Parsifal*, 1962–63; Preziosilla, *La Forza del Destino (The Force of Destiny)*, 1962–63; Berta (Marcellina), *Il Barbiere di Siviglia (The Barber of Seville)*, 1963–64; Dorabella, *Così fan tutte*, 1963–64; Khivria, *The Fair at Sorochinsk*, 1963–64; Mrs. Sedley, *Peter Grimes*, 1963–64;

Mute, *The Fantasticks,* 1963–64; Hostess of the Inn, *Boris Godunov,* 1964–65; Suzuki, *Madama Butterfly,* 1964–65; Zita, *Gianni Schicchi,* 1964–65

Freedlander, Fern: Dewman, *Hänsel und Gretel,* 2001–02

Freeland, Sally: Muffin, *A Wedding,* 2007–08

Freeman, Colenton: Aegisthus, *The Cry of Clytaemnestra,* 1979–80; Crab Man, *Porgy and Bess,* 1979–80; Frazier, *Porgy and Bess,* 1979–80; The Ringmaster, *The Bartered Bride,* 1979–80; Panait, *The Greek Passion,* 1980–81; The Duke of Mantua, *Rigoletto,* 1980–81

Freeze, Chris: Peter Grimes, *Peter Grimes,* 2003–04; Rodolfo, *La Bohème,* 2004–05

Frei, Adam: Pinellino, *Gianni Schicchi,* 1993–94

Frey, Leah Beth: Javotte, *Manon,* 1967–68; Flora Bervoix, *La Traviata,* 1968–69; Ortlinde, *Die Walküre,* 1969–70; Sister Angelica, *Il Trittico (A Triptych),* 1969–70

Fridlin, Nance: Clo-clo, *Die lustige Witwe (The Merry Widow),* 1949–50

Friedman, Deborah: Venere (Venus), *L'Orfeo,* 1987–88; First Lady, *Die Zauberflöte (The Magic Flute),* 1988–89; Magda de Civry, *La Rondine (The Swallow),* 1989–90

Friedman, Erik: Mr. Dashwood, *Little Women,* 2001–02; Baron Douphol, *La Traviata,* 2002–03; Frank, *Die Fledermaus (The Bat),* 2002–03; Major Holmes, *The Secret Garden,* 2003–04; Speaker of the Temple, *Die Zauberflöte (The Magic Flute),* 2004–05; Steven Kodaly, *She Loves Me,* 2004–05; Zaretsky, *Eugene Onegin,* 2004–05

Friel, Margaret: Donna Fulvia, *Love on Trial (La Pietra del Paragone),* 1969–70; Oscar, *Un Ballo in Maschera (A Masked Ball),* 1969–70

Fries, Carolyn: Ellen, *Oklahoma!,* 1997–98

Fries, Kathlyn: Hero, *Béatrice et Bénédict,* 1987–88; Anne Egerman, *A Little Night Music,* 1988–89; Norina, *Don Pasquale,* 1988–89; Fiordiligi, *Così fan tutte,* 1989–90; Magda de Civry, *La Rondine (The Swallow),* 1989–90; Musetta, *La Bohème,* 1989–90; Adina, *L'Elisir d'amore (The Elixir of Love),* 1990–91; The Marchesa Violante Onesti (Sandrina), *La Finta Giardiniera,* 1990–91

Friesen, Norman: Crebillon, *La Rondine (The Swallow),* 1959–60; The Postman, *The Most Happy Fella,* 1959–60

Fudge, Tamara Phillips: Princess Linetta, *The Love for Three Oranges,* 1980–81; Princess Nicoletta, *The Love for Three Oranges,* 1980–81

Fuller, Marjorie: Dame Quickly, *Falstaff,* 1956–57; Anna Leonowens, *The King and I,* 1957–58; Amelia's Friend, *Amelia Goes to the Ball,* 1957–58; Mrs. Herring, *Albert Herring,* 1957–58; Princess Eboli, *Don Carlos,* 1961–62;

Carmen, *Carmen,* 1962–63; Dame Hannah, *Ruddigore (The Witch's Curse),* 1962–63; First Mourner, *The Darkened City,* 1962–63

Fuller, William: The Idol, *The Ruby,* 1954–55; Titurel, *Parsifal,* 1954–55; Truffaldino, *Ariadne auf Naxos,* 1954–55; Capt. George Brackett, *South Pacific,* 1956–57

Fulton, Rachel: Voice of the Mother, *Les Contes d'Hoffmann (The Tales of Hoffmann),* 2002–03; Olga, *Die lustige Witwe (The Merry Widow),* 2003–04; Rose Lennox, *The Secret Garden,* 2003–04; First Lady, *Die Zauberflöte (The Magic Flute),* 2004–05

Fuselier, Kimberly: Trina Sieppe, *McTeague,* 1995–96; Donna Fiorilla, *Il Turco in Italia (The Turk in Italy),* 1996–97; Susanna, *Le Nozze di Figaro (The Marriage of Figaro),* 1997–98; Eurydice, *Orphée aux enfers (Orpheus in the Underworld),* 1998–99; Player, *Mass,* 1998–99

Futral, Cynthia: Betty Parris, *The Crucible,* 1987–88; Lisa, *La Sonnambula (The Sleepwalker),* 1985–86; Abigail Williams, *The Crucible,* 1987–88; Blonde, *Die Entführung aus dem Serail (The Abduction from the Seraglio),* 1987–88; Norina, *Don Pasquale,* 1988–89

Gailey, Matthew: Dickon, *The Secret Garden,* 2003–04; Rev. Horace Adams, *Peter Grimes,* 2003–04; Sam, *The Ballad of Baby Doe,* 2003–04; Arpad Laszlo, *She Loves Me,* 2004–05

Galchick, Donna: Dryad, *Ariadne auf Naxos,* 1969–70; A Slave, *Salome,* 1970–71; Grimgerde, *Die Walküre,* 1971–72

Galer, Suzanne: Diana Devereaux, *Of Thee I Sing,* 1987–88; Orfeo, *L'Orfeo,* 1987–88; Queen of the Night, *Die Zauberflöte (The Magic Flute),* 1988–89

Gallagher, Fulton: Count Almaviva, *Le Nozze di Figaro (The Marriage of Figaro),* 1962–63; Don Carlos of Vargas, *La Forza del Destino (The Force of Destiny),* 1962–63; Marcello, *La Bohème,* 1962–63; Priest, *The Darkened City,* 1962–63; Enrico, *Il Campanello di Notte (The Night Bell),* 1963–64; Pedrillo, *Die Entführung aus dem Serail (The Abduction from the Seraglio),* 1966–67; Tybalt, *Roméo et Juliette,* 1966–67

Gallagher, Patricia: Mary McLennon, *The Land Between the Rivers,* 1955–56; Despina, *Così fan tutte,* 1956–57

Gallagher, Robert: Pedro / Head Muleteer, *Man of La Mancha,* 1988–89; Prince James, *Jubilee,* 1991–92

Galloway, Melanie: Mary Turner, *Of Thee I Sing,* 1987–88; Paquette, *Candide,* 1987–88; La Ciesca, *Gianni Schicchi,* 1988–89

Gamber, Patricia: Nina, *Song of Norway*, 1951–52; Pamina, *Die Zauberflöte (The Magic Flute)*, 1953–54

Gamble, Polly: Sharon, *Finian's Rainbow*, 1969–70

Gamble, Richard: First Man of Paris, *Danton and Robespierre*, 1977–78; Priest, *Die Zauberflöte (The Magic Flute)*, 1977–78; Doctor Grenville, *La Traviata*, 1978–79; Luther, *Les Contes d'Hoffmann (The Tales of Hoffmann)*, 1978–79; Innkeeper, *Manon*, 1979–80; Count Ceprano, *Rigoletto*, 1980–81; Leandro, *The Love for Three Oranges*, 1980–81; Barney, *The Ballad of Baby Doe*, 1982–83; Marco, *Il Trittico (A Triptych)*, 1982–83; Bulgarian Soldier, *Candide*, 1983–84; Sailor, *Candide*, 1983–84; The Prefect of Constantinople, *Candide*, 1983–84

Gamez, Denise: Mother Goose, *The Rake's Progress*, 1986–87; Old Lady, *Candide*, 1987–88; Madame Armfeldt, *A Little Night Music*, 1988–89; Third Lady, *Die Zauberflöte (The Magic Flute)*, 1988–89; Voice of the Mother, *Les Contes d'Hoffmann (The Tales of Hoffmann)*, 1988–89; Zita, *Gianni Schicchi*, 1988–89; Emilia, *Otello*, 1989–90; Martha, *Faust*, 1989–90; Annina, *La Traviata*, 1990–91; Margaret, *Wozzeck*, 1990–91; Baba the Turk, *The Rake's Progress*, 1991–92; Suzuki, *Madama Butterfly*, 1991–92; Dame Quickly, *Falstaff*, 1992–93

Garabedian, Lillian: La Duchesse, *Candide*, 1957–58; Lola, *Cavalleria Rusticana*, 1957–58; Mrs. Herring, *Albert Herring*, 1957–58; Pilgrim Mother, *Candide*, 1957–58; Suzuki, *Madama Butterfly*, 1958–59; Ulrica, *Un Ballo in Maschera (A Masked Ball)*, 1958–59; Voice from Heaven, *Parsifal*, 1958–59

Garciacano, Gerardo: Dancaire, *Carmen*, 1998–99; Graf Dominik, *Arabella*, 1998–99; Marcello, *La Bohème*, 1999–2000; Pantalone, *The Love for Three Oranges*, 1999–2000

Gardner, Cheryl: Annie, *Porgy and Bess*, 1976–77; Tuptim, *The King and I*, 1996–97

Gardner, Susanne Marie: Marta, *The Sound of Music*, 2000–01; Amaryllis, *The Music Man*, 2001–02

Garner, Bea: Ludmila, *The Bartered Bride*, 2001–02

Garner, Luvenia: Clara, *Porgy and Bess*, 1979–80

Garrott, Alice: Shepherd Boy, *Tosca*, 1969–70; The Monitor of the Convent, *Il Trittico (A Triptych)*, 1969–70; A Page, *Manon Lescaut*, 1970–71; Herodias, *Salome*, 1970–71; Deianira, *Heracles*, 1971–72; Fricka, *Die Walküre*, 1971–72; Adelaide, *Arabella*, 1972–73; Frugola, *Il Trittico (A Triptych)*, 1972–73; Princess Bolokonsky, *Myshkin*, 1972–73; Princess Eboli, *Don Carlos*, 1972–73

Garst, John: Man in Armor, *Die Zauberflöte (The Magic Flute)*, 1988–89; Priest, *Die Zauberflöte (The Magic Flute)*, 1988–89

Garvin, Bradley: Baron Thunder-Ten-Tronck, *Candide*, 1987–88; Judge of the Inquisition, *Candide*, 1987–88; The Extortionist, *Candide*, 1987–88; Don Basilio, *Il Barbiere di Siviglia (The Barber of Seville)*, 1988–89; Simone, *Gianni Schicchi*, 1988–89; Colline, *La Bohème*, 1989–90; Don Alfonso, *Così fan tutte*, 1989–90; Mephistopheles, *Faust*, 1989–90; Doctor Grenville, *La Traviata*, 1990–91; Dr. Dulcamara, *L'Elisir d'amore (The Elixir of Love)*, 1990–91

Gastineau, Clare: The Child, *Wozzeck*, 1990–91; Trouble, *Madama Butterfly*, 1991–92

Gauger, Jill: Ethel Toffelmier, *The Music Man*, 1980–81; Aunt Eller, *Oklahoma!*, 1981–82

Geddert, Heidi: Sophia, *Tom Jones*, 1983–84

Gehrenbeck, Robert: M. Javelinot, *Dialogues des Carmélites*, 1997–98

Geiser, William: Cochenille, *Les Contes d'Hoffmann (The Tales of Hoffmann)*, 1947–48; Nathanael, *Les Contes d'Hoffmann (The Tales of Hoffmann)*, 1947–48

Gelfand, Benjamin: Doctor Grenville, *La Traviata*, 2002–03; Don Geronio, *Il Turco in Italia (The Turk in Italy)*, 2003–04; Benoit, *La Bohème*, 2004–05; Don Magnifico, *La Cenerentola (Cinderella)*, 2004–05; Sacristan, *Tosca*, 2004–05

Genaux, Vivica: Mrs. Dolly Gallagher Levi, *Hello, Dolly!*, 1991–92; Rosalia, *West Side Story*, 2002–03

Gent, Jillian: Pousette, *Manon*, 1993–94; Rivka, *Fiddler on the Roof*, 1994–95

Gentry, Larry: Edward Jarvis, *Lost in the Stars*, 1950–51

George, Vance: Archie Beaton, *Brigadoon*, 1961–62; The Boy, *The Fantasticks*, 1963–64

Gersten, Frederick: Simon Boccanegra, *Simon Boccanegra*, 1964–65; Dr. Malatesta, *Don Pasquale*, 1965–66; Escamillo, *Carmen*, 1965–66; Herr Von Faninal, *Der Rosenkavalier*, 1965–66

Geyer, Gwynne: Eliza Doolittle, *My Fair Lady*, 1979–80; Marenka, *The Bartered Bride*, 1979–80; Susanna, *Le Nozze di Figaro (The Marriage of Figaro)*, 1980–81

Gibson, Sue: Grimgerde, *Die Walküre*, 1971–72

Giering, Jane: Spirit, *Die Zauberflöte (The Magic Flute)*, 1982–83; Cunegonde, *Candide*, 1983–84; Sophia, *Tom Jones*, 1983–84

Gilbert, Barbara: Hanna Glawari, *Die lustige Witwe (The Merry Widow)*, 1983–84; Mrs. Honour, *Tom Jones*, 1983–84; Mimi, *La Bohème*, 1984–85; Micaëla, *Carmen*, 1984–85; Amina, *La Sonnambula (The Sleepwalker)*, 1985–86

Gilbert, Katherine: Samantha, *The Ballad of Baby Doe*, 1982–83; Clo-clo, *Die lustige Witwe (The Merry Widow)*, 1983–84; Woglinde, *Das Rheingold*, 1983–84

Gilbert, Robyn: Player, *Mass*, 1988–89; Spirit, *Die Zauberflöte (The Magic Flute)*, 1988–89; Suzy, *La Rondine (The Swallow)*, 1989–90; Margot, *Die lustige Witwe (The Merry Widow)*, 1990–91; Mother Goose, *The Rake's Progress*, 1991–92

Gilchrist, Juliet: Mrs. Paroo, *The Music Man*, 2001–02; Mrs. Alice Ford, *Falstaff*, 2003–04; Mrs. Webb, *Our Town*, 2005–06

Gill, Anne: Mrs. Medlock, *The Secret Garden*, 2003–04

Gill, Jennifer: Hata, *The Bartered Bride*, 2001–02; Muse, *Les Contes d'Hoffmann (The Tales of Hoffmann)*, 2002–03; Nicklausse, *Les Contes d'Hoffmann (The Tales of Hoffmann)*, 2002–03; Prince Orlofsky, *Die Fledermaus (The Bat)*, 2002–03

Gillas, John: Don Carlos, *Don Carlos*, 1972–73

Gillaspy, John: Billy Budd, *Billy Budd*, 1952–53; Papageno, *Die Zauberflöte (The Magic Flute)*, 1953–54; Curly, *Oklahoma!*, 1954–55; Dr. Falke, *Die Fledermaus (The Bat)*, 1954–55; Giorgio Germont, *La Traviata*, 1954–55; David, *Die Meistersinger von Nürnberg (The Mastersingers of Nuremberg)*, 1968–69

Gilligan, John: Waiter, *On the Town*, 1951–52

Gilliland, Patricia Johnson: Erika, *Vanessa*, 1974–75

Gilliland, Peter: Second Man, *Kiss Me, Kate*, 1973–74

Gillis, Peter: Pedrillo, *Die Entführung aus dem Serail (The Abduction from the Seraglio)*, 1981–82; Count Almaviva, *Il Barbiere di Siviglia (The Barber of Seville)*, 1982–83

Gillom, Dennis: A Lackey, *Ariadne auf Naxos*, 1969–70; Betto, *Il Trittico (A Triptych)*, 1969–70; First Gospeleer, *Finian's Rainbow*, 1969–70; Howard, *Finian's Rainbow*, 1969–70; King Philip II, *Don Carlos*, 1972–73; Talpa, *Il Trittico (A Triptych)*, 1972–73

Gilmore, Earl: Prince Shuisky, *Boris Godunov*, 1964–65; Remendado, *Carmen*, 1965–66; The Father Confessor, *Dialogues des Carmélites*, 1965–66

Gilmore, Gail: Frugola, *Il Trittico (A Triptych)*, 1972–73; Sister Osmina, *Il Trittico (A Triptych)*, 1972–73; The nursing sister from the infirmary, *Il Trittico (A Triptych)*, 1972–73; Carmen, *Carmen*, 1973–74

Gilmore, John: Narumov, *La Pique Dame (The Queen of Spades)*, 1968–69; Tailor's apprentice, *The Boys from Syracuse*, 1968–69; A Lamplighter, *Manon Lescaut*, 1970–71; Anatol, *Vanessa*, 1974–75; Belmonte, *Die Entführung aus dem Serail (The Abduction from the Seraglio)*, 1974–75; Marco Palmieri, *The Gondoliers*, 1974–75; Werther, *Werther*, 1975–76; Governor, *Candide*, 1976–77; Idamante, *Idomeneo*, 1976–77; Player, *Bernstein on Broadway*, 1976–77; Sam Polk, *Susannah*, 1976–77

Gilmore, Rachele: Ida, *Die Fledermaus (The Bat)*, 2002–03; Stella, *Les Contes d'Hoffmann (The Tales of Hoffmann)*, 2002–03

Giltner, Steven: First Deputy, *Finian's Rainbow*, 1969–70

Gingerich, Margaret: Mrs. Watkins, *Jubilee*, 1991–92

Gingery, Connie Jo: Fiametta, *The Gondoliers*, 1974–75; The McCourt family, *The Ballad of Baby Doe*, 1975–76; Flower Girl, *My Fair Lady*, 1979–80

Girardi, Sulie: Tenth Woman of Paris, *Danton and Robespierre*, 1977–78; Second Mourner, *The Darkened City*, 1978–79; Colombina, *Arlecchino*, 1979–80; Hata, *The Bartered Bride*, 1979–80; Mrs. McLean, *Susannah*, 1979–80; An Old Woman, *The Greek Passion*, 1980–81; Marcellina, *Le Nozze di Figaro (The Marriage of Figaro)*, 1980–81; Princess Clarissa, *The Love for Three Oranges*, 1980–81; Mistress Page (Frau Reich), *Die lustigen Weiber von Windsor (The Merry Wives of Windsor)*, 1981–82; Suzuki, *Madama Butterfly*, 1981–82; Berta (Marcellina), *Il Barbiere di Siviglia (The Barber of Seville)*, 1982–83; Third Lady, *Die Zauberflöte (The Magic Flute)*, 1982–83; Zita, *Il Trittico (A Triptych)*, 1982–83; Flosshilde, *Das Rheingold*, 1983–84; Hostess of the Inn, *Boris Godunov*, 1983–84; Old Lady, *Candide*, 1983–84

Gissendanner, Paulette: Gertrude, *Hänsel und Gretel*, 1982–83; The Abbess, *Il Trittico (A Triptych)*, 1982–83; The Antique Chair, *L'Enfant et les Sortilèges (The Bewitched Child)*, 1984–85; The Owl, *L'Enfant et les Sortilèges (The Bewitched Child)*, 1984–85; Juno, *The Tempest*, 1985–86

Gitter, Marshall: Juggler, *The Darkened City*, 1978–79

Given, Ruthie: Violin Student, *Street Scene*, 1949–50

Glann, John: Alidoro, *La Cenerentola (Cinderella)*, 2004–05; Louis, *A View from the Bridge*, 2004–05

Glanzberg, Susan: Maria, The Innkeeper's Wife, *Man of La Mancha*, 1988–89; Prince Orlofsky, *Die Fledermaus (The Bat)*, 1990–91

Glaze, Tommye Lou: Maid, *Amelia Goes to the Ball*, 1957–58; Kate Pinkerton, *Madama Butterfly*, 1958–59; Princess Linetta, *The Love for Three Oranges*, 1958–59; Page, *Parsifal*, 1959–60

Gleich, Cynthia: Guenevere, *Camelot*, 1968–69; Morgan le Fey, *Camelot*, 1968–69; Guenevere, *Camelot*, 1969–70

Glen, Jeremy: John, *Peter Grimes*, 1994–95; Solo Child, *La Bohème*, 1994–95; Louis Leonowens, *The King and I*, 1996–97

Gloden, Martha: Casilda, *The Gondoliers*, 1974–75

Gobles, Chris: Curio, *Giulio Cesare (Julius Caesar)*, 2002–03; Riff, *West Side Story*, 2002–03; Bogdanowitsch, *Die lustige Witwe (The Merry Widow)*, 2003–04; Luther, *Les Contes d'Hoffmann (The Tales of Hoffmann)*, 2007–08

Godshall, Rodney: Lunardo, *Quattro rusteghi (The Four Ruffians)*, 1966–67; Titurel, *Parsifal*, 1966–67; Dr. Wilhelm Reischmann, *Elegy for Young Lovers*, 1967–68; Ferrando, *Il Trovatore*, 1967–68; Mathieu, *Andrea Chénier*, 1967–68; Seneca, *L'Incoronazione di Poppea (The Coronation of Poppea)*, 1967–68; Titurel, *Parsifal*, 1967–68; Dr. Bartolo, *Le Nozze di Figaro (The Marriage of Figaro)*, 1968–69; Mustafa, *L'Italiana in Algeri (The Italian Girl in Algiers)*, 1968–69

Goen, Aaron: Constable Locke, *The Music Man*, 2001–02

Goldman, Emma: Giorgetta, *Il Trittico (A Triptych)*, 1972–73

Goldstein, Stuart: Desk Clerk of the Hotel, *Arabella*, 1972–73; Andres, *Les Contes d'Hoffmann (The Tales of Hoffmann)*, 1973–74; Cochenille, *Les Contes d'Hoffmann (The Tales of Hoffmann)*, 1973–74; Franz, *Les Contes d'Hoffmann (The Tales of Hoffmann)*, 1973–74; Pittichinaccio, *Les Contes d'Hoffmann (The Tales of Hoffmann)*, 1973–74; Virgil Thomson, *The Mother of Us All*, 1973–74; Student from Krakow, *Doktor Faust*, 1974–75

Goldthwaite, Thomas: Albert's manservant, *Werther*, 1961–62; Bruhlmann, *Werther*, 1961–62; Mr. Lundie, *Brigadoon*, 1961–62

Golliver, April: Madame Larina, *Eugene Onegin*, 1997–98; Carmen, *Carmen*, 1998–99; Third Lady, *Die Zauberflöte (The Magic Flute)*, 1998–99; Erika, *Vanessa*, 1999–2000; Princess Clarissa, *The Love for Three Oranges*, 1999–2000; Old Lady, *Candide*, 2000–01; Rosina, *Il Barbiere di Siviglia (The Barber of Seville)*, 2000–01

Gong, Dong-Jian: Prince Gremin, *Eugene Onegin*, 1988–89

Gonzalez, Enid: Anita, *West Side Story*, 1992–93; Berta (Marcellina), *Il Barbiere di Siviglia (The Barber of Seville)*, 1994–95

Gonzalez, Joseph: An Indian, *The Bartered Bride*, 1986–87

Good, Kathryn: Assistant Courtesan, *The Boys from Syracuse*, 1968–69

Goodenough, John: Claudio, *Béatrice et Bénédict*, 1987–88; Fiorello, *Il Barbiere di Siviglia (The Barber of Seville)*, 1988–89; Marco, *Gianni Schicchi*, 1988–89; Officer, *Il Barbiere di Siviglia (The Barber of Seville)*, 1988–89; Benoit, *La Bohème*, 1989–90; Perichaud, *La Rondine (The Swallow)*, 1989–90; Wagner, *Faust*, 1989–90; Frank, *Die Fledermaus (The Bat)*, 1990–91; Marquis D'Obigny, *La Traviata*, 1990–91; Wozzeck, *Wozzeck*, 1990–91; Judge, *Hello, Dolly!*, 1991–92; Rigoletto, *Rigoletto*, 1992–93; Sir John Falstaff, *Falstaff*, 1992–93

Goodmon, Jordan: Mary Lennox, *The Secret Garden*, 2003–04

Goodsell, Stephen: Keeper of the Madhouse, *The Rake's Progress*, 1986–87; The Buffoon, *The Legend of Tsar Saltan*, 1986–87; Sharpless, *Madama Butterfly*, 1987–88

Gorby, Drew: Baritone, *Carmina Burana*, 1991–92; Nick Shadow, *The Rake's Progress*, 1991–92; Prime Minister (Lord Wyndham), *Jubilee*, 1991–92; Count Ceprano, *Rigoletto*, 1992–93

Gordon, Joel: Aegeon, *The Boys from Syracuse*, 1968–69; Squire Dap, *Camelot*, 1968–69; Og, *Finian's Rainbow*, 1969–70

Gordon, John: Guccio, *Il Trittico (A Triptych)*, 1969–70; Song Vendor, *Il Trittico (A Triptych)*, 1969–70

Gordon, Michael: Porgy, *Porgy and Bess*, 1976–77

Gordon, Samuel: Parpignol, *La Bohème*, 1962–63; Second Suitor, *The Darkened City*, 1962–63; Simpleton, *Boris Godunov*, 1964–65; The Shepherd, *Oedipus Rex*, 1964–65

Gordon, Samuel: Somewhere solo, *West Side Story*, 1985–86; Richard Nixon, *Nixon in China*, 1994–95; Speaker of the Temple, *Die Zauberflöte (The Magic Flute)*, 1994–95; Lt. Joseph Cable, *South Pacific*, 1995–96; Cascada, *Die lustige Witwe (The Merry Widow)*, 1996–97; English Ambassador, *The Ghosts of Versailles*, 1996–97; Frank, *Die Fledermaus (The Bat)*, 1996–97; Sir Edward Ramsay, *The King and I*, 1996–97; The Poet, Prosdocimo, *Il Turco in Italia (The Turk in Italy)*, 1996–97

Gould, Patricia: Naiad, *Ariadne auf Naxos*, 1954–55; Fire, *L'Enfant et les Sortilèges (The Bewitched Child)*, 1955–56; Dewman, *Hänsel und Gretel*, 1956–57

Gover, Deborah: Countess Ceprano, *Rigoletto*, 1992–93; Gabrielle, *Die Teufel von Loudun (The Devils of Loudun)*, 1992–93

Graf, Werner: Klaas, *Die Entführung aus dem Serail (The Abduction from the Seraglio)*, 1951–52; The School Master, *A Parfait for Irene*, 1951–52; Dansker, *Billy Budd*, 1952–53; Nikitich, *Boris Godunov*, 1953–54; Antonio, *Le Nozze di Figaro (The Marriage of Figaro)*, 1955–56; Dr. Bartolo, *Le Nozze di Figaro (The Marriage of Figaro)*, 1955–56; Talpa, *Il Tabarro (The Cloak)*, 1955–56; The Sofa, *L'Enfant et les Sortilèges (The Bewitched Child)*, 1955–56; Alcindoro, *La Bohème*, 1957–58; Benoit, *La Bohème*, 1957–58; Colline, *La Bohème*, 1957–58; Don Magnifico, *La Cenerentola (Cinderella)*, 1957–58; Don Pasquale, *Don Pasquale*, 1957–58; Inquisition Guard, *Candide*, 1957–58; Prince Ivan, *Candide*, 1957–58; The Chief of Police, *Amelia Goes to the Ball*, 1957–58; LaRoche, *Capriccio*, 1958–59; Leporello, *Don Giovanni*, 1958–59; Samuel, *Un Ballo in Maschera (A Masked Ball)*, 1958–59; Sir John Falstaff, *Die lustigen Weiber von Windsor (The Merry Wives of Windsor)*, 1958–59

Grange, William: Henry Higgins, *My Fair Lady*, 1979–80; Ladas, *The Greek Passion*, 1980–81

Grant, Heidi: Blonde, *Die Entführung aus dem Serail (The Abduction from the Seraglio),* 1987–88

Gray, Greta: Grima, *Song of Norway,* 1951–52; Ivy, *On the Town,* 1951–52; Miss Anders, *Song of Norway,* 1951–52; Carrie Pipperidge, *Carousel,* 1952–53; Papagena, *Die Zauberflöte (The Magic Flute),* 1953–54; Adele, *Die Fledermaus (The Bat),* 1954–55; Zerbinetta, *Ariadne auf Naxos,* 1954–55

Gray, Heather: Mrs. Meg Page, *Falstaff,* 1992–93; Rosette, *Manon,* 1993–94; Secretary I, *Nixon in China,* 1994–95

Gray, Michael: John, *Peter Grimes,* 1987–88

Green, Jonathan R.: De Bretigny, *Manon,* 2006–07; Rigoletto, *Rigoletto,* 2007–08

Greenleaf, Chris: Sunny, *Finian's Rainbow,* 1969–70

Greenlee, Robert: Pilate, *Passion Play—Carmina Burana,* 1982–83

Greenspan, Leslie: Parishioner, *Canterbury Tales,* 1978–79

Greenwell, Kim: Wellgunde, *Das Rheingold,* 1983–84; Shepherd Figure in the Wallpaper, *L'Enfant et les Sortilèges (The Bewitched Child),* 1984–85

Greer, Gordon: Don Carlos, *Don Carlos,* 1972–73; Graf Elemer, *Arabella,* 1972–73; Knight, *Parsifal,* 1972–73; Man in Armor, *Die Zauberflöte (The Magic Flute),* 1972–73; Royal Herald, *Don Carlos,* 1972–73; Song Vendor, *Il Trittico (A Triptych),* 1972–73; Don Jose, *Carmen,* 1973–74; First Man, *Kiss Me, Kate,* 1973–74; Mario Cavaradossi, *Tosca,* 1973–74

Greer, Lauren: Mary, *The Ballad of Baby Doe,* 2003–04

Gregory, Norman: Photographer, *Street Scene,* 1960–61

Griffin, Jennifer: Gabriella, *La Rondine (The Swallow),* 1989–90; April, *Company,* 1990–91; Frou-Frou, *Die lustige Witwe (The Merry Widow),* 1990–91

Griffis, Edna: Yum-Yum, *The Mikado,* 1950–51

Griffith, Diane: Katisha, *The Mikado,* 1950–51; Kundry, *Parsifal,* 1950–51; Linda, *Lost in the Stars,* 1950–51; Maddalena, *Rigoletto,* 1950–51

Grimes, Robert: Rubberface, *Show Boat,* 1953–54

Grimes, W. Brandon: Rudolph, *Hello, Dolly!,* 1991–92

Grimm, Nancy: Virtue, *L'Incoronazione di Poppea (The Coronation of Poppea),* 1967–68

Grist, Reri: Elizabeth "Baby" Doe, *The Ballad of Baby Doe,* 1982–83

Grodecki, Deborah: Madame Larina, *Eugene Onegin,* 1974–75; Countess Charlotte Malcolm, *A Little Night Music,* 1975–76; Lisetta, *Il Mondo della Luna (The World on the Moon),* 1975–76; Adah, *Naughty Marietta,* 1977–78; Louise Danton, *Danton and Robespierre,* 1977–78; Shepherd Boy, *Tosca,* 1977–78; Governess, *The Turn of the Screw,* 1978–79; Musetta, *La Bohème,* 1979–80

Grohman, Bryon: Dr. Blind, *Die Fledermaus (The Bat),* 2002–03; Nathanael, *Les Contes d'Hoffmann (The Tales of Hoffmann),* 2002–03; Spalanzani, *Les Contes d'Hoffmann (The Tales of Hoffmann),* 2002–03; Don Narciso, *Il Turco in Italia (The Turk in Italy),* 2003–04; Don Ramiro, *La Cenerentola (Cinderella),* 2004–05

Gross, Douglas: Customs Officer, *La Bohème,* 1979–80

Gross, Robert: Rev. Horace Adams, *Peter Grimes,* 1963–64

Gross, William: Arturo Bucklaw, *Lucia di Lammermoor,* 1963–64; Joe, *La Fanciulla del West (The Girl of the Golden West),* 1963–64

Grosvenor, Susan: Musetta, *La Bohème,* 1970–71

Gruber, David: The McCourt family, *The Ballad of Baby Doe,* 1975–76; Captain, *The Scarlet Letter,* 1976–77; Coroner, *Porgy and Bess,* 1976–77; Official Registrar, *Madama Butterfly,* 1976–77; Lieutenant Governor Grandet, *Naughty Marietta,* 1977–78; Sciarrone, *Tosca,* 1977–78

Gruett, Jon: Maitland, *1600 Pennsylvania Avenue,* 1992–93; New York Delegate, *1600 Pennsylvania Avenue,* 1992–93

Grundheber, Franz: Bogdanowitsch, *Die lustige Witwe (The Merry Widow),* 1964–65; Knight, *Parsifal,* 1964–65; Masetto, *Don Giovanni,* 1964–65; Rangoni, *Boris Godunov,* 1964–65; Bogdanowitsch, *Die lustige Witwe (The Merry Widow),* 1965–66; Escamillo, *Carmen,* 1965–66; Herr Von Faninal, *Der Rosenkavalier,* 1965–66; Knight, *Parsifal,* 1965–66; Morales, *Carmen,* 1965–66; Rigoletto, *Rigoletto,* 1995–96; Wozzeck, *Wozzeck,* 1999–2000

Grundmann, Helmut: Count Monterone, *Rigoletto,* 1966–67; Klingsor, *Parsifal,* 1966–67; Maurizio, *Quattro rusteghi (The Four Ruffians),* 1966–67; Prince of Verona, *Roméo et Juliette,* 1966–67

Gruoner, Scott: Leo, *Tamerlano,* 1984–85; Tempter, *Murder in the Cathedral,* 1984–85; Morales, *Carmen,* 1984–85; Frank, *Die Fledermaus (The Bat),* 1985–86; Belcore, *L'Elisir d'amore (The Elixir of Love),* 1986–87; Krushina, *The Bartered Bride,* 1986–87

Grzywacz, Marianne: Nicklausse, *Les Contes d'Hoffmann (The Tales of Hoffmann),* 1959–60; The Fortune Teller, *La Rondine (The Swallow),* 1959–60

Guberna, Jorge Enrique: Romeo, *Roméo et Juliette,* 1966–67; The Duke of Mantua, *Rigoletto,* 1966–67; Turiddu, *Cavalleria Rusticana,* 1966–67; Chevalier des Grieux, *Manon,* 1967–68; Jenik, *The Bartered Bride,* 1967–68; Nero, *L'Incoronazione di Poppea (The Coronation of Poppea),* 1967–68; Gherman, *La Pique Dame (The Queen of Spades),* 1968–69; Lindoro, *L'Italiana in Algeri (The Italian Girl in Algiers),* 1968–69; Luigi, *Il Trittico (A Triptych),* 1969–70

Gudmundsdottir, Esther: Giovanna, *Rigoletto,* 1986–87; Ann Putnam, *The Crucible,* 1987–88

Gudmundsdottir, Thorunn: Rebecca Nurse, *The Crucible,* 1987–88

Guinez, Maria: Zerbinetta, *Ariadne auf Naxos,* 1969–70

Gulley, Sandrea: Sandman, *Hänsel und Gretel,* 1982–83

Gumbel, Roberta: Clara, *Porgy and Bess,* 1979–80; Delores-Sue Tobias, *Soldier Boy, Soldier,* 1982–83; Pamina, *Die Zauberflöte (The Magic Flute),* 1982–83; Tytania, *A Midsummer Night's Dream,* 1983–84

Gunlogson, Kirsten: Margarita, *West Side Story,* 1992–93; Giovanna, *Rigoletto,* 1995–96; Verginella, *La Périchole,* 1995–96; Lady Thiang, *The King and I,* 1996–97; Prince Orlofsky, *Die Fledermaus (The Bat),* 1996–97; Mrs. Meg Page, *Falstaff,* 1997–98

Gunter, Jane: Suzy, *La Rondine (The Swallow),* 1959–60; Voice of the Mother, *Les Contes d'Hoffmann (The Tales of Hoffmann),* 1959–60; Mrs. Olga Olsen, *Street Scene,* 1960–61; Mary, *Der Fliegende Holländer (The Flying Dutchman),* 1962–63

Gustafson, Phyllis: Katchen, *Werther,* 1961–62; Theobald, *Don Carlos,* 1961–62; Mercedes, *Carmen,* 1962–63

Guthier, Zachary: Trouble, *Madama Butterfly,* 2001–02

Gutschick, Alice: Gianetta, *L'Elisir d'amore (The Elixir of Love),* 1961–62

Gwaltney, Ivanna: Fyodor, *Boris Godunov,* 1953–54; Page, *Parsifal,* 1953–54; Spirit, *Die Zauberflöte (The Magic Flute),* 1953–54; Echo, *Ariadne auf Naxos,* 1954–55; Page, *Parsifal,* 1954–55; Ludmila, *The Bartered Bride,* 1955–56; Page, *Parsifal,* 1955–56; Mrs. Meg Page, *Falstaff,* 1956–57

Gwaltney, Jeff: A Jailer, *Dialogues des Carmélites,* 2004–05; Benvolio, *Roméo et Juliette,* 2005–06

Haas, Joseph: Don Carlos, *Don Carlos,* 1960–61; Man in Armor, *Die Zauberflöte (The Magic Flute),* 1960–61

Hache, Patrick: Antonio, *Le Nozze di Figaro (The Marriage of Figaro),* 1997–98; Zaretsky, *Eugene Onegin,* 1997–98; Fred Graham, *Kiss Me, Kate,* 1998–99; Second Man, *Kiss Me, Kate,* 1998–99

Hacker, Kathleen: Micaëla, *Carmen,* 1991–92; Susanna, *Le Nozze di Figaro (The Marriage of Figaro),* 1992–93

Haddawi, Jamie: Amaryllis, *The Music Man,* 1980–81

Haering, Ken: Count Ceprano, *Rigoletto,* 1974–75; Gretchen's Brother, *Doktor Faust,* 1974–75

Hagan, Anne: Samantha, *The Ballad of Baby Doe,* 1982–83; Frou-Frou, *Die lustige Witwe (The Merry Widow),* 1983–84

Hagel, Phyllis: Gilda, *Rigoletto,* 1950–51

Hagemeyer, Roxanne: Tessa, *The Gondoliers,* 1974–75; Countess Celimene, *A Little Night Music,* 1975–76; Desiree Armfeldt, *A Little Night Music,* 1975–76; Mary, *The Ballad of Baby Doe,* 1975–76; Silver Dollar (grown up), *The Ballad of Baby Doe,* 1975–76; Carrie Pipperidge, *Carousel,* 1976–77; Mrs. Gleaton, *Susannah,* 1976–77

Hagen, Donna: Ballet Maria, *West Side Story,* 1985–86

Hagen, Heidi: Papagena, *Die Zauberflöte (The Magic Flute),* 1977–78; Molly, *Canterbury Tales,* 1978–79; Mrs. Hayes, *Susannah,* 1979–80

Hagerman, Karen: Genevieve, *Pelléas et Mélisande,* 1976–77

Hahn, Monica: La Ciesca, *Gianni Schicchi,* 1988–89; Player, *Mass,* 1988–89; The Witch, *Hänsel und Gretel,* 1989–90; Joanne, *Company,* 1990–91

Haile, Richard: Graf Lamoral, *Arabella,* 1972–73; Priest, *Die Zauberflöte (The Magic Flute),* 1972–73; Titurel, *Parsifal,* 1972–73; Count Almaviva, *Le Nozze di Figaro (The Marriage of Figaro),* 1973–74; Crespel, *Les Contes d'Hoffmann (The Tales of Hoffmann),* 1973–74; Count Monterone, *Rigoletto,* 1974–75; Doctor Faust, *Doktor Faust,* 1974–75; Amfortas, *Parsifal,* 1975–76

Hakola, Melvin: Amonasro, *Aida,* 1963–64

Hale, Elizabeth: Rosette, *Manon,* 1979–80; Princess Linetta, *The Love for Three Oranges,* 1980–81; Effie, *The Ballad of Baby Doe,* 1982–83

Hale, Leslie: Beppe, *I Pagliacci,* 1966–67; Prince Shuisky, *Boris Godunov,* 1966–67; Tybalt, *Roméo et Juliette,* 1966–67

Hale, Richard: Cesare Angelotti, *Tosca,* 1973–74

Hale, Virgil: The Duke of Mantua, *Rigoletto,* 1950–51; Mr. Upfold, *Albert Herring,* 1957–58

Halili, Jeffrey: Ferrando, *Così fan tutte,* 2000–01; Jenik, *The Bartered Bride,* 2001–02

Halimic, Jasmina: Valencienne, *Die lustige Witwe (The Merry Widow),* 2003–04; Tatyana, *Eugene Onegin,* 2004–05

Halkovic, Anne: Princess Samahris of Turkestan, *Kismet,* 1989–90

Hall, Jeanette: Minnie, *La Fanciulla del West (The Girl of the Golden West),* 1963–64; Amelia Grimaldi (Maria Boccanegra), *Simon Boccanegra,* 1964–65; Kundry, *Parsifal,* 1965–66; Lady Macbeth, *Macbeth,* 1965–66; Madame Lidoine, *Dialogues des Carmélites,* 1965–66

Hall, Nancy: Arminy, *Carousel,* 1993–94; Nella, *Gianni Schicchi,* 1993–94; Ellen Orford, *Peter Grimes,* 1994–95; Trina Sieppe, *McTeague,* 1995–96; Tatyana, *Eugene Onegin,* 1997–98

Halvorson, David: Officer, *Il Barbiere di Siviglia (The Barber of Seville),* 1971–72

Ham, Antonia: Anita, *West Side Story,* 1992–93

Hamill, Pamela: A Tourier, *Il Trittico (A Triptych),* 1969–70

Hamilton, Anna Lee: Marguerite, *Faust,* 1955–56

Hamilton, Chris: Gabey, *On the Town,* 1951–52

Hamilton, Dwight: Butler at the Windsor Hotel, *The Ballad of Baby Doe,* 1975–76

Hamilton, Peter: Bill Calhoun, *Kiss Me, Kate,* 1951–52; Lucentio, *Kiss Me, Kate,* 1951–52

Hammans, Scott: Bartender, *My Fair Lady,* 1979–80; Constable, *My Fair Lady,* 1979–80; Constable Locke, *The Music Man,* 1980–81

Hammil, Pamela Ann: Amazon, *The Boys from Syracuse,* 1968–69

Hammond, Ivan: Policeman, *Street Scene,* 1960–61

Hammond, Janice: Alma March, *Little Women,* 2001–02

Hanna, Bruce: Messenger/Commissioner, *La Traviata,* 1968–69; Narumov, *La Pique Dame (The Queen of Spades),* 1968–69

Hansen, Randy: Bardolph, *Falstaff,* 1976–77; Couthon, *Danton and Robespierre,* 1977–78; The Devil, *The Night Before Christmas,* 1977–78

Hansen-Simmons, Amy: Gretel, *Hänsel und Gretel,* 1995–96

Hanson, Ernest: Editor, *Wonderful Town,* 1954–55; A vendor of songs, *Il Tabarro (The Cloak),* 1955–56; The Teapot, *L'Enfant et les Sortilèges (The Bewitched Child),* 1955–56; Seabee Richard West, *South Pacific,* 1956–57; Tommy Keeler, *Annie Get Your Gun,* 1956–57

Hapner, Justin: Tiger, *West Side Story,* 2002–03

Happel, Maryliese: Mrs. Hopkins, *My Fair Lady,* 1979–80

Harbin, William: King of Hesse, *Candide,* 1957–58; Martin, *Candide,* 1957–58; Very, Very Old Inquisitor, *Candide,* 1957–58

Harbuck, William: Guardsman, *Manon,* 1967–68; Krushina, *The Bartered Bride,* 1967–68

Hardesty, Lynne: Adele, *Die Fledermaus (The Bat),* 1962–63; Lucia, *Lucia di Lammermoor,* 1963–64; Serafina, *Il Campanello di Notte (The Night Bell),* 1963–64

Hardin, Annie: Miller's Wife, *Canterbury Tales,* 1978–79; The Wife of Bath, *Canterbury Tales,* 1978–79

Hardin, Fraser: The Summoner, *Canterbury Tales,* 1978–79

Hardin, Lance: Anxious, *West Side Story,* 1992–93

Hardy, Eric: Jacey Squires, *The Music Man,* 1980–81

Hardy, Wade: Alan, *Canterbury Tales,* 1978–79; Drunkard, *The Darkened City,* 1978–79; Officer of the Border Guard, *Boris Godunov,* 1978–79; Placebo, *Canterbury Tales,* 1978–79; The Merchant, *Canterbury Tales,* 1978–79; Voice from Inside, *The Darkened City,* 1978–79

Harkins, Robert: A Footman, *Vanessa,* 1974–75; A mute, *Die Entführung aus dem Serail (The Abduction from the Seraglio),* 1974–75; Nicholas, *Vanessa,* 1974–75; The Duke of Plaza-Toro, *The Gondoliers,* 1974–75

Harrelson, Robert: Dentist, *McTeague,* 1995–96; Spalanzani, *Les Contes d'Hoffmann (The Tales of Hoffmann),* 1995–96; The Music Master, *Ariadne auf Naxos,* 1996–97; Sir Joseph Porter, *HMS Pinafore,* 1997–98

Harrington, Jan: Marschallin's Chef, *Der Rosenkavalier,* 1965–66

Harris, Scott: Baby John, *West Side Story,* 2002–03

Harris, Stephanie: Papagena, *Die Zauberflöte (The Magic Flute),* 2004–05

Harris, Steve: Jailer, *Tosca,* 1973–74; T.T., *The Mother of Us All,* 1973–74

Harris, Theodore: Friar Laurence, *Roméo et Juliette,* 1966–67; Maurizio, *Quattro rusteghi (The Four Ruffians),* 1966–67; Osmin, *Die Entführung aus dem Serail (The Abduction from the Seraglio),* 1966–67

Harrison, René: Gossip 2, *The Ghosts of Versailles,* 1996–97; Blanche, *Dialogues des Carmélites,* 1997–98

Harrison, William: The Judge, *Lost in the Stars,* 1950–51; Pitkin, *On the Town,* 1951–52; Kuppelweiser, *Blossom Time,* 1952–53

Harrod, Joyce: Child's Mama, *L'Enfant et les Sortilèges (The Bewitched Child),* 1955–56; Bloody Mary, *South Pacific,* 1956–57; Lady Thiang, *The King and I,* 1957–58

Harrod, William: Goro, *Madama Butterfly,* 1958–59; M. Taupe, *Capriccio,* 1958–59; Dick McGann, *Street Scene,* 1960–61; Sam Kaplan, *Street Scene,* 1960–61; Harry Beaton, *Brigadoon,* 1961–62; Sandy Dean, *Brigadoon,* 1961–62

Harsh, Tamara: Princess Nicoletta, *The Love for Three Oranges,* 1993–94

Harshaw, Margaret: Kundry, *Parsifal,* 1962–63; Kundry, *Parsifal,* 1963–64; Princess Turandot, *Turandot,* 1964–65; Kundry, *Parsifal,* 1966–67; Kundry, *Parsifal,* 1967–68; Brünnhilde, *Die Walküre,* 1969–70

Hart, Brien: A Muleteer, *Man of La Mancha,* 1985–86; Juano, *West Side Story,* 1985–86; The "Horses," *Man of La Mancha,* 1985–86

Hartman, Bartha: Chava, *Fiddler on the Roof,* 1972–73; Tessa, *The Gondoliers,* 1974–75

Hartman, Jeannine: K.C., *West Side Story,* 1992–93

Hartschuh, Neil: Flute Player, *Der Rosenkavalier,* 1965–66

Hartwell, William: Al Alcaide, *La Forza del Destino (The Force of Destiny)*, 1962–63; Antonio, *Le Nozze di Figaro (The Marriage of Figaro)*, 1962–63; Guard, *The Darkened City*, 1962–63; Schaunard, *La Bohème*, 1962–63; Second Bearer, *The Darkened City*, 1962–63; Fabrizio, *Love on Trial (La Pietra del Paragone)*, 1969–70; Sacristan, *Tosca*, 1969–70; Geronte de Ravoir, *Manon Lescaut*, 1970–71; Schaunard, *La Bohème*, 1970–71; Rogoshin, *Myshkin*, 1972–73

Haskel, Jenean: Madrigal Singer, *Manon Lescaut*, 1970–71

Haskin, Howard: Borsa, *Rigoletto*, 1974–75; Father Chapelle, *The Ballad of Baby Doe*, 1975–76; Page, *Parsifal*, 1975–76; Schmidt, *Werther*, 1975–76; Sportin' Life, *Porgy and Bess*, 1976–77

Hatch, Ronald: The Imperial Commissioner, *Madama Butterfly*, 1958–59; Titurel, *Parsifal*, 1958–59

Hatfield, David: Baptista, *Kiss Me, Kate*, 1973–74; Harry Trevor, *Kiss Me, Kate*, 1973–74

Hauan, Kenneth: Goro, *Madama Butterfly*, 1987–88; Dr. Sanson Carrasco / The Duke, *Man of La Mancha*, 1988–89; Monostatos, *Die Zauberflöte (The Magic Flute)*, 1988–89; Spalanzani, *Les Contes d'Hoffmann (The Tales of Hoffmann)*, 1988–89; Kaspar, *Amahl and the Night Visitors*, 1990–91; Horace Vandergelder, *Hello, Dolly!*, 1991–92

Haulter, Christopher: Joe, *Oklahoma!*, 1997–98

Hauxwell, Janice: Woman with Hat/Duchess, *The Ghosts of Versailles*, 1996–97; Dame Quickly, *Falstaff*, 1997–98; Kate, *Oklahoma!*, 1997–98; Olga, *Eugene Onegin*, 1997–98; Adelaide, *Arabella*, 1998–99; Katherine, *Kiss Me, Kate*, 1998–99; Lilli Vanessi, *Kiss Me, Kate*, 1998–99; Baba the Turk, *The Rake's Progress*, 1999–2000; Zia Principessa, *Suor Angelica (Sister Angelica)*, 1999–2000; Mother Abbess, *The Sound of Music*, 2000–01

Havranek, Roger: A Monk, *Don Carlos*, 1961–62; Bailiff, *Werther*, 1961–62; Dr. Dulcamara, *L'Elisir d'amore (The Elixir of Love)*, 1961–62; Klingsor, *Parsifal*, 1961–62; Monk, *Don Carlos*, 1961–62; Snug, *A Midsummer Night's Dream*, 1961–62; The Beadle (and Jailer), *The Scarlet Letter*, 1961–62; Theseus, *A Midsummer Night's Dream*, 1961–62; Colline, *La Bohème*, 1962–63; Daland, *Der Fliegende Holländer (The Flying Dutchman)*, 1962–63; Figaro, *Le Nozze di Figaro (The Marriage of Figaro)*, 1962–63; Klingsor, *Parsifal*, 1962–63; Marquis of Calatrava, *La Forza del Destino (The Force of Destiny)*, 1962–63; Mayor, *The Darkened City*, 1962–63; Padre Guardiano, *La Forza del Destino (The Force of Destiny)*, 1962–63; Don Alfonso, *Così fan tutte*, 1963–64; Don Basilio, *Il Barbiere di Siviglia (The Barber of Seville)*, 1963–64; Gypsy, *The Fair at Sorochinsk*, 1963–64; Jake Wallace, *La Fanciulla del West (The Girl of the Golden West)*, 1963–64; Klingsor, *Parsifal*, 1963–64; Raimondo Bidebent, *Lucia di Lammermoor*, 1963–64; Swallow, *Peter Grimes*, 1963–64; The King, *Aida*, 1963–64; Fiesco (Andrea Grimaldi), *Simon Boccanegra*, 1964–65; Klingsor, *Parsifal*, 1964–65; Leporello, *Don Giovanni*, 1964–65; Pimen, *Boris Godunov*, 1964–65; Timur, *Turandot*, 1964–65; Tiresias, *Oedipus Rex*, 1964–65; Varlaam, *Boris Godunov*, 1964–65; Baron Ochs of Lerchenau, *Der Rosenkavalier*, 1965–66; Don Pasquale, *Don Pasquale*, 1965–66; Sarastro, *Die Zauberflöte (The Magic Flute)*, 1965–66; Zuniga, *Carmen*, 1965–66; Chief Anderson, *A Hoosier Tale*, 1966–67; Lunardo, *Quattro rusteghi (The Four Ruffians)*, 1966–67; Osmin, *Die Entführung aus dem Serail (The Abduction from the Seraglio)*, 1966–67; Pimen, *Boris Godunov*, 1966–67; Sparafucile, *Rigoletto*, 1966–67; Gurnemanz, *Parsifal*, 1967–68; Kezal, *The Bartered Bride*, 1967–68; Mephistopheles, *Mefistofele*, 1967–68; Seneca, *L'Incoronazione di Poppea (The Coronation of Poppea)*, 1967–68; Figaro, *Le Nozze di Figaro (The Marriage of Figaro)*, 1968–69; Mustafa, *L'Italiana in Algeri (The Italian Girl in Algiers)*, 1968–69; Nick Shadow, *The Rake's Progress*, 1968–69; Veit Pogner, *Die Meistersinger von Nürnberg (The Mastersingers of Nuremberg)*, 1968–69; Gianni Schicchi, *Il Trittico (A Triptych)*, 1969–70; Lycomedes, *Deidamia*, 1969–70; Macrobio, *Love on Trial (La Pietra del Paragone)*, 1969–70; Colline, *La Bohème*, 1970–71; Don Fernando, *Fidelio*, 1970–71; First Nazarene, *Salome*, 1970–71; Raimondo Bidebent, *Lucia di Lammermoor*, 1970–71; Rocco, *Fidelio*, 1970–71; Doctor Bartolo, *Il Barbiere di Siviglia (The Barber of Seville)*, 1971–72; Leporello, *Don Giovanni*, 1971–72; Mephistopheles, *Faust*, 1971–72; General Ivolgin, *Myshkin*, 1972–73; Graf Waldner, *Arabella*, 1972–73; King Philip II, *Don Carlos*, 1972–73; Sarastro, *Die Zauberflöte (The Magic Flute)*, 1972–73; The Doctor, *Wozzeck*, 1973–74; Prince Gremin, *Eugene Onegin*, 1974–75; Buonafede, *Il Mondo della Luna (The World on the Moon)*, 1975–76; Daland, *Der Fliegende Holländer (The Flying Dutchman)*, 1978–79; The Doctor, *Wozzeck*, 1981–82; Doctor Bartolo, *Il Barbiere di Siviglia (The Barber of Seville)*, 1988–89

Hawkins, Gaylord: Elderly Man, *Street Scene*, 1949–50; Man, *Street Scene*, 1949–50

Hawley, Ann: Kate, *The Ballad of Baby Doe*, 1982–83

Hawley, Janine: Porter of the Convent, *Il Trittico (A Triptych)*, 1982–83; Spirit, *Die Zauberflöte (The Magic Flute)*, 1982–83; The Monitor of the Convent, *Il Trittico (A Triptych)*, 1982–83; Beggar Woman, *Sweeney Todd*, 1983–84; Fyodor, *Boris Godunov*, 1983–84; Dorabella, *Così fan tutte*, 1984–85; Antonia / Alonso's Niece, *Man of La Mancha*, 1985–86

Hawn, David: Missail, *Boris Godunov*, 1983–84; Lillas Pastia, *Carmen*, 1984–85; Captain of the Inquisition, *Man of La Mancha*, 1985–86; Njegus, *Die lustige Witwe (The Merry Widow)*, 1990–91; Keeper of the Madhouse, *The Rake's Progress*, 1991–92

Hay, Beverly: Despina, *Così fan tutte*, 1977–78; Governess, *The Turn of the Screw*, 1978–79; Old Woman, *Canterbury Tales*, 1978–79

Hayes, Cassandra: Kate, *The Ballad of Baby Doe*, 1975–76; Bess, *Porgy and Bess*, 1976–77; Cio-Cio San, *Madama Butterfly*, 1976–77

Hayes, Edward: Paco / A Muleteer, *Man of La Mancha*, 1988–89; Father Bernard, *Candide*, 1993–94; Ali Hakim, *Oklahoma!*, 1997–98

Hayes, Michael: Hoffmann, *Les Contes d'Hoffmann (The Tales of Hoffmann)*, 2002–03

Hayes, Ted: Mayor, *Jubilee*, 1991–92; Professor Rexford, *Jubilee*, 1991–92

Haynes, Sam: The Girl's Father, *The Fantasticks*, 1963–64

Hays, Melissa: Mary, *The Dawn of the Poor King*, 1990–91

Hazelbauer, William: Knight, *Parsifal*, 1960–61; Priest, *Die Zauberflöte (The Magic Flute)*, 1960–61; Reverend Master John W. Wilson, *The Scarlet Letter*, 1960–61; Royal Herald, *Don Carlos*, 1960–61

Hazelrigg, Tulle: Mary Hildebrand, *Street Scene*, 1960–61

Heal, Leslie: Lisbon Woman, *Candide*, 2000–01; Pousette, *Manon*, 2001–02

Healy, Linda: Celestial Voice, *Don Carlos*, 1972–73; Nella, *Il Trittico (A Triptych)*, 1972–73; Sister Genevieve, *Il Trittico (A Triptych)*, 1972–73; Theobald, *Don Carlos*, 1972–73; Angel More, *The Mother of Us All*, 1973–74; Olympia, *Les Contes d'Hoffmann (The Tales of Hoffmann)*, 1973–74; Constanza, *Die Entführung aus dem Serail (The Abduction from the Seraglio)*, 1974–75

Heath, Joy Clarice: Annie, *Porgy and Bess*, 1979–80

Heaton, Diane: Spirit, *Die Zauberflöte (The Magic Flute)*, 1960–61

Hebert, Pamela: Guenevere, *Camelot*, 1968–69; Lisa, *La Pique Dame (The Queen of Spades)*, 1968–69; Morgan le Fey, *Camelot*, 1968–69; Floria Tosca, *Tosca*, 1969–70; Waltraute, *Die Walküre*, 1969–70; Leonore, *Fidelio*, 1970–71

Hebert, Rubye: Hippolyta, *A Midsummer Night's Dream*, 1961–62; First Mourner, *The Darkened City*, 1962–63; Marcellina, *Le Nozze di Figaro (The Marriage of Figaro)*, 1962–63; Auntie, *Peter Grimes*, 1963–64

Hedges, Don: The Doctor's Assistant, *L'Elisir d'amore (The Elixir of Love)*, 1986–87

Hedlund, Ronald: Governor of Buenos Aires, *Candide*, 1957–58; Sid, *Albert Herring*, 1957–58; Count Renato, *Un Ballo in Maschera (A Masked Ball)*, 1958–59

Heicher, Helen: Nimue, *Camelot*, 1969–70

Heidema, Betty: Lady, *Street Scene*, 1960–61; Nursemaid, *Street Scene*, 1960–61; Voice of the Cockerel, *Le Coq d'or (The Golden Cockerel)*, 1960–61

Heidenreich, Connie: Despinio, *The Greek Passion*, 1980–81; Apprentice Waiter, *The Excursions of Mr. Broucek*, 1981–82; Dewman, *Hänsel und Gretel*, 1982–83; Sister Genevieve, *Il Trittico (A Triptych)*, 1982–83; Olga, *Die lustige Witwe (The Merry Widow)*, 1983–84

Heilemann, Eleanor: Flora Bervoix, *La Traviata*, 1954–55; Laurey, *Oklahoma!*, 1954–55; Cherubino, *Le Nozze di Figaro (The Marriage of Figaro)*, 1955–56; Giorgetta, *Il Tabarro (The Cloak)*, 1955–56; Gertrude, *Hänsel und Gretel*, 1956–57

Hein, Karin: Laura Fitzgerald, *Jubilee*, 1991–92; Mrs. Rose, *Hello, Dolly!*, 1991–92

Heinzen, Nick: Spirit, *Die Zauberflöte (The Magic Flute)*, 2004–05; Mustardseed, *A Midsummer Night's Dream*, 2005–06

Heitzman, Michael: Baby John, *West Side Story*, 1985–86

Held, Helen: Kundry, *Parsifal*, 1955–56

Helding, Lynn: Orfeo, *L'Orfeo*, 1987–88

Hellman, Susan: Princess Nicoletta, *The Love for Three Oranges*, 1999–2000

Helm, Alicia: Lily, *Porgy and Bess*, 1979–80

Helppie, Kevin: Second Apprentice, *Wozzeck*, 1981–82

Helton, Melanie: Girl on the street, *Trouble in Tahiti*, 1976–77; Player, *Bernstein on Broadway*, 1976–77; Trio—soprano, *Trouble in Tahiti*, 1976–77; Frasquita, *Carmen*, 1977–78

Henderson, Marsha: Annie, *Porgy and Bess*, 1976–77

Henderson, Oliver: Dappertutto, *Les Contes d'Hoffmann (The Tales of Hoffmann)*, 2007–08

Hendricks, Andrew: Pluto, *Orphée aux enfers (Orpheus in the Underworld)*, 1992–93; Businessman, *Candide*, 1993–94; Dr. Pangloss, *Candide*, 1993–94; Pantalone, *The Love for Three Oranges*, 1993–94; Sage, *Candide*, 1993 94; Voltaire, *Candide*, 1993–94; Pelleas, *Pelléas et Mélisande*, 1994–95; Richard Nixon, *Nixon in China*, 1994–95; Don Andres, *La Périchole*, 1995–96; Guglielmo, *Così fan tutte*, 1995–96; Dr. Falke, *Die Fledermaus (The Bat)*, 1996–97; The Poet, Prosdocimo, *Il Turco in Italia (The Turk in Italy)*, 1996–97; Bill Calhoun, *Kiss Me, Kate*, 1998–99; Celebrant, *Mass*, 1998–99; Dandini, *La Cenerentola (Cinderella)*, 1998–99; Lucentio, *Kiss Me, Kate*, 1998–99; Leandro, *The Love for Three Oranges*, 1999–2000; Harry, *Jeppe*, 2002–03

Hendrix, Anntoinette: Joby, White House Staff, *1600 Pennsylvania Avenue*, 1992–93

Hendrix, Britt Nicole: Ngana, *South Pacific,* 1995–96; Louisa, *The Sound of Music,* 2000–01

Hendron, Suzanne: Luce, *The Boys from Syracuse,* 1968–69; Second Maid, *The Boys from Syracuse,* 1968–69

Henery, Diana: Page, *Parsifal,* 1967–68; Poppea, *L'Incoronazione di Poppea (The Coronation of Poppea),* 1967–68

Henry, Melinda: Luce, *The Boys from Syracuse,* 1968–69

Henry, Michael: Charlie Cowell, *The Music Man,* 2001–02

Hensley, Mary Alice: Voice of the Mother, *Les Contes d'Hoffmann (The Tales of Hoffmann),* 1947–48; Kundry, *Parsifal,* 1948–49; Kundry, *Parsifal,* 1949–50; Kundry, *Parsifal,* 1950–51; Maddalena, *Rigoletto,* 1950–51

Hensley, Steven: Bardolph, *Falstaff,* 1997–98; Will Parker, *Oklahoma!,* 1997–98; Gregory, *Kiss Me, Kate,* 1998–99; Orpheus, *Orphée aux enfers (Orpheus in the Underworld),* 1998–99; Paul, *Kiss Me, Kate,* 1998–99

Hensley, Tom: Tom, *Finian's Rainbow,* 1953–54

Herber, Lou: Helene, *Hin und Zurück (There and Back),* 1947–48; Stella, *Les Contes d'Hoffmann (The Tales of Hoffmann),* 1947–48; Flower Girl, *The New Moon,* 1949–50; Lulu, *The Jumping Frog of Calaveras County,* 1949–50; Mrs. Emma Jones, *Street Scene,* 1949–50; Mrs. Godfrey Van Dare, *The Firefly,* 1949–50; Zozo, *Die lustige Witwe (The Merry Widow),* 1949–50; Aurelia, *The Chocolate Soldier,* 1950–51; Grace Kumalo, *Lost in the Stars,* 1950–51

Hermance, Myron: Page, *Parsifal,* 1950–51

Hernandez, Tomas: Karpathy, *My Fair Lady,* 1979–80

Herold, Teresa S.: La Diva, *Jeppe,* 2002–03; Auntie, *Peter Grimes,* 2003–04; The Old Prioress, *Dialogues des Carmélites,* 2004–05

Herron, D. Keith: Henchman, *Arlecchino,* 1979–80

Hershberger, Virgil: Johannes Pafuri, *Lost in the Stars,* 1950–51

Hertling, Heather: Maid, *Of Thee I Sing,* 1987–88; Miss Benson, *Of Thee I Sing,* 1987–88; First Lady, *Die Zauberflöte (The Magic Flute),* 1988–89; Player, *Mass,* 1988–89; Sylviane, *Die lustige Witwe (The Merry Widow),* 1990–91

Herzberg, Jean: Mrs. Alice Ford, *Falstaff,* 1976–77; Micaëla, *Carmen,* 1977–78; Fiordiligi, *Così fan tutte,* 1978–79; Musetta, *La Bohème,* 1979–80; Susannah Polk, *Susannah,* 1979–80

Hess, Deborah: Mayor's Wife, *Jenůfa,* 1972–73; The Monitor of the Convent, *Il Trittico (A Triptych),* 1972–73

Hess, J. Harold: Andrew Johnson, *The Mother of Us All,* 1973–74; Don Basilio, *Le Nozze di Figaro (The Marriage of Figaro),* 1973–74; Nathanael, *Les Contes d'Hoffmann (The Tales of Hoffmann),* 1973–74; Spoletta, *Tosca,* 1973–74; The Captain, *Wozzeck,* 1973–74

Hesse, George: Klingsor, *Parsifal,* 1972–73; Knight, *Parsifal,* 1972–73; Mill Foreman, *Jenůfa,* 1972–73; Baron Scarpia, *Tosca,* 1973–74; Coppelius, *Les Contes d'Hoffmann (The Tales of Hoffmann),* 1973–74; Count Almaviva, *Le Nozze di Figaro (The Marriage of Figaro),* 1973–74; Dappertutto, *Les Contes d'Hoffmann (The Tales of Hoffmann),* 1973–74; Dr. Miracle, *Les Contes d'Hoffmann (The Tales of Hoffmann),* 1973–74; Lindorf, *Les Contes d'Hoffmann (The Tales of Hoffmann),* 1973–74; Eugene Onegin, *Eugene Onegin,* 1974–75; Marcello, *La Bohème,* 1974–75; Amfortas, *Parsifal,* 1975–76; Sharpless, *Madama Butterfly,* 1975–76; Doctor Seldon, *Carousel,* 1976–77; Golaud, *Pelléas et Mélisande,* 1976–77; Principal, *Carousel,* 1976–77; Sharpless, *Madama Butterfly,* 1976–77; Starkeeper, *Carousel,* 1976–77; Marcello, *La Bohème,* 1979–80

Hettinger, Karen: Madame Tallien, *Danton and Robespierre,* 1977–78; Third Lady, *Die Zauberflöte (The Magic Flute),* 1977–78

Heverly, Shanna: Clarice, *West Side Story,* 2002–03

Hewitt, Margaret: Jou-Jou, *Die lustige Witwe (The Merry Widow),* 1965–66; Fourth Sharecropper, *Finian's Rainbow,* 1969–70

Heyman, Stuart: Aide to President Arthur, *The Ballad of Baby Doe,* 1975–76

Hickman, Floyd: Erkmann, *Blossom Time,* 1952–53

Hicks, George: Lieutenant, *Doktor Faust,* 1974–75

Hicks, John: Choir boy, *Candide,* 1983–84

Hicks, Nettie: Micaëla, *Carmen,* 1965–66

Hicks, Patricia: Louise, *Carousel,* 1970–71

Hicks, Samuel: The Host of the Garter Inn, *Falstaff,* 1956–57; Bear Keeper, *Candide,* 1957–58; Parpignol, *La Bohème,* 1957–58; M. Taupe, *Capriccio,* 1958–59; Servant of Amelia, *Un Ballo in Maschera (A Masked Ball),* 1958–59; Slender (Spaerlich), *Die lustigen Weiber von Windsor (The Merry Wives of Windsor),* 1958–59; The Chief Magistrate, *Un Ballo in Maschera (A Masked Ball),* 1958–59; Cochenille, *Les Contes d'Hoffmann (The Tales of Hoffmann),* 1959–60; Knight, *Parsifal,* 1959–60; Student, *La Rondine (The Swallow),* 1959–60; Newcomer, *Street Scene,* 1960–61; Captain, *Simon Boccanegra,* 1964–65; Gherardo, *Gianni Schicchi,* 1964–65; Goro, *Madama Butterfly,* 1964–65; Remendado, *Carmen,* 1965–66; Missail, *Boris Godunov,* 1966–67; Spalanzani, *Les Contes d'Hoffmann (The Tales of Hoffmann),* 1973–74

Higginbotham, Carlton: Innkeeper, *Manon,* 1967–68; Samuel, *Un Ballo in Maschera (A Masked Ball),* 1969–70; Sciarrone, *Tosca,* 1969–70; A Monk, *Don Carlos,* 1972–73; Grand Inquisitor, *Don Carlos,* 1972–73

Higgins, Casey: Venus, *Orphée aux enfers (Orpheus in the Underworld),* 1998–99

Higgins, David: Captain, *Carousel,* 1970–71

Higgins, Howard: Trouble, *Madama Butterfly,* 1975–76; Trouble, *Madama Butterfly,* 1976–77; Winthrop Paroo, *The Music Man,* 1980–81; Squire Dap, *Camelot,* 1986–87

Hightower, Taylor: Boatswain, *HMS Pinafore,* 1997–98; Doctor Grenville, *La Traviata,* 1997–98; Thierry, *Dialogues des Carmélites,* 1997–98; Morales, *Carmen,* 1998–99; Priest, *Die Zauberflöte (The Magic Flute),* 1998–99; The Leader, *Down in the Valley,* 1998–99; The Preacher, *Down in the Valley,* 1998–99; Gianni Schicchi, *Gianni Schicchi,* 1999–2000; Captain Georg von Trapp, *The Sound of Music,* 2000–01; Dr. Dulcamara, *L'Elisir d'amore (The Elixir of Love),* 2000–01; Olin Blitch, *Susannah,* 2000–01; Peter, *Hänsel und Gretel,* 2001–02; Jeppe, *Jeppe,* 2002–03; Tolomeo, *Giulio Cesare (Julius Caesar),* 2002–03; Captain Balstrode, *Peter Grimes,* 2003–04; Don Pasquale, *Don Pasquale,* 2003–04

Hiken, Dana: Masha, *La Pique Dame (The Queen of Spades),* 1968–69

Hill, Agnes: An elegant lady, *The Scarlet Letter,* 1961–62

Hill, George: Barney, *The Ballad of Baby Doe,* 1975–76

Hill, Jean: Cobweb, *A Midsummer Night's Dream,* 1961–62

Hill, Karen: Virginia, *Oklahoma!,* 1981–82

Hill, Larry: Rawkins, *Finian's Rainbow,* 1969–70

Hill, Mary Ellen: Winnie Tate, *Annie Get Your Gun,* 1956–57

Hilliard, Kenneth: Nish, *Die lustige Witwe (The Merry Widow),* 1964–65; A mute, *Die Entführung aus dem Serail (The Abduction from the Seraglio),* 1966–67

Hills, Colin: Ambrogio, *Il Barbiere di Siviglia (The Barber of Seville),* 1980–81; Andonis, *The Greek Passion,* 1980–81; Eroshka, *Prince Igor,* 1980–81; Notary, *Don Pasquale,* 1980–81; Alfred, *Die Fledermaus (The Bat),* 1982–83

Himsel, Judy: Mae Jones, *Street Scene,* 1960–61; Spirit, *Die Zauberflöte (The Magic Flute),* 1960–61

Hindrelet, Katherine: Cis, *Albert Herring,* 1966–67; Lucietta, *Quattro rusteghi (The Four Ruffians),* 1966–67; Elizabeth Zimmer, *Elegy for Young Lovers,* 1967–68; Lady-in-waiting to the Empress, *L'Incoronazione di Poppea (The Coronation of Poppea),* 1967–68; Susanna, *Le Nozze di Figaro (The Marriage of Figaro),* 1968–69

Hindrichs, Emily: Madame Lidoine, *Dialogues des Carmélites,* 2004–05

Hinds, Walter: Innkeeper, *Manon Lescaut,* 1959–60; Knight, *Parsifal,* 1963–64

Hines, John: First Apprentice, *Wozzeck,* 1990–91; Narrator, *The Dawn of the Poor King,* 1990–91; Baritone, *Carmina Burana,* 1991–92; Escamillo, *Carmen,* 1991–92; Tonio, *I Pagliacci,* 1991–92; Trulove, *The Rake's Progress,* 1991–92; Ford, *Falstaff,* 1992–93

Hingtgen, Christina: Bielke, *Fiddler on the Roof,* 1994–95; Liat, *South Pacific,* 1995–96; Dodo, *Die lustige Witwe (The Merry Widow),* 1996–97

Hintz, Richard: Chevalier de St. Brioche, *Die lustige Witwe (The Merry Widow),* 1965–66

Hirschboeck, Noël: Cherubino, *Le Nozze di Figaro (The Marriage of Figaro),* 1973–74; Constance Fletcher, *The Mother of Us All,* 1973–74; Maddalena, *Rigoletto,* 1974–75

Hitt, James: Jailer, *Tosca,* 1969–70

Hoagland, Susan: Lauretta, *Gianni Schicchi,* 1964–65

Hobson, Seth: Clerk at the Clarendon Hotel, *The Ballad of Baby Doe,* 2003–04; Doorman at the Tabor Grand Theatre, *The Ballad of Baby Doe,* 2003–04; Father Chapelle, *The Ballad of Baby Doe,* 2003–04; Monostatos, *Die Zauberflöte (The Magic Flute),* 2004–05

Hocks, Ruth: Elizabeth of Valois, *Don Carlos,* 1961–62

Hodel, Jonathan: Borsa, *Rigoletto,* 1992–93; Father Mignon, *Die Teufel von Loudun (The Devils of Loudun),* 1992–93; Belmonte, *Die Entführung aus dem Serail (The Abduction from the Seraglio),* 1993–94; The Prince, *The Love for Three Oranges,* 1993–94; Count Almaviva, *Il Barbiere di Siviglia (The Barber of Seville),* 1994–95; Prince Tamino, *Die Zauberflöte (The Magic Flute),* 1994–95; Count Almaviva, *The Ghosts of Versailles,* 1996–97; Don Ottavio, *Don Giovanni,* 1996–97; Alfredo Germont, *La Traviata,* 1997–98; Fenton, *Falstaff,* 1997–98; Lensky, *Eugene Onegin,* 1997–98; Idomeneo, *Idomeneo,* 1998–99; Man in Armor, *Die Zauberflöte (The Magic Flute),* 1998–99; The Padre, *Man of La Mancha,* 1999–2000

Hodge, Kathy: Petra, *A Little Night Music,* 1988–89; The Housekeeper for Alonso, *Man of La Mancha,* 1988–89; Marriage arranger for Zubbediya, *Kismet,* 1989–90

Hodge, Mary Frances: The Armchair, *L'Enfant et les Sortilèges (The Bewitched Child),* 1955–56; Ensign Nellie Forbush, *South Pacific,* 1956–57

Hoeks, Ruth: Elizabeth of Valois, *Don Carlos,* 1961–62; Helena, *A Midsummer Night's Dream,* 1961–62; Hermia, *A Midsummer Night's Dream,* 1961–62

Hoffman, Daniel: Albert, *The Ballad of Baby Doe,* 1982–83; Guccio, *Il Trittico (A Triptych),* 1982–83; Marquis D'Obigny, *La Traviata,* 1983–84

Hoffman, Peggy: Servant of Buonafede, *Il Mondo della Luna (The World on the Moon)*, 1975–76

Hoffmann, Amanda: Javotte, *Manon*, 2001–02

Hohimer, Amy: Amaryllis, *The Music Man*, 1980–81

Hoke, Thomas: Lillas Pastia, *Carmen*, 1973–74; Giorgio, *The Gondoliers*, 1974–75

Holcenberg, David: Big Deal, *West Side Story*, 1985–86

Holcomb, Gloria: Julie Jordan, *Carousel*, 1952–53; First Lady, *Die Zauberflöte (The Magic Flute)*, 1953–54

Holiday, Richard: Boyar in Attendance, *Boris Godunov*, 1964–65; Pritschitsch, *Die lustige Witwe (The Merry Widow)*, 1964–65

Holland, Rachel: Madame Lidoine, *Dialogues des Carmélites*, 1997–98; First Lady, *Die Zauberflöte (The Magic Flute)*, 1998–99; Fata Morgana, *The Love for Three Oranges*, 1999–2000; Vanessa, *Vanessa*, 1999–2000; Fiordiligi, *Così fan tutte*, 2000–01; Cio-Cio San, *Madama Butterfly*, 2001–02; Marenka, *The Bartered Bride*, 2001–02; Donna Anna, *Don Giovanni*, 2002–03; Ellen Orford, *Peter Grimes*, 2003–04; Floria Tosca, *Tosca*, 2004–05

Holler, Peggy: Page, *Parsifal*, 1960–61; Spirit, *Die Zauberflöte (The Magic Flute)*, 1960–61

Holley, William: Amelia's Lover, *Amelia Goes to the Ball*, 1957–58; Lun Tha, *The King and I*, 1957–58; Rodolfo, *La Bohème*, 1957–58; Count Riccardo, *Un Ballo in Maschera (A Masked Ball)*, 1958–59; Don Ottavio, *Don Giovanni*, 1958–59; Lt. Pinkerton, *Madama Butterfly*, 1958–59; Chevalier des Grieux, *Manon Lescaut*, 1959–60; Hoffmann, *Les Contes d'Hoffmann (The Tales of Hoffmann)*, 1959–60; Ruggero Lastouc, *La Rondine (The Swallow)*, 1959–60; The Duke of Mantua, *Rigoletto*, 1959–60

Holliday, Thomas: Betto, *Gianni Schicchi*, 1964–65; Chernikofsky, *Boris Godunov*, 1964–65; Commendatore, *Don Giovanni*, 1964–65; Nikitich, *Boris Godunov*, 1964–65; Officer of the Border Guard, *Boris Godunov*, 1964–65; Pietro, *Simon Boccanegra*, 1964–65; The Bonze, *Madama Butterfly*, 1964–65; Second Commissioner, *Dialogues des Carmélites*, 1965–66; Footman, *Der Rosenkavalier*, 1965–66; Murderer, *Macbeth*, 1965–66; Priest, *Die Zauberflöte (The Magic Flute)*, 1965–66; Waiter, *Der Rosenkavalier*, 1965–66; Marullo, *Rigoletto*, 1966–67; Pasha Selim, *Die Entführung aus dem Serail (The Abduction from the Seraglio)*, 1966–67; Prince of Verona, *Roméo et Juliette*, 1966–67; Superintendant Budd, *Albert Herring*, 1966–67; Count des Grieux, *Manon*, 1967–68; Kezal, *The Bartered Bride*, 1967–68; Superintendant Budd, *Albert Herring*, 1967–68; Doctor Bartolo, *Il Barbiere di Siviglia (The Barber of Seville)*, 1971–72; Hunding, *Die Walküre*, 1971–72; Leporello, *Don Giovanni*, 1971–72;

Officer, *Il Barbiere di Siviglia (The Barber of Seville)*, 1971–72; Mill Foreman, *Jenůfa*, 1972–73; Papageno, *Die Zauberflöte (The Magic Flute)*, 1972–73; Fred Graham, *Kiss Me, Kate*, 1973–74; Petruchio, *Kiss Me, Kate*, 1973–74

Hollinger, Martin: Customs Officer, *La Bohème*, 1949–50; Knight, *Parsifal*, 1949–50

Holman, Kelli: Somewhere solo, *West Side Story*, 1985–86; Guenevere, *Camelot*, 1986–87

Holmes, Eugene: Commendatore, *Don Giovanni*, 1964–65; Creon, *Oedipus Rex*, 1964–65; Simon Boccanegra, *Simon Boccanegra*, 1964–65; Amfortas, *Parsifal*, 1965–66; Macbeth, *Macbeth*, 1965–66

Holmes, Jill: Adele, *Die Fledermaus (The Bat)*, 1996–97; Diana, *Orphée aux enfers (Orpheus in the Underworld)*, 1998–99

Holsapple, John: Alessio, *La Sonnambula (The Sleepwalker)*, 1985–86; Tiger, *West Side Story*, 1985–86; Sir Dinadan, *Camelot*, 1986–87

Holst, Kelly: A Favorite of the Governor, *Candide*, 2000–01; First Waitress, *Candide*, 2000–01; Sandman, *Hänsel und Gretel*, 2001–02; Olympia, *Les Contes d'Hoffmann (The Tales of Hoffmann)*, 2002–03

Holub, Albert: Musician, *Die Kluge (The Clever Girl)*, 1959–60; Deputy, *Don Carlos*, 1960–61; A Monk, *Don Carlos*, 1961–62; Cesare Angelotti, *Tosca*, 1961–62; Quince, *A Midsummer Night's Dream*, 1961–62

Holwerda, David: Don Carlos, *Don Carlos*, 1972–73; Parsifal, *Parsifal*, 1972–73; John Adams, *The Mother of Us All*, 1973–74; The Drum Major, *Wozzeck*, 1973–74

Holzfeind, Matthew: Frosch, *Die Fledermaus (The Bat)*, 2002–03

Holzmeier, Jana: Betty Parris, *The Crucible*, 1987–88

Honea, Richard: Page, *Parsifal*, 1972–73; Elder Gleaton, *Susannah*, 1976–77

Honn, Elisabeth: Chava, *Fiddler on the Roof*, 1994–95

Honnold, Julia Ann: Bianca, *Kiss Me, Kate*, 1951–52; Diana Dream, *On the Town*, 1951–52; Lois Lane, *Kiss Me, Kate*, 1951–52; Marquerita, *Song of Norway*, 1951–52; Sigrid, *Song of Norway*, 1951–52; Kundry, *Parsifal*, 1954–55

Honore, Jonathan: Don Jose, *Carmen*, 1991–92

Hooper, Anne Marie: Rose Maybud, *Ruddigore (The Witch's Curse)*, 1962–63

Hoover, Maya Frieman: Cio-Cio San, *Madama Butterfly*, 2001–02

Hoover, Robin: Topsy, *The King and I*, 1996–97

Hope, Adam: Heavenly Friend, *Carousel*, 1993–94; Matthew, *Carousel*, 1993–94

Hopkins, Joseph: Betto, *Gianni Schicchi*, 1993–94

Hopper, Alice: Ellen Orford, *Peter Grimes*, 1994–95; Ludmila, *The Bartered Bride*, 1994–95

Horist, Matthew: Moose, *West Side Story,* 1992–93; Normanno, *Lucia di Lammermoor,* 1993–94

Horne, Brian: The Chief Justice, *Of Thee I Sing,* 1987–88; Adam, *Die Teufel von Loudun (The Devils of Loudun),* 1992–93; Bardolph, *Falstaff,* 1992–93; Enoch Snow, *Carousel,* 1993–94; Truffaldino, *The Love for Three Oranges,* 1993–94; Man in Armor, *Die Zauberflöte (The Magic Flute),* 1994–95; Mao Tse-tung, *Nixon in China,* 1994–95

Horsman, Leonore: The Bat, *L'Enfant et les Sortilèges (The Bewitched Child),* 1955–56

Horton, Gary: Marcello, *La Bohème,* 1970–71

Horton, Sharon: Carrie Pipperidge, *Carousel,* 1970–71

Hoskins, Rachel: Gianetta, *L'Elisir d'amore (The Elixir of Love),* 1961–62

Hostetter, Dylan: Amahl, *Amahl and the Night Visitors,* 1990–91

Hostler, James: Anselmo / a Muleteer, *Man of La Mancha,* 1985–86

Hotz, William: Reggie, *Where's Charley?,* 1953–54

Houghton, Erin: Pitti-Sing, *The Mikado,* 2006–07; Sandman, *Hänsel und Gretel,* 2006–07; Security woman, *A Wedding,* 2007–08

House, Ronald: Nelson, *Porgy and Bess,* 1979–80; Jigger Craigin, *Carousel,* 1993–94

Howard, Diane: Barbarina, *Le Nozze di Figaro (The Marriage of Figaro),* 1980–81; A Novice, *Il Trittico (A Triptych),* 1982–83; Marie, *La Fille du régiment (The Daughter of the Regiment),* 1984–85

Howard, Emily: Sarah Good, *The Crucible,* 1987–88

Howard, Frank: Third Officer, *Candide,* 1957–58; Vinter, *Candide,* 1957–58; Servant of Amelia, *Un Ballo in Maschera (A Masked Ball),* 1958–59; The Chief Magistrate, *Un Ballo in Maschera (A Masked Ball),* 1958–59

Howard, Robert: Harlequin, *Ariadne auf Naxos,* 1954–55; Baldy, *The Land Between the Rivers,* 1955–56; Count Almaviva, *Le Nozze di Figaro (The Marriage of Figaro),* 1955–56; Mephistopheles, *Faust,* 1955–56; Charlie Davenport, *Annie Get Your Gun,* 1956–57; Dancaire, *Carmen,* 1956–57; Sir John Falstaff, *Falstaff,* 1956–57

Howard, Vernon: Bangle Man, *Kismet,* 1963–64; The Boy's Father, *The Fantasticks,* 1963–64; Wazir's Functionary, *Kismet,* 1963–64; Baron Mirko Zeta, *Die lustige Witwe (The Merry Widow),* 1965–66; Pritschitsch, *Die lustige Witwe (The Merry Widow),* 1965–66; Duke of Ephesus, *The Boys from Syracuse,* 1968–69

Howe, Fred: Scholar, *Der Rosenkavalier,* 1965–66; Frenchman, *Myshkin,* 1972–73

Howe, Martha J.: Effie, *The Ballad of Baby Doe,* 1975–76; Voice from Heaven, *Parsifal,* 1975–76

Howell, Fred: Pops, *Kiss Me, Kate,* 1973–74

Howell, John: Albazar, *Il Turco in Italia (The Turk in Italy),* 1996–97; Triquet, *Eugene Onegin,* 1997–98; Brack Weaver, *Down in the Valley,* 1998–99; Player, *Mass,* 1998–99

Howes, Robert: Arthur Jones, *Billy Budd,* 1952–53

Hrycelak, Steven: Fiorello, *Il Barbiere di Siviglia (The Barber of Seville),* 2005–06; Zuniga, *Carmen,* 2005–06; Dottor Bombasto, *Arlecchino,* 2006–07; Sparafucile, *Rigoletto,* 2007–08; William Williamson, *A Wedding,* 2007–08

Hu, Wayne: Graf Waldner, *Arabella,* 2006–07; Count Almaviva, *Le Nozze di Figaro (The Marriage of Figaro),* 2007–08

Hu, Yoon: Rainbowglory, *The Excursions of Mr. Broucek,* 1981–82

Hubbard, Bruce: Amantio di Nicolao, *Il Trittico (A Triptych),* 1972–73; Guccio, *Il Trittico (A Triptych),* 1972–73; Black Man, *The Mother of Us All,* 1973–74; Dancaire, *Carmen,* 1973–74; Schlemil, *Les Contes d'Hoffmann (The Tales of Hoffmann),* 1973–74; Second Man, *Kiss Me, Kate,* 1973–74; A Captain, *Eugene Onegin,* 1974–75; Marullo, *Rigoletto,* 1974–75; Schaunard, *La Bohème,* 1974–75; Albert, *Werther,* 1975–76; Pantalone, *The Love for Three Oranges,* 1975–76; Joe, *Show Boat,* 1984–85

Hubbs, Jennifer: Ensign Nellie Forbush, *South Pacific,* 1995–96

Hubert, Charlotte: Countess Ceprano, *Rigoletto,* 1974–75

Huckle, John Paul: Antonio, *Le Nozze di Figaro (The Marriage of Figaro),* 2001–02; Olin Britt, *The Music Man,* 2001–02; Commendatore, *Don Giovanni,* 2002–03; Pistol, *Falstaff,* 2003–04; Sarastro, *Die Zauberflöte (The Magic Flute),* 2004–05; Friar Laurence, *Roméo et Juliette,* 2005–06; Theseus, *A Midsummer Night's Dream,* 2005–06; Zuniga, *Carmen,* 2005–06; Commendatore, *Don Giovanni,* 2006–07; Count des Grieux, *Manon,* 2006–07

Hudson, Chad: Prince Rudolph, *Jubilee,* 1991–92

Huff, Joshua Phillip: Little Lud, *1600 Pennsylvania Avenue,* 1992–93; Tommy Djilas, *The Music Man,* 2001–02

Hughes, Sheldon: The Father Confessor, *Dialogues des Carmélites,* 1997–98; Idamante, *Idomeneo,* 1998–99; Anatol, *Vanessa,* 1999–2000; Nemorino, *L'Elisir d'amore (The Elixir of Love),* 2000–01; Vashek, *The Bartered Bride,* 2001–02

Huling, Vicky: Carrie Pipperidge, *Carousel,* 1970–71

Huls, Susan: Vivienne, *Oklahoma!,* 1981–82

Hulse, Charles: Phillip, *Kiss Me, Kate,* 1951–52

Hultgren, Lori: Boy, *Die Zauberflöte (The Magic Flute),* 1994–95; Secretary I, *Nixon in China,* 1994–95; Despina, *Così fan tutte,* 1995–96; Anna Leonowens, *The King and I,* 1996–97; Zaida, *Il Turco in Italia (The Turk in Italy),* 1996–97;

Laurey, *Oklahoma!,* 1997–98; Mother Marie of the Incarnation, *Dialogues des Carmélites,* 1997–98; Carmen, *Carmen,* 1998–99

Humble, Aaron: First Officer, *Candide,* 2000–01; Pedrillo, *Die Entführung aus dem Serail (The Abduction from the Seraglio),* 2003–04

Hunt, Jeremy: Celio, *The Love for Three Oranges,* 1999–2000; Figaro, *Il Barbiere di Siviglia (The Barber of Seville),* 2000–01; Guglielmo, *Così fan tutte,* 2000–01; Valentin, *Faust,* 2000–01; Krushina, *The Bartered Bride,* 2001–02; Lescaut, *Manon,* 2001–02; Giulio Cesare, *Giulio Cesare (Julius Caesar),* 2002–03; Count Danilo Danilovitch, *Die lustige Witwe (The Merry Widow),* 2003–04

Hunt, Julia: Nedda, *I Pagliacci,* 1991–92; Eurydice, *Orfeo ed Euridice,* 1992–93; Maria, *West Side Story,* 1992–93; Fata Morgana, *The Love for Three Oranges,* 1993–94

Hunt, Leah: Cunegonde, *Candide,* 2000–01; Lucia, *Lucia di Lammermoor,* 2001–02

Hunter, Bruce: Augure, *L'Orfeo,* 1987–88; Messenger, *Béatrice et Bénédict,* 1987–88; Doctor Bartolo, *Il Barbiere di Siviglia (The Barber of Seville),* 1988–89; Schlemil, *Les Contes d'Hoffmann (The Tales of Hoffmann),* 1988–89; The Innkeeper / The Governor, *Man of La Mancha,* 1988–89; Alcindoro, *La Bohème,* 1989–90; Benoit, *La Bohème,* 1989–90; Jawan, *Kismet,* 1989–90; Rambaldo Fernandez, *La Rondine (The Swallow),* 1989–90; Teucer, *The Cry of Clytaemnestra,* 1989–90; Virgil's Ghost, *Francesca da Rimini,* 1989–90

Huntley, Heath: Ambrogio, *Il Barbiere di Siviglia (The Barber of Seville),* 1963–64; Merchant, *Kismet,* 1963–64; A Jailer, *Dialogues des Carmélites,* 1965–66; M. Javelinot, *Dialogues des Carmélites,* 1965–66; Count Monterone, *Rigoletto,* 1966–67; Lord Capulet, *Roméo et Juliette,* 1966–67

Huntsman, Elliot: Prince Chulalongkorn, *The King and I,* 1996–97

Hurt, Phyllis: Zorah, *Ruddigore (The Witch's Curse),* 1962–63

Hurt, Weston: Junius, *The Rape of Lucretia,* 1999–2000; Belcore, *L'Elisir d'amore (The Elixir of Love),* 2000–01; Marullo, *Rigoletto,* 2000–01; Enrico Ashton, *Lucia di Lammermoor,* 2001–02; Sharpless, *Madama Butterfly,* 2001–02

Hutchens, James: First Deputy, *Finian's Rainbow,* 1953–54

Hutchinson Brown, Dorothy: Amelfa, *Le Coq d'or (The Golden Cockerel),* 1960–61

Hwang, Hoo Ryoung: Player, *Mass,* 1998–99; Lauretta, *Gianni Schicchi,* 1999–2000; Mimi, *La Bohème,* 1999–2000; Susanna, *Le Nozze di Figaro (The Marriage of Figaro),* 2001–02

Hwang, Jung Hyun: Albazar, *Il Turco in Italia (The Turk in Italy),* 2003–04

Ihde, Martha: A Novice, *Il Trittico (A Triptych),* 1972–73; Papagena, *Die Zauberflöte (The Magic Flute),* 1972–73; Shprintze, *Fiddler on the Roof,* 1972–73; Barbarina, *Le Nozze di Figaro (The Marriage of Figaro),* 1973–74

Ingham, Michael: Guglielmo, *Così fan tutte,* 1970–71; Ford, *Falstaff,* 1971–72

Ingram, Paula: Second Lady, *Die Zauberflöte (The Magic Flute),* 1982–83; Paquette, *Candide,* 1983–84; Diana, *Orphée aux enfers (Orpheus in the Underworld),* 1984–85; The Dragonfly, *L'Enfant et les Sortilèges (The Bewitched Child),* 1984–85; Aldonza / Dulcinea, *Man of La Mancha,* 1985–86; Maria, *West Side Story,* 1985–86

Ingram, Robert: Sorcerer, *The Boys from Syracuse,* 1968–69

Innecco, Alexandre: Master of Ceremonies, *The Love for Three Oranges,* 1993–94; Monostatos, *Die Zauberflöte (The Magic Flute),* 1994–95

Inoue, Koichi: The Fool, *Wozzeck,* 1990–91; Goro, *Madama Butterfly,* 1991–92

Ireland, Kathy: Princess Nicoletta, *The Love for Three Oranges,* 1975–76; Pamina, *Die Zauberflöte (The Magic Flute),* 1977–78

Irvin, Carolyn: Clara, *Porgy and Bess,* 1976–77

Irwin, Stanley: Silvano, *Un Ballo in Maschera (A Masked Ball),* 1969–70; Enrico Ashton, *Lucia di Lammermoor,* 1970–71; Keller, *Myshkin,* 1972–73

Irwin, Teresa L.: Countess Almaviva, *Le Nozze di Figaro (The Marriage of Figaro),* 1997–98

Isaacs, Gregory: Edmondo, *Manon Lescaut,* 1970–71; Fourth Jew, *Salome,* 1970–71; Lebedev, *Myshkin,* 1972–73

Isom, Sally: Jane, *Finian's Rainbow,* 1953–54; Ngana, *South Pacific,* 1956–57

Itkin, David: Father Bernard, *Candide,* 1987–88; Player, *Mass,* 1987–88; Victim of the Inquisition, *Candide,* 1987–88; Player, *Mass,* 1988–89

Iverson, Lyle: Al, *The Most Happy Fella,* 1959–60; The Cashier, *The Most Happy Fella,* 1959–60

Ivey, James: Morales, *Carmen,* 2005–06; Lescaut, *Manon,* 2006–07; Rigoletto, *Rigoletto,* 2007–08

Izzo, Maria: Countess Ceprano, *Rigoletto,* 1995–96; Florestine, *The Ghosts of Versailles,* 1996–97; Barbarina, *Le Nozze di Figaro (The Marriage of Figaro),* 1997–98

Jack, Dwight: Giuseppe, *La Traviata,* 1960–61; Harry Beaton, *Brigadoon,* 1961–62; Sandy Dean, *Brigadoon,* 1961–62; Aegeon, *The Boys from Syracuse,* 1968–69

Jackson, Ardis: Maid, *Amelia Goes to the Ball,* 1957–58; Thisbe, *La Cenerentola (Cinderella),* 1957–58

Jackson, Betty: Meg Brockie, *Brigadoon*, 1952–53; Nettie Fowler, *Carousel*, 1952–53; Hostess of the Inn, *Boris Godunov*, 1953–54; Julie, *Show Boat*, 1953–54; Meg Brockie, *Brigadoon*, 1953–54; Mrs. Beverly Smythe, *Where's Charley?*, 1953–54; Second Lady, *Die Zauberflöte (The Magic Flute)*, 1953–54; Prince Orlofsky, *Die Fledermaus (The Bat)*, 1954–55; The Composer, *Ariadne auf Naxos*, 1954–55

Jackson, Jack: Knight, *Parsifal*, 1948–49

Jackson, Leslie: Mingo, *Porgy and Bess*, 1979–80

Jackson, Richard: First Sharecropper, *Finian's Rainbow*, 1969–70; Preacher, *Finian's Rainbow*, 1969–70; Third Gospeleer, *Finian's Rainbow*, 1969–70

Jackson, Sheri: Zerlina, *Don Giovanni*, 1996–97; Sister Constance, *Dialogues des Carmélites*, 1997–98

Jackson, Sue: Page, *Rigoletto*, 1959–60; Sophie, *Werther*, 1961–62

Jacobs, Joan: Berta (Marcellina), *Il Barbiere di Siviglia (The Barber of Seville)*, 1971–72; Martha, *Faust*, 1971–72; Siegrune, *Die Walküre*, 1971–72

Jacot, Eleonore: Mrs. Sedley, *Peter Grimes*, 1994–95

Jacquez, Noelle: Gertrude, *Hänsel und Gretel*, 2006–07

Jaeger, Richard: Vincent Jones, *Street Scene*, 1949–50; Count Scharntoff, *Blossom Time*, 1952–53; David Bascomb, *Carousel*, 1952–53; Jeff Douglas, *Brigadoon*, 1952–53; Robust, *Finian's Rainbow*, 1953–54; Sir Francis Chesney, *Where's Charley?*, 1953–54; Steve, *Show Boat*, 1953–54; Chick Clark, *Wonderful Town*, 1954–55; The King, *The King and I*, 1957–58

Jakob, Jennifer: Rita Billingsley, *A Wedding*, 2007–08

James, Carolyne: Zita, *Gianni Schicchi*, 1964–65; Annina, *Der Rosenkavalier*, 1965–66; Mercedes, *Carmen*, 1965–66; Third Lady, *Die Zauberflöte (The Magic Flute)*, 1965–66; Lucia, *Cavalleria Rusticana*, 1966–67; Maddalena, *Rigoletto*, 1966–67; Margarita, *Quattro rusteghi (The Four Ruffians)*, 1966–67; Mrs. Herring, *Albert Herring*, 1966–67

James, Creighton: Remendado, *Carmen*, 1998–99; Gherardo, *Gianni Schicchi*, 1999–2000; Truffaldino, *The Love for Three Oranges*, 1999–2000; Ambrogio, *Il Barbiere di Siviglia (The Barber of Seville)*, 2000–01; Governor, *Candide*, 2000–01; Nemorino, *L'Elisir d'amore (The Elixir of Love)*, 2000–01; Jacey Squires, *The Music Man*, 2001–02; Laurie, *Little Women*, 2001–02; Gabriel von Eisenstein, *Die Fledermaus (The Bat)*, 2002–03; Belmonte, *Die Entführung aus dem Serail (The Abduction from the Seraglio)*, 2003–04; Prince Tamino, *Die Zauberflöte (The Magic Flute)*, 2004–05; Tony, *A View from the Bridge*, 2004–05

James, Eric: Sen. Robert E. Lyons, *Of Thee I Sing*, 1987–88

James, Kimberly Gratland: Mercedes, *Carmen*, 1998–99; Erika, *Vanessa*, 1999–2000; Princess Clarissa, *The Love for Three Oranges*, 1999–2000; Siebel, *Faust*, 2000–01; Cherubino, *Le Nozze di Figaro (The Marriage of Figaro)*, 2001–02; Jo, *Little Women*, 2001–02; Mrs. Sedley, *Peter Grimes*, 2003–04

Janda, Susan: Francisca, *West Side Story*, 1985–86

Jankowski, Gary: Bailiff, *The Crucible*, 1987–88; Francis X. Gilhooley, *Of Thee I Sing*, 1987–88; Osmin, *Die Entführung aus dem Serail (The Abduction from the Seraglio)*, 1987–88; Swallow, *Peter Grimes*, 1987–88; Crespel, *Les Contes d'Hoffmann (The Tales of Hoffmann)*, 1988–89; Sarastro, *Die Zauberflöte (The Magic Flute)*, 1988–89; Lodovico, *Otello*, 1989–90

Jao, Radmar: Nibbles, *West Side Story*, 1985–86

Jardim, Angela: Dewman, *Hänsel und Gretel*, 1982–83; Marie Antoinette, *The Ghosts of Versailles*, 1996–97; Tatyana, *Eugene Onegin*, 1997–98; Vanessa, *Vanessa*, 1999–2000

Jarrell, Crystal: Emily, *The Ballad of Baby Doe*, 2003–04; Olga, *Die lustige Witwe (The Merry Widow)*, 2003–04; Olga, *Eugene Onegin*, 2004–05

Jarvis, Kenneth: Indio, *West Side Story*, 2002–03

Jaworski, Warren: Baron Douphol, *La Traviata*, 1968–69; Cesare Angelotti, *Tosca*, 1969–70; Silvano, *Un Ballo in Maschera (A Masked Ball)*, 1969–70

Jeffers, Ann: Casilda, *The Gondoliers*, 1974–75; Page, *Rigoletto*, 1974–75

Jenkins, Deborah: Amy, *Company*, 1990–91

Jenkins, John: Policeman, *Albert Herring*, 1966–67

Jennings, Norman: Schaunard, *La Bohème*, 1957–58; Rambaldo Fernandez, *La Rondine (The Swallow)*, 1959–60

Jennings, Ronald: Amahl, *Amahl and the Night Visitors*, 1951–52

Jennings, Xan: Mrs. Ott, *Susannah*, 2007–08

Jens, Julianne: Ariadne/Prima Donna, *Ariadne auf Naxos*, 1969–70; Brünnhilde, *Die Walküre*, 1971–72

Jensen, Joaquina: Old woman, *Heracles*, 1971–72; Mayor's Wife, *Jenůfa*, 1972–73; Page, *Parsifal*, 1972–73; The Abbess, *Il Trittico (A Triptych)*, 1972–73; Zita, *Il Trittico (A Triptych)*, 1972–73; Gertrude Stein, *The Mother of Us All*, 1973–74; Jenny Reefer, *The Mother of Us All*, 1973–74

Jepson, Kristine: The Squirrel, *L'Enfant et les Sortilèges (The Bewitched Child)*, 1984–85; Juno, *The Tempest*, 1985–86; Mary, *Der Fliegende Holländer (The Flying Dutchman)*, 1985–86; Ludmila, *The Bartered Bride*, 1986–87; Maddalena, *Rigoletto*, 1986–87; Elizabeth Proctor, *The Crucible*, 1987–88

Jessup, Rene: Abraham Kaplan, *Street Scene*, 1960–61

Jewett, Marilyn: Aunt Eller, *Oklahoma!*, 1954–55; Mrs. Wade, *Wonderful Town*, 1954–55; Sarah Potts, *The Land Between the Rivers*, 1955–56

Jewsbury, Chad: Bill Bobstay, *HMS Pinafore*, 2005–06; Starveling, *A Midsummer Night's Dream*, 2005–06

Jhong, Bok-joo: Spirit, *Die Zauberflöte (The Magic Flute)*, 1972–73

Jimenez-Pons, Emilio: Bob Boles, *Peter Grimes*, 2003–04; The Chevalier, *Dialogues des Carmélites*, 2004–05

Johanson, Erik: Hoffmann, *Les Contes d'Hoffmann (The Tales of Hoffmann)*, 1988–89; Faust, *Faust*, 1989–90

Johns, Marnee: Juno, *Orphée aux enfers (Orpheus in the Underworld)*, 1992–93; Nettie Fowler, *Carousel*, 1993–94

Johnson, Arnold: Francisco, *The Tempest*, 1985–86; Second Commissioner, *Dialogues des Carmélites*, 1986–87

Johnson, Bessie: Queenie, *Show Boat*, 1953–54

Johnson, Bill: Man on the street, *Trouble in Tahiti*, 1976–77; Player, *Bernstein on Broadway*, 1976–77; Trio—baritone, *Trouble in Tahiti*, 1976–77

Johnson, Billie Jean: Wife of Lazarus, *The Darkened City*, 1978–79

Johnson, Carl: Attendant, *Don Carlos*, 1961–62; Orange Merchant, *Kismet*, 1963–64

Johnson, Christopher: Graf Dominik, *Arabella*, 2006–07; Breedley, *A Wedding*, 2007–08

Johnson, Diane: Bess, *Porgy and Bess*, 1979–80

Johnson, Elizabeth: Mrs. McLean, *Susannah*, 2000–01; Alisa, *Lucia di Lammermoor*, 2001–02

Johnson, Eric: Gastone, *La Traviata*, 1978–79; Curly, *Oklahoma!*, 1981–82; Betto, *Il Trittico (A Triptych)*, 1982–83; Doctor Bartolo, *Il Barbiere di Siviglia (The Barber of Seville)*, 1982–83; Joe, *The Most Happy Fella*, 1982–83; Man in Armor, *Die Zauberflöte (The Magic Flute)*, 1982–83; Fasolt, *Das Rheingold*, 1983–84; Quince, *A Midsummer Night's Dream*, 1983–84; Sweeney Todd, *Sweeney Todd*, 1983–84; Wotan, *Das Rheingold*, 1983–84

Johnson, Evelyn: La Ciesca, *Gianni Schicchi*, 1993–94

Johnson, Gale: Oscar, *Un Ballo in Maschera (A Masked Ball)*, 1975–76; Ilia, *Idomeneo*, 1976–77; Julie Jordan, *Carousel*, 1976–77; Player, *Bernstein on Broadway*, 1976–77; Despina, *Così fan tutte*, 1977–78; Queen of the Night, *Die Zauberflöte (The Magic Flute)*, 1977–78

Johnson, Jean: Senta, *Der Fliegende Holländer (The Flying Dutchman)*, 1978–79

Johnson, Jeremiah: Graf Waldner, *Arabella*, 2006–07; Peter, *Hänsel und Gretel*, 2006–07; Belcore, *L'Elisir d'amore (The Elixir of Love)*, 2007–08

Johnson, Judy: Naiad, *Ariadne auf Naxos*, 1969–70

Johnson, Kathy: Jano, *Jenůfa*, 1972–73; Spirit, *Die Zauberflöte (The Magic Flute)*, 1972–73

Johnson, Lynette: Olga, *Eugene Onegin*, 1974–75

Johnson, Mark: Count Monterone, *Rigoletto*, 1980–81; Leandro, *The Love for Three Oranges*, 1980–81; Officer, *Il Barbiere di Siviglia (The Barber of Seville)*, 1980–81; Sharpless, *Madama Butterfly*, 1981–82; Pasquale, *The Most Happy Fella*, 1982–83; Baron Mirko Zeta, *Die lustige Witwe (The Merry Widow)*, 1983–84; Demetrius, *A Midsummer Night's Dream*, 1983–84; The Beadle, *Sweeney Todd*, 1983–84

Johnson, Matt: Policeman, *Carousel*, 1993–94; Yussel, *Fiddler on the Roof*, 1994–95; Phra Alack, *The King and I*, 1996–97

Johnson, Michael: Odysseus, *The Cry of Clytaemnestra*, 1979–80; Wozzeck, *Wozzeck*, 1981–82; Herman, *The Most Happy Fella*, 1982–83; Figaro, *Il Barbiere di Siviglia (The Barber of Seville)*, 1982–83; Gianni Schicchi, *Il Trittico (A Triptych)*, 1982–83; Loge, *Das Rheingold*, 1983–84; Herald, *Murder in the Cathedral*, 1984–85

Johnson, Patsy: Page, *Parsifal*, 1972–73; Spirit, *Die Zauberflöte (The Magic Flute)*, 1972–73; Cherubino, *Le Nozze di Figaro (The Marriage of Figaro)*, 1973–74; Indiana Elliott, *The Mother of Us All*, 1973–74; Katherine, *Kiss Me, Kate*, 1973–74; Lilli Vanessi, *Kiss Me, Kate*, 1973–74

Johnson, Rebecca: Nettie Fowler, *Carousel*, 1970–71

Johnson, Roy: Hlabeni, *Lost in the Stars*, 1950–51; Nanki-Poo, *The Mikado*, 1950–51

Johnson, Scott: Mr. Lundie, *Brigadoon*, 1961–62; Frosch, *Die Fledermaus (The Bat)*, 1962–63; Crony, *The Fair at Sorochinsk*, 1963–64; Dr. Crabbe, *Peter Grimes*, 1963–64; The Old Actor, *The Fantasticks*, 1963–64

Johnson, Shallen: Mrs. Meg Page, *Falstaff*, 1997–98; Eurydice, *Orphée aux enfers (Orpheus in the Underworld)*, 1998–99

Johnson, Stephanie: Donna Anna, *Don Giovanni*, 1996–97; Countess Almaviva, *Le Nozze di Figaro (The Marriage of Figaro)*, 1997–98; Violetta Valery, *La Traviata*, 1997–98; Electra, *Idomeneo*, 1998–99; Marguerite, *Faust*, 2000–01; Marenka, *The Bartered Bride*, 2001–02

Johnson, Steven: David, *Company*, 1990–91; Kronkov, *Die lustige Witwe (The Merry Widow)*, 1990–91; Messenger/Commissioner, *La Traviata*, 1990–91; Servant, *La Traviata*, 1990–91; Barnaby Tucker, *Hello, Dolly!*, 1991–92; Dancaire, *Carmen*, 1991–92; Prince James, *Jubilee*, 1991–92; Action, *West Side Story*, 1992–93; Antonio, *Le Nozze di Figaro (The Marriage of Figaro)*,

1992–93; Marullo, *Rigoletto,* 1992–93; Pluto, *Orphée aux enfers (Orpheus in the Underworld),* 1992–93

Johnson, Sylvia: Page, *Parsifal,* 1956–57

Johnson, Thomas: Agent of the Inquisition, *Candide,* 1993–94; Slave Driver, *Candide,* 1993–94; Bogdanowitsch, *Die lustige Witwe (The Merry Widow),* 1996–97; Official Registrar, *Madama Butterfly,* 1996–97; Second Commissioner, *Dialogues des Carmélites,* 1997–98; Player, *Mass,* 1998–99

Johnson, Will: Seabee Morton Wise, *South Pacific,* 1956–57

Johnson, William: Jake, *Porgy and Bess,* 1979–80; Undertaker, *Porgy and Bess,* 1979–80; Wagner, *Faust,* 1981–82; Doorman at the Tabor Grand Theatre, *The Ballad of Baby Doe,* 1982–83; Main-Man Cruthfield, *Soldier Boy, Soldier,* 1982–83; Giorgio Germont, *La Traviata,* 1983–84; Puck, *A Midsummer Night's Dream,* 1983–84; Sweeney Todd, *Sweeney Todd,* 1983–84; Marcello, *La Bohème,* 1984–85; Tempter, *Murder in the Cathedral,* 1984–85; Prospero, *The Tempest,* 1985–86

Johnston, Dennis: Alcindoro, *La Bohème,* 1970–71; Don Fernando, *Fidelio,* 1970–71; Sergeant, *Manon Lescaut,* 1970–71

Johnston, Mary Jo: Floria Tosca, *Tosca,* 1969–70; Gerhilde, *Die Walküre,* 1969–70

Joiner, Rob: Huntsman, *Candide,* 2000–01

Jonas, Kimi: Kim (child), *Show Boat,* 1984–85

Jones, Carrie: Anybodys, *West Side Story,* 1985–86

Jones, David: Stuart Dalrymple, *Brigadoon,* 1952–53; Stuart Dalrymple, *Brigadoon,* 1953–54; Jake, *The Most Happy Fella,* 1959–60

Jones, Earl: Crespel, *Les Contes d'Hoffmann (The Tales of Hoffmann),* 1947–48; Jennie's father, *Down in the Valley,* 1947–48; The Mikado of Japan, *The Mikado,* 1950–51

Jones, Grace: Spirit, *Die Zauberflöte (The Magic Flute),* 1960–61; Ellen Orford, *Peter Grimes,* 1963–64; Liu, *Turandot,* 1964–65

Jones, J. Loren: Belmonte, *Die Entführung aus dem Serail (The Abduction from the Seraglio),* 1961–62; Kunz Volgelgesang, *Die Meistersinger von Nürnberg (The Mastersingers of Nuremberg),* 1961–62

Jones, Judy: Sarah, *The Ballad of Baby Doe,* 1975–76

Jones, Keith: Father Chapelle, *The Ballad of Baby Doe,* 1982–83; Herod, *Passion Play—Carmina Burana,* 1982–83; Chevalier de St. Brioche, *Die lustige Witwe (The Merry Widow),* 1983–84; Faun, *Candide,* 1983–84; Prince Shuisky, *Boris Godunov,* 1983–84

Jones, Mark: Valentin, *Faust,* 1989–90; Belcore, *L'Elisir d'amore (The Elixir of Love),* 1990–91; Dr. Falke, *Die Fledermaus (The Bat),* 1990–91; Giorgio

Germont, *La Traviata,* 1990–91; Roberto (Nardo), *La Finta Giardiniera,* 1990–91; Silvio, *I Pagliacci,* 1991–92; Snowboy, *West Side Story,* 1992–93

Jones, Neil: Sam, *The Ballad of Baby Doe,* 1975–76; Player, *Bernstein on Broadway,* 1976–77; Trio—tenor, *Trouble in Tahiti,* 1976–77; Monostatos, *Die Zauberflöte (The Magic Flute),* 1977–78; Servant, *Danton and Robespierre,* 1977–78; Andres, *Les Contes d'Hoffmann (The Tales of Hoffmann),* 1978–79; Boyar in Attendance, *Boris Godunov,* 1978–79; Cochenille, *Les Contes d'Hoffmann (The Tales of Hoffmann),* 1978–79; Franz, *Les Contes d'Hoffmann (The Tales of Hoffmann),* 1978–79; Pittichinaccio, *Les Contes d'Hoffmann (The Tales of Hoffmann),* 1978–79; Second Suitor, *The Darkened City,* 1978–79; Little Bat McLean, *Susannah,* 1979–80; Vashek, *The Bartered Bride,* 1979–80; Ovlor, *Prince Igor,* 1980–81; The Prince, *The Love for Three Oranges,* 1980–81; Yannakos, *The Greek Passion,* 1980–81; Chester A. Arthur, *The Ballad of Baby Doe,* 1982–83; Rinuccio, *Il Trittico (A Triptych),* 1982–83; Sam, *The Ballad of Baby Doe,* 1982–83; Candide, *Candide,* 1983–84

Jones, Pamela: Serena, *Porgy and Bess,* 1979–80; Frasquita, *Carmen,* 1991–92; Soprano, *Carmina Burana,* 1991–92

Jones, Randy: Bellboy, *Jubilee,* 1991–92; Bulgarian Soldier, *Candide,* 1993–94; Sailor, *Candide,* 1993–94

Jones, Ruby: Azucena, *Il Trovatore,* 1967–68; Bersi, *Andrea Chénier,* 1967–68; Mother Goose, *The Rake's Progress,* 1968–69

Jones, Scott: Third Mourner, *The Darkened City,* 1978–79

Jones, Ted: Nathaniel, *Kiss Me, Kate,* 1951–52; Mr. Gedge, *Albert Herring,* 1957–58

Jones, Wesley: Snowboy, *West Side Story,* 1992–93

Jorgensen, Michael: Asmodus, *Doktor Faust,* 1974–75

Jorgensen, Sally: Madrigal Singer, *Manon Lescaut,* 1970–71; Karolka, *Jenůfa,* 1972–73

Jose, Brian: Juano, *West Side Story,* 1992–93; Boris, *Fiddler on the Roof,* 1994–95; Schmeril, *Fiddler on the Roof,* 1994–95; The Interpreter, *The King and I,* 1996–97; Uncle Tom, *The King and I,* 1996–97

Joselson, Rachel: First Lady, *Die Zauberflöte (The Magic Flute),* 1977–78; Giulietta, *Les Contes d'Hoffmann (The Tales of Hoffmann),* 1978–79; Stella, *Les Contes d'Hoffmann (The Tales of Hoffmann),* 1978–79

Joshi, Georgina: Clorinda, *La Cenerentola (Cinderella),* 2004–05; Despina, *Così fan tutte,* 2005–06

Juarez, Ivan: Crespel, *Les Contes d'Hoffmann (The Tales of Hoffmann)*, 1995–96; Truffaldino, *Ariadne auf Naxos*, 1996–97; Marquis D'Obigny, *La Traviata*, 1997–98

Judge, Daniel: Betto, *Gianni Schicchi*, 1988–89; Luther, *Les Contes d'Hoffmann (The Tales of Hoffmann)*, 1988–89; The Innkeeper / The Governor, *Man of La Mancha*, 1988–89; Rambaldo Fernandez, *La Rondine (The Swallow)*, 1989–90; The Wazir of Police, *Kismet*, 1989–90; Baron Mirko Zeta, *Die lustige Witwe (The Merry Widow)*, 1990–91; Frosch, *Die Fledermaus (The Bat)*, 1990–91; Second Apprentice, *Wozzeck*, 1990–91

Julin, Jessica: Beatrice, *A View from the Bridge*, 2004–05

Jung, Jeannette (Junk): Rosina, *Il Barbiere di Siviglia (The Barber of Seville)*, 1971–72; Zdenka, *Arabella*, 1972–73; Olympia, *Les Contes d'Hoffmann (The Tales of Hoffmann)*, 1973–74; Susanna, *Le Nozze di Figaro (The Marriage of Figaro)*, 1973–74; Clarissa, *Il Mondo della Luna (The World on the Moon)*, 1975–76; Countess Celimene, *A Little Night Music*, 1975–76; Desiree Armfeldt, *A Little Night Music*, 1975–76; Elizabeth "Baby" Doe, *The Ballad of Baby Doe*, 1975–76

Justak, Nora: Ceres, *The Tempest*, 1985–86; Mother Marie of the Incarnation, *Dialogues des Carmélites*, 1986–87; Mrs. Sedley, *Peter Grimes*, 1987–88; Tituba, *The Crucible*, 1987–88

Kahl, Howard: Franz, *Les Contes d'Hoffmann (The Tales of Hoffmann)*, 1947–48; Robert, *Hin und Zurück (There and Back)*, 1947–48; Spalanzani, *Les Contes d'Hoffmann (The Tales of Hoffmann)*, 1947–48; Page, *Parsifal*, 1948–49; Alcindoro, *La Bohème*, 1949–50; Alexander, *The New Moon*, 1949–50; Benoit, *La Bohème*, 1949–50; Dick McGann, *Street Scene*, 1949–50; Guitar Player, *The Jumping Frog of Calaveras County*, 1949–50; John Thurston, *The Firefly*, 1949–50; Nish, *Die lustige Witwe (The Merry Widow)*, 1949–50; Arthur Jarvis, *Lost in the Stars*, 1950–51; Ko-Ko, *The Mikado*, 1950–51; Charley Wykeham, *Where's Charley?*, 1953–54; Jeff Douglas, *Brigadoon*, 1953–54; Jim, *Show Boat*, 1953–54; Monostatos, *Die Zauberflöte (The Magic Flute)*, 1953–54; Officer of the Border Guard, *Boris Godunov*, 1953–54; Og, *Finian's Rainbow*, 1953–54

Kahn, Rebecca: The Child, *L'Enfant et les Sortilèges (The Bewitched Child)*, 1984–85

Kaiser, Carl: Alfredo Germont, *La Traviata*, 1954–55; Faust, *Faust*, 1955–56

Kamara, Maria: Dewman, *Hänsel und Gretel*, 1995–96

Kampman, Thomas: A vendor of songs, *Il Tabarro (The Cloak)*, 1955–56; Amos, *The Land Between the Rivers*, 1955–56; Don Basilio, *Le Nozze di Figaro (The Marriage of Figaro)*, 1955–56; Don Curzio, *Le Nozze di Figaro (The Marriage of Figaro)*, 1955–56; The Frog, *L'Enfant et les Sortilèges (The Bewitched Child)*, 1955–56; Tinca, *Il Tabarro (The Cloak)*, 1955–56; Bardolph, *Falstaff*, 1956–57; Page, *Parsifal*, 1956–57; Remendado, *Carmen*, 1956–57

Kanne, Karen: Guitarist, *Man of La Mancha*, 1985–86

Kanowsky, Carl: Orson, *Too Many Sopranos*, 2006–07; William Williamson, *A Wedding*, 2007–08

Kanter, Lori: Ellen, *Oklahoma!*, 1981–82; Ida, *Die Fledermaus (The Bat)*, 1982–83; Meg, *The Ballad of Baby Doe*, 1982–83; Sister Osmina, *Il Trittico (A Triptych)*, 1982–83; Attendant to Cunegonde, *Candide*, 1983–84

Karlsond, Harriet: Susanna, *Le Nozze di Figaro (The Marriage of Figaro)*, 1968–69

Kass, Caron: The Chinese Cup, *L'Enfant et les Sortilèges (The Bewitched Child)*, 1984–85; Maria / The Innkeeper's Wife, *Man of La Mancha*, 1985–86

Kaufmann, Evelyn: Vivienne, *Oklahoma!*, 1954–55; Siebel, *Faust*, 1955–56; The Child, *L'Enfant et les Sortilèges (The Bewitched Child)*, 1955–56; Hansel, *Hänsel und Gretel*, 1956–57; Floria Tosca, *Tosca*, 1957–58; Lady Billows, *Albert Herring*, 1957–58; Mimi, *La Bohème*, 1957–58; Amelia, *Un Ballo in Maschera (A Masked Ball)*, 1958–59; Cio-Cio San, *Madama Butterfly*, 1958–59; Donna Elvira, *Don Giovanni*, 1958–59

Kazerouni, Joe: Jigger Craigin, *Carousel*, 1952–53; Novotny, *Blossom Time*, 1952–53

Kebl, Ellen: Mrs. Yellow Foot, *Annie Get Your Gun*, 1956–57

Keenan, John: Max, *The Most Happy Fella*, 1982–83

Keeton, Seth: Alidoro, *La Cenerentola (Cinderella)*, 1998–99; Colline, *La Bohème*, 1999–2000; Doctor Spinelloccio, *Gianni Schicchi*, 1999–2000; Trulove, *The Rake's Progress*, 1999–2000; Don Alfonso, *Così fan tutte*, 2000–01; Dr. Bartolo, *Le Nozze di Figaro (The Marriage of Figaro)*, 2001–02; Kezal, *The Bartered Bride*, 2001–02

Kehrer, David: The Doctor, *Vanessa*, 1974–75

Keith, Rebecca: Esmeralda, *The Bartered Bride*, 1994–95; Yniold, *Pelléas et Mélisande*, 1994–95

Kelder, Sarah: Nurse of the Children, *Boris Godunov*, 1983–84

Kelle, Elizabeth: Countess Ceprano, *Rigoletto*, 1950–51; Blonde, *Die Entführung aus dem Serail (The Abduction from the Seraglio)*, 1951–52; Claire, *On the Town*, 1951–52

Kelleher, Michael: Captain of the Inquisition, *Man of La Mancha*, 1988–89; Slave, *Die Zauberflöte (The Magic Flute)*, 1988–89; Chief Policeman, *Kismet*,

1989–90; Pratt, *1600 Pennsylvania Avenue*, 1992–93; Virginia Delegate, *1600 Pennsylvania Avenue*, 1992–93

Keller, Frederick: Micha, *The Bartered Bride*, 1979–80; Patriarcheas, *The Greek Passion*, 1980–81

Keller, Grace: Penny, *Carousel*, 1993–94; Guadalena, *La Périchole*, 1995–96; Papagena, *Die Zauberflöte (The Magic Flute)*, 1994–95

Keller, Rod: Pirate, *Candide*, 1993–94

Kelley, Erin: Dewman, *Hänsel und Gretel*, 2001–02; Player, *Putting It Together*, 2002–03; Zerlina, *Don Giovanni*, 2002–03; Elizabeth "Baby" Doe, *The Ballad of Baby Doe*, 2003–04; Lily Craven, *The Secret Garden*, 2003–04

Kellner, Herbert: Doctor Spinelloccio, *Il Trittico (A Triptych)*, 1972–73; Monostatos, *Die Zauberflöte (The Magic Flute)*, 1972–73; Motel, the Tailor, *Fiddler on the Roof*, 1972–73; Page, *Parsifal*, 1972–73; Parpignol, *La Bohème*, 1974–75

Kelly, Carol: Countess Ceprano, *Rigoletto*, 1959–60; Olympia, *Les Contes d'Hoffmann (The Tales of Hoffmann)*, 1959–60; Yvette, *La Rondine (The Swallow)*, 1959–60

Kelsay, Janet: Yum-Yum, *The Mikado*, 1950–51

Kemp, Robert: Another Servant, *Dialogues des Carmélites*, 1986–87; Thierry, *Dialogues des Carmélites*, 1986–87

Kendall, Gary: Governor Harrison, *A Hoosier Tale*, 1966–67; Count des Grieux, *Manon*, 1967–68; Foquier-Tinville, *Andrea Chénier*, 1967–68; Knight, *Parsifal*, 1967–68; Corporal of Police, *The Boys from Syracuse*, 1968–69; Dr. Bartolo, *Le Nozze di Figaro (The Marriage of Figaro)*, 1968–69; Trulove, *The Rake's Progress*, 1968–69; Lycomedes, *Deidamia*, 1969–70; Macrobio, *Love on Trial (La Pietra del Paragone)*, 1969–70; Samuel, *Un Ballo in Maschera (A Masked Ball)*, 1969–70; Colline, *La Bohème*, 1970–71; Don Alfonso, *Così fan tutte*, 1970–71; Don Fernando, *Fidelio*, 1970–71; Geronte de Ravoir, *Manon Lescaut*, 1970–71; Raimondo Bidebent, *Lucia di Lammermoor*, 1970–71; Rocco, *Fidelio*, 1970–71; Commendatore, *Don Giovanni*, 1971–72; Don Basilio, *Il Barbiere di Siviglia (The Barber of Seville)*, 1971–72; Mephistopheles, *Faust*, 1971–72

Kendall, William: Arthur, *Camelot*, 1968–69; Corporal of Police, *The Boys from Syracuse*, 1968–69; Duke of Ephesus, *The Boys from Syracuse*, 1968–69; Amantio di Nicolao, *Il Trittico (A Triptych)*, 1969–70; Arthur, *Camelot*, 1969–70; Captain, *Carousel*, 1970–71; David Bascomb, *Carousel*, 1970–71; Heavenly Friend, *Carousel*, 1970–71

Kenne, Charles: An Officer, *Dialogues des Carmélites*, 1965–66

Kennedy, Richard: Buzz, *Finian's Rainbow*, 1969–70; Geologist, *Finian's Rainbow*, 1969–70; Doctor Seldon, *Carousel*, 1970–71; Starkeeper, *Carousel*, 1970–71; Tinca, *Il Trittico (A Triptych)*, 1972–73; Duke of Parma, *Doktor Faust*, 1974–75

Kent, Sara: Hata, *The Bartered Bride*, 1955–56

Kerr, Brian: Crebillon, *La Rondine (The Swallow)*, 1989–90; Peter, *Company*, 1990–91; Pritschitsch, *Die lustige Witwe (The Merry Widow)*, 1990–91; Delaware Delegate, *1600 Pennsylvania Avenue*, 1992–93

Kerr, Deborah: Helena, *A Midsummer Night's Dream*, 1961–62

Kerrigan, Lindsay: Sandman, *Hänsel und Gretel*, 2006–07; Page, *Rigoletto*, 2007–08

Kerstetter, Caryn: Dewman, *Hänsel und Gretel*, 2006–07; Gianetta, *L'Elisir d'amore (The Elixir of Love)*, 2007–08; Muse, *Les Contes d'Hoffmann (The Tales of Hoffmann)*, 2007–08; Nicklausse, *Les Contes d'Hoffmann (The Tales of Hoffmann)*, 2007–08

Kessler, Ashley: The McCourt family, *The Ballad of Baby Doe*, 2003–04

Keston, John: Don Carlos, *Don Carlos*, 1961–62; Don Alvaro, *La Forza del Destino (The Force of Destiny)*, 1962–63; Don Jose, *Carmen*, 1962–63; Knight, *Parsifal*, 1962–63; Minstrel, *The Darkened City*, 1962–63; Richard Dauntless, *Ruddigore (The Witch's Curse)*, 1962–63

Ketcham, David: Benvolio, *Roméo et Juliette*, 1966–67; Page, *Parsifal*, 1966–67

Ketelsen, Kyle: Coppelius, *Les Contes d'Hoffmann (The Tales of Hoffmann)*, 1995–96; Dappertutto, *Les Contes d'Hoffmann (The Tales of Hoffmann)*, 1995–96; Dr. Miracle, *Les Contes d'Hoffmann (The Tales of Hoffmann)*, 1995–96; Don Giovanni, *Don Giovanni*, 1996–97; Selim, *Il Turco in Italia (The Turk in Italy)*, 1996–97; Figaro, *Le Nozze di Figaro (The Marriage of Figaro)*, 1997–98; Prince Gremin, *Eugene Onegin*, 1997–98; Don Magnifico, *La Cenerentola (Cinderella)*, 1998–99; Fred Graham, *Kiss Me, Kate*, 1998–99; Petruchio, *Kiss Me, Kate*, 1998–99

Kieffer, Deborah: Charlotte, *Werther*, 1961–62; Hermia, *A Midsummer Night's Dream*, 1961–62

Kiel, Don: Sheriff, *Finian's Rainbow*, 1953–54; Lonigan, *Wonderful Town*, 1954–55

Kiesgen, Meredith: Victoria, *A Wedding*, 2007–08

Kilgallin, Fred: Arturo Bucklaw, *Lucia di Lammermoor*, 1993–94

Kim, Hansu: Graf Elemer, *Arabella*, 1998–99; Andres, *Wozzeck*, 1999–2000; Baron Thunder-Ten-Tronck, *Candide*, 2000–01; Goro, *Madama Butterfly*, 2001–02; Normanno, *Lucia di Lammermoor*, 2001–02

Kim, Jungwoo: Speaker of the Temple, *Die Zauberflöte (The Magic Flute)*, 2004–05

Kim, You-Seong: Ilia, *Idomeneo,* 1998–99; Suor Genovieffa, *Suor Angelica (Sister Angelica),* 1999–2000

Kincade, Claire: Little Old Lady, *On the Town,* 1951–52

Kincaid, Elizabeth: The Baroness, *Candide,* 2000–01; Alisa, *Lucia di Lammermoor,* 2001–02; Rosette, *Manon,* 2001–02; Flora Bervoix, *La Traviata,* 2002–03; Alice Shaw, *The Secret Garden,* 2003–04

King, Darryl: The Imperial Commissioner, *Madama Butterfly,* 1996–97

King, James: Otello, *Otello,* 1989–90

King, Jasper: Amfortas, *Parsifal,* 1958–59; Don Giovanni, *Don Giovanni,* 1958–59; John Kent, *Roberta,* 1958–59; Master Ford (Herr Fluth), *Die lustigen Weiber von Windsor (The Merry Wives of Windsor),* 1958–59; Silvano, *Un Ballo in Maschera (A Masked Ball),* 1958–59; The Count, *Capriccio,* 1958–59; Amfortas, *Parsifal,* 1959–60; Count Monterone, *Rigoletto,* 1959–60; Dr. Miracle, *Les Contes d'Hoffmann (The Tales of Hoffmann),* 1959–60; Lescaut, *Manon Lescaut,* 1959–60; Deputy, *Don Carlos,* 1960–61; Klingsor, *Parsifal,* 1960–61; Man in Armor, *Die Zauberflöte (The Magic Flute),* 1960–61; Priest, *Die Zauberflöte (The Magic Flute),* 1960–61; Worshipful Master Bellingham, *The Scarlet Letter,* 1960–61

King, Jeremy: Second Cockney, *My Fair Lady,* 1979–80; Conductor, *The Music Man,* 1980–81

King, Joslyn: Caliban, *The Tempest,* 1985–86; Mary, *Der Fliegende Holländer (The Flying Dutchman),* 1985–86; Baba the Turk, *The Rake's Progress,* 1986–87; The Old Prioress, *Dialogues des Carmélites,* 1986–87; Gambling Lady, *Candide,* 1987–88; The Baroness, *Candide,* 1987–88; Ursula, *Béatrice et Bénédict,* 1987–88

King, Keith: Angelo, *The Boys from Syracuse,* 1968–69

King, Marilyn: Mrs. Anna Maurant, *Street Scene,* 1960–61; Princess Eboli, *Don Carlos,* 1960–61; Second Lady, *Die Zauberflöte (The Magic Flute),* 1960–61

King, Roy: Mario Cavaradossi, *Tosca,* 1969–70; Don Carlos, *Don Carlos,* 1972–73; Man in Armor, *Die Zauberflöte (The Magic Flute),* 1972–73; Matteo, *Arabella,* 1972–73; Rabbi, *Fiddler on the Roof,* 1972–73

King, Thomas: Chaplitsky, *La Pique Dame (The Queen of Spades),* 1968–69; An Officer, *Ariadne auf Naxos,* 1969–70

Kingery, Larry: Jimmie Curry, *110 in the Shade,* 1967–68; Jimmie Curry, *110 in the Shade,* 1968–69; Mordred, *Camelot,* 1968–69; Mordred, *Camelot,* 1969–70; Og, *Finian's Rainbow,* 1969–70

Kingsley, Edward: A Night Watchman, *Die Meistersinger von Nürnberg (The Mastersingers of Nuremberg),* 1961–62

Kinsey, Barbara: Elizabeth of Valois, *Don Carlos,* 1960–61; Hester Prynne, *The Scarlet Letter,* 1960–61; Mrs. Anna Maurant, *Street Scene,* 1960–61; Elizabeth of Valois, *Don Carlos,* 1961–62; Helena, *A Midsummer Night's Dream,* 1961–62; Hester Prynne, *The Scarlet Letter,* 1961–62

Kinzler, Marjorie: Clo-clo, *Die lustige Witwe (The Merry Widow),* 1965–66

Kirardi, Susan: Tenth Woman of Paris, *Danton and Robespierre,* 1977–78

Kiser, Betsy: Mrs. McLean, *Susannah,* 1976–77; Mrs. Meg Page, *Falstaff,* 1976–77; Nettie Fowler, *Carousel,* 1976–77; Mary, *Der Fliegende Holländer (The Flying Dutchman),* 1978–79

Kiser, Elizabeth: Dinah, *Trouble in Tahiti,* 1976–77; Pilgrim Mother, *Candide,* 1976–77; Player, *Bernstein on Broadway,* 1976–77; Carmen, *Carmen,* 1977–78; Gabrielle Danton, *Danton and Robespierre,* 1977–78; Dorabella, *Così fan tutte,* 1978–79; Muse, *Les Contes d'Hoffmann (The Tales of Hoffmann),* 1978–79; Nicklausse, *Les Contes d'Hoffmann (The Tales of Hoffmann),* 1978–79

Kleffer, Deborah: Flora Bervoix, *La Traviata,* 1960–61

Klein, Adam: Antonio, *The Tempest,* 1985–86; Erik, *Der Fliegende Holländer (The Flying Dutchman),* 1985–86; Old Grandfather, *The Legend of Tsar Saltan,* 1986–87; Judge Danforth, *The Crucible,* 1987–88; Peter Grimes, *Peter Grimes,* 1987–88

Kline, Kevin: File, *110 in the Shade,* 1967–68

Klink, David: Bartender, *A Wedding,* 2007–08

Klink, Matthias: Prince Tamino, *Die Zauberflöte (The Magic Flute),* 1994–95

Kloppenburg, Joseph "Bill": Alcindoro, *La Bohème,* 2007–08; Benoit, *La Bohème,* 2007–08; Elder McLean, *Susannah,* 2007–08

Kluck, Lisa: Sally, *Die Fledermaus (The Bat),* 1996–97

Kluegel, Elizabeth: Baccho (Bacchus), *L'Orfeo,* 1987–88; Fredrika Armfeldt, *A Little Night Music,* 1988–89; Olympia, *Les Contes d'Hoffmann (The Tales of Hoffmann),* 1988–89; Adina, *L'Elisir d'amore (The Elixir of Love),* 1990–91; Nanetta, *Falstaff,* 1992–93

Knaub, Richard: Khadja, *Die lustige Witwe (The Merry Widow),* 1949–50

Kness, Austin: Eddie, *A View from the Bridge,* 2004–05; Escamillo, *Carmen,* 2005–06; Don Giovanni, *Don Giovanni,* 2006–07; Unnamed Bass, *Too Many Sopranos,* 2006–07; Count Almaviva, *Le Nozze di Figaro (The Marriage of Figaro),* 2007–08

Kness, Karen: Queen of the Night, *Die Zauberflöte (The Magic Flute),* 2004–05; Miss Titmouse, *Too Many Sopranos,* 2006–07

Knight, Donald: First Commissioner, *Dialogues des Carmélites,* 1965–66; Malcolm, *Macbeth,* 1965–66; Guardsman, *Manon,* 1967–68

Knight, Robert: Jailer, *Tosca,* 1977–78; Soldier, *Danton and Robespierre,* 1977–78; King Arthur, *Canterbury Tales,* 1978–79; Pluto, *Canterbury Tales,* 1978–79

Knoll, David: John, *Peter Grimes,* 1963–64; Gherardino, *Gianni Schicchi,* 1964–65; Fleance, *Macbeth,* 1965–66; Kitchen Boy, *Der Rosenkavalier,* 1965–66; Harry, *Albert Herring,* 1966–67

Knoll, Eric: Trouble, *Madama Butterfly,* 1964–65

Knoll, Richard: Dick Johnson, *La Fanciulla del West (The Girl of the Golden West),* 1963–64; Peter Grimes, *Peter Grimes,* 1963–64; Radames, *Aida,* 1963–64; Gabriele Adorno, *Simon Boccanegra,* 1964–65; Lt. Pinkerton, *Madama Butterfly,* 1964–65; Parsifal, *Parsifal,* 1964–65; The Unknown Prince (Calaf), *Turandot,* 1964–65; Don Jose, *Carmen,* 1965–66; Italian Tenor, *Der Rosenkavalier,* 1965–66; Macduff, *Macbeth,* 1965–66; Prince Tamino, *Die Zauberflöte (The Magic Flute),* 1965–66; Canio, *I Pagliacci,* 1966–67; Parsifal, *Parsifal,* 1966–67; Andrea Chénier, *Andrea Chénier,* 1967–68; Faust, *Mefistofele,* 1967–68

Koesters, Johannes: Dr. Malatesta, *Don Pasquale,* 1980–81; Fotis, *The Greek Passion,* 1980–81

Kohalmy, Marika: Floria Tosca, *Tosca,* 1961–62; Donna Leonora, *La Forza del Destino (The Force of Destiny),* 1962–63; Micaëla, *Carmen,* 1962–63

Kohl, Amanda: Maid, *Manon,* 2006–07; Diana, *A Wedding,* 2007–08

Kohoutek, E. L.: Admiral DeJean, *The New Moon,* 1949–50; Fouchette, *The New Moon,* 1949–50; Intern, *Street Scene,* 1949–50; Jack Travers, *The Firefly,* 1949–50; Policeman, *Street Scene,* 1949–50

Kolbet, Jon: 3rd Muezzin, *Kismet,* 1989–90; Aegisthus, *The Cry of Clytaemnestra,* 1989–90; Bangle Man, *Kismet,* 1989–90; Imam, *Kismet,* 1989–90; Gabriel von Eisenstein, *Die Fledermaus (The Bat),* 1990–91; Belfiore, *La Finta Giardiniera,* 1990–91; Vicomte Camille di Rosillon, *Die lustige Witwe (The Merry Widow),* 1990–91; Tenor, *Carmina Burana,* 1991–92

Koontz, Elizabeth: Tytania, *A Midsummer Night's Dream,* 2005–06; Die Fiakermilli, *Arabella,* 2006–07; Pousette, *Manon,* 2006–07

Koopman, John: Geronte de Ravoir, *Manon Lescaut,* 1959–60; General Polkan, *Le Coq d'or (The Golden Cockerel),* 1960–61; Varlaam, *Boris Godunov,* 1966–67

Kopach, Diane: Flora, *The Turn of the Screw,* 1978–79

Korf, Geoffrey: Farfarello, *The Love for Three Oranges,* 1993–94

Korzec, Melissa: Player, *Putting It Together,* 2002–03; Claire Holmes, *The Secret Garden,* 2003–04

Kosacik, George: Master Page (Herr Reich), *Die lustigen Weiber von Windsor (The Merry Wives of Windsor),* 1958–59

Kowallis, Tod: Ferrando, *Così fan tutte,* 1984–85; Gabriel von Eisenstein, *Die Fledermaus (The Bat),* 1985–86; Tony, *West Side Story,* 1985–86; Tsaryevich Guidon, *The Legend of Tsar Saltan,* 1986–87; Benedick, *Béatrice et Bénédict,* 1987–88; Lt. Pinkerton, *Madama Butterfly,* 1987–88; Martin, *Candide,* 1987–88; Reverend Samuel Parris, *The Crucible,* 1987–88; The Governor of Cartagena, *Candide,* 1987–88; Faust, *Faust,* 1989–90; Paolo, *Francesca da Rimini,* 1989–90; Hoffmann, *Les Contes d'Hoffmann (The Tales of Hoffmann),* 1995–96; Lt. Pinkerton, *Madama Butterfly,* 1996–97; Alfredo Germont, *La Traviata,* 1997–98; Lensky, *Eugene Onegin,* 1997–98

Kowalski, Jane: Child's Mama, *L'Enfant et les Sortilèges (The Bewitched Child),* 1984–85; Mother Jeanne, *Dialogues des Carmélites,* 1986–87; Ann Putnam, *The Crucible,* 1987–88; The Baroness, *Candide,* 1987–88; Madame Vilmorac, *A Little Night Music,* 1988–89; Mrs. Segstrom, *A Little Night Music,* 1988–89; Bianca, *La Rondine (The Swallow),* 1989–90; Flora Bervoix, *La Traviata,* 1990–91; Giovanna, *Rigoletto,* 1992–93; Public Opinion, *Orphée aux enfers (Orpheus in the Underworld),* 1992–93

Kowalski, Linda: Ciesca, *Il Trittico (A Triptych),* 1972–73; Karolka, *Jenůfa,* 1972–73; Page, *Parsifal,* 1972–73; The Monitor of the Convent, *Il Trittico (A Triptych),* 1972–73; Indiana Elliott, *The Mother of Us All,* 1973–74; Muse, *Les Contes d'Hoffmann (The Tales of Hoffmann),* 1973–74; Nicklausse, *Les Contes d'Hoffmann (The Tales of Hoffmann),* 1973–74; Olga, *Eugene Onegin,* 1974–75; Erika, *Vanessa,* 1974–75

Kozacik, George: A Herald, *The Love for Three Oranges,* 1958–59; Second Tramp, *Die Kluge (The Clever Girl),* 1959–60

Kozar, John: Frank, *Brigadoon,* 1961–62

Kraabel, Amy: Velma, *West Side Story,* 1992–93; Venus, *Orphée aux enfers (Orpheus in the Underworld),* 1992–93; Paquette, *Candide,* 1993–94; Ensign Nellie Forbush, *South Pacific,* 1995–96

Kraeft, Kay: Annina, *La Traviata,* 1960–61

Kraft, Colleen: Venice Quartet 3, *Kiss Me, Kate,* 1998–99

Krajewska, Marian: Micaëla, *Carmen,* 1965–66; Octavian, *Der Rosenkavalier,* 1965–66

Krasovec, Kathryn: Valencienne, *Die lustige Witwe (The Merry Widow),* 1990–91; Angelina (Cinderella), *La Cenerentola (Cinderella),* 1991–92; Cherubino, *Le Nozze di Figaro (The Marriage of Figaro),* 1992–93

Kraus, Joseph: First Cockney, *My Fair Lady,* 1979–80

Krempp, Jeanne: Chava, *Fiddler on the Roof,* 1972–73; Anne Egerman, *A Little Night Music,* 1975–76; Kate, *The Ballad of Baby Doe,* 1975–76; Silver Dollar (grown up), *The Ballad of Baby Doe,* 1975–76

Kretchmar, Richard: Dr. Bartolo, *Le Nozze di Figaro (The Marriage of Figaro),* 1962–63; Frank, *Die Fledermaus (The Bat),* 1962–63; Zuniga, *Carmen,* 1962–63; Hobson, *Peter Grimes,* 1963–64; Jim Larkens, *La Fanciulla del West (The Girl of the Golden West),* 1963–64; The Wazir of Police, *Kismet,* 1963–64; Amantio di Nicolao, *Gianni Schicchi,* 1964–65; Guccio, *Gianni Schicchi,* 1964–65

Kreutz, Michael: Doc, *West Side Story,* 1985–86; Frosch, *Die Fledermaus (The Bat),* 1985–86; Figaro, *Le Nozze di Figaro (The Marriage of Figaro),* 1986–87; Micha, *The Bartered Bride,* 1986–87; Sir Sagramore, *Camelot,* 1986–87; Dr. Pangloss, *Candide,* 1987–88; Player, *Mass,* 1988–89

Krueger, George: Titurel, *Parsifal,* 1948–49; Gurnemanz, *Parsifal,* 1949–50; Gurnemanz, *Parsifal,* 1950–51; Gurnemanz, *Parsifal,* 1953–54; Pimen, *Boris Godunov,* 1953–54

Krueger, Kathryn: Woman, *Down in the Valley,* 1947–48; Nursemaid, *Street Scene,* 1949–50; Salvation Army Girl, *Street Scene,* 1949–50; Jane Ashton, *Brigadoon,* 1952–53; Jane Ashton, *Brigadoon,* 1953–54; Kundry, *Parsifal,* 1953–54; Third Lady, *Die Zauberflöte (The Magic Flute),* 1953–54

Krueger, Michael: Fafner, *Das Rheingold,* 1983–84; Customs Officer, *La Bohème,* 1984–85; Pete, *Show Boat,* 1984–85; Steve, *Show Boat,* 1984–85; Tempter, *Murder in the Cathedral,* 1984–85; The Armchair, *L'Enfant et les Sortilèges (The Bewitched Child),* 1984–85; Benedict, *The Tempest,* 1985–86; Leporello, *Don Giovanni,* 1985–86; Pedro / Head Muleteer, *Man of La Mancha,* 1985–86; Dr. Dulcamara, *L'Elisir d'amore (The Elixir of Love),* 1986–87; Kezal, *The Bartered Bride,* 1986–87; Reverend John Hale, *The Crucible,* 1987–88; Swallow, *Peter Grimes,* 1987–88; The Bonze, *Madama Butterfly,* 1987–88; The Grand Inquisitor, *Candide,* 1987–88; The Prefect of Police, *Candide,* 1987–88; Coppelius, *Les Contes d'Hoffmann (The Tales of Hoffmann),* 1988–89; Dappertutto, *Les Contes d'Hoffmann (The Tales of Hoffmann),* 1988–89; Don Pasquale, *Don Pasquale,* 1988–89; Dr. Miracle, *Les Contes d'Hoffmann (The Tales of Hoffmann),* 1988–89; Lindorf, *Les Contes d'Hoffmann (The Tales of Hoffmann),* 1988–89; Agamemnon, *The Cry of Clytaemnestra,* 1989–90; Iago, *Otello,* 1989–90; Giorgio Germont, *La Traviata,* 1990–91; Rigoletto, *Rigoletto,* 1992–93

Kruger, Mary: Siebel, *Faust,* 1989–90; Marie, *Wozzeck,* 1990–91; Rosalinda, *Die Fledermaus (The Bat),* 1990–91; Anne Trulove, *The Rake's Progress,* 1991–92; Cio-Cio San, *Madama Butterfly,* 1991–92; Donna Elvira, *Don Giovanni,* 1991–92

Krupski, Sharon: Sister Osmina, *Il Trittico (A Triptych),* 1969–70

Krygowski, Heather: Paquette, *Candide,* 2000–01

Kudriavchenko, Ekaterina: Francesca, *Francesca da Rimini,* 1989–90

Kuhar, Ursula Maria: Marcellina, *Le Nozze di Figaro (The Marriage of Figaro),* 2007–08; Mrs. Ott, *Susannah,* 2007–08

Kuhn, Timothy: De Bretigny, *Manon,* 2001–02; Don Giovanni, *Don Giovanni,* 2002–03

Kullman, Charles: Parsifal, *Parsifal,* 1956–57; Parsifal, *Parsifal,* 1958–59; Parsifal, *Parsifal,* 1960–61; Parsifal, *Parsifal,* 1962–63; Parsifal, *Parsifal,* 1963–64

Kutner, Michael: Washington Dandy, *The Ballad of Baby Doe,* 1975–76

Lackey, Herndon: Croupier, *Candide,* 1976–77; Dr. Pangloss, *Candide,* 1976–77; Player, *Bernstein on Broadway,* 1976–77; Prince Ivan, *Candide,* 1976–77; Sam, *Trouble in Tahiti,* 1976–77; Dancaire, *Carmen,* 1977–78; Papageno, *Die Zauberflöte (The Magic Flute),* 1977–78; Priest, *The Darkened City,* 1978–79

Lacombe, Manuel: Strawberry Man, *Street Scene,* 1949–50

LaCosse, Steven: Dante, *Francesca da Rimini,* 1989–90; Paul, *Company,* 1990–91; Giuseppe, *La Traviata,* 1990–91; The Captain, *Wozzeck,* 1990–91; Goro, *Madama Butterfly,* 1991–92; Sellem, *The Rake's Progress,* 1991–92; The King, *Jubilee,* 1991–92; Admiral Cockburn, *1600 Pennsylvania Avenue,* 1992–93; Auctioneer, *1600 Pennsylvania Avenue,* 1992–93; Chief Justice of the Supreme Court, *1600 Pennsylvania Avenue,* 1992–93; De Laubardemont, *Die Teufel von Loudun (The Devils of Loudun),* 1992–93; Dr. Caius, *Falstaff,* 1992–93; Krupke, *West Side Story,* 1992–93; Rhode Island Delegate, *1600 Pennsylvania Avenue,* 1992–93; Secretary of Senate, *1600 Pennsylvania Avenue,* 1992–93; Guillot de Morfontaine, *Manon,* 1993–94; Spoletta, *Tosca,* 1993–94; Truffaldino, *The Love for Three Oranges,* 1993–94; Vashek, *The Bartered Bride,* 1994–95

Lacy, Lee: First Sharecropper, *Finian's Rainbow,* 1953–54; Frank, *Show Boat,* 1953–54; Howard, *Finian's Rainbow,* 1953–54; Jack Chesney, *Where's Charley?,* 1953–54

Lacy, Stan: Clerk at the Clarendon Hotel, *The Ballad of Baby Doe,* 2003–04; Doorman at the Tabor Grand Theatre, *The Ballad of Baby Doe,* 2003–04; Father Chapelle, *The Ballad of Baby Doe,* 2003–04; First Commissioner, *Dialogues des Carmélites,* 2004–05

LaFleur, Lisa: Angelina (Cinderella), *La Cenerentola (Cinderella),* 2004–05; Carmen, *Carmen,* 2005–06; Hippolyta, *A Midsummer Night's Dream,* 2005–06

LaFuze, Thomas: Tailor, *The Boys from Syracuse,* 1968–69

Lamb, David: Chalmers, *Oklahoma!,* 1981–82; Doctor, *Of Thee I Sing,* 1987–88; Senate Clerk, *Of Thee I Sing,* 1987–88; First Beggar, *Kismet,* 1989–90; Pearl Merchant, *Kismet,* 1989–90

Lambard, Alison: Spirit, *Die Zauberflöte (The Magic Flute),* 1982–83

Lambert, Jane: Woman, *The Darkened City,* 1962–63

Lamble, Walter: An Officer, *Dialogues des Carmélites,* 1965–66; Leopold, *Der Rosenkavalier,* 1965–66; Sorcerer, *The Boys from Syracuse,* 1968–69

Lancaster, Thomas: Page, *Parsifal,* 1959–60; Pittichinaccio, *Les Contes d'Hoffmann (The Tales of Hoffmann),* 1959–60

Lance, Sally: Gianetta, *L'Elisir d'amore (The Elixir of Love),* 1961–62; Mustardseed, *A Midsummer Night's Dream,* 1961–62; Susanna, *Le Nozze di Figaro (The Marriage of Figaro),* 1962–63; Serafina, *Il Campanello di Notte (The Night Bell),* 1963–64

Landoe, Signe: Inez, *Il Trovatore,* 1967–68; Nella, *Il Trittico (A Triptych),* 1969–70; Nerea, *Deidamia,* 1969–70; Sister Dolcina, *Il Trittico (A Triptych),* 1969–70; The Composer, *Ariadne auf Naxos,* 1969–70; Musetta, *La Bohème,* 1970–71; Helmwige, *Die Walküre,* 1971–72; Mrs. Alice Ford, *Falstaff,* 1971–72

Lane, Beverly: Pearl, *The Scarlet Letter,* 1960–61

Lane, Charles: Peter, *Porgy and Bess,* 1976–77

Lane, Louise: Mrs. Squires, *The Music Man,* 1980–81

Lane, Susan: Laurey, *Oklahoma!,* 1981–82; Nella, *Il Trittico (A Triptych),* 1982–83

Lang, Kathryn: Princess Clarissa, *The Love for Three Oranges,* 1993–94; Hodel, *Fiddler on the Roof,* 1994–95; Melisande, *Pelléas et Mélisande,* 1994–95; Rosina, *Il Barbiere di Siviglia (The Barber of Seville),* 1994–95; Dorabella, *Così fan tutte,* 1995–96; Hansel, *Hänsel und Gretel,* 1995–96; The Composer, *Ariadne auf Naxos,* 1996–97; Angelina (Cinderella), *La Cenerentola (Cinderella),* 1998–99; Lucretia, *The Rape of Lucretia,* 1999–2000

Lang, Michael: Miles, *The Turn of the Screw,* 1978–79

Langan, David: Doctor Grenville, *La Traviata,* 1983–84; Nikitich, *Boris Godunov,* 1983–84; Officer of the Border Guard, *Boris Godunov,* 1983–84; Snug, *A Midsummer Night's Dream,* 1983–84; Colline, *La Bohème,* 1984–85; Don Alfonso, *Così fan tutte,* 1984–85; Commendatore, *Don Giovanni,* 1985–86; Count Rodolfo, *La Sonnambula (The Sleepwalker),* 1985–86; Gonzalo, *The Tempest,* 1985–86

Langan, Kevin: Count Carl-Magnus Malcolm, *A Little Night Music,* 1975–76; Kreonte, *The Love for Three Oranges,* 1975–76; The Imperial Commissioner, *Madama Butterfly,* 1975–76; Titurel, *Parsifal,* 1975–76; William Jennings Bryan, *The Ballad of Baby Doe,* 1975–76; Pistol, *Falstaff,* 1976–77; The Imperial Commissioner, *Madama Butterfly,* 1976–77; Cesare Angelotti, *Tosca,* 1977–78; Chub Korny, *The Night Before Christmas,* 1977–78; Don Alfonso, *Così fan tutte,* 1977–78; Sarastro, *Die Zauberflöte (The Magic Flute),* 1977–78; St. Just, *Danton and Robespierre,* 1977–78; Crespel, *Les Contes d'Hoffmann (The Tales of Hoffmann),* 1978–79; Daland, *Der Fliegende Holländer (The Flying Dutchman),* 1978–79; Don Alfonso, *Così fan tutte,* 1978–79; Mayor, *The Darkened City,* 1978–79; Pimen, *Boris Godunov,* 1978–79; Ajax, *The Cry of Clytaemnestra,* 1979–80; Commendatore, *Don Giovanni,* 1979–80

Langham, Edward: Albert, *The Ballad of Baby Doe,* 1975–76; Newsboy, *The Ballad of Baby Doe,* 1975–76; Freddy Eynsford-Hill, *My Fair Lady,* 1979–80

Langkamer, Andrea: Blessed Spirit, *Orfeo ed Euridice,* 1992–93

Langton, Sunny: Blonde, *Die Entführung aus dem Serail (The Abduction from the Seraglio),* 1974–75; Sophie, *Werther,* 1975–76

Lantz, Daniel: Mayor Shinn, *The Music Man,* 1980–81; Andrew Carnes, *Oklahoma!,* 1981–82

Large, John: Klingsor, *Parsifal,* 1959–60; Lindorf, *Les Contes d'Hoffmann (The Tales of Hoffmann),* 1959–60; Marullo, *Rigoletto,* 1959–60; Ramiro, *L'Heure espagnole (The Spanish Hour),* 1959–60; The King, *Die Kluge (The Clever Girl),* 1959–60; Deputy, *Don Carlos,* 1960–61; Mr. Frank Maurant, *Street Scene,* 1960–61; Papageno, *Die Zauberflöte (The Magic Flute),* 1960–61; The Beadle (and Jailer), *The Scarlet Letter,* 1960–61; Albert, *Werther,* 1961–62; Tommy Albright, *Brigadoon,* 1961–62

Larkins, Karen: Pantalis, *Mefistofele,* 1967–68

Larson, Cynthia: The Housekeeper for Alonso, *Man of La Mancha,* 1988–89

Larson, Juliana: Lucinda, *The Veil,* 1949–50; Mimi, *La Bohème,* 1949–50

Larson, Sue: Parassja, *The Fair at Sorochinsk,* 1963–64

LaRue, Margie: Maggie Anderson, *Brigadoon,* 1952–53; Rosi, *Blossom Time,* 1952–53

Lasher, John: Fiorello, *Il Barbiere di Siviglia (The Barber of Seville),* 1971–72

Lathrop, Arthur: Baron Thunder-Ten-Tronck, *Candide,* 2000–01; Elder Hayes, *Susannah,* 2000–01; Herr Zeller, *The Sound of Music,* 2000–01; Doc, *West Side Story,* 2002–03

Latta, Matthew: Flute, *A Midsummer Night's Dream,* 2005–06; Don Ottavio, *Don Giovanni,* 2006–07; Elder Gleaton, *Susannah,* 2007–08

Lau, Matthew: Benoit, *La Bohème,* 1979–80; Freddy Eynsford-Hill, *My Fair Lady,* 1979–80; Leporello, *Don Giovanni,* 1979–80; Lescaut, *Manon,* 1979–80; Figaro, *Le Nozze di Figaro (The Marriage of Figaro),* 1980–81

Lauer, Brian: Kurt, *The Sound of Music,* 2000–01

Lavengood, Patricia: Page, *Parsifal,* 1957–58; Donna Elvira, *Don Giovanni,* 1958–59

Laves, Ruth: Topsy, *The King and I,* 1957–58

Lawless, John: Snowboy, *West Side Story,* 1985–86

Lawrence, Barry: Gianni Schicchi, *Gianni Schicchi,* 1988–89

Lawson, Matthew: John, *Passion Play—Carmina Burana,* 1982–83

Lawyer, Harriet: Barbarina, *Le Nozze di Figaro (The Marriage of Figaro),* 1955–56; The Princess in the Storybook, *L'Enfant et les Sortilèges (The Bewitched Child),* 1955–56; Golde, *Fiddler on the Roof,* 1972–73

Layng, Judy: Cobweb, *A Midsummer Night's Dream,* 1961–62; Fiona MacLaren, *Brigadoon,* 1961–62; Sophie, *Werther,* 1961–62; Rose Maybud, *Ruddigore (The Witch's Curse),* 1962–63; Olga, *Die lustige Witwe (The Merry Widow),* 1964–65; Page, *Parsifal,* 1964–65; Ruzia, *Boris Godunov,* 1964–65; Olga, *Die lustige Witwe (The Merry Widow),* 1965–66; Ruzia, *Boris Godunov,* 1966–67

Lazarus, Roy: Gurnemanz, *Parsifal,* 1965–66; Sarastro, *Die Zauberflöte (The Magic Flute),* 1965–66

Lazich, Milton: Pinellino, *Gianni Schicchi,* 1964–65; Doctor, *Macbeth,* 1965–66; Man in Armor, *Die Zauberflöte (The Magic Flute),* 1965–66; Count Ceprano, *Rigoletto,* 1966–67; Old Chief Tetepachsit, *A Hoosier Tale,* 1966–67; Mathieu, *Andrea Chénier,* 1967–68; Micha, *The Bartered Bride,* 1967–68; Schmidt, *Andrea Chénier,* 1967–68; Hans Schwarz, *Die Meistersinger von Nürnberg (The Mastersingers of Nuremberg),* 1968–69; Marco, *Il Trittico (A Triptych),* 1969–70; Talpa, *Il Trittico (A Triptych),* 1969–70

Leach, Dennis: Coroner, *Porgy and Bess,* 1979–80; De Bretigny, *Manon,* 1979–80; Elder Ott, *Susannah,* 1979–80; Schaunard, *La Bohème,* 1979–80

Leadbetter, Sheila: Filipyevna, *Eugene Onegin,* 1988–89

Lease, Gus: Principal, *Carousel,* 1952–53; Schubert, *Blossom Time,* 1952–53

Lebherz, Louis: Daniel Webster, *The Mother of Us All,* 1973–74; Dr. Bartolo, *Le Nozze di Figaro (The Marriage of Figaro),* 1973–74; Second Apprentice, *Wozzeck,* 1973–74

Ledbetter, Victor: Guglielmo, *Così fan tutte,* 1984–85; Knight, *Murder in the Cathedral,* 1984–85; Don Giovanni, *Don Giovanni,* 1985–86; Miguel de Cervantes / Don Quixote, *Man of La Mancha,* 1985–86; John Proctor, *The Crucible,* 1987–88

Lee, Harry: First Priest of the Temple, *Die Zauberflöte (The Magic Flute),* 1994–95

Lee, Jack: Valentin, *Faust,* 1955–56

Lee, John: Cesare Angelotti, *Tosca,* 1957–58; Notary, *Don Pasquale,* 1977–78

Lee, Michael: Leon, *The Ghosts of Versailles,* 1996–97; Bardolph, *Falstaff,* 1997–98; Gastone, *La Traviata,* 1997–98; Idamante, *Idomeneo,* 1998–99; Prince Tamino, *Die Zauberflöte (The Magic Flute),* 1998–99; Male Chorus, *The Rape of Lucretia,* 1999–2000; The Captain, *Wozzeck,* 1999–2000

Lee, Neal: Alchemist, *Candide,* 1957–58; Knight, *Parsifal,* 1957–58

Lee, Rosalind: Player, *Mass,* 1998–99

Lee, Sang-Hyuk: The Teapot, *L'Enfant et les Sortilèges (The Bewitched Child),* 1984–85; Don Ottavio, *Don Giovanni,* 1985–86; Elvino, *La Sonnambula (The Sleepwalker),* 1985–86; Apollo, *L'Orfeo,* 1987–88; Ernesto, *Don Pasquale,* 1988–89

Lee, Sangwon: Echo, *Ariadne auf Naxos,* 1996–97

Lee, Teresa: Attendant to Cunegonde, *Candide,* 1983–84; Gambling Lady, *Candide,* 1983–84; Prospective Slave, *Candide,* 1983–84

Lee, Young Ju: Marquis D'Obigny, *La Traviata,* 2002–03; Pistol, *Falstaff,* 2003–04; Selim, *Il Turco in Italia (The Turk in Italy),* 2003–04; Prince Gremin, *Eugene Onegin,* 2004–05; Don Basilio, *Il Barbiere di Siviglia (The Barber of Seville),* 2005–06; Friar Laurence, *Roméo et Juliette,* 2005–06

Lee Aiken, Dava: Joan, *Street Scene,* 1949–50

Leemhuis, Kathryn: Dorabella, *Così fan tutte,* 2005–06; Hansel, *Hänsel und Gretel,* 2006–07; Tulip, *A Wedding,* 2007–08

Legaspi, Joseph: Second Commissioner, *Dialogues des Carmélites,* 2004–05; Innkeeper, *Manon,* 2006–07; Prince Yamadori, *Madama Butterfly,* 2006–07; Luther, *Les Contes d'Hoffmann (The Tales of Hoffmann),* 2007–08

Leggett, Paula: Gertie Cummings, *Oklahoma!,* 1981–82; Mrs. Lovett, *Sweeney Todd,* 1983–84; Julie, *Show Boat,* 1984–85

Lehman, Gary: Endimione, *L'Orfeo,* 1987–88; Judge of the Inquisition, *Candide,* 1987–88; Dr. Malatesta, *Don Pasquale,* 1988–89; Eugene Onegin, *Eugene Onegin,* 1988–89; Figaro, *Il Barbiere di Siviglia (The Barber of Seville),* 1988–89

Leibovich, Haggar: Queen of the Night, *Die Zauberflöte (The Magic Flute),* 2004–05

Lein, Melinda: Lauretta, *Gianni Schicchi,* 1993–94

Leithauser, Elise: Sullita, *West Side Story,* 1992–93

Lenhart, Tristan: The Child, *Wozzeck,* 1990–91; Ford's Page, *Falstaff,* 1992–93

Lentz, Daniel: Antonio, *Le Nozze di Figaro (The Marriage of Figaro),* 2007–08

Lentz, Karen: Nettie Fowler, *Carousel,* 1952–53; Spirit, *Die Zauberflöte (The Magic Flute),* 1953–54; Page, *Parsifal,* 1954–55; Page, *Parsifal,* 1955–56

Leonard, Virginia: The Girl, *The Fantasticks,* 1963–64; Sylviane, *Die lustige Witwe (The Merry Widow),* 1964–65

Leste, Julia: Shepherd Figure in the Wallpaper, *L'Enfant et les Sortilèges (The Bewitched Child),* 1984–85; Antonia / Alonso's Niece, *Man of La Mancha,* 1985–86

Lett, Jean: Nita, *Lost in the Stars,* 1950–51

Levar, Frank: Antonio, *Le Nozze di Figaro (The Marriage of Figaro),* 1980–81; Cloudy, *The Excursions of Mr. Broucek,* 1981–82

Levenburg, Iris: Flossie's pal, *On the Town,* 1951–52

L'Eveque, Celeste: Hata, *The Bartered Bride,* 1967–68

Leverenz, Andrew: Rev. Horace Adams, *Peter Grimes,* 1987–88

Levitt, Joseph: Page, *Parsifal,* 1975–76; Washington Dandy, *The Ballad of Baby Doe,* 1975–76; Bardolph, *Falstaff,* 1976–77; Remendado, *Carmen,* 1977–78; Spoletta, *Tosca,* 1977–78; Calchas, *The Cry of Clytaemnestra,* 1979–80; Little Bat McLean, *Susannah,* 1979–80; Truffaldino, *The Love for Three Oranges,* 1980–81; Yannakos, *The Greek Passion,* 1980–81; Kaufmann, *Jakob Lenz,* 1981–82; Mr. Matej Broucek, *The Excursions of Mr. Broucek,* 1981–82; Chester A. Arthur, *The Ballad of Baby Doe,* 1982–83; Sam, *The Ballad of Baby Doe,* 1982–83

Levitt, Marina: Marenka, *The Bartered Bride,* 1986–87

Levy, Henry: Konrad Nachtigall, *Die Meistersinger von Nürnberg (The Mastersingers of Nuremberg),* 1968–69

Levy, Offer: Count Ceprano, *Rigoletto,* 1986–87; Trulove, *The Rake's Progress,* 1986–87; Augure, *L'Orfeo,* 1987–88

Lewis, Fiona: Minerva, *Orphée aux enfers (Orpheus in the Underworld),* 1998–99; Queen of the Night, *Die Zauberflöte (The Magic Flute),* 1998–99

Lewis, James: Mr. Fletcher, *Wonderful Town,* 1954–55

Lewis, Richard: Frank, *Die Fledermaus (The Bat),* 1982–83; Marco, *Il Trittico (A Triptych),* 1982–83; Allworthy, *Tom Jones,* 1983–84; Baron Mirko Zeta, *Die lustige Witwe (The Merry Widow),* 1983–84; Marquis D'Obigny, *La Traviata,* 1983–84; Leo, *Tamerlano,* 1984–85

Lewis, Thomas: A Moravian, *A Hoosier Tale,* 1966–67

Leyrer, Linda: Nella, *Il Trittico (A Triptych),* 1982–83; Minerva, *Orphée aux enfers (Orpheus in the Underworld),* 1984–85; Lucia, *Lucia di Lammermoor,* 1993–94

Lickey, Harold: Pang, *Turandot,* 1964–65

Liddle, Ray: Marquis D'Obigny, *La Traviata,* 1978–79; The Boyar Khrushchev, *Boris Godunov,* 1978–79; Abbate Cospicuo, *Arlecchino,* 1979–80; Doctor Bartolo, *Il Barbiere di Siviglia (The Barber of Seville),* 1980–81; Don Pasquale, *Don Pasquale,* 1980–81; Dr. Bartolo, *Le Nozze di Figaro (The Marriage of Figaro),* 1980–81; Dr. Caius, *Die lustigen Weiber von Windsor (The Merry Wives of Windsor),* 1981–82; Jud Fry, *Oklahoma!,* 1981–82; Michele, *Il Trittico (A Triptych),* 1982–83; Tony, *The Most Happy Fella,* 1982–83; Sulpice, *La Fille du régiment (The Daughter of the Regiment),* 1984–85

Lidums, Skaidrite: Page, *Parsifal,* 1958–59

Lillethun, Joel: Motel, the Tailor, *Fiddler on the Roof,* 1972–73

Lim, Hongteak: Parpignol, *La Bohème,* 2007–08

Lindner, Elyssa: Bianca, *La Rondine (The Swallow),* 1959–60; Giulietta, *Les Contes d'Hoffmann (The Tales of Hoffmann),* 1959–60; An elegant lady, *The Scarlet Letter,* 1960–61; Countess of Eremberg, *Don Carlos,* 1960–61

Lindsay, Carmen: Mrs. Potter Potter, *Annie Get Your Gun,* 1956–57; Clorinda, *La Cenerentola (Cinderella),* 1957–58; Musetta, *La Bohème,* 1957–58; Amelia, *Un Ballo in Maschera (A Masked Ball),* 1958–59

Lindsay, Joshua: Matteo, *Arabella,* 2006–07; Hoffmann, *Les Contes d'Hoffmann (The Tales of Hoffmann),* 2007–08

Lindsey, Kate: Dolly, *Jeppe,* 2002–03; Mrs. Meg Page, *Falstaff,* 2003–04

Lipton, Martha: Amneris, *Aida,* 1963–64; Jocasta, *Oedipus Rex,* 1964–65; Magdalena, *Die Meistersinger von Nürnberg (The Mastersingers of Nuremberg),* 1968–69; Fricka, *Die Walküre,* 1969–70; The Princess, *Il Trittico (A Triptych),* 1969–70; Ulrica, *Un Ballo in Maschera (A Masked Ball),* 1969–70

Liscio, Paula: Amazon, *The Boys from Syracuse,* 1968–69; Pauline, *La Pique Dame (The Queen of Spades),* 1968–69

Lissek, Shira: Francisca, *West Side Story,* 1992–93; Shprintze, *Fiddler on the Roof,* 1994–95

Lister, Michael: Westphalian Soldier, *Candide,* 1993–94; Customs Officer, *La Bohème,* 1994–95; Yankel, the Grocer, *Fiddler on the Roof,* 1994–95

Little, David: Count Danilo Danilovitch, *Die lustige Witwe (The Merry Widow),* 1983–84; Donner, *Das Rheingold,* 1983–84; Jupiter, *Orphée aux enfers (Orpheus in the Underworld),* 1984–85; Ramiro, *L'Heure espagnole (The Spanish Hour),* 1984–85; Alonso, King of Naples, *The Tempest,* 1985–86; Dr. Falke, *Die Fledermaus (The Bat),* 1985–86; Rigoletto, *Rigoletto,* 1986–87

Livingston, Diana: Mrs. Anderssen, *A Little Night Music,* 1988–89; Nella, *Gianni Schicchi,* 1988–89; Electra, *The Cry of Clytaemnestra,* 1989–90; Gianetta, *L'Elisir d'amore (The Elixir of Love),* 1990–91; Serpetta, *La Finta Giardiniera,* 1990–91

Llewellyn, Susan: A Tourier, *Il Trittico (A Triptych),* 1972–73; Barena, *Jenůfa,* 1972–73

Lockard, Barbara: Mrs. Mullin, *Carousel,* 1952–53; Ellie, *Show Boat,* 1953–54; Sharon, *Finian's Rainbow,* 1953–54; Dryad, *Ariadne auf Naxos,* 1954–55; Kundry, *Parsifal,* 1955–56; Martha, *Faust,* 1955–56; Annie Oakley, *Annie*

Get Your Gun, 1956–57; Carmen, *Carmen,* 1956–57; Valencienne, *Die lustige Witwe (The Merry Widow),* 1965–66; Martha, *Mefistofele,* 1967–68; Nancy, *Albert Herring,* 1967–68; Baba the Turk, *The Rake's Progress,* 1968–69; Luce, *The Boys from Syracuse,* 1968–69; The Countess, *La Pique Dame (The Queen of Spades),* 1968–69; Marchesa Ortensia, *Love on Trial (La Pietra del Paragone),* 1969–70; Schwertleite, *Die Walküre,* 1969–70; The Princess, *Il Trittico (A Triptych),* 1969–70; Ulrica, *Un Ballo in Maschera (A Masked Ball),* 1969–70; Zita, *Il Trittico (A Triptych),* 1969–70; Nettie Fowler, *Carousel,* 1970–71; Mrs. Yepanchin, *Myshkin,* 1972–73; Madame Armfeldt, *A Little Night Music,* 1975–76

Lockhart, Howard: Marcello, *La Bohème,* 1949–50

Lockman, Jeffrey: Peter, *Hänsel und Gretel,* 1982–83; Servant, *The Ballad of Baby Doe,* 1982–83; Alberich, *Das Rheingold,* 1983–84; Dowling, *Tom Jones,* 1983–84; Messenger/Commissioner, *La Traviata,* 1983–84; A Tree, *L'Enfant et les Sortilèges (The Bewitched Child),* 1984–85; Alcindoro, *La Bohème,* 1984–85; Tempter, *Murder in the Cathedral,* 1984–85

Lockwood, Carolyn: Echo, *Ariadne auf Naxos,* 1954–55; Flora Bervoix, *La Traviata,* 1954–55

Lodge, Drusilla: Hannah, *Oklahoma!,* 1954–55; Cat, *L'Enfant et les Sortilèges (The Bewitched Child),* 1955–56; Despina, *Così fan tutte,* 1956–57; The Witch, *Hänsel und Gretel,* 1956–57; Clorinda, *La Cenerentola (Cinderella),* 1957–58; Floria Tosca, *Tosca,* 1957–58; Lady Billows, *Albert Herring,* 1957–58; Santuzza, *Cavalleria Rusticana,* 1957–58

Lofton, Lee: The Prince, *The Love for Three Oranges,* 1993–94; The Ringmaster, *The Bartered Bride,* 1994–95; Count Panatellas, *La Périchole,* 1995–96; Sheriff, *McTeague,* 1995–96; Lun Tha, *The King and I,* 1996–97; Scaramuccio, *Ariadne auf Naxos,* 1996–97

Logan, Brad: Second Man of Paris, *Danton and Robespierre,* 1977–78

LoMonaco, Jerome: Faust, *Faust,* 1971–72

Lonergan, Vincent: Gremio, *Kiss Me, Kate,* 1973–74; Remendado, *Carmen,* 1973–74; Spalanzani, *Les Contes d'Hoffmann (The Tales of Hoffmann),* 1973–74; Pedrillo, *Die Entführung aus dem Serail (The Abduction from the Seraglio),* 1974–75; Triquet, *Eugene Onegin,* 1974–75; Newsboy, *The Ballad of Baby Doe,* 1975–76; Goro, *Madama Butterfly,* 1976–77; Little Bat McLean, *Susannah,* 1976–77

Lonnberg, Charles: Mr. Lippo Fiorentino, *Street Scene,* 1960–61

Loomis, David: Alcindoro, *La Bohème,* 1957–58; Benoit, *La Bohème,* 1957–58

Loshkajian, Nancy: Frugola, *Il Trittico (A Triptych),* 1982–83; Praskovia, *Die lustige Witwe (The Merry Widow),* 1983–84; The Chinese Cup, *L'Enfant et les Sortilèges (The Bewitched Child),* 1984–85; The Marquise of Birkenfeld, *La Fille du régiment (The Daughter of the Regiment),* 1984–85; The Housekeeper for Alonso, *Man of La Mancha,* 1985–86; Hata, *The Bartered Bride,* 1986–87

Losure, Janie: Ado Annie Carnes, *Oklahoma!,* 1981–82

Louck, Steven: Fiorello, *Il Barbiere di Siviglia (The Barber of Seville),* 1956–57; Officer, *Il Barbiere di Siviglia (The Barber of Seville),* 1956–57; Prince Yamadori, *Madama Butterfly,* 1958–59

Loveland, Morgan: Fermina / A Servant Girl, *Man of La Mancha,* 1999–2000

Lover, Sandra: Kate Pinkerton, *Madama Butterfly,* 1958–59

Lovig, Linda: Barbarina, *Le Nozze di Figaro (The Marriage of Figaro),* 1962–63

Lovin, Richard: Will Parker, *Oklahoma!,* 1954–55

Low, Lorraine: Marcellina, *Le Nozze di Figaro (The Marriage of Figaro),* 1980–81

Lowe, Bernard: Camille Desmoulins, *Danton and Robespierre,* 1977–78; Vakula, *The Night Before Christmas,* 1977–78

Lowrie, John: Guitarist, *Man of La Mancha,* 1988–89

Lowry, Lisa: Sarah, *The Ballad of Baby Doe,* 2003–04

Loyd, Lavetta: Despina, *Così fan tutte,* 1963–64; Marsinah, *Kismet,* 1963–64; Valencienne, *Die lustige Witwe (The Merry Widow),* 1964–65; Page, *Parsifal,* 1965–66; Sister Constance, *Dialogues des Carmélites,* 1965–66; Spirit, *Die Zauberflöte (The Magic Flute),* 1965–66

Loyzelle, Henry: Welsh servant, *The Ballad of Baby Doe,* 1975–76; The Cook, *Canterbury Tales,* 1978–79

Lualdi, Brenda: Barbarina, *Le Nozze di Figaro (The Marriage of Figaro),* 1968–69; Second Maid, *The Boys from Syracuse,* 1968–69; Dryad, *Ariadne auf Naxos,* 1969–70; Second Lay Sister, *Il Trittico (A Triptych),* 1969–70

Lubbers, Rachael: Mercedes, *Carmen,* 2005–06

Lucas, Austin: Orestes as a child, *The Cry of Clytaemnestra,* 1989–90

Lucas, James: Animal Vendor, *Der Rosenkavalier,* 1965–66; Slave, *Die Zauberflöte (The Magic Flute),* 1965–66

Lucas, Noah: Moth, *A Midsummer Night's Dream,* 1983–84

Lucchese, Dawn: Zerlina, *Don Giovanni,* 1979–80

Ludden, Daniel: Dr. Bartolo, *Le Nozze di Figaro (The Marriage of Figaro),* 1986–87; Bailiff, *The Crucible,* 1987–88; A Captain, *Eugene Onegin,* 1988–89; Luther, *Les Contes d'Hoffmann (The Tales of Hoffmann),* 1988–89

Ludwig, David: Caiaphas, *Passion Play—Carmina Burana,* 1982–83; The Boyar Khrushchev, *Boris Godunov,* 1983–84

Lund, John: Stewpot, *South Pacific,* 1956–57

Lundberg, Mark: Detective, *Porgy and Bess,* 1979–80; Diomedes, *The Cry of Clytaemnestra,* 1979–80; Count Monterone, *Rigoletto,* 1980–81; Don Basilio, *Il Barbiere di Siviglia (The Barber of Seville),* 1980–81; Grigoris, *The Greek Passion,* 1980–81; Kreonte, *The Love for Three Oranges,* 1980–81; Prince Galitsky, *Prince Igor,* 1980–81; The Bonze, *Madama Butterfly,* 1981–82

Lundy, Alexis: Pamina, *Die Zauberflöte (The Magic Flute),* 2004–05; Micaëla, *Carmen,* 2005–06; Zdenka, *Arabella,* 2006–07

Lunney, Edward: Maximilian, *Candide,* 1957–58

Lusk, Franklin: Radames, *Aida,* 1963–64; Gabriele Adorno, *Simon Boccanegra,* 1964–65; Grigori (Dimitri, the Pretender), *Boris Godunov,* 1964–65; Oedipus, *Oedipus Rex,* 1964–65; Calaf, *Turandot,* 1964–65; The Chevalier, *Dialogues des Carmélites,* 1965–66

Lutzenhiser, Stuart: Edgardo, *Lucia di Lammermoor,* 1993–94; Rinuccio, *Gianni Schicchi,* 1993–94; Peter Grimes, *Peter Grimes,* 1994–95; Rodolfo, *La Bohème,* 1994–95; Piquillo, *La Périchole,* 1995–96; The Duke of Mantua, *Rigoletto,* 1995–96

Lyford, Richard: Count Ceprano, *Rigoletto,* 1986–87; Lion, *Candide,* 1987–88; Ned Keene, *Peter Grimes,* 1987–88; Prince Yamadori, *Madama Butterfly,* 1987–88; Recruiting Agent, *Candide,* 1987–88; Dr. Malatesta, *Don Pasquale,* 1988–89; Eugene Onegin, *Eugene Onegin,* 1988–89; Mr. Lindquist, *A Little Night Music,* 1988–89; Ruggero Lastouc, *La Rondine (The Swallow),* 1989–90; Alfredo Germont, *La Traviata,* 1990–91

Lynan, Charles: Joe, *The Most Happy Fella,* 1959–60; Harry Easter, *Street Scene,* 1960–61

Lynch, Nancy: Barbarina, *Le Nozze di Figaro (The Marriage of Figaro),* 1968–69

Lyndes, Nicole: Whore, *Candide,* 1993–94; Niece, *Peter Grimes,* 1994–95; Rosalinda, *Die Fledermaus (The Bat),* 1996–97

Lynge, Stephanie: Karen O'Kane, *Jubilee,* 1991–92

Lysack, Chris: Elder Hayes, *Susannah,* 2007–08; Hoffmann, *Les Contes d'Hoffmann (The Tales of Hoffmann),* 2007–08

Mabary, Sarah: Third Lady, *Die Zauberflöte (The Magic Flute),* 2004–05; Buttercup, *HMS Pinafore,* 2005–06; Hermia, *A Midsummer Night's Dream,* 2005–06; Mrs. Gibbs, *Our Town,* 2005–06; Adelaide, *Arabella,* 2006–07

Mace, Joseph: Waiter, *A Wedding,* 2007–08

Mack, Eileen: Lizette, *Naughty Marietta,* 1977–78; Papagena, *Die Zauberflöte (The Magic Flute),* 1977–78; Despina, *Così fan tutte,* 1978–79; May, *Canterbury Tales,* 1978–79

MacKay, Nancy: Georgette, *La Rondine (The Swallow),* 1959–60; Yvette, *La Rondine (The Swallow),* 1959–60; First Lady, *Die Zauberflöte (The Magic Flute),* 1960–61

MacLaren, Bruce: Diomedes, *The Cry of Clytaemnestra,* 1989–90; Peter, *Hänsel und Gretel,* 1989–90; Escamillo, *Carmen,* 1991–92; Tonio, *I Pagliacci,* 1991–92

Maddox, Patricia: Annina, *La Traviata,* 1954–55

Madonia, Dana: Zaneeta Shinn, *The Music Man,* 2001–02

Magdamo, Priscilla: Flora Bervoix, *La Traviata,* 1960–61

Magee, Carol: Spirit, *Die Zauberflöte (The Magic Flute),* 1965–66

Magee, Emily: Desdemona, *Otello,* 1989–90; Francesca, *Francesca da Rimini,* 1989–90; Arminda, *La Finta Giardiniera,* 1990–91; Violetta Valery, *La Traviata,* 1990–91; Donna Anna, *Don Giovanni,* 1991–92; Countess Almaviva, *Le Nozze di Figaro (The Marriage of Figaro),* 1992–93

Magnusson, Steinarr: Achilles, *The Cry of Clytaemnestra,* 1989–90; Gobin, *La Rondine (The Swallow),* 1989–90

Magrames, Georgia: Ellen, *Oklahoma!,* 1954–55; Berta (Marcellina), *Il Barbiere di Siviglia (The Barber of Seville),* 1956–57; Mercedes, *Carmen,* 1956–57; Lucia, *Cavalleria Rusticana,* 1957–58; Ulrica, *Un Ballo in Maschera (A Masked Ball),* 1958–59

Magruder, Charles: Don Basilio, *Il Barbiere di Siviglia (The Barber of Seville),* 1956–57; Titurel, *Parsifal,* 1956–57; Colline, *La Bohème,* 1957–58; Gurnemanz, *Parsifal,* 1957–58

Magruder, June: Fiordiligi, *Così fan tutte,* 1956–57; Mimi, *La Bohème,* 1957–58

Mahy, Daune: Countess Ceprano, *Rigoletto,* 1966–67; Marina, *Quattro rusteghi (The Four Ruffians),* 1966–67

Mahy, Kenneth: Amantio di Nicolao, *Gianni Schicchi,* 1964–65; The Imperial Commissioner, *Madama Butterfly,* 1964–65; Titurel, *Parsifal,* 1964–65; Governor Jennings, *A Hoosier Tale,* 1966–67; Krushina, *The Bartered Bride,* 1967–68; Lescaut, *Manon,* 1967–68; Wagner, *Mefistofele,* 1967–68

Maier, Helen: Antonio, *The Firefly,* 1949–50

Maiyo, Jean: Rosabella, *The Most Happy Fella,* 1959–60

Majstorovich, Nadja: An elegant lady, *The Scarlet Letter,* 1976–77

Malachesky, Mark: Paul, *Company,* 1990–91; Alidoro, *La Cenerentola (Cinderella),* 1991–92; Cornelius Hackl, *Hello, Dolly!,* 1991–92; Police Officer, *Jubilee,* 1991–92; Process Server, *Jubilee,* 1991–92; John Styx, *Orphée aux enfers (Orpheus* *in the Underworld),* 1992–93; Amantio di Nicolao, *Gianni Schicchi,* 1993–94; Celio, *The Love for Three Oranges,* 1993–94; Sciarrone, *Tosca,* 1993–94; Motel, the Tailor, *Fiddler on the Roof,* 1994–95

Malek, Angela: Dewman, *Hänsel und Gretel,* 1989–90; Soprano Page, *The Dawn of the Poor King,* 1990–91; Amor, *Orfeo ed Euridice,* 1992–93; Philippe, *Die Teufel von Loudun (The Devils of Loudun),* 1992–93

Malgieri, Jesse: The Bonze, *Madama Butterfly,* 2006–07; Antonio, *Le Nozze di Figaro (The Marriage of Figaro),* 2007–08; Count Monterone, *Rigoletto,* 2007–08

Malk, Samantha: Sandman, *Hänsel und Gretel,* 2001–02; Annina, *La Traviata,* 2002–03; Nanetta, *Falstaff,* 2003–04

Mallon, Kathleen: Player, *Bernstein on Broadway,* 1976–77

Mallory, Charlise: Carmen, *Carmen,* 1962–63; Frasquita, *Carmen,* 1962–63; Musetta, *La Bohème,* 1962–63; Niece, *Peter Grimes,* 1963–64

Malone, Carol: Despina, *Così fan tutte,* 1963–64

Maloy, John: Hank, *A Parfait for Irene,* 1951–52; Knight, *Parsifal,* 1951–52; Ralph, the Stage Manager, *Kiss Me, Kate,* 1951–52; Richard Nordraak, *Song of Norway,* 1951–52; Enoch Snow, *Carousel,* 1952–53; Maintop, *Billy Budd,* 1952–53; Parsifal, *Parsifal,* 1952–53; Cap'n Andy, *Show Boat,* 1953–54; Man in Armor, *Die Zauberflöte (The Magic Flute),* 1953–54; Parsifal, *Parsifal,* 1953–54; Rawkins, *Finian's Rainbow,* 1953–54; Alfred, *Die Fledermaus (The Bat),* 1954–55

Mangiameli, Kate: Bianca, *The Rape of Lucretia,* 1999–2000; Maddalena, *Rigoletto,* 2000–01; Meg, *Little Women,* 2001–02

Mann, Frederick C.: Carnival Boy, *Carousel,* 1970–71; The Fiddler, *Fiddler on the Roof,* 1972–73

Mann, Natalie: Susanna, *The Ghosts of Versailles,* 1996–97; Marcellina, *Le Nozze di Figaro (The Marriage of Figaro),* 1997–98; Aldonza / Dulcinea, *Man of La Mancha,* 1999–2000; Suor Angelica, *Suor Angelica (Sister Angelica),* 1999–2000

Mannino, Angela: Blonde, *Die Entführung aus dem Serail (The Abduction from the Seraglio),* 2003–04; Musetta, *La Bohème,* 2004–05; Despina, *Così fan tutte,* 2005–06; Miss Titmouse, *Too Many Sopranos,* 2006–07

Mannion, Elizabeth: Carmen, *Carmen,* 1965–66; Marina Mnishek, *Boris Godunov,* 1966–67; Baba the Turk, *The Rake's Progress,* 1968–69; Isabella, *L'Italiana in Algeri (The Italian Girl in Algiers),* 1968–69; The Countess, *La Pique Dame (The Queen of Spades),* 1968–69; Baronessa Clarissa, *Love on Trial (La Pietra del Paragone),* 1969–70; Sieglinde, *Die Walküre,* 1969–70; Sieglinde, *Die Walküre,* 1971–72; Kostelnicka, *Jenůfa,* 1972–73; Kundry, *Parsifal,* 1972–73; Princess Eboli, *Don Carlos,* 1972–73; Kundry, *Parsifal,* 1975–76

Manz, Tom: Nachum, *Fiddler on the Roof,* 1972–73

Marchant, Marilyn: Amelia, *Amelia Goes to the Ball,* 1957–58

Marchetich, Ray: Billy Bigelow, *Carousel,* 1952–53; Sailor, *Billy Budd,* 1952–53; Tommy Albright, *Brigadoon,* 1952–53

Markin, Tracy: Jenny, *Company,* 1990–91

Markle, Carolyn: Gabriella, *La Rondine (The Swallow),* 1959–60; Waitress, *The Most Happy Fella,* 1959–60

Marks, Siegrid: Frasquita, *Carmen,* 1991–92; Eurydice, *Orfeo ed Euridice,* 1992–93

Maroon, Brent: Student from Krakow, *Doktor Faust,* 1974–75; Cesare Angelotti, *Tosca,* 1977–78

Marshall, Jean: Frasquita, *Carmen,* 1956–57; Page, *Parsifal,* 1956–57; Italian Singer, *Capriccio,* 1958–59; Page, *Parsifal,* 1958–59; Smeraldina, *The Love for Three Oranges,* 1958–59; Frasquita, *Carmen,* 1962–63

Marshall, Richard: Policeman, *On the Town,* 1951–52

Martel, Sophie-Marie: Second Lady, *Die Zauberflöte (The Magic Flute),* 1994–95

Martin, Bruce: Fiesco, *Simon Boccanegra,* 1964–65; Simone, *Gianni Schicchi,* 1964–65; Tiresias, *Oedipus Rex,* 1964–65; Varlaam, *Boris Godunov,* 1964–65

Martin, Cheryl: Soprano Page, *The Dawn of the Poor King,* 1990–91; Princess Diana, *Jubilee,* 1991–92; Eurydice, *Orphée aux enfers (Orpheus in the Underworld),* 1992–93; Julie Jordan, *Carousel,* 1993–94; Manon Lescaut, *Manon,* 1993–94

Martin, Cory: Cupid, *Orphée aux enfers (Orpheus in the Underworld),* 1992–93; Pink Sheep, *Candide,* 1993–94

Martin, David: Simon, *Quattro rusteghi (The Four Ruffians),* 1966–67; Gregor Mittenhofer, *Elegy for Young Lovers,* 1967–68; Ottone, *L'Incoronazione di Poppea (The Coronation of Poppea),* 1967–68; Roger, *Andrea Chénier,* 1967–68; Figaro, *Le Nozze di Figaro (The Marriage of Figaro),* 1968–69; Fritz Kothner, *Die Meistersinger von Nürnberg (The Mastersingers of Nuremberg),* 1968–69; Nick Shadow, *The Rake's Progress,* 1968–69; Taddeo, *L'Italiana in Algeri (The Italian Girl in Algiers),* 1968–69; Tom of Warwick, *Camelot,* 1968–69; Tom of Warwick, *Camelot,* 1969–70

Martin, Heather: Marcellina, *Le Nozze di Figaro (The Marriage of Figaro),* 1997–98; Suor Dolcina, *Suor Angelica (Sister Angelica),* 1999–2000; Berta (Marcellina), *Il Barbiere di Siviglia (The Barber of Seville),* 2000–01

Martin, Ian: Trouble, *Madama Butterfly,* 1996–97

Martin, Timothy: Lensky, *Eugene Onegin,* 1988–89

Martinez, Eileen: Pearl, *The Scarlet Letter*, 1976–77; Olympia, *Les Contes d'Hoffmann (The Tales of Hoffmann)*, 1978–79; Iphygeneia, *The Cry of Clytaemnestra*, 1979–80

Martinez, Frank: Chino, *West Side Story*, 1985–86; Matthew Arnold Fulton, *Of Thee I Sing*, 1987–88

Martz, Chris: A Muleteer, *Man of La Mancha*, 1988–89

Mascari, Marie: Barbarina, *Le Nozze di Figaro (The Marriage of Figaro)*, 1992–93; Nanetta, *Falstaff*, 1992–93; Blonde, *Die Entführung aus dem Serail (The Abduction from the Seraglio)*, 1993–94

Mason, Abigail: Waitress, *The Most Happy Fella*, 1959–60

Masters, Marie: Mercedes, *Carmen*, 2005–06; Gretel, *Hänsel und Gretel*, 2006–07; Madame Pompous, *Too Many Sopranos*, 2006–07; Gilda, *Rigoletto*, 2007–08

Match, Michael: Sesto, *Giulio Cesare (Julius Caesar)*, 2002–03; Shepherd Boy, *Tosca*, 2004–05; The Witch, *Hänsel und Gretel*, 2006–07

Mathew, Jane: Second Woman of Paris, *Danton and Robespierre*, 1977–78

Matousek, Linda: Auntie, *Peter Grimes*, 1963–64; Dorabella, *Così fan tutte*, 1963–64; Priestess, *Aida*, 1963–64; Jocasta, *Oedipus Rex*, 1964–65; Marina Mnishek, *Boris Godunov*, 1964–65; Voice from Heaven, *Parsifal*, 1964–65; Carmen, *Carmen*, 1965–66; The Old Prioress, *Dialogues des Carmélites*, 1965–66; Voice from Heaven, *Parsifal*, 1965–66; Lola, *Cavalleria Rusticana*, 1966–67; Maddalena, *Rigoletto*, 1966–67; Mrs. Herring, *Albert Herring*, 1966–67; Voice from Heaven, *Parsifal*, 1966–67; Azucena, *Il Trovatore*, 1967–68; Mrs. Herring, *Albert Herring*, 1967–68; Ottavia, *L'Incoronazione di Poppea (The Coronation of Poppea)*, 1967–68

Mattei, Raul: Mario Cavaradossi, *Tosca*, 1977–78; Tallien, *Danton and Robespierre*, 1977–78; First Suitor, *The Darkened City*, 1978–79

Matthen, Paul: Hans Sachs, *Die Meistersinger von Nürnberg (The Mastersingers of Nuremberg)*, 1961–62; The Music Master, *Ariadne auf Naxos*, 1969–70; Amfortas, *Parsifal*, 1972–73

Matthews, Jonathan: Leandro, Cavalier, *Arlecchino*, 2006–07; Luigi, *A Wedding*, 2007–08; Nathanael, *Les Contes d'Hoffmann (The Tales of Hoffmann)*, 2007–08

Mattox, Judith: Cis, *Albert Herring*, 1966–67; Page, *Rigoletto*, 1966–67; Elvira, *L'Italiana in Algeri (The Italian Girl in Algiers)*, 1968–69

Maudry, Eléonore: Sandman, *Hänsel und Gretel*, 1995–96

Maultsby, Nancy: The Old Prioress, *Dialogues des Carmélites*, 1986–87; Elizabeth Proctor, *The Crucible*, 1987–88; Suzuki, *Madama Butterfly*, 1987–88; Judith, *Bluebeard's Castle*, 1988–89; Olga, *Eugene Onegin*, 1988–89; Emilia, *Otello*, 1989–90

Maxwell, Andrew: The Kralahome, *The King and I*, 1996–97

Maxwell, Marian: Jane, *Finian's Rainbow*, 1969–70

May, Gary: Zanni, *Il Mondo della Luna (The World on the Moon)*, 1975–76

May, Luis Giron: Coppelius, *Les Contes d'Hoffmann (The Tales of Hoffmann)*, 1978–79; Dr. Miracle, *Les Contes d'Hoffmann (The Tales of Hoffmann)*, 1978–79; Giorgio Germont, *La Traviata*, 1978–79

Mayberry, Brandon: Gideon March, *Little Women*, 2001–02; Raimondo Bidebent, *Lucia di Lammermoor*, 2001–02; Giulio Cesare, *Giulio Cesare (Julius Caesar)*, 2002–03

Mayer, Deborah: Gertrude, *Hänsel und Gretel*, 1989–90

Maynor, Kevin: Khan Konchak, *Prince Igor*, 1980–81; Sparafucile, *Rigoletto*, 1980–81; Rev. Thruston Norwood, *Soldier Boy, Soldier*, 1982–83

Mayo, Randy: Peter, *Hänsel und Gretel*, 1995–96; Frank, *Die Fledermaus (The Bat)*, 1996–97; Don Pasquale, *Don Pasquale*, 1997–98; Marquis D'Obigny, *La Traviata*, 1997–98; Don Magnifico, *La Cenerentola (Cinderella)*, 1998–99; Alcindoro, *La Bohème*, 1999–2000; Benoit, *La Bohème*, 1999–2000; The Innkeeper / The Governor, *Man of La Mancha*, 1999–2000

McAdams, Timothy: Player, *Mass*, 1987–88; Player, *Mass*, 1988–89; The Padre, *Man of La Mancha*, 1988–89; Chevalier de St. Brioche, *Die lustige Witwe (The Merry Widow)*, 1990–91

McCammon, Ruth: Girl, *Street Scene*, 1949–50; Young Shopgirl, *Street Scene*, 1949–50

McCarter, John: Max, *The Most Happy Fella*, 1959–60

McCarther, Sean: Graf Dominik, *Arabella*, 2006–07; Crespel, *Les Contes d'Hoffmann (The Tales of Hoffmann)*, 2007–08; Marullo, *Rigoletto*, 2007–08

McCarthy, Colleen: Player, *Mass*, 1987–88; Aldonza / Dulcinea, *Man of La Mancha*, 1988–89; Countess Charlotte Malcolm, *A Little Night Music*, 1988–89; Player, *Mass*, 1988–89; Lalume, *Kismet*, 1989–90; Mrs. Dolly Gallagher Levi, *Hello, Dolly!*, 1991–92

McCarthy, Lauren: Anita, *West Side Story*, 2002–03

McCarty, Cullen: Timony, *Carousel*, 1993–94; Nachum, *Fiddler on the Roof*, 1994–95; Luther Billis, *South Pacific*, 1995–96

McClain, Betsy: Jessie, *Annie Get Your Gun*, 1956–57

McClain, Joseph: Borsa, *Rigoletto*, 1966–67; Count Riccardo, *Quattro rusteghi (The Four Ruffians)*, 1966–67; Mr. Upfold, *Albert Herring*, 1966–67; An Incroyable, *Andrea Chénier*, 1967–68; Guillot de Morfontaine, *Manon*, 1967–68; Soldier of the Praetorian Guard, *L'Incoronazione di Poppea (The Coronation* of Poppea), 1967–68; The Ringmaster, *The Bartered Bride*, 1967–68; Don Basilio, *Le Nozze di Figaro (The Marriage of Figaro)*, 1968–69

McClellan, Jean: Clo-clo, *Die lustige Witwe (The Merry Widow)*, 1996–97; Lover George, *The King and I*, 1996–97

McClure, Gilda: Maid, *Of Thee I Sing*, 1987–88; Miss Benson, *Of Thee I Sing*, 1987–88; Victim of the Inquisition, *Candide*, 1987–88

McCluskey, Eric: Stage Manager, *Our Town*, 2005–06; Graf Elemer, *Arabella*, 2006–07

McComb, Richard: Alfredo Germont, *La Traviata*, 1968–69; Tom Rakewell, *The Rake's Progress*, 1968–69; Brighella, *Ariadne auf Naxos*, 1969–70; Mario Cavaradossi, *Tosca*, 1969–70; Edgardo, *Lucia di Lammermoor*, 1970–71; Second Jew, *Salome*, 1970–71; Don Ottavio, *Don Giovanni*, 1971–72; Knight, *Parsifal*, 1972–73; Laca, *Jenůfa*, 1972–73; Priest, *Die Zauberflöte (The Magic Flute)*, 1972–73; Mario Cavaradossi, *Tosca*, 1973–74; The Captain, *Wozzeck*, 1973–74; Lensky, *Eugene Onegin*, 1974–75; The Duke of Mantua, *Rigoletto*, 1974–75

McConnell, Cassandra: Boy, *Die Zauberflöte (The Magic Flute)*, 1994–95; Giulietta, *Les Contes d'Hoffmann (The Tales of Hoffmann)*, 1995–96

McConochy, Millicent: Sarah, *Finian's Rainbow*, 1953–54; Kundry, *Parsifal*, 1954–55; Laura, *The Ruby*, 1954–55; Rosalinda, *Die Fledermaus (The Bat)*, 1954–55; Violetta Valery, *La Traviata*, 1954–55

McCord, Kimberly: Naiad, *Ariadne auf Naxos*, 1996–97

McCormack, Sarah: Effie, *The Ballad of Baby Doe*, 2003–04; Filipyevna, *Eugene Onegin*, 2004–05

McCourt, James: Policeman, *On the Town*, 1951–52

McCoy, Steve: Mike, *Oklahoma!*, 1997–98

McCullough, Johnna: Strawberry Woman, *Porgy and Bess*, 1979–80

McCutchen, Gilbert: Slave, *Die Zauberflöte (The Magic Flute)*, 1953–54

McDaniel, Carolyne: Mrs. Meg Page, *Falstaff*, 1971–72

McDaniels, Marla: Black Woman, *The Mother of Us All*, 1973–74; Samantha, *The Ballad of Baby Doe*, 1975–76; Smeraldina, *The Love for Three Oranges*, 1975–76; Bess, *Porgy and Bess*, 1976–77

McDonald, John: A Steersman, *Der Fliegende Holländer (The Flying Dutchman)*, 1962–63; The Innkeeper / The Governor, *Man of La Mancha*, 1985–86; An Officer, *Dialogues des Carmélites*, 1986–87

McDonald, William: Gonzalvo, *L'Heure espagnole (The Spanish Hour)*, 1959–60; Sam Kaplan, *Street Scene*, 1960–61; Charlie Dalrymple, *Brigadoon*, 1961–62; David, *Die Meistersinger von Nürnberg (The Mastersingers of Nuremberg)*, 1961–62; Knight, *Parsifal*, 1961–62; Nemorino, *L'Elisir d'amore (The Elixir of Love)*, 1961–62; Oberon, *A Midsummer Night's Dream*, 1961–62; Chevalier des Grieux, *Manon*, 1967–68; Lucano, *L'Incoronazione di Poppea (The Coronation of Poppea)*, 1967–68; David, *Die Meistersinger von Nürnberg (The Mastersingers of Nuremberg)*, 1968–69; Lindoro, *L'Italiana in Algeri (The Italian Girl in Algiers)*, 1968–69; Tom Rakewell, *The Rake's Progress*, 1968–69; Bacchus/Tenor, *Ariadne auf Naxos*, 1969–70; Giocondo, *Love on Trial (La Pietra del Paragone)*, 1969–70; Rodolfo, *La Bohème*, 1970–71

McDonough, Dugg: Chaucer, *Canterbury Tales*, 1978–79

McElroy, Beverly: Annina, *La Traviata*, 1968–69

McEwen, Douglas: Baron Douphol, *La Traviata*, 1954–55; Knight, *Parsifal*, 1954–55

McFadden, Tara: Player, *Mass*, 1998–99

McFarland, Robert: Ford, *Falstaff*, 1976–77; Escamillo, *Carmen*, 1977–78; Robespierre, *Danton and Robespierre*, 1977–78; Giorgio Germont, *La Traviata*, 1978–79

McGarrity, Evelyn: Floria Tosca, *Tosca*, 1957–58; Kundry, *Parsifal*, 1957–58; Santuzza, *Cavalleria Rusticana*, 1957–58

McGee, Philip: Policeman, *Carousel*, 1976–77

McGhee, James: Second Crap Shooter, *The Jumping Frog of Calaveras County*, 1949–50

McGirr, Kira: Cherubino, *Le Nozze di Figaro (The Marriage of Figaro)*, 2007–08

McGowan, Joelyn: Mercedes, *Carmen*, 1965–66; Florence Pike, *Albert Herring*, 1966–67; Lola, *Cavalleria Rusticana*, 1966–67; Carolina von Kirchstetten, *Elegy for Young Lovers*, 1967–68; Florence Pike, *Albert Herring*, 1967–68; Ludmila, *The Bartered Bride*, 1967–68; Nancy, *Albert Herring*, 1967–68; Rosette, *Manon*, 1967–68

McGraw, William: Escamillo, *Carmen*, 1973–74; Eugene Onegin, *Eugene Onegin*, 1974–75; Rigoletto, *Rigoletto*, 1974–75; Dappertutto, *Les Contes d'Hoffmann (The Tales of Hoffmann)*, 1978–79; Lazarus, *The Darkened City*, 1978–79; Lindorf, *Les Contes d'Hoffmann (The Tales of Hoffmann)*, 1978–79

McIntosh, David: Captain, *The Firefly*, 1949–50; Harry Easter, *Street Scene*, 1949–50; Monsieur Beaunoir, *The New Moon*, 1949–50; Amfortas, *Parsifal*, 1950–51; James Jarvis, *Lost in the Stars*, 1950–51; Kasimir Popoff, *The Chocolate Soldier*, 1950–51; Marullo, *Rigoletto*, 1950–51; Father Grieg, *Song of Norway*, 1951–52; Fred Graham, *Kiss Me, Kate*, 1951–52; Petruchio, *Kiss Me, Kate*, 1951–52; Doctor Bartolo, *Il Barbiere di Siviglia (The Barber of Seville)*, 1963–64; Don Alfonso, *Così fan tutte*, 1963–64; Gianni Schicchi, *Gianni Schicchi*, 1964–65; Leporello, *Don Giovanni*, 1964–65; Varlaam, *Boris Godunov*, 1964–65; Pacuvio,

Love on Trial (La Pietra del Paragone), 1969–70; The Music Master, *Ariadne auf Naxos,* 1969–70; Benoit, *La Bohème,* 1974–75

McIntosh, Erin: Diane, *Finian's Rainbow,* 1969–70

McIver, Emary: Page, *Parsifal,* 1957–58; Don Ottavio, *Don Giovanni,* 1958–59; Fenton, *Die lustigen Weiber von Windsor (The Merry Wives of Windsor),* 1958–59; Italian Singer, *Capriccio,* 1958–59; Page, *Parsifal,* 1958–59; Truffaldino, *The Love for Three Oranges,* 1958–59; Chevalier des Grieux, *Manon Lescaut,* 1959–60; Edmondo, *Manon Lescaut,* 1959–60; Giuseppe, *The Most Happy Fella,* 1959–60; Gonzalvo, *L'Heure espagnole (The Spanish Hour),* 1959–60; Hoffmann, *Les Contes d'Hoffmann (The Tales of Hoffmann),* 1959–60; Prunier, *La Rondine (The Swallow),* 1959–60; The Duke of Mantua, *Rigoletto,* 1959–60

McKay, Ann: Nurse of the Children, *Boris Godunov,* 1953–54; Third Lady, *Die Zauberflöte (The Magic Flute),* 1953–54

McKee, Laurie Ann: Yente, *Fiddler on the Roof,* 1972–73

McKenzie, Arthur: Fiorello, *Il Barbiere di Siviglia (The Barber of Seville),* 1980–81; Cloudy, *The Excursions of Mr. Broucek,* 1981–82; Peter, *Hänsel und Gretel,* 1982–83

McKern, Corey: Customs Officer, *La Bohème,* 1999–2000; Dr. Sanson Carrasco / The Duke, *Man of La Mancha,* 1999–2000; Gianni Schicchi, *Gianni Schicchi,* 1999–2000; Nicholas, *Vanessa,* 1999–2000; Ambrogio, *Il Barbiere di Siviglia (The Barber of Seville),* 2000–01; Guglielmo, *Così fan tutte,* 2000–01; Wagner, *Faust,* 2000–01; Count Almaviva, *Le Nozze di Figaro (The Marriage of Figaro),* 2001–02; John Brooke, *Little Women,* 2001–02; Player, *Putting It Together,* 2002–03

McKesson, Joseph: McTeague, *McTeague,* 1995–96; Bacchus/Tenor, *Ariadne auf Naxos,* 1996–97; Begearss, *The Ghosts of Versailles,* 1996–97; Fred, *Oklahoma!,* 1997–98; Giuseppe, *La Traviata,* 1997–98; The Chevalier, *Dialogues des Carmélites,* 1997–98

McKinley, George: Belmonte, *Die Entführung aus dem Serail (The Abduction from the Seraglio),* 1951–52; Hortensio, *Kiss Me, Kate,* 1951–52; Kaspar, *Amahl and the Night Visitors,* 1951–52; Sailor, *On the Town,* 1951–52; Red Whiskers, *Billy Budd,* 1952–53

McKinley, Susan: Trouble, *Madama Butterfly,* 1987–88

McKinzie, Richard: Knight, *Parsifal,* 1948–49; Burton, *Lost in the Stars,* 1950–51; Massakroff, *The Chocolate Soldier,* 1950–51

McKnight, Emily: Despina, *Così fan tutte,* 1970–71; Nanetta, *Falstaff,* 1971–72

McLane, Tobin: Glad Hand, *West Side Story,* 1985–86; Sir Lionel, *Camelot,* 1986–87

McLeod, Wendy: Madame Larina, *Eugene Onegin,* 1988–89; Spirit, *Die Zauberflöte (The Magic Flute),* 1988–89

McNabb, Lenore: Cecily, *Where's Charley?,* 1953–54; Gertie Cummings, *Oklahoma!,* 1954–55

McNair, Sylvia: Manon Lescaut, *Manon,* 1979–80; Gilda, *Rigoletto,* 1980–81; Constanza, *Die Entführung aus dem Serail (The Abduction from the Seraglio),* 1981–82; Malinka, *The Excursions of Mr. Broucek,* 1981–82

McNamarra, Patricia: Ado Annie Carnes, *Oklahoma!,* 1954–55

McNeely, Darlene: Sister Mathilde, *Dialogues des Carmélites,* 1965–66

McQuerrey, Lawrence: Pish-Tush, *The Mikado,* 1950–51; Stephans, *The Chocolate Soldier,* 1950–51; Count Peppi, *Song of Norway,* 1951–52; Doctor Seldon, *Carousel,* 1952–53; Donald, *Billy Budd,* 1952–53; Starkeeper, *Carousel,* 1952–53; Papageno, *Die Zauberflöte (The Magic Flute),* 1953–54

McRath, Leah: Giulietta, *Les Contes d'Hoffmann (The Tales of Hoffmann),* 2007–08

McVey, Michael: First Commissioner, *Dialogues des Carmélites,* 1986–87; Sam Jenkins, *Of Thee I Sing,* 1987–88; Henrik Egerman, *A Little Night Music,* 1988–89

Mead, Jacquelyn: Julie, *The New Moon,* 1949–50; Mae Jones, *Street Scene,* 1949–50; Page, *Parsifal,* 1949–50; Page, *Parsifal,* 1950–51

Meadows, Christine: Augusta Tabor, *The Ballad of Baby Doe,* 1982–83; Rosina, *Il Barbiere di Siviglia (The Barber of Seville),* 1982–83; Hermia, *A Midsummer Night's Dream,* 1983–84; Carmen, *Carmen,* 1984–85

Meckalavage, Jan: Marguerite, *Faust,* 1955–56

Medina, Cody: Count des Grieux, *Manon,* 2006–07; Djura, *Arabella,* 2006–07; Saint Peter, *Too Many Sopranos,* 2006–07; Olin Blitch, *Susannah,* 2007–08; Snooks, *A Wedding,* 2007–08

Medwetz, Rebecca: Martha, *Faust,* 1981–82; Frugola, *Il Trittico (A Triptych),* 1982–83; Hansel, *Hänsel und Gretel,* 1982–83; Fricka, *Das Rheingold,* 1983–84; Nurse of the Children, *Boris Godunov,* 1983–84; Andronicus, *Tamerlano,* 1984–85; Carmen, *Carmen,* 1984–85; Teresa, *La Sonnambula (The Sleepwalker),* 1985–86

Meehan, Molly: Kate Pinkerton, *Madama Butterfly,* 1987–88; Aldonza / Dulcinea, *Man of La Mancha,* 1988–89

Megles, Meredith: Nettie Fowler, *Carousel,* 1993–94

Meisner, Zander: Mouthpiece, *West Side Story,* 2002–03

Melander, Karen: Cherubino, *Le Nozze di Figaro (The Marriage of Figaro),* 1962–63; Sweet Seller, *The Darkened City,* 1962–63; Madame Rosa, *Il Campanello di*

Notte (The Night Bell), 1963–64; Rosina, *Il Barbiere di Siviglia (The Barber of Seville),* 1963–64

Mellman, Laura: Anybodys, *West Side Story,* 2002–03

Memering, John: Sergeant of Police, *The Boys from Syracuse,* 1968–69

Menninga, Adam: Newsboy, *The Ballad of Baby Doe,* 2003–04

Mentzel, Michael: Blues Singer, *Mass,* 1998–99; Player, *Mass,* 1998–99; Farfarello, *The Love for Three Oranges,* 1999–2000; Marco, *Gianni Schicchi,* 1999–2000; Maximilian, *Candide,* 2000–01; Mr. Dashwood, *Little Women,* 2001–02; Nibbles, *West Side Story,* 2002–03; Nireno, *Giulio Cesare (Julius Caesar),* 2002–03; Barney, *The Ballad of Baby Doe,* 2003–04

Merren, Stephen: Ambrogio, *Il Barbiere di Siviglia (The Barber of Seville),* 1971–72

Merrick, Justin: Randolph, *A Wedding,* 2007–08

Merriman, Joan: Muse, *Les Contes d'Hoffmann (The Tales of Hoffmann),* 1947–48; Nicklausse, *Les Contes d'Hoffmann (The Tales of Hoffmann),* 1947–48; Page, *Parsifal,* 1948–49

Merriman, Thomas: Gurnemanz, *Parsifal,* 1948–49

Meskimen, Joe: Mute, *The Fantasticks,* 1963–64

Metzger, Charles: Huntsman, *Candide,* 2000–01; An Indian, *The Bartered Bride,* 2001–02; Don Curzio, *Le Nozze di Figaro (The Marriage of Figaro),* 2001–02

Meyer, David: De Bretigny, *Manon,* 1993–94; Captain Balstrode, *Peter Grimes,* 1994–95; Crespel, *Les Contes d'Hoffmann (The Tales of Hoffmann),* 1995–96; Dr. Malatesta, *Don Pasquale,* 1997–98; Dandini, *La Cenerentola (Cinderella),* 1998–99; Celio, *The Love for Three Oranges,* 1999–2000; Wozzeck, *Wozzeck,* 1999–2000; Doctor Bartolo, *Il Barbiere di Siviglia (The Barber of Seville),* 2000–01

Meyer, Stephen: Commendatore, *Don Giovanni,* 1985–86; Daland, *Der Fliegende Holländer (The Flying Dutchman),* 1985–86; Master of the Ship, *The Tempest,* 1985–86; Kezal, *The Bartered Bride,* 1986–87; Sir Sagramore, *Camelot,* 1986–87; Sparafucile, *Rigoletto,* 1986–87; Third Sailor, *The Legend of Tsar Saltan,* 1986–87; Somarone, *Béatrice et Bénédict,* 1987–88; The Bonze, *Madama Butterfly,* 1987–88; Bluebeard, *Bluebeard's Castle,* 1988–89; Don Pasquale, *Don Pasquale,* 1988–89; Zaretsky, *Eugene Onegin,* 1988–89; Colline, *La Bohème,* 1989–90

Michaels, Cary: Truffaldino, *The Love for Three Oranges,* 1975–76; Fenton, *Falstaff,* 1976–77; Goro, *Madama Butterfly,* 1976–77; Little Bat McLean, *Susannah,* 1976–77; First Speaker, *Danton and Robespierre,* 1977–78; The Devil, *The Night Before Christmas,* 1977–78; A Steersman, *Der Fliegende Holländer (The Flying Dutchman),* 1978–79

Michaels, Emily: Dolly Tate, *Annie Get Your Gun,* 1956–57

Mickel, Chiara: Elizabeth Tabor, *The Ballad of Baby Doe,* 1975–76

Mickel, Heather: Silver Dollar Tabor, *The Ballad of Baby Doe,* 1975–76

Mickel, Jennifer: Mrs. Higgins' Maid, *My Fair Lady,* 1979–80; Ado Annie Carnes, *Oklahoma!,* 1981–82

Mickel, Kathleen: Mrs. Eynsford-Hill, *My Fair Lady,* 1979–80

Mickley, James: Antonio, *The Gondoliers,* 1974–75

Mihalka, Toffer: Luther, *Les Contes d'Hoffmann (The Tales of Hoffmann),* 1995–96; A Wig Maker, *Ariadne auf Naxos,* 1996–97; Pritschitsch, *Die lustige Witwe (The Merry Widow),* 1996–97; Wilhelm, *The Ghosts of Versailles,* 1996–97; Don Curzio, *Le Nozze di Figaro (The Marriage of Figaro),* 1997–98; Will Parker, *Oklahoma!,* 1997–98; Brack Weaver, *Down in the Valley,* 1998–99; Haberdasher, *Kiss Me, Kate,* 1998–99; Venice Quartet 1, *Kiss Me, Kate,* 1998–99; Rinuccio, *Gianni Schicchi,* 1999–2000; Second Apprentice, *Wozzeck,* 1999–2000; Sellem, *The Rake's Progress,* 1999–2000; Borsa, *Rigoletto,* 2000–01

Milby, Debra: Margaret, *Wozzeck,* 1981–82; The Mistress of the Novices, *Il Trittico (A Triptych),* 1982–83

Miles, Jermaine: Chino, *West Side Story,* 2002–03

Millberg, Constance: Mrs. McLean, *Susannah,* 1976–77; Solokha, *The Night Before Christmas,* 1977–78

Miller, Cynthia: Marietta, *Naughty Marietta,* 1977–78

Miller, Elizabeth: Mimi, *La Bohème,* 1989–90

Miller, James: Snug, *A Midsummer Night's Dream,* 1961–62; Alcindoro, *La Bohème,* 1962–63; Antonio, *Le Nozze di Figaro (The Marriage of Figaro),* 1962–63; Benoit, *La Bohème,* 1962–63; Second Bearer, *The Darkened City,* 1962–63; Don Basilio, *Il Barbiere di Siviglia (The Barber of Seville),* 1963–64

Miller, Lisa: Eine Kartenaufschlaegerin, *Arabella,* 2006–07; Mrs. McLean, *Susannah,* 2007–08

Miller, Rodney: A Captain, *Eugene Onegin,* 1974–75; Customs Officer, *La Bohème,* 1974–75; Master of Ceremonies, *Doktor Faust,* 1974–75; Nicholas, *Vanessa,* 1974–75; Pasha Selim, *Die Entführung aus dem Serail (The Abduction from the Seraglio),* 1974–75; Johann, *Werther,* 1975–76; The King of Clubs, *The Love for Three Oranges,* 1975–76; William Jennings Bryan, *The Ballad of Baby Doe,* 1975–76; David Bascomb, *Carousel,* 1976–77; Elder McLean, *Susannah,* 1976–77; Heavenly Friend, *Carousel,* 1976–77; Roger Chillingworth, *The Scarlet Letter,* 1976–77

Miller, Sarah: Giulietta, *Les Contes d'Hoffmann (The Tales of Hoffmann)*, 1978–79; Stella, *Les Contes d'Hoffmann (The Tales of Hoffmann)*, 1978–79; Donna Anna, *Don Giovanni*, 1979–80; Electra, *The Cry of Clytaemnestra*, 1979–80

Miller, Susan: Niece, *Peter Grimes*, 1994–95; Gretel, *Hänsel und Gretel*, 1995–96; Gossip 2, *The Ghosts of Versailles*, 1996–97; Jou-Jou, *Die lustige Witwe (The Merry Widow)*, 1996–97; Susanna, *Le Nozze di Figaro (The Marriage of Figaro)*, 1997–98; Zdenka, *Arabella*, 1998–99

Miller, Tom: Damian, *Canterbury Tales*, 1978–79

Millevoi, Gina: Clorinda, *La Cenerentola (Cinderella)*, 1991–92; Rosalia, *West Side Story*, 1992–93; Carrie Pipperidge, *Carousel*, 1993–94

Milone, Marie-Paule: Aristeo, *L'Orfeo*, 1987–88

Mims, Marilyn: Mimi, *La Bohème*, 1984–85; Donna Elvira, *Don Giovanni*, 1985–86

Mindrum, Matthew: Glad Hand, *West Side Story*, 2002–03; Albert, *The Ballad of Baby Doe*, 2003–04; Footman at the wedding, *The Ballad of Baby Doe*, 2003–04; Alcindoro, *La Bohème*, 2004–05; Thierry, *Dialogues des Carmélites*, 2004–05

Minton, Alexa: Trouble, *Madama Butterfly*, 2006–07

Mishenkin, Arkady: Paolo, *Francesca da Rimini*, 1989–90

Missling, Darwin: Giocondo, *Love on Trial (La Pietra del Paragone)*, 1969–70; Dr. Caius, *Falstaff*, 1971–72; Ippolit, *Myshkin*, 1972–73

Mitch, Dale: Mr. Lundie, *Brigadoon*, 1952–53

Mitchell, Abigail: Javotte, *Manon*, 2006–07

Mitchell, Dayna: Ado Annie Carnes, *Oklahoma!*, 1997–98; Venice Quartet 4, *Kiss Me, Kate*, 1998–99

Mitchell, Mary: Annina, *La Traviata*, 1960–61

Mitchell, Patricia: Gretel, *Hänsel und Gretel*, 1956–57

Mix, LeAnn: Maria / The Innkeeper's Wife, *Man of La Mancha*, 1988–89; Ayah to Lalume, *Kismet*, 1989–90; Martha, *Faust*, 1989–90; Olga, *Die lustige Witwe (The Merry Widow)*, 1990–91

Mjolsnes, Mona: Electra as a child, *The Cry of Clytaemnestra*, 1989–90

Moffitt, Johanna: Countess Ceprano, *Rigoletto*, 2007–08

Monahan, Brent: Bushy, *The Ballad of Baby Doe*, 1975–76; Fredrik Egerman, *A Little Night Music*, 1975–76; Dr. Caius, *Falstaff*, 1976–77

Monette, Jeffrey: Aristocrat, *The Ghosts of Versailles*, 1996–97; Eugene Onegin, *Eugene Onegin*, 1997–98; Notary, *Don Pasquale*, 1997–98; Baptista, *Kiss Me, Kate*, 1998–99; Harry Trevor, *Kiss Me, Kate*, 1998–99; Pluto, *Orphée aux enfers (Orpheus in the Underworld)*, 1998–99; Junius, *The Rape of Lucretia*, 1999–2000; Schaunard, *La Bohème*, 1999–2000; Belcore, *L'Elisir d'amore (The Elixir*

of Love), 2000–01; Marullo, *Rigoletto*, 2000–01; Sharpless, *Madama Butterfly*, 2001–02; Dr. Falke, *Die Fledermaus (The Bat)*, 2002–03; Giorgio Germont, *La Traviata*, 2002–03

Monette, LaVergne: Brünnhilde, *Die Walküre*, 1971–72; Donna Elvira, *Don Giovanni*, 1971–72; Elizabeth of Valois, *Don Carlos*, 1972–73; First Lady, *Die Zauberflöte (The Magic Flute)*, 1972–73; Jenufa, *Jenůfa*, 1972–73

Monroe, Mark: Player, *Bernstein on Broadway*, 1976–77; Trio—tenor, *Trouble in Tahiti*, 1976–77

Monsour, David: Lt. Buzz Adams, *South Pacific*, 1956–57; Mac, *Annie Get Your Gun*, 1956–57; Hessian, *Candide*, 1957–58

Montané, Carlos: The Duke of Mantua, *Rigoletto*, 1986–87

Montgomery, Alan: Andres, *Les Contes d'Hoffmann (The Tales of Hoffmann)*, 1973–74; Cochenille, *Les Contes d'Hoffmann (The Tales of Hoffmann)*, 1973–74; Franz, *Les Contes d'Hoffmann (The Tales of Hoffmann)*, 1973–74; Pittichinaccio, *Les Contes d'Hoffmann (The Tales of Hoffmann)*, 1973–74; The Fool, *Wozzeck*, 1973–74; Virgil Thomson, *The Mother of Us All*, 1973–74; Triquet, *Eugene Onegin*, 1974–75

Montgomery, Kathryn: Donna Elvira, *Don Giovanni*, 1971–72; Iole, *Heracles*, 1971–72; Arabella, *Arabella*, 1972–73; Elizabeth of Valois, *Don Carlos*, 1972–73; Bianca, *Kiss Me, Kate*, 1973–74; Lillian Russell, *The Mother of Us All*, 1973–74; Lois Lane, *Kiss Me, Kate*, 1973–74; Marie, *Wozzeck*, 1973–74; Duchess of Parma, *Doktor Faust*, 1974–75; Vanessa, *Vanessa*, 1974–75; Amelia, *Un Ballo in Maschera (A Masked Ball)*, 1975–76; Cio-Cio San, *Madama Butterfly*, 1975–76; Electra, *Idomeneo*, 1976–77

Montgomery, May: Sister Genevieve, *Il Trittico (A Triptych)*, 1969–70

Moon, Jason: The Marquis de la Force, *Dialogues des Carmélites*, 1997–98; Arbace, *Idomeneo*, 1998–99; Marco, *Gianni Schicchi*, 1999–2000; Count Monterone, *Rigoletto*, 2000–01

Moon, Jye-Sung: Prince Yamadori, *Madama Butterfly*, 1996–97; Suleyman Pasha, *The Ghosts of Versailles*, 1996–97; Giorgio Germont, *La Traviata*, 1997–98

Mooney, Gwyneth: Spirit, *Die Zauberflöte (The Magic Flute)*, 1998–99

Moore, Charles: Flamand, *Capriccio*, 1958–59; Ruggero Lastouc, *La Rondine (The Swallow)*, 1959–60; The Duke of Mantua, *Rigoletto*, 1959–60; Sam Kaplan, *Street Scene*, 1960–61

Moore, Dale: Daland, *Der Fliegende Holländer (The Flying Dutchman)*, 1985–86

Moore, Eileen: Mary Magdalena, *Passion Play—Carmina Burana*, 1982–83; Sister Genevieve, *Il Trittico (A Triptych)*, 1982–83; Margot, *Die lustige Witwe (The Merry Widow)*, 1983–84

Moore, Eric: Kunz Volgelgesang, *Die Meistersinger von Nürnberg (The Mastersingers of Nuremberg)*, 1968–69

Moore, James: Marquis de Cascada, *Die lustige Witwe (The Merry Widow)*, 1983–84; Knight, *Murder in the Cathedral*, 1984–85; Dancaire, *Carmen*, 1984–85; Alessio, *La Sonnambula (The Sleepwalker)*, 1985–86; Riff, *West Side Story*, 1985–86; The Padre, *Man of La Mancha*, 1985–86; Second Sailor, *The Legend of Tsar Saltan*, 1986–87

Moore, Jeffrey: Jake, *Porgy and Bess*, 1976–77

Moore, Justin: A Jailer, *Dialogues des Carmélites*, 2004–05; Morales, *Carmen*, 2005–06; Don Giovanni, *Don Giovanni*, 2006–07; Official Registrar, *Madama Butterfly*, 2006–07; Belcore, *L'Elisir d'amore (The Elixir of Love)*, 2007–08; Marcello, *La Bohème*, 2007–08

Moore, Michael: An Abbé, *Andrea Chénier*, 1967–68

Moore, Previn: Monostatos, *Die Zauberflöte (The Magic Flute)*, 1982–83; Tinca, *Il Trittico (A Triptych)*, 1982–83; Mime, *Das Rheingold*, 1983–84; Snout, *A Midsummer Night's Dream*, 1983–84; Tobias Ragg, *Sweeney Todd*, 1983–84; A Peasant, *La Fille du régiment (The Daughter of the Regiment)*, 1984–85; Arithmetic, *L'Enfant et les Sortilèges (The Bewitched Child)*, 1984–85; Bajazet, *Tamerlano*, 1984–85; Charlie, *Show Boat*, 1984–85; Pluto, *Orphée aux enfers (Orpheus in the Underworld)*, 1984–85; The Frog, *L'Enfant et les Sortilèges (The Bewitched Child)*, 1984–85; Alfred, *Die Fledermaus (The Bat)*, 1985–86; Don Ottavio, *Don Giovanni*, 1985–86; Sancho Panza, *Man of La Mancha*, 1985–86; The Barber, *Man of La Mancha*, 1985–86; Nemorino, *L'Elisir d'amore (The Elixir of Love)*, 1986–87; Sellem, *The Rake's Progress*, 1986–87; The Ringmaster, *The Bartered Bride*, 1986–87

Moore, Roger: Robin, *Falstaff*, 1971–72; Paul, *Kiss Me, Kate*, 1973–74; Page, *A Little Night Music*, 1975–76; Enoch Snow, Jr., *Carousel*, 1976–77

Moore, Tracey: Aunt Eller, *Oklahoma!*, 1981–82; Siebel, *Faust*, 1981–82; Cleo, *The Most Happy Fella*, 1982–83; Mama McCourt, *The Ballad of Baby Doe*, 1982–83; Fyodor, *Boris Godunov*, 1983–84; Mrs. Lovett, *Sweeney Todd*, 1983–84; Mrs. Western, *Tom Jones*, 1983–84

Moran, Harriet: Cherubino, *Le Nozze di Figaro (The Marriage of Figaro)*, 1968–69; Page, *Parsifal*, 1968–69

More, Michael: Page, *Parsifal*, 1965–66; Page, *Parsifal*, 1967–68; Ruiz, *Il Trovatore*, 1967–68; Soldier of the Praetorian Guard, *L'Incoronazione di Poppea (The Coronation of Poppea)*, 1967–68

More, Peter: The Man who Dies, *The Fantasticks*, 1963–64

Morgan, Katharine: Jeanne, *Die Teufel von Loudun (The Devils of Loudun)*, 1992–93; Floria Tosca, *Tosca*, 1993–94

Morgan, Russel: Ambrogio, *Il Barbiere di Siviglia (The Barber of Seville)*, 1956–57

Morgan, Steven: Anselmo / a Muleteer, *Man of La Mancha*, 1999–2000

Morganstern, Jules: Buzz, *Finian's Rainbow*, 1953–54; Jake, *Show Boat*, 1953–54; Wilkinson, *Where's Charley?*, 1953–54

Morken, David: Max, *The Most Happy Fella*, 1959–60

Morrell, Patrice: Susanna Walcott, *The Crucible*, 1987–88

Morris, Brian: Jose / a Muleteer, *Man of La Mancha*, 1988–89

Morris, Hannah: Graduate, *Street Scene*, 1949–50; Lady, *Street Scene*, 1949–50

Morris, Jack: Bob Boles, *Peter Grimes*, 1963–64; Count Almaviva, *Il Barbiere di Siviglia (The Barber of Seville)*, 1963–64; The Caliph, *Kismet*, 1963–64; Knight, *Parsifal*, 1964–65; Rinuccio, *Gianni Schicchi*, 1964–65; Vicomte Camille di Rosillon, *Die lustige Witwe (The Merry Widow)*, 1964–65

Morris, Robert: Boyar in Attendance, *Boris Godunov*, 1953–54; Priest, *Die Zauberflöte (The Magic Flute)*, 1953–54; Prince Shuisky, *Boris Godunov*, 1953–54

Morris, Susan: Lady Anne, *Camelot*, 1968–69

Morrison, Ray: Cancian, *Quattro rusteghi (The Four Ruffians)*, 1966–67; Knight, *Parsifal*, 1966–67; Sparafucile, *Rigoletto*, 1966–67; Superintendant Budd, *Albert Herring*, 1966–67

Morrison, Richard: Dr. Falke, *Die Fledermaus (The Bat)*, 1982–83; Jesus, *Passion Play—Carmina Burana*, 1982–83

Morrison, Virginia: Spirit, *Die Zauberflöte (The Magic Flute)*, 1977–78; Ruzia, *Boris Godunov*, 1978–79; Esmeralda, *The Bartered Bride*, 1979–80; Javotte, *Manon*, 1979–80; Cherubino, *Le Nozze di Figaro (The Marriage of Figaro)*, 1980–81; Cleo, *The Most Happy Fella*, 1982–83; Lauretta, *Il Trittico (A Triptych)*, 1982–83; Helena, *A Midsummer Night's Dream*, 1983–84; Despina, *Così fan tutte*, 1984–85; Julie, *Show Boat*, 1984–85

Morrissey, Jeff: Iago, *Otello*, 1989–90; Lanciotto, *Francesca da Rimini*, 1989–90; Wozzeck, *Wozzeck*, 1990–91; Don Narciso, *Il Turco in Italia (The Turk in Italy)*, 1996–97

Mortensen, Rod: Slave, *Die Zauberflöte (The Magic Flute)*, 1965–66; A skipper, *Die Entführung aus dem Serail (The Abduction from the Seraglio)*, 1966–67

Morton, Joanna: Spirit, *Die Zauberflöte (The Magic Flute)*, 1998–99

Mosel, Stephen: Banquo, *Macbeth*, 1965–66; Titurel, *Parsifal*, 1965–66; Count Ceprano, *Rigoletto*, 1966–67; Friar Laurence, *Roméo et Juliette*, 1966–67

Mosser, Dennis: Old Man, *The Darkened City*, 1962–63

Mossholder, Lynelle: Dodo, *Die lustige Witwe (The Merry Widow)*, 1965–66

Moul, James: Figaro, *Le Nozze di Figaro (The Marriage of Figaro)*, 1955–56; Kezal, *The Bartered Bride*, 1955–56; Talpa, *Il Tabarro (The Cloak)*, 1955–56; Titurel, *Parsifal*, 1955–56; Traveler, *The Land Between the Rivers*, 1955–56; Major Gordon Lillie, *Annie Get Your Gun*, 1956–57; Sacristan, *Tosca*, 1957–58

Moulton, Andrew: Mikhail, *Fiddler on the Roof*, 1994–95; Yitzuk, *Fiddler on the Roof*, 1994–95

Mouney, Lauren: Barbarina, *Le Nozze di Figaro (The Marriage of Figaro)*, 2001–02

Mout, Edward: Fenton, *Falstaff*, 2003–04; Lensky, *Eugene Onegin*, 2004–05

Mowry, Mark: Ferrando, *Così fan tutte*, 1995–96; Gabriel von Eisenstein, *Die Fledermaus (The Bat)*, 1996–97; Ralph Rackstraw, *HMS Pinafore*, 1997–98; Idomeneo, *Idomeneo*, 1998–99; The Prince, *The Love for Three Oranges*, 1999–2000; Tom Rakewell, *The Rake's Progress*, 1999–2000

Moyer King, Marilyn: Kundry, *Parsifal*, 1958–59; Kundry, *Parsifal*, 1959–60

Mramor, Pat: Adele, *Die Fledermaus (The Bat)*, 1954–55; Ado Annie Carnes, *Oklahoma!*, 1954–55; Eileen Sherwood, *Wonderful Town*, 1954–55; Nedda, *I Pagliacci*, 1954–55; Esmeralda, *The Bartered Bride*, 1955–56; Susanna, *Le Nozze di Figaro (The Marriage of Figaro)*, 1955–56

Much, Marc: Waiter, *The Ballad of Baby Doe*, 1975–76

Mueller, Clare: Zerlina, *Don Giovanni*, 1985–86; Amore (Cupid), *L'Orfeo*, 1987–88; Bridget Booth, *The Crucible*, 1987–88; Antonia, *Les Contes d'Hoffmann (The Tales of Hoffmann)*, 1988–89; Pamina, *Die Zauberflöte (The Magic Flute)*, 1988–89; Rosina, *Il Barbiere di Siviglia (The Barber of Seville)*, 1988–89; Violetta Valery, *La Traviata*, 1990–91

Mulholland, James: Crespel, *Les Contes d'Hoffmann (The Tales of Hoffmann)*, 1959–60; Gurnemanz, *Parsifal*, 1959–60; Sparafucile, *Rigoletto*, 1959–60; King Dodon, *Le Coq d'or (The Golden Cockerel)*, 1960–61; King Philip II, *Don Carlos*, 1960–61; Mr. Frank Maurant, *Street Scene*, 1960–61; Priest, *Die Zauberflöte (The Magic Flute)*, 1960–61; Dr. Dulcamara, *L'Elisir d'amore (The Elixir of Love)*, 1961–62; Fritz Kothner, *Die Meistersinger von Nürnberg (The Mastersingers of Nuremberg)*, 1961–62; King Philip II, *Don Carlos*, 1961–62; Osmin, *Die Entführung aus dem Serail (The Abduction from the Seraglio)*, 1961–62; Sacristan, *Tosca*, 1961–62; Theseus, *A Midsummer Night's Dream*, 1961–62; Colline, *La Bohème*, 1962–63; Count Almaviva, *Le Nozze di Figaro (The Marriage of Figaro)*, 1962–63; Escamillo, *Carmen*, 1962–63; Figaro, *Le Nozze di Figaro (The Marriage of Figaro)*, 1962–63; Marquis of Calatrava, *La Forza del Destino (The Force of Destiny)*, 1962–63; Mayor, *The Darkened City*, 1962–63; Padre Guardiano, *La Forza del Destino (The Force of Destiny)*, 1962–63; The

Dutchman, *Der Fliegende Holländer (The Flying Dutchman)*, 1962–63; Titurel, *Parsifal*, 1962–63

Mullen, Fred: Officer Murphy, *Street Scene*, 1949–50; Policeman, *The Firefly*, 1949–50

Muller-Bergh, Christian: Father Mignon, *Die Teufel von Loudun (The Devils of Loudun)*, 1992–93

Mulvane, Forrest: Steve Sankey, *Street Scene*, 1949–50

Mumford, James: Crab Man, *Porgy and Bess*, 1976–77; Crown, *Porgy and Bess*, 1976–77; Frazier, *Porgy and Bess*, 1976–77; Crown, *Porgy and Bess*, 1979–80

Muntada, Maria Luisa: The nursing sister from the infirmary, *Il Trittico (A Triptych)*, 1982–83

Murakami, May: Papagena, *Die Zauberflöte (The Magic Flute)*, 1965–66

Murdoch, Caroline: Countess de Coigny, *Andrea Chénier*, 1967–68; Flora Bervoix, *La Traviata*, 1968–69; Ariadne/Prima Donna, *Ariadne auf Naxos*, 1969–70; Manon Lescaut, *Manon Lescaut*, 1970–71; Donna Anna, *Don Giovanni*, 1971–72

Murdock, Douglas: Chekalinsky, *La Pique Dame (The Queen of Spades)*, 1968–69; Don Curzio, *Le Nozze di Figaro (The Marriage of Figaro)*, 1968–69; An Officer, *Ariadne auf Naxos*, 1969–70; The Chief Magistrate, *Un Ballo in Maschera (A Masked Ball)*, 1969–70; Lichas, *Heracles*, 1971–72; Robert, *Company*, 1990–91

Murphy, Cassie: Mrs. Squires, *The Music Man*, 2001–02

Murphy, Kevin: Dr. Crabbe, *Peter Grimes*, 2003–04; Alfieri, *A View from the Bridge*, 2004–05; Colline, *La Bohème*, 2004–05; Sciarrone, *Tosca*, 2004–05; Don Alfonso, *Così fan tutte*, 2005–06; Dr. Gibbs, *Our Town*, 2005–06; Theseus, *A Midsummer Night's Dream*, 2005–06

Murphy, Sheila: Le Novizie (Prima), *Suor Angelica (Sister Angelica)*, 1999–2000; Le Novizie (Seconda), *Suor Angelica (Sister Angelica)*, 1999–2000; Despina, *Così fan tutte*, 2000–01; Susanna, *Le Nozze di Figaro (The Marriage of Figaro)*, 2001–02; Adele, *Die Fledermaus (The Bat)*, 2002–03; Blonde, *Die Entführung aus dem Serail (The Abduction from the Seraglio)*, 2003–04; Sister Constance, *Dialogues des Carmélites*, 2004–05

Murphy, Stuart: Slave, *Die Zauberflöte (The Magic Flute)*, 1953–54

Murphy, Thomas: Tom Jones, *Tom Jones*, 1983–84; Knight, *Murder in the Cathedral*, 1984–85; Parpignol, *La Bohème*, 1984–85; Borsa, *Rigoletto*, 1986–87

Murray, David: Baron Douphol, *La Traviata*, 1960–61; Worshipful Master Bellingham, *The Scarlet Letter*, 1960–61; Konrad Nachtigall, *Die Meistersinger von Nürnberg (The Mastersingers of Nuremberg)*, 1961–62; Starveling, *A*

Midsummer Night's Dream, 1961–62; Worshipful Master Bellingham, *The Scarlet Letter*, 1961–62

Musselwhite, Harry: Bouncer at the saloon, *The Ballad of Baby Doe*, 1975–76; Farfarello, *The Love for Three Oranges*, 1975–76; Titurel, *Parsifal*, 1975–76; Physician, *Pelléas et Mélisande*, 1976–77; Don Pasquale, *Don Pasquale*, 1977–78; Patsyuk, *The Night Before Christmas*, 1977–78; Rudolfo, *Naughty Marietta*, 1977–78; Sacristan, *Tosca*, 1977–78

Mussman, Alan: Schlemil, *Les Contes d'Hoffmann (The Tales of Hoffmann)*, 1978–79

Mutchler, Leslie: Filipyevna, *Eugene Onegin*, 1997–98; Smeraldina, *The Love for Three Oranges*, 1999–2000; Zia Principessa, *Suor Angelica (Sister Angelica)*, 1999–2000; Martha, *Faust*, 2000–01; Jo, *Little Women*, 2001–02

Myers, Denise: Serena, *Porgy and Bess*, 1979–80

Myers, Marie: Despinio, *The Greek Passion*, 1980–81

Myers, Rex: Bramble, *The Veil*, 1949–50

Myszkowski, John: Butler at the Windsor Hotel, *The Ballad of Baby Doe*, 1982–83; Agent of the Inquisition, *Candide*, 1983–84; Kronkov, *Die lustige Witwe (The Merry Widow)*, 1983–84; Mr. Western, *Tom Jones*, 1983–84; Rangoni, *Boris Godunov*, 1983–84; Hortensius, *La Fille du régiment (The Daughter of the Regiment)*, 1984–85; Guide, *Carmen*, 1984–85; Dr. Sanson Carrasco / The Duke, *Man of La Mancha*, 1985–86; Borsa, *Rigoletto*, 1986–87; Old Grandfather, *The Legend of Tsar Saltan*, 1986–87; Vashek, *The Bartered Bride*, 1986–87; Gherardo, *Gianni Schicchi*, 1988–89; Peter, *Company*, 1990–91

Myszkowski, Lin: A Tourier, *Il Trittico (A Triptych)*, 1982–83; The Princess in the Storybook, *L'Enfant et les Sortilèges (The Bewitched Child)*, 1984–85; Micaëla, *Carmen*, 1984–85; Nimue, *Camelot*, 1986–87

Nachtrab, Christopher: Puck, *A Midsummer Night's Dream*, 2005–06

Nadelmann, Noemi: The Bat, *L'Enfant et les Sortilèges (The Bewitched Child)*, 1984–85; Iris, *The Tempest*, 1985–86

Nagosky, Ann: Elizabeth Tabor, *The Ballad of Baby Doe*, 1982–83

Nailor, Chaz: Second Commissioner, *Dialogues des Carmélites*, 2004–05; Paris, *Roméo et Juliette*, 2005–06; Graf Lamoral, *Arabella*, 2006–07; Alcindoro, *La Bohème*, 2007–08; Benoit, *La Bohème*, 2007–08; Dr. Bartolo, *Le Nozze di Figaro (The Marriage of Figaro)*, 2007–08

Nakas, Vytas: Alcindoro, *La Bohème*, 1970–71; First Solider, *Salome*, 1970–71; Raimondo Bidebent, *Lucia di Lammermoor*, 1970–71; Pistol, *Falstaff*, 1971–72; Burdovsky, *Myshkin*, 1972–73

Naldi, Ronald: Mr. Daniel Buchanan, *Street Scene*, 1960–61; Page, *Parsifal*, 1960–61; Prince Tamino, *Die Zauberflöte (The Magic Flute)*, 1960–61; Reverend Master John W. Wilson, *The Scarlet Letter*, 1960–61; Lysander, *A Midsummer Night's Dream*, 1961–62; Nemorino, *L'Elisir d'amore (The Elixir of Love)*, 1961–62; Page, *Parsifal*, 1961–62; Pedrillo, *Die Entführung aus dem Serail (The Abduction from the Seraglio)*, 1961–62; A Steersman, *Der Fliegende Holländer (The Flying Dutchman)*, 1962–63; Alfred, *Die Fledermaus (The Bat)*, 1962–63; Minstrel, *The Darkened City*, 1962–63; Page, *Parsifal*, 1962–63; Rodolfo, *La Bohème*, 1962–63; Count Almaviva, *Il Barbiere di Siviglia (The Barber of Seville)*, 1963–64; Ferrando, *Così fan tutte*, 1963–64; Grisha, *The Fair at Sorochinsk*, 1963–64; Page, *Parsifal*, 1963–64; Don Ottavio, *Don Giovanni*, 1964–65; Lt. Pinkerton, *Madama Butterfly*, 1964–65; Page, *Parsifal*, 1964–65; Pong, *Turandot*, 1964–65; Rinuccio, *Gianni Schicchi*, 1964–65

Nall, Nancy: Noble Orphan, *Der Rosenkavalier*, 1965–66; Spirit, *Die Zauberflöte (The Magic Flute)*, 1965–66; Emmie, *Albert Herring*, 1966–67; Page, *Rigoletto*, 1966–67; Xenia, *Boris Godunov*, 1966–67; Love, *L'Incoronazione di Poppea (The Coronation of Poppea)*, 1967–68

Nall Brookshire, Adeline: Mrs. Laura Hildebrand, *Street Scene*, 1949–50

Narducci, Daniel: Count Carl-Magnus Malcolm, *A Little Night Music*, 1988–89; Miguel de Cervantes / Don Quixote, *Man of La Mancha*, 1988–89; Schlemil, *Les Contes d'Hoffmann (The Tales of Hoffmann)*, 1988–89; Montano, *Otello*, 1989–90; Public Poet, *Kismet*, 1989–90

Narviez, James: Player, *Mass*, 1988–89

Nathan, Gloria: Gertrude, *Hänsel und Gretel*, 1982–83; The Mistress of the Novices, *Il Trittico (A Triptych)*, 1982–83; Flosshilde, *Das Rheingold*, 1983–84; Andronicus, a Grecian Prince, *Tamerlano*, 1984–85

Naumenko, Aleksand: Virgil's Ghost, *Francesca da Rimini*, 1989–90

Navarra, Theresa: Page, *Parsifal*, 1950–51

Navarro, Abraham: Jamie, *West Side Story*, 1992–93

Navkal, Nikhil: Security man, *A Wedding*, 2007–08; Wilhelm, *Les Contes d'Hoffmann (The Tales of Hoffmann)*, 2007–08

Neal, Albert: Mingo, *Porgy and Bess*, 1976–77; Brighella, *Arlecchino*, 1979–80; Peter, *Porgy and Bess*, 1979–80; Don Basilio, *Le Nozze di Figaro (The Marriage of Figaro)*, 1980–81; Ewart Dunlop, *The Music Man*, 1980–81; Andres, *Wozzeck*, 1981–82; Pedrillo, *Die Entführung aus dem Serail (The Abduction from the Seraglio)*, 1981–82; Rainbowglory, *The Excursions of Mr. Broucek*, 1981–82; Merchant, *Passion Play—Carmina Burana*, 1982–83; Simpleton, *Boris Godunov*, 1983–84

Nechaev, Yuri: Lanciotto, *Francesca da Rimini,* 1989–90

Nedobeck, Mary: Peasant woman, *Boris Godunov,* 1964–65

Neeley, Thomasina: A Tourier, *Il Trittico (A Triptych),* 1982–83

Neely, James Bert: A Wig Maker, *Ariadne auf Naxos,* 1969–70; Cesare Angelotti, *Tosca,* 1969–70; Servant of Amelia, *Un Ballo in Maschera (A Masked Ball),* 1969–70; Lescaut, *Manon Lescaut,* 1970–71; Masetto, *Don Giovanni,* 1971–72; Pistol, *Falstaff,* 1971–72; Dr. Schneider, *Myshkin,* 1972–73

Neff, James: Dr. Neville Craven, *The Secret Garden,* 2003–04; Jacob, *The Ballad of Baby Doe,* 2003–04; Ned Keene, *Peter Grimes,* 2003–04; Pasha Selim, *Die Entführung aus dem Serail (The Abduction from the Seraglio),* 2003–04; The Host of the Garter Inn, *Falstaff,* 2003–04

Neff, Robert: Chief Policeman, *Kismet,* 1963–64

Nelson, Charles: Justinius, *Canterbury Tales,* 1978–79; Young Knight, *Canterbury Tales,* 1978–79; Elder Gleaton, *Susannah,* 1979–80; Ladas, *The Greek Passion,* 1980–81; Pasha Selim, *Die Entführung aus dem Serail (The Abduction from the Seraglio),* 1981–82

Nelson, Christopher: Monostatos, *Die Zauberflöte (The Magic Flute),* 2004–05; Parpignol, *La Bohème,* 2004–05; Ralph Rackstraw, *HMS Pinafore,* 2005–06; Remendado, *Carmen,* 2005–06; Arlecchino, *Arlecchino,* 2006–07; Borsa, *Rigoletto,* 2007–08; Donato, *A Wedding,* 2007–08

Nelson, Daniel: Augustine Moser, *Die Meistersinger von Nürnberg (The Mastersingers of Nuremberg),* 1961–62; Don Basilio, *Le Nozze di Figaro (The Marriage of Figaro),* 1962–63; Dr. Bartolo, *Le Nozze di Figaro (The Marriage of Figaro),* 1962–63; First Suitor, *The Darkened City,* 1962–63; Rodolfo, *La Bohème,* 1962–63; Edgardo, *Lucia di Lammermoor,* 1963–64; Ferrando, *Così fan tutte,* 1963–64; Grisha, *The Fair at Sorochinsk,* 1963–64; Rev. Horace Adams, *Peter Grimes,* 1963–64; Pong, *Turandot,* 1964–65; Brighella, *Ariadne auf Naxos,* 1969–70; Count Riccardo, *Un Ballo in Maschera (A Masked Ball),* 1969–70; Ulysses, *Deidamia,* 1969–70; Edgardo, *Lucia di Lammermoor,* 1970–71; First Jew, *Salome,* 1970–71; Fenton, *Falstaff,* 1971–72

Nelson, Falle: Inquisition Guard, *Candide,* 1957–58; The Imperial Commissioner, *Madama Butterfly,* 1958–59

Nelson, Linda Kay: Annina, *La Traviata,* 1978–79

Nelson, Nelda: Mimi, *La Bohème,* 1970–71; Second Lady, *Die Zauberflöte (The Magic Flute),* 1972–73; Carmen, *Carmen,* 1973–74; Giulietta, *Les Contes d'Hoffmann (The Tales of Hoffmann),* 1973–74; Gabrielle Danton, *Danton and Robespierre,* 1977–78; Solokha, *The Night Before Christmas,* 1977–78; Clytaemnestra, *The Cry of Clytaemnestra,* 1979–80; Augusta Tabor, *The Ballad of Baby Doe,* 1982–83; Ariel, *The Tempest,* 1985–86; Clytaemnestra, *The Cry of Clytaemnestra,* 1989–90

Nelson, Steve: Lescaut, *Manon,* 1979–80; Teucer, *The Cry of Clytaemnestra,* 1979–80

Nemerov, Karen: Angel (adult), *The Dawn of the Poor King,* 1990–91; Thisbe, *La Cenerentola (Cinderella),* 1991–92

Nesbitt, Douglas: Chasseur at Chez Maxim, *Die lustige Witwe (The Merry Widow),* 1964–65; Chasseur at Chez Maxim, *Die lustige Witwe (The Merry Widow),* 1965–66

Nesbitt, Nicholas: Arlecchino, *Arlecchino,* 2006–07; Nemorino, *L'Elisir d'amore (The Elixir of Love),* 2007–08; Sam Polk, *Susannah,* 2007–08

Netherly, Neil: Innkeeper, *Manon,* 1993–94; Marco, *Gianni Schicchi,* 1993–94; Marcello, *La Bohème,* 1994–95

Neufeld, Frances: Berta (Marcellina), *Il Barbiere di Siviglia (The Barber of Seville),* 1980–81; Giovanna, *Rigoletto,* 1980–81

Neufeld, Rudolph: Guardsman, *Manon,* 1979–80; Micha, *The Bartered Bride,* 1979–80; Ser Metteo del Sarto, *Arlecchino,* 1979–80; Kostandis, *The Greek Passion,* 1980–81; Pantalone, *The Love for Three Oranges,* 1980–81

Neuman, Jani: Zaneeta Shinn, *The Music Man,* 1980–81

Neumann, Vicki: Gertie Cummings, *Oklahoma!,* 1981–82

Newell, Patrick: Bernardo, *West Side Story,* 1992–93; Bontemps, *Die Teufel von Loudun (The Devils of Loudun),* 1992–93; Father Ambrose, *Die Teufel von Loudun (The Devils of Loudun),* 1992–93; Celio, *The Love for Three Oranges,* 1993–94; Cesare Angelotti, *Tosca,* 1993–94; Maximilian, *Candide,* 1993–94; Physician, *Pelléas et Mélisande,* 1994–95; Schaunard, *La Bohème,* 1994–95; Second Priest of the Temple, *Die Zauberflöte (The Magic Flute),* 1994–95; Don Pedro, *La Périchole,* 1995–96; Figaro, *The Ghosts of Versailles,* 1996–97; Captain Corcoran, *HMS Pinafore,* 1997–98

Nichols, Adam: Spirit, *Die Zauberflöte (The Magic Flute),* 2004–05

Nichols, Gayletha: Hata, *The Bartered Bride,* 1979–80; Berta Marcellina, *Il Barbiere di Siviglia (The Barber of Seville),* 1980–81; Konchakovna, *Prince Igor,* 1980–81; Suzuki, *Madama Butterfly,* 1981–82; Madame Lidoine, *Dialogues des Carmélites,* 1986–87

Nickel, Judy: Anne, *The Mother of Us All,* 1973–74; Voice of the Mother, *Les Contes d'Hoffmann (The Tales of Hoffmann),* 1973–74

Nickel, Stanley: Don Basilio, *Le Nozze di Figaro (The Marriage of Figaro),* 1973–74; John Adams, *The Mother of Us All,* 1973–74; Triquet, *Eugene Onegin,* 1974–75

Nicolson (Smith), Mark: Benedick, *Béatrice et Bénédict,* 1987–88

Nicosia, Judy: Siebel, *Faust,* 1971–72

Niemeyer, Jennifer: Pauline, *West Side Story,* 1992–93

Nilson, Eric: The Apparition of the Poet, Svatopluk Cech, *The Excursions of Mr. Broucek,* 1981–82; Officer, *Il Barbiere di Siviglia (The Barber of Seville),* 1982–83; Croupier, *Candide,* 1983–84; Don Issachar, *Candide,* 1983–84; Judge of the Inquisition, *Candide,* 1983–84

Nilsson, Margaret: Luna, *Jeppe,* 2002–03; Augusta Tabor, *The Ballad of Baby Doe,* 2003–04

Niwa, Frank: The Kralahome, *The King and I,* 1957–58

Noble, Timothy: Robespierre, *Danton and Robespierre,* 1977–78; Speaker of the Temple, *Die Zauberflöte (The Magic Flute),* 1977–78; Coppelius, *Les Contes d'Hoffmann (The Tales of Hoffmann),* 1978–79; Dappertutto, *Les Contes d'Hoffmann (The Tales of Hoffmann),* 1978–79; Dr. Miracle, *Les Contes d'Hoffmann (The Tales of Hoffmann),* 1978–79; Lazarus, *The Darkened City,* 1978–79; Lindorf, *Les Contes d'Hoffmann (The Tales of Hoffmann),* 1978–79; Rangoni, *Boris Godunov,* 1978–79; Agamemnon, *The Cry of Clytaemnestra,* 1979–80; Don Giovanni, *Don Giovanni,* 1979–80; Grigoris, *The Greek Passion,* 1980–81; Harold Hill, *The Music Man,* 1980–81; Igor, *Prince Igor,* 1980–81; Rigoletto, *Rigoletto,* 1980–81; Wotan, *Das Rheingold,* 1983–84; Sir John Falstaff, *Falstaff,* 1992–93; Sir John Falstaff, *Falstaff,* 1997–98; Sir John Falstaff, *Falstaff,* 2003–04; Tony, *The Most Happy Fella,* 2007–08

Noggle, Anna: Sarah, *The Ballad of Baby Doe,* 2003–04

Nolan, Margaret: Parishoner, *Canterbury Tales,* 1978–79; Proserpina, *Canterbury Tales,* 1978–79

Nold, Simone: Pamina, *Die Zauberflöte (The Magic Flute),* 1994–95

Nolen, Laura Vlasak: Maddalena, *Rigoletto,* 2000–01; Cecelia March, *Little Women,* 2001–02; Suzuki, *Madama Butterfly,* 2001–02; Giulietta, *Les Contes d'Hoffmann (The Tales of Hoffmann),* 2002–03; Prince Orlofsky, *Die Fledermaus (The Bat),* 2002–03

Nordhorn, Johanna: Colombina, *Arlecchino,* 2006–07; Antonia, *A Wedding,* 2007–08

Norman, Jerry: Laca, *Jenůfa,* 1972–73; Matteo, *Arabella,* 1972–73; Prince Tamino, *Die Zauberflöte (The Magic Flute),* 1972–73; Andres, *Wozzeck,* 1973–74; Don Jose, *Carmen,* 1973–74; Hoffmann, *Les Contes d'Hoffmann (The Tales of Hoffmann),* 1973–74

Norman, Penny: A Tourier, *Il Trittico (A Triptych),* 1972–73; Barena, *Jenůfa,* 1972–73; Grandma Tzeitel, *Fiddler on the Roof,* 1972–73; Nella, *Il Trittico (A Triptych),* 1972–73

Norman, Rebecca: Amelia's Maid, *Amelia Goes to the Ball,* 1957–58; Lisbon Woman, *Candide,* 1957–58; Venetian Lady, *Candide,* 1957–58; Princess Ninetta, *The Love for Three Oranges,* 1958–59

Norris, Paul: Newspaper Man, *Street Scene,* 1960–61

Norsworthy, Barbara Kathleen: Donna Anna, *Don Giovanni,* 1964–65

Norsworthy, Stanley: Don Giovanni, *Don Giovanni,* 1964–65; Paolo, *Simon Boccanegra,* 1964–65; The Messenger, *Oedipus Rex,* 1964–65

Northart, Leo: Sir Sagramore, *Camelot,* 1968–69

Norton, Joycelyn: Filipyevna, *Eugene Onegin,* 1974–75

Norton, Judith: Thisbe, *La Cenerentola (Cinderella),* 1998–99

Nossaman, Audrey: Katherine, *Kiss Me, Kate,* 1951–52; Lilli Vanessi, *Kiss Me, Kate,* 1951–52; Mother Grieg, *Song of Norway,* 1951–52; Eva, *Die Meistersinger von Nürnberg (The Mastersingers of Nuremberg),* 1961–62

Nowell, Janie: Shaindel, *Fiddler on the Roof,* 1972–73

Nuckols, Fava: Madame Vilmorac, *A Little Night Music,* 1975–76; Malla, *A Little Night Music,* 1975–76; Mrs. Mullin, *Carousel,* 1976–77

Oakden, Andrew: High Priest, *Idomeneo,* 1998–99; The Doctor, *Vanessa,* 1999–2000; Trulove, *The Rake's Progress,* 1999–2000; Rigoletto, *Rigoletto,* 2000–01; Enrico Ashton, *Lucia di Lammermoor,* 2001–02; Giorgio Germont, *La Traviata,* 2002–03

Oberholtzer, William: Fritz Kothner, *Die Meistersinger von Nürnberg (The Mastersingers of Nuremberg),* 1968–69; Haly, *L'Italiana in Algeri (The Italian Girl in Algiers),* 1968–69; Knight, *Parsifal,* 1968–69; Surin, *La Pique Dame (The Queen of Spades),* 1968–69; Phoenix, *Deidamia,* 1969–70; Enrico Ashton, *Lucia di Lammermoor,* 1970–71; Heracles, *Heracles,* 1971–72; Valentin, *Faust,* 1971–72; General Yepanchin, *Myshkin,* 1972–73; Wozzeck, *Wozzeck,* 1973–74; The Dutchman, *Der Fliegende Holländer (The Flying Dutchman),* 1978–79

Obery, Alice: Eighth Woman of Paris, *Danton and Robespierre,* 1977–78; Olympia, *Les Contes d'Hoffmann (The Tales of Hoffmann),* 1978–79; Zerlina, *Don Giovanni,* 1979–80; Rosina, *Il Barbiere di Siviglia (The Barber of Seville),* 1980–81

O'Brien, Julia: Papagena, *Die Zauberflöte (The Magic Flute),* 1994–95

O'Brien, Marcia: Carrie Pipperidge, *Carousel,* 1952–53; Amy Spettigue, *Where's Charley?,* 1953–54; Giorgetta, *Il Tabarro (The Cloak),* 1955–56; Mary

McLennon, *The Land Between the Rivers*, 1955–56; The Child, *L'Enfant et les Sortilèges (The Bewitched Child)*, 1955–56; Gretel, *Hänsel und Gretel*, 1956–57; Liat, *South Pacific*, 1956–57; Nanetta, *Falstaff*, 1956–57

O'Brien, Michelle: Kate Pinkerton, *Madama Butterfly*, 1981–82; Prince Orlofsky, *Die Fledermaus (The Bat)*, 1982–83; The Princess, *Il Trittico (A Triptych)*, 1982–83; Third Lady, *Die Zauberflöte (The Magic Flute)*, 1982–83; Fricka, *Das Rheingold*, 1983–84; Hippolyta, *A Midsummer Night's Dream*, 1983–84; Tamerlane, Emperor of the Tatars, *Tamerlano*, 1984–85

O'Connor, Shannon: Sima, *Fiddler on the Roof*, 1994–95; Gerhilde, *Die Walküre*, 1971–72; Jenufa, *Jenůfa*, 1972–73; Zdenka, *Arabella*, 1972–73

O'Hara, Katherine: Queen of the Night, *Die Zauberflöte (The Magic Flute)*, 1994–95; Olympia, *Les Contes d'Hoffmann (The Tales of Hoffmann)*, 1995–96

Olimpio-Ormenisan, Florin: Count Almaviva, *Il Barbiere di Siviglia (The Barber of Seville)*, 2005–06; Don Ottavio, *Don Giovanni*, 2006–07

Oliphant, Bernadine: Mimi, *La Bohème*, 1962–63

Olipra, Amy: Mrs. Sedley, *Peter Grimes*, 2003–04; Mother Jeanne, *Dialogues des Carmélites*, 2004–05

Olsen, Rees: Father Nordraak, *Song of Norway*, 1951–52

Olsen, Solveig: Lucia, *The Rape of Lucretia*, 1999–2000; Liesl, *The Sound of Music*, 2000–01; Lisbon Woman, *Candide*, 2000–01

Olsen, Thomas: Innkeeper, *Der Rosenkavalier*, 1965–66; Page, *Parsifal*, 1965–66; Slave, *Die Zauberflöte (The Magic Flute)*, 1965–66; Albert Herring, *Albert Herring*, 1966–67; Beppe, *I Pagliacci*, 1966–67; Filipeto, *Quattro rusteghi (The Four Ruffians)*, 1966–67; Albert Herring, *Albert Herring*, 1967–68; Valetto, *L'Incoronazione di Poppea (The Coronation of Poppea)*, 1967–68; Vashek, *The Bartered Bride*, 1967–68; Achilles, *Deidamia*, 1969–70

Olson, Daniel: Escamillo, *Carmen*, 1998–99; Customs Officer, *La Bohème*, 1999–2000; First Apprentice, *Wozzeck*, 1999–2000; Pantalone, *The Love for Three Oranges*, 1999–2000; Pedro / Head Muleteer, *Man of La Mancha*, 1999–2000

Olson, John: Big Deal, *West Side Story*, 2002–03

Olson, Philip: Ferrando, *Così fan tutte*, 1956–57; Knight, *Parsifal*, 1956–57; Lt. Joseph Cable, *South Pacific*, 1956–57; Don Ramiro, *La Cenerentola (Cinderella)*, 1957–58; Ernesto, *Don Pasquale*, 1957–58; Mr. Upfold, *Albert Herring*, 1957–58

Olson, Rachel: Auntie, *Peter Grimes*, 2003–04

Oltman, Sandra: Ciesca, *Il Trittico (A Triptych)*, 1982–83; Marie, *The Most Happy Fella*, 1982–83; The nursing sister from the infirmary, *Il Trittico (A Triptych)*, 1982–83

O'Malley, Brendan: Fred Graham, *Kiss Me, Kate*, 1998–99; Petruchio, *Kiss Me, Kate*, 1998–99

O'Neal, John: Pritschitsch, *Die lustige Witwe (The Merry Widow)*, 1990–91; Official Registrar, *Madama Butterfly*, 1991–92; Prince Yamadori, *Madama Butterfly*, 1991–92; Silvio, *I Pagliacci*, 1991–92; Marullo, *Rigoletto*, 1992–93

O'Neill, Daniel: Action, *West Side Story*, 2002–03

Ong, Ida: Cio-Cio San, *Madama Butterfly*, 1981–82

Opalach, Jan: A Lackey, *Ariadne auf Naxos*, 1969–70; Betto, *Il Trittico (A Triptych)*, 1972–73; The Mayor, *Jenůfa*, 1972–73; Titurel, *Parsifal*, 1972–73; Sacristan, *Tosca*, 1973–74

Oppelt, Laurie: Player, *Mass*, 1988–89

Ormos, Patrick: Don Alhambra del Bolero, *The Gondoliers*, 1974–75

Osborn, Mark: Second Muezzin, *Kismet*, 1989–90; Fig Seller, *Kismet*, 1989–90; Silk Merchant, *Kismet*, 1989–90

Osborn, Scott: Willie Maurant, *Street Scene*, 1960–61

Osborne, George: Baron Scarpia, *Tosca*, 1961–62; Belcore, *L'Elisir d'amore (The Elixir of Love)*, 1961–62; Bottom, *A Midsummer Night's Dream*, 1961–62; Knight, *Parsifal*, 1961–62; Rodrigo, *Don Carlos*, 1961–62

Osifchin, Matthew: Guccio, *Gianni Schicchi*, 1999–2000; Pinellino, *Gianni Schicchi*, 1999–2000; Lieutenant, *The Sound of Music*, 2000–01; Second Officer, *Candide*, 2000–01

Oskouie, Kelly: Marcellina, *Le Nozze di Figaro (The Marriage of Figaro)*, 1986–87; Auntie, *Peter Grimes*, 1987–88; Voice of the Mother, *Les Contes d'Hoffmann (The Tales of Hoffmann)*, 1988–89; Gertrude, *Hänsel und Gretel*, 1989–90

Ostertag, Maribeth: Shepherd Figure in the Wallpaper, *L'Enfant et les Sortilèges (The Bewitched Child)*, 1955–56; Berta (Marcellina), *Il Barbiere di Siviglia (The Barber of Seville)*, 1956–57; Louise, *Annie Get Your Gun*, 1956–57; Mercedes, *Carmen*, 1956–57; Sandman, *Hänsel und Gretel*, 1956–57; Angelina (Cinderella), *La Cenerentola (Cinderella)*, 1957–58; Anna Leonowens, *The King and I*, 1957–58; Nancy, *Albert Herring*, 1957–58; Shepherd Boy, *Tosca*, 1957–58; Clairon, *Capriccio*, 1958–59; Princess Clarissa, *The Love for Three Oranges*, 1958–59; Suzuki, *Madama Butterfly*, 1958–59

Ott, Quinto: Ambrogio, *Il Barbiere di Siviglia (The Barber of Seville)*, 2005–06; Prince of Verona, *Roméo et Juliette*, 2005–06

Otterman, Frank: Jigger Craigin, *Carousel*, 1970–71

Otwell, Kathleen: The Governess, *La Pique Dame (The Queen of Spades)*, 1968–69

Owen, Janice: Esmeralda, *The Bartered Bride,* 1967–68; Javotte, *Manon,* 1967–68; First Maid, *The Boys from Syracuse,* 1968–69

Ozer, Lynne: Milliner, *Der Rosenkavalier,* 1965–66

Pabon, Susan: Page, *Parsifal,* 1975–76; Princess Linetta, *The Love for Three Oranges,* 1975–76; Samantha, *The Ballad of Baby Doe,* 1975–76; Dorabella, *Così fan tutte,* 1977–78; First Woman of Paris, *Danton and Robespierre,* 1977–78; Mercedes, *Carmen,* 1977–78; Sixth Woman of Paris, *Danton and Robespierre,* 1977–78; The Tsaritsa, *The Night Before Christmas,* 1977–78; Hostess of the Inn, *Boris Godunov,* 1978–79; Mrs. Grose, *The Turn of the Screw,* 1978–79; Donna Elvira, *Don Giovanni,* 1979–80

Packard, Florence: Blanche, *Dialogues des Carmélites,* 1965–66; First Lady, *Die Zauberflöte (The Magic Flute),* 1965–66; Constanza, *Die Entführung aus dem Serail (The Abduction from the Seraglio),* 1966–67

Page, Paula: Nella, *Gianni Schicchi,* 1964–65; Annina, *Der Rosenkavalier,* 1965–66; Lady in Waiting, *Macbeth,* 1965–66; Mother Marie of the Incarnation, *Dialogues des Carmélites,* 1965–66; Third Lady, *Die Zauberflöte (The Magic Flute),* 1965–66; Nancy, *Albert Herring,* 1966–67; Stephano, *Roméo et Juliette,* 1966–67

Page, Robert: Jenkins, *The Firefly,* 1949–50; Alexius Spiridoff, *The Chocolate Soldier,* 1950–51; Eland, *Lost in the Stars,* 1950–51; Morales, *Carmen,* 1956–57; Customs Officer, *La Bohème,* 1957–58; Jailer, *Tosca,* 1957–58; Knight, *Parsifal,* 1957–58; Mr. Gedge, *Albert Herring,* 1957–58; Hans Foltz, *Die Meistersinger von Nürnberg (The Mastersingers of Nuremberg),* 1961–62

Paglin, Lisa: Fiametta, *The Gondoliers,* 1974–75

Paik, Eui Hyun: Priest, *Murder in the Cathedral,* 1984–85; Boatswain, *The Tempest,* 1985–86

Palay, Elliot: Baron Douphol, *La Traviata,* 1968–69; Betto, *Il Trittico (A Triptych),* 1969–70; Lancelot, *Camelot,* 1969–70; Chevalier des Grieux, *Manon Lescaut,* 1970–71; Narraboth, *Salome,* 1970–71

Palla, Joseph Nicholas: Ballet Tony, *West Side Story,* 1985–86; Toro, *West Side Story,* 1985–86; Simon of Legree, *The King and I,* 1996–97

Palmer, Arthur: Milkman, *Street Scene,* 1960–61; Policeman, *Street Scene,* 1960–61

Palmer, Gail: Gertrude, *Roméo et Juliette,* 1966–67

Palmer, Lanny: Lauretta, *Il Trittico (A Triptych),* 1969–70

Palmer, Thomas: Marcello, *La Bohème,* 1970–71; Ford, *Falstaff,* 1971–72

Palmer, Virginia: A Tourier, *Il Trittico (A Triptych),* 1982–83

Palmore, Gail: Mother Jeanne, *Dialogues des Carmélites,* 1965–66

Palsson, Bergthor: Doctor Grenville, *La Traviata,* 1983–84; Schelkalov, *Boris Godunov,* 1983–84; Theseus, *A Midsummer Night's Dream,* 1983–84; Tempter, *Murder in the Cathedral,* 1984–85; Masetto, *Don Giovanni,* 1985–86; The Marquis de la Force, *Dialogues des Carmélites,* 1986–87; Trulove, *The Rake's Progress,* 1986–87; Tsar Saltan, *The Legend of Tsar Saltan,* 1986–87

Palsson, Solrun: First Lay Sister, *Il Trittico (A Triptych),* 1982–83; Sister Lucilla, *Il Trittico (A Triptych),* 1982–83; Annina, *La Traviata,* 1983–84

Paltiel, Ellen: Gelosia, *L'Orfeo,* 1987–88

Panousis, Art: Sandy Dean, *Brigadoon,* 1953–54

Papakhian, Anahid: Irene Molloy, *Hello, Dolly!,* 1991–92; Esmeralda, *The Bartered Bride,* 1994–95

Papavassiliou, Stuart: Zaccheus, *Passion Play—Carmina Burana,* 1982–83

Papian, Sharon: Nurse of the Children, *Boris Godunov,* 1964–65; Zita, *Gianni Schicchi,* 1964–65; Mother Marie of the Incarnation, *Dialogues des Carmélites,* 1965–66; Third Lady, *Die Zauberflöte (The Magic Flute),* 1965–66; Florence Pike, *Albert Herring,* 1966–67; Margarita, *Quattro rusteghi (The Four Ruffians),* 1966–67; Florence Pike, *Albert Herring,* 1967–68; Martha, *Mefistofele,* 1967–68

Papps, George: Titurel, *Parsifal,* 1957–58; Count Ceprano, *Rigoletto,* 1959–60; The Jailer, *Die Kluge (The Clever Girl),* 1959–60

Parcher, William: Drunk, *Danton and Robespierre,* 1977–78; Escamillo, *Carmen,* 1977–78; Jailer, *Tosca,* 1977–78; Rudi Panko, *The Night Before Christmas,* 1977–78; Crespel, *Les Contes d'Hoffmann (The Tales of Hoffmann),* 1978–79; Don Alfonso, *Così fan tutte,* 1978–79; Mayor, *The Darkened City,* 1978–79; Miller, *Canterbury Tales,* 1978–79; Varlaam, *Boris Godunov,* 1978–79; Alfred P. Doolittle, *My Fair Lady,* 1979–80; Count des Grieux, *Manon,* 1979–80; Olin Blitch, *Susannah,* 1979–80; Ser Metteo del Sarto, *Arlecchino,* 1979–80; Figaro, *Il Barbiere di Siviglia (The Barber of Seville),* 1980–81

Park, Erica: Sister Mathilde, *Dialogues des Carmélites,* 1997–98

Park, Mi Young: Olympia, *Les Contes d'Hoffmann (The Tales of Hoffmann),* 2002–03

Park, Sae-Jung: The Imperial Commissioner, *Madama Butterfly,* 1981–82; An Indian, *The Bartered Bride,* 1986–87

Park, Soon Young: Ford, *Falstaff,* 2003–04; Notary, *Don Pasquale,* 2003–04; Baron Scarpia, *Tosca,* 2004–05; Marcello, *La Bohème,* 2004–05

Parker, Essic: Jim, *Porgy and Bess,* 1979–80

Parker, Wyatt: Mr. Gedge, *Albert Herring,* 1966–67

Parks, Julia: Dorabella, *Così fan tutte,* 1984–85; Mercedes, *Carmen,* 1984–85; Ariel, *The Tempest,* 1985–86; Prince Orlofsky, *Die Fledermaus (The Bat),*

1985–86; Cherubino, *Le Nozze di Figaro (The Marriage of Figaro)*, 1986–87; Mother Marie of the Incarnation, *Dialogues des Carmélites*, 1986–87

Parlier, Beth: Page, *Rigoletto*, 2000–01

Parly, Ticho: Curly, *Oklahoma!*, 1954–55; Robert Baker, *Wonderful Town*, 1954–55; Scott, *The Ruby*, 1954–55

Parr, Joseph: Amantio di Nicolao, *Il Trittico (A Triptych)*, 1969–70

Parry, Scott: Guard, *Down in the Valley*, 1998–99

Parsons, William: Governor's Aide, *Candide*, 1993–94; Judge of the Inquisition, *Candide*, 1993–94; Count Almaviva, *Il Barbiere di Siviglia (The Barber of Seville)*, 1994–95; Ottone, *Agrippina*, 1995–96; The Witch, *Hänsel und Gretel*, 1995–96

Partridge, James: Professor, *South Pacific*, 1956–57

Pass, Matthew: Longinus, *Passion Play—Carmina Burana*, 1982–83

Patterson, Elaine: Minnie, *Annie Get Your Gun*, 1956–57; The Frog, *L'Enfant et les Sortilèges (The Bewitched Child)*, 1984–85

Patterson, Kevin: Juan / a Muleteer, *Man of La Mancha*, 1988–89; Poet, *Bluebeard's Castle*, 1988–89; The Stage Manager, *1600 Pennsylvania Avenue*, 1992–93

Patterson, Matthew: Froh, *Das Rheingold*, 1983–84; Señor of Cadiz, *Candide*, 1983–84; Simpleton, *Boris Godunov*, 1983–84; Victim of the Inquisition, *Candide*, 1983–84; Westphalian Soldier, *Candide*, 1983–84; Arithmetic, *L'Enfant et les Sortilèges (The Bewitched Child)*, 1984–85; The Frog, *L'Enfant et les Sortilèges (The Bewitched Child)*, 1984–85; Adrian, *The Tempest*, 1985–86

Patterson, Susan: Asteria, *Tamerlano*, 1984–85; Marie, *La Fille du régiment (The Daughter of the Regiment)*, 1984–85

Patterson, Teresa: Auntie, *Peter Grimes*, 1987–88

Patton, Donald: Furniture Mover, *Street Scene*, 1949–50

Patton, Ronald: Frank, *Die Fledermaus (The Bat)*, 1962–63; Sir Roderic Murgatroyd, *Ruddigore (The Witch's Curse)*, 1962–63; Zuniga, *Carmen*, 1962–63; The Narrator, *The Fantasticks*, 1963–64; Chevalier de St. Brioche, *Die lustige Witwe (The Merry Widow)*, 1964–65; Marco, *Gianni Schicchi*, 1964–65; The Imperial Commissioner, *Madama Butterfly*, 1964–65; Chevalier de St. Brioche, *Die lustige Witwe (The Merry Widow)*, 1965–66

Paul, Ian: Washington Dandy, *The Ballad of Baby Doe*, 2003–04; First Commissioner, *Dialogues des Carmélites*, 2004–05

Pavlick, Elaine: Lizzie Curry, *110 in the Shade*, 1967–68; Isabella, *L'Italiana in Algeri (The Italian Girl in Algiers)*, 1968–69; Lizzie Curry, *110 in the Shade*, 1968–69; Magdalena, *Die Meistersinger von Nürnberg (The Mastersingers*

of Nuremberg), 1968–69; Ciesca, *Il Trittico (A Triptych)*, 1969–70; Nerea, *Deidamia*, 1969–70; Fiordiligi, *Così fan tutte*, 1970–71; Julie Jordan, *Carousel*, 1970–71; Marzelline, *Fidelio*, 1970–71; Nanetta, *Falstaff*, 1971–72; Zerlina, *Don Giovanni*, 1971–72

Paxton, Larry: Fouquier-Tinville, *Danton and Robespierre*, 1977–78; A Steersman, *Der Fliegende Holländer (The Flying Dutchman)*, 1978–79; Absalon, *Canterbury Tales*, 1978–79; Minstrel, *The Darkened City*, 1978–79; Peter Quint, *The Turn of the Screw*, 1978–79; Prince Shuisky, *Boris Godunov*, 1978–79; Prologue, *The Turn of the Screw*, 1978–79; The Clerk of Oxford, *Canterbury Tales*, 1978–79; Aegisthus, *The Cry of Clytaemnestra*, 1979–80; Jenik, *The Bartered Bride*, 1979–80; Rodolfo, *La Bohème*, 1979–80; Manolios, *The Greek Passion*, 1980–81; Vladimir, *Prince Igor*, 1980–81; Martin, *Candide*, 1983–84; The Governor of Cartagena, *Candide*, 1983–84

Payas, Nathan: The Duke of Mantua, *Rigoletto*, 2000–01; Guillot de Morfontaine, *Manon*, 2001–02; Don Ottavio, *Don Giovanni*, 2002–03

Payne, Betsy: Violet, *Wonderful Town*, 1954–55

Payne, Marilyn: Mistress Hibbins, *The Scarlet Letter*, 1960–61; Princess Eboli, *Don Carlos*, 1960–61; Third Lady, *Die Zauberflöte (The Magic Flute)*, 1960–61; Charlotte, *Werther*, 1961–62; Magdalena, *Die Meistersinger von Nürnberg (The Mastersingers of Nuremberg)*, 1961–62; Oberon, *A Midsummer Night's Dream*, 1961–62; Princess Eboli, *Don Carlos*, 1961–62

Payne, Robyn: Estella, *West Side Story*, 1992–93; Flautist, *Candide*, 1993–94; Rosette, *Manon*, 1993–94; Susan, *Carousel*, 1993–94

Payton, Donald: A Lamplighter, *Manon Lescaut*, 1970–71; Second Nazarene, *Salome*, 1970–71; Dr. Caius, *Falstaff*, 1971–72; Gherardo, *Il Trittico (A Triptych)*, 1972–73; Page, *Parsifal*, 1972–73; Royal Herald, *Don Carlos*, 1972–73; Tinca, *Il Trittico (A Triptych)*, 1972–73; Jo the Loiterer, *The Mother of Us All*, 1973–74; Remendado, *Carmen*, 1973–74; Cecco, *Il Mondo della Luna (The World on the Moon)*, 1975–76; Mr. Erlanson, *A Little Night Music*, 1975–76

Peacock, John: Lancelot, *Camelot*, 1969–70; Policeman, *Carousel*, 1970–71

Peacock, Joseph: Albazar, *Il Turco in Italia (The Turk in Italy)*, 1996–97; Don Curzio, *Le Nozze di Figaro (The Marriage of Figaro)*, 1997–98; Hortensio, *Kiss Me, Kate*, 1998–99

Peacock, Joseph: Mercury, *Orphée aux enfers (Orpheus in the Underworld)*, 1998–99

Pearl, Janice: Page, *Parsifal*, 1951–52; Blonde, *Die Entführung aus dem Serail (The Abduction from the Seraglio)*, 1951–52

Peden, Charis: Candace, *A Wedding*, 2007–08

Pedersen, Judith: A Novice, *Il Trittico (A Triptych),* 1969–70; Oscar, *Un Ballo in Maschera (A Masked Ball),* 1969–70; Despina, *Così fan tutte,* 1970–71; Aglaya, *Myshkin,* 1972–73

Peeler, Steven: Boatswain, *The Tempest,* 1985–86; Servant, *Dialogues des Carmélites,* 1986–87; Thierry, *Dialogues des Carmélites,* 1986–87; Maximilian, *Candide,* 1987–88; The French Ambassador, *Of Thee I Sing,* 1987–88

Pell, William: Roucher, *Andrea Chénier,* 1967–68; Haly, *L'Italiana in Algeri (The Italian Girl in Algiers),* 1968–69; Count Asdrubale, *Love on Trial (La Pietra del Paragone),* 1969–70; Phoenix, *Deidamia,* 1969–70

Pellinen, Peter: Slender (Spaerlich), *Die lustigen Weiber von Windsor (The Merry Wives of Windsor),* 1981–82; Lover, *Il Trittico (A Triptych),* 1982–83; Newsboy, *The Ballad of Baby Doe,* 1982–83; Old Silver Miner, *The Ballad of Baby Doe,* 1982–83; Slave, *Die Zauberflöte (The Magic Flute),* 1982–83; Song Vendor, *Il Trittico (A Triptych),* 1982–83; Washington Dandy, *The Ballad of Baby Doe,* 1982–83; Blifil, *Tom Jones,* 1983–84; Chevalier de St. Brioche, *Die lustige Witwe (The Merry Widow),* 1983–84; Snout, *A Midsummer Night's Dream,* 1983–84

Pender, Martha: Leonora, *Il Trovatore,* 1967–68

Penn, Hannah: Marcellina, *Le Nozze di Figaro (The Marriage of Figaro),* 2001–02; Cornelia, *Giulio Cesare (Julius Caesar),* 2002–03; Augusta Tabor, *The Ballad of Baby Doe,* 2003–04

Penn, Jeffrey: Morales, *Carmen,* 1977–78; Second Thug, *Danton and Robespierre,* 1977–78; Marquis D'Obigny, *La Traviata,* 1978–79; Schelkalov, *Boris Godunov,* 1978–79; Marcello, *La Bohème,* 1979–80

Peo, Ron: Varlaam, *Boris Godunov,* 1983–84; Don Inigo Gomez, *L'Heure espagnole (The Spanish Hour),* 1984–85; Knight, *Murder in the Cathedral,* 1984–85; Mars, *Orphée aux enfers (Orpheus in the Underworld),* 1984–85; The Clock, *L'Enfant et les Sortilèges (The Bewitched Child),* 1984–85; Escamillo, *Carmen,* 1984–85; Don Giovanni, *Don Giovanni,* 1985–86

Pepka, Edgar: Besac, *The New Moon,* 1949–50; Novakovich, *Die lustige Witwe (The Merry Widow),* 1949–50; Schaunard, *La Bohème,* 1949–50; Pish-Tush, *The Mikado,* 1950–51

Peplinski, Andrew: A Herald, *The Love for Three Oranges,* 1993–94

Peplinski, Leo: Slave, *Die Zauberflöte (The Magic Flute),* 1988–89; 4th Muezzin, *Kismet,* 1989–90

Pereira, Kenneth: Sharpless, *Madama Butterfly,* 2006–07; Marcello, *La Bohème,* 2007–08; Schlemil, *Les Contes d'Hoffmann (The Tales of Hoffmann),* 2007–08; Spalanzani, *Les Contes d'Hoffmann (The Tales of Hoffmann),* 2007–08

Perez, Ailyn: Despina, *Così fan tutte,* 2000–01; Esmeralda, *The Bartered Bride,* 2001–02

Perez, Antonio: Pantalone, *The Love for Three Oranges,* 1958–59; Count Monterone, *Rigoletto,* 1959–60; Pasquale, *The Most Happy Fella,* 1959–60

Periolat, Jeanne: Assistant Courtesan, *The Boys from Syracuse,* 1968–69

Perkins, Ellistine: Fata Morgana, *The Love for Three Oranges,* 1958–59; Waitress, *The Most Happy Fella,* 1959–60

Perkins, Joseph: Pepe, *West Side Story,* 2002–03

Perkins, Susanne: Clarice, *West Side Story,* 1992–93

Perrin, Mary Ann: Mrs. Higgins, *My Fair Lady,* 1979–80

Perry, Amanda: Sally, *Die Fledermaus (The Bat),* 1996–97; Diana, *Orphée aux enfers (Orpheus in the Underworld),* 1998–99

Perry, David: Peaseblossom, *A Midsummer Night's Dream,* 1983–84

Perry, Jean: Adelina, *Song of Norway,* 1951–52

Perry, Mary: Priestess, *Aida,* 1963–64

Person, Heidi: Lisette, *La Rondine (The Swallow),* 1989–90; Adele, *Die Fledermaus (The Bat),* 1990–91; Serpetta, *La Finta Giardiniera,* 1990–91

Pesdan, Cheryl: Tatyana, *Eugene Onegin,* 1988–89; Electra, *The Cry of Clytaemnestra,* 1989–90; Musetta, *La Bohème,* 1989–90; Marie, *Wozzeck,* 1990–91; Cio-Cio San, *Madama Butterfly,* 1991–92

Peters, Abigail: Rosette, *Manon,* 2006–07; Suzuki, *Madama Butterfly,* 2006–07; Voice of the Mother, *Les Contes d'Hoffmann (The Tales of Hoffmann),* 2007–08

Peters, Patricia: Helen, *Wonderful Town,* 1954–55

Peterson, Dana: Countess Ceprano, *Rigoletto,* 1992–93

Peterson, Michael: Old Man, *The Darkened City,* 1978–79; Borsa, *Rigoletto,* 1980–81; Oliver Hix, *The Music Man,* 1980–81

Pflieger, John: Marullo, *Rigoletto,* 1966–67; Paris, *Roméo et Juliette,* 1966–67

Philips, Shane: Baby John, *West Side Story,* 1992–93

Phillips, Bary: Jake, *Porgy and Bess,* 1976–77; Player, *Bernstein on Broadway,* 1976–77

Phillips, Debra: Nutrice, *L'Orfeo,* 1987–88; Angel (adult), *The Dawn of the Poor King,* 1990–91; Kate Pinkerton, *Madama Butterfly,* 1991–92; Zerlina, *Don Giovanni,* 1991–92

Phillips, Harvey: Mowgli (Charles Rausmiller), *Jubilee,* 1991–92

Phillips, Linda: Juliet, *Roméo et Juliette,* 1966–67; Lucietta, *Quattro rusteghi (The Four Ruffians),* 1966–67; Drusilla, *L'Incoronazione di Poppea (The Coronation of Poppea),* 1967–68; Hilda Mack, *Elegy for Young Lovers,* 1967–68

Phillips, Norman: Rigoletto, *Rigoletto,* 1986–87

Phillips, Tamara: Eliza Doolittle, *My Fair Lady*, 1979–80

Piche, Guy: Belmonte, *Die Entführung aus dem Serail (The Abduction from the Seraglio)*, 1951–52; Parsifal, *Parsifal*, 1951–52

Pickett, Lauren: Mrs. Gleaton, *Susannah*, 2007–08

Pickett, Rick: A Denver Politician, *The Ballad of Baby Doe*, 1975–76; Tom, *Un Ballo in Maschera (A Masked Ball)*, 1975–76; Elder Ott, *Susannah*, 1976–77; Jigger Craigin, *Carousel*, 1976–77; The Bonze, *Madama Butterfly*, 1976–77; Man in Armor, *Die Zauberflöte (The Magic Flute)*, 1977–78; Patsyuk, *The Night Before Christmas*, 1977–78; St. Just, *Danton and Robespierre*, 1977–78; Second Bearer, *The Darkened City*, 1978–79; Dottor Bombasto, *Arlecchino*, 1979–80

Pidduck, Chester: Don Curzio, *Le Nozze di Figaro (The Marriage of Figaro)*, 2001–02; Porter of the Seminary, *Manon*, 2001–02; Gastone, *La Traviata*, 2002–03; Albazar, *Il Turco in Italia (The Turk in Italy)*, 2003–04; Chevalier de St. Brioche, *Die lustige Witwe (The Merry Widow)*, 2003–04; Simon Stimson, *Our Town*, 2005–06

Piekarsky, Daniel: Candide, *Candide*, 1993–94; Borsa, *Rigoletto*, 1995–96

Pier, Christina: Dryad, *Ariadne auf Naxos*, 1996–97; Maestra dell Novizie, *Suor Angelica (Sister Angelica)*, 1999–2000; Dorabella, *Così fan tutte*, 2000–01; Countess Almaviva, *Le Nozze di Figaro (The Marriage of Figaro)*, 2001–02; Donna Elvira, *Don Giovanni*, 2002–03

Pierce, Alice: Eurydice, *Orphée aux enfers (Orpheus in the Underworld)*, 1984–85; Fire, *L'Enfant et les Sortilèges (The Bewitched Child)*, 1984–85; Iris, *The Tempest*, 1985–86; Lisa, *La Sonnambula (The Sleepwalker)*, 1985–86

Pierce, John: Ramiro, *L'Heure espagnole (The Spanish Hour)*, 1984–85; Tempter, *Murder in the Cathedral*, 1984–85; Prospero, *The Tempest*, 1985–86; Belcore, *L'Elisir d'amore (The Elixir of Love)*, 1986–87; Count Monterone, *Rigoletto*, 1986–87; Nick Shadow, *The Rake's Progress*, 1986–87; John Proctor, *The Crucible*, 1987–88

Pierson, David: Merchant of Ephesus, *The Boys from Syracuse*, 1968–69; Sir Dinadan, *Camelot*, 1969–70

Pilar, Nobleza: Queen of the Night, *Die Zauberflöte (The Magic Flute)*, 1965–66; Pousette, *Manon*, 1967–68

Pita, Jorge: Gastone, *La Traviata*, 1983–84; Rodolfo, *La Bohème*, 1984–85

Pittman, Reginald: Don Basilio, *Le Nozze di Figaro (The Marriage of Figaro)*, 1980–81; Ovlor, *Prince Igor*, 1980–81; Truffaldino, *The Love for Three Oranges*, 1980–81; Fenton, *Die lustigen Weiber von Windsor (The Merry Wives of Windsor)*, 1981–82; Alfred, *Die Fledermaus (The Bat)*, 1982–83; Clem, *The Most Happy Fella*, 1982–83; Prince Tamino, *Die Zauberflöte (The Magic Flute)*, 1982–83; Lysander, *A Midsummer Night's Dream*, 1983–84; Vicomte Camille di Rosillon, *Die lustige Witwe (The Merry Widow)*, 1983–84; The Caliph, *Kismet*, 1989–90

Pizzo, Andy: Willie Maurant, *Street Scene*, 1960–61

Plant, Walter: Jenik, *The Bartered Bride*, 1967–68; Knight, *Parsifal*, 1967–68; Lucano, *L'Incoronazione di Poppea (The Coronation of Poppea)*, 1967–68; Nergus, *Mefistofele*, 1967–68; Ruiz, *Il Trovatore*, 1967–68; Gherman, *La Pique Dame (The Queen of Spades)*, 1968–69; Gastone, *La Traviata*, 1968–69; Knight, *Parsifal*, 1968–69; Lover, *Il Trittico (A Triptych)*, 1969–70; Rinuccio, *Il Trittico (A Triptych)*, 1969–70; Rinuccio, *Il Trittico (A Triptych)*, 1972–73; Hoffmann, *Les Contes d'Hoffmann (The Tales of Hoffmann)*, 1973–74; Lensky, *Eugene Onegin*, 1974–75

Plate, Wilfried: Gabriele Adorno, *Simon Boccanegra*, 1964–65; Grigori (Dimitri, the Pretender), *Boris Godunov*, 1964–65; Don Jose, *Carmen*, 1965–66

Ploss, Shelley: Maid, *A Wedding*, 2007–08

Plourde, Jason: Marquis D'Obigny, *La Traviata*, 2002–03; Baron Mirko Zeta, *Die lustige Witwe (The Merry Widow)*, 2003–04; Swallow, *Peter Grimes*, 2003–04; William Jennings Bryan, *The Ballad of Baby Doe*, 2003–04; Don Magnifico, *La Cenerentola (Cinderella)*, 2004–05; The Marquis de la Force, *Dialogues des Carmélites*, 2004–05; Figaro, *Il Barbiere di Siviglia (The Barber of Seville)*, 2005–06; Sir Joseph Porter, *HMS Pinafore*, 2005–06

Plucinik, Mary Ann: The McCourt family, *The Ballad of Baby Doe*, 1975–76; Duenna, *Canterbury Tales*, 1978–79

Poeschl, Baerbl: Oscar, *Un Ballo in Maschera (A Masked Ball)*, 1975–76

Poffenberger, Jennifer: Dodo, *Die lustige Witwe (The Merry Widow)*, 1990–91; Sally, *Die Fledermaus (The Bat)*, 1990–91

Pohlhammer, James: Benoit, *La Bohème*, 1970–71; Captain in the Navy, *Manon Lescaut*, 1970–71

Poindexter, Jay: Robbins, *Porgy and Bess*, 1979–80

Poland, Ray: Soldier, *The Boys from Syracuse*, 1968–69; Customs Officer, *La Bohème*, 1970–71; Schaunard, *La Bohème*, 1970–71

Polichio, Marjorie: The Nightingale, *L'Enfant et les Sortilèges (The Bewitched Child)*, 1955–56

Polk, Rebecca: Zerbinetta, *Ariadne auf Naxos*, 1996–97

Pollock, Evelyn: Lucia, *Lucia di Lammermoor*, 2001–02; Marian Paroo, *The Music Man*, 2001–02; Violetta Valery, *La Traviata*, 2002–03

Polson, Pat: Noble Orphan, *Der Rosenkavalier*, 1965–66

Polzin, Don: Knight, *Parsifal*, 1953–54; Mityukh, *Boris Godunov*, 1953–54

Pomfret, Bonnie: Adele, *Die Fledermaus (The Bat),* 1985–86

Ponella, Tony: Spirit, *Die Zauberflöte (The Magic Flute),* 2004–05; Cobweb, *A Midsummer Night's Dream,* 2005–06

Pons, Emilio Jiminez: Elder Gleaton, *Susannah,* 2000–01; Normanno, *Lucia di Lammermoor,* 2001–02; Sesto, *Giulio Cesare (Julius Caesar),* 2002–03; The Fakir, *The Secret Garden,* 2003–04

Ponticelli, Elvira: Player, *Mass,* 1987–88; Fredrika Armfeldt, *A Little Night Music,* 1988–89

Pool, Gary: An Indian, *The Bartered Bride,* 1967–68; Balthasar Zorn, *Die Meistersinger von Nürnberg (The Mastersingers of Nuremberg),* 1968–69; Gherardo, *Il Trittico (A Triptych),* 1969–70; Spoletta, *Tosca,* 1969–70; Tinca, *Il Trittico (A Triptych),* 1969–70; The Dancing Master, *Manon Lescaut,* 1970–71; Bardolph, *Falstaff,* 1971–72

Poor, Mary: Lady Anne, *Camelot,* 1969–70; Naiad, *Ariadne auf Naxos,* 1969–70; Oscar, *Un Ballo in Maschera (A Masked Ball),* 1969–70; Lauretta, *Il Trittico (A Triptych),* 1972–73; Lover, *Il Trittico (A Triptych),* 1972–73; Sister Geneviève, *Il Trittico (A Triptych),* 1972–73; Angel More, *The Mother of Us All,* 1973–74

Popcheff, Louis: Jacques, *The New Moon,* 1949–50

Pope, Greta: Lily, *Porgy and Bess,* 1976–77

Popkin, Meera: Player, *Mass,* 1987–88; A Moorish Girl, *Man of La Mancha,* 1988–89; Player, *Mass,* 1988–89

Popp, Mary Jane: Adriana, *The Boys from Syracuse,* 1968–69

Poppino, Marilyn: Princess Clarissa, *The Love for Three Oranges,* 1980–81; Kedruta, *The Excursions of Mr. Broucek,* 1981–82; Margaret, *Wozzeck,* 1981–82; The Witch, *Hänsel und Gretel,* 1982–83; Zita, *Il Trittico (A Triptych),* 1982–83

Porter, Margaret: Waitress, *The Most Happy Fella,* 1959–60

Porter, Pamela: First Lady, *Die Zauberflöte (The Magic Flute),* 1972–73

Porterfield, Robyn: Angel, *West Side Story,* 1992–93

Portinga, Vada: Kate Pinkerton, *Madama Butterfly,* 1964–65; Frasquita, *Carmen,* 1965–66

Posell, George: Notary, *Il Barbiere di Siviglia (The Barber of Seville),* 1956–57; Notary, *Don Pasquale,* 1957–58; Abraham Kaplan, *Street Scene,* 1960–61; Andrew MacLaren, *Brigadoon,* 1961–62; Klaas, *Die Entführung aus dem Serail (The Abduction from the Seraglio),* 1961–62

Potter, Chase: John, *Peter Grimes,* 1994–95

Potter, Thomas: Antonio, *Le Nozze di Figaro (The Marriage of Figaro),* 1980–81; Pantalone, *The Love for Three Oranges,* 1980–81; Prince Yamadori, *Madama Butterfly,* 1981–82; Wuerfl, *The Excursions of Mr. Broucek,* 1981–82; Amantio

di Nicolao, *Il Trittico (A Triptych),* 1982–83; Dr. Falke, *Die Fledermaus (The Bat),* 1982–83

Poulos, Bonnie: Mary, *Der Fliegende Holländer (The Flying Dutchman),* 1962–63; Marcellina, *Le Nozze di Figaro (The Marriage of Figaro),* 1968–69

Powell, Alvy: Crown, *Porgy and Bess,* 1979–80

Powell, Greg: Dancaire, *Carmen,* 1977–78; Papageno, *Die Zauberflöte (The Magic Flute),* 1977–78; Second Speaker, *Danton and Robespierre,* 1977–78; Sir Harry Blake, *Naughty Marietta,* 1977–78

Powers, Mary: The Abbess, *Il Trittico (A Triptych),* 1969–70

Poyner, Deborah: Mama Sieppe, *McTeague,* 1995–96; Susanna, *The Ghosts of Versailles,* 1996–97; Mother Marie of the Incarnation, *Dialogues des Carmélites,* 1997–98; Suor Angelica, *Suor Angelica (Sister Angelica),* 1999–2000

Pratnicki, Marion: Eulalie MacKecknie Shinn, *The Music Man,* 1980–81; Giovanna, *Rigoletto,* 1980–81

Pratt, Nathan: Colin Craven, *The Secret Garden,* 2003–04; John, *Peter Grimes,* 2003–04; Spirit, *Die Zauberflöte (The Magic Flute),* 2004–05

Pressler, Ami: Trouble, *Madama Butterfly,* 1958–59

Pressler, Barbara: Giorgetta, *Il Trittico (A Triptych),* 1982–83; Valencienne, *Die lustige Witwe (The Merry Widow),* 1983–84

Pressler, James: Mr. Matej Broucek, *The Excursions of Mr. Broucek,* 1981–82; The Captain, *Wozzeck,* 1981–82

Price, Dwaine: Goro, *Madama Butterfly,* 1958–59; Borsa, *Rigoletto,* 1959–60

Price, Julia: The Bat, *L'Enfant et les Sortilèges (The Bewitched Child),* 1984–85

Priddy, John: Loge, *Das Rheingold,* 1983–84; Gaylord Ravenal, *Show Boat,* 1984–85; Sebastian, *The Tempest,* 1985–86; Reverend Samuel Parris, *The Crucible,* 1987–88

Pridgen, Shaunica: Consuelo, *West Side Story,* 2002–03

Prime, Krystal: Venus, *Orphée aux enfers (Orpheus in the Underworld),* 1992–93; Princess Nicoletta, *The Love for Three Oranges,* 1993–94

Prince, Melinda: Virginia, *Carousel,* 1993–94

Pringle, Catherine Carrier: Margot, *Die lustige Witwe (The Merry Widow),* 1996–97

Proctor, Daniel: Action, *West Side Story,* 1985–86; Bulgarian Soldier, *Candide,* 1987–88; Enforcer, *Candide,* 1987–88; Player, *Mass,* 1987–88; Player, *Mass,* 1988–89

Prokop, Jan: Mistress Anne Page (Anna Reich), *Die lustigen Weiber von Windsor (The Merry Wives of Windsor),* 1981–82; Adele, *Die Fledermaus (The Bat),*

1982–83; Papagena, *Die Zauberflöte (The Magic Flute)*, 1982–83; Johanna, *Sweeney Todd*, 1983–84

Provenzale, Nicholas: Prince Peter, *Jubilee*, 1991–92; Juan / a Muleteer, *Man of La Mancha*, 1999–2000; James, *Candide*, 2000–01; Player, *Putting It Together*, 2002–03; Count Danilo Danilovitch, *Die lustige Witwe (The Merry Widow)*, 2003–04; Lt. Peter Wright, *The Secret Garden*, 2003–04; Georg Nowack, *She Loves Me*, 2004–05

Pruett, Chris: Jaquino, *Fidelio*, 1970–71; Grigori (Dimitri, the Pretender), *Boris Godunov*, 1983–84

Pryor, Gwin: Julie Jordan, *Carousel*, 1952–53; Papagena, *Die Zauberflöte (The Magic Flute)*, 1953–54

Pugh, Guy: Notary, *Don Pasquale*, 1980–81

Pugh, James: Elder Hayes, *Susannah*, 1976–77; Fenton, *Falstaff*, 1976–77

Puglisi, Joseph: Guardsman, *Manon*, 2001–02

Purcell, Alicia: Maid, *Vanessa*, 1974–75; Mrs. Hayes, *Susannah*, 1976–77; Frasquita, *Carmen*, 1977–78; Second Lady, *Die Zauberflöte (The Magic Flute)*, 1977–78

Purvis, Derrick: Father Rangier, *Die Teufel von Loudun (The Devils of Loudun)*, 1992–93; Pistol, *Falstaff*, 1992–93; Cesare Angelotti, *Tosca*, 1993–94; Judge of the Inquisition, *Candide*, 1993–94; Kreonte, *The Love for Three Oranges*, 1993–94; Osmin, *Die Entführung aus dem Serail (The Abduction from the Seraglio)*, 1993–94; Simone, *Gianni Schicchi*, 1993–94; Arkel, *Pelléas et Mélisande*, 1994–95; Hobson, *Peter Grimes*, 1994–95; Don Alfonso, *Così fan tutte*, 1995–96; Emile DeBeque, *South Pacific*, 1995–96

Pye, Edith: A young girl, *Heracles*, 1971–72; Jano, *Jenůfa*, 1972–73; Sister Angelica, *Il Trittico (A Triptych)*, 1972–73; Micaëla, *Carmen*, 1973–74

Quale, Signe: First Lady, *Die Zauberflöte (The Magic Flute)*, 1953–54

Quinn, John: Hermann, *Les Contes d'Hoffmann (The Tales of Hoffmann)*, 1973–74

Raab, Katherine: Uncle Tom, *The King and I*, 1957–58

Rabbitt, Ashleigh: Naiad, *Ariadne auf Naxos*, 1996–97; Barbarina, *Le Nozze di Figaro (The Marriage of Figaro)*, 1997–98

Rabiner, Ellen: Cherubino, *Le Nozze di Figaro (The Marriage of Figaro)*, 1980–81; Siebel, *Faust*, 1981–82; Beggar Woman, *Sweeney Todd*, 1983–84

Radder, Megan: Gretel, *Hänsel und Gretel*, 2006–07; Yum-Yum, *The Mikado*, 2006–07; Gilda, *Rigoletto*, 2007–08

Rademaker, Debra: Giulia, *The Gondoliers*, 1974–75

Radke, Sara: Countess Ceprano, *Rigoletto*, 2007–08

Radulescu, Paul: Figaro, *Il Barbiere di Siviglia (The Barber of Seville)*, 1994–95

Ragains, Diana: Waitress, *The Most Happy Fella*, 1959–60; Jenny Hildebrand, *Street Scene*, 1960–61

Ragan, Kari: Lolo, *Die lustige Witwe (The Merry Widow)*, 1990–91

Rahming, Gregory: Barbary Pirate, *Candide*, 1983–84; Lion, *Candide*, 1983–84; Puck, *A Midsummer Night's Dream*, 1983–84; Corporal, *La Fille du régiment (The Daughter of the Regiment)*, 1984–85; Don Inigo Gomez, *L'Heure espagnole (The Spanish Hour)*, 1984–85; Priest, *Murder in the Cathedral*, 1984–85; Zuniga, *Carmen*, 1984–85; Count Rodolfo, *La Sonnambula (The Sleepwalker)*, 1985–86; Leporello, *Don Giovanni*, 1985–86; Pedro / Head Muleteer, *Man of La Mancha*, 1985–86; The Innkeeper / The Governor, *Man of La Mancha*, 1985–86; Dr. Dulcamara, *L'Elisir d'amore (The Elixir of Love)*, 1986–87

Rajunas, Lydia: Annina, *La Traviata*, 1983–84

Rakestraw, John: Peter, *Passion Play—Carmina Burana*, 1982–83

Ramirez, Rafael: Normanno, *Lucia di Lammermoor*, 1993–94

Ramlet, James: Man in Armor, *Die Zauberflöte (The Magic Flute)*, 1977–78; Official, *Danton and Robespierre*, 1977–78; Zuniga, *Carmen*, 1977–78; Pimen, *Boris Godunov*, 1978–79; Dottor Bombasto, *Arlecchino*, 1979–80; Dr. Bartolo, *Le Nozze di Figaro (The Marriage of Figaro)*, 1980–81; The King of Clubs, *The Love for Three Oranges*, 1980–81; Osmin, *Die Entführung aus dem Serail (The Abduction from the Seraglio)*, 1981–82; Sir John Falstaff, *Die lustigen Weiber von Windsor (The Merry Wives of Windsor)*, 1981–82; Sarastro, *Die Zauberflöte (The Magic Flute)*, 1982–83; William Jennings Bryan, *The Ballad of Baby Doe*, 1982–83; Snug, *A Midsummer Night's Dream*, 1983–84

Rampaso, Luciano: Luigi, *Il Trittico (A Triptych)*, 1972–73

Rampy, David: Panait, *The Greek Passion*, 1980–81; Lt. Pinkerton, *Madama Butterfly*, 1981–82; The Captain, *Wozzeck*, 1981–82; The Harper, *The Excursions of Mr. Broucek*, 1981–82; Gabriel von Eisenstein, *Die Fledermaus (The Bat)*, 1982–83; Luigi, *Il Trittico (A Triptych)*, 1982–83; Man in Armor, *Die Zauberflöte (The Magic Flute)*, 1982–83

Randall, Nicholas: Aide to President Arthur, *The Ballad of Baby Doe*, 1982–83

Raney, Pamela: Lottie, *Show Boat*, 1984–85

Raskas, Shirley: Rosina, *Il Barbiere di Siviglia (The Barber of Seville)*, 1956–57

Rathbun, James: Phra Alack, *The King and I*, 1957–58

Ratliff, Roberta: Fritzi Kranz, *Blossom Time*, 1952–53

Rawlings, Carol: Louisa Giovanni, *Song of Norway*, 1951–52; Lucy, *On the Town*, 1951–52; Page, *Parsifal*, 1951–52; Kundry, *Parsifal*, 1952–53

Rawlins, Emily: Second Lady, *Die Zauberflöte (The Magic Flute),* 1965–66; Santuzza, *Cavalleria Rusticana,* 1966–67; Helen of Troy, *Mefistofele,* 1967–68; Marenka, *The Bartered Bride,* 1967–68; Poppea, *L'Incoronazione di Poppea (The Coronation of Poppea),* 1967–68; Lisa, *La Pique Dame (The Queen of Spades),* 1968–69; Violetta Valery, *La Traviata,* 1968–69

Rawlins, Harriet: Nimue, *Camelot,* 1968–69; Alisa, *Lucia di Lammermoor,* 1970–71; Berta (Marcellina), *Il Barbiere di Siviglia (The Barber of Seville),* 1971–72; The Mistress of the Novices, *Il Trittico (A Triptych),* 1972–73; Zita, *Il Trittico (A Triptych),* 1972–73; Hattie, *Kiss Me, Kate,* 1973–74; Susan B. Anthony, *The Mother of Us All,* 1973–74

Ray, David: Candide, *Candide,* 2000–01; Goro, *Madama Butterfly,* 2001–02; Laurie, *Little Women,* 2001–02; Alfred, *Die Fledermaus (The Bat),* 2002–03

Ray, Jean: Gilda, *Rigoletto,* 1950–51

Ray, Robert: Andres, *Les Contes d'Hoffmann (The Tales of Hoffmann),* 1947–48; Pittichinaccio, *Les Contes d'Hoffmann (The Tales of Hoffmann),* 1947–48

Ray, Sandra: Sitzi Kranz, *Blossom Time,* 1952–53

Raymond, Brad: Dancaire, *Carmen,* 2005–06; De Bretigny, *Manon,* 2006–07; Sharpless, *Madama Butterfly,* 2006–07

Read, Constance: Adele, *Die Fledermaus (The Bat),* 1962–63; Susanna, *Le Nozze di Figaro (The Marriage of Figaro),* 1962–63

Reading, Carrie: Emily, *The Ballad of Baby Doe,* 2003–04; Sylviane, *Die lustige Witwe (The Merry Widow),* 2003–04; Madame Larina, *Eugene Onegin,* 2004–05; Stephano, *Roméo et Juliette,* 2005–06

Ream, Richard: Joe, *Street Scene,* 1949–50

Rebilas, Richard: Master Ford (Herr Fluth), *Die lustigen Weiber von Windsor (The Merry Wives of Windsor),* 1981–82; Papageno, *Die Zauberflöte (The Magic Flute),* 1982–83; Anthony Hope, *Sweeney Todd,* 1983–84; Mr. Western, *Tom Jones,* 1983–84; Lancelot, *Camelot,* 1986–87; Tsar Saltan, *The Legend of Tsar Saltan,* 1986–87

Redd, Paula: Maria, *Porgy and Bess,* 1976–77; Old Lady Pereperchikha, *The Night Before Christmas,* 1977–78; Prostitute, *Danton and Robespierre,* 1977–78; First Mourner, *The Darkened City,* 1978–79; Hostess of the Inn, *Boris Godunov,* 1978–79; Clytaemnestra, *The Cry of Clytaemnestra,* 1979–80; Maria, *Porgy and Bess,* 1979–80

Redding, Michael: Farfarello, *The Love for Three Oranges,* 1999–2000; Elder McLean, *Susannah,* 2000–01; Oliver Hix, *The Music Man,* 2001–02; Baron Douphol, *La Traviata,* 2002–03

Reddy, Leah: The Baroness, *Candide,* 2000–01

Redick, Janice: Adriana, *The Boys from Syracuse,* 1968–69; Deidamia, *Deidamia,* 1969–70; Lucia, *Lucia di Lammermoor,* 1970–71; Marguerite, *Faust,* 1971–72; Rosina, *Il Barbiere di Siviglia (The Barber of Seville),* 1971–72

Reece, Arley: Don Alvaro, *La Forza del Destino (The Force of Destiny),* 1962–63; Lillas Pastia, *Carmen,* 1962–63

Reed, Gilbert: The Wild Horse, *Annie Get Your Gun,* 1956–57

Reed, Keith: Count Almaviva, *Le Nozze di Figaro (The Marriage of Figaro),* 1986–87; Captain Balstrode, *Peter Grimes,* 1987–88; Leonato, *Béatrice et Bénédict,* 1987–88; Pasha Selim, *Die Entführung aus dem Serail (The Abduction from the Seraglio),* 1987–88; Coppelius, *Les Contes d'Hoffmann (The Tales of Hoffmann),* 1988–89; Dappertutto, *Les Contes d'Hoffmann (The Tales of Hoffmann),* 1988–89; Dr. Miracle, *Les Contes d'Hoffmann (The Tales of Hoffmann),* 1988–89; Fredrik Egerman, *A Little Night Music,* 1988–89; Lindorf, *Les Contes d'Hoffmann (The Tales of Hoffmann),* 1988–89; Man in Armor, *Die Zauberflöte (The Magic Flute),* 1988–89; Speaker of the Temple, *Die Zauberflöte (The Magic Flute),* 1988–89

Reed, Nancy: Eliza, *The King and I,* 1957–58; Maggie Anderson, *Brigadoon,* 1961–62

Reed, Tim: Slim, *Oklahoma!,* 1997–98

Reeder, William: Rodolfo, *La Bohème,* 1970–71; Count Almaviva, *Il Barbiere di Siviglia (The Barber of Seville),* 1971–72; Faust, *Faust,* 1971–72; Ganya, *Myshkin,* 1972–73; Prince Tamino, *Die Zauberflöte (The Magic Flute),* 1972–73; Steva, *Jenůfa,* 1972–73

Reese, Jean: Sister Angelica, *Il Trittico (A Triptych),* 1972–73; Antonia, *Les Contes d'Hoffmann (The Tales of Hoffmann),* 1973–74; Countess Almaviva, *Le Nozze di Figaro (The Marriage of Figaro),* 1973–74

Reeve, Scott: Squire Dap, *Camelot,* 1969–70; Customs Officer, *La Bohème,* 1970–71; Schaunard, *La Bohème,* 1970–71; Wagner, *Faust,* 1971–72; Andreas, *Carmen,* 1973–74; Chris the Citizen, *The Mother of Us All,* 1973–74; Morales, *Carmen,* 1973–74; Giuseppe Palmieri, *The Gondoliers,* 1974–75; Marcello, *La Bohème,* 1974–75; The Doctor, *Vanessa,* 1974–75; Zaretsky, *Eugene Onegin,* 1974–75

Rehm, John: City Marshall, *Street Scene,* 1960–61

Rei, Annalisa: Annina, *La Traviata,* 1990–91

Reid, Kay: Kate Pinkerton, *Madama Butterfly,* 1987–88

Reiff, Peder: Desk Clerk of the Hotel, *Arabella,* 1998–99; Morales, *Carmen,* 1998–99; Peters, *Down in the Valley,* 1998–99; Player, *Mass,* 1998–99; Rock Singer, *Mass,* 1998–99; Jose / a Muleteer, *Man of La Mancha,* 1999–2000; Schaunard,

La Bohème, 1999–2000; Fiorello, *Il Barbiere di Siviglia (The Barber of Seville)*, 2000–01; Officer, *Il Barbiere di Siviglia (The Barber of Seville)*, 2000–01

Reighley, Kurt: Bertrand, *A Little Night Music*, 1988–89; Page, *A Little Night Music*, 1988–89; First Muezzin, *Kismet*, 1989–90; Parpignol, *La Bohème*, 1989–90; Silk Merchant, *Kismet*, 1989–90

Reina, Mark: Ferone, *Candide*, 1976–77; Man on the street, *Trouble in Tahiti*, 1976–77; Player, *Bernstein on Broadway*, 1976–77; Trio—baritone, *Trouble in Tahiti*, 1976–77

Reinhart, Jerry: Corelli, *The Firefly*, 1949–50; Mr. Lippo Fiorentino, *Street Scene*, 1949–50; Spaniard, *The New Moon*, 1949–50; Waiter, *Die lustige Witwe (The Merry Widow)*, 1949–50; Borsa, *Rigoletto*, 1950–51; Page, *Parsifal*, 1950–51; Actor, *On the Town*, 1951–52; Bimmy, *On the Town*, 1951–52; Einar, *Song of Norway*, 1951–52; Pedrillo, *Die Entführung aus dem Serail (The Abduction from the Seraglio)*, 1951–52; S. Uperman, *On the Town*, 1951–52; Second Man, *Kiss Me, Kate*, 1951–52; Tito, *Song of Norway*, 1951–52; Tom, *On the Town*, 1951–52

Reininghaus, Marlene: Rossweisse, *Die Walküre*, 1969–70

Remak, Henry: Concierge, *Arabella*, 1972–73; Klaas, *Die Entführung aus dem Serail (The Abduction from the Seraglio)*, 1974–75; The Old Knight, *Canterbury Tales*, 1978–79

Renkin, Helen: Page, *Parsifal*, 1952–53

Renne, Mary Ann: Musician, *Die Kluge (The Clever Girl)*, 1959–60; Blonde, *Die Entführung aus dem Serail (The Abduction from the Seraglio)*, 1961–62; Peaseblossom, *A Midsummer Night's Dream*, 1961–62; Maid, *Il Campanello di Notte (The Night Bell)*, 1963–64

Renneisen, William: Brakeman, *The Most Happy Fella*, 1982–83; Barbary Pirate, *Candide*, 1983–84; Schelkalov, *Boris Godunov*, 1983–84; Victim of the Inquisition, *Candide*, 1983–84

Rettmer, Brenda: Frasquita, *Carmen*, 1962–63; Donna Elvira, *Don Giovanni*, 1964–65; Kate Pinkerton, *Madama Butterfly*, 1964–65; Nella, *Gianni Schicchi*, 1964–65; Praskovia, *Die lustige Witwe (The Merry Widow)*, 1964–65

Rey, Beatrice: Girl, *Street Scene*, 1949–50; Graduate, *Street Scene*, 1949–50

Rey, Timothy: Coley, White House Staff, *1600 Pennsylvania Avenue*, 1992–93; Mr. Simoleon the Left End Man, *1600 Pennsylvania Avenue*, 1992–93; Rhinestone Lilly, *1600 Pennsylvania Avenue*, 1992–93

Reyes, Dulce: Marcellina, *Le Nozze di Figaro (The Marriage of Figaro)*, 1986–87; Mrs. Sedley, *Peter Grimes*, 1987–88; Suzuki, *Madama Butterfly*, 1987–88; Tituba, *The Crucible*, 1987–88; Olga, *Eugene Onegin*, 1988–89; Clytaemnestra, *The Cry of Clytaemnestra*, 1989–90

Reynolds, McCarry: John, *Peter Grimes*, 2003–04

Reynolds, Morris: Gremio, *Kiss Me, Kate*, 1951–52; Jigger Craigin, *Carousel*, 1952–53; Klingsor, *Parsifal*, 1952–53; Second Mate, *Billy Budd*, 1952–53; Pete, *Show Boat*, 1953–54; Schelkalov, *Boris Godunov*, 1953–54; Woody, *Finian's Rainbow*, 1953–54

Reynolds, Myrna: Lalume, *Kismet*, 1963–64

Rhee, Hyorim: Spirit, *Die Zauberflöte (The Magic Flute)*, 1988–89

Rhie, Yungee: Olympia, *Les Contes d'Hoffmann (The Tales of Hoffmann)*, 2007–08

Rhodes, Damen: Claudio, *Béatrice et Bénédict*, 1987–88

Rhodes, Matthew: Carpenter's Mate, *HMS Pinafore*, 2005–06

Rhodes, Paul: Fiorello, *Il Barbiere di Siviglia (The Barber of Seville)*, 1971–72; Graf Dominik, *Arabella*, 1972–73; Pinellino, *Il Trittico (A Triptych)*, 1972–73; Chris the Citizen, *The Mother of Us All*, 1973–74; Wozzeck, *Wozzeck*, 1973–74; Guglielmo, *Così fan tutte*, 1977–78; Panas, *The Night Before Christmas*, 1977–78; Andonis, *The Greek Passion*, 1980–81; Cord Elam, *Oklahoma!*, 1981–82; The Drum Major, *Wozzeck*, 1981–82

Rhodes, William: Osmin, *Die Entführung aus dem Serail (The Abduction from the Seraglio)*, 1974–75; Rigoletto, *Rigoletto*, 1974–75; Buonafede, *Il Mondo della Luna (The World on the Moon)*, 1975–76; Count Carl-Magnus Malcolm, *A Little Night Music*, 1975–76; Count Renato, *Un Ballo in Maschera (A Masked Ball)*, 1975–76; Billy Bigelow, *Carousel*, 1976–77; Sir John Falstaff, *Falstaff*, 1976–77

Ribbens, Sarah: First Lady, *Die Zauberflöte (The Magic Flute)*, 1998–99

Rice, Colette: Fiordiligi, *Così fan tutte*, 1989–90

Rice, Jennifer: Boy, *Die Zauberflöte (The Magic Flute)*, 1994–95; Dewman, *Hänsel und Gretel*, 1995–96; Echo, *Ariadne auf Naxos*, 1996–97; Josephine, *HMS Pinafore*, 1997–98; Cupid, *Orphée aux enfers (Orpheus in the Underworld)*, 1998–99; Player, *Mass*, 1998–99; Female Chorus, *The Rape of Lucretia*, 1999–2000; Susannah Polk, *Susannah*, 2000–01

Rice, Laura: Old Lady Pereperchikha, *The Night Before Christmas*, 1977–78; Nurse of the Children, *Boris Godunov*, 1978–79; Ludmila, *The Bartered Bride*, 1979–80; Mrs. Ott, *Susannah*, 1979–80; Konchakovna, *Prince Igor*, 1980–81

Richards, Jane: Ensign Dinah Murphy, *South Pacific*, 1956–57

Richards, Jerry: Indian Priest, *The Ruby*, 1954–55

Richards, Kurt: A Footman, *Vanessa*, 1974–75

Richards, Mig: Lolo, *Die lustige Witwe (The Merry Widow)*, 1949–50

Richards, Mildred: Page, *Parsifal*, 1949–50; Nadina, *The Chocolate Soldier*, 1950–51

Richards, Paul: Page, *Parsifal,* 1952–53; Page, *Parsifal,* 1953–54; Beppe, *I Pagliacci,* 1954–55; Gabriel von Eisenstein, *Die Fledermaus (The Bat),* 1954–55; Page, *Parsifal,* 1954–55; Don Curzio, *Le Nozze di Figaro (The Marriage of Figaro),* 1955–56; Page, *Parsifal,* 1955–56

Richardson, Alexandra: Electra as a child, *The Cry of Clytaemnestra,* 1979–80

Richardson, Gabriella: Orestes as a child, *The Cry of Clytaemnestra,* 1979–80

Richardson, Marcy: Pousette, *Manon,* 2001–02; Donna Fiorilla, *Il Turco in Italia (The Turk in Italy),* 2003–04

Richardson, Thomas: Ashby, *La Fanciulla del West (The Girl of the Golden West),* 1963–64; Doctor Bartolo, *Il Barbiere di Siviglia (The Barber of Seville),* 1963–64; Don Alfonso, *Così fan tutte,* 1963–64; Hobson, *Peter Grimes,* 1963–64

Richter, Wilburt: Frosch, *Die Fledermaus (The Bat),* 1954–55; The Major Domo, *Ariadne auf Naxos,* 1954–55; Will Parker, *Oklahoma!,* 1954–55; The Little Old Man, *L'Enfant et les Sortilèges (The Bewitched Child),* 1955–56; Vashek, *The Bartered Bride,* 1955–56; Foster Wilson, *Annie Get Your Gun,* 1956–57

Rickards, Steven: Marat, *Danton and Robespierre,* 1977–78; Oberon, *A Midsummer Night's Dream,* 1983–84

Ricks, Valerie: Hazel, *Show Boat,* 1984–85

Riegel, Lisa: Fermina / A Servant Girl, *Man of La Mancha,* 1988–89; Third Wife, *Bluebeard's Castle,* 1988–89; Sandman, *Hänsel und Gretel,* 1989–90; Angel (adult), *The Dawn of the Poor King,* 1990–91; Minnie Fay, *Hello, Dolly!,* 1991–92; Princess Diana, *Jubilee,* 1991–92

Riemenschneider, Mark: Lt. Ian Shaw, *The Secret Garden,* 2003–04; Vicomte Camille di Rosillon, *Die lustige Witwe (The Merry Widow),* 2003–04

Rights, Marilyn: Kundry, *Parsifal,* 1951–52; Mother, *Amahl and the Night Visitors,* 1951–52

Riley, Jessica: Virginia, *Oklahoma!,* 1997–98; Jennie Parsons, *Down in the Valley,* 1998–99; La Badessa, *Suor Angelica (Sister Angelica),* 1999–2000; Mother Goose, *The Rake's Progress,* 1999–2000; Sister Sophia, *The Sound of Music,* 2000–01; Hansel, *Hänsel und Gretel,* 2001–02; Effie, *The Ballad of Baby Doe,* 2003–04; Mother Marie of the Incarnation, *Dialogues des Carmélites,* 2004–05

Ringham, William: Stage Doorman, *Kiss Me, Kate,* 1951–52

Rio, James: Menelaus, *The Cry of Clytaemnestra,* 1989–90; Kaspar, *Amahl and the Night Visitors,* 1990–91; Eric Dare, *Jubilee,* 1991–92; Sellem, *The Rake's Progress,* 1991–92

Risley, Patricia: Hata, *The Bartered Bride,* 1986–87; Middle Sister, later Tkachikha, *The Legend of Tsar Saltan,* 1986–87; Nimue, *Camelot,* 1986–87; Gelosia, *L'Orfeo,* 1987–88; Countess Charlotte Malcolm, *A Little Night Music,* 1988–89; Madame Vilmorac, *A Little Night Music,* 1988–89; Mrs. Segstrom, *A Little Night Music,* 1988–89; Third Lady, *Die Zauberflöte (The Magic Flute),* 1988–89; Hansel, *Hänsel und Gretel,* 1989–90; The Cavaliere Ramiro, *La Finta Giardiniera,* 1990–91; Valencienne, *Die lustige Witwe (The Merry Widow),* 1990–91; Angelina (Cinderella), *La Cenerentola (Cinderella),* 1991–92

Ritchie, Timothy: Alfred, *Die Fledermaus (The Bat),* 1996–97; Goro, *Madama Butterfly,* 1996–97; Vicomte Camille di Rosillon, *Die lustige Witwe (The Merry Widow),* 1996–97; Fenton, *Falstaff,* 1997–98; Don Jose, *Carmen,* 1998–99; Man in Armor, *Die Zauberflöte (The Magic Flute),* 1998–99

Rittenhouse, Kelly: Consuelo, *West Side Story,* 1992–93

Riutta, Matt: Messenger, *Jubilee,* 1991–92; The Usher, *Jubilee,* 1991–92; North Carolina Delegate, *1600 Pennsylvania Avenue,* 1992–93

Rivenq, Nicolas: Boyar in Attendance, *Boris Godunov,* 1983–84; The Boyar Khrushchev, *Boris Godunov,* 1983–84; Jupiter, *Orphée aux enfers (Orpheus in the Underworld),* 1984–85; Schaunard, *La Bohème,* 1984–85; Excamillo, *Carmen,* 1984–85; Frank, *Die Fledermaus (The Bat),* 1985–86

Rivera, Wayne: Normanno, *Lucia di Lammermoor,* 1963–64; Trinidad, *La Fanciulla del West (The Girl of the Golden West),* 1963–64; Marquis de Croissant, *Die lustige Witwe (The Merry Widow),* 1964–65; First Commissioner, *Dialogues des Carmélites,* 1965–66; First Chief, *A Hoosier Tale,* 1966–67; Borsa, *Rigoletto,* 1966–67; Filipeto, *Quattro rusteghi (The Four Ruffians),* 1966–67

Rivera-Gonzalez, Jesus: Arturo Bucklaw, *Lucia di Lammermoor,* 1993–94; Parpignol, *La Bohème,* 1994–95; Don Ottavio, *Don Giovanni,* 1996–97; Triquet, *Eugene Onegin,* 1997–98; John Styx, *Orphée aux enfers (Orpheus in the Underworld),* 1998–99; Parpignol, *La Bohème,* 1999–2000

Robbins, Joseph: Schlemil, *Les Contes d'Hoffmann (The Tales of Hoffmann),* 1959–60

Roberts, Anne: Maddalena, *Rigoletto,* 1959–60; Nicklausse, *Les Contes d'Hoffmann (The Tales of Hoffmann),* 1959–60; Suzy, *La Rondine (The Swallow),* 1959–60

Roberts, Michelle: Rosalia, *West Side Story,* 1992–93

Roberts, Quincy: Blues Singer, *Mass,* 1998–99; Thomas Bouche, *Down in the Valley,* 1998–99; Amantio di Nicolao, *Gianni Schicchi,* 1999–2000; Kreonte, *The Love for Three Oranges,* 1999–2000; Sparafucile, *Rigoletto,* 2000–01; Kezal, *The Bartered Bride,* 2001–02; The Bonze, *Madama Butterfly,* 2001–02; Crespel, *Les Contes d'Hoffmann (The Tales of Hoffmann),* 2002–03; Luther, *Les Contes d'Hoffmann (The Tales of Hoffmann),* 2002–03; Hobson, *Peter Grimes,* 2003–04;

Osmin, *Die Entführung aus dem Serail (The Abduction from the Seraglio)*, 2003–04

Robinson, Douglas: The Prince, *The Love for Three Oranges*, 1975–76; Pelleas, *Pelléas et Mélisande*, 1976–77

Robinson, Harold: Deputy, *Don Carlos*, 1961–62; Dr. Falke, *Die Fledermaus (The Bat)*, 1962–63; Robin Oakapple / Sir Ruthven Murgatroyd, *Ruddigore (The Witch's Curse)*, 1962–63; The Narrator, *The Fantasticks*, 1963–64; Baron Mirko Zeta, *Die lustige Witwe (The Merry Widow)*, 1965–66

Robinson, Kristen: Niece #1, *Peter Grimes*, 2003–04; Clorinda, *La Cenerentola (Cinderella)*, 2004–05

Robinson, Linda: Princess Nicoletta, *The Love for Three Oranges*, 1958–59

Robinson, Tad: Customs Officer, *La Bohème*, 1979–80

Robinson, Thelma: Second Mourner, *The Darkened City*, 1962–63

Robinson, Twyla: Fiordiligi, *Così fan tutte*, 1995–96; Donna Elvira, *Don Giovanni*, 1996–97; Mrs. Alice Ford, *Falstaff*, 1997–98; Arabella, *Arabella*, 1998–99

Robison, Richard: Rambaldo Fernandez, *La Rondine (The Swallow)*, 1959–60; Ramiro, *L'Heure espagnole (The Spanish Hour)*, 1959–60; Prince Afron, *Le Coq d'or (The Golden Cockerel)*, 1960–61

Rocchio, Michael: Assistant to the Hairdresser, *Manon Lescaut*, 1970–71; Gianni Schicchi, *Il Trittico (A Triptych)*, 1972–73; Tevye, *Fiddler on the Roof*, 1972–73; Anthony Comstock, *The Mother of Us All*, 1973–74; Schaunard, *La Bohème*, 1974–75; Klingsor, *Parsifal*, 1975–76; Mr. Lindquist, *A Little Night Music*, 1975–76; Pantalone, *The Love for Three Oranges*, 1975–76

Rock, Carollyn: Sylviane, *Die lustige Witwe (The Merry Widow)*, 1996–97; Zerlina, *Don Giovanni*, 1996–97; Nanetta, *Falstaff*, 1997–98; Micaëla, *Carmen*, 1998–99

Rockhold, Julie: First Lay Sister, *Il Trittico (A Triptych)*, 1982–83; Sister Lucilla, *Il Trittico (A Triptych)*, 1982–83

Rockman, Matthew: Trouble, *Madama Butterfly*, 1981–82

Roderick, James: Page, *Parsifal*, 1948–49

Rodger, John: Jankel, *Arabella*, 2006–07; Leandro, *Arlecchino*, 2006–07; The Duke of Mantua, *Rigoletto*, 2007–08

Rodman, Fontaine: Aide to President Arthur, *The Ballad of Baby Doe*, 1975–76

Rodriguez, Mario: Executioner, *Candide*, 1993–94; Guccio, *Gianni Schicchi*, 1993–94; Lion, *Candide*, 1993–94; Officer, *Il Barbiere di Siviglia (The Barber of Seville)*, 1994–95

Rodriguez, Sandra: Terracita, *West Side Story*, 1992–93

Roemer, Katya: Ninth Woman of Paris, *Danton and Robespierre*, 1977–78

Rogel, Alvin: Trabucco, *La Forza del Destino (The Force of Destiny)*, 1962–63

Rogers, Bruce: The Ringmaster, *The Bartered Bride*, 1967–68

Rogers, Carol: Maid, *Quattro rusteghi (The Four Ruffians)*, 1966–67; Love, *L'Incoronazione di Poppea (The Coronation of Poppea)*, 1967–68; Cherubino, *Le Nozze di Figaro (The Marriage of Figaro)*, 1968–69; Page, *Parsifal*, 1968–69

Rogers, Georgia: Curra, *La Forza del Destino (The Force of Destiny)*, 1962–63; Nella, *Gianni Schicchi*, 1964–65; Sylviane, *Die lustige Witwe (The Merry Widow)*, 1965–66; Alexandra, *Myshkin*, 1972–73

Rogers, Jean: Flower Girl, *Blossom Time*, 1952–53

Rogers, Katherine: Maud Dunlop, *The Music Man*, 1980–81; Norina, *Don Pasquale*, 1980–81; Blonde, *Die Entführung aus dem Serail (The Abduction from the Seraglio)*, 1981–82; Elizabeth "Baby" Doe, *The Ballad of Baby Doe*, 1982–83

Rogers, Scott: Herman Ortel, *Die Meistersinger von Nürnberg (The Mastersingers of Nuremberg)*, 1968–69

Rogister, Evan: Welko, *Arabella*, 1998–99; Betto, *Gianni Schicchi*, 1999–2000; Kreonte, *The Love for Three Oranges*, 1999–2000; Voltaire (Pangloss, Cacambo, Martin, Galley Slave), *Candide*, 2000–01; De Bretigny, *Manon*, 2001–02

Roland, Sophie: Luna, *Jeppe*, 2002–03; Voice of the Mother, *Les Contes d'Hoffmann (The Tales of Hoffmann)*, 2002–03; Dame Quickly, *Falstaff*, 2003–04; The Old Prioress, *Dialogues des Carmélites*, 2004–05; Carmen, *Carmen*, 2005–06

Rollo, Anita: Lucia, *The Rape of Lucretia*, 1999–2000; Adina, *L'Elisir d'amore (The Elixir of Love)*, 2000–01; Amy, *Little Women*, 2001–02

Roman, Judy: Bianca, *Kiss Me, Kate*, 1973–74; Lois Lane, *Kiss Me, Kate*, 1973–74

Romig, Clifton: Don Pedro, *Béatrice et Bénédict*, 1987–88; Hobson, *Peter Grimes*, 1987–88; Crespel, *Les Contes d'Hoffmann (The Tales of Hoffmann)*, 1988–89; Frid, *A Little Night Music*, 1988–89; Sarastro, *Die Zauberflöte (The Magic Flute)*, 1988–89; Simone, *Gianni Schicchi*, 1988–89; Ajax, *The Cry of Clytaemnestra*, 1989–90; Alcindoro, *La Bohème*, 1989–90; Lodovico, *Otello*, 1989–90; Balthasar, *Amahl and the Night Visitors*, 1990–91; The Doctor, *Wozzeck*, 1990–91

Rorex, Michael: Slender (Spaerlich), *Die lustigen Weiber von Windsor (The Merry Wives of Windsor)*, 1981–82; Don Ottavio, *Don Giovanni*, 1991–92; Fenton, *Falstaff*, 1992–93; Chevalier des Grieux, *Manon*, 1993–94; Jenik, *The Bartered Bride*, 1994–95

Rose, Bridget: Boy, *Die Zauberflöte (The Magic Flute)*, 1994–95

Rose, Rachel: Mrs. Soames, *Our Town*, 2005–06

Roseberry, Lynn: Older Sister, later Povarikha, *The Legend of Tsar Saltan*, 1986–87

Roselli, Christopher: Herald, *Otello,* 1989–90; Majordomo, *La Rondine (The Swallow),* 1989–90; Rabonnier, *La Rondine (The Swallow),* 1989–90; Baron Douphol, *La Traviata,* 1990–91; Frank, *Die Fledermaus (The Bat),* 1990–91; Melchior, *Amahl and the Night Visitors,* 1990–91; Don Giovanni, *Don Giovanni,* 1991–92; Sharpless, *Madama Butterfly,* 1991–92; Count Almaviva, *Le Nozze di Figaro (The Marriage of Figaro),* 1992–93; Baron Scarpia, *Tosca,* 1993–94; Enrico Ashton, *Lucia di Lammermoor,* 1993–94; Lescaut, *Manon,* 1993–94

Rosen, Carol: A Princess of Ababu, *Kismet,* 1963–64; Dodo, *Die lustige Witwe (The Merry Widow),* 1964–65

Rosenquist, Tiffany: La Conversa, *Suor Angelica (Sister Angelica),* 1999–2000; Maria, *The Sound of Music,* 2000–01; Paquette, *Candide,* 2000–01; Beth, *Little Women,* 2001–02; Maria, *West Side Story,* 2002–03; Zerlina, *Don Giovanni,* 2002–03; Zaida, *Il Turco in Italia (The Turk in Italy),* 2003–04; Rosina, *Il Barbiere di Siviglia (The Barber of Seville),* 2005–06

Rosier, Elise: Barbarina, *Le Nozze di Figaro (The Marriage of Figaro),* 1986–87

Roskin, Jessica: Marriage arranger for Samahris, *Kismet,* 1989–90

Ross, Barbara: Fyodor, *Boris Godunov,* 1964–65

Ross, Christine: Mistress Page (Frau Reich), *Die lustigen Weiber von Windsor (The Merry Wives of Windsor),* 1981–82

Ross, Elizabeth Lyra: Lily, *Porgy and Bess,* 1976–77; Spirit, *Die Zauberflöte (The Magic Flute),* 1977–78

Ross, Louis: Enoch Snow, Jr., *Carousel,* 1952–53

Ross, Michael: Charlie Hildebrand, *Street Scene,* 1949–50; Cabin Boy, *Billy Budd,* 1952–53

Ross Mitchell, Mary: Annina, *La Traviata,* 1960–61

Rossi-Lemeni, Nicola: Boris Godunov, *Boris Godunov,* 1983–84

Ross-Johnson, Emily: Niece #2, *Peter Grimes,* 2003–04

Rothmuller, Marko: Amfortas, *Parsifal,* 1956–57; Sixtus Beckmesser, *Die Meistersinger von Nürnberg (The Mastersingers of Nuremberg),* 1961–62; Amfortas, *Parsifal,* 1962–63; Sixtus Beckmesser, *Die Meistersinger von Nürnberg (The Mastersingers of Nuremberg),* 1968–69; Gianni Schicchi, *Il Trittico (A Triptych),* 1972–73; Tevye, *Fiddler on the Roof,* 1972–73

Roush, Jeffrey: Andrew Carnes, *Oklahoma!,* 1981–82

Rousseau, Lisa: Elizabeth Tabor, *The Ballad of Baby Doe,* 1975–76

Rowan, Glenn: Giuseppe, *La Traviata,* 1954–55; Andrew McLennon, *The Land Between the Rivers,* 1955–56; Micha, *The Bartered Bride,* 1955–56

Rowe, Mary Jane: Robin, *Falstaff,* 1956–57; Simon of Legree, *The King and I,* 1957–58

Rowell, Annette: Mrs. Olga Olsen, *Street Scene,* 1960–61

Rowen, Glenn: A Wig Maker, *Ariadne auf Naxos,* 1954–55; Dr. Falke, *Die Fledermaus (The Bat),* 1954–55; Figaro, *Le Nozze di Figaro (The Marriage of Figaro),* 1955–56; The Clock, *L'Enfant et les Sortilèges (The Bewitched Child),* 1955–56; Tinca, *Il Tabarro (The Cloak),* 1955–56; Doctor Bartolo, *Il Barbiere di Siviglia (The Barber of Seville),* 1956–57

Rowland, Jane: Sister Mathilde, *Dialogues des Carmélites,* 1965–66; Spirit, *Die Zauberflöte (The Magic Flute),* 1965–66; Giovanna, *Rigoletto,* 1966–67; Page, *Parsifal,* 1966–67

Rowland, Theodore: Dappertutto, *Les Contes d'Hoffmann (The Tales of Hoffmann),* 1959–60; Knight, *Parsifal,* 1959–60; Perichaud, *La Rondine (The Swallow),* 1959–60; Rigoletto, *Rigoletto,* 1959–60; Giorgio Germont, *La Traviata,* 1960–61; Rodrigo, *Don Carlos,* 1960–61; Macbeth, *Macbeth,* 1965–66

Rowlett, Herman: Dumas, *Andrea Chénier,* 1967–68

Roy, Suzanne: Lady Billows, *Albert Herring,* 1967–68

Rucker, Joan: Second Sharecropper, *Finian's Rainbow,* 1969–70

Ruetz, Robert: Don Jose, *Carmen,* 1956–57; Fenton, *Falstaff,* 1956–57; Mario Cavaradossi, *Tosca,* 1957–58

Ruhle, Deborah: Arithmetic, *L'Enfant et les Sortilèges (The Bewitched Child),* 1955–56; Barbarina, *Le Nozze di Figaro (The Marriage of Figaro),* 1955–56; Dewman, *Hänsel und Gretel,* 1956–57; Liat, *South Pacific,* 1956–57

Ruiz, Naomi: Zerlina, *Don Giovanni,* 2006–07; Antonia, *A Wedding,* 2007–08

Rumple, Cindy: Snookie, *110 in the Shade,* 1967–68

Rundle, Richard: Paco / A Muleteer, *Man of La Mancha,* 1999–2000

Rusnak, Jerri: Sister Mathilde, *Dialogues des Carmélites,* 1986–87; Berta (Marcellina), *Il Barbiere di Siviglia (The Barber of Seville),* 1988–89; Praskovia, *Die lustige Witwe (The Merry Widow),* 1990–91; Marcellina, *Le Nozze di Figaro (The Marriage of Figaro),* 1992–93; Alisa, *Lucia di Lammermoor,* 1993–94

Russell, Rebecca: Beatrice, *Béatrice et Bénédict,* 1987–88; Dorabella, *Così fan tutte,* 1989–90

Russell, Richard: Maximilian, *Candide,* 1983–84; Njegus, *Die lustige Witwe (The Merry Widow),* 1983–84; Gonzalvo, *L'Heure espagnole (The Spanish Hour),* 1984–85; Orpheus, *Orphée aux enfers (Orpheus in the Underworld),* 1984–85; The Duke of Krackenthorp, *La Fille du régiment (The Daughter of the Regiment),* 1984–85; Dr. Blind, *Die Fledermaus (The Bat),* 1985–86; The Padre, *Man of La Mancha,* 1985–86; Trinculo, *The Tempest,* 1985–86; Sellem, *The Rake's Progress,* 1986–87; The Father Confessor, *Dialogues des Carmélites,* 1986–87; Ezekiel Cheever, *The Crucible,* 1987–88

Russey, James: Ferrando, *Così fan tutte*, 1970–71; Normanno, *Lucia di Lammermoor*, 1970–71; Fenton, *Falstaff*, 1971–72; Count of Lerma, *Don Carlos*, 1972–73

Russo, Amanda: Marcellina, *Le Nozze di Figaro (The Marriage of Figaro)*, 2007–08

Rustay, Betsy: Jenny's friend, *Street Scene*, 1960–61

Rustay, Mary: Waitress, *The Most Happy Fella*, 1959–60

Ruszala, Joanna: Donna Anna, *Don Giovanni*, 2006–07; Mimi, *La Bohème*, 2007–08

Ruzzier, Guido: Guillot, *Eugene Onegin*, 1974–75

Ryan, Christopher: Second Ancestor, *Ruddigore (The Witch's Curse)*, 1962–63

Ryan, Paul: Wilhelm, *The Ghosts of Versailles*, 1996–97

Ryberg, William: Marullo, *Rigoletto*, 1980–81; Miroslav the Goldsmith, *The Excursions of Mr. Broucek*, 1981–82; Giuseppe, *The Most Happy Fella*, 1982–83; Man in Armor, *Die Zauberflöte (The Magic Flute)*, 1982–83

Rychak, Jean: Berta (Marcellina), *Il Barbiere di Siviglia (The Barber of Seville)*, 1963–64; Niece, *Peter Grimes*, 1963–64; Page, *Parsifal*, 1963–64; La Ciesca, *Gianni Schicchi*, 1964–65; Page, *Parsifal*, 1964–65

Ryken, Frank: Hortensio, *Kiss Me, Kate*, 1973–74

Saalbach, Valerie: A Novice, *Il Trittico (A Triptych)*, 1972–73; Lover, *Il Trittico (A Triptych)*, 1972–73; Spirit, *Die Zauberflöte (The Magic Flute)*, 1972–73

Sabo, Marlee Jo: Despina, *Così fan tutte*, 1963–64; Niece, *Peter Grimes*, 1963–64; Valencienne, *Die lustige Witwe (The Merry Widow)*, 1964–65; Zerlina, *Don Giovanni*, 1964–65

Sadeghpour, Mitra: Gertie Cummings, *Oklahoma!*, 1997–98; Frasquita, *Carmen*, 1998–99; Juno, *Orphée aux enfers (Orpheus in the Underworld)*, 1998–99; Antonia / Alonso's Niece, *Man of La Mancha*, 1999–2000; Nella, *Gianni Schicchi*, 1999–2000

Sadlier, David: Elder Hayes, *Susannah*, 2000–01; Ewart Dunlop, *The Music Man*, 2001–02; Guillot de Morfontaine, *Manon*, 2001–02; Jenik, *The Bartered Bride*, 2001–02; Tony, *West Side Story*, 2002–03; Rodolpho, *A View from the Bridge*, 2004–05

Safsten, Kaarin: Madame Lidoine, *Dialogues des Carmélites*, 1997–98; Electra, *Idomeneo*, 1998–99; Fata Morgana, *The Love for Three Oranges*, 1999–2000; Marie, *Wozzeck*, 1999–2000; Fiordiligi, *Così fan tutte*, 2000–01; Eulalie MacKecknie Shinn, *The Music Man*, 2001–02

Salinas, Michael: Businessman, *Candide*, 1993–94; Count des Grieux, *Manon*, 1993–94; Dr. Pangloss, *Candide*, 1993–94; Sacristan, *Tosca*, 1993–94; Sage, *Candide*, 1993–94; The King of Clubs, *The Love for Three Oranges*, 1993–94; Voltaire, *Candide*, 1993–94; Fiorello, *Il Barbiere di Siviglia (The Barber of Seville)*, 1994–95; Micha, *The Bartered Bride*, 1994–95; Claudius, *Agrippina*, 1995–96; Emile DeBeque, *South Pacific*, 1995–96; Don Geronio, *Il Turco in Italia (The Turk in Italy)*, 1996–97; Louis XVI, *The Ghosts of Versailles*, 1996–97; The King, *The King and I*, 1996–97; Dr. Bartolo, *Le Nozze di Figaro (The Marriage of Figaro)*, 1997–98; Pistol, *Falstaff*, 1997–98

Salonis, Clarke: Third Tramp, *Die Kluge (The Clever Girl)*, 1959–60; Henry Davis, *Street Scene*, 1960–61; Knight, *Parsifal*, 1960–61; Monk, *Don Carlos*, 1960–61

Samarzea, Brian: Calchas, *The Cry of Clytaemnestra*, 1989–90; Captain of the Inquisition, *Man of La Mancha*, 1999–2000; Chester A. Arthur, *The Ballad of Baby Doe*, 2003–04; Mayor of Leadville, *The Ballad of Baby Doe*, 2003–04; Old Silver Miner, *The Ballad of Baby Doe*, 2003–04

Samarzea, Kelly: Woman with Hat/Duchess, *The Ghosts of Versailles*, 1996–97; Dame Quickly, *Falstaff*, 1997–98; Adelaide, *Arabella*, 1998–99; Third Lady, *Die Zauberflöte (The Magic Flute)*, 1998–99; Old Baroness, *Vanessa*, 1999–2000; The Housekeeper for Alonso, *Man of La Mancha*, 1999–2000

Samels, Robert: Coppelius, *Les Contes d'Hoffmann (The Tales of Hoffmann)*, 2002–03; Leporello, *Don Giovanni*, 2002–03; Don Pasquale, *Don Pasquale*, 2003–04; Selim, *Il Turco in Italia (The Turk in Italy)*, 2003–04; William Jennings Bryan, *The Ballad of Baby Doe*, 2003–04; Marco, *A View from the Bridge*, 2004–05; Bottom, *A Midsummer Night's Dream*, 2005–06; Dr. Gibbs, *Our Town*, 2005–06

Samms, Margaret: Aunt Minnie, *Roberta*, 1958–59

Sams, Susan: Old Lady, *Candide*, 1983–84; Sylviane, *Die lustige Witwe (The Merry Widow)*, 1983–84; Ellie, *Show Boat*, 1984–85; The Owl, *L'Enfant et les Sortilèges (The Bewitched Child)*, 1984–85

Samuelsen, Roy: Amfortas, *Parsifal*, 1961–62; Baron Scarpia, *Tosca*, 1961–62; Count Almaviva, *Le Nozze di Figaro (The Marriage of Figaro)*, 1962–63; Don Carlos of Vargas, *La Forza del Destino (The Force of Destiny)*, 1962–63; Lazarus, *The Darkened City*, 1962–63; The Dutchman, *Der Fliegende Holländer (The Flying Dutchman)*, 1962–63; Amfortas, *Parsifal*, 1963–64; Amonasro, *Aida*, 1963–64; Captain Balstrode, *Peter Grimes*, 1963–64; Enrico Ashton, *Lucia di Lammermoor*, 1963–64; Figaro, *Il Barbiere di Siviglia (The Barber of Seville)*, 1963–64; Jack Rance, *La Fanciulla del West (The Girl of the Golden West)*, 1963–64; Solopy Tcherevik, *The Fair at Sorochinsk*, 1963–64; A Mandarin, *Turandot*, 1964–65; Amfortas, *Parsifal*, 1964–65; Boris Godunov, *Boris Godunov*, 1964–65; Creon, *Oedipus Rex*, 1964–65; Don Giovanni, *Don Giovanni*, 1964–65;

Ping, *Turandot*, 1964–65; Simon Boccanegra, *Simon Boccanegra*, 1964–65; Escamillo, *Carmen*, 1965–66; Macbeth, *Macbeth*, 1965–66; Amfortas, *Parsifal*, 1966–67; Lord Capulet, *Roméo et Juliette*, 1966–67; Rigoletto, *Rigoletto*, 1966–67; Tonio, *I Pagliacci*, 1966–67; William Conner, *A Hoosier Tale*, 1966–67; Amfortas, *Parsifal*, 1967–68; Charles Gérard, *Andrea Chénier*, 1967–68; Count di Luna, *Il Trovatore*, 1967–68; Amfortas, *Parsifal*, 1968–69; Count Almaviva, *Le Nozze di Figaro (The Marriage of Figaro)*, 1968–69; Hans Sachs, *Die Meistersinger von Nürnberg (The Mastersingers of Nuremberg)*, 1968–69; Prince Yeletsky, *La Pique Dame (The Queen of Spades)*, 1968–69; Michele, *Il Trittico (A Triptych)*, 1969–70; Wotan, *Die Walküre*, 1969–70; Don Pizarro, *Fidelio*, 1970–71; Jokanaan, *Salome*, 1970–71; Don Giovanni, *Don Giovanni*, 1971–72; Sir John Falstaff, *Falstaff*, 1971–72; Grand Inquisitor, *Don Carlos*, 1972–73; Gurnemanz, *Parsifal*, 1972–73; Baron Scarpia, *Tosca*, 1973–74; Doctor Faust, *Doktor Faust*, 1974–75; Baron Scarpia, *Tosca*, 1977–78; Don Alfonso, *Così fan tutte*, 1977–78; The Dutchman, *Der Fliegende Holländer (The Flying Dutchman)*, 1978–79; The Dutchman, *Der Fliegende Holländer (The Flying Dutchman)*, 1985–86

Sanabria, Pamela: A Novice, *Il Trittico (A Triptych)*, 1969–70; Echo, *Ariadne auf Naxos*, 1969–70; Lover, *Il Trittico (A Triptych)*, 1969–70

Sandberg, Kirsten: Graziella, *West Side Story*, 1992–93

Sandburg, Donald: Windy, *Show Boat*, 1953–54; Speedy Valenti, *Wonderful Town*, 1954–55

Sandel, Leann: Esmeralda, *The Bartered Bride*, 1986–87; Nedda, *I Pagliacci*, 1991–92

Sanders, Margaret: La Cercatrice (Prima), *Suor Angelica (Sister Angelica)*, 1999–2000

Sanders, Scott: Ambrogio, *Il Barbiere di Siviglia (The Barber of Seville)*, 1994–95

Sanderson, Clay: Schrank, *West Side Story*, 2002–03

Sanford, Linda: The Witch, *Hänsel und Gretel*, 1956–57

Sarago, Brandon: Gee-Tar, *West Side Story*, 1992–93

Sarakatsannis, Melanie: Fermina / A Servant Girl, *Man of La Mancha*, 1985–86; Margarita, *West Side Story*, 1985–86; Susanna, *Le Nozze di Figaro (The Marriage of Figaro)*, 1986–87; Hero, *Béatrice et Bénédict*, 1987–88; Mary Warren, *The Crucible*, 1987–88; Player, *Mass*, 1987–88; Pamina, *Die Zauberflöte (The Magic Flute)*, 1988–89; Player, *Mass*, 1988–89; Cassandra, *The Cry of Clytaemnestra*, 1989–90; Despina, *Così fan tutte*, 1989–90; Gilda, *Rigoletto*, 1992–93

Sarapoff, Jessica: Baccho (Bacchus), *L'Orfeo*, 1987–88

Sare, William: Handsome Charlie, *La Fanciulla del West (The Girl of the Golden West)*, 1963–64; Ned Keene, *Peter Grimes*, 1963–64; Guccio, *Gianni Schicchi*, 1964–65; Mityukh, *Boris Godunov*, 1964–65; Footman, *Der Rosenkavalier*, 1965–66; Waiter, *Der Rosenkavalier*, 1965–66; Nikitich, *Boris Godunov*, 1966–67; De Bretigny, *Manon*, 1967–68; Roucher, *Andrea Chénier*, 1967–68

Satin, Sheldon: Gaylord Ravenal, *Show Boat*, 1953–54; Second Sharecropper, *Finian's Rainbow*, 1953–54; Gabriel von Eisenstein, *Die Fledermaus (The Bat)*, 1954–55; Scaramuccio, *Ariadne auf Naxos*, 1954–55

Sattely, Virginia: The Maid, *Jenůfa*, 1972–73

Sauder, Ann: Praskovia, *Die lustige Witwe (The Merry Widow)*, 2003–04; Second Lady, *Die Zauberflöte (The Magic Flute)*, 2004–05; Dorabella, *Così fan tutte*, 2005–06; Hansel, *Hänsel und Gretel*, 2006–07

Saunders, Allen: A Herald, *The Love for Three Oranges*, 1993–94; Doctor Spinelloccio, *Gianni Schicchi*, 1993–94; Doctor Bartolo, *Il Barbiere di Siviglia (The Barber of Seville)*, 1994–95; Lazar Wolf, *Fiddler on the Roof*, 1994–95; Man in Armor, *Die Zauberflöte (The Magic Flute)*, 1994–95; Swallow, *Peter Grimes*, 1994–95; Claudius, *Agrippina*, 1995–96; Papa Sieppe, *McTeague*, 1995–96; Baron Mirko Zeta, *Die lustige Witwe (The Merry Widow)*, 1996–97; Don Geronio, *Il Turco in Italia (The Turk in Italy)*, 1996–97; Dr. Bartolo, *Le Nozze di Figaro (The Marriage of Figaro)*, 1997–98; Graf Waldner, *Arabella*, 1998–99; Jupiter, *Orphée aux enfers (Orpheus in the Underworld)*, 1998–99; Man in Armor, *Die Zauberflöte (The Magic Flute)*, 1998–99; Priest, *Die Zauberflöte (The Magic Flute)*, 1998–99; The Doctor, *Wozzeck*, 1999–2000; The King of Clubs, *The Love for Three Oranges*, 1999–2000; Count Monterone, *Rigoletto*, 2000–01; Doctor Bartolo, *Il Barbiere di Siviglia (The Barber of Seville)*, 2000–01; Sparafucile, *Rigoletto*, 2000–01

Saunderson, Lisa: Countess Almaviva, *Le Nozze di Figaro (The Marriage of Figaro)*, 1980–81; Marguerite, *Faust*, 1981–82; Rosina, *Il Barbiere di Siviglia (The Barber of Seville)*, 1982–83

Savage, Charles: Zanni, *Il Mondo della Luna (The World on the Moon)*, 1975–76

Savage, Vera: Hanna Glawari, *Die lustige Witwe (The Merry Widow)*, 2003–04; Pamina, *Die Zauberflöte (The Magic Flute)*, 2004–05; Fiordiligi, *Così fan tutte*, 2005–06; Donna Elvira, *Don Giovanni*, 2006–07

Savridi, Polyna: Gilda, *Rigoletto*, 1966–67; Nedda, *I Pagliacci*, 1966–67

Sawawaki, Michiharu: Ford, *Falstaff*, 1992–93; Mannoury, *Die Teufel von Loudun (The Devils of Loudun)*, 1992–93

Scaggs, Jonathan: Baron Elberfeld, *The Sound of Music*, 2000–01

Scammon, Vera: Antonia, *Les Contes d'Hoffmann (The Tales of Hoffmann)*, 1947–48; Marianne Beaunoir, *The New Moon*, 1949–50; Mimi, *La Bohème*, 1949–50; Nina, *The Firefly*, 1949–50; Nursemaid, *Street Scene*, 1949–50; Salvation Army Girl, *Street Scene*, 1949–50; Constanza, *Die Entführung aus dem Serail (The Abduction from the Seraglio)*, 1951–52; Violetta Valery, *La Traviata*, 1960–61; Rosalinda, *Die Fledermaus (The Bat)*, 1962–63; Rosina, *Il Barbiere di Siviglia (The Barber of Seville)*, 1963–64

Scamon, Sherrill: Kim (child), *Show Boat*, 1953–54

Scarbrough, Jerry: Notary, *Don Pasquale*, 1957–58

Schaefer, Lisa: Lady Anne, *Camelot*, 1986–87

Schaffer, Jean: Ngana, *South Pacific*, 1995–96

Schaible, Charlotte: The nursing sister from the infirmary, *Il Trittico (A Triptych)*, 1969–70; Ortlinde, *Die Walküre*, 1971–72

Schaible, Robert: Doctor Grenville, *La Traviata*, 1968–69

Schaldenbrand, Christopher: Papageno, *Die Zauberflöte (The Magic Flute)*, 1988–89; Schaunard, *La Bohème*, 1989–90; Baron Douphol, *La Traviata*, 1990–91; Narrator, *The Dawn of the Poor King*, 1990–91; Don Giovanni, *Don Giovanni*, 1991–92; Sharpless, *Madama Butterfly*, 1991–92

Schall, Richard: Second Workman, *On the Town*, 1951–52; Einar, *Song of Norway*, 1951–52; Figment, *On the Town*, 1951–52; Gunnar, *Song of Norway*, 1951–52; Harrison Howell, *Kiss Me, Kate*, 1951–52; Ibsen, *Song of Norway*, 1951–52; Night Club M.C., *On the Town*, 1951–52; Andrew MacLaren, *Brigadoon*, 1952–53; Mr. Kranz, *Blossom Time*, 1952–53; Andrew MacLaren, *Brigadoon*, 1953–54; Missail, *Boris Godunov*, 1953–54; Frosch, *Die Fledermaus (The Bat)*, 1954–55; Gastone, *La Traviata*, 1954–55; Scaramuccio, *Ariadne auf Naxos*, 1954–55

Schapman, Marc: Bardolph, *Falstaff*, 2003–04; Mike, *A View from the Bridge*, 2004–05; Spoletta, *Tosca*, 2004–05; George Gibbs, *Our Town*, 2005–06; Ralph Rackstraw, *HMS Pinafore*, 2005–06; Chevalier des Grieux, *Manon*, 2006–07; Nelson Deadly, *Too Many Sopranos*, 2006–07

Schauble, Kent: First Commissioner, *Dialogues des Carmélites*, 1997–98

Scheerer, Gretchen: Amelia's Maid, *Amelia Goes to the Ball*, 1957–58; Venetian Lady, *Candide*, 1957–58

Schendel, William: Ambrose Kemper, *Hello, Dolly!*, 1991–92

Schier, David: Beelzebub, *Doktor Faust*, 1974–75

Schildkret, David: Doctor Spinelloccio, *Il Trittico (A Triptych)*, 1982–83; Dr. Blind, *Die Fledermaus (The Bat)*, 1982–83

Schimmer, Russel: Elder McLean, *Susannah*, 2000–01

Schlanbusch, Lewis: Captain, *The Scarlet Letter*, 1976–77; Policeman, *Carousel*, 1976–77; Florenz, *Naughty Marietta*, 1977–78; Baron Douphol, *La Traviata*, 1978–79; Abbate Cospicuo, *Arlecchino*, 1979–80; Masetto, *Don Giovanni*, 1979–80; Dr. Malatesta, *Don Pasquale*, 1980–81; Figaro, *Il Barbiere di Siviglia (The Barber of Seville)*, 1980–81; Sharpless, *Madama Butterfly*, 1981–82

Schleuter, Scott: Moishe, *Fiddler on the Roof*, 1994–95

Schmidt, Heidi: Iphygeneia, *The Cry of Clytaemnestra*, 1989–90

Schmidt, Karl: Man in Armor, *Die Zauberflöte (The Magic Flute)*, 1965–66; Thierry, *Dialogues des Carmélites*, 1965–66; Micha, *The Bartered Bride*, 1967–68; Schmidt, *Andrea Chénier*, 1967–68; Second Soldier, *Salome*, 1970–71

Schneider, Keith: Megairus, *Doktor Faust*, 1974–75; The McCourt family, *The Ballad of Baby Doe*, 1975–76

Schneller, Cecile: Musician, *Die Kluge (The Clever Girl)*, 1959–60; Page, *Rigoletto*, 1959–60; Shirley Kaplan, *Street Scene*, 1960–61

Schoepflin, Frederick: Erik, *Der Fliegende Holländer (The Flying Dutchman)*, 1978–79

Schrader, Jonathan: Benoit, *La Bohème*, 1994–95; Krushina, *The Bartered Bride*, 1994–95; Don Pedro, *La Périchole*, 1995–96; Lesbo, *Agrippina*, 1995–96; Luther, *Les Contes d'Hoffmann (The Tales of Hoffmann)*, 1995–96; The Music Master, *Ariadne auf Naxos*, 1996–97; Baron Douphol, *La Traviata*, 1997–98; Captain Corcoran, *HMS Pinafore*, 1997–98

Schreiner, Norman Frederick: Paris, *Roméo et Juliette*, 1966–67; A Messenger, *Il Trovatore*, 1967–68; An Abbé, *Andrea Chénier*, 1967–68; Guillot de Morfontaine, *Manon*, 1967–68; Augustine Moser, *Die Meistersinger von Nürnberg (The Mastersingers of Nuremberg)*, 1968–69; Chaplitsky, *La Pique Dame (The Queen of Spades)*, 1968–69; Gastone, *La Traviata*, 1968–69; Sellem, *The Rake's Progress*, 1968–69; Scaramuccio, *Ariadne auf Naxos*, 1969–70; The Chief Magistrate, *Un Ballo in Maschera (A Masked Ball)*, 1969–70; The Dancing Master, *Ariadne auf Naxos*, 1969–70; Hyllus, *Heracles*, 1971–72; Priest, *Die Zauberflöte (The Magic Flute)*, 1972–73; Steva, *Jenůfa*, 1972–73; Lensky, *Eugene Onegin*, 1974–75

Schrock, Scharmal: Marianne Leitmetzerin, *Der Rosenkavalier*, 1965–66; Lady Billows, *Albert Herring*, 1966–67; Lady Billows, *Albert Herring*, 1967–68

Schub, Kathryn: Barbarina, *Le Nozze di Figaro (The Marriage of Figaro)*, 1980–81

Schuba, Peter: Hunding, *Die Walküre*, 1969–70; Tom, *Un Ballo in Maschera (A Masked Ball)*, 1969–70; Truffaldino, *Ariadne auf Naxos*, 1969–70

Schubert, Cecile: Thillite, *Kiss Me, Kate*, 1973–74

Schubert, Nancy: Marcellina, *Le Nozze di Figaro (The Marriage of Figaro)*, 1955–56; Sarah Potts, *The Land Between the Rivers*, 1955–56; The Chinese Cup,

L'Enfant et les Sortilèges (The Bewitched Child), 1955–56; Annie Oakley, *Annie Get Your Gun*, 1956–57; Carmen, *Carmen*, 1956–57; Ensign Nellie Forbush, *South Pacific*, 1956–57

Schuette, Patrick: Snowboy, *West Side Story*, 2002–03

Schulte, Nelda: Ruth Putnam, *The Crucible*, 1987–88

Schultz, Thomas: Nathanael, *Les Contes d'Hoffmann (The Tales of Hoffmann)*, 1959–60; Page, *Parsifal*, 1959–60; Student, *La Rondine (The Swallow)*, 1959–60; Mr. Daniel Buchanan, *Street Scene*, 1960–61

Schumacher, John: Ajax, *The Cry of Clytaemnestra*, 1989–90; Bogdanowitsch, *Die lustige Witwe (The Merry Widow)*, 1990–91; Zuniga, *Carmen*, 1991–92; Dr. Bartolo, *Le Nozze di Figaro (The Marriage of Figaro)*, 1992–93; Agent of the Inquisition, *Candide*, 1993–94; Baron Thunder-Ten-Tronck, *Candide*, 1993–94; Pasha Prefect, *Candide*, 1993–94

Schumacher, William: A Muleteer, *Man of La Mancha*, 1988–89; Montano, *Otello*, 1989–90; Commendatore, *Don Giovanni*, 1991–92; Zuniga, *Carmen*, 1991–92; Figaro, *Le Nozze di Figaro (The Marriage of Figaro)*, 1992–93; The President, *1600 Pennsylvania Avenue*, 1992–93; Count des Grieux, *Manon*, 1993–94

Schurger, Aaron: Tenorio / a Muleteer, *Man of La Mancha*, 1988–89

Schutz, Paul: Footman, *Annie Get Your Gun*, 1956–57

Schwartzkopf, Michael: Dromio of Ephesus, *The Boys from Syracuse*, 1968–69; Noah Curry, *110 in the Shade*, 1968–69

Schwein, Margaret: La Cercatrice (Seconda), *Suor Angelica (Sister Angelica)*, 1999–2000; La Ciesca, *Gianni Schicchi*, 1999–2000; Marcellina, *Le Nozze di Figaro (The Marriage of Figaro)*, 2001–02

Schwenzfeier, Judith: Noble Orphan, *Der Rosenkavalier*, 1965–66; Maid, *Manon*, 1967–68; The Governess, *La Pique Dame (The Queen of Spades)*, 1968–69; Zulma, *L'Italiana in Algeri (The Italian Girl in Algiers)*, 1968–69; Marchesa Ortensia, *Love on Trial (La Pietra del Paragone)*, 1969–70; Zita, *Il Trittico (A Triptych)*, 1969–70; Berta (Marcellina), *Il Barbiere di Siviglia (The Barber of Seville)*, 1971–72; Dame Quickly, *Falstaff*, 1971–72; Martha, *Faust*, 1971–72

Scott, Brian: First Bearer, *The Darkened City*, 1978–79; Vashek, *The Bartered Bride*, 1979–80; Borsa, *Rigoletto*, 1980–81; Goro, *Madama Butterfly*, 1981–82; The Fool, *Wozzeck*, 1981–82; Mercury, *Orphée aux enfers (Orpheus in the Underworld)*, 1984–85; The Teapot, *L'Enfant et les Sortilèges (The Bewitched Child)*, 1984–85; Torquemada, *L'Heure espagnole (The Spanish Hour)*, 1984–85; Dr. Blind, *Die Fledermaus (The Bat)*, 1985–86; Sancho Panza, *Man of La Mancha*, 1985–86; The Barber, *Man of La Mancha*, 1985–86; Trinculo, *The Tempest*, 1985–86

Scott, Dan: Priest, *Die Zauberflöte (The Magic Flute)*, 1953–54

Scott, Daniel: A Lackey, *Ariadne auf Naxos*, 1954–55; Doctor Grenville, *La Traviata*, 1954–55; A Tree, *L'Enfant et les Sortilèges (The Bewitched Child)*, 1955–56; Antonio, *Le Nozze di Figaro (The Marriage of Figaro)*, 1955–56; Dr. Bartolo, *Le Nozze di Figaro (The Marriage of Figaro)*, 1955–56; Traveler, *The Land Between the Rivers*, 1955–56; Don Alfonso, *Così fan tutte*, 1956–57; Pawnee's Messenger, *Annie Get Your Gun*, 1956–57; Pistol, *Falstaff*, 1956–57; Trainman, *Annie Get Your Gun*, 1956–57; Zuniga, *Carmen*, 1956–57

Scott, David: Angus MacGregor, *Brigadoon*, 1952–53; Enoch Snow, *Carousel*, 1952–53; Knight, *Parsifal*, 1952–53; Angus MacGregor, *Brigadoon*, 1953–54; Knight, *Parsifal*, 1953–54; Priest, *Die Zauberflöte (The Magic Flute)*, 1953–54; Second Gospeleer, *Finian's Rainbow*, 1953–54; Vallon, *Show Boat*, 1953–54; Andrew Carnes, *Oklahoma!*, 1954–55; Frank, *Die Fledermaus (The Bat)*, 1954–55; Harlequin, *Ariadne auf Naxos*, 1954–55; The Wreck, *Wonderful Town*, 1954–55

Scott, Mariellen: Frasquita, *Carmen*, 1956–57; Lady Richmond, *Candide*, 1957–58

Scott, Sheri Lee: Mrs. Pearce, *My Fair Lady*, 1979–80

Scott, Thelma: Mascha, *The Chocolate Soldier*, 1950–51

Seaberg, Edward: Marquis de Cascada, *Die lustige Witwe (The Merry Widow)*, 1983–84; Slave Driver, *Candide*, 1983–84; Starveling, *A Midsummer Night's Dream*, 1983–84

Seader, Kate: Trouble, *Madama Butterfly*, 2001–02

Searles, David: Antonio, *Le Nozze di Figaro (The Marriage of Figaro)*, 1968–69; Keeper of the Madhouse, *The Rake's Progress*, 1968–69; Surin, *La Pique Dame (The Queen of Spades)*, 1968–69; Titurel, *Parsifal*, 1968–69; Fabrizio, *Love on Trial (La Pietra del Paragone)*, 1969–70; Truffaldino, *Ariadne auf Naxos*, 1969–70; Don Alfonso, *Così fan tutte*, 1970–71; Colline, *La Bohème*, 1974–75; Master of Ceremonies, *Doktor Faust*, 1974–75

Searles, Jenny: First Lady, *Die Zauberflöte (The Magic Flute)*, 2004–05; Helena, *A Midsummer Night's Dream*, 2005–06

Sears, John: The Ringmaster, *The Bartered Bride*, 2001–02; Gastone, *La Traviata*, 2002–03; Pedrillo, *Die Entführung aus dem Serail (The Abduction from the Seraglio)*, 2003–04

Secunde, Nadine: Hester Prynne, *The Scarlet Letter*, 1976–77; Fiordiligi, *Così fan tutte*, 1977–78; Floria Tosca, *Tosca*, 1977–78; Marina Mnishek, *Boris Godunov*, 1978–79; Senta, *Der Fliegende Holländer (The Flying Dutchman)*, 1978–79

Seibel, Peggy: Blonde, *Die Entführung aus dem Serail (The Abduction from the Seraglio)*, 1966–67

Selke, Emily: The Child, *Wozzeck*, 1981–82; Trouble, *Madama Butterfly*, 1981–82; Silver Dollar Tabor, *The Ballad of Baby Doe*, 1982–83

Sellers, Bruce: Priest, *Die Zauberflöte (The Magic Flute)*, 1977–78; Nathanael, *Les Contes d'Hoffmann (The Tales of Hoffmann)*, 1978–79; Third Suitor, *The Darkened City*, 1978–79; Don Curzio, *Le Nozze di Figaro (The Marriage of Figaro)*, 1980–81

Seltenright, Ruth Joy: Peep-Bo, *The Mikado*, 1950–51

Sengelaub, Jack: Spirit, *Die Zauberflöte (The Magic Flute)*, 2004–05

Senger, Reuven: Caronte (Charon), *L'Orfeo*, 1987–88; Andres, *Les Contes d'Hoffmann (The Tales of Hoffmann)*, 1988–89; Cochenille, *Les Contes d'Hoffmann (The Tales of Hoffmann)*, 1988–89; Franz, *Les Contes d'Hoffmann (The Tales of Hoffmann)*, 1988–89; Monostatos, *Die Zauberflöte (The Magic Flute)*, 1988–89; Pittichinaccio, *Les Contes d'Hoffmann (The Tales of Hoffmann)*, 1988–89; Prunier, *La Rondine (The Swallow)*, 1989–90

Sentgeorge, Jacob: Vashek, *The Bartered Bride*, 2001–02; Don Ottavio, *Don Giovanni*, 2002–03; Capt. Albert Lennox, *The Secret Garden*, 2003–04; Rev. Horace Adams, *Peter Grimes*, 2003–04; Sam, *The Ballad of Baby Doe*, 2003–04; Ladislav Sipos, *She Loves Me*, 2004–05; Gabriel, *Too Many Sopranos*, 2006–07; Ko-Ko, *The Mikado*, 2006–07

Serrano, Silfredo: Giove (Jupiter), *L'Orfeo*, 1987–88; Nathanael, *Les Contes d'Hoffmann (The Tales of Hoffmann)*, 1988–89; Roderigo, *Otello*, 1989–90; Chevalier de St. Brioche, *Die lustige Witwe (The Merry Widow)*, 1990–91; The Fool, *Wozzeck*, 1990–91

Serviss, James: Melchior, *Amahl and the Night Visitors*, 1951–52; Osmin, *Die Entführung aus dem Serail (The Abduction from the Seraglio)*, 1951–52; Bull, *The Ruby*, 1954–55

Severin, William: The Ringmaster, *The Bartered Bride*, 1955–56

Sezerman, Ayse: Bianca, *La Rondine (The Swallow)*, 1989–90; Gianetta, *L'Elisir d'amore (The Elixir of Love)*, 1990–91

Shaalan, Sherif: Sparafucile, *Rigoletto*, 1986–87; Reverend John Hale, *The Crucible*, 1987–88

Shade, Nancy: Leonora, *Il Trovatore*, 1967–68; Madeleine de Coigny, *Andrea Chénier*, 1967–68; Violetta Valery, *La Traviata*, 1968–69; Amelia, *Un Ballo in Maschera (A Masked Ball)*, 1969–70; Giorgetta, *Il Trittico (A Triptych)*, 1969–70; Sister Angelica, *Il Trittico (A Triptych)*, 1969–70; Mimi, *La Bohème*, 1970–71; Musetta, *La Bohème*, 1970–71; Salome, *Salome*, 1970–71

Shadwick, Angie: Martha, *Faust*, 2000–01; Meg, *Little Women*, 2001–02; Rosette, *Manon*, 2001–02; La Diva, *Jeppe*, 2002–03

Shannon, Pamela: Florestine, *The Ghosts of Versailles*, 1996–97

Shapiro, Rita: Blonde, *Die Entführung aus dem Serail (The Abduction from the Seraglio)*, 1981–82; Adele, *Die Fledermaus (The Bat)*, 1982–83; Papagena, *Die Zauberflöte (The Magic Flute)*, 1982–83; Sylviane, *Die lustige Witwe (The Merry Widow)*, 1983–84

Shaughnessy, Michael: Corporal of Police, *The Boys from Syracuse*, 1968–69; Dromio of Syracuse, *The Boys from Syracuse*, 1968–69

Shay, Earl: Second Beggar, *Kismet*, 1963–64; Servant to the Widow, *Kismet*, 1963–64; A Doctor, *Arabella*, 1972–73

Shea, Joanne: Hata, *The Bartered Bride*, 1967–68; Maid, *Manon*, 1967–68; Page, *Parsifal*, 1967–68; A Tourier, *Il Trittico (A Triptych)*, 1969–70

Shealy, Joyce: Donna Leonora, *La Forza del Destino (The Force of Destiny)*, 1962–63; Wife of Lazarus, *The Darkened City*, 1962–63; Aida, *Aida*, 1963–64; Minnie, *La Fanciulla del West (The Girl of the Golden West)*, 1963–64; Amelia Grimaldi (Maria Boccanegra), *Simon Boccanegra*, 1964–65; Kundry, *Parsifal*, 1964–65; Princess Turandot, *Turandot*, 1964–65; Lady Macbeth, *Macbeth*, 1965–66; The Princess (Feldmarschallin) von Werdenberg, *Der Rosenkavalier*, 1965–66

Shearer, Elizabeth: Middle Sister, later Tkachikha, *The Legend of Tsar Saltan*, 1986–87

Shearer, Mary: Helmwige, *Die Walküre*, 1971–72; Sister Dolcina, *Il Trittico (A Triptych)*, 1972–73; Sister Lucilla, *Il Trittico (A Triptych)*, 1972–73; The Maid, *Jenůfa*, 1972–73; Frasquita, *Carmen*, 1973–74; Julie Jordan, *Carousel*, 1976–77; Melisande, *Pelléas et Mélisande*, 1976–77; Louise Danton, *Danton and Robespierre*, 1977–78; Pamina, *Die Zauberflöte (The Magic Flute)*, 1977–78; Queen Guenevere, *Canterbury Tales*, 1978–79; The Prioress, *Canterbury Tales*, 1978–79

Shearon, Michael: Marco, *Gianni Schicchi*, 1988–89

Sheehan, David: Owgoost, *McTeague*, 1995–96

Sheehan, Jack: Finian, *Finian's Rainbow*, 1953–54; Mr. Lundie, *Brigadoon*, 1953–54; Ali Hakim, *Oklahoma!*, 1954–55; Chief Sitting Bull, *Annie Get Your Gun*, 1956–57; Dr. Pangloss, *Candide*, 1957–58; Voltaire, *Candide*, 1957–58; , *The Most Happy Fella*, 1959–60; Jeff Douglas, *Brigadoon*, 1961–62

Sheehan, Michael: Owgoost, *McTeague*, 1995–96

Shelley, Eric: Tom, *Oklahoma!*, 1997–98

Shemanski, Mark: Dr. Crabbe, *Peter Grimes*, 1987–88

Sheppard, Edna: Mrs. Mkize, *Lost in the Stars*, 1950–51

Sherman, Robert: Col. W. F. Cody (Buffalo Bill), *Annie Get Your Gun*, 1956–57

Sherrill, Donald: Count Almaviva, *Le Nozze di Figaro (The Marriage of Figaro)*, 1986–87

Shetnev, Orville: Count Monterone, *Rigoletto*, 1950–51

Sheya, Aaron: Gherardo, *Gianni Schicchi*, 1993–94; Customs Officer, *La Bohème*, 1994–95; Rev. Horace Adams, *Peter Grimes*, 1994–95; Chevalier de St. Brioche, *Die lustige Witwe (The Merry Widow)*, 1996–97; Priest, *Die Zauberflöte (The Magic Flute)*, 1998–99

Shibata, Itsuko: Mimi, *La Bohème*, 1994–95; Antonia, *Les Contes d'Hoffmann (The Tales of Hoffmann)*, 1995–96; Cio-Cio San, *Madama Butterfly*, 1996–97

Shideler, Sarah: Page, *Parsifal*, 1961–62; Prince Orlofsky, *Die Fledermaus (The Bat)*, 1962–63

Shields, Erin: Player, *Mass*, 1998–99

Shikowitz, Ross: Albert, *The Ballad of Baby Doe*, 2003–04; Cascada, *Die lustige Witwe (The Merry Widow)*, 2003–04; Footman at the wedding, *The Ballad of Baby Doe*, 2003–04; Thierry, *Dialogues des Carmélites*, 2004–05

Shin, Dong Won: Rodolfo, *La Bohème*, 1999–2000

Shin, Kyung Wook: Harlequin, *Ariadne auf Naxos*, 1969–70; Pacuvio, *Love on Trial (La Pietra del Paragone)*, 1969–70; Sacristan, *Tosca*, 1969–70; Benoit, *La Bohème*, 1970–71; Innkeeper, *Manon Lescaut*, 1970–71; The Host of the Garter Inn, *Falstaff*, 1971–72; Doctor Spinelloccio, *Il Trittico (A Triptych)*, 1972–73; Klingsor, *Parsifal*, 1972–73; Papageno, *Die Zauberflöte (The Magic Flute)*, 1972–73; Sacristan, *Tosca*, 1973–74; The Bonze, *Madama Butterfly*, 1975–76

Shin, Min Jung: Mrs. Ott, *Susannah*, 2000–01

Shin, Yoon Soo: The Duke of Mantua, *Rigoletto*, 1995–96; Lt. Pinkerton, *Madama Butterfly*, 1996–97; Rinuccio, *Gianni Schicchi*, 1999–2000; Rodolfo, *La Bohème*, 1999–2000; The Duke of Mantua, *Rigoletto*, 2000–01; Chevalier des Grieux, *Manon*, 2001–02; Lt. Pinkerton, *Madama Butterfly*, 2001–02

Shinall, Vernon: Superintendant Budd, *Albert Herring*, 1957–58; Commendatore, *Don Giovanni*, 1958–59; Gurnemanz, *Parsifal*, 1958–59; Master Page (Herr Reich), *Die lustigen Weiber von Windsor (The Merry Wives of Windsor)*, 1958–59; The Bonze, *Madama Butterfly*, 1958–59; Sparafucile, *Rigoletto*, 1959–60

Shine, Betty: Fata Morgana, *The Love for Three Oranges*, 1980–81; Marie, *Wozzeck*, 1981–82; The Witch, *Hänsel und Gretel*, 1982–83

Shipps, Lindsay: Sister Mathilde, *Dialogues des Carmélites*, 2004–05

Shirk, Terry: Royal Herald, *Don Carlos*, 1961–62; Spoletta, *Tosca*, 1961–62; Nergus, *Mefistofele*, 1967–68

Shirley, Daniel: Joe, *Our Town*, 2005–06; Tybalt, *Roméo et Juliette*, 2005–06; Enrico Carouser, *Too Many Sopranos*, 2006–07; Guillot de Morfontaine, *Manon*, 2006–07; Dino, *A Wedding*, 2007–08

Shirley, Hazel: Giulietta, *Les Contes d'Hoffmann (The Tales of Hoffmann)*, 1947–48; Kundry, *Parsifal*, 1948–49; Kundry, *Parsifal*, 1949–50; Mrs. Anna Maurant, *Street Scene*, 1949–50; Sybil Van Dare, *The Firefly*, 1949–50

Shirley, Helen: Jenny Hildebrand, *Street Scene*, 1949–50

Shirn, Carolyn: Sarah Good, *The Crucible*, 1987–88; Vittoria (Victory), *L'Orfeo*, 1987–88

Shivers, Lisa: The McCourt family, *The Ballad of Baby Doe*, 1982–83

Shoaff, Judy: Frou-Frou, *Die lustige Witwe (The Merry Widow)*, 1964–65

Shoemaker, Cecil: Butler, *My Fair Lady*, 1979–80; Jim, *Show Boat*, 1984–85

Shoupe, Carol: Newcomer, *Street Scene*, 1960–61

Shriner, Christine: Musetta, *La Bohème*, 1974–75

Shriner, Deborah: Pearl, *The Scarlet Letter*, 1960–61; Pearl, *The Scarlet Letter*, 1961–62; Spirit, *Die Zauberflöte (The Magic Flute)*, 1965–66; Courtesan, *The Boys from Syracuse*, 1968–69

Shriner, Diana: Snookie, *110 in the Shade*, 1967–68; Courtesan, *The Boys from Syracuse*, 1968–69; Fatima, *The Boys from Syracuse*, 1968–69; Snookie, *110 in the Shade*, 1968–69

Shriner, William: Klingsor, *Parsifal*, 1956–57; Parsifal, *Parsifal*, 1961–62; Siegmund, *Die Walküre*, 1969–70; Billy Bigelow, *Carousel*, 1970–71; Siegmund, *Die Walküre*, 1971–72; The Drum Major, *Wozzeck*, 1973–74

Shuffle, John: Henry B., *The Mother of Us All*, 1973–74; Jacob, *The Ballad of Baby Doe*, 1975–76; Arbace, *Idomeneo*, 1976–77; Bacio Bazzini, *Candide*, 1976–77; Maximilian, *Candide*, 1976–77; Pilgrim Father, *Candide*, 1976–77; Player, *Bernstein on Broadway*, 1976–77; Sam, *Trouble in Tahiti*, 1976–77

Shur, Adda: Princess Ninetta, *The Love for Three Oranges*, 1980–81; Malinka, *The Excursions of Mr. Broucek*, 1981–82; Rosalinda, *Die Fledermaus (The Bat)*, 1982–83; Marina Mnishek, *Boris Godunov*, 1983–84

Shutt, Cynthia: Jenny's friend, *Street Scene*, 1960–61; Countess of Eremberg, *Don Carlos*, 1961–62

Sibbersen, Kristin: Spirit, *Die Zauberflöte (The Magic Flute)*, 1982–83; Mrs. Western, *Tom Jones*, 1983–84

Sick, Mark: The Pastor, *Werther*, 1961–62

Siebert, Glenn: Prince Tamino, *Die Zauberflöte (The Magic Flute)*, 1977–78; Ferrando, *Così fan tutte*, 1978–79; Peter Quint, *The Turn of the Screw*, 1978–79; Prologue, *The Turn of the Screw*, 1978–79; Second Suitor, *The Darkened City*, 1978–79; Don Ottavio, *Don Giovanni*, 1979–80; Orestes, *The Cry of Clytaemnestra*, 1979–80

Siegle, Laurence: Dr. Caius, *Die lustigen Weiber von Windsor (The Merry Wives of Windsor),* 1958–59

Sievers, David: An Indian, *The Bartered Bride,* 2001–02; Dr. Blind, *Die Fledermaus (The Bat),* 2002–03; Ben Weatherstaff, *The Secret Garden,* 2003–04; Dr. Caius, *Falstaff,* 2003–04; Triquet, *Eugene Onegin,* 2004–05

Sigmon, David: Second Commissioner, *Dialogues des Carmélites,* 1997–98; Mars, *Orphée aux enfers (Orpheus in the Underworld),* 1998–99; Doctor Spinelloccio, *Gianni Schicchi,* 1999–2000; Keeper of the Madhouse, *The Rake's Progress,* 1999–2000; Count Ceprano, *Rigoletto,* 2000–01; Dr. Bartolo, *Le Nozze di Figaro (The Marriage of Figaro),* 2001–02; Micha, *The Bartered Bride,* 2001–02

Sikora, Daniela: Queen of the Night, *Die Zauberflöte (The Magic Flute),* 1982–83

Silva, Leonard: Official Registrar, *Madama Butterfly,* 2001–02

Silver, FrankieLynn: Sister Constance, *Dialogues des Carmélites,* 1986–87

Silverboerg, Thomas: Reverend Master John W. Wilson, *The Scarlet Letter,* 1976–77

Simmons, Amy Hansen: Pat Nixon, *Nixon in China,* 1994–95

Simmons, David: Andres, *Les Contes d'Hoffmann (The Tales of Hoffmann),* 1995–96; Cochenille, *Les Contes d'Hoffmann (The Tales of Hoffmann),* 1995–96; Franz, *Les Contes d'Hoffmann (The Tales of Hoffmann),* 1995–96; Luther Billis, *South Pacific,* 1995–96; Pittichinaccio, *Les Contes d'Hoffmann (The Tales of Hoffmann),* 1995–96

Simmons, Kristopher: Photographer, *A Wedding,* 2007–08

Simmons, Lisa: Esmeralda, *The Bartered Bride,* 1979–80

Simmons, Renee: Queenie, *Show Boat,* 1984–85

Simmons, Todd: The Host of the Garter Inn, *Falstaff,* 1992–93

Simms, Brian: Man with Guitar, *Show Boat,* 1984–85; Jose / a Muleteer, *Man of La Mancha,* 1985–86

Sims, Tom: Alec, *Finian's Rainbow,* 1953–54; Man in Armor, *Die Zauberflöte (The Magic Flute),* 1953–54; Sciarrone, *Tosca,* 1957–58

Sims, Wayne: Whirling Dervish, *Kismet,* 1989–90

Sisk, Robert: Mr. George Jones, *Street Scene,* 1949–50; Knight, *Parsifal,* 1950–51; Gregory, *Kiss Me, Kate,* 1951–52; Knight, *Parsifal,* 1951–52

Six, Scott: Dr. Caius, *Falstaff,* 1997–98; John Styx, *Orphée aux enfers (Orpheus in the Underworld),* 1998–99; Matteo, *Arabella,* 1998–99; Male Chorus, *The Rape of Lucretia,* 1999–2000; Sancho Panza, *Man of La Mancha,* 1999–2000; Sam Polk, *Susannah,* 2000–01; Edgardo, *Lucia di Lammermoor,* 2001–02; Lt. Pinkerton, *Madama Butterfly,* 2001–02

Skiba, Scott: Baron Mirko Zeta, *Die lustige Witwe (The Merry Widow),* 2003–04; Captain Balstrode, *Peter Grimes,* 2003–04; Horace Tabor, *The Ballad of Baby Doe,* 2003–04; Eugene Onegin, *Eugene Onegin,* 2004–05; Marco, *A View from the Bridge,* 2004–05; Escamillo, *Carmen,* 2005–06; Mandryka, *Arabella,* 2006–07

Skinner, Philip: Wuerfl, *The Excursions of Mr. Broucek,* 1981–82; Don Basilio, *Il Barbiere di Siviglia (The Barber of Seville),* 1982–83; Horace Tabor, *The Ballad of Baby Doe,* 1982–83; Joe, *The Most Happy Fella,* 1982–83; Speaker of the Temple, *Die Zauberflöte (The Magic Flute),* 1982–83; Bottom, *A Midsummer Night's Dream,* 1983–84; Donner, *Das Rheingold,* 1983–84; Beckett, *Murder in the Cathedral,* 1984–85; Don Alfonso, *Così fan tutte,* 1984–85

Skinner, Stephen: Master Page (Herr Reich), *Die lustigen Weiber von Windsor (The Merry Wives of Windsor),* 1981–82; The Doctor, *Wozzeck,* 1981–82; Sarastro, *Die Zauberflöte (The Magic Flute),* 1982–83; Fafner, *Das Rheingold,* 1983–84; Judge Turpin, *Sweeney Todd,* 1983–84; Quince, *A Midsummer Night's Dream,* 1983–84

Skretkowicz, Kinga: Princess Nicoletta, *The Love for Three Oranges,* 1999–2000; Gretel, *Hänsel und Gretel,* 2001–02; Adele, *Die Fledermaus (The Bat),* 2002–03; Donna Fiorilla, *Il Turco in Italia (The Turk in Italy),* 2003–04

Skrevanos, Renee: Page, *Parsifal,* 1975–76; Princess Nicoletta, *The Love for Three Oranges,* 1975–76; Madame Tallien, *Danton and Robespierre,* 1977–78; Mercedes, *Carmen,* 1977–78; Spirit, *Die Zauberflöte (The Magic Flute),* 1977–78

Skusnichenko, Pyotr: Paolo, *Francesca da Rimini,* 1989–90

Slagel, Donald: Fred Cullen, *Street Scene,* 1949–50; Absalom Kumalo, *Lost in the Stars,* 1950–51; Count Ceprano, *Rigoletto,* 1950–51; Baptista, *Kiss Me, Kate,* 1951–52; Harry Trevor, *Kiss Me, Kate,* 1951–52; Klingsor, *Parsifal,* 1951–52; Little Old Man, *On the Town,* 1951–52; Servant, *Amahl and the Night Visitors,* 1951–52

Slater, Myron: Parsifal, *Parsifal,* 1957–58; Rodolfo, *La Bohème,* 1957–58; Turiddu, *Cavalleria Rusticana,* 1957–58; Graf Elemer, *Arabella,* 1972–73; Thaddeus Stevens, *The Mother of Us All,* 1973–74

Sliger, Charles: Ike Skidmore, *Oklahoma!,* 1981–82; Wagner, *Faust,* 1981–82; Frank, *Die Fledermaus (The Bat),* 1982–83; The Cashier, *The Most Happy Fella,* 1982–83; Bulgarian Soldier, *Candide,* 1983–84; Sailor, *Candide,* 1983–84

Small, Eric: Adam, *Die Teufel von Loudun (The Devils of Loudun),* 1992–93; Don Basilio, *Le Nozze di Figaro (The Marriage of Figaro),* 1992–93; Gherardo, *Gianni Schicchi,* 1993–94; Vashek, *The Bartered Bride,* 1994–95; Andres, *Wozzeck,*

1999–2000; Count Almaviva, *Il Barbiere di Siviglia (The Barber of Seville),* 2000–01; Chevalier des Grieux, *Manon,* 2001–02

Smartt, Michael: Jankel, *Arabella,* 1972–73; Schlemil, *Les Contes d'Hoffmann (The Tales of Hoffmann),* 1973–74; Count Monterone, *Rigoletto,* 1974–75; Student from Krakow, *Doktor Faust,* 1974–75; Count Renato, *Un Ballo in Maschera (A Masked Ball),* 1975–76; Porgy, *Porgy and Bess,* 1976–77; Porgy, *Porgy and Bess,* 1979–80; Rigoletto, *Rigoletto,* 1980–81; Jakob Lenz, *Jakob Lenz,* 1981–82

Smith, Alice Jane: Meg Brockie, *Brigadoon,* 1952–53

Smith, Alma Jean: Giorgetta, *Il Trittico (A Triptych),* 1972–73; Antonia, *Les Contes d'Hoffmann (The Tales of Hoffmann),* 1973–74; Countess Almaviva, *Le Nozze di Figaro (The Marriage of Figaro),* 1973–74

Smith, Coleman: Balthasar Zorn, *Die Meistersinger von Nürnberg (The Mastersingers of Nuremberg),* 1961–62

Smith, DaMar: Reverend Bushrod, *1600 Pennsylvania Avenue,* 1992–93

Smith, David: Enrico Ashton, *Lucia di Lammermoor,* 1963–64; Fiorello, *Il Barbiere di Siviglia (The Barber of Seville),* 1963–64; Sonora Slim, *La Fanciulla del West (The Girl of the Golden West),* 1963–64

Smith, David W.: The Drum Major, *Wozzeck,* 1990–91; Canio, *I Pagliacci,* 1991–92; Remendado, *Carmen,* 1991–92; Bardolph, *Falstaff,* 1992–93; Don Curzio, *Le Nozze di Figaro (The Marriage of Figaro),* 1992–93; Guillot de Morfontaine, *Manon,* 1993–94; Pedrillo, *Die Entführung aus dem Serail (The Abduction from the Seraglio),* 1993–94; Bob Boles, *Peter Grimes,* 1994–95; Brighella, *Ariadne auf Naxos,* 1996–97; The Dancing Master, *Ariadne auf Naxos,* 1996–97

Smith, Dawn: Ortlinde, *Die Walküre,* 1971–72

Smith, Ed: Indian Priest, *The Ruby,* 1954–55

Smith, Ethel: Mrs. Laura Hildebrand, *Street Scene,* 1960–61

Smith, Eugene: Jenik, *The Bartered Bride,* 1955–56

Smith, Gene: Luigi, *Il Tabarro (The Cloak),* 1955–56

Smith, Greg: Wagner, *Faust,* 1989–90; Baron Mirko Zeta, *Die lustige Witwe (The Merry Widow),* 1990–91; Dr. Falke, *Die Fledermaus (The Bat),* 1990–91; Larry, *Company,* 1990–91; Alidoro, *La Cenerentola (Cinderella),* 1991–92; The King, *Jubilee,* 1991–92

Smith, Larry G.: Mordcha, *Fiddler on the Roof,* 1972–73

Smith, Linda: Carmen, *Carmen,* 1962–63; Marcellina, *Le Nozze di Figaro (The Marriage of Figaro),* 1962–63; Preziosilla, *La Forza del Destino (The Force of Destiny),* 1962–63; Alisa, *Lucia di Lammermoor,* 1963–64; Khivria, *The Fair at Sorochinsk,* 1963–64; Mrs. Sedley, *Peter Grimes,* 1963–64; Wowkle, *La Fanciulla del West (The Girl of the Golden West),* 1963–64

Smith, Malcolm: Grand Inquisitor, *Don Carlos,* 1960–61; Gurnemanz, *Parsifal,* 1960–61; Monk, *Don Carlos,* 1960–61; Roger Chillingworth, *The Scarlet Letter,* 1960–61; Sarastro, *Die Zauberflöte (The Magic Flute),* 1960–61; Grand Inquisitor, *Don Carlos,* 1961–62; Gurnemanz, *Parsifal,* 1961–62; Osmin, *Die Entführung aus dem Serail (The Abduction from the Seraglio),* 1961–62; Roger Chillingworth, *The Scarlet Letter,* 1961–62; Veit Pogner, *Die Meistersinger von Nürnberg (The Mastersingers of Nuremberg),* 1961–62; Titurel, *Parsifal,* 1963–64; Commendatore, *Don Giovanni,* 1964–65; Gurnemanz, *Parsifal,* 1964–65; Pimen, *Boris Godunov,* 1964–65; Timur, *Turandot,* 1964–65

Smith, Margaret: Blonde, *Die Entführung aus dem Serail (The Abduction from the Seraglio),* 1966–67; Lady-in-waiting to the Empress, *L'Incoronazione di Poppea (The Coronation of Poppea),* 1967–68

Smith, Mary Jean: Mary, *Finian's Rainbow,* 1953–54

Smith, Mary Winston: Strawberry Woman, *Porgy and Bess,* 1976–77

Smith, Norman: Dr. Wilhelm Reischmann, *Elegy for Young Lovers,* 1967–68; Dumas, *Andrea Chénier,* 1967–68; Ferrando, *Il Trovatore,* 1967–68

Smith, Pamela: Maggie Anderson, *Brigadoon,* 1961–62; Princess Samahris of Turkestan, *Kismet,* 1963–64; Lolo, *Die lustige Witwe (The Merry Widow),* 1965–66

Smith, Paul: An Officer, *Ariadne auf Naxos,* 1996–97; Louis XVI, *The Ghosts of Versailles,* 1996–97; Doctor Grenville, *La Traviata,* 1997–98; Graf Lamoral, *Arabella,* 1998–99; Jupiter, *Orphée aux enfers (Orpheus in the Underworld),* 1998–99

Smith, Perry: Andrew Johnson, *The Mother of Us All,* 1973–74

Smith, Peter: Amfortas, *Parsifal,* 1949–50; Dr. Betts, *The Veil,* 1949–50; Man, *Street Scene,* 1949–50; Marcello, *La Bohème,* 1949–50; Robert, *The New Moon,* 1949–50

Smith, Randall: Mime, *Das Rheingold,* 1983–84; Tempter, *Murder in the Cathedral,* 1984–85; Don Jose, *Carmen,* 1984–85; A Steersman, *Der Fliegende Holländer (The Flying Dutchman),* 1985–86; The Chevalier, *Dialogues des Carmélites,* 1986–87

Smith, Robert: Candide, *Candide,* 1976–77; Player, *Bernstein on Broadway,* 1976–77; Remendado, *Carmen,* 1977–78; The Deacon, *The Night Before Christmas,* 1977–78; Prince Shuisky, *Boris Godunov,* 1978–79

Smith, Robin: Giovanna, *Rigoletto,* 2007–08; Voice of the Mother, *Les Contes d'Hoffmann (The Tales of Hoffmann),* 2007–08

Smith, Roger: Elder Ott, *Susannah,* 1979–80; Footman, *My Fair Lady,* 1979–80

Smith, Ronald: Photographer, *Street Scene*, 1960–61; Workman, *Street Scene*, 1960–61; Undertaker, *Porgy and Bess*, 1976–77

Smith, S. Kendrick: Henry, *1600 Pennsylvania Avenue*, 1992–93; Uncle Sam the Interlocutor, *1600 Pennsylvania Avenue*, 1992–93

Smith, Timothy: Count Panatellas, *La Périchole*, 1995–96; Spalanzani, *Les Contes d'Hoffmann (The Tales of Hoffmann)*, 1995–96; Chevalier de St. Brioche, *Die lustige Witwe (The Merry Widow)*, 1996–97; Dr. Blind, *Die Fledermaus (The Bat)*, 1996–97; Goro, *Madama Butterfly*, 1996–97; Ralph Rackstraw, *HMS Pinafore*, 1997–98; Orpheus, *Orphée aux enfers (Orpheus in the Underworld)*, 1998–99

Smith (Nicolson), Mark: Ferdinand, *The Tempest*, 1985–86; Nemorino, *L'Elisir d'amore (The Elixir of Love)*, 1986–87; Tom Rakewell, *The Rake's Progress*, 1986–87; Tsaryevich Guidon, *The Legend of Tsar Saltan*, 1986–87

Snider, Jeffrey: Marullo, *Rigoletto*, 1980–81; Second Apprentice, *Wozzeck*, 1981–82; Officer, *Il Barbiere di Siviglia (The Barber of Seville)*, 1982–83; Jonas Fogg, *Sweeney Todd*, 1983–84; Rangoni, *Boris Godunov*, 1983–84; Cap'n Andy, *Show Boat*, 1984–85; Windy, *Show Boat*, 1984–85; Dancaire, *Carmen*, 1984–85

Snider, William: Constable, *Der Rosenkavalier*, 1965–66

Sniderwin, George: Master of Ceremonies, *La Pique Dame (The Queen of Spades)*, 1968–69; Ulrich Eisslinger, *Die Meistersinger von Nürnberg (The Mastersingers of Nuremberg)*, 1968–69

Snoddy, Martha: Sister Dolcina, *Il Trittico (A Triptych)*, 1972–73; Sister Lucilla, *Il Trittico (A Triptych)*, 1972–73; Spirit, *Die Zauberflöte (The Magic Flute)*, 1972–73; Isabel Wentworth, *The Mother of Us All*, 1973–74

Snodgrass, Daniel: An Old Man, *Eugene Onegin*, 1988–89; Hermann, *Les Contes d'Hoffmann (The Tales of Hoffmann)*, 1988–89; Pinellino, *Gianni Schicchi*, 1988–89; De Cerisay, *Die Teufel von Loudun (The Devils of Loudun)*, 1992–93; Prince Henri de Conde, *Die Teufel von Loudun (The Devils of Loudun)*, 1992–93

Snow, Greg: Waiter, *Of Thee I Sing*, 1987–88

Snowden, Julia: Giovanna, *Rigoletto*, 2007–08

Snyder, Audrey: Mrs. McLean, *Susannah*, 2007–08; Nettie/Aunt Bea, *A Wedding*, 2007–08

Snyder, Richard: Captain, *The Scarlet Letter*, 1960–61; General Polkan, *Le Coq d'or (The Golden Cockerel)*, 1960–61; Man in Armor, *Die Zauberflöte (The Magic Flute)*, 1960–61; Mr. Carl Olsen, *Street Scene*, 1960–61; Quince, *A Midsummer Night's Dream*, 1961–62; Old Adam Goodheart, *Ruddigore (The Witch's Curse)*, 1962–63; Josef Mauer, *Elegy for Young Lovers*, 1967–68

Soddy, Julie: Flora Bervoix, *La Traviata*, 1983–84; Coryphee, *Murder in the Cathedral*, 1984–85; Public Opinion, *Orphée aux enfers (Orpheus in the Underworld)*, 1984–85; The Marquise of Birkenfeld, *La Fille du régiment (The Daughter of the Regiment)*, 1984–85

Sohn, Hyoun-soo: Siebel, *Faust*, 2000–01; Hansel, *Hänsel und Gretel*, 2001–02; Suzuki, *Madama Butterfly*, 2001–02; Muse, *Les Contes d'Hoffmann (The Tales of Hoffmann)*, 2002–03; Nicklausse, *Les Contes d'Hoffmann (The Tales of Hoffmann)*, 2002–03; Zaida, *Il Turco in Italia (The Turk in Italy)*, 2003–04; Olga, *Eugene Onegin*, 2004–05

Solano, Ulises: Lun Tha, *The King and I*, 1996–97; The Fool, *Wozzeck*, 1999–2000

Soller, Robert: Dr. Wilson, *Street Scene*, 1949–50; Dr. Wilson, *Street Scene*, 1960–61; Officer Murphy, *Street Scene*, 1960–61

Solley, Marvin: The Mayor, *A Parfait for Irene*, 1951–52

Soman, Bharati: Gianetta, *L'Elisir d'amore (The Elixir of Love)*, 2000–01

Somerville, Judy: Parassja, *The Fair at Sorochinsk*, 1963–64

Sommer, Michael: Shears, *Finian's Rainbow*, 1969–70; Sheriff, *Finian's Rainbow*, 1969–70

Sorisio, Linda: Olga, *Die lustige Witwe (The Merry Widow)*, 1983–84

Sowers, Richard: Jailer, *Tosca*, 1973–74; A Herald, *The Love for Three Oranges*, 1975–76; Rangoni, *Boris Godunov*, 1978–79

Spade, Samuel: Guccio, *Gianni Schicchi*, 1999–2000; Pinellino, *Gianni Schicchi*, 1999–2000; Elder Ott, *Susannah*, 2000–01; Count des Grieux, *Manon*, 2001–02; Friedrich Bhaer, *Little Women*, 2001–02; Achilla, *Giulio Cesare (Julius Caesar)*, 2002–03; Jacob, *The Ballad of Baby Doe*, 2003–04; Sacristan, *Tosca*, 2004–05; Schaunard, *La Bohème*, 2004–05; Mr. Webb, *Our Town*, 2005–06

Spain, Catherine: Marta, *Company*, 1990–91

Spangler, Lora: Irene Molloy, *Hello, Dolly!*, 1991–92

Spann, Annette: Dame Quickly, *Falstaff*, 1976–77; Serena, *Porgy and Bess*, 1976–77

Spannuth, Russell: Henry, *Finian's Rainbow*, 1953–54

Sparks, Peggy: Zaneeta Shinn, *The Music Man*, 1980–81

Spaulding, Craig: Sir Dinadan, *Camelot*, 1968–69; Third Sharecropper, *Finian's Rainbow*, 1969–70

Specht, Sybille: The Composer, *Ariadne auf Naxos*, 1996–97

Spina, Julianna: Baroness Elberfeld, *The Sound of Music*, 2000–01

Spivey, Orman: Marquis D'Obigny, *La Traviata*, 1954–55

Sponseller, Christopher: Dappertutto, *Les Contes d'Hoffmann (The Tales of Hoffmann)*, 2002–03; Bardolph, *Falstaff*, 2003–04; Bob Boles, *Peter Grimes*,

2003–04; Washington Dandy, *The Ballad of Baby Doe*, 2003–04; Lensky, *Eugene Onegin*, 2004–05; Matteo, *Arabella*, 2006–07

Sporleder, Anita: Faye, *Oklahoma!*, 1981–82

Springer, Jeffrey: Gastone, *La Traviata*, 1978–79; Jess, *Oklahoma!*, 1981–82; Westphalian Soldier, *Candide*, 1983–84; Remendado, *Carmen*, 1984–85; Don Basilio, *Le Nozze di Figaro (The Marriage of Figaro)*, 1986–87; First Sailor, *The Legend of Tsar Saltan*, 1986–87; Bob Boles, *Peter Grimes*, 1987–88; Judge Danforth, *The Crucible*, 1987–88; Cassio, *Otello*, 1989–90; Rodolfo, *La Bohème*, 1989–90; Alfred, *Die Fledermaus (The Bat)*, 1990–91; Lt. Pinkerton, *Madama Butterfly*, 1991–92; Mario Cavaradossi, *Tosca*, 2004–05

Springer, Stanley: Man in Armor, *Die Zauberflöte (The Magic Flute)*, 1977–78; Gastone, *La Traviata*, 1978–79; Spalanzani, *Les Contes d'Hoffmann (The Tales of Hoffmann)*, 1978–79; Third Mourner, *The Darkened City*, 1978–79; Elder Hayes, *Susannah*, 1979–80; Menelaus, *The Cry of Clytaemnestra*, 1979–80

Sroufe, Jeffrey: Antonio, *Le Nozze di Figaro (The Marriage of Figaro)*, 1986–87; Baron Thunder-Ten-Tronck, *Candide*, 1987–88; Francis Nurse, *The Crucible*, 1987–88; Judge of the Inquisition, *Candide*, 1987–88; Slave Driver, *Candide*, 1987–88; Somarone, *Béatrice et Bénédict*, 1987–88

St. Laurent, Mark: Newsboy, *The Ballad of Baby Doe*, 1982–83; Washington Dandy, *The Ballad of Baby Doe*, 1982–83; Priest, *Murder in the Cathedral*, 1984–85; The Armchair, *L'Enfant et les Sortilèges (The Bewitched Child)*, 1984–85; Gonzalo, Tutor to the King, *The Tempest*, 1985–86

Staff, Charles: Frank, *Brigadoon*, 1952–53; Harmonica Player, *Finian's Rainbow*, 1953–54; Drunk, *Wonderful Town*, 1954–55

Stafford, Frank: Bound, *The Veil*, 1949–50; Page, *Parsifal*, 1949–50

Stahl, Earl: Sandy Dean, *Brigadoon*, 1952–53

Stahl, Fred: Marquis D'Obigny, *La Traviata*, 1968–69

Stalas, Alexandra: Stella, *Les Contes d'Hoffmann (The Tales of Hoffmann)*, 1973–74; Mrs. Anderssen, *A Little Night Music*, 1975–76

Stankiewicz, Sarah: Cousin Hebe, *HMS Pinafore*, 2005–06

Stanley, Charles: Announcer, *On the Town*, 1951–52; Mr. Ratcliffe, *Billy Budd*, 1952–53

Stanley, Elizabeth: Player, *Mass*, 1998–99

Stapleton, Ian: Marquis de Croissant, *Die lustige Witwe (The Merry Widow)*, 1964–65; Missail, *Boris Godunov*, 1964–65

Stapp, Gregory: Colline, *La Bohème*, 1979–80

Stapp, Olivia: Deianira, *Heracles*, 1971–72

Staring, Laura: Suor Osmina, *Suor Angelica (Sister Angelica)*, 1999–2000

Starkey, David: Frank Lippencott, *Wonderful Town*, 1954–55; Ike Skidmore, *Oklahoma!*, 1954–55; Faust, *Faust*, 1955–56; Page, *Parsifal*, 1955–56; Count Almaviva, *Il Barbiere di Siviglia (The Barber of Seville)*, 1956–57; Ferrando, *Così fan tutte*, 1956–57; Page, *Parsifal*, 1956–57; Ernesto, *Don Pasquale*, 1957–58; Amelia's Lover, *Amelia Goes to the Ball*, 1957–58

Starkey, David (son): Don Basilio, *Le Nozze di Figaro (The Marriage of Figaro)*, 1992–93; Elson, *1600 Pennsylvania Avenue*, 1992–93; Glad Hand, *West Side Story*, 1992–93; John Styx, *Orphée aux enfers (Orpheus in the Underworld)*, 1992–93; South Carolina Delegate, *1600 Pennsylvania Avenue*, 1992–93; Alcindoro, *La Bohème*, 1994–95; Ned Keene, *Peter Grimes*, 1994–95

Starkey, Ruth: Mistress Hibbins, *The Scarlet Letter*, 1976–77; Mrs. Ott, *Susannah*, 1976–77

Starks, Eric: Indio, *West Side Story*, 1992–93

Starnes, Christia: Eine Kartenaufschlaegerin, *Arabella*, 2006–07

Staton, Sue: Mrs. Coburg, *Blossom Time*, 1952–53

Statsenko, Boris: Lanciotto, *Francesca da Rimini*, 1989–90; Virgil's Ghost, *Francesca da Rimini*, 1989–90

Stauber, Rebecca: Minerva, *Orphée aux enfers (Orpheus in the Underworld)*, 1998–99; La Cercatrice (Prima), *Suor Angelica (Sister Angelica)*, 1999–2000; Mrs. Gleaton, *Susannah*, 2000–01

Stavely, Starla: Sospetto, *L'Orfeo*, 1987–88; Lauretta, *Gianni Schicchi*, 1988–89

Stavrou, Thei: Maestro dell Novizie, *Suor Angelica (Sister Angelica)*, 1999–2000

Stebbe, John: Notary, *La Fille du régiment (The Daughter of the Regiment)*, 1984–85

Steckbeck, Mary Ann: Julie, *Show Boat*, 1953–54

Steele, Robert: Policeman, *Carousel*, 1970–71

Steenerson, Anna: Elizabeth "Baby" Doe, *The Ballad of Baby Doe*, 2003–04; Blanche, *Dialogues des Carmélites*, 2004–05; Emily, *Our Town*, 2005–06; Josephine, *HMS Pinafore*, 2005–06; Juliet, *Roméo et Juliette*, 2005–06; Just Jeanette, *Too Many Sopranos*, 2006–07

Steigerwald, Gary Lee: Photographer, *The Ballad of Baby Doe*, 1982–83

Steinberg, Sharon: Pousette, *Manon*, 1979–80

Steiner, William: Station Master, *Lost in the Stars*, 1950–51; The Mikado of Japan, *The Mikado*, 1950–51; Titurel, *Parsifal*, 1950–51

Steingraber, Thor: Mouthpiece, *West Side Story*, 1985–86; Mordred, *Camelot*, 1986–87; Alexander Throttlebottom, *Of Thee I Sing*, 1987–88

Stelman, Laura: Papagena, *Die Zauberflöte (The Magic Flute)*, 2004–05; Frasquita, *Carmen*, 2005–06; The Sandman, *Too Many Sopranos*, 2006–07

Stephan, Erwin: Otello, *Otello,* 1989–90

Stephan, Naomi: Giovanna, *Rigoletto,* 1959–60

Stephens, Beverly: Cinders, *L'Enfant et les Sortilèges (The Bewitched Child),* 1955–56

Stephens, David: Starveling, *A Midsummer Night's Dream,* 1983–84

Stephenson, Elizabeth: Senta, *Der Fliegende Holländer (The Flying Dutchman),* 1985–86; Madame Lidoine, *Dialogues des Carmélites,* 1986–87

Stephenson, Michelle: Minerva, *Orphée aux enfers (Orpheus in the Underworld),* 1992–93; Carrie Pipperidge, *Carousel,* 1993–94; Shepherd Boy, *Tosca,* 1993–94; Madame Mao, *Nixon in China,* 1994–95; Niece, *Peter Grimes,* 1994–95; Die Fiakermilli, *Arabella,* 1998–99; Queen of the Night, *Die Zauberflöte (The Magic Flute),* 1998–99

Stephenson, Peggy: Cherubino, *Le Nozze di Figaro (The Marriage of Figaro),* 1986–87; Beatrice, *Béatrice et Bénédict,* 1987–88; Countess Celimene, *A Little Night Music,* 1988–89; Desiree Armfeldt, *A Little Night Music,* 1988–89; Muse, *Les Contes d'Hoffmann (The Tales of Hoffmann),* 1988–89; Nicklausse, *Les Contes d'Hoffmann (The Tales of Hoffmann),* 1988–89

Stevens, Barbara: Shepherd Figure in the Wallpaper, *L'Enfant et les Sortilèges (The Bewitched Child),* 1955–56; Cunegonde, *Candide,* 1957–58; Norina, *Don Pasquale,* 1957–58; Italian Singer, *Capriccio,* 1958–59; Oscar, *Un Ballo in Maschera (A Masked Ball),* 1958–59; Stephanie, *Roberta,* 1958–59; Zerlina, *Don Giovanni,* 1958–59; Gilda, *Rigoletto,* 1959–60

Stevens, Michelle: Spirit, *Die Zauberflöte (The Magic Flute),* 1982–83; Lolo, *Die lustige Witwe (The Merry Widow),* 1983–84

Stevens, Sally: Second Lady, *Die Zauberflöte (The Magic Flute),* 1982–83

Stevenson, Deanna: Suzuki, *Madama Butterfly,* 1964–65; Carmen, *Carmen,* 1965–66; Mercedes, *Carmen,* 1965–66; Page, *Parsifal,* 1965–66; The Old Prioress, *Dialogues des Carmélites,* 1965–66; Nancy, *Albert Herring,* 1966–67

Stevenson, John: 3rd Beggar, *Kismet,* 1963–64; Nish, *Die lustige Witwe (The Merry Widow),* 1964–65; Bill Starbuck, *110 in the Shade,* 1967–68; De Bretigny, *Manon,* 1967–68; Antipholus of Syracuse, *The Boys from Syracuse,* 1968–69; Bill Starbuck, *110 in the Shade,* 1968–69

Stevenson, Lanelle: Hanna Glawari, *Die lustige Witwe (The Merry Widow),* 1964–65; Zerlina, *Don Giovanni,* 1964–65; Hanna Glawari, *Die lustige Witwe (The Merry Widow),* 1965–66; Lavinia Conner, *A Hoosier Tale,* 1966–67; Miss Wordsworth, *Albert Herring,* 1966–67; Stephano, *Roméo et Juliette,* 1966–67; Miss Wordsworth, *Albert Herring,* 1967–68

Stewart, Bonnie: Spirit, *Die Zauberflöte (The Magic Flute),* 1953–54; Violetta Valery, *La Traviata,* 1954–55; Countess Almaviva, *Le Nozze di Figaro (The Marriage of Figaro),* 1955–56; Marenka, *The Bartered Bride,* 1955–56

Stewart, Stephanie: Brigitta, *The Sound of Music,* 2000–01

Stewart, Vickie: Amazon, *The Boys from Syracuse,* 1968–69

Stickle, Laura: Meg, *The Ballad of Baby Doe,* 2003–04

Stickler, Larry: Officer, *Il Barbiere di Siviglia (The Barber of Seville),* 1971–72

Stiles, Patricia: Margaret, *Wozzeck,* 1999–2000

Stilwell, Richard: Guglielmo, *Così fan tutte,* 1963–64; Jack Rance, *La Fanciulla del West (The Girl of the Golden West),* 1963–64; Officer, *Il Barbiere di Siviglia (The Barber of Seville),* 1963–64; Don Giovanni, *Don Giovanni,* 1964–65; Paolo, *Simon Boccanegra,* 1964–65; Sharpless, *Madama Butterfly,* 1964–65; Klingsor, *Parsifal,* 1965–66; The Marquis de la Force, *Dialogues des Carmélites,* 1965–66

Stinson, Jonathan: John Brooke, *Little Women,* 2001–02; Lescaut, *Manon,* 2001–02; Harry, *Jeppe,* 2002–03; Masetto, *Don Giovanni,* 2002–03; Ned Keene, *Peter Grimes,* 2003–04; Njegus, *Die lustige Witwe (The Merry Widow),* 2003–04; Eugene Onegin, *Eugene Onegin,* 2004–05

Stinson, Scott: Welsh servant, *The Ballad of Baby Doe,* 1982–83

Stofft, Joan: Blonde, *Die Entführung aus dem Serail (The Abduction from the Seraglio),* 1961–62

Stofft Evans, Joan: Adina, *L'Elisir d'amore (The Elixir of Love),* 1961–62; Blonde, *Die Entführung aus dem Serail (The Abduction from the Seraglio),* 1961–62; Tytania, *A Midsummer Night's Dream,* 1961–62

Stokes, Emily: Buffy, *A Wedding,* 2007–08

Stoll, Laurie: Young girl, *110 in the Shade,* 1967–68; Young girl, *110 in the Shade,* 1968–69; Bielke, *Fiddler on the Roof,* 1972–73; Fredrika Armfeldt, *A Little Night Music,* 1975–76

Stone, Larry: Third Deputy, *Finian's Rainbow,* 1969–70

Stone, Monte: Dr. Pangloss, *Candide,* 1987–88; Martin, *Candide,* 1987–88; Preacher, *Mass,* 1987–88; The Governor of Cartagena, *Candide,* 1987–88; Preacher, *Mass,* 1988–89

Stone, Paula: Amy, *Company,* 1990–91; Minnie Fay, *Hello, Dolly!,* 1991–92

Stone, Sarah: Gertrude, *Roméo et Juliette,* 2005–06

Stonecipher, Dale: Stephan Kumalo, *Lost in the Stars,* 1950–51; First Workman, *On the Town,* 1951–52

Stonecypher, Velda: Giovanna, *Rigoletto,* 1959–60; Mrs. Laura Hildebrand, *Street Scene,* 1960–61; Amneris, *Aida,* 1963–64

Storck, Stefan: Figaro, *Il Barbiere di Siviglia (The Barber of Seville),* 1994–95; Papageno, *Die Zauberflöte (The Magic Flute),* 1994–95

Storey, Randall: Bruhlmann, *Werther,* 1975–76; Footman at the wedding, *The Ballad of Baby Doe,* 1975–76; Policeman, *Porgy and Bess,* 1976–77

Storm, Tiffany: Karen O'Kane, *Jubilee,* 1991–92

Stoudt, Ryan: Moose, *West Side Story,* 2002–03

Stout, Donald: Herman Ortel, *Die Meistersinger von Nürnberg (The Mastersingers of Nuremberg),* 1961–62

Stout, Johnnie: Slave Girl, *Kismet,* 1963–64

Stout, Kimberly: Bianca, *Kiss Me, Kate,* 1998–99; Lois Lane, *Kiss Me, Kate,* 1998–99

Strain, Ike: Novice, *Billy Budd,* 1952–53; Young Man, *Boris Godunov,* 1953–54

Strain, John: Man with Guitar, *Show Boat,* 1953–54

Stratton, Roger: Second Beggar, *Kismet,* 1989–90

Strauss, Chloe: Peaseblossom, *A Midsummer Night's Dream,* 2005–06

Strauss, Danielle: Giunone, *L'Orfeo,* 1987–88; Lauretta, *Gianni Schicchi,* 1988–89; Despina, *Così fan tutte,* 1989–90

Strebing, Mary: Blanche, *Dialogues des Carmélites,* 1965–66; Juliet, *Roméo et Juliette,* 1966–67; Marina, *The Four Ruffians,* 1966–67; Margaret, *Mefistofele,* 1966–67

Strejc, Kristen: Voice of the Dawn, *The Dawn of the Poor King,* 1990–91; Micaëla, *Carmen,* 1991–92

Strempel, Eileen: Queen of the Night, *Die Zauberflöte (The Magic Flute),* 1988–89; Adele, *Die Fledermaus (The Bat),* 1990–91

Strong, Alvin: Mingo, *Porgy and Bess,* 1976–77

Strother, Martin: Diomedes, *The Cry of Clytaemnestra,* 1979–80; Porgy, *Porgy and Bess,* 1979–80; The Sacristan of St. Vitus's Cathedral, *The Excursions of Mr. Broucek,* 1981–82; Talpa, *Il Trittico (A Triptych),* 1982–83

Stuart, Lila: Blanche, *Dialogues des Carmélites,* 1965–66; Carmen, *Carmen,* 1965–66; First Lady, *Die Zauberflöte (The Magic Flute),* 1965–66; The Princess (Feldmarschallin) von Werdenberg, *Der Rosenkavalier,* 1965–66; Felice, *Quattro rusteghi (The Four Ruffians),* 1966–67; Gilda, *Rigoletto,* 1966–67; Mekinges, *A Hoosier Tale,* 1966–67; Santuzza, *Cavalleria Rusticana,* 1966–67; Madeleine de Coigny, *Andrea Chénier,* 1967–68; Marenka, *The Bartered Bride,* 1967–68; Margaret, *Mefistofele,* 1967–68; Senta, *Der Fliegende Holländer (The Flying Dutchman),* 1985–86

Stuart, Val: Ernesto, *Don Pasquale,* 1965–66; Italian Tenor, *Der Rosenkavalier,* 1965–66; Macduff, *Macbeth,* 1965–66; Prince Tamino, *Die Zauberflöte (The Magic Flute),* 1965–66; Valzacchi, *Der Rosenkavalier,* 1965–66; Vicomte Camille di Rosillon, *Die lustige Witwe (The Merry Widow),* 1965–66; Albert Herring, *Albert Herring,* 1966–67; Belmonte, *Die Entführung aus dem Serail (The Abduction from the Seraglio),* 1966–67; Pedrillo, *Die Entführung aus dem Serail (The Abduction from the Seraglio),* 1966–67; The Duke of Mantua, *Rigoletto,* 1966–67; The Prophet, *A Hoosier Tale,* 1966–67; Turiddu, *Cavalleria Rusticana,* 1966–67; Albert Herring, *Albert Herring,* 1967–68; Nero, *L'Incoronazione di Poppea (The Coronation of Poppea),* 1967–68; Vashek, *The Bartered Bride,* 1967–68

Stubblefield, Kenneth: First Mate, *Billy Budd,* 1952–53; Monostatos, *Die Zauberflöte (The Magic Flute),* 1953–54; Dr. Blind, *Die Fledermaus (The Bat),* 1954–55

Stucki, Brian: Belmonte, *Die Entführung aus dem Serail (The Abduction from the Seraglio),* 2003–04; Don Narciso, *Il Turco in Italia (The Turk in Italy),* 2003–04; Ernesto, *Don Pasquale,* 2003–04; Don Ramiro, *La Cenerentola (Cinderella),* 2004–05; Ferrando, *Così fan tutte,* 2005–06

Stuempfle, Michael: Knight, *Parsifal,* 1975–76

Stutts, Berkley: Alfred, *Die Fledermaus (The Bat),* 1985–86; Lodovico, *The Tempest,* 1985–86; Don Curzio, *Le Nozze di Figaro (The Marriage of Figaro),* 1986–87; Vashek, *The Bartered Bride,* 1986–87; Candide, *Candide,* 1987–88; Triquet, *Eugene Onegin,* 1988–89; Ferrando, *Così fan tutte,* 1989–90; Orestes, *The Cry of Clytaemnestra,* 1989–90

Su, Tzu-Yuan: The Fiddler, *Fiddler on the Roof,* 1994–95

Suarez, Axania: Ernestina, *Hello, Dolly!,* 1991–92

Such, John: Andreas, *Carmen,* 1977–78; Priest, *The Darkened City,* 1978–79; Schaunard, *La Bohème,* 1979–80

Suhre, Gretchen: Giulia, *The Gondoliers,* 1974–75

Sulich, Steve: Francesco, *The Gondoliers,* 1974–75

Sullivan, Robert: The "Horses," *Man of La Mancha,* 1988–89; Joseph, *The Dawn of the Poor King,* 1990–91

Summer, Robert: Malcolm, *Macbeth,* 1965–66; Monostatos, *Die Zauberflöte (The Magic Flute),* 1965–66; Priest, *Die Zauberflöte (The Magic Flute),* 1965–66; Struhan, *Der Rosenkavalier,* 1965–66; Boyar in Attendance, *Boris Godunov,* 1966–67

Summers, Franklin: Al, *The Most Happy Fella,* 1959–60; Crespel, *Les Contes d'Hoffmann (The Tales of Hoffmann),* 1959–60; The Peasant, *Die Kluge (The Clever Girl),* 1959–60; Titurel, *Parsifal,* 1959–60; Grand Inquisitor, *Don Carlos,* 1960–61; King Philip II, *Don Carlos,* 1960–61; Monk, *Don Carlos,*

1960–61; Sarastro, *Die Zauberflöte (The Magic Flute),* 1960–61; Titurel, *Parsifal,* 1960–61; Hans Schwarz, *Die Meistersinger von Nürnberg (The Mastersingers of Nuremberg),* 1961–62

Summers, Sarah: Anya, *Fiddler on the Roof,* 1994–95

Summerville, Judy: Mad Margaret, *Ruddigore (The Witch's Curse),* 1962–63

Summerville Johnson, Judy: Niece, *Peter Grimes,* 1963–64; Tzeital, *Fiddler on the Roof,* 1972–73

Sumners, John: The Chevalier, *Dialogues des Carmélites,* 2004–05; Don Jose, *Carmen,* 2005–06; Romeo, *Roméo et Juliette,* 2005–06

Surface, Scott: A Captain, *Eugene Onegin,* 1997–98; A Jailer, *Dialogues des Carmélites,* 1997–98; Messenger/Commissioner, *La Traviata,* 1997–98

Svejcar, Eric: The Ringmaster, *The Bartered Bride,* 1994–95; Andres, *Les Contes d'Hoffmann (The Tales of Hoffmann),* 1995–96; Cochenille, *Les Contes d'Hoffmann (The Tales of Hoffmann),* 1995–96; Franz, *Les Contes d'Hoffmann (The Tales of Hoffmann),* 1995–96; Pittichinaccio, *Les Contes d'Hoffmann (The Tales of Hoffmann),* 1995–96

Swain, David: Kronkov, *Die lustige Witwe (The Merry Widow),* 2003–04; Washington Dandy, *The Ballad of Baby Doe,* 2003–04; Alidoro, *La Cenerentola (Cinderella),* 2004–05; Cesare Angelotti, *Tosca,* 2004–05; Colline, *La Bohème,* 2004–05; Jailer, *Tosca,* 2004–05; Doctor Bartolo, *Il Barbiere di Siviglia (The Barber of Seville),* 2005–06; Lord Capulet, *Roméo et Juliette,* 2005–06; Dottor Bombasto, *Arlecchino,* 2006–07

Swan, Anita: Smeraldina, *The Love for Three Oranges,* 1975–76

Swaney, Jake: Robin, *Falstaff,* 2003–04

Swaney, Susan: Cunegonde, *Candide,* 1993–94; Madame Mao, *Nixon in China,* 1994–95; Tzeital, *Fiddler on the Roof,* 1994–95; Rosina, *The Ghosts of Versailles,* 1996–97

Swart, Jack: Luther Billis, *South Pacific,* 1956–57

Swedarsky, Louis: Archie Beaton, *Brigadoon,* 1961–62; Jawan, *Kismet,* 1963–64; The Girl's Father, *The Fantasticks,* 1963–64

Swedish, Ann: Zulma, *L'Italiana in Algeri (The Italian Girl in Algiers),* 1968–69; Baronessa Clarissa, *Love on Trial (La Pietra del Paragone),* 1969–70; The Composer, *Ariadne auf Naxos,* 1969–70; Dorabella, *Così fan tutte,* 1970–71; Mrs. Meg Page, *Falstaff,* 1971–72; Siebel, *Faust,* 1971–72; Siegrune, *Die Walküre,* 1971–72; Marie, *Myshkin,* 1972–73

Swedish, Eileen: Ciesca, *Il Trittico (A Triptych),* 1972–73; Golde, *Fiddler on the Roof,* 1972–73; Frasquita, *Carmen,* 1973–74; Giulietta, *Les Contes d'Hoffmann (The Tales of Hoffmann),* 1973–74; Henrietta M., *The Mother of Us All,* 1973–74; Stella, *Les Contes d'Hoffmann (The Tales of Hoffmann),* 1973–74

Sweeney, William: Dancaire, *Carmen,* 1956–57; Peter, *Hänsel und Gretel,* 1956–57; Alfio, *Cavalleria Rusticana,* 1957–58; Amfortas, *Parsifal,* 1957–58; Inquisition Guard, *Candide,* 1957–58; Prince Ivan, *Candide,* 1957–58

Swennes, Kim: Apprentice Waiter, *The Excursions of Mr. Broucek,* 1981–82

Swerling, Jeremy: The Village Peddler, *L'Elisir d'amore (The Elixir of Love),* 1986–87

Swetnam, Gwendolyn: The McCourt family, *The Ballad of Baby Doe,* 1982–83

Swezey, Wayne: Guard, *The Darkened City,* 1962–63

Swift, Page: Fricka, *Die Walküre,* 1971–72; Mrs. Meg Page, *Falstaff,* 1971–72; Kostelnicka, *Jenůfa,* 1972–73; Kundry, *Parsifal,* 1972–73; Margaret, *Wozzeck,* 1973–74; Augusta Tabor, *The Ballad of Baby Doe,* 1975–76; Fata Morgana, *The Love for Three Oranges,* 1975–76

Swyers, Howard: Player, *Mass,* 1998–99; Thomas Bouche, *Down in the Valley,* 1998–99; Betto, *Gianni Schicchi,* 1999–2000; Fiorello, *Il Barbiere di Siviglia (The Barber of Seville),* 2000–01; Officer, *Il Barbiere di Siviglia (The Barber of Seville),* 2000–01; Count Almaviva, *Le Nozze di Figaro (The Marriage of Figaro),* 2001–02; Mayor Shinn, *The Music Man,* 2001–02; Prince Yamadori, *Madama Butterfly,* 2001–02; The Imperial Commissioner, *Madama Butterfly,* 2001–02; Dr. Falke, *Die Fledermaus (The Bat),* 2002–03; Sir John Falstaff, *Falstaff,* 2003–04; Baron Scarpia, *Tosca,* 2004–05; Ser Metteo del Sarto, *Arlecchino,* 2006–07

Syler, Ross: Willie, *Die lustige Witwe (The Merry Widow),* 1949–50

Sylvester, Michael: The Duke of Mantua, *Rigoletto,* 1974–75; Count Riccardo, *Un Ballo in Maschera (A Masked Ball),* 1975–76; Lt. Pinkerton, *Madama Butterfly,* 1975–76; Werther, *Werther,* 1975–76; Idomeneo, *Idomeneo,* 1976–77; Lt. Pinkerton, *Madama Butterfly,* 1976–77; Ernesto, *Don Pasquale,* 1977–78; First Thug, *Danton and Robespierre,* 1977–78; Rodolfo, *La Bohème,* 1979–80

Szajko, Suzanne: Ciesca, *Il Trittico (A Triptych),* 1969–70

Tadlock, David: Nikitich, *Boris Godunov,* 1983–84; Officer of the Border Guard, *Boris Godunov,* 1983–84; Second Apprentice, *Wozzeck,* 1990–91

Talley, Michael: Count Riccardo, *Un Ballo in Maschera (A Masked Ball),* 1975–76; Idomeneo, *Idomeneo,* 1976–77; Lt. Pinkerton, *Madama Butterfly,* 1976–77; Don Jose, *Carmen,* 1977–78; Ernesto, *Don Pasquale,* 1977–78; Alfredo Germont, *La Traviata,* 1978–79; Erik, *Der Fliegende Holländer (The Flying Dutchman),* 1978–79; Hoffmann, *Les Contes d'Hoffmann (The Tales of Hoffmann),* 1978–79

Tanguay, Amanda: Terracita, *West Side Story,* 2002–03

Tarachow, Glen: Whirling Dervish, *Kismet,* 1989–90

Tassell, Brad: Gee-Tar, *West Side Story,* 1985–86; Pellinore, *Camelot,* 1986–87

Tatara, Cynthia: Mad Margaret, *Ruddigore (The Witch's Curse),* 1962–63

Tavenner, Teddy: Suzette, *The Firefly,* 1949–50

Taverner, Angela: Amor, *Orfeo ed Euridice,* 1992–93; Blonde, *Die Entführung aus dem Serail (The Abduction from the Seraglio),* 1993–94

Taylor, Dana: Harry, *My Fair Lady,* 1979–80

Taylor, Kathleen: Cat, *L'Enfant et les Sortilèges (The Bewitched Child),* 1984–85

Taylor, Kyra: Electra as a child, *The Cry of Clytaemnestra,* 1989–90

Taylor, Marilyn: Countess Almaviva, *Le Nozze di Figaro (The Marriage of Figaro),* 1986–87; Ellen Orford, *Peter Grimes,* 1987–88; Antonia, *Les Contes d'Hoffmann (The Tales of Hoffmann),* 1988–89; Marguerite, *Faust,* 1989–90

Taylor, Mark: Mike, *Oklahoma!,* 1981–82

Taylor, Meredith: Pousette, *Manon,* 2006–07; Barbarina, *Le Nozze di Figaro (The Marriage of Figaro),* 2007–08

Taylor, Patricia: Mrs. Gleaton, *Susannah,* 1976–77; Second Lady, *Die Zauberflöte (The Magic Flute),* 1977–78; The Weaver's Wife, *The Night Before Christmas,* 1977–78

Taylor, Robert: Priest, *Die Zauberflöte (The Magic Flute),* 1960–61; Graf Lamoral, *Arabella,* 1998–99; Zuniga, *Carmen,* 1998–99; Alcindoro, *La Bohème,* 1999–2000; Benoit, *La Bohème,* 1999–2000; Leandro, *The Love for Three Oranges,* 1999–2000; Simone, *Gianni Schicchi,* 1999–2000; Mephistopheles, *Faust,* 2000–01; The Bonze, *Madama Butterfly,* 2001–02

Taylor, Stephen: Ciccio, *The Most Happy Fella,* 1982–83

Taylor, William: Joe, *Show Boat,* 1953–54; Klingsor, *Parsifal,* 1953–54; Woody, *Finian's Rainbow,* 1953–54; Dr. Falke, *Die Fledermaus (The Bat),* 1954–55; Klingsor, *Parsifal,* 1954–55; The Music Master, *Ariadne auf Naxos,* 1954–55

Teal, Betty: Margot, *Die lustige Witwe (The Merry Widow),* 1949–50

Templet, Jill: A young Polovtsian maiden, *Prince Igor,* 1980–81

Tenhumberg, Timothy: Barker, *1600 Pennsylvania Avenue,* 1992–93; Maryland Delegate, *1600 Pennsylvania Avenue,* 1992–93

Terrell, Carol: Niece, *Peter Grimes,* 1987–88; Madame Merville, *A Little Night Music,* 1988–89; Mrs. Nordstrom, *A Little Night Music,* 1988–89; Lisette, *La Rondine (The Swallow),* 1989–90

Terrell, Katherine: Rosette, *Manon,* 2006–07

Thevenot, Trent: A Jailer, *Dialogues des Carmélites,* 1986–87

Thiele, Don: Budney, *Where's Charley?,* 1953–54; Indian Priest, *The Ruby,* 1954–55; Duca, *Candide,* 1957–58; Hessian, *Candide,* 1957–58

Thomas, DeVera: Susan, *Company,* 1990–91; Donna Elvira, *Don Giovanni,* 1991–92

Thomas, Diann: Susan B. Anthony, *The Mother of Us All,* 1973–74

Thomas, Eugene: Pedro / Head Muleteer, *Man of La Mancha,* 1988–89; Dancaire, *Carmen,* 1991–92; Prince Yamadori, *Madama Butterfly,* 1991–92; Count Ceprano, *Rigoletto,* 1992–93; De Cerisay, *Die Teufel von Loudun (The Devils of Loudun),* 1992–93; Prince Henri de Conde, *Die Teufel von Loudun (The Devils of Loudun),* 1992–93; Mordcha, *Fiddler on the Roof,* 1994–95; Guglielmo, *Così fan tutte,* 1995–96; Count Danilo Danilovitch, *Die lustige Witwe (The Merry Widow),* 1996–97

Thomas, Jason Matthew: Don Curzio, *Le Nozze di Figaro (The Marriage of Figaro),* 2007–08

Thomas, Nathan: Jake, *Show Boat,* 1984–85; Merlyn, *Camelot,* 1986–87

Thomas, Nova: Spirit, *Die Zauberflöte (The Magic Flute),* 1977–78; Fyodor, *Boris Godunov,* 1978–79; Mimi, *La Bohème,* 1979–80; Susannah Polk, *Susannah,* 1979–80; Yaroslavna, *Prince Igor,* 1980–81; Cio-Cio San, *Madama Butterfly,* 1981–82; Giorgetta, *Il Trittico (A Triptych),* 1982–83; Sister Angelica, *Il Trittico (A Triptych),* 1982–83

Thomas, Rita: Countess Ceprano, *Rigoletto,* 1980–81

Thompson, Benjamin: Jim, White House Staff, *1600 Pennsylvania Avenue,* 1992–93

Thompson, Carmen: Kathy, *Company,* 1990–91

Thompson, Jacqueline: Valencienne, *Die lustige Witwe (The Merry Widow),* 2003–04

Thompson, Patricia: Hata, *The Bartered Bride,* 2001–02; Cornelia, *Giulio Cesare (Julius Caesar),* 2002–03; Dame Quickly, *Falstaff,* 2003–04; Filipyevna, *Eugene Onegin,* 2004–05; Berta (Marcellina), *Il Barbiere di Siviglia (The Barber of Seville),* 2005–06; Adelaide, *Arabella,* 2006–07

Thompson, Paul: Archie Beaton, *Brigadoon,* 1952–53; Iron Tail, *Annie Get Your Gun,* 1956–57

Thompson, Ronald: Nathanael, *Les Contes d'Hoffmann (The Tales of Hoffmann),* 1973–74

Thompson, Sumner: Harlequin, *Ariadne auf Naxos,* 1996–97; Count Almaviva, *Le Nozze di Figaro (The Marriage of Figaro),* 1997–98; The Leader, *Down in the Valley,* 1998–99; The Preacher, *Down in the Valley,* 1998–99; Tarquinius, *The Rape of Lucretia,* 1999–2000; Wagner, *Faust,* 2000–01

Thomson, Marka: Child, *The Ballad of Baby Doe,* 1982–83

Thomure, Jennifer: Kim (child), *Show Boat,* 1984–85

Thorn, Linda: Pamina, *Die Zauberflöte (The Magic Flute),* 1965–66; Sister Constance, *Dialogues des Carmélites,* 1965–66; Emmie, *Albert Herring,* 1966–67; Gilda, *Rigoletto,* 1974–75

Thornton, John: Policeman, *Amelia Goes to the Ball,* 1957–58

Thueson, Diane: Antonia, *Les Contes d'Hoffmann (The Tales of Hoffmann),* 1995–96; Rosina, *The Ghosts of Versailles,* 1996–97; Valencienne, *Die lustige Witwe (The Merry Widow),* 1996–97; Nanetta, *Falstaff,* 1997–98; Arabella, *Arabella,* 1998–99; Anne Trulove, *The Rake's Progress,* 1999–2000; Marguerite, *Faust,* 2000–01

Tichenor, Katherine: Petra, *A Little Night Music,* 1988–89

Tiedemann, Patrice: La Ciesca, *Gianni Schicchi,* 1993–94; Berta (Marcellina), *Il Barbiere di Siviglia (The Barber of Seville),* 1994–95; First Lady, *Die Zauberflöte (The Magic Flute),* 1994–95; Agrippina, *Agrippina,* 1995–96; Mastrilla, *La Périchole,* 1995–96; Sylviane, *Die lustige Witwe (The Merry Widow),* 1996–97

Tilson, Scott: Prince Yamadori, *Madama Butterfly,* 1996–97; Zaretsky, *Eugene Onegin,* 1997–98

Timms, Patti: Bloodhound, *The King and I,* 1957–58

Tippey, James: Titurel, *Parsifal,* 1953–54; Varlaam, *Boris Godunov,* 1953–54; Amfortas, *Parsifal,* 1954–55; Frank, *Die Fledermaus (The Bat),* 1954–55; Jud Fry, *Oklahoma!,* 1954–55; Robert Baker, *Wonderful Town,* 1954–55; Escamillo, *Carmen,* 1956–57; Ford, *Falstaff,* 1956–57; Frank Butler, *Annie Get Your Gun,* 1956–57; Baron Scarpia, *Tosca,* 1957–58

Tischler, Mark: Gofer, *Kiss Me, Kate,* 1973–74

Tisheff, Stephanie: Gertrude Stein, *The Mother of Us All,* 1973–74; Giovanna, *Rigoletto,* 1974–75; Maid, *Vanessa,* 1974–75

Todhunter, Susan: Echo, *Ariadne auf Naxos,* 1969–70; Adelaida, *Myshkin,* 1972–73

Tomlin, Gary: Buzz, *Finian's Rainbow,* 1969–70; Geologist, *Finian's Rainbow,* 1969–70

Tonne, Keith: Reverend Master John W. Wilson, *The Scarlet Letter,* 1976–77; Monostatos, *Die Zauberflöte (The Magic Flute),* 1977–78; Rudolfo, *Naughty Marietta,* 1977–78; Silas Slick, *Naughty Marietta,* 1977–78; Spoletta, *Tosca,* 1977–78; Andres, *Les Contes d'Hoffmann (The Tales of Hoffmann),* 1978–79; Cochenille, *Les Contes d'Hoffmann (The Tales of Hoffmann),* 1978–79; First Suitor, *The Darkened City,* 1978–79; Franz, *Les Contes d'Hoffmann (The Tales of Hoffmann),* 1978–79; Pittichinaccio, *Les Contes d'Hoffmann (The Tales of Hoffmann),* 1978–79; Simpleton, *Boris Godunov,* 1978–79; Leandro, *Arlecchino,* 1979–80

Torres, Mark: Servant, *The Ballad of Baby Doe,* 1975–76; Zanni, *Il Mondo della Luna (The World on the Moon),* 1975–76

Torres, Regina: La Suor Zelatrice, *Suor Angelica (Sister Angelica),* 1999–2000; Mrs. Gleaton, *Susannah,* 2000–01; Ludmila, *The Bartered Bride,* 2001–02

Townsend, Clifford: Geologist, *Finian's Rainbow,* 1969–70; Second Gospeleer, *Finian's Rainbow,* 1969–70

Tozzi, Giorgio: Tevye, *Fiddler on the Roof,* 1994–95

Tracy, Neal: Crespel, *Les Contes d'Hoffmann (The Tales of Hoffmann),* 1973–74; Dancaire, *Carmen,* 1973–74; Donald Gallup, *The Mother of Us All,* 1973–74; Antonio, *The Gondoliers,* 1974–75

Trager, Kevin: A Captain, *Eugene Onegin,* 1997–98; Boatswain, *HMS Pinafore,* 1997–98; The Marquis de la Force, *Dialogues des Carmélites,* 1997–98; Arbace, *Idomeneo,* 1998–99; Papageno, *Die Zauberflöte (The Magic Flute),* 1998–99

Trainer, Alison: Poppea, *Agrippina,* 1995–96

Traub, Donald: First Musician, *On the Town,* 1951–52; 3rd Workman, *On the Town,* 1951–52

Travis, Elizabeth: Mrs. Teale, *Roberta,* 1958–59

Trego, Brian: Elder Gleaton, *Susannah,* 1979–80; Menelaus, *The Cry of Clytaemnestra,* 1979–80; Michelis, *The Greek Passion,* 1980–81; The Drum Major, *Wozzeck,* 1981–82

Treitz, Mary: Countess Almaviva, *Le Nozze di Figaro (The Marriage of Figaro),* 1962–63

Trent, David: Governor, *Candide,* 1993–94; Man in Armor, *Die Zauberflöte (The Magic Flute),* 1994–95; Mao Tse-tung, *Nixon in China,* 1994–95; Don Jose, *Carmen,* 1998–99; The Drum Major, *Wozzeck,* 1999–2000

Trester, Grace: Mimi, *La Bohème,* 1957–58; Mistress Alice Ford (Frau Fluth), *Die lustigen Weiber von Windsor (The Merry Wives of Windsor),* 1958–59; The Countess, *Capriccio,* 1958–59; Mekinges, *A Hoosier Tale,* 1966–67

Trester Jones, Grace: Antonia, *Les Contes d'Hoffmann (The Tales of Hoffmann),* 1959–60; Gilda, *Rigoletto,* 1959–60; Manon Lescaut, *Manon Lescaut,* 1959–60; Lucia, *Lucia di Lammermoor,* 1963–64; Cio-Cio San, *Madama Butterfly,* 1964–65; Helen of Troy, *Mefistofele,* 1967–68

Troyer, Jerry: David Bascomb, *Carousel,* 1970–71; Heavenly Friend, *Carousel,* 1970–71; Jigger Craigin, *Carousel,* 1970–71

Trubitt, Hiliard: Klaas, *Die Entführung aus dem Serail (The Abduction from the Seraglio),* 1987–88

Truhel, Jeremy: Elder Gleaton, *Susannah,* 2000–01; Arturo Bucklaw, *Lucia di Lammermoor,* 2001–02; Don Basilio, *Le Nozze di Figaro (The Marriage of*

Figaro), 2001–02; Nathanael, *Les Contes d'Hoffmann (The Tales of Hoffmann),* 2002–03; Player, *Putting It Together,* 2002–03; Spalanzani, *Les Contes d'Hoffmann (The Tales of Hoffmann),* 2002–03

Tully, John: Lt. Joseph Cable, *South Pacific,* 1956–57; Sir Edward Ramsay, *The King and I,* 1957–58

Turnage, Wayne: A Jailer, *Dialogues des Carmélites,* 1965–66; Commissary of the Police, *Der Rosenkavalier,* 1965–66; M. Javelinot, *Dialogues des Carmélites,* 1965–66; Papageno, *Die Zauberflöte (The Magic Flute),* 1965–66; Servant, *Macbeth,* 1965–66

Turner, John: Second Deputy, *Finian's Rainbow,* 1953–54; The Boyar Khrushchev, *Boris Godunov,* 1953–54; Brighella, *Ariadne auf Naxos,* 1954–55; Dr. Blind, *Die Fledermaus (The Bat),* 1954–55; Franz, *Les Contes d'Hoffmann (The Tales of Hoffmann),* 1959–60; The Donkey Man, *Die Kluge (The Clever Girl),* 1959–60; Mr. Lippo Fiorentino, *Street Scene,* 1960–61; Old Astrologer, *Le Coq d'or (The Golden Cockerel),* 1960–61

Turner, Randal: Masetto, *Don Giovanni,* 1985–86; Riff, *West Side Story,* 1985–86; A Jailer, *Dialogues des Carmélites,* 1986–87; John P. Wintergreen, *Of Thee I Sing,* 1987–88; Sharpless, *Madama Butterfly,* 1987–88; Betto, *Gianni Schicchi,* 1988–89; Figaro, *Il Barbiere di Siviglia (The Barber of Seville),* 1988–89; Guglielmo, *Così fan tutte,* 1989–90; Marcello, *La Bohème,* 1989–90; Valentin, *Faust,* 1989–90

Turner, Richard: Henri, *South Pacific,* 1956–57

Tuttle, Nathan: Cord Elam, *Oklahoma!,* 1997–98

Uhlin, Leigh: A Princess of Ababu, *Kismet,* 1989–90

Ulmer, Michal: Hershel, *Fiddler on the Roof,* 1994–95

Ulrich, Walter: Chief of Staff, *Of Thee I Sing,* 1987–88; Guide, *Of Thee I Sing,* 1987–88; Momo (Momus), *L'Orfeo,* 1987–88; Prince Yamadori, *Madama Butterfly,* 1987–88; Notary, *Don Pasquale,* 1988–89; Sancho Panza, *Man of La Mancha,* 1988–89; Omar, *Kismet,* 1989–90; David, *Company,* 1990–91; Frosch, *Die Fledermaus (The Bat),* 1990–91

Urban, Elizabeth: Countess Ceprano, *Rigoletto,* 1995–96; Kate Pinkerton, *Madama Butterfly,* 1996–97

Urbina, Mark: Morales, *Carmen,* 1991–92; Chino, *West Side Story,* 1992–93; First Gambler, *Candide,* 1993–94; Heresy Agent, *Candide,* 1993–94; Pantalone, *The Love for Three Oranges,* 1993–94; Fiorello, *Il Barbiere di Siviglia (The Barber of Seville),* 1994–95

Urreiztieta, Arizeder: Celio, *The Love for Three Oranges,* 1980–81; Skula, *Prince Igor,* 1980–81; Dr. Caius, *Die lustigen Weiber von Windsor (The Merry Wives of Windsor),* 1981–82; Betto, *Il Trittico (A Triptych),* 1982–83; Judas, *Passion Play—Carmina Burana,* 1982–83

Uschkrat, Betsy: Juliet, *Roméo et Juliette,* 2005–06; Manon Lescaut, *Manon,* 2006–07; Adina, *L'Elisir d'amore (The Elixir of Love),* 2007–08; Susannah Polk, *Susannah,* 2007–08

Uselman, James: Knight, *Parsifal,* 1965–66; Major-domo of Faninal, *Der Rosenkavalier,* 1965–66; Man in Armor, *Die Zauberflöte (The Magic Flute),* 1965–66; Waiter, *Der Rosenkavalier,* 1965–66; Knight, *Parsifal,* 1966–67; Mr. Upfold, *Albert Herring,* 1966–67; Mr. Upfold, *Albert Herring,* 1967–68; Kunz Volgelgesang, *Die Meistersinger von Nürnberg (The Mastersingers of Nuremberg),* 1968–69

Uthup, Joe: Robin, *Falstaff,* 1997–98; Player, *Mass,* 1998–99; Solo Child, *La Bohème,* 1999–2000

Vacano, Florence: Inez, *The Gondoliers,* 1974–75

Vail, Kris: Lieutenant, *Doktor Faust,* 1974–75; Sam, *The Ballad of Baby Doe,* 1975–76; The Prince, *The Love for Three Oranges,* 1975–76; Dr. Caius, *Falstaff,* 1976–77; Prince Tamino, *Die Zauberflöte (The Magic Flute),* 1977–78; Tallien, *Danton and Robespierre,* 1977–78

Valentine, Rebeckah: Annina, *La Traviata,* 1997–98; Mother Jeanne, *Dialogues des Carmélites,* 1997–98; Spirit, *Die Zauberflöte (The Magic Flute),* 1998–99; Mother Goose, *The Rake's Progress,* 1999–2000

Van Arsdale, Mark: Donato, *A Wedding,* 2007–08; Sam Polk, *Susannah,* 2007–08

van der Ploeg, Lisa: Mercedes, *Carmen,* 1991–92; Orpheus, *Orfeo ed Euridice,* 1992–93; Princess Clarissa, *The Love for Three Oranges,* 1993–94; Auntie, *Peter Grimes,* 1994–95; Genevieve, *Pelléas et Mélisande,* 1994–95; Hata, *The Bartered Bride,* 1994–95; Maddalena, *Rigoletto,* 1995–96; Maria Miranda Macapa, *McTeague,* 1995–96; Suzuki, *Madama Butterfly,* 1996–97

Van Doren, Evan: Friedrich, *The Sound of Music,* 2000–01

Van Eck, Kate: La Suora Infermiera, *Suor Angelica (Sister Angelica),* 1999–2000

Van Epps, John: Guglielmo, *Così fan tutte,* 1956–57; Knight, *Parsifal,* 1956–57

Van Hecke, Holly: Papagena, *Die Zauberflöte (The Magic Flute),* 1972–73; Barbarina, *Le Nozze di Figaro (The Marriage of Figaro),* 1973–74; Blonde, *Die Entführung aus dem Serail (The Abduction from the Seraglio),* 1974–75; Gianetta, *The Gondoliers,* 1974–75

Van Meter, Mary: Pink Sheep, *Candide,* 1993–94; Malke, *Fiddler on the Roof,* 1994–95

Van Meter, Tiffany: Pink Sheep, *Candide,* 1993–94

Van Ness, Valda: Waltraute, *Die Walküre,* 1971–72

Van Nuys, Edward: Paulus, *Lost in the Stars,* 1950–51

van Renterghem, Deborah: Proserpina, *L'Orfeo,* 1987–88

Van Way, Nolan: Marquis D'Obigny, *La Traviata,* 1954–55; Andrew McLennon, *The Land Between the Rivers,* 1955–56; Knight, *Parsifal,* 1955–56; Krushina, *The Bartered Bride,* 1955–56; Emile DeBeque, *South Pacific,* 1956–57; Escamillo, *Carmen,* 1956–57; Figaro, *Il Barbiere di Siviglia (The Barber of Seville),* 1956–57; Frank Butler, *Annie Get Your Gun,* 1956–57

Vanderford, Heidi: Eine Kartenaufschlaegerin, *Arabella,* 1998–99; Lucretia, *The Rape of Lucretia,* 1999–2000; Dorabella, *Così fan tutte,* 2000–01; Cecelia March, *Little Women,* 2001–02

Vanderhoof, Jessica: Mama McCourt, *The Ballad of Baby Doe,* 2003–04; Third Lady, *Die Zauberflöte (The Magic Flute),* 2004–05; Gertrude, *Roméo et Juliette,* 2005–06

Vanelle, Louis: Hoffmann, *Les Contes d'Hoffmann (The Tales of Hoffmann),* 1947–48

Vannerette, Edith: Gilda, *Rigoletto,* 1974–75; Elizabeth "Baby" Doe, *The Ballad of Baby Doe,* 1975–76; Flaminia, *Il Mondo della Luna (The World on the Moon),* 1975–76; Lucille, *Danton and Robespierre,* 1977–78; Violetta Valery, *La Traviata,* 1978–79

Vaughn, Meghann: Hippolyta, *A Midsummer Night's Dream,* 2005–06; Gertrude, *Hänsel und Gretel,* 2006–07; Muse, *Les Contes d'Hoffmann (The Tales of Hoffmann),* 2007–08; Nicklausse, *Les Contes d'Hoffmann (The Tales of Hoffmann),* 2007–08

Vaughn, Virgil: Crab Man, *Porgy and Bess,* 1976–77; Nelson, *Porgy and Bess,* 1976–77; Sportin' Life, *Porgy and Bess,* 1979–80

Vavilov, Alexey: Dante, *Francesca da Rimini,* 1989–90; Beppe, *I Pagliacci,* 1991–92

Vayo, J. Paula: Mrs. Paroo, *The Music Man,* 1980–81

Velho, Homero: Marco, *Gianni Schicchi,* 1993–94; Avram, *Fiddler on the Roof,* 1994–95; Ned Keene, *Peter Grimes,* 1994–95; Pallante, *Agrippina,* 1995–96; Figaro, *The Ghosts of Versailles,* 1996–97; Harlequin, *Ariadne auf Naxos,* 1996–97; Sir Joseph Porter, *HMS Pinafore,* 1997–98; Papageno, *Die Zauberflöte (The Magic Flute),* 1998–99; Maximilian, *Candide,* 2000–01

Vendever, Joy: Peasant woman, *Boris Godunov,* 1966–67

Veneracion, Andrea: Mrs. Greta Fiorentino, *Street Scene,* 1960–61

Ver Hoven, Victoria: Anne Egerman, *A Little Night Music,* 1975–76; Spirit, *Die Zauberflöte (The Magic Flute),* 1977–78

Verner, Donald: Baron Douphol, *La Traviata,* 1983–84

Vernon, Rebecca: The Antique Chair, *L'Enfant et les Sortilèges (The Bewitched Child),* 1984–85; Iphygeneia, *The Cry of Clytaemnestra,* 1989–90; Voice of the Dawn, *The Dawn of the Poor King,* 1990–91

Vertesi, Cam: Pritschitsch, *Die lustige Witwe (The Merry Widow),* 2003–04; The McCourt family, *The Ballad of Baby Doe,* 2003–04

Vessels, William: Dr. Caius, *Die lustigen Weiber von Windsor (The Merry Wives of Windsor),* 1958–59; Kreonte, *The Love for Three Oranges,* 1958–59; Major-Domo, *Capriccio,* 1958–59; Masetto, *Don Giovanni,* 1958–59; Prince Yamadori, *Madama Butterfly,* 1958–59; Clem, *The Most Happy Fella,* 1959–60; Don Inigo Gomez, *L'Heure espagnole (The Spanish Hour),* 1959–60; Geronte de Ravoir, *Manon Lescaut,* 1959–60; Luther, *Les Contes d'Hoffmann (The Tales of Hoffmann),* 1959–60; Perichaud, *La Rondine (The Swallow),* 1959–60; Spalanzani, *Les Contes d'Hoffmann (The Tales of Hoffmann),* 1959–60; Nish, *Die lustige Witwe (The Merry Widow),* 1965–66; Mr. Gedge, *Albert Herring,* 1966–67; Officer of the Border Guard, *Boris Godunov,* 1966–67; Simon, *Quattro rusteghi (The Four Ruffians),* 1966–67; Mr. Gedge, *Albert Herring,* 1967–68

Vibbert, Victoria: Eleventh Woman of Paris, *Danton and Robespierre,* 1977–78; Thisbe, *La Cenerentola (Cinderella),* 1991–92; Marcellina, *Le Nozze di Figaro (The Marriage of Figaro),* 1992–93

Vicens, Alex: Edgardo, *Lucia di Lammermoor,* 2001–02

Viehe, Gary: Third Suitor, *The Darkened City,* 1962–63

Vigilante, Simone: Public Opinion, *Orphée aux enfers (Orpheus in the Underworld),* 1998–99; Second Lady, *Die Zauberflöte (The Magic Flute),* 1998–99; Maria / The Innkeeper's Wife, *Man of La Mancha,* 1999–2000; Zita, *Gianni Schicchi,* 1999–2000

Villanueva, David: Dentist, *McTeague,* 1995–96

Villeneuve, Lucile: Marie, *The Most Happy Fella,* 1959–60

Vincent, Edward: Amantio di Nicolao, *Il Trittico (A Triptych),* 1972–73; Guccio, *Il Trittico (A Triptych),* 1972–73

Vincent, Joshua: First Commissioner, *Dialogues des Carmélites,* 1997–98; Don Basilio, *Le Nozze di Figaro (The Marriage of Figaro),* 1997–98; First Man, *Kiss Me, Kate,* 1998–99; High Priest, *Idomeneo,* 1998–99; Player, *Mass,* 1998–99; Rock Singer, *Mass,* 1998–99; Truffaldino, *The Love for Three Oranges,* 1999–2000; Candide, *Candide,* 2000–01

Vinzant, Valerie: The Sandman, *Too Many Sopranos*, 2006–07; Susanna, *Le Nozze di Figaro (The Marriage of Figaro)*, 2007–08

Vogel, Donald: Titurel, *Parsifal*, 1949–50; William, *The Veil*, 1949–50; John Kumalo, *Lost in the Stars*, 1950–51; Klingsor, *Parsifal*, 1950–51; Pooh-Bah, *The Mikado*, 1950–51; Sparafucile, *Rigoletto*, 1950–51; Balthasar, *Amahl and the Night Visitors*, 1951–52; Osmin, *Die Entführung aus dem Serail (The Abduction from the Seraglio)*, 1951–52; The Professor, *A Parfait for Irene*, 1951–52; Titurel, *Parsifal*, 1951–52; John Claggart, *Billy Budd*, 1952–53; Titurel, *Parsifal*, 1952–53; Sarastro, *Die Zauberflöte (The Magic Flute)*, 1953–54; Big Billie Potts, *The Land Between the Rivers*, 1955–56; Klingsor, *Parsifal*, 1955–56

Vogler, Paul: Dandini, *La Cenerentola (Cinderella)*, 1991–92; Horse Guard, *Jubilee*, 1991–92; Grandier, *Die Teufel von Loudun (The Devils of Loudun)*, 1992–93; Massachusetts Delegate, *1600 Pennsylvania Avenue*, 1992–93; Scott, *1600 Pennsylvania Avenue*, 1992–93; De Bretigny, *Manon*, 1993–94; Rabbi, *Fiddler on the Roof*, 1994–95

Voights, Richard: Geologist, *Finian's Rainbow*, 1953–54; Shears, *Finian's Rainbow*, 1953–54

Volak, Renee: Gianetta, *L'Elisir d'amore (The Elixir of Love)*, 1986–87; Niece, *Peter Grimes*, 1987–88; Gretel, *Hänsel und Gretel*, 1989–90; Mimi, *La Bohème*, 1989–90; Hanna Glawari, *Die lustige Witwe (The Merry Widow)*, 1990–91; Anne Trulove, *The Rake's Progress*, 1991–92; Mrs. Alice Ford, *Falstaff*, 1992–93; Somewhere solo, *West Side Story*, 1992–93

Volek, Joan: Norina, *Don Pasquale*, 1965–66

Volek Gersten, Joan: Queen of the Night, *Die Zauberflöte (The Magic Flute)*, 1965–66; Sophie, *Der Rosenkavalier*, 1965–66

Volovna, Marla: Mother, *Amahl and the Night Visitors*, 1990–91; Baba the Turk, *The Rake's Progress*, 1991–92

Volpe, Peter: First Apprentice, *Wozzeck*, 1981–82; Master Page (Herr Reich), *Die lustigen Weiber von Windsor (The Merry Wives of Windsor)*, 1981–82; Man in Armor, *Die Zauberflöte (The Magic Flute)*, 1982–83; Simone, *Il Trittico (A Triptych)*, 1982–83; William Jennings Bryan, *The Ballad of Baby Doe*, 1982–83; Fasolt, *Das Rheingold*, 1983–84; Pimen, *Boris Godunov*, 1983–84; Theseus, *A Midsummer Night's Dream*, 1983–84; Beckett, *Murder in the Cathedral*, 1984–85; Colline, *La Bohème*, 1984–85

von Eckhardt, Marina: Maid, *Quattro rusteghi (The Four Ruffians)*, 1966–67

Vowan, Ruth: The Nightingale, *L'Enfant et les Sortilèges (The Bewitched Child)*, 1984–85; Amina, *La Sonnambula (The Sleepwalker)*, 1985–86; Adina, *L'Elisir d'amore (The Elixir of Love)*, 1986–87; Gilda, *Rigoletto*, 1986–87

Vrenios, Elizabeth: Niece, *Peter Grimes*, 1963–64; Valencienne, *Die lustige Witwe (The Merry Widow)*, 1964–65; Papagena, *Die Zauberflöte (The Magic Flute)*, 1965–66

Vrenios, Ernest: Don Curzio, *Le Nozze di Figaro (The Marriage of Figaro)*, 1962–63; First Bearer, *The Darkened City*, 1962–63; Third Mourner, *The Darkened City*, 1962–63; Afansy Ivanovich, *The Fair at Sorochinsk*, 1963–64; Arturo Bucklaw, *Lucia di Lammermoor*, 1963–64; Harry, *La Fanciulla del West (The Girl of the Golden West)*, 1963–64; Don Ottavio, *Don Giovanni*, 1964–65; Page, *Parsifal*, 1964–65; The Shepherd, *Oedipus Rex*, 1964–65; Vicomte Camille di Rosillon, *Die lustige Witwe (The Merry Widow)*, 1964–65; Prince Tamino, *Die Zauberflöte (The Magic Flute)*, 1965–66; Valzacchi, *Der Rosenkavalier*, 1965–66; Romeo, *Roméo et Juliette*, 1966–67; Beppe, *I Pagliacci*, 1966–67

Vruno, Donna: Fruma-Sarah, *Fiddler on the Roof*, 1972–73

Wade, Ralph: Knight, *Parsifal*, 1958–59; Edmondo, *Manon Lescaut*, 1959–60

Waechter, Thomas: Musician, *Die Kluge (The Clever Girl)*, 1959–60

Waggener, Dawn: Constanza, *Die Entführung aus dem Serail (The Abduction from the Seraglio)*, 1993–94; First Lady, *Die Zauberflöte (The Magic Flute)*, 1994–95; Fiordiligi, *Così fan tutte*, 1995–96; La Périchole, *La Périchole*, 1995–96; Hanna Glawari, *Die lustige Witwe (The Merry Widow)*, 1996–97; Blanche, *Dialogues des Carmélites*, 1997–98; Violetta Valery, *La Traviata*, 1997–98

Waggoner, David: Steve Sankey, *Street Scene*, 1960–61

Wagner, Janice: Epicier, *Candide*, 1957–58; Florence Pike, *Albert Herring*, 1957–58; Lady Cutely, *Candide*, 1957–58

Wagner, Richard: Public Poet, *Kismet*, 1963–64; Gianni Schicchi, *Gianni Schicchi*, 1964–65; Masetto, *Don Giovanni*, 1964–65; The Bonze, *Madama Butterfly*, 1964–65; Notary, *Der Rosenkavalier*, 1965–66; Papageno, *Die Zauberflöte (The Magic Flute)*, 1965–66; Servant, *Macbeth*, 1965–66; The Marquis de la Force, *Dialogues des Carmélites*, 1965–66

Wake, Arthur: The Professor, *Hin und Zurück (There and Back)*, 1947–48

Wakefield, Mary: Sharon, *Finian's Rainbow*, 1969–70; Sister Genevieve, *Il Trittico (A Triptych)*, 1969–70; Julie Jordan, *Carousel*, 1970–71; Mimi, *La Bohème*, 1970–71

Walden, Debbie: Grace, *Street Scene*, 1949–50

Walker, Catherine: Frou-Frou, *Die lustige Witwe (The Merry Widow)*, 1996–97

Walker, John: Alfredo Germont, *La Traviata*, 1960–61; Prince Tamino, *Die Zauberflöte (The Magic Flute)*, 1960–61; Belmonte, *Die Entführung aus dem Serail (The Abduction from the Seraglio)*, 1961–62; Charlie Dalrymple,

Brigadoon, 1961–62; David, *Die Meistersinger von Nürnberg (The Mastersingers of Nuremberg)*, 1961–62; Lysander, *A Midsummer Night's Dream*, 1961–62; Mario Cavaradossi, *Tosca*, 1961–62; Nemorino, *L'Elisir d'amore (The Elixir of Love)*, 1961–62; Werther, *Werther*, 1961–62

Walker, Karen: Muse, *Les Contes d'Hoffmann (The Tales of Hoffmann)*, 1978–79; Nicklausse, *Les Contes d'Hoffmann (The Tales of Hoffmann)*, 1978–79; Sweet Seller, *The Darkened City*, 1978–79

Walker, Nancy: Pamina, *Die Zauberflöte (The Magic Flute)*, 1982–83

Walker, Richard: Elder Hayes, *Susannah*, 1979–80; Guillot de Morfontaine, *Manon*, 1979–80; Odysseus, *The Cry of Clytaemnestra*, 1979–80; Andres, *Wozzeck*, 1981–82; Lt. Pinkerton, *Madama Butterfly*, 1981–82; Mazal, *The Excursions of Mr. Broucek*, 1981–82; Count Almaviva, *Il Barbiere di Siviglia (The Barber of Seville)*, 1982–83; Giuseppe, *The Most Happy Fella*, 1982–83; Pirelli, *Sweeney Todd*, 1983–84

Wall, Elise: Mrs. Hayes, *Susannah*, 1976–77; Dorabella, *Così fan tutte*, 1978–79; Fyodor, *Boris Godunov*, 1978–79

Wall, Stephen: Clerk at the Clarendon Hotel, *The Ballad of Baby Doe*, 1975–76; Knight, *Parsifal*, 1975–76; Mayor of Leadville, *The Ballad of Baby Doe*, 1975–76; The Chief Magistrate, *Un Ballo in Maschera (A Masked Ball)*, 1975–76

Wallace, Star: Suor Dolcina, *Suor Angelica (Sister Angelica)*, 1999–2000

Walnut, Frank: Sailor, *On the Town*, 1951–52

Walsh, Daniel: Albert, *Werther*, 1961–62; Demetrius, *A Midsummer Night's Dream*, 1961–62; Dr. Falke, *Die Fledermaus (The Bat)*, 1962–63; Lazarus, *The Darkened City*, 1962–63; Gypsy, *The Fair at Sorochinsk*, 1963–64; Alfio, *Cavalleria Rusticana*, 1966–67; Mercutio, *Roméo et Juliette*, 1966–67; Rangoni, *Boris Godunov*, 1966–67; Sid, *Albert Herring*, 1966–67; Silvio, *I Pagliacci*, 1966–67

Walstrum, Eve: Nellie, *Annie Get Your Gun*, 1956–57; Clo-clo, *Die lustige Witwe (The Merry Widow)*, 1964–65

Walstrum, Martha: Parthy Ann Hawkes, *Show Boat*, 1953–54

Walters, Kathryn: Mary Hildebrand, *Street Scene*, 1949–50

Walters, Ruth: Solo Child, *La Bohème*, 1984–85

Walton, Ronald: Cecil, *Where's Charley?*, 1953–54; Cmdr. William Harbison, *South Pacific*, 1956–57

Wankier, Suzette: Amelia, *Un Ballo in Maschera (A Masked Ball)*, 1969–70; Fiordiligi, *Così fan tutte*, 1970–71; Manon Lescaut, *Manon Lescaut*, 1970–71; Mrs. Alice Ford, *Falstaff*, 1971–72; Cio-Cio San, *Madama Butterfly*, 1975–76

Wapinsky, Tamara: Donna Anna, *Don Giovanni*, 2002–03; Ellen Orford, *Peter Grimes*, 2003–04; Beatrice, *A View from the Bridge*, 2004–05

Ward, Clifton: Mityukh, *Boris Godunov*, 1966–67

Ward, James: Keeper of the Madhouse, *The Rake's Progress*, 1986–87; M. Javelinot, *Dialogues des Carmélites*, 1986–87; Bontemps, *Die Teufel von Loudun (The Devils of Loudun)*, 1992–93

Ward, Leo: Young Man, *Boris Godunov*, 1964–65; Monostatos, *Die Zauberflöte (The Magic Flute)*, 1965–66; Young Man, *Boris Godunov*, 1966–67

Warden, Jeff: Bertrand, *A Little Night Music*, 1975–76

Warfield, Jean: Old Lady, *Street Scene*, 1960–61; Puck, *A Midsummer Night's Dream*, 1961–62

Waring, Sally: Jean MacLaren, *Brigadoon*, 1961–62

Warren, Charles: Jared, *Lost in the Stars*, 1950–51

Warren, Gregory: Monostatos, *Die Zauberflöte (The Magic Flute)*, 1998–99; Pamina, *Die Zauberflöte (The Magic Flute)*, 1998–99

Washington, Stephanie: Rita Billingsley, *A Wedding*, 2007–08

Waters, Laura: Musetta, *La Bohème*, 2007–08

Watson, Allison: Buttercup, *HMS Pinafore*, 1997–98; Zita, *Gianni Schicchi*, 1999–2000; Giovanna, *Rigoletto*, 2000–01; Mrs. Ott, *Susannah*, 2000–01; Alma March, *Little Women*, 2001–02

Watson, Catherine: Claire, *Die Teufel von Loudun (The Devils of Loudun)*, 1992–93; Princess Linetta, *The Love for Three Oranges*, 1993–94; Mrs. Sedley, *Peter Grimes*, 1994–95; Secretary III, *Nixon in China*, 1994–95; Yente, *Fiddler on the Roof*, 1994–95; Bloody Mary, *South Pacific*, 1995–96; Juno, *Agrippina*, 1995–96; Narciso, *Agrippina*, 1995–96; Prince Orlofsky, *Die Fledermaus (The Bat)*, 1996–97; Zita, *Gianni Schicchi*, 1999–2000

Watson, Rachel: Frau Zeller, *The Sound of Music*, 2000–01; Gianetta, *L'Elisir d'amore (The Elixir of Love)*, 2000–01

Watters, Boyd: Gherardino, *Il Trittico (A Triptych)*, 1972–73

Watters, Clark: Doctor Bartolo, *Il Barbiere di Siviglia (The Barber of Seville)*, 1971–72; Graf Waldner, *Arabella*, 1972–73; Lazar Wolf, *Fiddler on the Roof*, 1972–73; Simone, *Il Trittico (A Triptych)*, 1972–73; The Mayor, *Jenůfa*, 1972–73; Dr. Bartolo, *Le Nozze di Figaro (The Marriage of Figaro)*, 1973–74; Harrison Howell, *Kiss Me, Kate*, 1973–74; Luther, *Les Contes d'Hoffmann (The Tales of Hoffmann)*, 1973–74; Ulysses S. Grant, *The Mother of Us All*, 1973–74; Don Alhambra del Bolero, *The Gondoliers*, 1974–75; Bailiff, *Werther*, 1975–76; Jacob, *The Ballad of Baby Doe*, 1975–76; Kreonte, *The Love for Three Oranges*, 1975–76; Prince Yamadori, *Madama Butterfly*, 1975–76; David Bascomb,

Carousel, 1976–77; Elder Ott, *Susannah,* 1976–77; Pistol, *Falstaff,* 1976–77; Sacristan, *Tosca,* 1977–78; Blacksmith, *Canterbury Tales,* 1978–79; The Host, *Canterbury Tales,* 1978–79; Don Basilio, *Il Barbiere di Siviglia (The Barber of Seville),* 1980–81

Watters, Cynthia: Rosalinda, *Die Fledermaus (The Bat),* 1996–97; Norina, *Don Pasquale,* 1997–98; Ilia, *Idomeneo,* 1998–99; Katherine, *Kiss Me, Kate,* 1998–99; Lilli Vanessi, *Kiss Me, Kate,* 1998–99; Female Chorus, *The Rape of Lucretia,* 1999–2000; Susannah Polk, *Susannah,* 2000–01

Watters, Sean: Pepe, *West Side Story,* 1992–93

Watts, Ralph: Antipholus of Ephesus, *The Boys from Syracuse,* 1968–69; Antonio, *Le Nozze di Figaro (The Marriage of Figaro),* 1968–69; File, *110 in the Shade,* 1968–69

Wayne, Lilian: Coryphee, *Murder in the Cathedral,* 1984–85

Weathers, C. William: Mr. Appopolous, *Wonderful Town,* 1954–55

Weathers, Frankie: Infant Casmira, *Candide,* 1957–58; Cio-Cio San, *Madama Butterfly,* 1958–59; Oscar, *Un Ballo in Maschera (A Masked Ball),* 1958–59; Queen of the Night, *Die Zauberflöte (The Magic Flute),* 1960–61

Weaver, Janet: Fifi, *Die lustige Witwe (The Merry Widow),* 1949–50

Webb, Anthony: Graf Elemer, *Arabella,* 2006–07; Elder Hayes, *Susannah,* 2007–08; Luigi, *A Wedding,* 2007–08

Webb, Malcolm: Trouble, *Madama Butterfly,* 1975–76

Webb III, Charles H.: Trouble, *Madama Butterfly,* 1976–77

Webster, Douglas: Herman, *The Most Happy Fella,* 1982–83; Clerk at the Clarendon Hotel, *The Ballad of Baby Doe,* 1982–83; Newsboy, *The Ballad of Baby Doe,* 1982–83; The McCourt family, *The Ballad of Baby Doe,* 1982–83; Allworthy, *Tom Jones,* 1983–84; Cat, *L'Enfant et les Sortilèges (The Bewitched Child),* 1984–85; Priest, *Murder in the Cathedral,* 1984–85; Celebrant, *Mass,* 1987–88; Celebrant, *Mass,* 1988–89

Wedemeyer, Ellen: Princess Linetta, *The Love for Three Oranges,* 1993–94; Boy, *Die Zauberflöte (The Magic Flute),* 1994–95; Secretary II, *Nixon in China,* 1994–95

Weede, Richard: Bosun, *Billy Budd,* 1952–53

Weeks, Anne: Olympia, *Les Contes d'Hoffmann (The Tales of Hoffmann),* 1947–48; The Maid, *Hin und Zurück (There and Back),* 1947–48; Page, *Parsifal,* 1948–49

Weigel, Johan: Alfred, *Die Fledermaus (The Bat),* 1996–97; Begearss, *The Ghosts of Versailles,* 1996–97; The Chevalier, *Dialogues des Carmélites,* 1997–98; Matteo, *Arabella,* 1998–99; Remendado, *Carmen,* 1998–99; Anatol, *Vanessa,* 1999–2000; Tom Rakewell, *The Rake's Progress,* 1999–2000; Faust, *Faust,* 2000–01

Weigel, Richard: Annibale, *The Gondoliers,* 1974–75; Elder Gleaton, *Susannah,* 1976–77

Weiner, Sarah: A Tourier, *Il Trittico (A Triptych),* 1982–83

Weinius, Michael: Jeppe, *Jeppe,* 2002–03

Weinland, Thomas: Charlie Cowell, *The Music Man,* 1980–81

Weinman, Richard: Spettigue, *Where's Charley?,* 1953–54

Weisman, Constance: Aunt Emily, *A Parfait for Irene,* 1951–52

Weiss, Carlyle: Lt. Pinkerton, *Madama Butterfly,* 1958–59; The Prince, *The Love for Three Oranges,* 1958–59; Prunier, *La Rondine (The Swallow),* 1959–60; The Doctor, *The Most Happy Fella,* 1959–60

Weiss, Ira: Notary, *Il Barbiere di Siviglia (The Barber of Seville),* 1971–72

Weissmann, Nadine: Baba the Turk, *The Rake's Progress,* 1999–2000; Old Baroness, *Vanessa,* 1999–2000

Welch, Christi: Amore (Cupid), *L'Orfeo,* 1987–88; Spirit, *Die Zauberflöte (The Magic Flute),* 1988–89

Welch, James: Brack Weaver, *Down in the Valley,* 1947–48

Welker, Marla: Yniold, *Pelléas et Mélisande,* 1976–77

Wellman, Dennis: Don Anchise, *La Finta Giardiniera,* 1990–91; Vicomte Camille di Rosillon, *Die lustige Witwe (The Merry Widow),* 1990–91; Don Ramiro, *La Cenerentola (Cinderella),* 1991–92; Mario Cavaradossi, *Tosca,* 1993–94

Wells, Mark: Servant, *La Traviata,* 1978–79

Wells, Matthew: Andres, *Les Contes d'Hoffmann (The Tales of Hoffmann),* 2007–08; Cochenille, *Les Contes d'Hoffmann (The Tales of Hoffmann),* 2007–08; Franz, *Les Contes d'Hoffmann (The Tales of Hoffmann),* 2007–08; Little Bat McLean, *Susannah,* 2007–08; Pittichinaccio, *Les Contes d'Hoffmann (The Tales of Hoffmann),* 2007–08

Welsh, John: Marquis D'Obigny, *La Traviata,* 1960–61; A Surgeon, *La Forza del Destino (The Force of Destiny),* 1962–63

Wepner, Franklyn: Pinellino, *Il Trittico (A Triptych),* 1969–70

Westcott, Julia: Francisca, *West Side Story,* 2002–03

Westfall, David: Innkeeper, *Manon,* 1967–68; Page, *Parsifal,* 1967–68; Antipholus of Ephesus, *The Boys from Syracuse,* 1968–69

Westphal, Jayne: Flossie, *On the Town,* 1951–52

Weyandt, Michael: Mercutio, *Roméo et Juliette,* 2005–06; Lescaut, *Manon,* 2006–07

Whaley, Lynn Alan: Bill Calhoun, *Kiss Me, Kate,* 1973–74; Lucentio, *Kiss Me, Kate,* 1973–74; Luiz, *The Gondoliers,* 1974–75; Bushy, *The Ballad of Baby Doe,* 1975–76; Henrik Egerman, *A Little Night Music,* 1975–76; Marat, *Danton and*

Robespierre, 1977–78; John, *Canterbury Tales*, 1978–79; The Squire, *Canterbury Tales*, 1978–79

Whaley, Skip: Harry, *Albert Herring*, 1966–67

Wheeler, Mark: Noah Curry, *110 in the Shade*, 1967–68; Pierre Fléville, *Andrea Chénier*, 1967–68; Antipholus of Syracuse, *The Boys from Syracuse*, 1968–69; Sir Lionel, *Camelot*, 1968–69; Woody, *Finian's Rainbow*, 1969–70; Principal, *Carousel*, 1970–71

Whelan, Ralph: Milkman, *Street Scene*, 1949–50

Whinston, Pamela: Papagena, *Die Zauberflöte (The Magic Flute)*, 1960–61; Moth, *A Midsummer Night's Dream*, 1961–62; Barbarina, *Le Nozze di Figaro (The Marriage of Figaro)*, 1962–63; Rose Maybud, *Ruddigore (The Witch's Curse)*, 1962–63

White, Allen: Handsome Harry, *Street Scene*, 1960–61; Old Astrologer, *Le Coq d'or (The Golden Cockerel)*, 1960–61; Strawberry Man, *Street Scene*, 1960–61

White, Carmund: Dr. Caius, *Falstaff*, 2003–04; Simon Stimson, *Our Town*, 2005–06; Snout, *A Midsummer Night's Dream*, 2005–06; Goro, *Madama Butterfly*, 2006–07; Guillot de Morfontaine, *Manon*, 2006–07; Borsa, *Rigoletto*, 2007–08; Don Basilio, *Le Nozze di Figaro (The Marriage of Figaro)*, 2007–08

White, Jay: Shepherd Boy, *Tosca*, 1993–94; Mendel, *Fiddler on the Roof*, 1994–95; Secretary III, *Nixon in China*, 1994–95

White, John Paul: Commendatore, *Don Giovanni*, 1971–72; Don Basilio, *Il Barbiere di Siviglia (The Barber of Seville)*, 1971–72; A Monk, *Don Carlos*, 1972–73; Graf Lamoral, *Arabella*, 1972–73; Grand Inquisitor, *Don Carlos*, 1972–73; Sarastro, *Die Zauberflöte (The Magic Flute)*, 1972–73; Crespel, *Les Contes d'Hoffmann (The Tales of Hoffmann)*, 1973–74; Figaro, *Le Nozze di Figaro (The Marriage of Figaro)*, 1973–74; Osmin, *Die Entführung aus dem Serail (The Abduction from the Seraglio)*, 1974–75; Prince Gremin, *Eugene Onegin*, 1974–75; Sparafucile, *Rigoletto*, 1974–75

White, Laura: A Favorite of the Governor, *Candide*, 1983–84; Victim of the Inquisition, *Candide*, 1983–84; Giulietta, *Les Contes d'Hoffmann (The Tales of Hoffmann)*, 1988–89; Madame Larina, *Eugene Onegin*, 1988–89; Estella, *West Side Story*, 2002–03

White, Richard: Ford, *Falstaff*, 1976–77; Dr. Malatesta, *Don Pasquale*, 1977–78; Speaker of the Temple, *Die Zauberflöte (The Magic Flute)*, 1977–78; Guglielmo, *Così fan tutte*, 1978–79

White, Stewart: Schlemil, *Les Contes d'Hoffmann (The Tales of Hoffmann)*, 1947–48; The Philosopher, *Hin und Zurück (There and Back)*, 1947–48

White, Wendy: Mama McCourt, *The Ballad of Baby Doe*, 1975–76; Princess Clarissa, *The Love for Three Oranges*, 1975–76; Dame Quickly, *Falstaff*, 1976–77; Dinah, *Trouble in Tahiti*, 1976–77; Nettie Fowler, *Carousel*, 1976–77; Old Lady, *Candide*, 1976–77; Player, *Bernstein on Broadway*, 1976–77; Suzuki, *Madama Butterfly*, 1976–77; Carmen, *Carmen*, 1977–78

Whitener, Joshua: Josh, *Jeppe*, 2002–03; Vicomte Camille di Rosillon, *Die lustige Witwe (The Merry Widow)*, 2003–04; Mike, *A View from the Bridge*, 2004–05; Lysander, *A Midsummer Night's Dream*, 2005–06; Nanki-Poo, *The Mikado*, 2006–07; Dino, *A Wedding*, 2007–08; Nemorino, *L'Elisir d'amore (The Elixir of Love)*, 2007–08

Whiteside, Norman: Monostatos, *Die Zauberflöte (The Magic Flute)*, 1972–73; Song Vendor, *Il Trittico (A Triptych)*, 1972–73; Andres, *Les Contes d'Hoffmann (The Tales of Hoffmann)*, 1973–74; Cochenille, *Les Contes d'Hoffmann (The Tales of Hoffmann)*, 1973–74; Franz, *Les Contes d'Hoffmann (The Tales of Hoffmann)*, 1973–74; Pittichinaccio, *Les Contes d'Hoffmann (The Tales of Hoffmann)*, 1973–74; Spoletta, *Tosca*, 1973–74; Marco Palmieri, *The Gondoliers*, 1974–75

Whitmer, Carolyn: Angel, *The King and I*, 1957–58

Whitten, Kristi: Jennie, *Carousel*, 1993–94; Pamina, *Die Zauberflöte (The Magic Flute)*, 1998–99

Wible, Rosalee: Beggar, *Candide*, 1957–58

Wicker, Vernon: Bailiff, *Werther*, 1961–62; Bottom, *A Midsummer Night's Dream*, 1961–62; Deputy, *Don Carlos*, 1961–62; Titurel, *Parsifal*, 1961–62; Dr. Bartolo, *Le Nozze di Figaro (The Marriage of Figaro)*, 1962–63; Escamillo, *Carmen*, 1962–63; Fra Melitone, *La Forza del Destino (The Force of Destiny)*, 1962–63; Knight, *Parsifal*, 1962–63; Leader of Penitents, *The Darkened City*, 1962–63; Don Annibale Pistachio, *Il Campanello di Notte (The Night Bell)*, 1963–64; Solopy Tcherevik, *The Fair at Sorochinsk*, 1963–64

Wickson, Jason: Goro, *Madama Butterfly*, 2006–07; Elder Gleaton, *Susannah*, 2007–08; Rodolfo, *La Bohème*, 2007–08

Wieczorek, Todd: Friedrich Bhaer, *Little Women*, 2001–02; Doctor Grenville, *La Traviata*, 2002–03; A Denver Politician, *The Ballad of Baby Doe*, 2003–04; Bouncer at the saloon, *The Ballad of Baby Doe*, 2003–04; Cascada, *Die lustige Witwe (The Merry Widow)*, 2003–04; Cesare Angelotti, *Tosca*, 2004–05; Eddie, *A View from the Bridge*, 2004–05; Jailer, *Tosca*, 2004–05; Dick Deadeye, *HMS Pinafore*, 2005–06

Wieler, Fred: A Serenader, *Doktor Faust*, 1974–75

Wier, Max: Colline, *La Bohème*, 2007–08; Sparafucile, *Rigoletto*, 2007–08

Wiest, Joan: Petra, *A Little Night Music,* 1975–76; Princess Ninetta, *The Love for Three Oranges,* 1975–76; Carrie Pipperidge, *Carousel,* 1976–77

Wilburn, Christopher: Stage Manager, *Our Town,* 2005–06

Wilder, A.E.: Jolidon, *Die lustige Witwe (The Merry Widow),* 1949–50; Smiley, *The Jumping Frog of Calaveras County,* 1949–50

Wilder, Jan: Pamina, *Die Zauberflöte (The Magic Flute),* 1953–54

Wiley, David: Customs Officer, *La Bohème,* 1989–90

Wiley, Gerald: Baron Thunder-Ten-Tronck, *Candide,* 1957–58; Lawyer, *Candide,* 1957–58; Marquis, *Candide,* 1957–58

Wilkey, Jay: Don Giovanni, *Don Giovanni,* 1958–59; Leandro, *The Love for Three Oranges,* 1958–59; Master Ford (Herr Fluth), *Die lustigen Weiber von Windsor (The Merry Wives of Windsor),* 1958–59; Olivier, *Capriccio,* 1958–59; Ciccio, *The Most Happy Fella,* 1959–60; Parsifal, *Parsifal,* 1959–60; Rigoletto, *Rigoletto,* 1959–60

Wilkinson, Anita: Child's Mama, *L'Enfant et les Sortilèges (The Bewitched Child),* 1984–85

Wilkinson, Jean: Gretel, *Hänsel und Gretel,* 1982–83; Hanna Glawari, *Die lustige Witwe (The Merry Widow),* 1983–84; Donna Elvira, *Don Giovanni,* 1985–86; Marenka, *The Bartered Bride,* 1986–87

Williams, Albert: Lancelot, *Camelot,* 1968–69; Shears, *Finian's Rainbow,* 1969–70

Williams, Clifford: Messenger, *Heracles,* 1971–72; A Monk, *Don Carlos,* 1972–73; Simone, *Il Trittico (A Triptych),* 1972–73; Talpa, *Il Trittico (A Triptych),* 1972–73; Antonio, *Le Nozze di Figaro (The Marriage of Figaro),* 1973–74; Ulysses S. Grant, *The Mother of Us All,* 1973–74; Alcindoro, *La Bohème,* 1974–75; Benoit, *La Bohème,* 1974–75; Wagner, *Doktor Faust,* 1974–75

Williams, Connie: Martha, *Passion Play—Carmina Burana,* 1982–83; Spirit, *Die Zauberflöte (The Magic Flute),* 1982–83; Pink Sheep, *Candide,* 1983–84; Cupid, *Orphée aux enfers (Orpheus in the Underworld),* 1984–85; Fire, *L'Enfant et les Sortilèges (The Bewitched Child),* 1984–85; Little Bat McLean, *Susannah,* 2000–01

Williams, Daniel: First Officer, *Candide,* 2000–01; Little Bat McLean, *Susannah,* 2000–01

Williams, Delores: Hattie, *Kiss Me, Kate,* 1973–74

Williams, Janet: Wellgunde, *Das Rheingold,* 1983–84; Musetta, *La Bohème,* 1984–85; Venus, *Orphée aux enfers (Orpheus in the Underworld),* 1984–85; Frasquita, *Carmen,* 1984–85; Donna Anna, *Don Giovanni,* 1985–86; Younger Sister, *The Legend of Tsar Saltan,* 1986–87

Williams, John: Crown, *Porgy and Bess,* 1976–77

Williams, Joyce: The Mistress of the Novices, *Il Trittico (A Triptych),* 1972–73; Third Lady, *Die Zauberflöte (The Magic Flute),* 1972–73; Muse, *Les Contes d'Hoffmann (The Tales of Hoffmann),* 1973–74; Nicklausse, *Les Contes d'Hoffmann (The Tales of Hoffmann),* 1973–74; Tatyana, *Eugene Onegin,* 1974–75; Vanessa, *Vanessa,* 1974–75

Williams, Maria: Constanza, *Die Entführung aus dem Serail (The Abduction from the Seraglio),* 1993–94; Marenka, *The Bartered Bride,* 1994–95; Mimi, *La Bohème,* 1994–95; Cio-Cio San, *Madama Butterfly,* 1996–97

Williams, Pamela: Zita, *Gianni Schicchi,* 1993–94; Genevieve, *Pelléas et Mélisande,* 1994–95; Hata, *The Bartered Bride,* 1994–95; Hansel, *Hänsel und Gretel,* 1995–96; Voice of the Mother, *Les Contes d'Hoffmann (The Tales of Hoffmann),* 1995–96

Williams, Ruth: Girl on the street, *Trouble in Tahiti,* 1976–77; Player, *Bernstein on Broadway,* 1976–77; Trio—soprano, *Trouble in Tahiti,* 1976–77; Shepherd Boy, *Tosca,* 1977–78; The Weaver's Wife, *The Night Before Christmas,* 1977–78; Antonia, *Les Contes d'Hoffmann (The Tales of Hoffmann),* 1978–79; Mimi, *La Bohème,* 1979–80; Yaroslavna, *Prince Igor,* 1980–81; Cio-Cio San, *Madama Butterfly,* 1987–88

Williamson, Lisa: Mrs. Alice Ford, *Falstaff,* 1992–93; Lucia, *Lucia di Lammermoor,* 1993–94; Musetta, *La Bohème,* 1994–95; Gilda, *Rigoletto,* 1995–96; Anna Leonowens, *The King and I,* 1996–97; Donna Fiorilla, *Il Turco in Italia (The Turk in Italy),* 1996–97; Norina, *Don Pasquale,* 1997–98

Willis, Diane: Filipyevna, *Eugene Onegin,* 1974–75; Lisetta, *Il Mondo della Luna (The World on the Moon),* 1975–76; Suzuki, *Madama Butterfly,* 1975–76; Mrs. Ott, *Susannah,* 1976–77; Suzuki, *Madama Butterfly,* 1976–77

Willits, Linda: Assistant Courtesan, *The Boys from Syracuse,* 1968–69; Guenevere, *Camelot,* 1969–70

Willke, Dietrich: Tenorio / a Muleteer, *Man of La Mancha,* 1999–2000

Willoughby, Jay: Coppelius, *Les Contes d'Hoffmann (The Tales of Hoffmann),* 1959–60; Dappertutto, *Les Contes d'Hoffmann (The Tales of Hoffmann),* 1959–60; Dr. Miracle, *Les Contes d'Hoffmann (The Tales of Hoffmann),* 1959–60; Joe, *The Most Happy Fella,* 1959–60; Lindorf, *Les Contes d'Hoffmann (The Tales of Hoffmann),* 1959–60; Marullo, *Rigoletto,* 1959–60; The King, *Die Kluge (The Clever Girl),* 1959–60; Amfortas, *Parsifal,* 1960–61; Giorgio Germont, *La Traviata,* 1960–61; Rodrigo, *Don Carlos,* 1960–61; Baron Scarpia, *Tosca,* 1961–62; Belcore, *L'Elisir d'amore (The Elixir of Love),* 1961–62; Demetrius, *A Midsummer Night's Dream,* 1961–62; Pasha Selim, *Die Entführung aus* dem Serail (*The Abduction from the Seraglio*), 1961–62; Rodrigo, *Don Carlos,* 1961–62; Tommy Albright, *Brigadoon,* 1961–62

Wills, Jennifer: Gossip 1, *The Ghosts of Versailles,* 1996–97; Josephine, *HMS Pinafore,* 1997–98; Laurey, *Oklahoma!,* 1997–98; Papagena, *Die Zauberflöte (The Magic Flute),* 1998–99

Willy, Jeannette: Kundry, *Parsifal,* 1961–62

Wilmes, John: Alexander Throttlebottom, *Of Thee I Sing,* 1987–88

Wilson, Bayard: Crebillon, *La Rondine (The Swallow),* 1959–60; Luther, *Les Contes d'Hoffmann (The Tales of Hoffmann),* 1959–60; Spalanzani, *Les Contes d'Hoffmann (The Tales of Hoffmann),* 1959–60; The Mule Man, *Die Kluge (The Clever Girl),* 1959–60; Harry Easter, *Street Scene,* 1960–61; Papageno, *Die Zauberflöte (The Magic Flute),* 1960–61; Prince Afron, *Le Coq d'or (The Golden Cockerel),* 1960–61; Jailer, *Tosca,* 1961–62; A Surgeon, *La Forza del Destino (The Force of Destiny),* 1962–63; Dancaire, *Carmen,* 1962–63; Servant, *The Darkened City,* 1962–63

Wilson, Bert: Servant, *La Traviata,* 1960–61

Wilson, Blake: Angel, *Passion Play—Carmina Burana,* 1982–83

Wilson, Candace: A Page, *Manon Lescaut,* 1970–71; Rosswiesse, *Die Walküre,* 1971–72; Eine Kartenaufschlaegerin, *Arabella,* 1972–73; Sister Osmina, *Il Trittico (A Triptych),* 1972–73; The nursing sister from the infirmary, *Il Trittico (A Triptych),* 1972–73; Theobald, *Don Carlos,* 1972–73; Third Lady, *Die Zauberflöte (The Magic Flute),* 1972–73

Wilson, Gran: Camille Desmoulins, *Danton and Robespierre,* 1977–78; Vakula, *The Night Before Christmas,* 1977–78; Ferrando, *Così fan tutte,* 1978–79; Simpleton, *Boris Godunov,* 1978–79; Chevalier des Grieux, *Manon,* 1979–80; The Duke of Mantua, *Rigoletto,* 1980–81

Wilson, Harold: Pistol, *Falstaff,* 1997–98; Prince Gremin, *Eugene Onegin,* 1997–98; Alidoro, *La Cenerentola (Cinderella),* 1998–99; Sarastro, *Die Zauberflöte (The Magic Flute),* 1998–99; Voice of Neptune, *Idomeneo,* 1998–99; Zuniga, *Carmen,* 1998–99; Collatinus, *The Rape of Lucretia,* 1999–2000; First Apprentice, *Wozzeck,* 1999–2000; Mephistopheles, *Faust,* 2000–01; Count des Grieux, *Manon,* 2001–02

Wilson, Holly: Kate Pinkerton, *Madama Butterfly,* 1996–97; Cherubino, *Le Nozze di Figaro (The Marriage of Figaro),* 1997–98; Flora Bervoix, *La Traviata,* 1997–98; Angelina (Cinderella), *La Cenerentola (Cinderella),* 1998–99; Rosina, *Il Barbiere di Siviglia (The Barber of Seville),* 2000–01

Wilson, Julie: Meg Brockie, *Brigadoon,* 1961–62

Wilson, Karen: Spirit, *Die Zauberflöte (The Magic Flute),* 1960–61; Cherubino, *Le Nozze di Figaro (The Marriage of Figaro),* 1962–63; An Old Indian Woman, *A Hoosier Tale,* 1966–67; Fyodor, *Boris Godunov,* 1966–67

Wilson, Lara: Third Lady, *Die Zauberflöte (The Magic Flute),* 1994–95; Maddalena, *Rigoletto,* 1995–96

Wilson, Martin: Remendado, *Carmen,* 1991–92; Master of Ceremonies, *The Love for Three Oranges,* 1993–94

Wilson, Neil: Billie, *Roberta,* 1958–59; Joe, *The Most Happy Fella,* 1959–60; Mr. Frank Maurant, *Street Scene,* 1960–61; Tommy Albright, *Brigadoon,* 1961–62

Wilson, Pat: Hildy, *On the Town,* 1951–52; Irene, *A Parfait for Irene,* 1951–52

Wineman, Margaret: Dolly, *Show Boat,* 1984–85

Winger, Lisa: The Dragonfly, *L'Enfant et les Sortilèges (The Bewitched Child),* 1984–85; Caliban, *The Tempest,* 1985–86; Rosalia, *West Side Story,* 1985–86; Baba the Turk, *The Rake's Progress,* 1986–87

Wininger, Jessica: Trouble, *Madama Butterfly,* 1987–88

Winkler, Kristine: Clorinda, *La Cenerentola (Cinderella),* 1998–99; Pamina, *Die Zauberflöte (The Magic Flute),* 1998–99; Lauretta, *Gianni Schicchi,* 1999–2000; Musetta, *La Bohème,* 1999–2000; Gilda, *Rigoletto,* 2000–01; Gretel, *Hänsel und Gretel,* 2001–02

Winold, Hans Peter: The Child, *Wozzeck,* 1973–74

Winslow, Jane: Cupid, *Orphée aux enfers (Orpheus in the Underworld),* 1984–85; The Duchess of Krackenthorp, *La Fille du régiment (The Daughter of the Regiment),* 1984–85

Winslow, Matthew: Second Gambler, *Candide,* 1993–94; Servant of Maximilian, *Candide,* 1993–94; The Grand Inquisitor, *Candide,* 1993–94; Count Ceprano, *Rigoletto,* 1995–96; Papa Sieppe, *McTeague,* 1995–96; The Imperial Commissioner, *Madama Butterfly,* 1996–97; Dancaire, *Carmen,* 1998–99

Winsor, Caleb: Don Basilio, *Le Nozze di Figaro (The Marriage of Figaro),* 2007–08

Winter, Heather: Maud Dunlop, *The Music Man,* 2001–02; Player, *Putting It Together,* 2002–03

Winter, Susan: Katchen, *Werther,* 1975–76; Xenia, *Boris Godunov,* 1978–79

Wintermann, Bridget: Die Fiakermilli, *Arabella,* 1998–99

Winters, Glenn: Djura, *Arabella,* 1972–73; Hermann, *Les Contes d'Hoffmann (The Tales of Hoffmann),* 1973–74

Winzenried, Kirsten: Mama McCourt, *The Ballad of Baby Doe,* 1982–83

Wirenius, Lawrence: Pony Express Rider, *La Fanciulla del West (The Girl of the Golden West),* 1963–64

Wise, Patricia: Hanna Glawari, *Die lustige Witwe (The Merry Widow)*, 1996–97

Wisk, Bradley: Chevalier de St. Brioche, *Die lustige Witwe (The Merry Widow)*, 2003–04

Witakowski, Thomas: Farfarello, *The Love for Three Oranges*, 1980–81; Kostandis, *The Greek Passion*, 1980–81; Official Registrar, *Madama Butterfly*, 1981–82; Fiorello, *Il Barbiere di Siviglia (The Barber of Seville)*, 1982–83; Pharisee, *Passion Play—Carmina Burana*, 1982–83; Priest, *Die Zauberflöte (The Magic Flute)*, 1982–83; Alberich, *Das Rheingold*, 1983–84; Bottom, *A Midsummer Night's Dream*, 1983–84; Don Issachar, *Candide*, 1983–84; Judge of the Inquisition, *Candide*, 1983–84; Benoit, *La Bohème*, 1984–85; Cat, *L'Enfant et les Sortilèges (The Bewitched Child)*, 1984–85; Nick Shadow, *The Rake's Progress*, 1986–87

Witkowski, Miroslaw: Commendatore, *Don Giovanni*, 2006–07; Guardsman, *Manon*, 2006–07; The Bonze, *Madama Butterfly*, 2006–07; Colline, *La Bohème*, 2007–08; Dr. Bartolo, *Le Nozze di Figaro (The Marriage of Figaro)*, 2007–08

Witte, Leonore: Donna Anna, *Don Giovanni*, 1958–59; Mistress Alice Ford (Frau Fluth), *Die lustigen Weiber von Windsor (The Merry Wives of Windsor)*, 1958–59; The Countess, *Capriccio*, 1958–59; Gilda, *Rigoletto*, 1959–60

Witten, Mary: Countess Ceprano, *Rigoletto*, 1980–81; Marie, *Wozzeck*, 1981–82; First Lady, *Die Zauberflöte (The Magic Flute)*, 1982–83; Freia, *Das Rheingold*, 1983–84

Wittich, Lois: Peasant woman, *Boris Godunov*, 1964–65; Marianne Leitmetzerin, *Der Rosenkavalier*, 1965–66

Wittman, Duane: Dr. Blind, *Die Fledermaus (The Bat)*, 1996–97; The Father Confessor, *Dialogues des Carmélites*, 1997–98

Witzke, Ronald: Mars, *Orphée aux enfers (Orpheus in the Underworld)*, 1992–93; Gianni Schicchi, *Gianni Schicchi*, 1993–94; Jigger Craigin, *Carousel*, 1993–94; Captain Balstrode, *Peter Grimes*, 1994–95; Chou En-lai, *Nixon in China*, 1994–95; Golaud, *Pelléas et Mélisande*, 1994–95

Wolf, Carol: Dorabella, *Così fan tutte*, 1956–57; Hansel, *Hänsel und Gretel*, 1956–57; Mrs. Meg Page, *Falstaff*, 1956–57

Wolf, Marcia: Countess Almaviva, *Le Nozze di Figaro (The Marriage of Figaro)*, 1962–63; Wife of Lazarus, *The Darkened City*, 1962–63

Wolf, Sally: Lucille, *Danton and Robespierre*, 1977–78; Queen of the Night, *Die Zauberflöte (The Magic Flute)*, 1977–78; Miss Jessel, *The Turn of the Screw*, 1978–79; Iphygeneia, *The Cry of Clytaemnestra*, 1979–80; Manon Lescaut, *Manon*, 1979–80

Wolfersteig, Eloise: Marie, *The Most Happy Fella*, 1959–60; Lady, *Street Scene*, 1960–61; Nursemaid, *Street Scene*, 1960–61; Second Lady, *Die Zauberflöte (The Magic Flute)*, 1960–61

Wolfson, Charles: Mendel, *Fiddler on the Roof*, 1972–73

Wood, Judy: Sister Dolcina, *Il Trittico (A Triptych)*, 1969–70

Wood, Richard: Street Dancer, *Kismet*, 1963–64

Woodruff, Linda: Ayah to Princess Zubbediya, *Kismet*, 1963–64; Gertrude, *Roméo et Juliette*, 1966–67

Woods, Wanda: Mrs. Kranz, *Blossom Time*, 1952–53

Woollen, Jacobsen: Gherardino, *Gianni Schicchi*, 1999–2000; The Child, *Wozzeck*, 1999–2000

Woolridge, Warren: Nanki-Poo, *The Mikado*, 1950–51

Workman, Stanley: Man in Armor, *Die Zauberflöte (The Magic Flute)*, 1988–89; Priest, *Die Zauberflöte (The Magic Flute)*, 1988–89; Odysseus, *The Cry of Clytaemnestra*, 1989–90; Roderigo, *Otello*, 1989–90; Don Anchise, *La Finta Giardiniera*, 1990–91; Nemorino, *L'Elisir d'amore (The Elixir of Love)*, 1990–91

Worra, Caroline: Nella, *Gianni Schicchi*, 1993–94; Marenka, *The Bartered Bride*, 1994–95; Agrippina, *Agrippina*, 1995–96; Mastrilla, *La Périchole*, 1995–96; Donna Elvira, *Don Giovanni*, 1996–97; Mrs. Alice Ford, *Falstaff*, 1997–98

Worth, Andrew: Amahl, *Amahl and the Night Visitors*, 1990–91

Wozniak, Anthony: Whirling Dervish, *Kismet*, 1989–90

Wrancher, Elizabeth: Kundry, *Parsifal*, 1951–52; Mrs. Jones, *A Parfait for Irene*, 1951–52; Bellabruna, *Blossom Time*, 1952–53; Kundry, *Parsifal*, 1952–53; Mrs. Mullin, *Carousel*, 1952–53; Kundry, *Parsifal*, 1953–54; Queen of the Night, *Die Zauberflöte (The Magic Flute)*, 1953–54; Ariadne/Prima Donna, *Ariadne auf Naxos*, 1954–55; Floria Tosca, *Tosca*, 1961–62; Senta, *Der Fliegende Holländer (The Flying Dutchman)*, 1962–63; Kundry, *Parsifal*, 1968–69

Wright, Benjamin: Miles, *The Turn of the Screw*, 1978–79

Wright, Carole: Gerhilde, *Die Walküre*, 1971–72; Page, *Parsifal*, 1972–73; The Abbess, *Il Trittico (A Triptych)*, 1972–73

Wright, Daniel: Hermann, *Les Contes d'Hoffmann (The Tales of Hoffmann)*, 1959–60; Attendant, *Don Carlos*, 1960–61; Mr. George Jones, *Street Scene*, 1960–61; Slave, *Die Zauberflöte (The Magic Flute)*, 1960–61; Attendant, *Don Carlos*, 1961–62; Baron Scarpia, *Tosca*, 1961–62; Deputy, *Don Carlos*, 1961–62; Sciarrone, *Tosca*, 1961–62; Al Alcaide, *La Forza del Destino (The Force of Destiny)*, 1962–63; Alcindoro, *La Bohème*, 1962–63; Benoit, *La Bohème*, 1962–63; Billy Jackrabbit, *La Fanciulla del West (The Girl of the Golden West)*, 1963–64

Wright, Elayne: Dame Quickly, *Falstaff*, 1956–57; Sandman, *Hänsel und Gretel*, 1956–57; Florence Pike, *Albert Herring*, 1957–58; Old Lady, *Candide*, 1957–58; Thisbe, *La Cenerentola (Cinderella)*, 1957–58

Wright, Gene: Fiesco (Andrea Grimaldi), *Simon Boccanegra*, 1964–65

Wright, Steven: Boatswain, *Carousel*, 1993–94; Carnival Boy, *Carousel*, 1993–94; Dancing Agent, *Candide*, 1993–94; Dancing Boy, *Candide*, 1993–94; Sasha, *Fiddler on the Roof*, 1994–95

Wright, Thomas: Attendant, *Don Carlos*, 1960–61; Balloon Man, *Street Scene*, 1960–61; Slave, *Die Zauberflöte (The Magic Flute)*, 1960–61; Workman, *Street Scene*, 1960–61; Attendant, *Don Carlos*, 1961–62

Wrzesien, Dan: Pasha Selim, *Die Entführung aus dem Serail (The Abduction from the Seraglio)*, 1951–52; The Police Chief, *A Parfait for Irene*, 1951–52; Tommy Albright, *Brigadoon*, 1953–54

Wu, Shuang: Sandman, *Hänsel und Gretel*, 1982–83; The Nightingale, *L'Enfant et les Sortilèges (The Bewitched Child)*, 1984–85

Wycoff, Valerie: Zerlina, *Don Giovanni*, 1991–92; Gabrielle, *Die Teufel von Loudun (The Devils of Loudun)*, 1992–93

Wylie, Alice: Eliza, *The King and I*, 1996–97

Wylie, Ted David: Lictor, *L'Incoronazione di Poppea (The Coronation of Poppea)*, 1967–68; Pierre Fléville, *Andrea Chénier*, 1967–68

Wyman, Stephen: Sanson, *Danton and Robespierre*, 1977–78

Xia, Heng: Mother Jeanne, *Dialogues des Carmélites*, 2004–05; Stephano, *Roméo et Juliette*, 2005–06; Suzuki, *Madama Butterfly*, 2006–07

Yache, Tara: Second Lady, *Die Zauberflöte (The Magic Flute)*, 1994–95; Stella, *Les Contes d'Hoffmann (The Tales of Hoffmann)*, 1995–96; Dryad, *Ariadne auf Naxos*, 1996–97; Olga, *Die lustige Witwe (The Merry Widow)*, 1996–97

Yager, Leda: Barbarina, *Le Nozze di Figaro (The Marriage of Figaro)*, 1986–87; Euridice, *L'Orfeo*, 1987–88; Mary Warren, *The Crucible*, 1987–88; Pink Sheep, *Candide*, 1987–88; Mrs. Anderssen, *A Little Night Music*, 1988–89

Yarzebinski, Daniel: Sam, *Our Town*, 2005–06

Yates, Alice: The Squirrel, *L'Enfant et les Sortilèges (The Bewitched Child)*, 1955–56

Yates, Charmaine: Clara, *Porgy and Bess*, 1976–77

Yeats, William: An Officer, *Ariadne auf Naxos*, 1954–55; Knight, *Parsifal*, 1954–55; Jenik, *The Bartered Bride*, 1955–56; Little Billie Potts, *The Land Between the Rivers*, 1955–56; Parsifal, *Parsifal*, 1955–56; The Teapot, *L'Enfant et les Sortilèges (The Bewitched Child)*, 1955–56

Yechout, Cheryl: Susan, *Finian's Rainbow*, 1969–70

Yeldell, Carolyn: Amelia, *Un Ballo in Maschera (A Masked Ball)*, 1969–70; Helmwige, *Die Walküre*, 1969–70; The Mistress of the Novices, *Il Trittico (A Triptych)*, 1969–70

Yenne, Vernon: Hessian, *Candide*, 1957–58; Page, *Parsifal*, 1957–58; Policeman, *Amelia Goes to the Ball*, 1957–58; Page, *Parsifal*, 1958–59; Slender (Spaerlich), *Die lustigen Weiber von Windsor (The Merry Wives of Windsor)*, 1958–59; Andres, *Les Contes d'Hoffmann (The Tales of Hoffmann)*, 1959–60; Franz, *Les Contes d'Hoffmann (The Tales of Hoffmann)*, 1959–60; Jake, *The Most Happy Fella*, 1959–60; Student, *La Rondine (The Swallow)*, 1959–60; Torquemada, *L'Heure espagnole (The Spanish Hour)*, 1959–60; Dick McGann, *Street Scene*, 1960–61; Monostatos, *Die Zauberflöte (The Magic Flute)*, 1960–61; Mr. Daniel Buchanan, *Street Scene*, 1960–61; Prince Guidon, *Le Coq d'or (The Golden Cockerel)*, 1960–61; Don Curzio, *Le Nozze di Figaro (The Marriage of Figaro)*, 1962–63; Dr. Blind, *Die Fledermaus (The Bat)*, 1962–63; First Bearer, *The Darkened City*, 1962–63; Page, *Parsifal*, 1962–63; Third Mourner, *The Darkened City*, 1962–63; Spiridione, *Il Campanello di Notte (The Night Bell)*, 1963–64

Yoder, Kate: Hannah Snow, *Carousel*, 1993–94

Yoke, Mary: First Lay Sister, *Il Trittico (A Triptych)*, 1972–73; Countess Ceprano, *Rigoletto*, 1974–75; Vittoria, *The Gondoliers*, 1974–75

Yoo, Hee Jung: Nanetta, *Falstaff*, 2003–04; Sister Constance, *Dialogues des Carmélites*, 2004–05

Yoon, Jung Nan: Cio-Cio San, *Madama Butterfly*, 2006–07; Mimi, *La Bohème*, 2007–08

York, Karri: Nero, *Agrippina*, 1995–96

Youell, Barbara: Second Lady, *Die Zauberflöte (The Magic Flute)*, 1953–54

Young, Brian: First Beggar, *Kismet*, 1963–64; Chief Spy, *Kismet*, 1963–64

Young, Cristiane: Erda, *Das Rheingold*, 1983–84; Hostess of the Inn, *Boris Godunov*, 1983–84; Public Opinion, *Orphée aux enfers (Orpheus in the Underworld)*, 1984–85; Tamerlane, Emperor of the Tatars, *Tamerlano*, 1984–85

Young, Eugene: Marquis of Calatrava, *La Forza del Destino (The Force of Destiny)*, 1962–63; Ashby, *La Fanciulla del West (The Girl of the Golden West)*, 1963–64; Fiorello, *Il Barbiere di Siviglia (The Barber of Seville)*, 1963–64

Young, Karen: Kate Pinkerton, *Madama Butterfly*, 1981–82; Maria Mater, *Passion Play—Carmina Burana*, 1982–83; Prince Orlofsky, *Die Fledermaus (The Bat)*, 1982–83; The Princess, *Il Trittico (A Triptych)*, 1982–83; Oberon, *A Midsummer Night's Dream*, 1983–84; Erda, *Das Rheingold*, 1983–84

Young, Keith: Indio, *West Side Story*, 1985–86; Luis, *West Side Story*, 1992–93

Young, Kenneth: Omar, *Kismet*, 1963–64; Baron Mirko Zeta, *Die lustige Witwe (The Merry Widow)*, 1964–65; Papageno, *Die Zauberflöte (The Magic Flute)*, 1965–66

Young, Melanie: Celestial Voice, *Don Carlos*, 1972–73; Die Fiakermilli, *Arabella*, 1972–73; Queen of the Night, *Die Zauberflöte (The Magic Flute)*, 1972–73

Young, Sybil: Zerbinetta, *Ariadne auf Naxos*, 1969–70

Young-Holliday, Melanie: Katherine, *Kiss Me, Kate*, 1973–74; Lilli Vanessi, *Kiss Me, Kate*, 1973–74; Lillian Russell, *The Mother of Us All*, 1973–74

Youngquist, Heather: Dewman, *Hänsel und Gretel*, 2006–07; Gianetta, *L'Elisir d'amore (The Elixir of Love)*, 2007–08; Tulip, *A Wedding*, 2007–08

Yule, Donald: Don Magnifico, *La Cenerentola (Cinderella)*, 1957–58; Judge of the Inquisition, *Candide*, 1957–58; Old Inquisitor, *Candide*, 1957–58; Pilgrim Father, *Candide*, 1957–58; Superintendant Budd, *Albert Herring*, 1957–58; The Chief of Police, *Amelia Goes to the Ball*, 1957–58; The Prefect of Police, *Candide*, 1957–58; Huck Haines, *Roberta*, 1958–59; Klingsor, *Parsifal*, 1958–59; LaRoche, *Capriccio*, 1958–59; Leporello, *Don Giovanni*, 1958–59; Sir John Falstaff, *Die lustigen Weiber von Windsor (The Merry Wives of Windsor)*, 1958–59; The King of Clubs, *The Love for Three Oranges*, 1958–59; Tom, *Un Ballo in Maschera (A Masked Ball)*, 1958–59

Zachry, Lauren: Yniold, *Pelléas et Mélisande*, 1994–95; Poppea, *Agrippina*, 1995–96

Zadroga, Daniel: The Professor, *L'Elisir d'amore (The Elixir of Love)*, 1986–87

Zahara, Rebecca: Fata Morgana, *The Love for Three Oranges*, 1975–76; Petra, *A Little Night Music*, 1975–76; Servant of Buonafede, *Il Mondo della Luna (The World on the Moon)*, 1975–76

Zaieck, Rebecca: Mimi, *La Bohème*, 1974–75

Zara, Meridith: The Armchair, *L'Enfant et les Sortilèges (The Bewitched Child)*, 1955–56

Zarchy, Jennifer: Sister Dolcina, *Il Trittico (A Triptych)*, 1982–83

Zarr, Wayne: Count of Lerma, *Don Carlos*, 1960–61; Toni Reischmann, *Elegy for Young Lovers*, 1967–68

Zastrow, Joyce: Fiona MacLaren, *Brigadoon*, 1952–53; Kate, *Where's Charley?*, 1953–54

Zawisza, Philip: Bernardo, *West Side Story*, 1985–86; Stephano, *The Tempest*, 1985–86; Figaro, *Le Nozze di Figaro (The Marriage of Figaro)*, 1986–87; Micha, *The Bartered Bride*, 1986–87; Player, *Mass*, 1987–88; Recruiting Agent, *Candide*, 1987–88; Miguel de Cervantes / Don Quixote, *Man of La Mancha*, 1988–89; Papageno, *Die Zauberflöte (The Magic Flute)*, 1988–89; Player, *Mass*, 1988–89; Guglielmo, *Così fan tutte*, 1989–90; Peter, *Hänsel und Gretel*, 1989–90; Nick Shadow, *The Rake's Progress*, 1991–92

Zeffiro, William: Harold Hill, *The Music Man*, 1980–81

Zellmer, Peter: Rinuccio, *Il Trittico (A Triptych)*, 1972–73; First Man, *Kiss Me, Kate*, 1973–74; Giuseppe Palmieri, *The Gondoliers*, 1974–75; Goro, *Madama Butterfly*, 1975–76; Enoch Snow, *Carousel*, 1976–77; Welko, *Arabella*, 1972–73

Zetty, Claude: Customs Officer, *La Bohème*, 1949–50

Zhang, Jing: Mimi, *La Bohème*, 2004–05; Micaëla, *Carmen*, 2005–06; Cio-Cio San, *Madama Butterfly*, 2006–07; Antonia, *Les Contes d'Hoffmann (The Tales of Hoffmann)*, 2007–08

Zimmer, Christina: Maid, *A Wedding*, 2007–08

Zimmer, Robert: Big Deal, *West Side Story*, 1992–93

Zimmerman, Aaron: A-Rab, *West Side Story*, 1992–93

Zimmerman, Sara: Spirit, *Die Zauberflöte (The Magic Flute)*, 1965–66; Amazon, *The Boys from Syracuse*, 1968–69

Zini-Jones, Kendall: Candace, *A Wedding*, 2007–08; Stella, *Les Contes d'Hoffmann (The Tales of Hoffmann)*, 2007–08

Zoch, Janice: Peasant woman, *Boris Godunov*, 1966–67

Zook, Benjamin: Paco / A Muleteer, *Man of La Mancha*, 1985–86

Zorn, Elizabeth: Buddha, *The King and I*, 1957–58

Zorn, Lisa: Shepherd Figure in the Wallpaper, *L'Enfant et les Sortilèges (The Bewitched Child)*, 1984–85

Zungu, Thami: Colline, *La Bohème*, 1994–95; Speaker of the Temple, *Die Zauberflöte (The Magic Flute)*, 1994–95; Schlemil, *Les Contes d'Hoffmann (The Tales of Hoffmann)*, 1995–96

Zvetkova, Mariana: Voice of the Mother, *Les Contes d'Hoffmann (The Tales of Hoffmann)*, 1995–96; Ariadne/Prima Donna, *Ariadne auf Naxos*, 1996–97

Appendix 4

Opera Production Artists

Artist Name, Opera Name, Academic Year of Performance

CONDUCTOR

Agler, David: *A Wedding,* 2007–08

Altenbach, Andrew: *Così fan tutte,* 2005–06

Armenian, Raffi: *Die Entführung aus dem Serail (The Abduction from the Seraglio),* 1993–94

Baldner, Thomas: *Arlecchino,* 1979–80; *The Bartered Bride,* 1979–80; 1994–95; *Boris Godunov,* 1978–79; 1983–84; *Così fan tutte,* 1984–85; *The Crucible,* 1987–88; *The Cry of Clytaemnestra,* 1979–80; 1989–90; *Danton and Robespierre,* 1977–78; *The Darkened City,* 1978–79; *Das Rheingold,* 1983–84; *Der Fliegende Holländer (The Flying Dutchman),* 1978–79; 1985–86; *Die Entführung aus dem Serail (The Abduction from the Seraglio),* 1981–82; *Die Fledermaus (The Bat),* 1982–83; 1990–91; *Die lustige Witwe (The Merry Widow),* 1990–91; *Die lustigen Weiber von Windsor (The Merry Wives of Windsor),* 1981–82; *Die Teufel von Loudun (The Devils of Loudun),* 1992–93; *Die Zauberflöte (The Magic Flute),* 1977–78; 1988–89; *Don Giovanni,* 1996–97; *Francesca da Rimini,* 1989–90; *The Ghosts of Versailles,* 1996–97; *Gianni Schicchi,* 1993–94; *Hänsel und Gretel,* 1982–83; 1989–90; 2001–02; *Idomeneo,* 1998–99; *Il Barbiere di Siviglia (The Barber of Seville),* 1980–81; 1988–89; *Jakob Lenz,* 1981–82; *La Bohème,* 1979–80; 1989–90; *La Fille du régiment (The Daughter of the Regiment),* 1984–85; *Le Nozze di Figaro (The Marriage of Figaro),* 1980–81; 1986–87; 1997–98; *The Love for Three Oranges,* 1980–81; *Madama Butterfly,* 1987–88; *McTeague,* 1995–96; *Murder in the Cathedral,* 1984–85; *Peter Grimes,* 1994–95; *The Rake's Progress,* 1991–92; *Rigoletto,* 1992–93; *Suor Angelica (Sister Angelica),* 1999–2000; *The Tempest,* 1985–86; *Wozzeck,* 1990–91

Balkwill, Bryan: *Amahl and the Night Visitors,* 1990–91; *Il Barbiere di Siviglia (The Barber of Seville),* 1982–83; *Béatrice et Bénédict,* 1987–88; *Bluebeard's Castle,* 1988–89; *Carmen,* 1977–78; *Così fan tutte,* 1978–79; *The Dawn of the Poor King,* 1990–91; *Don Giovanni,* 1979–80; 1991–92; *Don Pasquale,* 1988–89; *The Excursions of Mr. Broucek,* 1981–82; *Falstaff,* 1976–77; 1992–93; *Francesca da Rimini,* 1989–90; *Gianni Schicchi,* 1988–89; *The Greek Passion,* 1980–81; *Il Trittico (A Triptych),* 1982–83; *La Cenerentola (Cinderella),* 1991–92; *La Bohème,* 1984–85; *La Finta Giardiniera,* 1990–91; *La Rondine (The Swallow),* 1989–90; *La Sonnambula (The Sleepwalker),* 1985–86; *La Traviata,* 1983–84; *The Legend of Tsar Saltan,* 1986–87; *L'Enfant et les Sortilèges (The Bewitched Child),* 1984–85; *Les Contes d'Hoffmann (The Tales of Hoffmann),* 1978–79; *L'Heure espagnole (The Spanish Hour),* 1984–85; *Manon,* 1979–80; *A Midsummer Night's Dream,* 1983–84; *The Night Before Christmas,* 1977–78; *Otello,* 1989–90; *Peter Grimes,* 1987–88; *Prince Igor,* 1980–81; *The Rake's Progress,* 1986–87; *Rigoletto,* 1980–81; *Susannah,* 1979–80; *The Turn of the Screw,* 1978–79; *Wozzeck,* 1981–82

Barrett, Michael: *Candide,* 2000–01; *Putting It Together,* 2002–03; *West Side Story,* 2002–03

Behr, Randall: *Dialogues des Carmélites,* 2004–05; *Il Turco in Italia (The Turk in Italy),* 2003–04

Binkley, Thomas: *L'Orfeo,* 1987–88; *Passion Play—Carmina Burana,* 1982–83

Biss, Paul: *Così fan tutte,* 1995–96; 2000–01; *Die Entführung aus dem Serail (The Abduction from the Seraglio),* 1987–88; *Die Zauberflöte (The Magic Flute),*

1994–95; *HMS Pinafore*, 1997–98; *La Cenerentola (Cinderella)*, 1998–99; *L'Elisir d'amore (The Elixir of Love)*, 1990–91; *Le Nozze di Figaro (The Marriage of Figaro)*, 1992–93; *Les Contes d'Hoffmann (The Tales of Hoffmann)*, 1988–89; *The Love for Three Oranges*, 1999–2000; *Madama Butterfly*, 1996–97; *The Rape of Lucretia*, 1999–2000; *Rigoletto*, 1986–87

Boncompagni, Elio: *Orphée aux enfers (Orpheus in the Underworld)*, 1992–93

Bradshaw, Richard: *Tamerlano*, 1984–85

Buswell, James: *Die Zauberflöte (The Magic Flute)*, 1982–83; *Don Giovanni*, 1985–86

Carciófolo, Jorge: *L'Elisir d'amore (The Elixir of Love)*, 2007–08

Colombo, Pierre: *Faust*, 1981–82

Contino, Fiora: *Un Ballo in Maschera (A Masked Ball)*, 1975–76; *Così fan tutte*, 1977–78; *Deidamia*, 1969–70; *Die Entführung aus dem Serail (The Abduction from the Seraglio)*, 1974–75; *Don Carlos*, 1972–73; *Faust*, 1971–72; *La Bohème*, 1970–71; *Le Nozze di Figaro (The Marriage of Figaro)*, 1973–74; *L'Incoronazione di Poppea (The Coronation of Poppea)*, 1967–68; *L'Italiana in Algeri (The Italian Girl in Algiers)*, 1968–69; *The Mother of Us All*, 1973–74; *Porgy and Bess*, 1976–77; *Rigoletto*, 1974–75; *Tosca*, 1977–78; *Il Trittico (A Triptych)*, 1972–73; *Il Trovatore*, 1967–68; *Werther*, 1975–76

Crutchfield, Will: *Le Nozze di Figaro (The Marriage of Figaro)*, 2007–08

Dalal, Zane: *Hänsel und Gretel*, 1989–90

de Leone, Carmon: *The Lion and Androcles*, 1972–73

Effron, David: *The Ballad of Baby Doe*, 2003–04; *The Bartered Bride*, 2001–02; *Carmen*, 1998–99; *Dialogues des Carmélites*, 1997–98; *Don Giovanni*, 2006–07; *Eugene Onegin*, 2004–05; *Falstaff*, 2003–04; *Giulio Cesare (Julius Caesar)*, 2002–03; *Jeppe*, 2002–03; *La Bohème*, 2007–08; *La Rondine (The Swallow)*, 2009–10; *La Traviata*, 2008–09; *Les Contes d'Hoffmann (The Tales of Hoffmann)*, 2007–08; *Madama Butterfly*, 2006–07; *Manon*, 2001–02; *A Midsummer Night's Dream*, 2005–06; *Our Town*, 2005–06; *Peter Grimes*, 2003–04; *Rigoletto*, 2000–01; *Roméo et Juliette*, 2005–06; *Wozzeck*, 1999–2000

Evans, Harold: *Eugene Onegin*, 1974–75

Fagen, Arthur: *L'Italiana in Algeri (The Italian Girl in Algiers)*, 2009–10

Fanning, Franklin: *Il Barbiere di Siviglia (The Barber of Seville)*, 1963–64; *Street Scene*, 1960–61

Fisher, Rob: *West Side Story*, 2009–10

Flatt, Adam: *Die Entführung aus dem Serail (The Abduction from the Seraglio)*, 1993–94

Fuerstner, Carl: *Die lustige Witwe (The Merry Widow)*, 1964–65; *Il Barbiere di Siviglia (The Barber of Seville)*, 1963–64; *La Fanciulla del West (The Girl of the Golden West)*, 1963–64

Gibson, Mark: *Carmen*, 2005–06; *Don Giovanni*, 2002–03; *Die Zauberflöte (The Magic Flute)*, 2009–10

Handt, Herbert: *I Pagliacci*, 1991–92

Harms, Gunnar: *Orphée aux enfers (Orpheus in the Underworld)*, 1992–93

Harrington, Jan: *Faust*, 1989–90; *Nixon in China*, 1994–95; *Orfeo ed Euridice*, 1992–93

Harvey, Raymond: *The Mikado*, 2006–07

Herz, Hermann: *Il Barbiere di Siviglia (The Barber of Seville)*, 1956–57

Hoffman, Ernst: *Amahl and the Night Visitors*, 1951–52; *The Bartered Bride*, 1955–56; *Billy Budd*, 1952–53; *Blossom Time*, 1952–53; *Boris Godunov*, 1953–54; *Brigadoon*, 1952–53; 1953–54; *Carousel*, 1952–53; *The Chocolate Soldier*, 1950–51; *Die Entführung aus dem Serail (The Abduction from the Seraglio)*, 1951–52; *Die lustige Witwe (The Merry Widow)*, 1949–50; *Die Zauberflöte (The Magic Flute)*, 1953–54; *Down in the Valley*, 1947–48; *Finian's Rainbow*, 1953–54; *The Firefly*, 1949–50; *Hin und Zurück (There and Back)*, 1947–48; *The Jumping Frog of Calaveras County*, 1949–50; *Kiss Me, Kate*, 1951–52; *La Bohème*, 1949–50; *Les Contes d'Hoffmann (The Tales of Hoffmann)*, 1947–48; *Lost in the Stars*, 1950–51; *The Mikado*, 1950–51; *The New Moon*, 1949–50; *On the Town*, 1951–52; *I Pagliacci*, 1954–55; *A Parfait for Irene*, 1951–52; *Parsifal*, 1948–49; 1949–50; 1950–51; 1952–53; 1953–54; 1954–55; *Rigoletto*, 1950–51; *The Ruby*, 1954–55; *Show Boat*, 1953–54; *Song of Norway*, 1951–52; *Street Scene*, 1949–50; *The Veil*, 1949–50; *Where's Charley?*, 1953–54; *Wonderful Town*, 1954–55

Itkin, David: *Peter Grimes*, 1987–88

Izquierdo, Juan Pablo: *Elegy for Young Lovers*, 1967–68; *Manon*, 1967–68; *The Rake's Progress*, 1968–69

Janas, Mark: *Bernstein on Broadway*, 1976–77; *Trouble in Tahiti*, 1976–77

Kaufmann, Walter: *A Hoosier Tale*, 1966–67

Kitsopoulos, Constantine: *The Most Happy Fella*, 2008–09

Kodjian, Varoujan: *La Traviata*, 1978–79

Kozma, Tibor: *Aida*, 1963–64; *Albert Herring*, 1957–58; *Amelia Goes to the Ball*, 1957–58; *Arabella*, 1972–73; *Ariadne auf Naxos*, 1969–70; *The Ballad of Baby Doe*, 1975–76; *The Bartered Bride*, 1967–68; *Così fan tutte*, 1956–57; 1970–71; *The Darkened City*, 1962–63; *Der Fliegende Holländer (The Flying Dutchman)*, 1962–63; *Dialogues des Carmélites*, 1965–66; *Die Kluge (The Clever Girl)*, 1959–60; *Die Meistersinger von Nürnberg (The Mastersingers of Nuremberg)*, 1961–62;

Die Zauberflöte (The Magic Flute), 1972–73; *Doktor Faust*, 1974–75; *Don Carlos*, 1960–61; 1961–62; 1972–73; *Don Giovanni*, 1958–59; 1964–65; 1971–72; *Eugene Onegin*, 1974–75; *The Fair at Sorochinsk*, 1963–64; *Falstaff*, 1971–72; *Gianni Schicchi*, 1964–65; *Heracles*, 1971–72; *Il Campanello di Notte (The Night Bell)*, 1963–64; *Il Mondo della Luna (The World on the Moon)*, 1975–76; *La Bohème*, 1957–58; 1962–63; *La Cenerentola (Cinderella)*, 1957–58; *La Pique Dame (The Queen of Spades)*, 1968–69; *La Rondine (The Swallow)*, 1959–60; *La Traviata*, 1960–61; *L'Elisir d'amore (The Elixir of Love)*, 1961–62; *Le Nozze di Figaro (The Marriage of Figaro)*, 1962–63; 1968–69; *Les Contes d'Hoffmann (The Tales of Hoffmann)*, 1973–74; *The Love for Three Oranges*, 1958–59; *Madama Butterfly*, 1958–59; *Mefistofele*, 1967–68; *A Midsummer Night's Dream*, 1961–62; *Oedipus Rex*, 1964–65; *Parsifal*, 1965–66; 1966–67; 1967–68; *Rigoletto*, 1959–60; 1966–67; *Roméo et Juliette*, 1966–67; *Salome*, 1970–71; *The Scarlet Letter*, 1960–61; 1961–62; *Simon Boccanegra*, 1964–65; *Tosca*, 1973–74; *Un Ballo in Maschera (A Masked Ball)*, 1969–70; *Vanessa*, 1974–75

Krachmalnik, Samuel: *Don Pasquale*, 1977–78

Krasnapolsky, Yuri: *Lucia di Lammermoor*, 1993–94

Larkin, Christopher: *Susannah*, 2000–01

Lee, Everett: *Idomeneo*, 1976–77

Lesniak, James: *Down in the Valley*, 1998–99

Lord, Stephen: *Rigoletto*, 2007–08

Lumpkin, William: *A View from the Bridge*, 2004–05

Mandeal, Cristian: *Madama Butterfly*, 1991–92

Mauceri, John: *Candide*, 1976–77

Morrow, Lynne: *Mass*, 1998–99

Mueller, Leo: *Carmen*, 1956–57

Nikolaev, Leonid V.: *Francesca da Rimini*, 1989–90

Noe, Kevin: *Arlecchino*, 2006–07; *Too Many Sopranos*, 2006–07

Palló, Imre: *Arabella*, 1998–99; *Ariadne auf Naxos*, 1996–97; *Die Entführung aus dem Serail (The Abduction from the Seraglio)*, 2003–04; *Die lustige Witwe (The Merry Widow)*, 1996–97; 2003–04; *Die Zauberflöte (The Magic Flute)*, 1998–99; *Don Pasquale*, 1997–98; 2003–04; *Falstaff*, 1997–98; *Faust*, 2000–01; *Hänsel und Gretel*, 1995–96; *Il Barbiere di Siviglia (The Barber of Seville)*, 1994–95; 2000–01; *Il Turco in Italia (The Turk in Italy)*, 1996–97; *La Bohème*, 1999–2000; 2004–05; *La Cenerentola (Cinderella)*, 2004–05; *La Périchole*, 1995–96; *La Traviata*, 1997–98; *L'Elisir d'amore (The Elixir of Love)*, 2000–01; *Le Nozze di Figaro (The Marriage of Figaro)*, 2001–02; *Les Contes d'Hoffmann (The Tales of Hoffmann)*, 2002–03; *Lucia di Lammermoor*, 2001–02; *Madama Butterfly*,

2001–02; *Manon*, 1993–94; *Orphée aux enfers (Orpheus in the Underworld)*, 1998–99; *Pelléas et Mélisande*, 1994–95; *The Rake's Progress*, 1999–2000; *Rigoletto*, 1995–96; *Tosca*, 2004–05; *Vanessa*, 1999–2000

Palomo, Lorenzo: *Tosca*, 1993–94

Porco, Robert: *The Bartered Bride*, 1986–87; *Candide*, 1987–88; 1993–94; *Carmen*, 1991–92; *Carmina Burana*, 1991–92; *Così fan tutte*, 1989–90; *Dialogues des Carmélites*, 1986–87; *Die Fledermaus (The Bat)*, 1985–86; 1996–97; *Die lustige Witwe (The Merry Widow)*, 1983–84; *Don Pasquale*, 1980–81; *Eugene Onegin*, 1988–89; 1997–98; *Jubilee*, 1991–92; *La Bohème*, 1994–95; *La Traviata*, 1990–91; *Les Contes d'Hoffmann (The Tales of Hoffmann)*, 1995–96; *A Little Night Music*, 1988–89; *Madama Butterfly*, 1981–82; *Man of La Mancha*, 1985–86; *Mass*, 1987–88; 1988–89; 1998–99; *Orphée aux enfers (Orpheus in the Underworld)*, 1984–85; *Soldier Boy, Soldier*, 1982–83; *Sweeney Todd*, 1983–84; *Tom Jones*, 1983–84; *West Side Story*, 1985–86; 1992–93

Priddy, John: *Boris Godunov*, 1983–84; *L'Elisir d'amore (The Elixir of Love)*, 1986–87

Rieling, Dale: *The Secret Garden*, 2003–04; *She Loves Me*, 2004–05

Ritchie, Stanley: *Agrippina*, 1995–96; *L'Orfeo*, 1987–88; *Tom Jones*, 1983–84

Satanowski, Robert: *The Scarlet Letter*, 1976–77

Saye, Theo: *The Tempest*, 1985–86

Schwartzkopf, Michael: *The King and I*, 1996–97; *Kiss Me, Kate*, 1998–99; *Man of La Mancha*, 1999–2000; *The Music Man*, 2001–02; *Oklahoma!*, 1997–98; *The Sound of Music*, 2000–01

Scott, William Fred: *Hänsel und Gretel*, 2006–07

Segal, Uriel: *Die Zauberflöte (The Magic Flute)*, 2004–05; *Il Barbiere di Siviglia (The Barber of Seville)*, 2005–06

Seibel, Klauspeter: *Arabella*, 2006–07

Sidlin, Murry: *The Love for Three Oranges*, 1993–94

Slon, Michael: *Mass*, 1998–99

Smith, Henry Charles: *Love on Trial (La Pietra del Paragone)*, 1969–70

Smith, Steven: *Susannah*, 2007–08

Solomon, Izler: *Turandot*, 1964–65

St. Leger, Frank: *Ruddigore (The Witch's Curse)*, 1962–63

Stahl, Edwin: *Manon Lescaut*, 1959–60; *The Most Happy Fella*, 1959–60

Stoll, Robert E.: *110 in the Shade*, 1967–68; 1968–69; *1600 Pennsylvania Avenue*, 1992–93; *The Boys from Syracuse*, 1968–69; *Brigadoon*, 1961–62; *Camelot*, 1968–69; 1969–70; 1986–87; *Candide*, 1983–84; *Canterbury Tales*, 1978–79; *Carousel*, 1970–71; 1976–77; 1993–94; *Company*, 1990–91; *Fiddler on the Roof*,

1972–73; 1994–95; *Finian's Rainbow*, 1969–70; *The Gondoliers*, 1974–75; *Hello, Dolly!*, 1991–92; *Kismet*, 1989–90; *Kiss Me, Kate*, 1973–74; *A Little Night Music*, 1975–76; *Man of La Mancha*, 1988–89; *The Most Happy Fella*, 1982–83; *The Music Man*, 1980–81; *My Fair Lady*, 1979–80; *Naughty Marietta*, 1977–78; *Of Thee I Sing*, 1987–88; *Oklahoma!*, 1981–82; *Peter Grimes*, 1977–78; *Show Boat*, 1984–85; *South Pacific*, 1995–96

Taylor, Ted: *Die Fledermaus (The Bat)*, 2002–03; *Little Women*, 2001–02

Tellez, Carmen: *Eugene Onegin*, 1988–89

Vacano, Wolfgang: *Albert Herring*, 1966–67; 1967–68; *Annie Get Your Gun*, 1956–57; *Ariadne auf Naxos*, 1954–55; *Boris Godunov*, 1964–65; 1966–67; *Candide*, 1957–58; *Capriccio*, 1958–59; *Carmen*, 1962–63; 1965–66; 1973–74; *Cavalleria Rusticana*, 1957–58; 1966–67; *Così fan tutte*, 1963–64; *Der Rosenkavalier*, 1965–66; *Die Entführung aus dem Serail (The Abduction from the Seraglio)*, 1961–62; 1966–67; *Die Fledermaus (The Bat)*, 1954–55; 1962–63; *Die lustigen Weiber von Windsor (The Merry Wives of Windsor)*, 1958–59; *Die Meistersinger von Nürnberg (The Mastersingers of Nuremberg)*, 1968–69; *Die Walküre*, 1969–70; 1971–72; *Die Zauberflöte (The Magic Flute)*, 1960–61; 1965–66; *Don Pasquale*, 1957–58; 1965–66; *Eugene Onegin*, 1974–75; *Falstaff*, 1956–57; *Faust*, 1955–56; *Fidelio*, 1970–71; *Hänsel und Gretel*, 1956–57; *Il Barbiere di Siviglia (The Barber of Seville)*, 1971–72; *Il Tabarro (The Cloak)*, 1955–56; *Il Trittico (A Triptych)*, 1969–70; *I Pagliacci*, 1966–67; *Jenůfa*, 1972–73; *La Bohème*, 1974–75; *La Fanciulla del West (The Girl of the Golden West)*, 1963–64; *La Forza del Destino (The Force of Destiny)*, 1962–63; *The King and I*, 1957–58; *The Land Between the Rivers*, 1955–56; *La Traviata*, 1954–55; 1968–69; *Le Coq d'or (The Golden Cockerel)*, 1960–61; *L'Enfant et les Sortilèges (The Bewitched Child)*, 1955–56; *Le Nozze di Figaro (The Marriage of Figaro)*, 1955–56; *Les Contes d'Hoffmann (The Tales of Hoffmann)*, 1959–60; 1973–74; *L'Heure espagnole (The Spanish Hour)*, 1959–60; *The Love for Three Oranges*, 1975–76; *Lucia di Lammermoor*, 1963–64; 1970–71; *Macbeth*, 1965–66; *Madama Butterfly*, 1964–65; 1975–76; 1976–77; *Manon Lescaut*, 1959–60; 1970–71; *The Most Happy Fella*, 1959–60; *Oklahoma!*, 1954–55; *Parsifal*, 1955–56; 1956–57; 1957–58; 1958–59; 1959–60; 1960–61; 1961–62; 1962–63; 1963–64; 1964–65; 1968–69; 1972–73; 1975–76; *Pelléas et Mélisande*, 1976–77; *Peter Grimes*, 1963–64; *Quattro rusteghi (The Four Ruffians)*, 1966–67; *Roberta*, 1958–59; *South Pacific*, 1956–57; *Street Scene*, 1960–61; *Susannah*, 1976–77; *Tosca*, 1957–58; 1961–62; 1969–70; *Un Ballo in Maschera (A Masked Ball)*, 1958–59; *Werther*, 1961–62; *Wozzeck*, 1973–74

Webb, Charles H., Jr.: *Andrea Chénier*, 1967–68; *The Ballad of Baby Doe*, 1982–83; *Die lustige Witwe (The Merry Widow)*, 1965–66; *Kismet*, 1963–64; *Porgy and Bess*, 1979–80

Wedow, Gary Thor: *Giulio Cesare (Julius Caesar)*, 2008–09

White, John Reeves: *Myshkin*, 1972–73

White, Steven: *La Traviata*, 2002–03

Wood, Robert: *HMS Pinafore*, 2005–06; *The Love for Three Oranges (Lyubov k Tryom Apelsinam)*, 2008–09

Zollman, Ronald: *Cendrillon*, 2008–09; *Manon*, 2006–07; *Roméo et Juliette*, 2009–10

STAGE DIRECTOR

Alexander, Carlos: *The Excursions of Mr. Broucek*, 1981–82

Alexander, Chris: *Les Contes d'Hoffmann (The Tales of Hoffmann)*, 2007–08

Allen, Ross: *110 in the Shade*, 1967–68; 1968–69; *Albert Herring*, 1957–58; *Amelia Goes to the Ball*, 1957–58; *Andrea Chénier*, 1967–68; *Annie Get Your Gun*, 1956–57; *Arabella*, 1972–73; *Ariadne auf Naxos*, 1969–70; *The Ballad of Baby Doe*, 1975–76; 1982–83; *The Bartered Bride*, 1979–80; 1986–87; *Boris Godunov*, 1953–54; 1964–65; 1966–67; 1978–79; *The Boys from Syracuse*, 1968–69; *Brigadoon*, 1953–54; 1961–62; *Camelot*, 1968–69; 1969–70; *Candide*, 1957–58; 1983–84; 1987–88; *Canterbury Tales*, 1978–79; *Capriccio*, 1958–59; *Carmen*, 1962–63; 1973–74; 1977–78; *Così fan tutte*, 1956–57; 1977–78; 1978–79; *The Crucible*, 1987–88; *Das Rheingold*, 1983–84; *Deidamia*, 1969–70; *Dialogues des Carmélites*, 1965–66; 1986–87; *Der Fliegende Holländer (The Flying Dutchman)*, 1985–86; *Der Rosenkavalier*, 1965–66; *Die Entführung aus dem Serail (The Abduction from the Seraglio)*, 1961–62; 1974–75; 1987–88; *Die Fledermaus (The Bat)*, 1962–63; 1982–83; 1985–86; *Die lustige Witwe (The Merry Widow)*, 1964–65; 1965–66; 1983–84; *Die lustigen Weiber von Windsor (The Merry Wives of Windsor)*, 1981–82; *Die Meistersinger von Nürnberg (The Mastersingers of Nuremberg)*, 1961–62; *Die Zauberflöte (The Magic Flute)*, 1953–54; 1960–61; 1965–66; 1982–83; *Don Carlos*, 1960–61; 1961–62; 1972–73; *Don Giovanni*, 1958–59; 1971–72; *Don Pasquale*, 1977–78; *Elegy for Young Lovers*, 1967–68; *The Fair at Sorochinsk*, 1963–64; *Falstaff*, 1971–72; 1976–77; *The Fantasticks*, 1963–64; *Faust*, 1955–56; 1971–72; 1981–82; *Fidelio*, 1970–71; *Finian's Rainbow*, 1953–54; *Gianni Schicchi*, 1964–65; *The Gondoliers*, 1974–75; *The Greek Passion*, 1980–81; *Hänsel und Gretel*, 1956–57; *Heracles*, 1971–72; *A Hoosier Tale*, 1966–67; *Idomeneo*, 1976–77; *Il Barbiere di Siviglia (The Barber of*

Seville), 1963–64; 1980–81; *Il Campanello di Notte (The Night Bell)*, 1963–64; *Il Mondo della Luna (The World on the Moon)*, 1975–76; *Il Tabarro (The Cloak)*, 1955–56; *I Pagliacci*, 1966–67; *Il Trittico (A Triptych)*, 1969–70; 1972–73; 1982–83; *Il Trovatore*, 1967–68; *Jakob Lenz*, 1981–82; *Kismet*, 1963–64; *Kiss Me, Kate*, 1973–74; *La Bohème*, 1970–71; *La Cenerentola (Cinderella)*, 1957–58; *La Fanciulla del West (The Girl of the Golden West)*, 1963–64; *La Fille du régiment (The Daughter of the Regiment)*, 1984–85; *La Pique Dame (The Queen of Spades)*, 1968–69; *La Traviata*, 1954–55; *La Rondine (The Swallow)*, 1959–60; *Le Coq d'or (The Golden Cockerel)*, 1960–61; *L'Elisir d'amore (The Elixir of Love)*, 1961–62; 1986–87; *L'Enfant et les Sortilèges (The Bewitched Child)*, 1955–56; 1984–85; *Le Nozze di Figaro (The Marriage of Figaro)*, 1962–63; *Les Contes d'Hoffmann (The Tales of Hoffmann)*, 1959–60; *L'Heure espagnole (The Spanish Hour)*, 1984–85; *L'Incoronazione di Poppea (The Coronation of Poppea)*, 1967–68; *The Lion and Androcles*, 1972–73; *L'Italiana in Algeri (The Italian Girl in Algiers)*, 1968–69; *A Little Night Music*, 1975–76; *The Love for Three Oranges*, 1975–76; 1980–81; *Love on Trial (La Pietra del Paragone)*, 1969–70; *Lucia di Lammermoor*, 1963–64; *Madama Butterfly*, 1958–59; 1964–65; 1981–82; *Man of La Mancha*, 1985–86; *Manon*, 1979–80; *Manon Lescaut*, 1959–60; 1970–71; *Mefistofele*, 1967–68; *The Most Happy Fella*, 1959–60; 1982–83; *The Mother of Us All*, 1973–74; *My Fair Lady*, 1979–80; *Myshkin*, 1972–73; *The Night Before Christmas*, 1977–78; *Oklahoma!*, 1954–55; *Orphée aux enfers (Orpheus in the Underworld)*, 1984–85; *Parsifal*, 1953–54; 1954–55; 1955–56; 1956–57; 1957–58; 1958–59; 1959–60; *Passion Play—Carmina Burana*, 1982–83; *Peter Grimes*, 1963–64; *Porgy and Bess*, 1976–77; 1979–80; *Quattro rusteghi (The Four Ruffians)*, 1966–67; *The Rake's Progress*, 1968–69; 1986–87; *Rigoletto*, 1966–67; 1974–75; 1980–81; *Roberta*, 1958–59; *Roméo et Juliette*, 1966–67; *Ruddigore (The Witch's Curse)*, 1962–63; *Salome*, 1970–71; *Show Boat*, 1953–54; *South Pacific*, 1956–57; *Street Scene*, 1960–61; *Susannah*, 1976–77; 1979–80; *The Tempest*, 1985–86; *Tom Jones*, 1983–84; *The Turn of the Screw*, 1978–79; *Vanessa*, 1974–75; *Werther*, 1961–62; *Where's Charley?*, 1953–54; *Wonderful Town*, 1954–55; *Wozzeck*, 1973–74; 1981–82

Alley, Laura: *Carmen*, 1998–99; *Hänsel und Gretel*, 2006–07

Atherton, James: *La Bohème*, 1984–85; *Don Giovanni*, 1985–86

Bergasse, Joshua: *West Side Story*, 2009–10

Binkley, Thomas: *L'Orfeo*, 1987–88

Brody, Alan: *Soldier Boy, Soldier*, 1982–83

Busch, Hans: *Aida*, 1963–64; *Albert Herring*, 1966–67; 1967–68; *Amahl and the Night Visitors*, 1951–52; *Ariadne auf Naxos*, 1954–55; *The Bartered Bride*, 1955–56; 1967–68; *Billy Budd*, 1952–53; *Carmen*, 1965–66; *Carousel*, 1970–71; 1976–77; *Cavalleria Rusticana*, 1966–67; *Les Contes d'Hoffmann (The Tales of Hoffmann)*, 1947–48; 1973–74; 1978–79; *Così fan tutte*, 1963–64; 1970–71; *Danton and Robespierre*, 1977–78; *The Darkened City*, 1962–63; 1978–79; *Der Fliegende Holländer (The Flying Dutchman)*, 1962–63; 1978–79; *Die Entführung aus dem Serail (The Abduction from the Seraglio)*, 1951–52; 1966–67; *Die Fledermaus (The Bat)*, 1954–55; *Die lustigen Weiber von Windsor (The Merry Wives of Windsor)*, 1958–59; *Die Walküre*, 1969–70; 1971–72; *Die Zauberflöte (The Magic Flute)*, 1972–73; 1977–78; *Doktor Faust*, 1974–75; *Don Giovanni*, 1964–65; *Don Pasquale*, 1957–58; 1965–66; *Down in the Valley*, 1947–48; *Eugene Onegin*, 1974–75; *Falstaff*, 1956–57; *Fiddler on the Roof*, 1972–73; *Finian's Rainbow*, 1969–70; *Hin und Zurück (There and Back)*, 1947–48; *Il Barbiere di Siviglia (The Barber of Seville)*, 1956–57; 1971–72; *I Pagliacci*, 1954–55; *Jenůfa*, 1972–73; *The Jumping Frog of Calaveras County*, 1949–50; *The King and I*, 1957–58; *Die Kluge (The Clever Girl)*, 1959–60; *La Bohème*, 1949–50; 1962–63; 1974–75; 1989–90; *La Forza del Destino (The Force of Destiny)*, 1962–63; *La Traviata*, 1960–61; 1968–69; *Le Nozze di Figaro (The Marriage of Figaro)*, 1955–56; 1968–69; 1973–74; *The Land Between the Rivers*, 1955–56; *L'Heure espagnole (The Spanish Hour)*, 1959–60; *The Love for Three Oranges*, 1958–59; *Macbeth*, 1965–66; *Madama Butterfly*, 1975–76; 1976–77; *Manon*, 1967–68; *A Midsummer Night's Dream*, 1961–62; *Naughty Marietta*, 1977–78; *Oedipus Rex*, 1964–65; *A Parfait for Irene*, 1951–52; *Parsifal*, 1948–49; 1949–50; 1950–51; 1952–53; 1960–61; 1961–62; 1962–63; 1963–64; 1964–65; 1965–66; 1966–67; 1967–68; 1968–69; 1972–73; 1975–76; *Pelléas et Mélisande*, 1976–77; *Peter Grimes*, 1977–78; *Rigoletto*, 1950–51; *Rigoletto*, 1959–60; *The Ruby*, 1954–55; *The Scarlet Letter*, 1960–61; 1961–62; 1976–77; *Simon Boccanegra*, 1964–65; *Tosca*, 1961–62; 1969–70; 1973–74; 1977–78; *Turandot*, 1964–65; *Un Ballo in Maschera (A Masked Ball)*, 1958–59; 1969–70; 1975–76; *The Veil*, 1949–50

Capobianco, Tito: *La Bohème*, 2007–08; *Die lustige Witwe (The Merry Widow)*, 2003–04; *Don Giovanni*, 2006–07; *La Traviata*, 2008–09; *Lucia di Lammermoor*, 2001–02, 2009–10; *Rigoletto*, 2000–01

Carra, Lawrence: *The Chocolate Soldier*, 1950–51; *Lost in the Stars*, 1950–51; *The Mikado*, 1950–51

Cazan, Ken: *Il Turco in Italia (The Turk in Italy)*, 2003–04

Cesbron, Jacques: *Orfeo ed Euridice*, 1992–93

Clark, Mark Ross: *Dialogues des Carmélites*, 1997–98; *Die Zauberflöte (The Magic Flute)*, 1998–99; *Down in the Valley*, 1998–99; *Il Barbiere di Siviglia (The Barber* of Seville), 2000–01; *La Bohème*, 1999–2000; *La Traviata*, 1997–98; 2002–03; *Madama Butterfly*, 2001–02

Danner, Dorothy: *Tosca*, 2004–05

Diamond, Tom: *Giulio Cesare (Julius Caesar)*, 2008–09

DiFonzo, Michael: *Carousel*, 1993–94; *West Side Story*, 1992–93

Eddleman, Jack: *Candide*, 1993–94; *Don Pasquale*, 1980–81; *Fiddler on the Roof*, 1994–95; *The King and I*, 1996–97; *Mass*, 1987–88; 1988–89; 1998–99; *The Music Man*, 1980–81; *Oklahoma!*, 1981–82; 1997–98; *West Side Story*, 1985–86

Ehrman, Michael: *The Ballad of Baby Doe*, 2003–04; *Faust*, 1989–90; *Le Nozze di Figaro (The Marriage of Figaro)*, 2007–08; *Manon*, 2006–07; *Roméo et Juliette*, 2005–06, 2009–10; *Susannah*, 2007–08

Fellbom, Claes: *Jeppe*, 2002–03

Field, Jonathon: *Carmen*, 2005–06

Ganakas, Greg: *The Secret Garden*, 2003–04

Gately, David: *Gianni Schicchi*, 1993–94; *Manon*, 2001–02

Girard, Dale Anthony: *Faust*, 2000–01

Gracis, Patrizia: *La Périchole*, 1995–96

Graham, Colin: *A Midsummer Night's Dream*, 2005–06; *Peter Grimes*, 2003–04

Grundheber, Franz: *Wozzeck*, 1999–2000

Guttman, Irving: *La Cenerentola (Cinderella)*, 1998–99

Haagensen, Erik: *1600 Pennsylvania Avenue*, 1992–93

Hadjimichev, Mihail: *Die Meistersinger von Nürnberg (The Mastersingers of Nuremberg)*, 1968–69

Hawthorne, Raymond: *Madama Butterfly*, 1996–97

Holliday, Thomas: *Die lustige Witwe (The Merry Widow)*, 1996–97; *South Pacific*, 1995–96

Hudson, Chuck: *Cendrillon*, 2008–09

Igesz, Bodo: *Don Giovanni*, 1979–80; *Eugene Onegin*, 1997–98; *La Bohème*, 1979–80; *Le Nozze di Figaro (The Marriage of Figaro)*, 1980–81; *Prince Igor*, 1980–81

Kellner, Herbert: *Così fan tutte*, 2000–01

Kullman, Charles: *Cavalleria Rusticana*, 1957–58; *La Bohème*, 1957–58; *Tosca*, 1957–58

LaCosse, Steven: *Carousel*, 1993–94

Lesenger, Jay: *The Bartered Bride*, 2001–02

Liotta, Vincent: *Arabella*, 1998–99; 2006–07; *Ariadne auf Naxos*, 1996–97; *Arlecchino*, 2006–07; *Camelot*, 1986–87; *Candide*, 2000–01; *Così fan tutte*, 1995–96; 2005–06; *Die Zauberflöte (The Magic Flute)*, 2004–05; *Don Giovanni*, 1996–97; 2002–03; *Don Pasquale*, 1997–98; 2003–04; *Falstaff*, 1997–98;

2003–04; *The Ghosts of Versailles*, 1996–97; *Gianni Schicchi*, 1999–2000; *Hänsel und Gretel*, 2001–02; *HMS Pinafore*, 1997–98; 2005–06; *Idomeneo*, 1998–99; *Il Turco in Italia (The Turk in Italy)*, 1996–97; *Kiss Me, Kate*, 1998–99; *La Cenerentola (Cinderella)*, 2004–05; *La Rondine (The Swallow)*, 2009–10; *L'Elisir d'amore (The Elixir of Love)*, 2000–01; *Le Nozze di Figaro (The Marriage of Figaro)*, 1997–98; 2001–02; *Les Contes d'Hoffmann (The Tales of Hoffmann)*, 1995–96; 2002–03; *L'Italiana in Algeri (The Italian Girl in Algiers)*, 2009–10; *Little Women*, 2001–02; *The Love for Three Oranges*, 1999–2000; *Man of La Mancha*, 1999–2000; *McTeague*, 1995–96; *Die lustigen Weiber von Windsor (The Merry Wives of Windsor)*, 2008–09; *The Mikado*, 2006–07; *The Most Happy Fella*, 2008–09; *The Music Man*, 2001–02; *Of Thee I Sing*, 1987–88; *Orphée aux enfers (Orpheus in the Underworld)*, 1998–99; *Our Town*, 2005–06; *Putting It Together*, 2002–03; *The Rake's Progress*, 1999–2000; *The Rape of Lucretia*, 1999–2000; *Rigoletto*, 1995–96; 2007–08; *She Loves Me*, 2004–05; *Show Boat*, 1984–85; *The Sound of Music*, 2000–01; *Suor Angelica (Sister Angelica)*, 1999–2000; *Susannah*, 2000–01; *Sweeney Todd*, 1983–84; *Too Many Sopranos*, 2006–07; *Vanessa*, 1999–2000; *A View from the Bridge*, 2004–05; *A Wedding*, 2007–08

Lockwood, Carolyn: *Lucia di Lammermoor*, 1970–71

Lucas, James: *Amahl and the Night Visitors*, 1990–91; *The Bartered Bride*, 1994–95; *Béatrice et Bénédict*, 1987–88; *Bluebeard's Castle*, 1988–89; *Carmen*, 1991–92; *Company*, 1990–91; *Così fan tutte*, 1989–90; *The Cry of Clytaemnestra*, 1989–90; *The Dawn of the Poor King*, 1990–91; *Die Entführung aus dem Serail (The Abduction from the Seraglio)*, 1993–94; *Die Fledermaus (The Bat)*, 1990–91; *Die Teufel von Loudun (The Devils of Loudun)*, 1992–93; *Die Zauberflöte (The Magic Flute)*, 1988–89; *Don Pasquale*, 1988–89; *Falstaff*, 1992–93; *Francesca da Rimini*, 1989–90; *Gianni Schicchi*, 1988–89; *Hello, Dolly!*, 1991–92; *I Pagliacci*, 1991–92; *Jubilee*, 1991–92; *Kismet*, 1989–90; *La Cenerentola (Cinderella)*, 1991–92; *La Finta Giardiniera*, 1990–91; *La Rondine (The Swallow)*, 1989–90; *La Sonnambula (The Sleepwalker)*, 1985–86; *La Traviata*, 1990–91; *Le Nozze di Figaro (The Marriage of Figaro)*, 1986–87; *Les Contes d'Hoffmann (The Tales of Hoffmann)*, 1988–89; *A Little Night Music*, 1988–89; *The Love for Three Oranges*, 1993–94; *Madama Butterfly*, 1987–88; 1991–92; *Man of La Mancha*, 1988–89; *Manon*, 1993–94; *Orphée aux enfers (Orpheus in the Underworld)*, 1992–93; *Otello*, 1989–90; *Peter Grimes*, 1987–88; *Rigoletto*, 1992–93; *Tosca*, 1993–94; *Wozzeck*, 1990–91

Maizel, Yefim: *Eugene Onegin*, 2004–05

Major, Joshua: *Die lustige Witwe (The Merry Widow)*, 1990–91

McKneely, Joey: *West Side Story*, 2002–03

Merrill, Nathaniel: *La Traviata,* 1978–79

Middleton, James: *Agrippina,* 1995–96

Montel, Michael: *La Bohème,* 1994–95

Moody, Richard: *Die lustige Witwe (The Merry Widow),* 1949–50

Moore, Aubrey: *Blossom Time,* 1952–53; *Brigadoon,* 1952–53; *Carousel,* 1952–53

Morelock, David: *Hänsel und Gretel,* 1995–96; *Il Barbiere di Siviglia (The Barber of Seville),* 1988–89; *L'Elisir d'amore (The Elixir of Love),* 1990–91; *Nixon in China,* 1994–95; *Pelléas et Mélisande,* 1994–95; *Peter Grimes,* 1994–95; *Rigoletto,* 1986–87; *Werther,* 1975–76

Muni, Nicholas: *The Love for Three Oranges (Lyubov k Tryom Apelsinam),* 2008–09; *Madama Butterfly,* 2006–07

Pallo, Constanze: *Il Barbiere di Siviglia (The Barber of Seville),* 1994–95

Pfeiffer, David: *Die Zauberflöte (The Magic Flute),* 1994–95

Pollock, Michael: *Carmen,* 1956–57

Porter, Andrew: *Die Entführung aus dem Serail (The Abduction from the Seraglio),* 1981–82; *The Rake's Progress,* 1991–92; *Tamerlano,* 1984–85

Rossi–Lemeni, Nicola: *Boris Godunov,* 1983–84; *Eugene Onegin,* 1988–89; *Il Barbiere di Siviglia (The Barber of Seville),* 1982–83; *The Legend of Tsar Saltan,* 1986–87; *Murder in the Cathedral,* 1984–85

Röthlisberger, Max: *Arlecchino,* 1979–80; *The Cry of Clytaemnestra,* 1979–80; *Doktor Faust,* 1974–75; *Hänsel und Gretel,* 1982–83; 1989–90; *A Midsummer Night's Dream,* 1983–84

Russell, Walter S.: *The Firefly,* 1949–50; *The New Moon,* 1949–50; *Street Scene,* 1949–50

Shain, Carl: *Kiss Me, Kate,* 1951–52; *On the Town,* 1951–52; *Song of Norway,* 1951–52

Sinclair, Andrew: *L'Elisir d'amore (The Elixir of Love),* 2007–08

Steingraber, Thor: *Die Fledermaus (The Bat),* 2002–03

Strasfogel, Ian: *Così fan tutte,* 1984–85; *La Traviata,* 1983–84

Sundine, Stephanie: *La Bohème,* 2004–05

Thompson, Robin: *Bernstein on Broadway,* 1976–77; *Trouble in Tahiti,* 1976–77

Thompson, Tazewell: *Dialogues des Carmélites,* 2004–05

Tozzi, Giorgio: *Don Giovanni,* 1991–92; *Le Nozze di Figaro (The Marriage of Figaro),* 1992–93; *Lucia di Lammermoor,* 1993–94

Verzatt, Marc: *Die Fledermaus (The Bat),* 1996–97

Vizioli, Stefano: *Die Entführung aus dem Serail (The Abduction from the Seraglio),* 2003–04; *Giulio Cesare (Julius Caesar),* 2002–03

Walker Castaldo, Kay: *Il Barbiere di Siviglia (The Barber of Seville),* 2005–06

Zhdanov, Vladimir F.: *Francesca da Rimini,* 1989–90

Zvulun, Tomer: *Die Zauberflöte (The Magic Flute),* 2009–10

CHOREOGRAPHER

Adam, Jennifer: *Roméo et Juliette,* 2005–06

Alley, Laura: *Hänsel und Gretel,* 2006–07

Bergasse, Joshua: *The Most Happy Fella,* 2008–09; *West Side Story,* 2009–10

Beriozoff, Nicolas: *The Bartered Bride,* 1979–80; *Manon,* 1979–80; *Prince Igor,* 1980–81

Bonnefoux, Jean-Pierre: *The Bartered Bride,* 1986–87; *Camelot,* 1986–87; *Die Fledermaus (The Bat),* 1985–86; *Eugene Onegin,* 1988–89; *La Rondine (The Swallow),* 1989–90; *La Sonnambula (The Sleepwalker),* 1985–86; *Nixon in China,* 1994–95; *Rigoletto,* 1986–87, 1995–96; *The Tempest,* 1985–86

Buzzell, Diane: *Die Fledermaus (The Bat),* 2002–03; *The Music Man,* 2001–02

Cesbron, Jacques: *Amahl and the Night Visitors,* 1990–91; *The Bartered Bride,* 1994–95; 2001–02; *Carmen,* 1998–99; *Carmina Burana,* 1991–92; *Carousel,* 1993–94; *The Dawn of the Poor King,* 1990–91; *Die Fledermaus (The Bat),* 1990–91; *Die lustige Witwe (The Merry Widow),* 1990–91; *Eugene Onegin,* 1997–98; *Faust,* 1989–90; *Kismet,* 1989–90; *La Traviata,* 1990–91; *L'Elisir d'amore (The Elixir of Love),* 1990–91; *L'Orfeo,* 1987–88; *Man of La Mancha,* 1988–89; 1999–2000; *Orfeo ed Euridice,* 1992–93; *Rigoletto,* 1992–93; 2000–01

Clifford, Jacqueline: *Mefistofele,* 1967–68

Cope, Garrett: *Die lustige Witwe (The Merry Widow),* 1949–50

Crane, Dean: *Kiss Me, Kate,* 1973–74

Davies, Dudley: *Die Fledermaus (The Bat),* 1982–83; *Die lustige Witwe (The Merry Widow),* 1983–84; *The Most Happy Fella,* 1982–83

de Anguera, Marguerite: *Blossom Time,* 1952–53; *Boris Godunov,* 1953–54; *Brigadoon,* 1952–53; *Carousel,* 1952–53; *Finian's Rainbow,* 1953–54; *Parsifal,* 1952–53; 1953–54; *Show Boat,* 1953–54; *Where's Charley?,* 1953–54

Derby, Kenneth: *A Midsummer Night's Dream,* 1983–84

DiFonzo, Michael: *West Side Story,* 1992–93

Eddleman, Jack: *Candide,* 1993–94; *Fiddler on the Roof,* 1994–95; *The King and I,* 1996–97; *Mass,* 1998–99; *The Music Man,* 1980–81; *Oklahoma!,* 1981–82; 1997–98; *West Side Story,* 1985–86

Faesi, Chris: *Giulio Cesare (Julius Caesar),* 2008–09

Foss-Pittman, Kathryn: *Carousel,* 1993–94

Fox, Jane: *Parsifal,* 1948–49; 1949–50; 1950–51; 1951–52; *Rigoletto,* 1950–51

Ganakas, Greg: *The Secret Garden*, 2003–04

Gavers, Mattlyn: *I Pagliacci*, 1966–67; *Macbeth*, 1965–66; *Rigoletto*, 1966–67; *Roméo et Juliette*, 1966–67

Gelfer, Steven: *Finian's Rainbow*, 1969–70

Hall, Stephanie: *Mass*, 1987–88; 1988–89; 1998–99

Hamilton, Peter: *Kiss Me, Kate*, 1951–52; *On the Town*, 1951–52; *Song of Norway*, 1951–52

Hancock, Jory: *Boris Godunov*, 1983–84; *Camelot*, 1986–87

Leggett, Paula: *Show Boat*, 1984–85

Lesenger, Jay: *Eugene Onegin*, 1974–75

Liotta, Vincent: *Arlecchino*, 2006–07; *HMS Pinafore*, 2005–06; *La Cenerentola (Cinderella)*, 2004–05; *She Loves Me*, 2004–05; *Too Many Sopranos*, 2006–07

Lowe, Melissa: *Orphée aux enfers (Orpheus in the Underworld)*, 1984–85

Mann, Fred C.: *Carousel*, 1970–71

McKneely, Joey: *West Side Story*, 2002–03

Melville, Kenneth: *Eugene Onegin*, 1974–75; *Faust*, 1971–72; *Le Nozze di Figaro (The Marriage of Figaro)*, 1973–74

Oukhtomsky, Wladimir: *Faust*, 1971–72

Pagels, Jurgen: *Carmen*, 1973–74; 1977–78; *Don Giovanni*, 1971–72

Palla, Joseph: *Die lustige Witwe (The Merry Widow)*, 1996–97; *Orphée aux enfers (Orpheus in the Underworld)*, 1998–99

Paskevska, Anna: *My Fair Lady*, 1979–80; *Naughty Marietta*, 1977–78; *Peter Grimes*, 1977–78

Peck, Leslie: *Faust*, 2000–01; *Hänsel und Gretel*, 2001–02

Peterman, Julia: *Carmen*, 2005–06; *Il Barbiere di Siviglia (The Barber of Seville)*, 2005–06

Phillips, Bary: *Bernstein on Broadway*, 1976–77; *Trouble in Tahiti*, 1976–77

Pinney, George: *Jubilee*, 1991–92; *The Sound of Music*, 2000–01

Reed, Gilbert: *Aida*, 1963–64; *Annie Get Your Gun*, 1956–57; *The Bartered Bride*, 1967–68; *Brigadoon*, 1961–62; *Capriccio*, 1958–59; *Carmen*, 1956–57; 1965–66; *Die lustige Witwe (The Merry Widow)*, 1965–66; *Die lustigen Weiber von Windsor (The Merry Wives of Windsor)*, 1958–59; *Don Giovanni*, 1958–59; *Falstaff*, 1956–57; *Hänsel und Gretel*, 1956–57; *The King and I*, 1957–58; *Kismet*, 1963–64; *La Forza del Destino (The Force of Destiny)*, 1962–63; *La Traviata*, 1960–61; *La Cenerentola (Cinderella)*, 1957–58; *Le Coq d'or (The Golden Cockerel)*, 1960–61; *Les Contes d'Hoffmann (The Tales of Hoffmann)*, 1959–60; *The Love for Three Oranges*, 1958–59; *Manon*, 1967–68; *The Most Happy Fella*, 1959–60; *Parsifal*, 1957–58; 1958–59; *Rigoletto*, 1959–60; *Roberta*, 1958–59;

South Pacific, 1956–57; *Street Scene*, 1960–61; *Un Ballo in Maschera (A Masked Ball)*, 1958–59

Russell, Colin: *Carousel*, 1976–77

Schwartz, Grace: *Le Nozze di Figaro (The Marriage of Figaro)*, 2007–08

Sorah, Jan: *Show Boat*, 1984–85

Sparrow, Patricia: *The Bartered Bride*, 1955–56; *Die Fledermaus (The Bat)*, 1954–55; *Faust*, 1955–56; *Il Tabarro (The Cloak)*, 1955–56; *La Traviata*, 1954–55; *L'Enfant et les Sortilèges (The Bewitched Child)*, 1955–56; *Le Nozze di Figaro (The Marriage of Figaro)*, 1955–56; *Oklahoma!*, 1954–55; *Parsifal*, 1954–55; 1955–56; *Wonderful Town*, 1954–55

Stowell, Kent: *Un Ballo in Maschera (A Masked Ball)*, 1969–70

Sullivan, Robert: *1600 Pennsylvania Avenue*, 1992–93; *La Périchole*, 1995–96; *Le Nozze di Figaro (The Marriage of Figaro)*, 1992–93; *Orphée aux enfers (Orpheus in the Underworld)*, 1992–93; *South Pacific*, 1995–96

Svetlova, Marina: *Don Giovanni*, 1971–72; *Faust*, 1971–72; 1981–82; *La Traviata*, 1978–79; *Salome*, 1970–71; *Un Ballo in Maschera (A Masked Ball)*, 1975–76

Tevlin, Michael: *The Gondoliers*, 1974–75

Vernon, Michael: *Cendrillon*, 2008–09; *Die lustigen Weiber von Windsor (The Merry Wives of Windsor)*, 2008–09; *Manon*, 2006–07; *Rigoletto*, 2007–08; *A Wedding*, 2007–08

Verzatt, Marc: *Die Fledermaus (The Bat)*, 1996–97

Wang, Guoping: *Don Giovanni*, 2006–07; *Eugene Onegin*, 2004–05

Watters, Sean: *1600 Pennsylvania Avenue*, 1992–93

Watts, Jonathan: *Boris Godunov*, 1964–65; *Die lustige Witwe (The Merry Widow)*, 1964–65

Weidenbener, Diana: *Down in the Valley*, 1998–99

Wood, Richard: *The Boys from Syracuse*, 1968–69; *Die Meistersinger von Nürnberg (The Mastersingers of Nuremberg)*, 1968–69

York, Jennifer: *The Excursions of Mr. Broucek*, 1981–82

Young, Derrick: *Company*, 1990–91

SET DESIGNER

Anania, Michael: *Carousel*, 1993–94

Ascareggi, James: *Finian's Rainbow*, 1969–70

Beck, Peter Dean: *The Mikado*, 2006–07

Burns Stevens, Robert: *Kiss Me, Kate*, 1951–52; *On the Town*, 1951–52; *Song of Norway*, 1951–52

Crayon, H. M.: *Billy Budd,* 1952–53; *Rigoletto,* 1950–51; *Roberta,* 1958–59

Cristini, C. Mario: *Aida,* 1963–64; *Carmen,* 1965–66; *Cavalleria Rusticana,* 1966–67; *The Darkened City,* 1962–63; *Deidamia,* 1969–70; *Der Fliegende Holländer (The Flying Dutchman),* 1962–63; *Der Rosenkavalier,* 1965–66; *Dialogues des Carmélites,* 1965–66; *Die Kluge (The Clever Girl),* 1959–60; *Die lustige Witwe (The Merry Widow),* 1965–66; *Die Meistersinger von Nürnberg (The Mastersingers of Nuremberg),* 1961–62; 1968–69; *Die Walküre,* 1969–70; 1971–72; *Don Giovanni,* 1964–65; *Don Pasquale,* 1965–66; *The Fair at Sorochinsk,* 1963–64; *Heracles,* 1971–72; *A Hoosier Tale,* 1966–67; *Il Barbiere di Siviglia (The Barber of Seville),* 1963–64; *Il Campanello di Notte (The Night Bell),* 1963–64; *Il Trittico (A Triptych),* 1969–70; 1972–73; *Il Trovatore,* 1967–68; *I Pagliacci,* 1966–67; *La Bohème,* 1962–63; *La Fanciulla del West (The Girl of the Golden West),* 1963–64; *La Forza del Destino (The Force of Destiny),* 1962–63; *La Pique Dame (The Queen of Spades),* 1968–69; *Le Coq d'or (The Golden Cockerel),* 1960–61; *L'Elisir d'amore (The Elixir of Love),* 1961–62; *Le Nozze di Figaro (The Marriage of Figaro),* 1968–69; 1973–74; *L'Incoronazione di Poppea (The Coronation of Poppea),* 1967–68; *The Love for Three Oranges,* 1958–59; *Manon,* 1967–68; *Manon Lescaut,* 1970–71; *Mefistofele,* 1967–68; *A Midsummer Night's Dream,* 1961–62; *Parsifal,* 1960–61; 1961–62; 1962–63; 1963–64; 1964–65; 1965–66; 1966–67; 1967–68; 1968–69; 1972–73; 1975–76; *Peter Grimes,* 1963–64; *Quattro rusteghi (The Four Ruffians),* 1966–67; *The Rake's Progress,* 1968–69; *Rigoletto,* 1966–67; *The Scarlet Letter,* 1960–61; 1961–62; *Simon Boccanegra,* 1964–65; *Tosca,* 1961–62; *Turandot,* 1964–65; *Un Ballo in Maschera (A Masked Ball),* 1969–70; 1975–76; *Werther,* 1961–62

Dahlstrom, Robert: *Bluebeard's Castle,* 1988–89

Dimitrov, Antonin: *Die Zauberflöte (The Magic Flute),* 1972–73; *Don Carlos,* 1972–73; *Don Giovanni,* 1971–72; *Faust,* 1971–72; *Il Barbiere di Siviglia (The Barber of Seville),* 1971–72; *Jenůfa,* 1972–73

Edmunds, Kate: *Kismet,* 1989–90

Elder, Eldon: *Die lustigen Weiber von Windsor (The Merry Wives of Windsor),* 1958–59

Fouchard, James: *Kiss Me, Kate,* 1998–99; *The Music Man,* 2001–02

Forrester, William: *La Rondine (The Swallow),* 2009–10; *The Most Happy Fella,* 2008–09

Gallagher, Edward: *Albert Herring,* 1957–58; *Annie Get Your Gun,* 1956–57; *The Bartered Bride,* 1955–56; *Cavalleria Rusticana,* 1957–58; *Faust,* 1955–56; *Hänsel und Gretel,* 1956–57; *Il Barbiere di Siviglia (The Barber of Seville),* 1956–57; *The King and I,* 1957–58; *La Bohème,* 1957–58; *The Land Between the Rivers,* 1955–56; *L'Enfant et les Sortilèges (The Bewitched Child),* 1955–56; *Le Nozze di Figaro (The Marriage of Figaro),* 1955–56; *Parsifal,* 1955–56; 1956–57; 1957–58; 1958–59; 1959–60; *Tosca,* 1957–58

Hendrickson, George W.: *Blossom Time,* 1952–53; *Brigadoon,* 1952–53; 1953–54; *Carousel,* 1952–53

Higgins, C. David: *1600 Pennsylvania Avenue,* 1992–93; *Agrippina,* 1995–96; *Amahl and the Night Visitors,* 1990–91; *The Ballad of Baby Doe,* 2003–04; *Candide,* 1983–84; 1987–88; 1993–94; 2000–01; *Canterbury Tales,* 1978–79; *Carmina Burana,* 1991–92; *Cendrillon,* 2008–09; *La Cenerentola (Cinderella),* 1991–92; 1998–99; 2004–05; *Company,* 1990–91; *The Love for Three Oranges (Lyubov k Tryom Apelsinam),* 2008–09; *The Crucible,* 1987–88; *Das Rheingold,* 1983–84; *The Dawn of the Poor King,* 1990–91; *Dialogues des Carmélites,* 1986–87; 1997–98; 2004–05; *Die Fledermaus (The Bat),* 1982–83; 1985–86; 1990–91; 1996–97; 2002–03; *Die lustige Witwe (The Merry Widow),* 2003–04; *Die lustigen Weiber von Windsor (The Merry Wives of Windsor),* 1981–82; *Die Teufel von Loudun (The Devils of Loudun),* 1992–93; *Don Carlos,* 1972–73; *Don Giovanni,* 2006–07; *Fiddler on the Roof,* 1972–73; *The Ghosts of Versailles,* 1996–97; *The Gondoliers,* 1974–75; *HMS Pinafore,* 1997–98; 2005–06; *Il Barbiere di Siviglia (The Barber of Seville),* 1980–81; 1982–83; 1988–89; 1994–95; 2000–01; 2005–06; *I Pagliacci,* 1991–92; *Jeppe,* 2002–03; *Kiss Me, Kate,* 1973–74; *La Bohème,* 2007–08; *La Rondine (The Swallow),* 1989–90; *La Traviata,* 1978–79; 1983–84; 1990–91; 1997–98; 2002–03; *L'Elisir d'amore (The Elixir of Love),* 1986–87; 1990–91; *Le Nozze di Figaro (The Marriage of Figaro),* 1997–98; *Les Contes d'Hoffmann (The Tales of Hoffmann),* 1988–89; 1995–96; 2002–03; 2007–08; *A Little Night Music,* 1988–89; *L'Orfeo,* 1987–88; *The Love for Three Oranges,* 1993–94; 1999–2000; *Lucia di Lammermoor,* 2001–02, 2009–10; *Madama Butterfly,* 2006–07; *Manon,* 1979–80; *Mass,* 1987–88; 1988–89; 1998–99; *A Midsummer Night's Dream,* 2005–06; *Murder in the Cathedral,* 1984–85; *Naughty Marietta,* 1977–78; *Nixon in China,* 1994–95; *Our Town,* 2005–06; *Peter Grimes,* 1977–78; *The Rape of Lucretia,* 1999–2000; *Rigoletto,* 2007–08; *Roméo et Juliette,* 2005–06; 2009–10; *The Secret Garden,* 2003–04; *Show Boat,* 1984–85; *Susannah,* 1976–77; 1979–80; 2000–01; 2007–08; *West Side Story,* 1985–86; 1992–93; 2002–03; *Die Zauberflöte (The Magic Flute),* 2009–10

Jones, Howard C.: *Hello, Dolly!,* 1991–92

Mack, Harold F.: *110 in the Shade,* 1967–68; 1968–69; *Arabella,* 1972–73; *Bernstein on Broadway,* 1976–77; *The Boys from Syracuse,* 1968–69; *Carousel,* 1970–71; 1976–77; *The Fantasticks,* 1963–64; *Fiddler on the Roof,* 1994–95; *The Lion and Androcles,* 1972–73; *A Little Night Music,* 1975–76; *Man of La*

Mancha, 1985–86; 1988–89; *Of Thee I Sing*, 1987–88; *Tosca*, 1969–70; 1973–74; 1977–78; *Trouble in Tahiti*, 1976–77; *Vanessa*, 1974–75

Martin, Paul: *Brigadoon*, 1961–62

Mulder, James: *La Bohème*, 1979–80

Munier, Leon L.: *Carmen*, 1956–57; *Così fan tutte*, 1956–57; *Falstaff*, 1956–57

Nomikos, Andreas: *Albert Herring*, 1966–67; 1967–68; *Amelia Goes to the Ball*, 1957–58; *Andrea Chénier*, 1967–68; *Ariadne auf Naxos*, 1969–70; *The Bartered Bride*, 1967–68; *Boris Godunov*, 1964–65; 1966–67; *Candide*, 1957–58; *Capriccio*, 1958–59; *Carmen*, 1962–63; *Così fan tutte*, 1963–64; *Die Entführung aus dem Serail (The Abduction from the Seraglio)*, 1961–62; 1966–67; *Die Fledermaus (The Bat)*, 1962–63; *Die Zauberflöte (The Magic Flute)*, 1960–61; 1965–66; *Don Carlos*, 1960–61; 1961–62; *Don Giovanni*, 1958–59; *Elegy for Young Lovers*, 1967–68; *Fidelio*, 1970–71; *Gianni Schicchi*, 1964–65; *Kismet*, 1963–64; *La Bohème*, 1970–71; *La Cenerentola (Cinderella)*, 1957–58; *La Rondine (The Swallow)*, 1959–60; *La Traviata*, 1960–61; 1968–69; *Le Nozze di Figaro (The Marriage of Figaro)*, 1962–63; *Les Contes d'Hoffmann (The Tales of Hoffmann)*, 1959–60; *L'Heure espagnole (The Spanish Hour)*, 1959–60; *L'Italiana in Algeri (The Italian Girl in Algiers)*, 1968–69; *Love on Trial (La Pietra del Paragone)*, 1969–70; *Lucia di Lammermoor*, 1963–64; 1970–71; *Macbeth*, 1965–66; *Madama Butterfly*, 1958–59; 1964–65; *Manon Lescaut*, 1959–60; *The Most Happy Fella*, 1959–60; *Myshkin*, 1972–73; *Oedipus Rex*, 1964–65; *Rigoletto*, 1959–60; *Roméo et Juliette*, 1966–67; *Salome*, 1970–71; *Street Scene*, 1960–61; *Tosca*, 1961–62

O'Hearn, Robert: *Arabella*, 1998–99; 2006–07; *Ariadne auf Naxos*, 1996–97; *Arlecchino*, 2006–07; *Carmen*, 1991–92; 1998–99; 2005–06; *The Cry of Clytaemnestra*, 1989–90; *Die Entführung aus dem Serail (The Abduction from the Seraglio)*, 2003–04; *Die lustigen Weiber von Windsor (The Merry Wives of Windsor)*, 2008–09; *Die Zauberflöte (The Magic Flute)*, 2004–05; *Don Pasquale*, 1997–98; 2003–04; *Eugene Onegin*, 1988–89; 1997–98; 2004–05; *Falstaff*, 1992–93; 1997–98; 2003–04; *Francesca da Rimini*, 1989–90; *Giulio Cesare (Julius Caesar)*, 2002–03; 2008–09; *Idomeneo*, 1998–99; *Il Turco in Italia (The Turk in Italy)*, 1996–97; 2003–04; *Jubilee*, 1991–92; *La Finta Giardiniera*, 1990–91; *La Périchole*, 1995–96; *L'Elisir d'amore (The Elixir of Love)*, 2000–01; 2007–08; *Le Nozze di Figaro (The Marriage of Figaro)*, 2001–02; 2007–08; *Little Women*, 2001–02; *Manon*, 1993–94; 2001–02; 2006–07; *McTeague*, 1995–96; *Orfeo ed Euridice*, 1992–93; *Otello*, 1989–90; *Pelléas et Mélisande*, 1994–95; *Peter Grimes*, 1987–88; 1994–95; 2003–04; *Putting It Together*, 2002–03; *She Loves Me*, 2004–

05; *Too Many Sopranos*, 2006–07; *Tosca*, 1993–94; *Vanessa*, 1999–2000; *A View from the Bridge*, 2004–05; *A Wedding*, 2007–08; *Wozzeck*, 1990–91; 1999–2000

Payne, Woodward: *Brigadoon*, 1961–62

Philips, Marvin J.: *Ariadne auf Naxos*, 1954–55; *Boris Godunov*, 1953–54; *Die Fledermaus (The Bat)*, 1954–55; *Die Zauberflöte (The Magic Flute)*, 1953–54; *Finian's Rainbow*, 1953–54; *La Traviata*, 1954–55; *I Pagliacci*, 1954–55; *Oklahoma!*, 1954–55; *The Ruby*, 1954–55; *Show Boat*, 1953–54; *Where's Charley?*, 1953–54; *Wonderful Town*, 1954–55

Popcheff, Louis: *The Firefly*, 1949–50; *The New Moon*, 1949–50; *Street Scene*, 1949–50

Rolf, (first name unknown): *Parsifal*, 1948–49; *Parsifal*, 1949–50

Roth, Wolfgang: *Down in the Valley*, 1947–48

Röthlisberger, Max, Jean Sokol, Jack Stewart, James Mulder: *La Bohème*, 1974–75

Röthlisberger, Max: *Arlecchino*, 1979–80; *The Ballad of Baby Doe*, 1975–76; 1982–83; *The Bartered Bride*, 1979–80; 1986–87; 1994–95; 2001–02; *Béatrice et Bénédict*, 1987–88; *Boris Godunov*, 1978–79; *Boris Godunov*, 1983–84; *Carmen*, 1973–74; 1977–78; *Così fan tutte*, 1977–78; 1978–79; 1984–85; 1989–90; 1995–96; 2000–01; 2005–06; *The Cry of Clytaemnestra*, 1979–80; *Danton and Robespierre*, 1977–78; *The Darkened City*, 1978–79; *Der Fliegende Holländer (The Flying Dutchman)*, 1978–79; 1985–86; *Die Entführung aus dem Serail (The Abduction from the Seraglio)*, 1974–75; 1981–82; 1987–88; 1993–94; *Die lustige Witwe (The Merry Widow)*, 1983–84; 1990–91; 1996–97; *Die Zauberflöte (The Magic Flute)*, 1977–78; 1982–83; 1988–89; 1994–95; 1998–99; *Doktor Faust*, 1974–75; *Don Giovanni*, 1979–80; 1985–86; 1991–92; 1996–97; 2002–03; *Don Pasquale*, 1977–78; 1980–81; 1988–89; *Eugene Onegin*, 1974–75; *The Excursions of Mr. Broucek*, 1981–82; *Faust*, 1981–82; 1989–90; 2000–01; *Gianni Schicchi*, 1988–89; 1993–94; 1999–2000; *The Greek Passion*, 1980–81; *Hänsel und Gretel*, 1982–83; 1989–90; 1995–96; 2001–02; 2006–07; *Idomeneo*, 1976–77; *Il Mondo della Luna (The World on the Moon)*, 1975–76; *Il Trittico (A Triptych)*, 1982–83; *Jakob Lenz*, 1981–82; *La Bohème*, 1984–85; 1989–90; 1994–95; 1999–2000; 2004–05; *La Fille du régiment (The Daughter of the Regiment)*, 1984–85; *La Sonnambula (The Sleepwalker)*, 1985–86; *The Legend of Tsar Saltan*, 1986–87; *L'Enfant et les Sortilèges (The Bewitched Child)*, 1984–85; *Le Nozze di Figaro (The Marriage of Figaro)*, 1980–81; 1986–87; 1992–93; *Les Contes d'Hoffmann (The Tales of Hoffmann)*, 1973–74; 1978–79; *L'Heure espagnole (The Spanish Hour)*, 1984–85; *The Love for Three Oranges*, 1975–76; 1980–81; *Madama Butterfly*, 1975–76; 1976–77; 1981–82; 1987–88; 1991–92; 1996–97; 2001–02;

2006–07; *A Midsummer Night's Dream*, 1983–84; *The Mother of Us All*, 1973–74; *The Night Before Christmas*, 1977–78; *Orphée aux enfers (Orpheus in the Underworld)*, 1984–85; 1992–93; 1998–99; *Passion Play—Carmina Burana*, 1982–83; *Pelléas et Mélisande*, 1976–77; *Porgy and Bess*, 1976–77; 1979–80; *Prince Igor*, 1980–81; *The Rake's Progress*, 1986–87; 1991–92; 1999–2000; *Rigoletto*, 1974–75; 1980–81; 1986–87; 1992–93; 1995–96; 2000–01; 2007–08; *The Scarlet Letter*, 1976–77; *Soldier Boy, Soldier*, 1982–83; *Suor Angelica (Sister Angelica)*, 1999–2000; *Tamerlano*, 1984–85; *The Tempest*, 1985–86; *Tom Jones*, 1983–84; *The Turn of the Screw*, 1978–79; *Wozzeck*, 1973–74; 1981–82

Russell, Walter S.: *The Jumping Frog of Calaveras County*, 1949–50; *The Veil*, 1949–50

Scammon, Richard C.: *La Bohème*, 1949–50; *Die lustige Witwe (The Merry Widow)*, 1949–50

Schmidt, Douglas: *The Most Happy Fella*, 1982–83

Schroder, William: *Die lustige Witwe (The Merry Widow)*, 2003–04

Shortt, Paul: *L'Italiana in Algeri (The Italian Girl in Algiers)*, 2009–10; *South Pacific*, 1995–96

Smith, Mark: *Die lustigen Weiber von Windsor (The Merry Wives of Windsor)*, 2008–09; *Down in the Valley*, 1998–99

Smith, Oliver: *My Fair Lady*, 1979–80

Sokol, Jean: *La Bohème*, 1979–80

Sollors, Daniel: *Camelot*, 1968–69; 1969–70; *Così fan tutte*, 1970–71; *Falstaff*, 1971–72; 1976–77

Sormani, Angelo: *Werther*, 1975–76

Stevens, Robert Burns: *Amahl and the Night Visitors*, 1951–52; *A Parfait for Irene*, 1951–52

Stewart, Jack: *La Bohème*, 1979–80

Taylor, Theda: *The Chocolate Soldier*, 1950–51; *Lost in the Stars*, 1950–51; *The Mikado*, 1950–51

Warfield, Jean: *Ruddigore (The Witch's Curse)*, 1962–63

Williams, Robert T.: *Man of La Mancha*, 1999–2000

Winter, Harold: *Il Tabarro (The Cloak)*, 1955–56

Yeargan, Michael: *Tosca*, 2004–05

LIGHTING DESIGNER

Bae, Namok: *Orphée aux enfers (Orpheus in the Underworld)*, 1992–93

Brown, Leslie: *The Ballad of Baby Doe*, 1982–83; *Die Fledermaus (The Bat)*, 1982–83

Buchanan, Jonet: *L'Elisir d'amore (The Elixir of Love)*, 1986–87

Burns Stevens, Robert: *Kiss Me, Kate*, 1951–52; *Song of Norway*, 1951–52

Busch, C. Frederick: *Rigoletto*, 1986–87

Busch, Hans: *Parsifal*, 1948–49

Cohen, Marc: *La Fanciulla del West (The Girl of the Golden West)*, 1963–64

Cristini, C. Mario: *The Love for Three Oranges*, 1958–59; *Die lustige Witwe (The Merry Widow)*, 1965–66

Dailey, Linda: *Die lustige Witwe (The Merry Widow)*, 1990–91

Duffin, Gerard: *Amahl and the Night Visitors*, 1990–91; *Bluebeard's Castle*, 1988–89; *Candide*, 1987–88; 1993–94; *Così fan tutte*, 1984–85; *The Dawn of the Poor King*, 1990–91; *Die Zauberflöte (The Magic Flute)*, 1988–89; *Gianni Schicchi*, 1988–89; *La Rondine (The Swallow)*, 1989–90; *La Sonnambula (The Sleepwalker)*, 1985–86; *Le Nozze di Figaro (The Marriage of Figaro)*, 1986–87; 1992–93; *Madama Butterfly*, 1991–92; *The Rake's Progress*, 1991–92

Duro, Julie: *Il Barbiere di Siviglia (The Barber of Seville)*, 2005–06; *Manon*, 2006–07; *Roméo et Juliette*, 2009–10

Esposito, Giovanni: *Die Entführung aus dem Serail (The Abduction from the Seraglio)*, 1961–62; *Die Meistersinger von Nürnberg (The Mastersingers of Nuremberg)*, 1961–62; *Don Carlos*, 1961–62; *A Midsummer Night's Dream*, 1961–62; *Parsifal*, 1961–62; *The Scarlet Letter*, 1961–62; *Tosca*, 1961–62; *Werther*, 1961–62

Floyd, Mark: *Il Barbiere di Siviglia (The Barber of Seville)*, 1982–83

Gaiser, Gary: *Die lustige Witwe (The Merry Widow)*, 1949–50

Gallagher, Edward: *Faust*, 1955–56; *Il Barbiere di Siviglia (The Barber of Seville)*, 1956–57; *The Land Between the Rivers*, 1955–56; *L'Enfant et les Sortilèges (The Bewitched Child)*, 1955–56; *Le Nozze di Figaro (The Marriage of Figaro)*, 1955–56; *Parsifal*, 1955–56

Hatch, Jeremy: *Die Zauberflöte (The Magic Flute)*, 1998–99; *Hänsel und Gretel*, 1995–96; *HMS Pinafore*, 1997–98; *Il Barbiere di Siviglia (The Barber of Seville)*, 2000–01; *La Bohème*, 1999–2000; *La Cenerentola (Cinderella)*, 1998–99

Hogue, Donald: *Parsifal*, 1956–57; *South Pacific*, 1956–57

Holt, Michael: *Down in the Valley*, 1998–99; *Faust*, 2000–01

Horn, Andrew: *Die Fledermaus (The Bat)*, 1996–97

Jones, Ted W.: *Aida*, 1963–64; *Amelia Goes to the Ball*, 1957–58; *Brigadoon*, 1961–62; *Candide*, 1957–58; *Capriccio*, 1958–59; *Cavalleria Rusticana*, 1957–58; *Die Kluge (The Clever Girl)*, 1959–60; *Die Zauberflöte (The Magic Flute)*, 1960–61; *Don Carlos*, 1960–61; *Don Giovanni*, 1958–59; *Il Barbiere di Siviglia (The Barber of Seville)*, 1963–64; *La Bohème*, 1957–58; *La Cenerentola (Cinderella)*, 1963–64;

1957–58; *Le Coq d'or (The Golden Cockerel)*, 1960–61; *Les Contes d'Hoffmann (The Tales of Hoffmann)*, 1959–60; *La Rondine (The Swallow)*, 1959–60; *La Traviata*, 1960–61; *L'Heure espagnole (The Spanish Hour)*, 1959–60; *Lucia di Lammermoor*, 1963–64; *Madama Butterfly*, 1958–59; 1964–65; *Manon Lescaut*, 1959–60; *The Most Happy Fella*, 1959–60; *Parsifal*, 1957–58; 1958–59; 1959–60; 1960–61; 1963–64; 1964–65; *Rigoletto*, 1959–60; *The Scarlet Letter*, 1960–61; *Street Scene*, 1960–61

Kaffenberger, William: *Wonderful Town*, 1954–55

Klages, William: *Myshkin*, 1972–73

Lott, Robert: *The Crucible*, 1987–88

Martin, Paul: *Carmen*, 1962–63; *The Darkened City*, 1962–63; *Die Fledermaus (The Bat)*, 1962–63; *Der Fliegende Holländer (The Flying Dutchman)*, 1962–63; *The Fair at Sorochinsk*, 1963–64; *La Bohème*, 1962–63; *La Forza del Destino (The Force of Destiny)*, 1962–63; *L'Elisir d'amore (The Elixir of Love)*, 1961–62; *Le Nozze di Figaro (The Marriage of Figaro)*, 1962–63; *Parsifal*, 1962–63

Mero, Patrick: *Die lustigen Weiber von Windsor (The Merry Wives of Windsor)*, 2008–09; *La Bohème*, 2004–05; *Tosca*, 2004–05

Moser, James: *Ariadne auf Naxos*, 1954–55; *Die Fledermaus (The Bat)*, 1954–55; *Finian's Rainbow*, 1953–54; *I Pagliacci*, 1954–55; *The Ruby*, 1954–55; *Show Boat*, 1953–54; *Where's Charley?*, 1953–54

Mroczek, Damen: *Hänsel und Gretel*, 2001–02

Munier, Leon L.: *Falstaff*, 1956–57

Murphy, Stuart: *Hänsel und Gretel*, 1956–57

Oberle, John: *Show Boat*, 1984–85

Philips, Marvin J.: *Oklahoma!*, 1954–55

Piedmont, Tilman: *Il Barbiere di Siviglia (The Barber of Seville)*, 1994–95; *Così fan tutte*, 1995–96; *Die Entführung aus dem Serail (The Abduction from the Seraglio)*, 1993–94; *Die Fledermaus (The Bat)*, 2002–03; *Die lustige Witwe (The Merry Widow)*, 1996–97; *La Traviata*, 1997–98; 2002–03; *Madama Butterfly*, 2001–02

Randall, Nicholas: *Candide*, 1983–84; *La Traviata*, 1983–84

Rusnak, Alan: *The Bartered Bride*, 1994–95

Schwandt, Michael: *Arabella*, 2006–07; *Arlecchino*, 2006–07; *The Ballad of Baby Doe*, 2003–04; *Carmen*, 1998–99; 2005–06; *Carousel*, 1993–94; *Cendrillon*, 2008–09; *Company*, 1990–91; *Les Contes d'Hoffmann (The Tales of Hoffmann)*, 1995–96; 2002–03; *Così fan tutte*, 2005–06; *Dialogues des Carmélites*, 2004–05; *Die lustige Witwe (The Merry Widow)*, 2003–04; *Die Zauberflöte (The Magic Flute)*, 1994–95; 2004–05; *Don Giovanni*, 1991–92; 1996–97; 2002–03;

2006–07; *Don Pasquale*, 2003–04; *Eugene Onegin*, 1997–98; *Falstaff*, 1992–93; 1997–98; 2003–04; *Faust*, 1989–90; *Fiddler on the Roof*, 1994–95; *Gianni Schicchi*, 1993–94; *Giulio Cesare (Julius Caesar)*, 2002–03; 2008–09; *Hänsel und Gretel*, 2006–07; *Hello, Dolly!*, 1991–92; *HMS Pinafore*, 2005–06; *Il Barbiere di Siviglia (The Barber of Seville)*, 1988–89; *Il Turco in Italia (The Turk in Italy)*, 2003–04; *Jeppe*, 2002–03; *The King and I*, 1996–97; *Kiss Me, Kate*, 1998–99; *La Bohème*, 1989–90; 1994–95; *La Cenerentola (Cinderella)*, 2004–05; *L'Elisir d'amore (The Elixir of Love)*, 1990–91; 2000–01; 2007–08; *Le Nozze di Figaro (The Marriage of Figaro)*, 2007–08; *Little Women*, 2001–02; *Lucia di Lammermoor*, 1993–94; *Lucia di Lammermoor*, 2001–02; *Madama Butterfly*, 1996–97; 2006–07; *Man of La Mancha*, 1999–2000; *Manon*, 2001–02; *Mass*, 1998–99; *A Midsummer Night's Dream*, 2005–06; *The Mikado*, 2006–07; *The Most Happy Fella*, 2008–09; *The Music Man*, 2001–02; *Oklahoma!*, 1997–98; *Our Town*, 2005–06; *Peter Grimes*, 2003–04; *The Rake's Progress*, 1999–2000; *Rigoletto*, 1992–93; 1995–96; 2000–01; 2007–08; *Roméo et Juliette*, 2005–06; *The Secret Garden*, 2003–04; *She Loves Me*, 2004–05; *The Sound of Music*, 2000–01; *South Pacific*, 1995–96; *Susannah*, 2000–01; 2007–08; *Too Many Sopranos*, 2006–07; *A View from the Bridge*, 2004–05; *A Wedding*, 2007–08; *West Side Story*, 1992–93; 2002–03; *Wozzeck*, 1999–2000

Siegle, Lawrence: *Roberta*, 1958–59

Slagel, Donald: *The Mikado*, 1950–51

Soller, Robert: *Rigoletto*, 1950–51

Somerfeld, Mark: *Eugene Onegin*, 2004–05

Stebbins, Timothy: *La Cenerentola (Cinderella)*, 1991–92; *Die Fledermaus (The Bat)*, 1990–91

Steele, Barry: *La Bohème*, 2007–08; *The Light in the Piazza*, 2009–10

Taylor, Theda: *Lost in the Stars*, 1950–51

Walsh, Tim: *La Bohème*, 1984–85; *La Fille du régiment (The Daughter of the Regiment)*, 1984–85

Welch, M. David: *Die Fledermaus (The Bat)*, 1985–86; *West Side Story*, 1985–86

White, Allen R.: *110 in the Shade*, 1967–68; 1968–69; *1600 Pennsylvania Avenue*, 1992–93; *Agrippina*, 1995–96; *Albert Herring*, 1966–67; 1967–68; *Andrea Chénier*, 1967–68; *Arabella*, 1998–99; *Ariadne auf Naxos*, 1969–70; 1996–97; *Arlecchino*, 1979–80; *The Ballad of Baby Doe*, 1975–76; *The Bartered Bride*, 1967–68; 1979–80; 1986–87; *Béatrice et Bénédict*, 1987–88; *Bernstein on Broadway*, 1976–77; *Boris Godunov*, 1966–67; 1978–79; 1983–84; *The Boys from Syracuse*, 1968–69; *Camelot*, 1968–69; 1969–70; 1986–87; *Candide*, 2000–01; *Canterbury Tales*, 1978–79; *Carmen*, 1977–78; 1991–92; *Carmina*

Burana, 1991–92; *Carousel*, 1970–71; 1986–87; *Così fan tutte*, 1970–71; 1978–79; 1989–90; 2000–01; *The Cry of Clytaemnestra*, 1979–80; 1989–90; *Danton and Robespierre*, 1977–78; *The Darkened City*, 1978–79; *Das Rheingold*, 1983–84; *Deidamia*, 1969–70; *Der Fliegende Holländer (The Flying Dutchman)*, 1978–79; 1985–86; *Dialogues des Carmélites*, 1986–87; 1997–98; *Die lustige Witwe (The Merry Widow)*, 1983–84; *Die lustigen Weiber von Windsor (The Merry Wives of Windsor)*, 1958–59; 1981–82; *Die Meistersinger von Nürnberg (The Mastersingers of Nuremberg)*, 1968–69; *Die Teufel von Loudin (The Devils of Loudon)*, 1992–93; *Doktor Faust*, 1974–75; *Don Carlos*, 1972–73; *Don Giovanni*, 1971–72; 1979–80; 1985–86; *Don Pasquale*, 1977–78; 1980–81; 1988–89; 1997–98; *Elegy for Young Lovers*, 1967–68; *Die Entführung aus dem Serail (The Abduction from the Seraglio)*, 1974–75; 1981–82; 1987–88; 2003–04; *Die Walküre*, 1969–70; 1971–72; *Die Zauberflöte (The Magic Flute)*, 1972–73; 1977–78; 1982–83; *Eugene Onegin*, 1974–75; 1988–89; *Falstaff*, 1971–72; 1976–77; *Faust*, 1971–72; 1981–82; *Fiddler on the Roof*, 1972–73; *Finian's Rainbow*, 1969–70; *Francesca da Rimini*, 1989–90; *The Ghosts of Versailles*, 1996–97; *Gianni Schicchi*, 1999–2000; *The Gondoliers*, 1974–75; *The Greek Passion*, 1980–81; *Hänsel und Gretel*, 1982–83; 1989–90; *Heracles*, 1971–72; *A Hoosier Tale*, 1966–67; *Idomeneo*, 1976–77; 1998–99; *Il Barbiere di Siviglia (The Barber of Seville)*, 1971–72; 1980–81; *Il Trittico (A Triptych)*, 1969–70; 1972–73; 1982–83; *Il Trovatore*, 1967–68; *Il Turco in Italia (The Turk in Italy)*, 1996–97; *I Pagliacci*, 1991–92; *Jakob Lenz*, 1981–82; *Jenůfa*, 1972–73; *Jubilee*, 1991–92; *Kismet*, 1989–90; *Kiss Me, Kate*, 1973–74; *La Finta Gardiniera (The Pretend Gardener)*, 1990–91; *La Pique Dame (The Queen of Spades)*, 1968–69; *La Périchole*, 1995–96; *La Traviata*, 1968–69; 1978–79; 1990–91; *The Legend of Tsar Saltan*, 1986–87; *L'Enfant et les Sortilèges (The Bewitched Child)*, 1984–85; *Le Nozze di Figaro (The Marriage of Figaro)*, 1968–69; 1980–81; 1997–98; 2001–02; *Les Contes d'Hoffmann (The Tales of Hoffmann)*, 1973–74; 1978–79; 1988–89; 2002–03; *L'Heure espagnole (The Spanish Hour)*, 1984–85; *L'Incoronazione di Poppea (The Coronation of Poppea)*, 1967–68; *The Lion and Androcles*, 1972–73; *L'Italiana in Algeri (The Italian Girl in Algiers)*, 1968–69; *A Little Night Music*, 1975–76; 1988–89; *L'Orfeo*, 1987–88; *The Love for Three Oranges*, 1980–81; 1993–94 ; *Love on Trial (La Pietra del Paragone)*, 1969–70; *Lucia di Lammermoor*, 1970–71; *Madama Butterfly*, 1975–76; 1976–77; 1981–82; 1987–88; *Man of La Mancha*, 1985–86; 1988–89; *Manon*, 1993–94; *Manon Lescaut*, 1970–71; *Mass*, 1987–88; 1988–89; *McTeague*, 1995–96; *Mefistofele*, 1967–68; *A Midsummer Night's Dream*, 1983–84; *The Most Happy Fella*, 1982–83; *The Mother of Us All*, 1973–74; *Murder in the Cathedral*, 1984–85;

The Music Man, 1980–81; *My Fair Lady*, 1979–80; *Naughty Marietta*, 1977–78; *The Night Before Christmas*, 1977–78; *Nixon in China*, 1994–95; *Of Thee I Sing*, 1987–88; *Oklahoma!*, 1981–82; *Orfeo ed Euridice*, 1992–93; *Orphée aux enfers (Orpheus in the Underworld)*, 1984–85; 2001–02; *Otello*, 1989–90; *Parsifal*, 1968–69; 1972–73; 1975–76; *Passion Play—Carmina Burana*, 1982–83; *Pelléas et Mélisande*, 1976–77; 1994–95; *Peter Grimes*, 1987–88; 1994–95; *Porgy and Bess*, 1976–77; 1979–80; *Prince Igor*, 1980–81; *Putting It Together*, 2002–03; *The Rake's Progress*, 1968–69; 1986–87; *The Rape of Lucretia*, 1999–2000; *Rigoletto*, 1966–67; 1974–75; *Roméo et Juliette*, 1966–67; *Salome*, 1970–71; *The Scarlet Letter*, 1960–61; *Soldier Boy, Soldier*, 1982–83; *Suor Angelica (Sister Angelica)*, 1999–2000; *Susannah*, 1976–77; 1979–80; *Sweeney Todd*, 1983–84; *Tamerlano*, 1984–85; *The Tempest*, 1985–86; *Tom Jones*, 1983–84; *Tosca*, 1969–70; 1973–74; 1977–78; 1993–94; *Trouble in Tahiti*, 1976–77; *The Turn of the Screw*, 1978–79; *Un Ballo in Maschera (A Masked Ball)*, 1969–70; 1975–76; *Vanessa*, 1974–75; 1999–2000; *Werther*, 1975–76; *Wozzeck*, 1973–74; 1981–82; 1990–91

Winter, Harold: *The Bartered Bride*, 1955–56; *Il Tabarro (The Cloak)*, 1955–56

Worley, Jane: *Boris Godunov*, 1953–54; *Parsifal*, 1952–53; 1953–54

Wright, Anne: *The Bartered Bride*, 2001–02

Zoeller, Mary: *Tom Jones*, 1983–84

CHORUS MASTER

Alireti, Cinthia: *Madama Butterfly*, 2006–07

Allbritten, James: *The Cry of Clytaemnestra*, 1989–90; *Francesca da Rimini*, 1989–90; *La Bohème*, 1989–90; *Otello*, 1989–90

Alston, John: *The Legend of Tsar Saltan*, 1986–87; *L'Elisir d'amore (The Elixir of Love)*, 1986–87; *Of Thee I Sing*, 1987–88

Bagwell, James: *Die Fledermaus (The Bat)*, 1996–97; *Die lustige Witwe (The Merry Widow)*, 1996–97; *The Ghosts of Versailles*, 1996–97; *Les Contes d'Hoffmann (The Tales of Hoffmann)*, 1995–96

Bain, Wilfred C.: *Parsifal*, 1948–49

Bayless, Eugene: *Amelia Goes to the Ball*, 1957–58; *Annie Get Your Gun*, 1956–57; *Blossom Time*, 1952–53; *Boris Godunov*, 1953–54; *Brigadoon*, 1952–53; 1953–54; *Candide*, 1957–58; *Carousel*, 1952–53; *Die Fledermaus (The Bat)*, 1954–55; *Don Giovanni*, 1964–65; *Don Pasquale*, 1957–58; *Faust*, 1955–56; *Finian's Rainbow*, 1953–54; *Il Barbiere di Siviglia (The Barber of Seville)*, 1956–57; *The King and I*, 1957–58; *Kiss Me, Kate*, 1951–52; *La Bohème*, 1957–58; *La Cenerentola (Cinderella)*, 1957–58; *The Land Between the Rivers*, 1955–56; *La*

Traviata, 1954–55; *Lost in the Stars*, 1950–51; *Manon Lescaut*, 1959–60; *The Most Happy Fella*, 1959–60; *On the Town*, 1951–52; *Parsifal*, 1955–56; 1956–57; 1957–58; 1963–64; 1964–65; 1966–67; *Roberta*, 1958–59; *Show Boat*, 1953–54; *South Pacific*, 1956–57; *Tosca*, 1957–58; *Where's Charley?*, 1953–54

Bennett, Alan: *Die lustige Witwe (The Merry Widow)*, 1990–91; *L'Orfeo*, 1987–88

Bennett, Dwight: *Eugene Onegin*, 1974–75

Bidlack, Jerry: *Die Zauberflöte (The Magic Flute)*, 1972–73; *Don Carlos*, 1972–73; *Jenůfa*, 1972–73; *Il Trittico (A Triptych)*, 1972–73

Bowles, Kenneth: *Amahl and the Night Visitors*, 1990–91; *The Dawn of the Poor King*, 1990–91

Breland, Barron: *Carmen*, 2005–06; *HMS Pinafore*, 2005–06; *Il Turco in Italia (The Turk in Italy)*, 2003–04; *The Mikado*, 2006–07

Briscoe, Roger: *La Traviata*, 1968–69; *Le Nozze di Figaro (The Marriage of Figaro)*, 1968–69

Broeker, Angela: *Mass*, 1988–89

Brown, Ryan: *Così fan tutte*, 2005–06; *Die Zauberflöte (The Magic Flute)*, 2004–05; *Don Giovanni*, 2006–07; *Our Town*, 2005–06

Buckwalter, Henry: *Le Nozze di Figaro (The Marriage of Figaro)*, 1973–74; *Les Contes d'Hoffmann (The Tales of Hoffmann)*, 1973–74; *The Mother of Us All*, 1973–74; *Tosca*, 1973–74; *Wozzeck*, 1973–74

Burleigh, Betsy: *Carmen*, 1991–92; *I Pagliacci*, 1991–92; *Jubilee*, 1991–92

Burnim, Mellonee: *Porgy and Bess*, 1976–77; 1979–80

Butler, J. Kevin: *Show Boat*, 1984–85

Butterman, Michael: *La Cenerentola (Cinderella)*, 1991–92; *Die Zauberflöte (The Magic Flute)*, 1994–95; *Peter Grimes*, 1994–95

Calabrese, Alfred: *Béatrice et Bénédict*, 1987–88; *Dialogues des Carmélites*, 1986–87; *Die Entführung aus dem Serail (The Abduction from the Seraglio)*, 1987–88; *Don Giovanni*, 1985–86

Cassel, David: *Deidamia*, 1969–70; *Fidelio*, 1970–71; *La Bohème*, 1970–71; *Love on Trial (La Pietra del Paragone)*, 1969–70; *Lucia di Lammermoor*, 1970–71; *Manon Lescaut*, 1970–71; *Tosca*, 1969–70; 1977–78; *Un Ballo in Maschera (A Masked Ball)*, 1969–70

Chamberlain, Bruce: *Die Zauberflöte (The Magic Flute)*, 1977–78; *Tosca*, 1977–78

Cheah, Phillip: *Così fan tutte*, 2000–01; *Le Nozze di Figaro (The Marriage of Figaro)*, 2001–02; *Little Women*, 2001–02

Clark, Larrie: *Falstaff*, 1956–57; *Hänsel und Gretel*, 1956–57

Cole, Daniel: *HMS Pinafore*, 1997–98; *Kiss Me, Kate*, 1998–99

Contino, Fiora: *Boris Godunov*, 1966–67; *Der Fliegende Holländer (The Flying Dutchman)*, 1962–63; *The Fair at Sorochinsk*, 1963–64; *Il Campanello di Notte (The Night Bell)*, 1963–64; *Il Mondo della Luna (The World on the Moon)*, 1975–76; *La Bohème*, 1962–63; *La Forza del Destino (The Force of Destiny)*, 1962–63; *L'Elisir d'amore (The Elixir of Love)*, 1961–62; *The Love for Three Oranges*, 1975–76; *Turandot*, 1964–65; *Un Ballo in Maschera (A Masked Ball)*, 1975–76; *Werther*, 1975–76

Corbin, Patricia: *Le Nozze di Figaro (The Marriage of Figaro)*, 1992–93; *Orphée aux enfers (Orpheus in the Underworld)*, 1992–93

Cowen, Graeme: *Die Entführung aus dem Serail (The Abduction from the Seraglio)*, 1974–75; *Doktor Faust*, 1974–75; *Eugene Onegin*, 1974–75; *La Bohème*, 1974–75; *Rigoletto*, 1974–75

Deeg, David: *Die lustige Witwe (The Merry Widow)*, 1964–65

Dixon, Michael: *The Bartered Bride*, 1979–80; *Der Fliegende Holländer (The Flying Dutchman)*, 1978–79; *Don Giovanni*, 1979–80; *Don Pasquale*, 1980–81; *The Greek Passion*, 1980–81; *Il Barbiere di Siviglia (The Barber of Seville)*, 1980–81; *Le Nozze di Figaro (The Marriage of Figaro)*, 1980–81; *The Love for Three Oranges*, 1980–81; *Manon*, 1979–80; *Porgy and Bess*, 1979–80; *Rigoletto*, 1980–81

Dyachkov, Kirill Y.: *Madama Butterfly*, 2001–02

Effron, David: *Ruddigore (The Witch's Curse)*, 1962–63

Elliot, Paul: *Agrippina*, 1995–96

Espina, Noni: *The Firefly*, 1949–50; *Street Scene*, 1949–50

Fanning, Franklin: *Parsifal*, 1963–64

Fentress, Stephen: *Der Fliegende Holländer (The Flying Dutchman)*, 1985–86; *The Tempest*, 1985–86

Fleischer, Randy: *Boris Godunov*, 1983–84; *Così fan tutte*, 1984–85; *Die lustige Witwe (The Merry Widow)*, 1983–84; *La Traviata*, 1983–84; *L'Enfant et les Sortilèges (The Bewitched Child)*, 1984–85; *L'Heure espagnole (The Spanish Hour)*, 1984–85; *Murder in the Cathedral*, 1984–85; *Orphée aux enfers (Orpheus in the Underworld)*, 1984–85

Flight, Paul: *The Rake's Progress*, 1991–92

Fuerstner, Carl: *Così fan tutte*, 1963–64; *Il Barbiere di Siviglia (The Barber of Seville)*, 1963–64; *La Fanciulla del West (The Girl of the Golden West)*, 1963–64; *Lucia di Lammermoor*, 1963–64

Gallagher, Fulton: *Die Entführung aus dem Serail (The Abduction from the Seraglio)*, 1966–67; *Rigoletto*, 1966–67; *Roméo et Juliette*, 1966–67

Gee, Bradford: *La Rondine (The Swallow)*, 1989–90

Gehrenbeck, Robert: *Il Barbiere di Siviglia (The Barber of Seville)*, 2000–01

Goetze, Mary: *Hänsel und Gretel*, 1982–83; 1989–90

Gray, William Jon: *Dialogues des Carmélites*, 2004–05; *Eugene Onegin*, 2004–05; *La Périchole*, 1995–96; *Manon*, 2001–02; *Peter Grimes*, 2003–04; *Susannah*, 2007–08; *A View from the Bridge*, 2004–05

Grove, Eugene: *Parsifal*, 1950–51

Hardy, Mark: *Don Pasquale*, 1997–98; *Il Turco in Italia (The Turk in Italy)*, 1996–97; *The King and I*, 1996–97; *Le Nozze di Figaro (The Marriage of Figaro)*, 1997–98; *Oklahoma!*, 1997–98

Harler, Alan: *Carousel*, 1976–77; *Danton and Robespierre*, 1977–78; *Falstaff*, 1976–77; *Idomeneo*, 1976–77; *Madama Butterfly*, 1976–77; *Parsifal*, 1975–76; *Pelléas et Mélisande*, 1976–77; *The Scarlet Letter*, 1976–77; *Susannah*, 1976–77

Harrington, Jan: *The Bartered Bride*, 1967–68; *Boris Godunov*, 1978–79; *Danton and Robespierre*, 1977–78; *Die Entführung aus dem Serail (The Abduction from the Seraglio)*, 1993–94; *Die Teufel von Loudun (The Devils of Loudun)*, 1992–93; *Falstaff*, 1971–72; *La Pique Dame (The Queen of Spades)*, 1968–69; *Madama Butterfly*, 1975–76; *The Rake's Progress*, 1968–69; 1986–87; *Vanessa*, 1974–75

Harsh, Tamara: *Lucia di Lammermoor*, 1993–94; *Manon*, 1993–94

Hejduk, James: *Il Trovatore*, 1967–68; *L'Incoronazione di Poppea (The Coronation of Poppea)*, 1967–68; *Manon*, 1967–68

Henry, Roger: *Die Fledermaus (The Bat)*, 2002–03; *Die lustige Witwe (The Merry Widow)*, 2003–04; *The Music Man*, 2001–02; *West Side Story*, 2002–03

Holland, Geoffrey: *L'Elisir d'amore (The Elixir of Love)*, 1990–91

Hornibrook, Wallace: *Mefistofele*, 1967–68

Hunt, Robert: *Madama Butterfly*, 1991–92

Irwin, Frederick: *Arabella*, 1998–99; *Gianni Schicchi*, 1999–2000; *Suor Angelica (Sister Angelica)*, 1999–2000

Johnson, Hugh B.: *Aida*, 1963–64; *Capriccio*, 1958–59; *Carmen*, 1956–57; 1962–63; *The Darkened City*, 1962–63; *Die Entführung aus dem Serail (The Abduction from the Seraglio)*, 1961–62; *Die Fledermaus (The Bat)*, 1962–63; *Die lustigen Weiber von Windsor (The Merry Wives of Windsor)*, 1958–59; *Die Meistersinger von Nürnberg (The Mastersingers of Nuremberg)*, 1961–62; *Die Zauberflöte (The Magic Flute)*, 1960–61; *Don Carlos*, 1960–61; 1961–62; *Don Giovanni*, 1958–59; *Gianni Schicchi*, 1964–65; *La Rondine (The Swallow)*, 1959–60; *La Traviata*, 1960–61; *Le Coq d'or (The Golden Cockerel)*, 1960–61; *Le Nozze di Figaro (The Marriage of Figaro)*, 1962–63; *Les Contes d'Hoffmann (The Tales of Hoffmann)*, 1959–60; *The Love for Three Oranges*, 1958–59; *Madama Butterfly*, 1958–59; 1964–65; *A Midsummer Night's Dream*, 1961–62; *The Most Happy Fella*, 1959–60; *Oedipus Rex*, 1964–65; *Parsifal*, 1958–59; 1959–60; 1960–61; 1961–62; 1962–63; 1963–64; *Rigoletto*, 1959–60; *The Scarlet Letter*, 1960–61; 1961–62; *Street Scene*, 1960–61; *Tosca*, 1961–62

Kallembach, James: *The Ballad of Baby Doe*, 2003–04; *La Traviata*, 2002–03

Keltner, Karen: *The Ballad of Baby Doe*, 1975–76

Kleiman, Marjorie: *Il Barbiere di Siviglia (The Barber of Seville)*, 1971–72; *Così fan tutte*, 1970–71; *Don Giovanni*, 1971–72

Kleinknecht, Daniel: *Rigoletto*, 1986–87

Krueger, George F.: *110 in the Shade*, 1967–68; 1968–69; *The Bartered Bride*, 1955–56; *Billy Budd*, 1952–53; *The Boys from Syracuse*, 1968–69; *Camelot*, 1968–69; 1969–70; *Die lustige Witwe (The Merry Widow)*, 1949–50; *Down in the Valley*, 1947–48; *Elegy for Young Lovers*, 1967–68; *Fiddler on the Roof*, 1972–73; *Finian's Rainbow*, 1969–70; *Hin und Zurück (There and Back)*, 1947–48; *Le Nozze di Figaro (The Marriage of Figaro)*, 1955–56; *The New Moon*, 1949–50; *Oklahoma!*, 1954–55; *Parsifal*, 1948–49; 1955–56; 1958–59; 1964–65; 1966–67; 1967–68; 1968–69; 1972–73; *Wonderful Town*, 1954–55

Kuzma, Marika: *Così fan tutte*, 1989–90

Larkin, Christopher: *Candide*, 1983–84

Leonard, John: *Le Nozze di Figaro (The Marriage of Figaro)*, 2007–08

Loomis, David: *Così fan tutte*, 1956–57

Louer, Michelle: *Faust*, 2000–01

Loux, Jennifer: *Il Barbiere di Siviglia (The Barber of Seville)*, 2005–06; *Manon*, 2006–07; *Roméo et Juliette*, 2005–06

Maclary, Edward: *The Ballad of Baby Doe*, 1982–83; *Die Zauberflöte (The Magic Flute)*, 1982–83; *Faust*, 1981–82; *Il Barbiere di Siviglia (The Barber of Seville)*, 1982–83; *Il Trittico (A Triptych)*, 1982–83; *Soldier Boy, Soldier*, 1982–83

McGovern, Paul: *Così fan tutte*, 1995–96; *McTeague*, 1995–96; *Nixon in China*, 1994–95; *Rigoletto*, 1995–96; *South Pacific*, 1995–96

McKinley, Frank: *Amahl and the Night Visitors*, 1951–52; *A Parfait for Irene*, 1951–52; *Parsifal*, 1951–52

McQuerrey, Lawrence: *Parsifal*, 1952–53; 1953–54

Morrow, Lynne: *Candide*, 2000–01; *Die Zauberflöte (The Magic Flute)*, 1998–99; *L'Elisir d'amore (The Elixir of Love)*, 2000–01; *The Love for Three Oranges*, 1999–2000; *Mass*, 1998–99; *Rigoletto*, 2000–01; *The Sound of Music*, 2000–01; *Susannah*, 2000–01; *Vanessa*, 1999–2000

Moser, Sarah E.: *Hello, Dolly!*, 1991–92

Moses, Don V.: *The Darkened City*, 1962–63; *Die Meistersinger von Nürnberg (The Mastersingers of Nuremberg)*, 1968–69; *Heracles*, 1971–72; *Il Barbiere di Siviglia*

(*The Barber of Seville*), 1963–64; *Peter Grimes*, 1963–64; *Simon Boccanegra*, 1964–65

Moyer, Philip: *Arabella*, 2006–07

Nelson, Eric: *Le Nozze di Figaro (The Marriage of Figaro)*, 1986–87; *Madama Butterfly*, 1987–88; *Peter Grimes*, 1987–88

Ng, Jonathan: *Down in the Valley*, 1998–99

O'Neal, Melinda: *La Bohème*, 1979–80

Oriatti, Michael: *Don Pasquale*, 2003–04

Plissey, Bethany: *Hänsel und Gretel*, 2001–02

Porco, Robert: *The Bartered Bride*, 1986–87; *Candide*, 1987–88; 1993–94; *Company*, 1990–91; *Die Fledermaus (The Bat)*, 1985–86; *The Greek Passion*, 1980–81; *La Bohème*, 1984–85

Prestinari, Charles: *The Bartered Bride*, 2001–02; *Don Giovanni*, 2002–03; *Les Contes d'Hoffmann (The Tales of Hoffmann)*, 2002–03; *Lucia di Lammermoor*, 2001–02

Pritchard, Lee H.: *Don Carlos*, 1972–73

Pugh, Frank: *A Hoosier Tale*, 1966–67

Roe, Richard Allen: *Don Giovanni*, 1991–92; *Wozzeck*, 1990–91

Ross, Allan A.: *Der Rosenkavalier*, 1965–66; *Dialogues des Carmélites*, 1965–66; *Die Meistersinger von Nürnberg (The Mastersingers of Nuremberg)*, 1968–69; *Die Zauberflöte (The Magic Flute)*, 1965–66; *Don Carlos*, 1972–73; *Don Pasquale*, 1965–66; *Macbeth*, 1965–66

Schwartzkopf, Michael: *Carmen*, 1998–99; *La Bohème*, 2004–05

Shantz, Timothy: *Falstaff*, 2003–04; *La Cenerentola (Cinderella)*, 2004–05; *Tosca*, 2004–05

Simons, Harriet: *Don Carlos*, 1961–62

Sinor, Eugenia: *A Midsummer Night's Dream*, 1983–84

Sloane, Ben: *Die lustige Witwe (The Merry Widow)*, 1965–66

Slon, Michael: *Dialogues des Carmélites*, 1997–98; *Eugene Onegin*, 1997–98; *Idomeneo*, 1998–99; *La Bohème*, 1999–2000; *La Cenerentola (Cinderella)*, 1998–99; *La Traviata*, 1997–98; *Madama Butterfly*, 1996–97; *Mass*, 1998–99; *Orphée aux enfers (Orpheus in the Underworld)*, 1998–99; *The Rake's Progress*, 1999–2000; *Wozzeck*, 1999–2000

Stahl, Edwin: *Un Ballo in Maschera (A Masked Ball)*, 1958–59

Stark, Eric: *La Bohème*, 1994–95; *Tosca*, 1993–94

Stoll, Robert E.: *Boris Godunov*, 1964–65; 1983–84; *Carmen*, 1965–66; 1973–74; 1977–78; *Faust*, 1971–72; 1989–90; *Kismet*, 1963–64; *Parsifal*, 1965–66; *Porgy and Bess*, 1976–77; *Prince Igor*, 1980–81

Stuempfle, Michael: *Kiss Me, Kate*, 1973–74

Swaney, Susan: *Hänsel und Gretel*, 1995–96

Tang-Yuk, Richard: *The Bartered Bride*, 1994–95; *Falstaff*, 1992–93; *The Love for Three Oranges*, 1993–94; *Orfeo ed Euridice*, 1992–93; *Rigoletto*, 1992–93

Taylor, Dana: *Kismet*, 1989–90

Tellez, Carmen: *Die Zauberflöte (The Magic Flute)*, 1988–89; *Don Pasquale*, 1988–89; *Eugene Onegin*, 1988–89; *Sweeney Todd*, 1983–84

Thayer, Lucinda: *Boris Godunov*, 1978–79

Trautwein, George: *Parsifal*, 1960–61; *La Traviata*, 1960–61

Tsouva, Vasiliki: *La Bohème*, 2007–08; *L'Elisir d'amore (The Elixir of Love)*, 2007–08; *Les Contes d'Hoffmann (The Tales of Hoffmann)*, 2007–08

Ueda, Aya: *Il Barbiere di Siviglia (The Barber of Seville)*, 1994–95

Urias, Marcelo: *Die Entführung aus dem Serail (The Abduction from the Seraglio)*, 2003–04; *Giulio Cesare (Julius Caesar)*, 2002–03; *Jeppe*, 2002–03

Vacano, Wolfgang: *Parsifal*, 1951–52; 1953–54; 1954–55; *Die Zauberflöte (The Magic Flute)*, 1953–54

Van Buskirk, Carl: *La Bohème*, 1949–50; *Parsifal*, 1949–50

Weller, Lawrence: *The Darkened City*, 1978–79; *Les Contes d'Hoffmann (The Tales of Hoffmann)*, 1978–79

Wesby, Roger: *Die Fledermaus (The Bat)*, 1990–91

Winters, Donald: *Parsifal*, 1952–53

Witakowski, Thomas: *Die Entführung aus dem Serail (The Abduction from the Seraglio)*, 1981–82; *Die Fledermaus (The Bat)*, 1982–83; *Die lustigen Weiber von Windsor (The Merry Wives of Windsor)*, 1981–82; *The Excursions of Mr. Broucek*, 1981–82; *Madama Butterfly*, 1981–82; *The Most Happy Fella*, 1982–83; *Wozzeck*, 1981–82

Yonkman, Jerry: *La Fille du régiment (The Daughter of the Regiment)*, 1984–85; *La Sonnambula (The Sleepwalker)*, 1985–86

Zerkle, Paula: *Il Barbiere di Siviglia (The Barber of Seville)*, 1988–89; *Les Contes d'Hoffmann (The Tales of Hoffmann)*, 1988–89

Marianne Williams Tobias is a cum laude graduate of Harvard University Longy School of Music, and the University of Minnesota, where she earned an MFA and DMA. She has done postdoctoral work with Menahem Pressler at the Indiana University Jacobs School of Music. Author of *Classical Music Without Fear* (Indiana University Press, 2003), Tobias is a seasoned pianist, public radio commentator, lecturer, and writer, and currently serves as program annotator for the Indianapolis Symphony Orchestra. She lives and performs regularly in Indianapolis.

George Calder is Professor of Music Emeritus at the Indiana University Jacobs School of Music, where he served as Executive Administrator of IU Opera Theater from 1968 to 1997. Calder was present for the transition from the limited East Hall to the even more restrictive University Middle School, and then to the new and modern Musical Arts Center. Before coming to IU, Calder studied and worked in Germany and Austria, where he served as a répétiteur in Mannheim. He retired in 1997 and graciously returned from retirement to serve as acting Opera Administrator in 2001.

Nancy J. Guyer served as Production Administrative Assistant at Indiana University Opera Theater for six years. She received a B.A. in German and Sociology from Wheaton College and is a certified event planner. She currently lives in Fort Pierce, Florida, with her husband and two daughters.

C. David Higgins is Professor of Music, Chair of Opera Studies, and a master scenic designer at the Indiana University Jacobs School of Music, where he has worked since the opening of the MAC in 1971. His design credits include the Ballet San Juan de Puerto Rico, Canton Ballet, Detroit Symphony, Dorset Opera (England), Icelandic National Theater, Korean National Ballet, Korean National Opera, Louisville Opera, Memphis Opera, San Antonio Festival, Sarasota Ballet, Seoul City Opera, Teatro la Paz de Belem, and the Teatro National de São Paulo.

Charles H. Webb is Dean Emeritus of the Indiana University Jacobs School of Music, where he served in various capacities from 1960 as Instructor of Music through his retirement as Dean in 1997. During his tenure Webb maintained an active performance schedule as both conductor and pianist, including appearances with many Jacobs School faculty members, including Josef Gingold, Janos Starker, Margaret Harshaw, Reri Grist, James Pellerite, and Harvey Phillips, among others. In 2004 he was appointed by Colin Powell to the Congressional Committee to Advise the Secretary of State on Cultural Diplomacy. He was also named a Living Legend of the State of Indiana by the Indiana Historical Society.

Editor: Jane Behnken
Managing Editor: Miki Bird
Production Director: Bernadette Zoss
Text and Jacket Designer: Pamela Rude
Composition: Pamela Rude and Tony Brewer
Printer: Four Colour Imports, Everbest